THE IMMIGRATION DEBATE

Studies on the Economic, Demographic, and Fiscal Effects of Immigration

James P. Smith and Barry Edmonston, Editors

Panel on the Demographic and Economic Impacts of Immigration

Committee on Population

and

Committee on National Statistics

Commission on Behavioral and Social Sciences and Education

National Research Council

NATIONAL ACADEMY PRESS
Washington, D.C.   1998

NATIONAL ACADEMY PRESS • 2101 Constitution Avenue, NW • Washington, DC 20418

NOTICE: The project that is the subject of this report was approved by the Governing Board of the National Research Council, whose members are drawn from the councils of the National Academy of Sciences, the National Academy of Engineering, and the Institute of Medicine. The members of the committee responsible for the report were chosen for their special competences and with regard for appropriate balance.

This report has been reviewed by a group other than the authors according to procedures approved by a Report Review Committee consisting of members of the National Academy of Sciences, the National Academy of Engineering, and the Institute of Medicine.

This study was supported by Order No. 95-55 between the National Academy of Sciences and the U.S. Commission on Immigration Reform. Any opinions, findings, conclusions, or recommendations expressed in this publication are those of the author(s) and do not necessarily reflect the view of the organizations or agencies that provided support for this project.

Library of Congress Cataloging-in-Publication Data

The immigration debate : studies on the economic, demographic, and fiscal effects of immigration / James P. Smith and Barry Edmonston, editors.

    p. cm.

Includes bibliographical references.

    ISBN 0-309-05998-4 (pbk.)

    1. United States—Emigration and immigration—Economic aspects.

2. United States—Emigration and immigration—Case studies I.

Smith, James P. (James Patrick), 1943- II. Edmonston, Barry.

    JV6471 .I445 1998

    330.973—ddc21   97-45468

Additional copies of this report are available from:

National Academy Press

2101 Constitution Avenue NW

Washington, DC 20418

Call 800-624-6242 or 202-334-3313 (in the Washington Metropolitan Area).

This report is also available online at **http://www.nap.edu**

Printed in the United States of America

PANEL ON DEMOGRAPHIC AND ECONOMIC IMPACTS OF IMMIGRATION

JAMES P. SMITH (*Chair*), RAND, Santa Monica, California

ALAN J. AUERBACH, Department of Economics, University of California, Berkeley

GEORGE J. BORJAS, John F. Kennedy School of Government, Harvard University

THOMAS ESPENSHADE, Office of Population Research, Princeton University

RICHARD FREEMAN, Department of Economics, Harvard University, and Labor Studies, National Bureau of Economic Research

JOHN F. GEWEKE, Department of Economics, University of Minnesota, Minnneapolis

CHARLES HIRSCHMAN, Department of Sociology, University of Washington

ROBERT INMAN, Department of Finance, Wharton School of Business, University of Pennsylvania

GUILLERMINA JASSO, Department of Sociology, New York University

RONALD D. LEE, Departments of Demography and Economics, University of California, Berkeley

MARY WATERS, Department of Sociology, Harvard University

FINIS R. WELCH, Department of Economics, Texas A&M University

BARRY EDMONSTON, *Study Director*

KRISTIN McCUE, *Research Associate*

JOEL ROSENQUIST, *Senior Project Assistant*

CONTRIBUTORS

JAY BHATTACHARYA, Department of Economics, Stanford University

SUSAN B. CARTER, Department of Economics, University of California, Riverside

MICHAEL S. CLUNE, Department of Demography, University of California, Berkeley

THOMAS J. ESPENSHADE, Department of Sociology and Office of Population Research, Princeton University

WILLIAM H. FREY, Population Studies Center, University of Michigan, Ann Arbor

EDWARD FUNKHOUSER, Department of Economics, University of California, Santa Barbara

DEBORAH L. GARVEY, Department of Economics, Princeton University

JOHN HAGAN, Faculty of Law, University of Toronto, Canada

RONALD D. LEE, Departments of Demography and Economics, University of California, Berkeley

KAO-LEE LIAW, Department of Geography, McMaster University, Ontario, Canada

THOMAS MaCURDY, Department of Economics and Senior Fellow, The Hoover Institution

TIMOTHY W. MILLER, Department of Demography, University of California, Berkeley

THOMAS NECHYBA, Department of Economics, Stanford University

ALBERTO PALLONI, Department of Sociology, University of Wisconsin, Madison

JAMES P. SMITH, RAND, Santa Monica, California

RICHARD SUTCH, Departments of Economics and History and Institute of Business and Economic Research, University of California, Berkeley

DANIEL TREFLER, Institute for Policy Analysis, University of Toronto, and Harris School of Public Policy, University of Chicago

STEPHEN J. TREJO, Department of Economics, University of California, Santa Barbara

Acknowledgments

In 1990, Congress appointed a bipartisan Commission on Immigration Reform to review the nation's immigration policies and laws. In turn, the commission asked the National Research Council to convene a panel of experts to assess the demographic, economic, and fiscal consequences of immigration. The panel was not asked to answer all the current questions about immigration or to recommend policy. Rather, the goal was to improve the scientific foundation for public discussion and policy making around a few key issues. In 1997, the panel released its report, entitled *The New Americans: Economic, Demographic, and Fiscal Effects of Immigration*, which contains its main findings and conclusions. This companion volume contains the detailed background papers that the panel commissioned along the way.

This book is the product of a great deal of hard work by a set of dedicated authors, to whom I am very grateful. In addition, I thank the U.S. Commission on Immigration Reform for its financial support and commission staff members Susan Forbes Martin, Lindsay Lowell, and David Howell for their efforts during the development of the project. At the National Research Council, Barbara Boyle Torrey, executive director of the Commission on Behavioral and Social Sciences and Education, was an important source of help and encouragement. The work took place under the general direction of John Haaga and Miron Straf. Barry Edmonston provided a constant intellectual and managerial presence, aided by several other current and former staff members including Kristin McCue, Karen Foote, and Barney Cohen. Elaine McGarraugh skillfully edited the manuscript. LaTanya Johnson prepared the papers for publication. I thank them all.

James P. Smith, *Chair*
Panel on the Demographic and Economic Impacts of Immigration

ix

The National Academy of Sciences is a private, nonprofit, self-perpetuating society of distinguished scholars engaged in scientific and engineering research, dedicated to the furtherance of science and technology and to their use for the general welfare. Upon the authority of the charter granted to it by the Congress in 1863, the Academy has a mandate that requires it to advise the federal government on scientific and technical matters. Dr. Bruce M. Alberts is president of the National Academy of Sciences.

The National Academy of Engineering was established in 1964, under the charter of the National Academy of Sciences, as a parallel organization of outstanding engineers. It is autonomous in its administration and in the selection of its members, sharing with the National Academy of Sciences the responsibility for advising the federal government. The National Academy of Engineering also sponsors engineering programs aimed at meeting national needs, encourages education and research, and recognizes the superior achievements of engineers. Dr. William A. Wulf is president of the National Academy of Engineering.

The Institute of Medicine was established in 1970 by the National Academy of Sciences to secure the services of eminent members of appropriate professions in the examination of policy matters pertaining to the health of the public. The Institute acts under the responsibility given to the National Academy of Sciences by its congressional charter to be an adviser to the federal government and, upon its own initiative, to identify issues of medical care, research, and education. Dr. Kenneth I. Shine is president of the Institute of Medicine.

The National Research Council was organized by the National Academy of Sciences in 1916 to associate the broad community of science and technology with the Academy's purposes of furthering knowledge and advising the federal government. Functioning in accordance with general policies determined by the Academy, the Council has become the principal operating agency of both the National Academy of Sciences and the National Academy of Engineering in providing services to the government, the public, and the scientific and engineering communities. The Council is administered jointly by both Academies and the Institute of Medicine. Dr. Bruce M. Alberts and Dr. William A. Wulf are chairman and vice chairman, respectively, of the National Research Council.

Contents

THE IMMIGRATION DEBATE

1

Introduction

James P. Smith

While America remains a nation of immigrants, its two-century-old debate about the wisdom of immigration continues unabated. Many people have expressed concerns about the effects of immigration on the economic prospects of the native born, on the rate at which our population is growing, on fiscal balances at all levels of government, and on the ability of immigrants to integrate into the social fabric of the nation.

Responding to these renewed concerns, Congress created the bipartisan U.S. Commission on Immigration Reform to recommend changes in immigration policy. In 1995 the Commission asked the National Research Council (NRC) to convene an expert panel to assess the demographic, economic, and fiscal consequences of immigration. This 12-member panel of demographers, economists, and sociologists was asked to address three key questions of the effect of immigration on

- the future size and composition of the U.S. population,
- the U.S economy and its workers, and
- the fiscal balances of federal, state, and local governments.

In answering these broad questions, the NRC panel—which I chaired—faced some complex theoretical and empirical issues. Where the existing literature was found to be deficient, the panel decided to commission a series of background papers to break some important new conceptual or empirical ground. These papers were presented and discussed at a conference held in September 1996 in Washington, DC. The topics addressed at that conference included the labor market role of female immigrants (Funkhouser and Trejo), a historical perspective on immigration (Carter and Sutch), a theoretical framework for addressing fiscal impacts of immigration (MaCurdy, Nechyba, and Bhattacharya), the association of immigration with criminal activity (Hagan and Palloni), and the theoretical labor market impact of international immigration and trade (Trefler). Many of the findings of these papers influenced the panel's final report, which was published in October 1997.[1] Revised versions of these conference papers are included in this volume.

In addition to these commissioned papers, the panel also decided to initiate some original research of its own. For its work on the fiscal impact of immigration, we relied on an ongoing study of New Jersey being conducted by one of the panel members (Garvey and Espenshade) and started our own case study of California (Clune). The final results from both case studies are also part of this volume. In addition to these annual budget estimates for two key immigrant states, the panel conducted a study of the national longitudinal effects of immigration (Lee and Miller). A part of that research project is included in this volume. Finally, the panel heard a series of presentations from an ongoing study of the effects of immigration on internal migration (Frey and Liaw). Internal migration is a central issue that arises in evaluating labor market impacts of immigration.

These essays served as important background for the NRC panel's deliberations and our final report. In addition, I believe that they stand on their own as scientific contributions on a critical policy issue not only in the United States but throughout most of the world. Because immigration touches sensitive issues and provokes strong emotional reactions, such dispassionate scientific research is all the more valuable.

THE FISCAL EFFECTS OF IMMIGRATION

Nowhere did our panel find the existing literature more lacking than on the fiscal effects of immigration. Although significant gaps remained, there were long and rich traditions of scholarship on the other two main questions—the economic and demographic impacts of immigration. Not so for the fiscal impacts. Instead, only a handful of existing empirical studies were available. Many of these represented not science but advocacy from both sides of the immigration debate. These studies often offered an incomplete accounting of either the full list of taxpayer costs and benefits by ignoring some programs and taxes while including others. More important, the conceptual foundation of this research was rarely explicitly stated, offering opportunities to tilt the research toward the desired result.

---

[1]See *The New Americans: Economic, Demographic, and Fiscal Effects of Immigration,* James P. Smith and Barry Edmonston (editors), National Academy Press, 1997.

From the panel's viewpoint, however, the most serious problem was that existing fiscal impact studies did not even appear to be addressing the key policy-relevant question—what is the taxpayer cost or benefit to native-born Americans of letting an additional immigrant into this country?

Our first priority then was to obtain a coherent conceptual framework in which to understand the issues involving the cost to native-born taxpayers of expanding or contracting the flow of immigrants. The chapter "An Economic Framework for Assessing the Fiscal Impacts of Immigration," by Thomas MaCurdy, Thomas Nechyba, and Jay Bhattacharya, provides such a framework. The authors posit a minimum set of factors that must be explicitly included in the framework. One of their most important admonitions is that fiscal impact studies must be multi-period. One reason is that both taxes and expenditures are extremely sensitive to age. If an immigrant arrives at an age at which his or her taxes are temporarily high and receipt of government benefits is temporarily low, the immigrant will look like a bonus to taxpayers. However, this could all be negated in the next period if expenditures rise and taxes fall.

One critical distinction in the government sector involves the separation of spending into three categories—public goods, interest on debt, and all others. In the extreme, immigrants do not increase spending on the first two categories but they do on the third. Fiscal impact studies should also be comprehensive in their treatment of expenditures and taxes. Compared with the native born, immigrant households are relatively heavy users of some government services, such as schools and income-conditioned transfer programs, and relatively light users of other government services, such as Social Security and Medicare. A corollary of this comprehensiveness requirement is that all sectors of government—federal, state, and local—should be included when analyzing fiscal impacts. Some programs—such as Social Security and Medicare—are concentrated at one level of government (federal) whereas other programs—e.g., schools—are the primary responsibility of other levels of government (state and local).

Fiscal impact studies must be explicit in their assumptions about who ends up paying taxes (tax incidence) and about the cost of providing government services (marginal versus average cost). A common mistake is to assume that those who end up paying a tax are the same people from whom the tax is collected.

One enduring salient fact about immigration into the United States involves geographic concentration. Immigrants have always moved to relatively few places, settling where they have family, friends, or fellow countrymen. Most immigrants still live in a handful of states and in less than a dozen cities. This geographic concentration means that any state or local fiscal effects of immigration (through taxes and government expenditures) may also be concentrated in a few states. With this in mind, our panel relied on fiscal impact studies in two of the important immigrant states—New Jersey and California. The New Jersey study is summarized in "Fiscal Impacts of Immigrant and Native Households: A

New Jersey Case Study" by Deborah L. Garvey and Thomas J. Espenshade. The California study is outlined in Michael S. Clune's contribution "The Fiscal Impacts of Immigrants: A California Case Study."

One reason why undertaking fiscal impact studies in two immigrant states turned out to be so fortuitous is that there exists a great deal of heterogeneity among the major immigrant states. Some dimensions of that heterogeneity is illustrated in Table 1-1, which highlights some key demographic and economic differences. Although they are both classified as "immigrant" states, one-fourth of all Californian households are headed by immigrants, compared with about one in seven in New Jersey. The ethnic composition of immigrants is also vastly different. The dominant ethnic ancestries in New Jersey are Europeans and Canadians, whereas Latin Americans, particularly those from Mexico, are a majority of all foreign-born Californians. Similarly, compared with foreign-born households residing in New Jersey, immigrant-headed households in California have much lower incomes and many more children. These differences say a lot about what the eventual taxpayer impact will be.

In their chapter, Garvey and Espenshade take a "bottom-up" approach to net fiscal impacts. Largely using governmental administrative data on program costs and tax collections, a "top-down" approach simply allocates prorated shares of spending or taxes to each household. One limitation of this approach is that it can not speak to the reasons for variation across households. By building up the estimates from the household level, we are able to understand which household-level attributes are responsible for the differences in net fiscal impacts that emerge.

Estimates from Garvey and Espenshade are derived from micro-level data for New Jersey obtained from the 1990 decennial census. The census provides a wealth of information on the demographic and economic characteristics of the residents. These data were supplemented with state-level data on actual program

TABLE 1-1   Profile of the Two Major Immigrant States

	New Jersey		California	
% foreign born	14		25	
% of immigrants who are				
European-Canadian	47		12	
Latin American	28		56	
Asian	20		25	
	Native Born	Immigrant	Native Born	Immigrant
Mean Household Income	$61,966	$58,372	$50,518	$37,878
# of children	.63	.81	.64	1.37
% on AFDC	3	3	5	10

SOURCE: *The New Americans: Economic, Demographic, and Fiscal Effects of Immigration*, James P. Smith and Barry Edmonston (editors), National Academy Press, 1997.

expenditures. Garvey and Espenshade report that in general immigrant households were more costly than native households. On both the expenditure and the tax side, however, this discrepancy was small compared with the differences that existed among immigrants. European households received relatively fewer state expenditures, whereas Asian and especially Latin-American immigrant households received state benefits well in excess of the foreign-born average.

Michael Clune examines the federal, state, and local fiscal impacts of immigrant households in California for FY 1995. Household-level data were obtained from the 1995 Current Population Survey (CPS) so that receipt and amount of government services can be divided into 25 categories and taxes into 13 separate categories. Supplemental data sources are used for services (police, fire, prisons, etc.) not included in the CPS files, and expenditure totals are scaled to match administrative records. Households were classified by their nativity, age, and ethnicity. As was true for Garvey and Espenshade, explicit incidence assumptions were made for all taxes.

One of the more difficult issues facing fiscal impact studies comes from recognizing that resident households are not the only sector either paying taxes or receiving benefits. The two most important examples are tourists (who pay sales taxes) and the corporate sector (business taxes). During their stay, tourists gain by their use of roads, police, and fire. The corporate sector also gains through these provisions. There is little hard evidence on the relation of these benefits to taxes so that some simplifying assumption must be made. Clune assumes that on net they are a wash, so that the household sector also obtains benefits equal to the taxes they pay.

Immigrant and native-born households in California differ on both the tax and government expenditure side. Across all sectors of government, however, total costs of the benefits obtained by immigrant and native-born households were actually quite similar. For example, in California, native-born households received $22,021, whereas immigrant-headed households were given $25,943 in all government benefits in FY 1995. This similarity in total government benefits hides considerable diversity in individual categories. As a general rule, those programs in which immigrants receive fewer benefits than native-born households are predominately at the federal level (e.g., Social Security and Medicare), whereas programs in which immigrants receive proportionately more benefits are at the state and local level (e.g., education). The same diversity exists for within-immigrant comparisons. Although Hispanic immigrants are heavy users of public education, Asian immigrants have much higher take-up rates for Supplemental Security Income. These program-by-program differences in take-up rates among immigrants and between immigrants and the native born is a strong argument that government benefits must be measured in a comprehensive way.

The differences between immigrant and native-born households are much larger on the tax side. Clune reports that immigrant-headed households pay 69 percent as much in taxes as do native-born households. The net result is that immigrant households in California receive considerably more in government services than they pay in taxes. That difference is made up by native-born households paying more in taxes than they obtain in benefits. This "fiscal burden" is particularly high among older immigrant households and among Hispanics is particularly high.

There is much confusion about what annual fiscal impact studies such as those in New Jersey and California actually measure. For immigrant-headed households, these studies measure the difference between the costs of all government services received minus the value of all taxes paid during a particular year. In the case of both New Jersey and California, immigrant-headed households receive more in government benefits than they pay in taxes. Because state and local government budgets must balance on an annual basis, this deficit among immigrant-headed households requires that there is a corresponding surplus among native-born households. That is, native-born households must be paying more in taxes than they are receiving in government benefits. The best way of thinking about these annual fiscal impact studies is that they measure the annual net transfer at that unit of government from native-born households to immigrant households so as to balance the books. For reasons explained below, they do not directly measure the net fiscal impact of adding another immigrant.

Table 1-2 provides comparable summary measures of these annual fiscal impact studies for these two states. In both states, immigrant-headed households receive on average net transfers from the government sector. These transfers are considerably smaller in New Jersey, largely because immigrant households there are economically better off and have fewer children (and thus less need for schools). These net transfers to immigrant households must be paid by native-born households in those states.

This "fiscal burden" is $229 per native-born New Jersey household and $1,174 per native-born California household. The much larger tax burden in California stems from the larger net transfer to immigrant households in that state as well as the larger fraction of households that are headed by an immigrant.

Ronald D. Lee and Timothy W. Miller's chapter, "The Current Fiscal Impact of Immigrants and Their Descendants: Beyond the Immigrant Household," continues their innovative work on estimating the fiscal impacts of immigrants. It begins by defining a number of conceptual ways in which immigrant fiscal impacts can be calculated. In contrast to annual budget estimates, the first method,

TABLE 1-2   Average Government Benefits Minus Taxes Paid

Immigrant-Headed Households		Native-Born-Headed Households	
New Jersey	California	New Jersey	California
1,484	3,463	−229	−1,174

SOURCE: *The New Americans: Economic, Demographic, and Fiscal Effects of Immigration*, James P. Smith and Barry Edmonston (editors), National Academy Press, 1997.

the "longitudinal formulation," addresses the policy-relevant question of what the taxpayer costs are of adding or subtracting another immigrant. To put it simply, the longitudinal formulation calculates all current and future taxes and all current and future government spending attributable to a new immigrant and his or her descendants. This approach forces the analyst to make explicit assumptions about the future course of many uncertain events. To illustrate with just one example, some assumption has to be made about the timing and magnitude of the resolution of the federal budget deficit when the baby boom generation retires. Because there is no way of avoiding making some assumptions and the inherent uncertainties cannot be dismissed, simulations under alternative assumption scenarios are recommended.

The other approaches that Lee and Miller analyze are all variants of cross-sectional annual budget computations. For a given year, they all ask some counterfactual questions—what if I took away one immigrant ("immigrant only"), one immigrant-headed household, including any native-born children in that household ("immigrant household"), and one immigrant household and any living descendants of this household, including native-born children who head households ("concurrent descendants")? The immigrant-only computation ignores all costs (especially schooling) and taxes associated with native-born children who are living in the immigrant's household. Such costs would certainly seem a consequence of immigration.

The immigrant household concept includes these costs and all others attributable to native-born second-generation children as long as they remain in the immigrant household. However, it ignores all costs and especially all taxes paid by the second generation when they form households of their own. These taxes are also the consequence of immigration. To remedy that problem, the descendent generation approach adds all government benefits received and taxes paid by the second and third generation as long as the first-generation immigrant from whom they descended is still alive. These three approaches can all be computed from annual cross-sectional experiments that are meant in part to account for some aspect of the bias inherent in the cross-sectional annual calculation. Although the authors still favor the longitudinal formulation, they argue that, among the cross-sectional annual budget estimates, the concurrent descendants approach is probably the least biased among the cross-sectional alternatives.

The basic bottom line of the concurrent descendant formulation is that immigrants are a net taxpayer benefit to native-born households. This net benefit takes place exclusively at the federal level and not at the state level. Consequently, residents of some immigrant-intensive states (such as California) experience higher taxes due to immigration.

Lee and Miller also provide an interesting comparison among the three annual budget approaches. They demonstrate that the most frequently used methodology—immigrant households—is the only one that produces a negative immigrant fiscal impact.

LABOR MARKET STUDIES

Much of the recent research on immigration has been unabashedly empirical. Daniel Trefler's chapter, "Immigrants and Natives in General Equilibrium Trade Models," sketches the theoretical implications of immigration on national welfare, wages, and trade flows. A strength of Trelfer's treatment is that it illustrates the strong parallels that exist between international immigration and international trade. For example, unskilled labor in other countries can affect wages in the United States either by migrating here or by producing goods that are imported to this country. It should be no surprise, then, that the pro and con arguments about the North American Free Trade Agreement mimic so closely those arguments advanced in the immigration debate.

A basic implication of trade between nations is the prediction that prices of inputs used in production (including labor) should converge internationally. The "factor price equalization" puzzle is that, in spite of greatly expanding trade, no such convergence seems to have taken place. In some new research, Trefler attempts to test whether some wage convergence exists if workers across different countries are "standardized" by their industry of employment (hopefully capturing some unobservables connected with productivity) or proxies for their skill or human capital.

His empirical results indicate that industry controls may well matter. If fixed employment weights are used, within-industry variances in wages declined noticeably between 1964 and 1991. However, controls for human capital differences across countries (e.g., education) do little to explain the lack of wage convergence across countries over time. This may not be surprising in light of Juhn, Murphy, and Pierce's (1993) finding that the bulk of rising wage inequality in the United States over time took place within age-education cells.[2] If skill differentiation within these cells is still large, our ability to fully standardize across countries may be quite limited.

The final question addressed by Trefler concerns the extent to which international trade has contributed to the declining incomes of less skilled workers in the United States. Immigration often receives the primary blame for rising wage inequality, but there are other plausible culprits. In addition to immigration, the other prominent candidates include skill-biased technological change and declining capital prices. Trefler argues that the conventional view downgrades the role of international trade, because trade is not important enough as it represents only 20 percent of the American work force. This assessment may be premature. For example, Trefler found that, relative to the domestic United States work force, the amount of labor with no or little education involved in imports to the United States has grown rapidly. This "effective" increase in the supply of low-skilled

---

[2]Chinhui Juhn, Kevin M. Murphy, and Brooks Pierce, "Wage Inequality and the Rise in Returns to Skill," *Journal of Political Economy*, Vol. 101, May 1993, pp. 410-442.

labor is so large that it must have played some role in the declining wages of the less skilled.

Virtually all existing empirical research on the labor market effects on immigration has dealt with men. Whether the question concerned life-cycle or generational assimilation of the immigrants themselves or the impacts of immigrants on native-born workers, with very few exceptions, only male immigrants and male native-born workers have been studied. Because the numbers of male and female immigrants into the United States are roughly the same, this is a strange situation indeed. To begin to retrieve some balance, our panel asked Edward Funkhouser and Stephen J. Trejo to conduct a parallel analysis for immigrant women. Their chapter, "Labor Market Outcomes of Female Immigrants in the United States," does just that.

Using micro data from the 1980 and 1990 U.S. decennial censuses, these researchers examine employment and wage patterns for immigrant women. In the first generation, most immigrants arrive with, live near, and marry people from their own background. Consequently, the broad trends in the attributes of female immigrants should closely parallel those of male immigrants. For example, similar to their male counterparts, female immigrants are less educated than native-born American women, a gap that has been growing over time.

Funkhouser and Trejo also examine the question of economic assimilation, an issue that has attracted a considerable amount of research interest for male immigrants. One special factor that must be considered when addressing these questions for women is that their comparison group—native-born American women—has also been undergoing significant structural labor market changes in recent decades. Labor force participation rates have increased dramatically among women in the past three decades and female wages have risen steadily, even relative to those of men. Therefore, immigrant women are being compared with a moving target—native-born American women—whose own labor market position is steadily improving.

Given the rapid rise in employment rates among native-born women, it is not surprising that the employment gap (compared with the native born) of new cohorts of female immigrants has been steadily rising. However, after an initial period of adjustment in the United States, Funkhouser and Trejo report that this employment gap diminishes significantly. The big unknown in these patterns concerns the employment rates of immigrant women before they came to America. Without knowing that crucial piece of information, we do not know whether the event of immigration to the United States lowered or raised the probability of their employment.

A very similar pattern exists with wages—widening wage gaps as new cohorts arrive and a diminution of those wage gaps with native-born women over time. These wage patterns closely mirror those found by numerous authors for men. The major exception to finding a significant amount of wage assimilation involves both Mexican men and Mexican women. Unlike the case for men, the declining relative position of female immigrants over time appears to have little to do with shifts in national origin. Instead, they are largely attributable to such human capital variables as education and English language ability.

HISTORICAL, DEMOGRAPHIC, AND SOCIAL CONSEQUENCES

Immigration to the United States is nothing new. Although many industrial countries today are experiencing immigration flows that exceed those into the United States, international immigration reaches far deeper into our history. This historical experience provides an abundance of data about how well or poorly immigrants have done and what their impact has been on native-born Americans. Susan B. Carter and Richard Sutch's chapter, "The Economic and Demographic Consequences of Immigration to the United States: Quantitative Historical Perspectives," provides a comprehensive summary and interpretation of that evidence.

Seen through a historical lens, there are many striking similarities and differences between today's immigrants and their predecessors. Although the absolute number of current immigrants rivals the peak levels at the beginning of the twentieth century, expressed relative to the size of the existing U.S. population, current immigration is far more modest. While immigration continues to attract the young, immigration at the beginning of this century was disproportionately male. In contrast, current immigration flows are roughly equal between men and women, a reflection of the important role family reunification plays in the current U.S. immigration preference system. Although strong conclusions must be tempered by the limitations of the data, the skills of immigrants at the beginning of the century appear to be in the middle of those of native-born Americans. The historical evidence is also supportive of life-cycle and generational assimilation of immigrants.

A far more difficult question is what role immigration played in the rapid economic growth of the American economy in the last half of the nineteenth century and the first half of the twentieth century. Although Carter and Sutch do not claim to definitely settle this question, they perform a useful service by clarifying and, where possible, quantifying the possible mechanisms through which immigration can alter economic growth. Among other things, these mechanisms include differential savings behavior, participation in inventive activity, and the exploitation of economies of scale.

One issue that has dominated the current immigration debate far more than its historical predecessors involves the fiscal effects of immigration. There are probably two reasons why that is so. First, the size of government at all levels is much higher today than it was during other periods of sustained immigration. Second, especially at the federal level, the impacts of earlier waves of immigration were probably quite positive. A big contribution of Carter and Sutch is their identification of the importance of pensions for Civil War veterans in the federal budget. All immigrants who arrived after this war paid into this system but would never qualify for benefits. Given this program and the public goods nature of some federal benefits, it is difficult to see how immigrants could end up as a net taxpayer burden at the federal level.

Much less historical evidence exists on taxpayer effects at the state and local levels, especially in those places where immigrants lived. As Carter and Sutch point out, and as remains true today, the answer probably lies primarily in education. Although immigrants were young and had more children, two mitigating factors were that school attendance rates for immigrant children were lower and immigrants were heavy users of private and parochial schools. Additional research on this issue deserves high priority.

The fear that immigrants contribute to high levels of crime is a recurrent theme in American history. In spite of the prominence of this issue, measuring the effect of immigration on crime is mired in a statistical maze. A limitation of existing crime statistics is that immigrant status of the perpetrator or victim is not known. A second more generic limitation is that statistics on crime and criminal acts can be two quite different phenomena. Many crimes are not reported, and, if reported, those who commit them are often not apprehended, convicted, or imprisoned. Data on characteristics of the prison population may be highly selective relative to the attributes of those who commit crimes.

John Hagan and Alberto Palloni take up these issues in their chapter, "Immigration and Crime in the United States." They point out that the recent fourth wave of increased immigration coincided with a dramatic increase in violent crime rates, increasing public perceptions that immigration and crime are closely linked. But the biases inherent in immigration statistics and the strong selectivity of the process at all stages makes an inference of causation extremely problematic. Working on data from El Paso and San Diego, they are able to show that prison statistics that seem very negative about immigrants could easily reflect lower rates of participation of immigrants in criminal activity. Until we obtain better methods of collecting data at all stages of criminal activity, strong conclusions about immigration and crime are unwarranted.

Immigrants are extremely concentrated geographically, with about three in every four living in only six states. This concentration raises the possibility that fiscal impacts of immigrants could vary considerably across states and localities. Similarly, labor market effects of immigration could also be more pronounced in those places where immigrants live. The direct increases in labor supply attributable to immigration, especially for unskilled labor, are much higher in immigrant-intensive areas than in the nation as a whole.

The expectation of larger economic impacts in those local areas with many immigrants rest on strong assumptions about both the demand and the supply sides of the labor market. First, the elasticity of demand for labor must be similar at the local and national level. This is very unlikely to be true. Demand curves tend to be more elastic the better are the available substitutes. The availability of substitutes for unskilled labor in Los Angeles, for example, is inherently much larger than for unskilled labor in the United States. Unskilled labor in all other labor markets constitutes to some degree a substitute for similar workers in Los Angeles. The implication is that the demand curve for unskilled labor must be much more elastic than the demand curve for unskilled labor defined at the national level. With very elastic demand curves at the local level, wages cannot fall very much as a consequence of the arrival of immigrants.

There are also supply-side adjustments that may mitigate any strong local labor market wage changes. The key issue is whether immigration affects patterns of net migration of native-born Americans across geographic boundaries. If low-skilled immigrants into California simply increase out-migration flows from California of domestic low-skilled workers or reduce the number of similarly skilled in-migrants into California, the size of the "supply" effects induced by immigration is considerably muted. Similarly, any wage effects caused by immigration will not be limited to California but will be dispersed across the country. This question of the internal migration reactions to immigration is the subject of William H. Frey and Kao-Lee Liaw's chapter, "The Impact of Recent Immigration on Population Redistribution Within the United States."

Frey and Liaw demonstrate that immigrants continue to locate in the same relatively few places. For example, just ten metropolitan areas accounted for two-thirds of all immigrant growth. In contrast, domestic migrants are far more eclectic in their choices of where to live. In recent years, domestic migrants have tended to relocate in places other than those attracting immigrants. Moreover, there exists considerable out-migration from high-immigration states, especially among less-skilled natives. For example, between 1990 and 1995, net immigration into Los Angeles was 792,712, whereas net internal migration was –1,095,455. During these years, internal migrants were attracted instead to the economically booming areas of the Sun Belt and the South.

Although the primary motivation for these internal migrants was the "pull" of the attractive economic circumstances in booming areas, the question Frey and Liaw pose is to what extent immigration also influenced these internal flows. This possibility is suggested by the fact that the out-migration from immigration-intensive areas was also concentrated among less-skilled native-born residents. Because it is difficult to control for all other confounding factors, causation is a very tricky business. In particular, demand shocks vary considerably across areas in very complex ways. With that important caveat in mind, Frey and Liaw conclude that immigration did induce out-migration of native-born workers. For people with a high school education or less, Frey and Liaw estimate that California would lose 51 net internal migrants for every 100 similarly skilled international migrants who arrived during the last five years.

2

An Economic Framework for Assessing the Fiscal Impacts of Immigration

Thomas MaCurdy, Thomas Nechyba, and Jay Bhattacharya

INTRODUCTION

By 1994, almost 1 in 11 U.S. residents were foreign born. More than 9 million of these 23 million immigrants entered the United States in the past decade alone. As the immigration level rises, concerns are growing over the extra burden immigrants place on the government through their use of services such as welfare, health care, and schools. In reaction, states and the federal government have moved to limit the availability of services to both legal and illegal immigrants. The new welfare reform is the latest example. This legislation bars illegal immigrants from virtually all public benefits. It also bars or permits states to bar legal immigrants from major federal programs including cash welfare, food stamps, Medicaid, and Supplemental Security Income, although these provisions are currently under challenge.

Such anti-immigrant measures have been fueled in part by a growing number of studies that attempt to quantify the fiscal impact of immigration. Closely linked to literature on rates of immigrant participation in welfare and other social services, these studies try to carefully account for the taxes contributed and benefits received by immigrants at the federal, state, or local level. The exact items included vary widely. For example, most studies account for use of social services, health care, and schools, but others also consider services such as libraries, highways, community colleges, and parks. Similarly, most count immigrant payments to income taxes and often sales taxes, but others also include contributions to excise taxes, motor vehicle fees, even lottery revenues. Finally, the techniques for assigning the dollar amounts are quite different, such as assigning average service use and average tax versus tracking actual use through administrative records. Not surprisingly, the resulting calculations reach quite different conclusions, some finding net costs of immigrants, others finding net benefits. In the absence of a systematic methodology, it is difficult to evaluate the competing claims.

In this chapter we propose a basic economic framework for evaluating the fiscal impact of immigrants, addressing the complicated issues of demographic characteristics, skill levels, multiple levels of government, and the dynamic effects of a changing population. Although immigrants are the principal example for this framework, it has application beyond the immigration debate. In reality, immigration is merely population growth with particular population characteristics. The model seeks to separate these two aspects: expanding population and the change in population characteristics. The same framework could be used to model other population changes such as a baby boom. Immigration is a special case primarily because it can be influenced more easily by policy choices.

In the second section we set out our basic economic framework for assessing the fiscal impacts of population growth. The third section begins with the specification of a "neutrality proposition" that identifies an economic environment that makes population growth fiscally neutral. In that section we explore the factors that are relevant in evaluating the consequences of different patterns of growth, distinguishing between population increases arising from uniform shifts in all groups and disproportionate increases in particular groups, such as the elderly or the unskilled. In the fourth section we look at the particular nature of U.S. population growth due to immigration, applying the results of the third section to unveil the types of fiscal costs and benefits likely to accompany immigration. Finally, in the fifth section we review how the existing literature fits into our framework, permitting us to surmise the costs and benefits improperly assessed or missed in these various studies.

ECONOMIC FRAMEWORK

In this section we develop an elementary economic model for analyzing population growth in general and immigration in particular. Although our proposed model may at first appear more complex than necessary, we believe it is the simplest possible framework that can address the basic issues faced by researchers attempting to conduct fiscal impact studies of immigration. For reasons detailed below, we conclude that at a minimum the model must include the following features:

(a) multiple periods,
(b) three generations,
(c) workers distinguished by high and low skills,
(d) two consumption goods categorized by the level of sales tax,

   (e)   an underlying model of production and consumption, and

   (f)   a government sector detailed enough to capture the major categories of spending and taxation.

In the following three subsections we provide the reasons for introducing these complexities and explain the role of these six features within the basic structure of the model. In the fourth subsection we explore some special concerns in using this general framework for fiscal impact studies of immigration relating fiscal trade-offs across periods and different levels of government.

Multiple Generations and the Composition of the Work Force

The first three elements of the model involve the composition of the population across time. There are three generations of agents living simultaneously in each period: the young (J), the middle aged (M), and the elderly (E). The work force is composed exclusively of the middle aged, and they are divided into high-skilled (h) and low-skilled (ℓ) workers. In conjunction with capital (K), the workers in the M generation produce current income (through the process described in the following subsection). Generation M consumes part of its labor earning and saves the remainder for consumption in the next period. The middle aged also provide for the young generation's consumption. The elderly consume from their holdings of capital (and government transfers). After every period, each generation advances, with E exiting the model and a new generation of J entering the model.

Income, Production, and Consumption

Aggregate income (Y) is produced through a production function f which takes the two types of labor as well as capital as its arguments; that is,

$$Y = f(\ell, h, K).$$

Throughout most of this chapter, we assume that this production function is constant returns to scale. Each type of M (high skilled and low skilled) is endowed with one unit of labor that is sold at the market wage. Wage rates are equal to the marginal product of labor, and the sum of wages is denoted by W. Similarly, the rental rate r is equal to the marginal product of capital. Income from capital is thus rK.

Total consumption (C) by agents in the model is divided into two categories: C_0 (which is taxed at the normal sales tax rate) and C_e (which is subject to an additional excise tax), so that

$$C = C_0 + C_e.$$

Generation J does not earn income; it is sustained by generation M. The remainder of generation M's after-tax income is savings invested to provide for income in the next period. Generation E's consumption is funded by reductions in its capital holdings.

Let total tax revenues be equal to T (which is divided into its components in the following subsection). By definition,

$$Y = W + rK = C + \Delta K + T.$$

Government Sector

We now more fully incorporate the government sector into the model. To start, we treat this sector as one unit. In the fourth subsection, we consider the additional complications arising from the federal structure particular to the United States. The government sector taxes the various aspects of economic activity (consumption, wages, rental income) and spends resources on the production of "public" goods and on direct transfer payments to individuals in the economy. Our model considers each of these areas of government activity—public goods spending (G_p), spending on transfer payments (G_x), and collection of tax revenues (G_t)—by focusing on the characteristics of these activities that are relevant for thinking about the fiscal impact of population growth and immigration on government finances and on current taxpayers. To complete the model and to ensure that the accounting identities hold, we then add a fourth government activity, the management of public debt (G_d), that includes both making current interest payments and issuing sufficient bonds to cover any shortfall in current revenues. The various aspects of the government sector are summarized in Table 2-1.

G_p: Spending on Public Goods

In studying the fiscal impact of population growth and immigration, two characteristics of government spending on public goods are particularly relevant. First, relatively few of the goods produced by the government sector are pure public goods, in the sense that the cost of providing the same level of the good is invariant to the size of the population. Broadly speaking, we can therefore divide government expenditures on public goods into two stylized categories: *pure public goods* (P_p) that we define as goods subject to little or no crowding (e.g., national defense) and impure public goods or *public services* (P_S) that we define as goods that are subject to a substantial amount of crowding (public safety, education). This distinction is important in the analysis of the fiscal impact of population growth (through immigration or other means), because population growth entails additional spending only on public services. It should be kept in mind that crowding in public services can be *nonanonymous*, in which case not only the total number but the characteristics of those consuming the service

TABLE 2-1 Government Sector = (G_p, G_x, G_t, G_d)

Government Activity	Subcategory	Examples	Role in Fiscal Impact Study
G_p - "Public" Goods Production	P_P - Pure Public Goods	National Defense	Not Relevant
	P_S - Public Services		
	P_C - Public Cons.	Waste Disposal, Corrections,	ΔP_C from Increased Pop.
	P_I - Public Invest.	Education, Infrastructure	ΔP_I minus Future Benefit
			Note: Crowding may be *non-anonymous*, and *population externalities* may be a factor.
G_x - Transfers	X_Y - Income Based T.	Welfare, Medicaid	ΔX_Y (Single Period Analysis)
	X_{NY} - Age Based T.	Social Security, Medicare	ΔX_{NY} (Multiple Period)
G_t - Tax Revenues	$\tau_w W$ - Wage Tax	Payroll Tax, Pers. Income T.	Assumptions about tax incidence are important for taxpayer perspective; effect on tax bases matters for govt finance perspective
	$\tau_k rK$ - Capital Tax	Pers. Income T., Prop. Tax	
	$\tau_C C$ - Consumption Tax	General Sales Tax	
	$\tau_e C_e$ -Excise Tax	Tobacco, Gas, Alcohol, Housing	
G_d - Debt Management	rD - Interest Expense		Not Relevant

matter. For example, some school children require more resources than others. Also, *population externalities* of new population groups may be negative or positive, causing previous levels of services to become more or less expensive for the original population. (In public schools, for example, peer effects are thought to play an important role in school outcomes. Thus, the introduction of a "bad" peer group requires additional resources to keep the quality of schooling the same for the original population.)

Second, studies on the fiscal impact of immigration must recognize that some public services are *investments* from the government's and the native taxpayer's perspectives in the sense that current expenditures on these services increase future tax receipts from the immigrant populations. Based on the degree of investment involved, we subdivide the category of public services into *public consumption services* (P_C) and *public investment services* (P_I). Spending on public education, for example, can be thought of as an input in the production process that provides skills to the current J generation which then has implications for the distribution of skill levels in the future M generation work force. A higher-skilled labor force in the future implies higher incomes and consumption levels as well as increased savings and capital accumulation, all of which are taxed by the government. Spending on education therefore entails current costs and future benefits for the government sector, which implies that the long-run net fiscal impact of this type of spending differs from its instantaneous short-run impact on current government budgets. Other types of public services, such as most municipal services, serve primarily as current consumption and contain little or no investment.

Government spending on public goods (G_p) is therefore divided (on the basis of crowding) into spending on pure public goods (P_P) and spending on public services (P_S), and public services are further divided (on the basis of the degree of investment) into public consumption (P_C) and investment (P_I) services. Although the degree and kind of crowding (and the resulting distinction between pure public goods and public services) have implications regarding *which* types of government expenditures to consider in calculating costs of immigration, the degree of investment in public service activity (and the resulting distinction between P_C and P_I) have implications regarding *how* such costs must enter the analysis.

G_x: Spending on Transfers

Much of today's government activity, however, has little to do with providing public goods and services and merely involves transfers from one population group to another. Transfer payments can be in the form of cash payments (Social Security, welfare), in-kind programs (Medicare, Medicaid, food stamps), or implicit tax exemptions (home mortgage deductions). In general, they fall into one of two broad categories: *income-based transfers* (X_Y) and *non-income-based transfers* (X_{NY}). Income-based transfers include general assistance programs for the poor (Medicaid, food stamps) but may also include transfers to middle-class taxpayers in the form of such tax expenditures as the home mortgage deduction. Non-income-based transfers, on the other hand, include mainly programs that transfer resources based on age (such as Social Security and Medicare). The distinction between these two categories of transfers will become particularly relevant when we discuss the difference between general population growth and selective population growth through immigration.

G_t: Tax Revenues

Our model includes four broad categories of taxes: taxes on *wages* (W), *rents* (rK), *general sales* or consumption (C), and *consumption of specific goods* (C_e). Each of these activities is taxed at a specific rate (τ_w, τ_k, τ_s, and τ_e, respectively), yielding total tax revenues

$$T = \tau_w W + \tau_k rK + \tau_s C + \tau_e C_e.$$

In the United States, most tax revenues come from personal income taxes, payroll taxes, corporate income taxes, general sales taxes, excise taxes, and property taxes, each of which can be viewed as a combination of the taxes introduced above. Personal income taxes are generally assumed to fall on W and K, payroll taxes on W, and corporate income taxes on K (i.e., on all capital, not just corporate capital). General sales taxes are borne by consumers in proportion to their total expenditures on C, whereas excise taxes are borne by those consumers who consume C_e. (See Pechman, 1985, for a detailed discussion of assumptions leading to these tax incidence implications.) Finally, the property tax is borne by K, C, and W (see Mieszkowski and Zodrow, 1983; Aaron, 1975; Hamilton, 1975).

G_d: Closing the Government Sector with Public Debt Management

For the accounting identities to hold, we also include interest payments on current debt (r*D where D is the value of outstanding government debt) as one of the expenditures incurred by the government sector. Furthermore, deficit financing (ΔD) covers any shortfall between current government revenues and expenses. Thus, total government revenues are equal to ($T+\Delta D$), whereas total government expenditures are equal to ($P_P + P_I + P_C + X_Y + X_{NY} + rD$). By definition,

$$T+\Delta D = P_P + P_I + P_C + X_Y + X_{NY} + rD.$$

For simplicity, from now on we assume that the government budget is balanced ($\Delta D = 0$) in each period, although we allow for the existence of debt (D>0) and interest payments (rD>0).

The Role of Costs and Benefits in Fiscal Impact
Studies of Population Growth

To determine the net fiscal impact of immigration (or any type of population change) within the context of the model presented above, three important elements must be explicitly addressed: (1) the definition of "costs" and "benefits," (2) the role of multiple periods in the analysis, and (3) the perspectives of different levels of governments in a federal system. Some conclusions regarding the first two issues are summarized in the last column of Table 2-1; those relating to the federal nature of the U.S. government sector are summarized below in Table 2-5.

Definition of Costs and Benefits

Our task in this chapter is to describe the fiscal consequences of changing population sizes and characteristics. The first critical step in this endeavor involves explicitly defining both the benefits and the costs of population changes. Fiscal impact studies have implicitly used different combinations of benefit and cost definitions, resulting in impact estimates that differ both in size and in interpretation. Costs, for example, have been defined as either

(1) the increase in total government expenditures resulting from the population change or
(2) the cost of government goods and services consumed by the new population,

whereas benefits have been defined as either

(1') the increase in total tax revenues resulting from the population change or
(2') the value of taxes paid by the new population group.

If all government expenditures were pure transfers (X_Y and X_{NY}), definitions (1) and (2) would be identical; that is, the cost of the transfers to the new population group would be exactly equal to the increase in the total government budget. Suppose, however, that the government also produces pure public goods (P_P). Then a population increase does not increase costs as defined by (1) but it does entail costs as defined by (2). Thus, some fiscal impact studies count part of national defense spending, for example, as a cost of immigration, whereas others do not. Similarly, the first definition of benefits ignores tax incidence and is concerned only with the impact on overall tax revenues (and thus the impact on tax bases), whereas the second definition concerns itself with the amount of taxes actually *paid* by the new population. Thus, the latter definition of benefits must be explicit about tax incidence assumptions.

Different combinations of these definitions not only lead to vastly different fiscal impact estimates, but they also view the problem from very different perspectives. Table 2-2 summarizes these perspectives. From a government finance

TABLE 2-2   Summary of Perspectives

| Expenditures | Revenues | |
	Definition (1')	Definition (2')
Definition (1)	Government Finance Perspective	Native Taxpayer Perspective
Definition (2)		New Taxpayer Perspective

perspective, for example, the benefit of a population change is simply the increase in tax revenues resulting from this change, whereas the cost is the increase in government expenditures. Thus,

Net Benefit to Government = (1') − (1).

On the other hand, from the native taxpayers' point of view, the *net* benefit of a population change is the difference between after-tax income with and without the population change (assuming government services for the original population remain constant). This involves both the change in before-tax incomes and the change in taxes paid by the native population, where the latter is a function of the increase in government expenses due to the new population minus the tax revenues *paid* by that population. In the case of immigration, for example, the net benefit to native taxpayers involves both the effect of immigration on native incomes and the additional tax burden (which may be negative) incurred by natives to finance the net fiscal drain (which may similarly be negative) of immigrants on the government. Thus,

Net Benefit to Taxpayers = Δ(Native Before-Tax Incomes) + (2') − (1).

Finally, the fiscal impact on the new population could also be considered. In the case of immigration, this involves comparing incomes of immigrants in the United States with the incomes the immigrants would have earned in their native countries. More precisely, the fiscal impact of immigration from this perspective is equal to the change in the immigrants' before-tax income resulting from immigration plus the net benefit they receive from government services; that is,

Net Benefit to Immigrants = Δ(Immigrant Before-Tax Incomes) + (2) − (2').[1]

Because the stated purpose of most fiscal impact studies of immigration is to calculate the net fiscal impact of immigration on U.S. taxpayers or government finances, definition (1) is the appropriate definition of costs (as it appears in both the "Net Government Benefit" and the "Net Taxpayer Benefit" equations). This implies that *pure public goods (P_p) and interest on debt (rD) are not relevant to calculating the fiscal impact of immigration* because the addition of further popu-

---

[1]This assumes that the immigrants would be obtaining zero net benefit from the tax/expenditure system in their country of origin.

lation groups does not add to those government expenditures. Therefore, out of total government expenditures $(P_P+P_I+P_C+X_Y+X_{NY}+rD)$ only public services (P_I+P_C) and transfers (X_Y+X_{NY}) represent legitimate categories of government expenses to be counted as costs of population growth (and immigration).

Although the definition of costs is the same from either the taxpayer or the government finance perspective, the definition of benefits differs between the two. The first definition (1') ignores tax incidence and focuses on total tax receipts, whereas the second definition (2') ignores total tax receipts and focuses on tax incidence. Most fiscal studies of immigration attempt to ascertain the impact on taxpayers rather than on government finances, which implies that (2') is usually the appropriate definition of benefits. Still, fiscal impact studies have also been commissioned by local and state governments that may be more interested in the final impact on balance sheets rather than the degree to which immigrants are actually paying for additional tax revenues. In the former case, assumptions about tax incidence matter, whereas in the latter case assumptions about behavioral changes leading to tax base changes matter.

The Need for Multi-Period Analysis

It is inappropriate to view the fiscal impact of population changes and immigration in a static one-period model. The age of the new population group has important implications for its impact on the economy (and thus the income of the current population) as well as its net impact on government finances. The three age groups in our model (J, M, E) each play a different role in the economy. To calculate the benefits and costs of an increase in any one of these age groups, both the present and the future must be taken into account—unless the increase occurs among E (who have no future role in the economy) or there is an expectation that the increased population will ultimately leave the economy before it becomes part of E (by returning to their country of origin, for example). We consider the impact of population growth among the three age groups in some detail in the third section of this chapter. For now, we merely stress the necessity of a multi-period analysis on both the expenditure and the revenue sides, given populations of different ages.

Table 2-3 divides major areas of government expenditure into the broad categories defined in our model, indicating the age groups the spending programs mainly target. It is clear from the table that public consumption services are rarely age specific, whereas public investment services can be age specific, particularly education programs. Similarly, the bulk of income-based transfers—in terms of budgetary outlays, Medicaid—are not age specific, whereas the non-income-based transfer programs generally are age specific. In principle then, most of P_C and X_Y could be analyzed within single periods. These expenditures are consumed today with few implications for the future (except that those con-

TABLE 2-3   Public Expenditures by All Levels of Government

Government Activity	Specific to J	Specific to M	Specific to E	Not Age Specific
P_P - Pure Public Goods				National Defense
				Int. Relations
P_C - Public Consumption Services				Environment
				Govt. Administ.
				Judiciary,
				Corrections,
				Police, Fire,
				Municipal
				Services
P_I - Public Investment Services	Education Head Start Tuition Subsidies	Job Training		Infrastructure
X_Y - Income Based Transfers	AFDC Child Nutrition (Head Start) (Tuition Subsidies)	AFDC Job Training		SSI, Medicaid Food Stamps Housing Assistance
X_{NY} - Non-Income Based Transfers	(Education)	Unemployment	Social Security Medicare Retirement Benefits	

suming income-based transfers today may be more likely to also consume them tomorrow).

Non-income-based transfers (X_{NY}), on the other hand, generally occur only in one specific period during the lifetime of an agent. In the case of Social Security, for example, if the growth in the population occurs in M, there is no Social Security expense today, but there will be an additional expense tomorrow when today's M becomes tomorrow's E. If new members of the M generation remain in the country as they become elderly, their expected future Social Security benefits must clearly be considered.

Similarly, public investment services (P_I) involve expense today, but the government sector will receive additional tax revenues in the future as a direct result of the expense. Thus, spending on education for J, for example, costs today but produces higher incomes (and thus income tax revenues) in the future when today's J becomes tomorrow's M. The share of P_I to be counted as a cost of population growth in J must therefore be reduced by the expected (discounted) future payoff from this expense. Expenditures on both public investment services and non-income-based transfers thus require a multi-period perspective.

The need for this multi-period perspective becomes even clearer when revenues and expenditures are considered simultaneously. On the revenue side, Table 2-4 divides U.S. taxes into the categories in our model based on the genera-

TABLE 2-4   Major Taxes for All Levels of Government

Government Activity	Specfic to J	Specific to M	Specific to E	Not Age Specific
Wage (W) Tax		Personal Income Tax Payroll Tax (Property Tax)		
Capital (K) Tax		Personal Income Tax Property Tax Corporate Income Tax	Personal Income Tax Property Tax Corporate Income Tax Estate Tax	
Consumption (C) Tax				General Sales Tax (Property Tax)
Excise (C$_e$) Tax		Alcohol, Tobacco Products	Alcohol, Tobacco Products	Gasoline, Tariffs

NOTE: Those publicly provided services that are funded directly through user fees can be left out of the analysis if neither the expense nor the user fee is counted. Examples include postal services, utilities, some public parks, etc.

tions that pay the taxes. Note that the J generation pays little tax although it consumes large categories of expenditures (education in particular). Yet it would clearly be unreasonable to argue that an increase in the J population carries with it only costs and no benefits for the current population. On the other hand, the M generation pays a large share of total taxes (payroll taxes in particular) while consuming few large budget expenditures. Finally, the E generation, although still paying a substantial amount in taxes, consumes the bulk of non-income-based transfers.

In general, tax payments from new populations and government expenditures caused by their presence are not well matched over time. The total tax benefit of population growth in any particular generation involves the calculation of tax payments as the generation passes through all age groups, especially through M into E, parallel to the multi-period calculation on the expenditure side.

Finally, from the perspective of both the government and the native taxpayer, the fiscal impact of immigration is linked closely to the future path of current tax bases. From the government perspective, tax bases matter because changes in these bases change expected tax revenues. From the taxpayer perspective, changes in bases matter in the sense that they involve changes in the before-tax incomes of current residents. An increase in the J population today, for example, has implications concerning the path of consumption, savings, and incomes in the future. These considerations are by definition multi-period in nature and are discussed further in the third section of this chapter.

The View from Different Levels of Government in a Federal System

Until now, we have discussed government as one unitary sector. In the United States, of course, the government sector is divided among federal, state, and local branches, each of which has different expenditure priorities and revenue bases. Furthermore, a complex web of fiscal interaction among the different levels of government has evolved (and is continuing to evolve). Fiscal impact studies will therefore differ depending on whether they are undertaken from a local, state, or national perspective. For brevity and conceptual clarity, we distinguish here between only lower-level (local) and higher-level (national) governments. There are three fundamental aspects in which the analysis differs for these two levels of government. First, local governments are subject to migration pressures whereas higher-level governments are relatively immune to such forces. Second, intergovernmental transfers create additional costs and benefits for the different levels of government. Third, generally speaking, each level of government does not account for the impact its activities have on the other levels of government. Conclusions from this section are summarized in Table 2-5.

Migration. Migration (of individuals as well as capital) is the central issue studied by economists who focus on local public finance. For our purposes, internal migration is important for the calculation of both costs and benefits of

TABLE 2-5　The View from Different Levels of Government in a Federal System

	Level of Government	
	Lower Level	Higher Level
Migration	Multi-period analysis for P_I, X_{NY}, and tax revenue becomes problematic as new populations may migrate in the future. Migration of existing tax bases may exacerbate externalities	Multi-period analysis for P_I, X_{NY}, and tax revenue becomes problematic as new populations may exit the country in the future.
Intergovernmental Transfers	Additional revenue source for grants that are based on population sizes and characteristics	Additional cost for grants that are based on population sizes and characteristics
Intergovernmental Externalities	Discount P_I by future tax benefits only to the extent that future *local* tax revenues rise as a result of P_I	Discount P_I by future tax benefits only to the extent that future *national* tax revenues rise as a result of P_I

immigration to local governments and taxpayers. On the cost side, P_P, rD, P_C, and X_Y are treated exactly as they have been up until now, but P_I and X_{NY} are now treated differently because of their multi-period nature. More precisely, P_I may involve investments that yield future increases in tax payments, but, at the time that those future tax payments are made, the new population member may no longer reside in the local jurisdiction that incurred the expense. In that case, from the local perspective, P_I then becomes a public consumption service (P_C). Public education serves as a good example. A local school district may invest resources to educate an immigrant child. But by the time the child becomes an adult who pays more in taxes due to higher skills resulting from the education received, he will likely reside outside that school district. In fact, because mobility increases with education, the more the local government invests, the less likely it is to see a future tax benefit from this investment.

Similarly, some elements of X_{NY} require a revised analysis because their multi-period nature affects the different levels of government differently. For example, if an immigrant arrives in the M generation and returns to his original country in the E generation, the national government's costs will be considerably less than it would have been had he or she not returned—there will be no outlays for Social Security or Medicare in his old age.

Similar issues arise on the benefit side. Generally, a multi-period calculation of expected tax revenues from the new population is appropriate, but local governments cannot as easily count on the new population remaining in its jurisdiction throughout the population's life cycle. In addition, the migration of *current* tax bases must be considered. An increase in a certain population group within one local jurisdiction may cause a native population group to leave for another jurisdiction or may attract new native populations into the jurisdiction. Such migrations of native populations may increase negative or positive externality (peer) effects. Consider the impact of the addition of "low" peer group students into a local school district. This increases the cost of maintaining the same quality local public schooling and may cause some "high" peer group students to opt for different school districts or private schools. The exit of this peer group then worsens the initial negative externality of the population change.

Intergovernmental Transfers. The existence of intergovernmental transfers (typically from higher- to lower-level governments) creates additional revenue and cost sources not represented in the unitary government sector analysis (as in Table 2-1). Block grants that are invariant to population size clearly are unaffected by increases in population groups in certain geographic areas, but grants that are based on population size and characteristics (per pupil state aid, for example) may be affected by immigration.[2] With these intergovernmental transfers in the model, the

---

[2] A well-publicized debate concerning the extent to which certain types of support such as welfare should be provided to immigrants is currently ongoing.

arrival of additional population groups creates additional revenues for local governments and additional costs for national (or state) governments. From a higher-level government perspective, these are real costs of immigration that must be included in the analysis, whereas from a local government perspective, they represent revenues that are just as real. Averaging over taxpayers, the two cancel out, and the unitary government approach is still appropriate.

Intergovernmental Externalities. Finally we return to the treatment of public investment services (P_I). Even in the absence of migration effects, the treatment of P_I from the perspective of any particular level of government is different from the treatment of P_I from the perspective of an average taxpayer in the sense that each level of government will underestimate the investment impact of the public service. That is, even in the absence of migration, both the lower- and higher-level government perspectives dictate that the current expense of P_I on the new population be discounted only to the extent that the investment generates future tax revenues for *that* level of government. An average taxpayer perspective, on the other hand, would count the investment impact on *all* levels of government.

FISCAL CONSEQUENCES OF POPULATION GROWTH

The model we provided in the second section sets up our framework for evaluating the consequences of population growth. We need to account for two distinct effects: the *direct effects* of population change on government expenditures and tax revenues and the *indirect effects* of population change on tax bases through its effects on wages, consumption, and savings. The indirect impact on tax bases is important from both the taxpayer and the government perspective (as was outlined above). From the perspective of native taxpayers, the underlying changes in wages, consumption, and savings alter the before-tax incomes of the native population. From the perspective of the government, the resulting tax base change alters the size of total tax revenues. We return in this discussion to the view of government as a unitary sector, with the understanding that the factors discussed above in the second section are important when considering the fiscal impact on particular levels of government.

We begin our evaluation of the fiscal impact of population growth with a benchmark case in which population growth is neutral, that is, it has no net fiscal impact. We derive six conditions for this neutrality result. In the remainder of this section we discuss the key role of each of these six conditions. Table 2-6 summarizes these results.

A Benchmark Case

Our model contains three different generations (J, M, and E) and two different types of workers (who make up the M generation). Altogether, the population

TABLE 2-6   Impact on Per Capita Expenditures and Per Capita Revenues

Condition Violated	Impact on Per Capita Expenditures		Impact on Per Capita Revenues	
	Current Period	Future Period	Current Period	Future Period
Condition (1)				
- $P_P>0$ or $rD>0$	Decrease	Decrease	No Change	No Change
Condition (2)				
- IRS	No Change (or decrease)	No Change (or increase)	Increase	Increase
- DRS	No change (or increase)	No Change (or increase)	Decrease	Decrease
Condition (3)				
- MC of P_S rising	Increase	Increase	No Change	No Change
- MC of P_S falling	Decrease	Decrease	No Change	No Change
Condition (4)				
- Higher Savings	No Change	Ambiguous	Decrease	Increase
- Lower Savings	No Change	Ambiguous	Increase	Decrease
Condition (5)				
- High Skills	Decrease in X_Y Ambiguous ΔP_I	Decrease in X_Y, Increase in X_{NY}	Increase	Increase
- Low Skills	Increase in X_Y Ambiguous ΔP_I	Increase in X_Y, Decrease in X_{NY}	Decrease	Decrease
Condition (6)				
- J - the young	Increase in P_I, X_Y Decrease in X_{NY}	Decrease in P_I Decrease in X_{NY}	Decrease	Increase
- M - the middle aged	Decrease in P_I Decrease in X_{NY}	Decrease in P_I Increase in X_{NY}	Increase	Ambiguous
- E- the elderly	Decrease in P_I Increase in X_{NY}	No Change	Ambiguous	None

consists of four types: the young (J), unskilled middle-aged workers (l), skilled middle-aged workers (h), and the elderly (E). If all four population groups increase in the same proportion, and if the consumption and savings behavior of the new population is identical to that of the original population, then capital (K) will also increase by the same proportion as the population groups. (The new members of M have the same savings behavior, and the new members of E bring equivalent levels of K with them and draw on their savings in the same manner as the existing E generation.)

If the production function *(f)* is constant returns to scale, total income (Y) increases by the same proportion as the population, and, because capital per worker remains the same, wage income per worker (for both high- and low-skilled labor) remains constant. Therefore, W grows in the same proportion as the population, as does the capital income (rK).

With the consumption patterns of the new population identical to those of the original population, equal income implies identical consumption behavior. This in turn implies that C and C_e also rise in the same proportions as the population. Thus, when population growth is uniform and the new population shares the behavior patterns of the old, and when the aggregate production function has constant returns to scale, all tax bases stay the same in per capita terms.

If, in addition, the marginal cost of providing public consumption and investment services to additional agents is constant and equal to average cost, then P_C, P_I, X_Y, and X_{NY} also rise in exact proportion to the population. Because P_P and rD remain unaffected by increases in the population, uniform population growth then has the net fiscal benefit of helping to fund the "fixed cost" of pure public goods and payments on the debt. As spending on P_P and rD goes to zero, this net fiscal benefit also goes to zero. We therefore arrive at the following observation:

Neutrality Proposition

If (1) spending on pure public goods and interest on the debt is zero;

(2) the aggregate production function (f) has constant returns to scale;

(3) the marginal cost of providing public services to additional agents of similar type (J, l, h, and E) is constant and equal to average cost;

(4) the consumption and savings patterns of the new population are identical to those of the original population;

(5) population growth of workers is uniform in l and h; and

(6) population growth is uniform in J, M, and E, then the net fiscal benefit of population growth is zero.

In the remainder of this section, we investigate the consequences of relaxing each of the conditions above in the context of the model developed in the second section. We first maintain the assumption of completely uniform population growth [conditions (5) and (6)] and consider the impact of weakening the economic conditions, (1) through (4). This is the task in the following subsection. We then turn to the immigration case, investigating the consequences of weakening the uniform population growth assumptions. In particular, we consider in the subsection on "condition (5)" a nonuniform change in the skill distribution within the M generation, a violation of condition (5). Then in the subsection on "condition (6)" we analyze the impact of a nonuniform change in the age distribution, a violation of condition (6).

Uniform Increase in Population

In this subsection, we consider violations of the first four conditions of the neutrality proposition, still assuming uniform population growth across J, l, h, and E. As we consider each of the four violations in turn, we assume that the other three conditions hold. First, we relax only the assumption of zero spending on pure public goods and on interest on debt. Second, we relax the assumption of constant returns to scale technology. Third, we allow for differences in the marginal cost of providing public services to the old and new populations. And finally, we allow for differences in the consumption and savings behavior of the old and new populations.

Condition (1): Expenditures on Pure Public Goods and Interest on the Debt

What is the fiscal effect of a new population group if the government has positive expenditures either on debt interest payments (rD) or on projects with a pure public good (P_p) component [assuming neutrality conditions (2) through (6) continue to hold]? As already noted, because these government expenditures are not subject to crowding, they can be viewed as "fixed" expenditures. (Note that interest payments on the debt are, in this sense, identical to expenditures on pure public goods.) Given no change in the private side of the economy, uniform population growth then leaves per person tax revenues unchanged while per person government expenditures fall. These facts together imply that the introduction of a new population has a net fiscal benefit.

Condition (2): Returns to Scale

Now consider replacing the assumption of a constant returns to scale technology with one of an increasing returns to scale technology, leaving all other assumptions in place. As population growth increases the scale of production, productivity and thus real wages and rents increase. Income rises for both the M generation (earning W) and the E generation (receiving rK). Current consumption rises for E, as the elderly consume out of rents. Both current consumption and savings increase for M.

In this scenario, the tax base, consisting of W, rK, and C, grows faster than the population. (C_0 definitely increases whereas C_e increases unless these goods are inferior.) Because savings increase, future tax revenues from rK also increase. Therefore, from both the government and the original taxpayer perspective, increasing returns to scale technology means that uniform population growth will have a positive net fiscal impact in both the current and the future period.[3] The opposite is true for the case of decreasing returns to scale.

Condition (3): The Marginal Cost of Providing Public Services

Next we consider violating condition (3) again with all other neutrality conditions met. This condition could be violated either because of the presence of a

---

[3]An additional secondary effect is that the demand for certain government activities (such as income-based transfers) declines as incomes rise.

fixed cost to providing the public service (in which case the average cost per person is declining even if the marginal cost is constant) or because the marginal cost is not constant. Any fixed-cost component to providing the public service is identical to a pure public goods component and can therefore be considered a violation of condition (1) (discussed above.) We therefore consider here violations of condition (3) that involve zero fixed costs; that is, we focus on cases in which the marginal cost of extending public services to new populations is not constant. Clearly, if marginal costs rise as populations increase, the net fiscal impact of population growth becomes negative, and if marginal costs fall as populations increase, the net fiscal impact of growth is positive (assuming that all other neutrality conditions hold).

Marginal costs may be nonconstant for many reasons. We consider here three cases in which this is true. First, the input cost schedules faced by local governments may be either increasing or decreasing. For example, suppose that a local government provides a service that requires inputs that it purchases from private providers that offer quantity discounts. Then the marginal cost of providing the service may decline as population increases because input prices fall as the population rises. Conversely, input prices may rise due to a scarcity of resources.

Second, the technology of producing the public service may be such that marginal costs are nonconstant even if input prices are constant. Suppose a school building in a local school district can accommodate additional students, but it becomes increasingly difficult as the student population increases. Then the marginal cost of extending services rises because of the nature (technology) of the public service.[4]

In the previous two cases, population changes cause changes in marginal costs regardless of the particular characteristics of the populations themselves. In the third case, the new population groups may have characteristics that require greater or fewer expenditures. For example, consider a rise in per pupil costs of public education because the new population requires special services, such as bilingual education. Then the higher marginal costs are a direct result of the new population's characteristics (lack of native language skills). The role of such differential characteristics that impact the degree of crowding in public services is discussed in more detail in the fourth section of this chapter.[5]

---

[4]If, in addition, there is some critical threshold after which a new school must be built, the marginal cost of accommodating additional students in classrooms may drop before it rises again as the student population increases further. Thus, the marginal cost may rise until it drops sharply only to rise again. Threshold effects of this kind are discussed further in the fourth section of this chapter.

[5]If the new and old populations are distinguishable, it is feasible to treat them as different population types even if they are otherwise identical to the original population. In this case, political mandates may alter the marginal costs of providing services to the new population. For example, legislation such as California's Proposition 187 and recent welfare and immigration reforms prohibit certain immigrant groups (i.e., illegal immigrants) from using many public services. If enforced, such legislation could effectively reduce to zero the marginal cost of these public services for the new population group.

Finally, we note that there are other examples of changing marginal costs that are not violations of condition (3). Condition (3) requires that the marginal cost of providing public services is constant *for each population type (i.e., J, l, h, and E),* which implies that the increase in the cost of providing public services as a whole remains constant so long as population growth is uniform. Nonuniform population growth will necessarily entail different changes in the overall cost of providing public services because some services are targeted specifically at certain generations (as, for example, education) (see Table 2-3). This, however, does not violate condition (3) but rather conditions (5) and (6).

Condition (4): Differing Consumption and Savings Patterns

Suppose again that all other neutrality conditions hold, but that the new population has different savings and consumption patterns from the native population—a violation of condition (4). This could manifest itself in three different ways: first, the new population may have either a higher or a lower propensity to save. Second, the new population may have higher or lower initial capital holdings. And third, the new population may engage in consumption (or savings) outside the national economy (for example, some immigrant groups send substantial funds to families in their original countries). In the last case, whereas taxes on W are unaffected, tax revenues on consumption (or capital) will be lower and the fiscal impact of the population growth will be negative. We concentrate here, however, on the first two cases and will assume for now that the new population consumes and saves exclusively in the domestic economy.

First, suppose that the new population has a higher propensity to save. Recall in our model that current income is divided between current consumption and savings which become next period's capital. Therefore, the dynamic nature of our model becomes important when condition (4) does not hold. In the first period, per capita consumption is lower as per capita savings rise. Because the current supplies of labor and capital are unaffected by this savings decision, there is no effect on wages or rents. Therefore, the current tax revenues, based on W, rK, and C, decline per capita and the new population appears to incur net fiscal costs. However, this decision also has a fiscal impact in the next period. K is now higher than it would have been. As long as the supply of labor is unchanged, the assumption of constant returns to scale technology (and perfect competition) means that production will rise, but the relative increase in K compared with L will lower rents (r) and raise wages (W). Overall, income and thus tax revenues will rise, although the original now-elderly generation will have lower income than they would have otherwise (because their contribution to K is unchanged but rents have fallen). Conversely, M generation workers will have higher incomes than they would have otherwise. In this way, total tax revenues rise in the future period but the income shares and thus tax incidence change.[6] Combining the effects for the two periods, the future increase in income tax (and sales tax) revenues should outweigh the current loss in sales taxes. The opposite conclusion holds if the new population has a higher propensity to consume. By the same logic, current sales tax revenues rise, but future production falls, the future elderly are better off, future workers are worse off, and future income and sales tax revenues are lowered by more than this period's gain.

Second, suppose that the new population holds more capital at the beginning of the period than the original population. Then effects in the current period will be similar to the effects described in the above paragraph for the next period. In other words, if per worker capital rises this period, wages (W) rise and rents (r) fall. Overall income and tax revenues rise in the current period, but the elderly among the original population will be worse off (because of lower rents), whereas workers in the M generation will be better off. The opposite clearly holds if the new population arrives with lower capital holdings than the original population.

Condition (5): Nonuniform Increase in Low- and High-Skilled Workers

Until now we have considered only uniform population growth. That is, we have assumed that the entering population is identical to the original population along all relevant dimensions. In the terms of our model, the relevant characteristics are age and skill mix. However, many concerns about immigration arise precisely out of the differences (in these dimensions) between the immigrant and the native populations. Here and in the following subsection we relax the uniform population growth assumptions in conditions (5) and (6), again maintaining all other neutrality conditions.

First, we evaluate the impact of population growth that is nonuniform in the skill levels of workers. Although population grows uniformly *across* generations, the proportion of generation M that has a high level of skills (h) grows faster than the proportion that has a low level of skills (l). We use this example throughout this subsection; however, the results are essentially symmetric if we reverse high skilled and low skilled.

High-skilled workers differ from low-skilled workers in one key way: they have higher marginal productivity and higher wages. In the current period, this means their income is higher and thus their consumption and savings are also likely to be higher. From a government perspective, they generate higher income

---

[6]The impact this has on government expenditures is ambiguous. In the current period, little change in per capita expenditures will occur because wages and incomes remain constant. In the next period, however, the elderly are worse off whereas the middle aged are better off. This may either increase or decrease government spending per person depending on the relative magnitude of these effects.

and sales tax revenues but they are ineligible for income-based transfers (X_Y). If they consume public services in equal proportion to the rest of the population, this implies that high-skilled workers are greater net contributors than the average taxpayer. This conclusion is even more certain if taxes are progressive. Therefore, a disproportionate increase in high-skilled workers is a net fiscal benefit in the current period so long as their use of public services is similar to the rest of the population.[7]

The impact of high-skilled workers, however, goes beyond their own income. To the degree that high-skilled workers are complements for low-skilled workers and for capital, the disproportionate increase in high-skilled workers will lower the wages of the native high-skilled workers, raise the wages of low-skilled workers, and raise the rents accruing to the elderly. This will have an additional benefit for tax revenues, tempered by the lower income of the native high-skilled population. Income inequality is also reduced.

Higher income today also has a number of impacts in the future. First, higher savings today increase future capital, which implies that an increase in the proportion of high-skilled workers increases future income for the elderly and for next period's workers (following the argument in "condition (4)" above). Today's M generation also provides for the consumption of the young. Because socioeconomic background is a crucial predictor of a child's success, we may also expect the children of high-skilled parents to be disproportionately likely to be high skilled themselves. If so, this factor augments the beneficial fiscal impact of today's high-skilled workers in future periods. Finally, to the extent that higher-income workers are entitled to higher Social Security benefits in the future, transfer payments to the elderly in the next period will increase by a greater proportion than current population growth.[8]

Condition (6): Nonuniform Increase Among Age Groups

Our model also permits population growth to be nonuniform across the three generations. Here we hold to conditions (1) through (5), but now relax the final condition and consider differential growth across J, M, and E. We first investi-

---

[7]The main public service that may be consumed in greater proportion by the high skilled is public education for their children. On the one hand, their children are likely to provide positive externalities due to their peer quality. This would mean that lower per pupil spending would yield similar quality education for the original population. On the other hand, high-skilled parents are likely to demand better schools and are thus likely to settle in high-spending school districts. This would imply that additional spending on public schools may increase in greater proportions than if population growth was uniform. Whether total spending on public services rises faster or slower than population growth is therefore ambiguous. For a more detailed discussion on problems in determining education expenditures due to immigration, see "Disproportionately Large Increases in J" below.

[8]The overall impact on the Social Security system, however, is likely to be positive because the increase in payroll taxes in the current period is likely to outweigh the increase in Social Security obligations in the next period. See, for example, Boskin et al. (1987).

gate the impact of higher growth rates in E, then consider higher growth rates in M and finally in J. We look in some detail at the special issues regarding the fiscal impact of education funding.

Disproportionately Large Increases in E

Suppose all population growth occurred among the elderly. Looking back at Tables 2-3 and 2-4, it is easy to see which expenditures and taxes are affected. On the tax side, the elderly pay taxes on capital (K) and consumption (C, C_e) but not on wages (W). Whether this implies an increase in overall tax revenues that is larger or smaller than the rate of population growth is unclear. It depends on the rise in capital that accompanies the increase in E as well as the consumption patterns of the new members of the E generation.[9] Furthermore, the extent to which the inflow of additional K increases income and thus tax revenues from current residents similarly depends on the size of the increase in K (as discussed above).

On the expenditure side, the elderly use public consumption services in proportions similar to the rest of the population but crowd public investment services (particularly education services) significantly less. On the other hand, they receive disproportionately large transfers, especially the non-income-based transfers that are almost exclusively paid to E (Social Security, Medicare). An increase in E therefore implies disproportionately *lower increases in spending on public services* (in particular public investment services) and disproportionately *higher spending on transfer payments*. Overall, whether the net fiscal impact of a disproportionate increase in E is positive or negative is an empirical issue.

Disproportionately Large Increases in M

Now suppose instead that population growth occurred entirely in the M generation (and that the skill proportions in the population remain constant). Again, Tables 2-3 and 2-4 help us determine the immediate fiscal impact of disproportionate growth in M. On the revenue side, members of M pay taxes on the largest tax bases in the model, particular payroll taxes on W. On the expenditure side, whereas M is likely to crowd public consumption services in similar proportions to the rest of the population, members of M cause less crowding in public investment services (receiving no education). They also receive government transfers in significantly smaller proportions than people from other generations (because income-based transfers are relatively minor in size compared with the non-income-based transfers for E). Thus, in the current period, an increase in M requires proportionately fewer government expenditures, but disproportionately increasing government revenues.

---

[9]The relatively large role of payroll taxes, however, makes it likely that overall tax revenues from the elderly are substantially smaller than those from the M generation.

In the next period, however, the M generation becomes the E generation, and all the issues discussed for the elderly apply. In particular, an increase in the M generation today implies a disproportionately large increase in E in the future. This brings with it a disproportionately large increase in non-income-based transfer payments (Social Security, Medicare) in the next period as well as a likely decline in revenues (as the generation ceases earning wages and paying taxes on W).

In addition to the direct effects considered above, however, there may be significant indirect effects of disproportionate population growth in the M generation. In particular, although we have assumed throughout most of this chapter that M begins with no capital holdings and generates growth in capital through its savings, population growth in M (through selective immigration) may increase K as the immigrant group brings capital with them. In the former scenario in which the new M population starts without any capital holdings, the growth in the M generation increases the labor supply unaccompanied by an increase in K. As discussed under "condition (4)" above, the marginal product of labor falls and the wages of the original population are depressed. This causes declines in the (per person) tax base W (important for the government perspective) and declines in the incomes of native M residents (important for the taxpayer perspective), although it increases the rents received by E. In the latter scenario in which the new M population brings new capital holdings, however, a growth in M may be accompanied by substantial growth in K, which may mitigate or offset these effects. The growth in capital that accompanies the growth in the labor force M is therefore of potential importance.

Disproportionately Large Increases in J

Finally, suppose that the entire population growth occurs in J. Because the only taxes on the young are based on their consumption, tax revenues in the current period will grow less than the population growth rate. On the expenditure side, the young crowd public consumption services in similar proportions to the rest of the population. However, as the main recipients of public investment services (i.e., education), disproportionate growth in J clearly causes crowding in P_I. (We discuss this issue in detail below.) The young also consume a disproportionately large share of income-based transfers, although they consume little in the way of non-income-based transfers. A disproportionately large increase in J therefore implies a disproportionately large increase in government expenditures and a disproportionately small increase in government revenues in the current period.

In the future, however, the young become workers and eventually become the elderly. Thus, an increase in J today implies an increase in M in the next period and an increase in E two periods hence. Thus, in the next period the considerations suggested above in "Disproportionately Large Increases in M" become applicable, and in the period after that, the considerations above in

"Disportionately Large Increases in E" play a role. These multi-period effects all need to be taken into account in a fiscal impact study that attempts to find the present discounted fiscal benefits of population growth in J.

The Special Case of Education. Probably the most difficult task facing those conducting fiscal impact studies of population growth in general and growth of generation J in particular is to adequately treat expenditures on education. The difficulties arise from a lack of agreement in the education literature on the nature of the education production process as well as the presence of diverse and complicated public funding mechanisms. More precisely, researchers face three obstacles. First, varying estimates of the value added by education spending make it difficult to measure the expected future fiscal payoff from expanding educational services to the new population. Second, whether education is viewed as investment or consumption, crowding costs are difficult to estimate because of uncertainty regarding both the value added by spending and by peer quality. Third, because the financing of public education is shared by all levels of government (in ways that depend on the state or locality under consideration), cost estimates will vary depending on which government perspective is taken.

Overcoming the first two obstacles depends critically on an accurate measurement of the value added by public school spending. The degree to which current spending affects future wages is the key to any future fiscal benefits from educational expenditures. Furthermore, this measurement is crucial in determining the extent of additional resources needed when J increases to keep education quality constant for the original population.[10] For example, if class sizes were irrelevant in producing quality education, population growth in J could occur without the need for additional expenditures on teacher salaries. On the other hand, if class size mattered greatly, additional population growth would require hiring more faculty. Unfortunately, scholars studying primary and secondary education remain deeply divided regarding the role of financial resources in creating quality public education.[11]

---

[10]Strictly speaking, what is required to overcome the first obstacle differs from what is required to overcome the second. In particular, the *actual* value added by spending on public education is needed for the first obstacle, whereas *parental perceptions* regarding this quantity are needed for the second. That is, the extent to which additional spending on public education takes place (through the political process) clearly depends on parental perceptions regarding the value of public education spending. The extent to which this spending has future payoffs, on the other hand, depends on actual value added, not parental perceptions. We implicitly assume here that parental perceptions and actual value added coincide.

[11]Hanushek (1986) surveys the literature linking test scores to educational inputs and finds little evidence that public resources spent on primary and secondary education contribute significantly to educational outcomes. Parental socioeconomic status and education level seem to dominate. Card and Krueger (1992), on the other hand, find significant returns to public school spending in labor markets (which would imply higher income and consumption tax revenues in the future). Their conclusions, however, have been questioned in work by Betts (1995) and Heckman et al. (1996).

The likely existence of population externalities (peer effects) in education creates additional complexities. To estimate accurately the increase in current expenditures on education resulting from an increase in J, researchers must estimate the additional cost of public education *holding constant the quality of education received by the original population.* Even if financial inputs play a minor role, peer effects are widely speculated to be a significant input into the education production process. (Coleman, 1966, first highlighted this effect.) Thus, population growth in J may alter the inputs in the public school system simply because peer quality is one of those inputs. If, for example, population growth within J entailed positive externalities, then this population growth would reduce the cost of providing a given quality of education to the original population. Similarly, negative population externalities imply increasing per person expenditures to maintain the same quality. These externalities are generally thought to be positive for high-ability children (who come in disproportionate numbers from high-income households) and negative for low-ability children (who come in disproportionate numbers from low-income households), but the empirical literature is still far from agreement on the *magnitude* of these effects.[12]

Thus, although the role of both financial resources and peer quality in the education production process is controversial, assumptions in these areas are key in obtaining cost estimates for fiscal impact studies. To estimate the cost of extending public education to particular immigrant groups, these studies must *explicitly or implicitly* take a position on both peer effects and financial inputs. Given the unresolved state of the education debate, completeness may require studies to consider the fiscal impacts under several different assumptions about the role of both financial resources and peer effects in the education production process.[13]

Additional complications for fiscal impact studies arise out of the complex government interaction that produces public education in the United States. Different states have different degrees of centralization, with some financing education primarily at the local level and others financing all marginal expenses at the

---

[12]Summers and Wolfe (1977), for example, find evidence that less able students benefit from more able peers whereas high-ability students are not nearly as affected by the presence of low-ability students. Henderson et al. (1978), on the other hand, find empirical support for peer effects that are equally present for both high- and low-ability groups. The whole enterprise of measuring peer effects, however, has not been well developed and faces many econometric hurdles [see, for example, Evans et al. (1992) and Manski (1993)].

[13]Additional complications particular to population growth from immigration involve such issues as bilingual and bicultural education (which may be required by state supreme courts for certain types of immigrant children). Furthermore, crowding may involve threshold effects (for general population growth as well as growth through immigration); that is, public education may involve little or no additional costs for one more student, but it may involve substantial costs if large population growth is concentrated in small areas. Finally, children with special needs (such as the disabled) clearly require additional resources. These issues are dealt with in more detail in the fourth section of this chapter.

state level. As we discussed in the second section, the difficulty for evaluation depends on which government's perspective the fiscal impact study takes. For example, determining the future fiscal benefit of providing public education to the new population becomes less of an issue when the study takes a local government perspective, because, from that perspective, it is likely that most future tax benefits will accrue to other districts due to migration of future workers.

The basic empirical question regarding the impact of finances and peer effects in education remains, however, because of the second obstacle discussed above. At the same time, this local perspective leaves out important national taxpayer benefits that a more national perspective would wish to take into account. Similarly, the complex state and federal grant programs that support public education in local communities create revenues from a local perspective and costs from a state and national perspective whenever the total level of the grant is based (at least in part) on the total student population within a locality. Finally, if population growth is localized, threshold effects may play an important role; that is, a modest amount of growth may require no additional school buildings, whereas more vigorous growth may well call for such fixed expenditures. Thus, the marginal cost of small increases in local populations (of J) may be small, whereas the marginal cost of larger increases in these populations may be significantly more than proportionately larger.

CHARACTERISTICS OF IMMIGRANTS

As developed above, our model provides a framework for evaluating the fiscal impact of population growth. This section considers in some detail how this model can be used to think about the fiscal impact of U.S. immigration. More precisely, we analyze the ways in which U.S. population growth through immigration violates the crucial neutrality conditions (3) through (6).[14] Each violation deals with a particular set of characteristics of immigrant populations that differs in some critical way from those assumed in the neutrality proposition, as well as from those of U.S. natives. Violations of condition (6), for example, involve the characteristics of the age distribution of immigrants versus those of natives, whereas violations of (5) pertain to the distribution of skill levels among immigrant workers versus native workers. Violations of (4) deal with the differences in consumption and savings behavior between natives and immigrants, and violations of condition (3) relate to the specific characteristics of immigrants that cause the marginal cost of providing public services to be nonconstant or different from the marginal cost of extending the same services to natives. We consider these violations in descending order [i.e., starting with violations of condition (6) and ending with violations of condition (3)].

---

[14]Conditions (1) and (2) have nothing to do with population growth per se. Condition (1) is clearly violated as both public goods spending and interest on the debt are positive.

As we work through these four cases, we discuss not only the relevant characteristics of immigrants, but also the implication of these characteristics for major categories of government expenditures. Where available, we present data on the crucial differences between U.S. natives and immigrants to the United States. Our list is not comprehensive, but it surely contains many of the characteristics critical to calculating the fiscal impacts of immigration on various levels of government and taxpayers in the United States. We largely focus on differences between newly arrived immigrant cohorts and natives rather than on immigrants as a whole, because most politically feasible immigration policy reforms focus on the former group.

Not surprisingly, our analysis suggests that immigration is unlikely to be fiscally neutral because the immigrant population violates all the assumptions in our neutrality proposition. Furthermore, our analysis indicates that much of the data and calculations necessary to make a thorough accounting of the fiscal impacts are not yet available in the literature.

Violations of Condition (6): Age Composition of Immigrants

The age distribution of immigrants is an important determinant of the net fiscal impact of immigration at all levels of government. The evidence summarized below indicates that the age composition of immigrants living in the United States differs significantly from that of natives. We rely on the analysis of the second and third sections in this chapter to highlight some of the likely fiscal consequences of this age shift for major public expenditure programs targeted at specific age groups, in particular education and Social Security benefits (see Table 2-3). We also present some evidence from the literature on how immigrants compare with natives in their use of public services and receipt of age-targeted transfer payments. Finally, we conclude with a discussion of the impact of family composition, a characteristic that is closely related to age distribution. In particular, the family composition of immigrant populations has important implications for income-based transfer programs and tax benefits.

The Age Distribution of Arriving Cohorts

There are three main reasons for the difference in the age distribution of immigrants and natives. First, the age distribution of newly arrived immigrants does not reproduce the native age distribution. This distribution is extremely sensitive to both immigration policy and conditions in other countries that determine the worldwide "supply" of immigrants. Second, immigrants have different mortality rates from natives.[15] The mortality rate will depend on, among other

---

[15]Also, immigrants have different fertility rates from natives. Although this factor is clearly important, we ignore the impact of fertility rates in the remainder of our analysis because the children born in this country to immigrant parents are native citizens of the United States and therefore are included in the age distribution for natives.

TABLE 2-7   Distribution of 1994 Native Ages Versus Immigrant Ages (1994 arrival cohort)

| Gender | Age Range | % of Population | |
		Immigrant	Native
Male	0-9 yrs	12.19	14.41
	10-19 yrs	20.84	13.57
	20-29 yrs	22.02	13.93
	30-39 yrs	19.13	16.09
	40-49 yrs	10.75	12.73
	50-59 yrs	7.99	8.64
	60-69 yrs	4.59	6.72
	70-79 yrs	2.10	12.00
	80+ yrs	0.39	1.92
Female	0-9 yrs	9.93	13.92
	10-19 yrs	17.52	12.70
	20-29 yrs	24.18	13.92
	30-39 yrs	20.44	16.97
	40-49 yrs	11.21	13.68
	50-59 yrs	7.36	10.38
	60-69 yrs	5.84	8.79
	70-79 yrs	2.69	6.72
	80+ yrs	0.82	2.93

SOURCE: U.S. Immigration and Naturalization Service (1996).

things, the country of origin and race distribution of the immigrant cohort, as well as the dietary and health habits of its members, none of which need match the characteristics of natives. Third, return or remigration is common in the immigrant community, whereas emigration is rare among natives.[16]

Table 2-7 presents the age density by sex of natives and the immigrant cohort that arrived in 1994. The newly arrived immigrants are generally younger than natives, with 55 percent of the males and 52 percent of the females less than 30 years of age, compared with 42 and 41 percent for native males and females, respectively. Seven percent of the newly arrived immigrant group is over 60 years old compared with 21 percent of the native population. Forty-six percent of the cohort is male, which is consistent with historical standards (U.S. Immigration and Naturalization Service, 1996:22).

---

[16] The age distribution also helps determine other immigrant characteristics of interest, as well as being determined by them. For example, the age density for the immigrant population is linked mechanically to the family composition (size, number of children, marital status) of the newly arrived immigrant cohort. In turn, the immigrant family composition helps determine remigration probabilities, which is itself in the equation for the age distribution of the remaining immigrants. To give a concrete example, immigrant groups consisting of single young men are far more likely to return to their country of origin (Sowell, 1981).

TABLE 2-8   Age Distribution of Immigrant by Arrival Cohort (1985-1994)

Age	% of Arrival Cohort									
	1985	1986	1987	1988	1989	1990	1991	1992	1993	1994
0-9 yrs	12.4	12.2	11.7	10.8	7.2	5.6	4.7	9.9	11.3	11.6
10-19 yrs	17.3	17.2	16.9	15.9	16.9	14.4	9.6	17.3	19.2	19.2
20-29 yrs	30.7	29.1	28.6	27.1	25.8	29.6	40.3	27.4	24.2	23.5
30-39 yrs	19.4	20.0	20.3	21.5	26.8	27.7	25.1	21.9	20.8	20.0
40-49 yrs	8.4	8.7	9.6	11.1	12.1	12.0	10.9	10.8	10.8	11.0
50-59 yrs	5.8	6.2	6.4	7.00	6.3	6.0	5.4	6.4	6.6	6.9
60-69 yrs	4.1	4.5	4.5	4.7	3.6	3.4	2.9	4.4	4.9	5.2
70-79 yrs	1.6	1.8	1.7	1.7	1.3	1.1	0.93	1.6	1.8	2.1
80+ yrs	0.32	0.38	0.33	0.36	0.26	0.27	0.20	0.37	0.43	0.52

SOURCE: U.S. Immigration and Naturalization Service (1996).

Table 2-8 shows how the age density of newly arrived immigrant cohorts has changed from 1985 to 1994. The 1994 and 1993 cohorts were slightly older than cohorts arriving prior to 1989, with a slightly higher percentage of middle-aged and elderly immigrants.[17] Relative to the native population, the new immigrant cohorts have a higher proportion of young (J) and middle aged (M).

Although new cohorts of immigrants tend to be younger than the native population, the set of all immigrants in the United States is not as young as one might believe looking at just the cohort-specific age profiles. Using data from the 1980 Census, Borjas (1990) reports that 27.3 and 11.2 percent of natives and immigrants, respectively, were under the age of 17. The percent over 64 years of age was 10.6 and 21.2 of natives and immigrants, respectively. This discrepancy with the cohort profiles arises because, at the time of the 1980 Census, the set of all immigrants consisted largely of those who had arrived earlier in the century (Blau, 1986). Since then, immigration reform has significantly increased the size of the more recent cohorts. Therefore, one would expect the age distribution of all immigrants to be younger than before.

Mortality and Remigration Rates

As highlighted in the third section of this chapter, fiscal impact calculations need to follow these new immigrants through the life cycle, *unless the immigrants leave due to mortality or return migration.* Unfortunately, there are few data on remigration rates, especially for recent immigrant waves, available in the

[17]1989-1991 are anomalous years. In these years, many of the "newly arrived" immigrants were in fact newly legalized immigrants who had been in the United States illegally since at least 1982. These immigrants, legalized under the 1986 Immigration Reform and Control Act, included a lower percentage of children, more 20-39 year olds, and fewer 60+ year olds than any of the other years in the series. In 1991, 66.4 percent of the new immigrant cohort was male (U.S. Immigration and Naturalization Service, 1996:22).

literature (Borjas, 1994). Recent studies focus only on particular ethnic groups rather than all immigrants (e.g., Ramos, 1992). In an older study, Warren and Peck (1980) report that one third of all immigrants return to their home country within ten years of arrival. Similarly, there are few data on immigrant mortality rates (Simon, 1989:86). The absence of these important data makes any attempt at estimating the long-term fiscal impacts of immigration problematic, as immigrants are likely to differ from natives significantly in both respects. In addition to determining the age distribution of immigrants, these data influence the calculation of the fiscal impact of immigration in other ways. For example, ignoring selective return migration of immigrants who do poorly in the U.S. economy (and thus contribute little in taxes while using income-based transfers) would negatively bias the estimate of the net long-term fiscal impact of an immigrant cohort.

Implications for Public Services and Age-Based Transfer Payments

As discussed in the third section and illustrated in Table 2-3, the main *age-based* expenditure programs are public education for generation J and Social Security (and Medicare) for generation E.[18] Neither of these is means tested, which means that expenditures are driven mainly by the age distribution of the population.

As shown above, although the new cohorts of immigrants are much younger than the native population, the set of immigrants as a whole is older in the 1980 Census (due to immigration earlier in the century). Thus, it is not surprising to find that immigrant families received proportionally more than natives from social insurance programs (mainly Social Security, but also unemployment insurance and worker's compensation) in 1975. Table 2-9, taken from Blau (1984), demonstrates this finding. Furthermore, Table 2-10, taken from Simon (1984), shows that each cohort of immigrants receives less money from Social Security than do natives, although older cohorts receive more. Of course, part of this lower participation rate by later cohorts arises because a larger percentage are not old enough to retire.

The tendency for the most recent cohorts to be slightly older than the cohorts arriving in the 1980s has interesting implications for both the burden to and the support of Social Security now and in the future. A greater influx of middle-aged immigrants (M) means a greater tax base to fund Social Security now. At the same time, it means larger obligations on the system in the future. A larger intake of elderly immigrants (E) does nothing to assist in funding Social Security, and it strictly enlarges the program's obligations in the near future—assuming these elderly immigrants are able to meet employment qualifications.

---

[18]For a discussion of how differential mortality rates affect the lifetime incidence of Social Security, see Garrett (1995).

TABLE 2-9   Receipt of Transfers per Household in 1975, Immigrants and Natives

Type of Program	Male Heads		Female Heads	
	Natives	Immigrants	Natives	Immigrants
Average payments (all families)				
Welfare	$73	$93	$416	$295
Social Insurance	$979	$1505	$1095	$1411
Percent participating				
Welfare	4.6%	5.5%	21.1%	14.7%
Social Insurance	36.5%	45.6%	44.9%	57.5%
Average payments (program participants only)				
Welfare	$1585	$1684	$1974	$2002
Social Insurance	$2680	$3301	$2437	$2454

SOURCE: Blau (1984, Table 1) - Calculated from the 1975 Survey of Income and Education (U.S. Bureau of the Census). Welfare includes public assistance, AFDC, and SSI. Social insurance includes Social Security, railroad retirement program, unemployment insurance, workers' compensation, and veterans' programs.

As with Social Security, government expenditures on education for any particular group depend critically on the age distribution of that group. The expenditures on public schooling for immigrants depend on three factors: the number of immigrants less than 18 years of age, their probability of attending publicly funded schools, and the average or marginal expenditures per immigrant child who does attend. Newly arrived immigrant cohorts have a higher percentage of young, whereas the set of all immigrants has a lower percentage of young than does the native population. The relative probability of attending public school presumably can be calculated from available data, but we were unable to find it in the published literature.

TABLE 2-10   Receipt of Social Security Dollars Per Capita in 1975 by Natives and Immigrant Cohorts

Arrival Cohort	Social Security Receipts
Natives	$735
1974	$3
1973	$49
1972	$127
1971	$5
1970	$34
1965-69	$152
1960-64	$326
1950-59	$424

SOURCE: Adapted from Simon (1984, Table 1). Calculated from the 1975 Survey of Income and Education (U.S. Bureau of the Census).

The marginal expenditures per immigrant student typically are assumed to be the same as for native children in the fiscal impact studies we reviewed, either explicitly or implicitly (see, for example Clark et al., 1994, and Garvey and Espenshade, 1996). However, this assumption is likely to be incorrect, given the costs of bilingual education and the crowding and peer group externalities that may be generated by having concentrated immigrant populations.

The Impact of Family Composition on Income-Based Transfers and Tax Benefits

Family structure and composition, although closely related to the age distribution, are of particular interest when examining the fiscal impacts of population growth, partially because of tax and transfer program rules and partially because family structure relates to other important behaviors. Of course, family composition is influenced by policy—family reunification has been at the heart of U.S. immigration rules since 1965.

From the tax side, family composition determines the contribution of immigrants to the various revenue sources. Both earned incomes and tax rules are dependent on family size. For example, married men earn higher wages than comparable single men, perhaps due to productivity differences between the two groups (see, for example, Kermit, 1992, or Neumark and Korenman, 1988). Family composition, especially the presence of children, is also an important eligibility criterion most income-based transfer programs. In the specific case of immigrants, family composition also affects remigration rates, changing the age distribution and eventual use of non-income-based transfers. These are just a few examples of the mechanisms through which fiscal impacts may change due to the composition of immigrant families.

Unfortunately, the main literature on the role of family composition on the fiscal impacts of immigrants focuses solely on immigrant use of social services, of the type discussed below under "Violation of Condition (5)." We do know that most immigrants have family members already in the United States: 465,000 of 687,907 immigrant visas issued in 1987 were issued on the basis of family reunification, not including immediate relatives of adult U.S. citizens. Based on Immigration and Naturalization Services (INS) data, most adult immigrants are married. Table 2-11 presents the marital status of the 1987 and 1994 arrival cohorts by sex reported by the INS (U.S. Immigration and Naturalization Service, 1996). In these cohorts, just over half of all immigrants are married. Because 20-30 percent of these immigrants are under the age of 20 and therefore most likely single, this means that the large majority of the adults in these two cohorts are married. The publicly reported INS data do not indicate how many of the married immigrants arrived with their spouses. Using data from the 1970 and 1980 censuses, Borjas and Bronars (1991) estimate that 71.8 percent of U.S. couples with at least one immigrant spouse migrated together. (The remainder

TABLE 2-11   Marital Status of 1987 and 1994 Immigrant Cohorts

	Marital Status	% of Arrival Cohort	
		1987	1994
All Immigrants	Single	43.00	44.11
	Married	52.79	52.03
	Widowed	2.52	2.27
	Divorced	1.57	1.37
	Separated	0.12	0.21
Male Immigrants	Single	46.07	49.81
	Married	51.76	48.28
	Widowed	0.75	0.70
	Divorced	1.33	1.03
	Separated	0.08	0.19
Female Immigrants	Single	39.93	39.20
	Married	53.81	55.28
	Widowed	4.28	3.62
	Divorced	1.82	1.67
	Separated	0.16	0.24

SOURCE: U.S. Immigration and Naturalization Service (1987, 1996).

were married after the arrival of the immigrant or the other spouse migrated at least five years after the initial immigrant.) In addition, they report that about 60-70 percent of immigrants in these censuses migrated within a five-year interval of a relative. Canadian, German, and Irish immigrants are more likely to have migrated alone than Mexicans, Koreans, or Filipinos.

Violations of Condition (5): Differences in Human Capital

In the third section we consider the factors relevant in assessing the fiscal impact when the new population differs in skill level or human capital, suggesting how these factors might be potentially significant. Here we draw on findings in the literature demonstrating that immigrants to the United States do in fact differ from natives both in the human capital they bring with them and in their propensity to invest in human capital once here. Not only does this factor alter the income distribution of the overall population, producing all of the consequences on the tax base outlined in our discussion above, but it also influences the amounts paid out in income-based transfers.

Educational Attainment of Immigrants

Human capital differences include such important attributes as education (quality and quantity), job market experience, occupational choice, industry-specific skills, English language skills, and occasionally other special abilities and talents. As with the immigrant age distribution, the human capital mix of immigrants has been changing over time for two reasons. First, newly arrived immigrants have changed on this dimension over time, and second, immigrants differ from natives in their subsequent acquisition of various types of human capital. The literature on the human capital of immigrants is extensive and has been reviewed elsewhere (Borjas, 1994). We summarize below some of the main facts from this literature that are pertinent to the fiscal impact of immigration.

Table 2-12, based on data from Funkhouser and Trejo (1995), presents the distribution of years of schooling by age for native and immigrant males between 18 and 61 years old, calculated from linked Current Population Survey (CPS) data sets from 1979 to 1989. Immigrants are considered collectively and by arrival cohort. In general, immigrants are less educated than natives. By 1989, the least educated immigrants were those cohorts that had arrived in the early 1980s, with more recent cohorts appearing somewhat more educated. Although years of education can only increase for individuals over time, no immigrant cohort, except those from 1987 to 1989, has monotonically increasing years of education over time, an artifact perhaps of sampling error or remigration. Educational attainment in the year of arrival, as well as propensity to acquire education once in the United States, varies significantly by national origin. With some exceptions, European, African, and Asian immigrants, for example, tend to have more education than South American immigrants (see Borjas, 1994:Table 2-8). Of course, years of education do not take into account the quality of schooling relative to schooling in the United States. Even if the quality abroad is on a par with U.S. schools, education abroad may not be equally renumerative in the U.S.

TABLE 2-12   Mean Years of Schooling of Natives and Immigrants by Arrival Cohort (1979-1989)

	CPS Survey Year				
	1979	1983	1986	1988	1989
Natives	12.5	12.71	12.86	12.97	13.03
All Immigrants	11.36	11.86	11.38	11.64	11.69
Immigrant Cohort					
pre-1960	11.99	12.67	12.29	12.66	12.46
1960-64	11.85	11.63	12.29	12.29	12.94
1965-69	11.43	12.28	11.95	12.71	11.93
1970-74	11.03	11.44	11.28	11.49	11.72
1975-79	10.67	11.63	11.16	11.47	11.49
1980-81	—	11.62	10.53	10.49	11.04
1982-84	—	11.35	11.34	11.53	11.00
1985-86	—	—	10.43	11.75	11.32
1987-89	—	—	—	11.09	11.92

SOURCE: Funkhouser and Trejo (1995). Males aged 18-61 from Nov. 1979, April 1983, June 1986, and Nov. 1989 CPS tapes. Sampling weights were used.

labor market. Nevertheless, education is an important indicator of labor market outcomes.

Another important skill for the U.S. labor market is the ability to speak English fluently. Table 2-13 (derived from Chiswick, 1992) shows by country of origin the percent of immigrants in the 1980 Census who spoke fluent English. Although we commonly accept that English is a necessary job skill, there is no study directly examining how much investment in English language education in the United States improves labor market outcomes for all non-English-speaking immigrant groups. McManus (1985) shows that Hispanic men who do not speak English well earn 31.8 percent less than Hispanic men who speak it fluently, although this penalty decreases when it is adjusted for other variables. We reproduce his results in Table 2-14. Of course, lack of English fluency affects the fiscal impact calculation not only through the job market, but also through the need to provide bilingual education for young immigrants, although there is debate regarding whether such special educational treatment is beneficial (see Chavez, 1992:297-298).

Labor Market Outcomes for Immigrants

For fiscal studies, the most relevant measure of labor productivity is the hourly wage. This is also one of the most studied aspects of immigrant-native differences. As reported by Borjas (1994), the consensus in the literature is that, based on wages, the 1980s saw a large decrease in the labor market skills ("quality") of the immigrants relative to immigrants in the 1970s or 1960s. Table 2-15, taken from Borjas (1994), shows the wage of successive cohorts of newly arrived immigrants relative to native workers by age over time, calculated from 1970,

TABLE 2-13   Percent of Immigrant Group Fluent in English, 1980 Census

Birthplace	% Fluent
Europe	87.54
Asia	
Vietnam	70.75
Philippines	95.09
China	75.56
South Asia	98.11
Other Asia	80.83
America	
Mexico	48.30
Cuba	64.71
Other America	75.62
Africa	97.31

SOURCE: Chiswick (1992). Fluency is defined by whether English is spoken at home or, if not, whether English is spoken well or very well.

TABLE 2-14   Weekly Wages of Hispanic Men by
English Proficiency as a Percentage of Weekly Wages of
English-Fluent Hispanic Men, 1975

English Proficiency	Relative Weekly Wage
Fluent Reference Group	100%
Very Well	90
Well	83
Not Well	68

SOURCE: McManus (1985).

1980, and 1990 census data. There has been a significant shift down in the wage of successive cohorts over time (although we note that the self-employed are excluded from these figures). For example, the cohort arriving between 1970 and 1974 who were between ages 25 and 34 in 1980 made 11 percent less than contemporary natives, whereas the cohort aged 25-34 in 1980-1984 made 18.6 percent less.

TABLE 2-15   Percentage Wage Differential Between Immigrant and Native Men by Age Group and Arrival Cohort (1970-1990)

Cohort	Age Group	Year 1970	1980	1990
All Immigrants		0.9	−9.2	−15.2
1985-89 Arrivals	25-34 in 1990	—	—	−23
	35-44 in 1990	—	—	−28.6
	45-54 in 1990	—	—	−36.2
1980-84 Arrivals	25-34 in 1990	—	—	−18.6
	35-44 in 1990	—	—	−25.3
	45-54 in 1990	—	—	−34
1975-79 Arrivals	25-34 in 1980	—	−21.3	−15.5
	35-44 in 1980	—	−24.9	−24.1
	45-54 in 1980	—	−29.8	−26.3
1970-74 Arrivals	25-34 in 1980	—	−11.4	−11.8
	35-44 in 1980	—	−17.7	−16.4
	45-54 in 1980	—	−26	−20.7
1965-69 Arrivals	15-24 in 1970	—	−4.6	−6.9
	25-34 in 1970	−12	−5.9	−2.5
	35-44 in 1970	−15.9	−15.3	−8.8
	45-54 in 1970	−22.5	−21.1	—
1960-64 Arrivals	15-24 in 1970	—	1.1	4.2
	25-34 in 1970	3.1	−0.3	−0.2
	35-44 in 1970	−6	−6.7	1.1
	45-54 in 1970	11.1	−10.8	—

SOURCE: Calculations based on Borjas (1994)—Subsample of Census 1970, 1980, and 1990 of men aged 25-64 who work in the civilian sector, are not self-employed, and do not reside in group quarters.

Using more recent data, Funkhouser and Trejo (1995) link CPS data sets to measure how the wages of newer immigrant cohorts changed over the 1980s relative to natives. Table 2-16, taken from their paper, shows the difference between mean log hourly wages of immigrants and natives by arrival cohort and time. For newly arrived cohorts, this difference moved toward zero over the 1980s. In 1983, for those who arrived in 1982 or 1983, the difference was –0.395, whereas in 1986, for those arriving in 1985 or 1986 it was -0.371. By 1988, the 1987 and 1988 arrival cohorts had the smallest (absolute) value of this difference in the 1980s, –0.341. In other words, cohorts arriving in the late 1980s did better relative to natives than did the early 1980s cohorts.

There are important limitations to the use of relative hourly wages to track labor market skills of immigrant cohorts. It ignores, for example, self-employment. This is especially important in fiscal impact studies because the self-employed face different tax rates than do wage and salary workers, and they are likely to have different demographic and behavioral characteristics. The focus on hourly wages similarly ignores other important labor market characteristics such as labor force participation and hours of work. As Sowell (1981) notes, the history of immigration is replete with examples of newly arrived immigrant cohorts who start out at low wages, but work long hours to earn their living.

Finally, Table 2-17 shows the distribution of occupations of newly arrived immigrant cohorts of all ages in 1987 and 1994. The large percentage of immigrants not reporting an occupation is explained partly by the presence of children in the cohort; in 1987 29 percent of the arrival cohort was under age 20, whereas in 1994 there were 31 percent under age 20. Accounting for this fact implies that 7 percent more of the 1994 cohort report an occupation than the 1987 cohort. We

TABLE 2-16   Mean Log Hourly Earnings of Immigrant Cohort Relative to Natives by Cohort and CPS Survey Year

Cohort	CPS Survey Year				
	1979	1983	1986	1988	1989
All Immigrants	–0.096	–0.04	–0.134	–0.13	–0.12
pre-1960	0.137	0.263	0.228	0.165	0.228
1960-64	0.037	0.099	0.161	0.105	0.163
1965-69	–0.079	0.063	0.047	0.057	0.071
1970-74	–0.205	–0.11	–0.09	–0.06	0
1975-79	–0.354	–0.19	–0.222	–0.21	–0.17
1980-81	—	–0.33	–0.366	–0.31	–0.28
1982-84	—	–0.4	–0.432	–0.25	–0.33
1985-86	—	—	–0.371	–0.29	–0.35
1987-89	—	—	—	–0.34	–0.26

SOURCE: Funkhouser and Trejo (1995). Sample includes male wage and salary workers aged 18-61 for whom earnings data are available. Hours earnings are computed as the ratio of usual weekly earnings to usual weekly hours of work. Sampling weights are used in the calculation.

TABLE 2-17   Occupational Distribution of 1987 and 1994
Immigrant Arrival Cohorts

| | % of Arrival Cohort | |
Occupation	1987	1994
Professional/Technical Specialty	8.4	7.0
Executive, Administrative, and Managerial	3.4	3.6
Sales	1.6	2.1
Administrative Support	2.7	3.5
Precision Production, Craft, and Repair	3.1	4.5
Operator, Fabricator, and Laborer	8.4	9.2
Farming, Forestry, and Fishing	1.9	2.0
Service	6.3	8.3
No occupation or not reported	64.3	59.8

SOURCE: U.S. Immigration and Naturalization Service (1987, 1996).

see from the table that there are proportionately more service workers and laborers in the 1994 cohort, whereas there are more professional workers in the 1987 cohort. This supports other evidence in the literature that the more recent immigrants work in the lower-skilled occupations.

Together, these findings suggest that recent immigrant groups more negatively impact the fiscal balance sheet than previous immigrant groups did, relative to natives. They have lower earnings and their children are likely to require more public education services. Their skill level, measured by hourly wages, is less relative to natives than it was before the 1960s, although it rose over the 1980s. Years of education for recent immigrant groups lag behind natives, although there was an increase in this figure in the late 1980s. There is apparently a significant economic incentive for non-English-speaking immigrants to acquire English language instruction, although there remains a significant proportion of immigrants who arrive without this ability.

U.S. Immigration Policy and Human Capital

The skill level of immigrants is, of course, partially determined by U.S. immigration policy. Although most immigrants enter the United States based on the principle of family reunification, approximately 140,000 people per year are admitted based on "employment-based preferences." Table 2-18 shows the immigration limits set by law in 1994 for those entering under employment-based preferences, as well as the actual number that were admitted. Priority workers have first preference and include executives of corporations and researchers of outstanding ability and their family members. The second preference is reserved for professionals with advanced degrees or extraordinary ability (as defined by the INS). The third preference includes Chinese students entering under the

TABLE 2-18   Employment-Based Preference Limits in U.S. Immigration Law
and Actual Number of Immigrants Admitted by Preference Category, 1994
Arrival Cohort

Preference	Description	1994 Limits	# immigrants admitted
First	Priority Workers	40,918	21,053
Second	Professionals	40,918	14,432
Third	Skilled and Unskilled Workers	40,918	76,956
Fourth	Special Immigrants	10,230	10,406
Fifth	Investors	10,229	444

SOURCE: U.S. Immigration and Naturalization Service (1996). Unfilled visas from higher categories can be used for lower preferences.

Chinese Student Protection Act, as well as other skilled and unskilled workers.
The fourth preference category, "special immigrants," consists mostly of reli-
gious workers. Very few people entered under the fifth preference category of
"investors" (U.S. Immigration and Naturalization Service, 1996).[19]

Implications for Income-Based Transfers

As noted in the third section, differential skill levels among workers have
implications for income-based transfers that are typically consumed only by low-
skilled workers and their families. Immigration policy has featured prominently
in recent debates on welfare reform.

Borjas (1990) reports that 9.1 percent of all immigrants in the 1980 Census
received welfare, whereas 8.0 percent of all natives did. He defines a family as
receiving welfare if at least one member participated in a cash program: AFDC,
old-age assistance, general assistance, or Supplemental Security Income (non-
income-based, social insurance programs such as Medicare and unemployment
insurance are excluded).   Table 2-19, taken from Borjas and Trejo (1991), shows
immigrant participation in welfare in the 1970 and 1980 censuses broken down
by arrival cohort, age, and sex of household head. Female-headed immigrant
households tend to participate less in welfare, and male-headed immigrant households tend to participate slightly more than do analogous native households.
Welfare participation by both natives and immigrants rose from 1970 to 1980.
Borjas and Trejo (1991) stress the fact that younger cohorts of immigrants tend to
use public services more than do older cohorts, holding years since migration
constant.

Borjas and Hilton (1996), using the Survey of Income and Program Participation find that the gap between immigrant and native families in the probability
of welfare use grew only slightly over the 1980s. The gap in participation in

---

[19]An additional 1,586 special agricultural workers immigrated to the United States in 1994.

TABLE 2-19   Native and Immigrant Welfare Participation Rates by Age, Cohort, and Sex of Household Head

Age Group/ Census Year	% Natives	% All Immigrants	% in Migration Years			
			1965-69	1960-64	1950-59	Before 1950
All Households						
18-34 in 1970	5.2	3.9	3.2	4.3	4.8	3.5
28-34 in 1980	6.5	6.9	7.5	7.3	5.8	6.6
35-49 in 1970	4.5	4.5	5.8	5.4	4.1	3.8
45-59 in 1980	7.2	7.3	10.1	8.8	6.2	6.4
50+ in 1970	7.5	6.8	12.2	13.3	6.5	6.5
60+ in 1980	10.8	11.0	27.1	19.5	11.0	10.0
Male-Headed Households						
18-34 in 1970	2.5	2.6	2.4	2.9	2.8	2.4
28-34 in 1980	3.3	4.2	4.8	4.6	3.3	3.5
35-49 in 1970	2.8	3.4	4.6	4.5	3.0	2.5
45-59 in 1980	4.8	5.6	8.2	6.8	4.5	4.6
50+ in 1970	5.3	5.4	10.8	10.7	5.2	5.0
60+ in 1980	7.9	9.1	21.7	14.7	8.4	8.3
Female-Headed Households						
18-34 in 1970	20.3	11.5	8.1	12.2	16.0	9.7
28-34 in 1980	18.4	16.7	17.6	16.9	15.0	17.5
35-49 in 1970	15.9	11.1	13.1	11.0	11.0	10.3
45-59 in 1980	15.7	12.9	16.1	15.5	11.7	11.3
50+ in 1970	12.9	10.8	17.9	22.3	11.6	9.7
60+ in 1980	14.9	13.8	37.7	29.0	16.4	12.3

SOURCE: Borjas and Trejo (1991, Table 2). Calculated from the 1970 & 1980 U.S. Census.

noncash programs (such as Medicaid, food stamps, and housing assistance) has grown as well, although not by much in any particular program. They report that when welfare use is defined as participation in either cash or noncash programs, the immigrant-native gap grew by about 4 percentage points from 1984 to 1991.

Table 2-20, taken from Simon (1984), reports per capita receipts from welfare for natives and immigrants by arrival cohort. He calculates these figures from the 1975 Survey of Income and Education. He finds that most immigrant cohorts receive less welfare money per capita than do natives, except for the newest cohorts. Blau (1984), using the same data source, calculates the average payout per family for immigrants and natives and finds that male-headed immigrant families use slightly more, and female-headed immigrant families use significantly less than do natives. We note, however, that female-headed families receive between three and four times as much money per family than do male-headed families. When Blau (1984) looks at payouts per family, given welfare program participation, she finds that immigrants tend to receive slightly more than do natives. Table 2-9 shows these figures from Blau (1984). These dif-

TABLE 2-20   Amount of Transfer Payments Received Per Capita in 1975 by Natives and Immigrant Arrival Cohorts

Arrival Cohort	Public Welfare	Supplemental Security	AFDC	Food Stamps
Natives	$108	$46	$45	$11
1974	$131	$91	$91	$15
1973	$47	$63	$6	$7
1972	$85	$38	$164	$12
1971	$189	$16	$13	$17
1970	$100	$50	$11	$16
1965-69	$191	$86	$18	$12
1960-64	$91	$69	$18	$12
1950-59	$122	$31	$50	$11

SOURCE: Adapted from Simon (1984, Table 1). Calculated from the 1975 Survey of Income and Education (U.S. Bureau of the Census).

ferences disappear after she controls for various demographic and economic variables.

The balance of evidence seems to indicate that immigrant participation in welfare programs is slightly higher than native participation and that the gap has grown with the newer cohorts. Because welfare programs are funded by federal, state, and local governments, this outcome has critical consequences on how immigration alters the fiscal circumstances of governments at different levels.

Violations of Condition (4): Consumption and Savings Behavior

In the third section we describe the fundamental role of consumption and savings behavior by immigrant groups. Immigrants to the United States are likely to differ substantially from natives in their consumption and savings patterns. They bring from their home countries cultural habits and tastes that persist, often over generations (Sowell, 1994). Behaviors arise from an interaction of these cultural habits with the incentives generated by institutions in the United States. Thus, although immigrants' consumption and savings patterns may change in the United States relative to their countrymen in their homeland, there is little reason to expect that they will reproduce native patterns.

Nevertheless, little work has been done exploring immigrant savings and consumption patterns. For example, Simon (1989:87) reflects on the fiscal impacts of immigrant savings behavior, but he reports that "this research has not yet been done." Because immigrants are younger than natives, Simon speculates that life-cycle considerations would lead them to save more than natives. On the other hand, he recognizes that wealth and human capital differences may work in the opposite direction. Family size and bequest motives may represent yet another source of divergence in savings rates of natives and immigrants.

In the absence of research in this area, most fiscal impact studies ignore likely differences between immigrants and natives in consumption when calculating sales taxes paid by immigrants. Diverse studies of both illegal and legal immigrants, several of which are reviewed in the final section of this chapter, all assume that immigrants consume in the same proportions as natives in the same income category. This assumption, although understandable given the lack of data, is untenable given cultural differences between natives and immigrants. For example, immigrants commonly send a significant part of their earnings back to family members in their country of origin. These remittance payments contribute to neither sales tax revenues nor to U.S. savings or investments. (They may however contribute to the wealth or human capital of future immigrants.) As already noted, calculations of immigrant contributions to both current and future tax revenues critically depend on a better understanding of these behavioral traits.

Violations of Condition (3): Characteristics Impacting Expenditures and Taxes

Our discussion in the third section suggest that the characteristics of the new population groups may cause the marginal costs of extending public services to be higher or lower than average expenditures for the native population. This subsection explores two characteristics of immigrant populations that may in fact contribute to such higher marginal costs (and have important implications elsewhere). We highlight the role of parental education and socioeconomic status in public education crowding, and we discuss the problems for researchers that have been raised by the location choices of immigrant groups.

Parental Education, Socioeconomic Status, and Cultural Factors in Education

Immigrants' skills and education levels play an important role in the provision of education for their children. The best predictor of educational outcomes for children is parental education and socioeconomic status. Thus, parental characteristics play a crucial role in the amount of crowding and externality effects experienced by public schools from increases in the student population. Separately, low parental education levels and low fluency in English among immigrant parents induce greater funds to be spent on bilingual and bicultural education.[20] As revealed in Table 2-13, immigrant groups from different countries of origin have substantially different fluency rates and thus cause substantially different levels of crowding in public schools. Finally, cultural factors stressing such values as work and individual achievement differ greatly among immigrants

---

[20]Although there is a debate regarding the effectiveness of various forms of bilingual education, some form of bilingual (and sometimes bicultural) education is required in many states by state supreme courts.

from different countries (Sowell, 1994). Borjas (1992) finds empirical support in the National Longitudinal Survey of Youth for the notion that "ethnic capital" plays an important role in the labor market and education outcomes of immigrant children, separately from the effect of parental human capital mentioned above. The role of culture, socioeconomic status, and parental human capital in determining differential rates of crowding in public schools, as well as in the use of other public services, are clearly significant and should play a prominent part in any fiscal impact study.

Location Choice of Immigrants

Immigrants do not locate themselves uniformly across the United States. The concentration of immigrants in certain geographic sectors may give rise to important threshold effects that would not appear if population growth were uniform. Although immigrant children might be absorbed easily into public schools if they were spread uniformly across the United States, this is clearly not the case when immigrant groups concentrate in a select number of states and their school districts are faced with massive fixed expenditures to accommodate those students.

Past waves of U.S. immigrants often stayed in the first port where they arrived. For example, Irish, Italian, Jewish, and Puerto Ricans concentrated in New York and other port cities of arrival in successive waves over the nineteenth and twentieth centuries (Sowell, 1981). Today, the top four immigrant recipient states—California, New York, Florida, and Texas—receive nearly 60 percent of all new immigrants. Table 2-21, based on INS data, shows the state of intended residence of the 1987 and 1994 arrival cohorts. During this seven-year period, the top five states' share of new immigrants declined slightly, from 67 to 64 percent.

Once immigrants arrive in the United States, they tend to migrate across state lines more frequently than do natives of the same age and ethnicity (see Bartel,

TABLE 2-21   Intended Location of 1987 and 1994 Immigrant Arrival Cohorts

	% of Arrival Cohort	
State	1987	1994
California	26.79	25.92
New York	18.98	17.95
Florida	9.09	7.22
Texas	7.04	6.98
New Jersey	5.13	5.48
Illinois	4.32	5.27
Other States	28.65	31.18

SOURCE: U.S. Immigration and Naturalization Service (1987, 1996).

1989:Table 7). Bartel (1989) also finds that it is the more highly educated immigrants who are more likely to move away from cities with a high concentration of immigrants of the same nationality. Finally, she finds that immigrants are more likely than natives to live in standard metropolitan statistical areas (SMSAs), and that whereas immigrants may move, they tend to move to other SMSAs.

As we noted above in several different contexts, residential choice and probability of migration are important in determining current and future impacts of immigration. Congestion and externalities in the use of public goods will also be more serious concerns where immigrants are concentrated. It is not accidental that it is the states and localities that absorb the highest volume of immigrants, and especially illegal immigrants, that have commissioned reports calculating the net fiscal impacts of immigration on their appropriate level of government. (In the next section, we briefly review the recent fiscal impact reports commissioned by Los Angeles and San Diego counties, California, and Texas.) The location of the new immigrants and the consequent congestion problems are dependent on many of the characteristics of immigrants that we discussed above, including education level and national origin mix, and are likely to change over time, further necessitating a dynamic framework when evaluating the fiscal impact of immigration.

CONCLUSION

In this section, we review a number of recent fiscal impact studies through the lens of the economic framework developed in this chapter. This is not intended to be a comprehensive examination of the literature; Rothman and Espenshade (1992) already offer an extensive survey of the cost-benefit studies of immigration. Instead, we use this section to illustrate some of the shortfalls of analyses done without a comprehensive theoretical structure.

Table 2-22 presents a summary of seven recent studies of the fiscal impact of immigration. The four sections of the table compare and contrast the studies, based on the population considered, the revenue sources and expenditure categories counted and their final "bottom-line" estimate. Using very different accounting strategies, most of the studies reach the conclusion that the immigrant groups considered are a net fiscal drain on the government.

These seven studies define their targeted immigrant populations based on differing legal definitions and geographical areas. Most include illegal immigrants; two consider solely this group. Others add in recent immigrants, amnesty immigrants (Immigration Reform and Control Act legalized), and the citizen children of illegal immigrants in some combination. One considers all legal immigrants. Because many of these studies were sponsored by agencies at various levels of government, the geographical areas run the gamut from counties (Los Angeles County and San Diego County) to states (California, Texas, New Jersey among others) to the entire United States. As we discussed above, the

TABLE 2-22 Summary of Fiscal Impact Studies

Study	Stewart, et al. (1992)	Parker & Rea (1993)	Huddle (1994)	Romero, Chang & Parker (1994)	Garvey & Espenshade (1996)	Clark, et al (1994)	Huddle (1993)
Population							
Illegal Immigrants	Yes	Yes	Yes	Yes	Unspecified	Yes	Yes
Legal Immigrants	post-1980 amnesty aliens, children of illegals	No	Post-1970 immigrants amnesty aliens	citizen children of illegals	Yes	No	post-1970 immigrants & amnesty aliens
Scope	LA County	SD County	Texas	California	New Jersey	CA,FL,TX,NY, IL,AZ,& NJ	U.S.
Population Size	2.3 Million	220 K	1.9 Million	1.7 Million	39 K	Various[7]	19.3 Million
Revenue Sources							
Fed. Income Tax	Yes[1]	No	Yes	Yes	No	No	Yes[2]
State Income Tax	Yes[1]	Yes	Yes	Yes	Yes	Yes	Yes[2]
Sales Taxes	Yes[1]	Yes	?	Yes	Yes	Yes	Yes[2]
Property Taxes	Yes[1]	No	?	Yes	Yes	Yes	Yes[2]
Excise Taxes	Yes[1]	Yes[4]	Yes[3]	?	Yes	No	Yes[2]
Payroll Taxes	Yes[1]	Yes	No	No	?	No	No
Immigrant-owned business Taxes	No	No	No	No	No	No	No
Expenditures							
Medicaid & county health	Yes	Yes[4]	Yes	Yes[1]	Yes[1]	Yes[5]	Yes
Social Services & Welfare	Yes	Yes	Yes	Yes	Yes[1]	No	Yes
Educational costs	Yes[1]	Yes	Yes[6]	Yes[1]	Yes[1]	Yes[1]	Yes[1]

Public housing	No	No	Yes	No	?	No	Yes
Costs of criminal courts	Yes	Yes	Yes	No	?	No	Yes
Incarceration costs	No	Yes	Yes	Yes[1]	?	Yes	Yes
Local public goods - parks, etc.	No	No	No	Yes[1]	Yes	No	No
Bilingual Education	No	No	Yes	No	No	No	Yes
Local "environmental costs"	No	No	No	Yes	?	No	No
Student Aid	No	No	Yes	No	No	No	Yes
Social Security	No	No	No	No	No	No	No
Medicare	No	No	No	No	No	No	No
Earned Income Tax Credit	No	No	No	No	No	No	No
Fiscal costs associated with native job displacement	No	Yes	Yes	No	No	No	Yes
Revenues (Billions)	$0.14[10]	$0.06	$1.47	$0.74	See note 8	See note 9	$283
Costs (Billions)	$0.95[10]	$0.30	$6.15	$3.4	See note 8	See note 9	$952

Final Estimates

[1]Estimates rely on comparisons with observably similar demographic groups. (Comparison group varies by study).

[2]Extrapolated from LA County tax receipts, and multiplied by an arbitrary "adjustment factor."

[3]Assumes immigrants and natives consume these services at the same rate.

[4]Assumes immigrants and natives consume these services at the same rate for some of the services in the category.

[5]Emergency services only.

[6]Unclear/ difficult to ascertain from description of methodology in paper.

[7]Several different population size estimates are calculated and compared in this study. They vary depending on assumptions and data sources.

[8]Final results are broken down by demographic groups and level of government - no single figure is presented. Net fiscal impact per immigrant household at state level varies between -$1000 and -$3000.

[9]Varies by state and different demographic/behavioral assumptions used.

[10]The study reports revenues and costs for other levels of government as well.

choice of government perspective will change the conclusions of the study; the characteristics of the specific new population considered will also change the outcomes.

Our first condition for population growth to be fiscally neutral is that expenditures on pure public goods and on public debt be zero. If these expenditures are positive, we conclude that population growth has a positive fiscal impact, all else being equal. Of course, these expenditures are positive. The studies in Table 2-22 treat these "fixed" public expenditures in one of two ways. They either ignore fixed public expenditures altogether, implicitly assigning zero benefit from immigration for these categories and thus biasing downward the impact estimate. Or they assign the per capita expenditures on these items as costs rather than benefits, which leads to an even larger negative bias. None of the studies attempt to calculate the benefit derived from immigration in "diluting" the base of payment for these pure public goods, even for major categories of expenditures as the debt, national defense, current Social Security transfers,[21] science research, and so on. How these benefits ought to be dealt with depends on which perspective the researcher takes and the level of government considered. It is obviously legitimate for a study on the county-level fiscal impacts of immigration to exclude the "dilution" benefit from federal programs. Nevertheless, some attempt should be made to estimate to what extent the goods and services provided by the county are pure public goods and count the effects appropriately. Some of the confusion would be eliminated if studies used marginal costs rather than average costs. The studies uniformly prefer the former, perhaps in order to maintain tractability.

Although they do not explicitly consider returns to scale (our second neutrality condition), these studies focus exclusively on the direct effects of immigration on government finances, ignoring the indirect effects, especially the impact of immigrants on the income of the original population. Huddle's two studies (1993, 1994) are the exception. He estimates the number of native workers "displaced" by immigrants from their jobs and then calculates how much this unemployment would negatively impact government finances.[22] All of the studies, including Huddle's, ignore the possibility that immigration might expand the job opportunities for natives in the long run, perhaps by new business creation, increased specialization, or a demand effect. In effect, they ignore the possibility that increasing returns to scale might hold. Of course, the empirical question of whether there are positive scale economies present in the American economy that can be exploited with immigration, or negative scale economies that suffer with

---

[21]Because U.S. residents must work 40 quarters to qualify for Social Security benefits, the current costs of Social Security are "fixed" from the perspective of newly arrived immigrants (see Simon, 1989).

[22]Passel (1994) vehemently attacks Huddle for ignoring or misreading the literature on the effects of immigration on native workers.

the increased population, is unresolved. Nevertheless, as our framework suggests, these effects are likely to be important in the calculation of fiscal impact.

Our neutrality proposition is also violated if the new and old populations have differing consumption and savings patterns. These seven studies attempt to estimate the effect of differing consumption patterns, but none discuss savings behavior. Remittances are discussed as a loss of sales and excise tax revenue. Taxes on immigrant-owned businesses are completely ignored. Although these studies do try to distinguish immigrant and native consumption patterns, they are less careful about distinguishing between immigrant groups. Several of the studies on illegal immigration assume that immigrants consume their income in the same way as other, more easily observable, legal immigrant demographic groups. Parker and Rea (1993), however, conducted a small-scale survey of illegal immigrants in San Diego County that includes questions about their consumption patterns. Unfortunately, because the illegal immigrants are identified mainly through their workplace, the sample chosen by Parker and Rea is not likely to be representative. Without better data, future fiscal impact studies of illegal immigration are likely to find this problematic as well.

All the studies, in at least some of their calculations, assume that immigrants and demographically similar elements of the native population share the same propensity to use government services. This is particularly true when calculating immigrants' share of the costs of public schools, where per pupil costs are generally assumed to be the same as for natives. Rothman and Espenshade (1992) find the same assumption in all of the fiscal impact studies that they review. The only exceptions are again Huddle's two studies, which include the costs of bilingual education. None attempt to estimate crowding externalities induced by large influxes of immigrants on the use of these public services. It seems reasonable to guess that including the correct marginal costs and allowing for crowding externalities would increase the estimate of the fiscal costs. However, this omission could bias the results in either direction and may depend on the precise immigrant group being considered (due to language, culture, and socioeconomic differences).

Ultimately, a serious shortcoming of these studies is the static model used for calculation. All existing studies ignore some critical intertemporal effects that impinge on how certain taxes and transfers should be counted. As our framework demonstrates, the current and future period effects could have opposing impacts on the fiscal costs and benefits of immigration. Many of the elements discussed in our synthesis have a dynamic component that should not be ignored. For example, education expenditures on immigrant children are invariably counted as a cost in the accounting schemes of the various papers. However, they are also an investment designed to make the young generation more productive in the future. Thus, the extra education expenditures result in future higher fiscal inflows that should be counted in the analysis at an appropriate discount rate. Another prominent example is payroll taxes, such as FICA, which is used to finance Social

Security, that are left completely out of most of the studies. If these taxes are viewed as forced savings for retirement, then their omission from the analysis is justified. Alternatively, if, as we argue, they are intergenerational transfers from the middle-aged generation to the elderly generation, then the effect of the new population on these fiscal revenues and expenditures should be accounted for in some manner. Finally, the focus on consumption ignores the role of savings and its potential impact on future revenues, especially if they help the economy to grow in the future.

Clearly, there is much work left to be done to acquire accurate estimates of the fiscal impacts of immigration at any level of government. Many gaps exist in our basic knowledge of the economic behavior of immigrants, both legal and illegal. This chapter seeks to improve our understanding of the theoretical under-pinnings of fiscal impact calculations. In doing so, it potentially provides a road map of the necessary future steps for empirical research.

ACKNOWLEDGMENTS

This project was undertaken at the request of the Commission on Behavioral and Social Sciences and Education of the National Research Council (NRC). We gratefully acknowledge support from National Institutes of Health (NIH) grant HD32055-02. Opinions stated in this document are those of the authors and do not necessarily represent any official position or policy. We benefited greatly from Margaret O'Brien-Strain who helped us extensively with both the ideas and the editing of this chapter. Selen Opcin also provided editing assistance.

REFERENCES

Aaron, Henry.
  1975   *Who Pays the Property Tax?* Washington, D.C.: The Brookings Institution.
Bartel, Ann P.
  1989   "Where Do the New U.S. Immigrants Live?" *Journal of Labor Economics* 7(4):371-391.
Betts, Julian.
  1995   "Does School Quality Matter? Evidence from the National Longitudinal Survey of Youth."
          Review of Economics and Statistics 77:231-250.
Blau, Francine D.
  1984   "The Use of Transfer Payments by Immigrants." *Industrial and Labor Relations Review*
          37(2):222-239.
Blau, Francine D.
  1986   "Immigration and the U.S. Taxpayer." Pp. 89-110 in *1986 Essays on Legal and Illegal
          Immigration*, S. Pozo, ed. Kalamazoo, Mich.: W.E. Upjohn Institute for Employment
          Research.
Borjas, George J.
  1990   *Friends or Strangers: The Impact of Immigrants on the U.S. Economy.* New York:
          Basic Books.

Borjas, George J.
1992 "Ethnic Capital and Intergenerational Mobility." *Quarterly Journal of Economics* 107(1):123-150.

Borjas, George J.
1994 "The Economics of Immigration." *Journal of Economic Literature* 32:1667-1717.

Borjas, George J., and Stephen G. Bronars.
1991 "Immigration and the Family." *Journal of Labor Economics* 9(2):123-148.

Borjas, George J., and Richard B. Freeman, eds.
1992 *Immigration and the Work Force: Economic Consequences for the United States and Source Areas.* Chicago: University of Chicago Press.

Borjas, George J., and Lynette Hilton.
1996 "Immigration and the Welfare State: Immigrant Participation in Means-Tested Entitlement Programs." *Quarterly Journal of Economics* 111:575-604.

Borjas, George J., and Stephen J. Trejo.
1991 "Immigrant Participation in the Welfare System." *Industrial and Labor Relations Review* 44(2):195-211.

Boskin, Michael J., Lawrence J. Kotlikoff, Douglas J. Puffert, and John B. Shoven.
1987 "Social Security: A Financial Appraisal Across and Within Generations." *National Tax Journal* 40(3):19-34.

Card, David, and Alan Krueger.
1992 "Does School Quality Matter? Returns to Education and the Characteristics of Public Schools in the United States." *Journal of Political Economy* 100:1-40.

Chavez, Linda.
1992 "Commentary on Part Three." Pp. 297-299 in *Immigration, Language, and Ethnicity*, Barry R. Chiswick, ed. Washington, D.C.: American Enterprise Institute.

Chiswick, Barry R.
1978 "The Effect of Americanization on the Earnings of Foreign-Born Men." *Journal of Political Economy* 86(5):897-921.

Chiswick, Barry R., ed.
1992 *Immigration, Language, and Ethnicity: Canada and the United States.* Washington D.C.: American Enterprise Institute.

Clark, Rebecca L., Jeffrey S. Passel, Wendy N. Zimmerman, and Michael E. Fix, with Taynia L. Mann, and Rosalind E. Berkowitz.
1994 "Fiscal Impacts of Undocumented Aliens: Selected Estimates for Seven States." Unpublished document, The Urban Institute, Washington, D.C.

Coleman, James S.
1966 *Equality of Educational Opportunity.* Washington D.C.: U.S. Government Printing Office.

Evans, W., Wallace Oates, and Robert Schwab.
1992 "Measuring Peer Group Effects: A Study of Teenage Behavior." *Journal of Political Economy* 100:968-991.

Funkhouser, Edward, and Stephen J. Trejo.
1995 "The Labor Market Skills of Recent Male Immigrants: Evidence from the Current Population Surveys." *Industrial and Labor Relations Review* 48(4):792-811.

Garrett, Daniel M.
1995 "The Effects of Differential Mortality Rates on the Progressivity of Social Security." *Economic Inquiry* 33:457-475.

Garvey, Deborah L., and Thomas J. Espenshade.
1996 "State and Local Fiscal Impacts of New Jersey's Immigrant and Native Households." Unpublished document, Princeton University, Princeton, N.J.

Hamilton, B.
   1975   "Zoning and Property Taxes in a System of Local Governments." *Urban Studies.* 12:205-
           211.
Hanushek, Eric.
   1986   "The Economics of Schooling: Production and Efficiency in Public Schools." *Journal of
           Economic Literature* 24:1147-1117.
Heckman, James, A. Layne-Farrar, and P. Todd.
   1996   "Does Measured School Quality Really Matter? Understanding the Empirical and Eco-
           nomic Foundations of the Evidence." Working paper, University of Chicago, Chicago, Ill.
Henderson, Vernon, Peter Mieszkowski, and Y. Sauvageau.
   1978   "Peer Group Effects and Educational Production Functions." *Journal of Public Econom-
           ics* 10:97-106.
Huddle, Donald.
   1993   "The Costs of Immigration." Unpublished document, Rice University, Houston, Texas.
Huddle, Donald.
   1994   "The Net Costs of Immigration to Texas." Unpublished document, Rice University,
           Houston, Texas.
Kermit, D.
   1992   "Does Marriage Make Men More Productive?" *Economic Research Center/NORC Popu-
           lation Research Center Discussion Paper* 38:92-92.
Manski, Charles.
   1993   "Identification of Endogenous Social Effects: The Reflection Problem." *Review of Eco-
           nomic Studies* 60:531-542.
McManus, Walter S.
   1985   "Labor Market Costs of Language Disparity: An Interpretation of Hispanic Earnings
           Differences." *American Economic Review* 75(4):818-827.
Mieszkowski, Peter, and George Zodrow.
   1983   "The Incidence of the Property Tax: The Benefit View versus the New View." In *Local
           Provision of Public Services: The Tiebout Model after 25 Years*, G. Zodrow, ed. New
           York: Academic Press.
Neumark, David B., and Sanders D. Korenman.
   1988   "Does Marriage Really Make Men More Productive?" Working paper, Board of Gover-
           nors of the Federal Reserve System, Finance and Economics Discussion Paper Series 29,
           p. 59.
Parker, Richard A., and Louis M. Rea.
   1993   "Illegal Immigration in San Diego County: An Analysis of Costs and Revenues." Un-
           published document, California State Senate Special Committee on Border Issues, Sacra-
           mento.
Passel, Jeffrey S.
   1994   "Immigrants and Taxes: A Reappraisal of Huddle's 'The Cost of Immigrants.'" Unpub-
           lished document, The Urban Institute, Washington, D.C.
Pechman, Joseph A.
   1985   *Who Paid the Taxes, 1966-85.* Washington, D.C.: The Brookings Institution.
Pozo, Susan, ed.
   1986   *1986 Essays on Legal and Illegal Immigration.* Papers presented in a seminar series
           conducted by the Department of Economics at Western Michigan University. Kalamazoo,
           Mich: W.E. Upjohn Institute for Employment Research.
Ramos, Fernando A.
   1992   "Out-Migration and Return Migration of Puerto Ricans." Pp. 49-66 in *Immigration and
           the Work Force,* George Borjas and Richard Freeman, eds. Chicago: University of Chi-
           cago Press.

Romero, Phillip J., Andrew J. Chang, and Theresa Parker.
  1994. "Shifting the Costs of a Failed Federal Policy: The Net Fiscal Impact of Illegal Immigrants in California." Unpublished document, California Governor's Office of Planning and Research, Sacramento.
Rothman, Eric S., and Thomas J. Espenshade.
  1992 "Fiscal Impacts of Immigration to the United States." *Population Index* 58(3):381-415.
Simon, Julian L.
  1984 "Immigrants, Taxes, and Welfare in the United States." *Population and Development Review* 10(1):55-69.
Simon, Julian L.
  1989 *The Economic Consequences of Immigration.* Cambridge, Mass: Basil Blackwell.
Sowell, Thomas.
  1981 *Ethnic America: A History.* New York: Basic Books.
Sowell, Thomas.
  1994 *Race and Culture: A World View.* New York: Harper Collins, Basic Books.
Stewart, William, F. Gascoigne, Mark Bannister, R. Wayne et. al.
  1992 "Impact of Undocumented Persons and Other Immigrants on Costs, Revenues, and Services in Los Angeles County." Unpublished document, Los Angeles County ISD, Los Angeles, Calif.
Summers, A., and B. Wolfe.
  1977 "Do Schools Make a Difference?" *American Economic Review* 67(4):639-652.
U.S. Immigration and Naturalization Service.
  1987 *Statistical Yearbook of the Immigration and Naturalization Service, 1986.* Washington, D.C.: U.S. Government Printing Office.
U.S. Immigration and Naturalization Service.
  1996 *Statistical Yearbook of the Immigration and Naturalization Service, 1994.* Washington, D.C.: U.S. Government Printing Office.
Warren, Robert, and Jennifer M. Peck.
  1980 "Foreign-Born Emigration from the United States: 1960-1970." *Demography* 17(1):71-84.

3

Fiscal Impacts of Immigrant and Native Households: A New Jersey Case Study

Deborah L. Garvey and Thomas J. Espenshade

INTRODUCTION

Studies of the economic impacts of immigration on receiving countries have focused primarily on the labor market consequences of immigrants. For example, how are the wages and employment opportunities of native-born Americans affected by the growing presence of foreign workers in local area labor markets? Much of the available research has concentrated on identifying potential adverse impacts for native minority workers (including women, blacks, and Latinos) and quantifying the change in either native workers' wages or their employment prospects (Abowd and Freeman, 1991; Borjas and Freeman, 1992; Borjas, 1994). Considerably less effort has been expended by economists in estimating the fiscal impacts of immigrants or in evaluating how these effects compare with the governmental benefits received and taxes paid by the native-born population. Indeed, these issues are barely mentioned in two recent review papers by Friedberg and Hunt (1995a, 1995b).

Examining the impacts of immigrants from a budgetary perspective involves estimating their revenue contributions to federal, state, and local governments; estimating the benefits they receive from each level of government in return; and then determining the degree to which the two amounts differ at each jurisdictional level. If revenues provided by a household exceed government expenditures on that household, the household is considered to be a net fiscal asset or gain to other taxpayers. If, on the other hand, fiscal costs exceed the revenues generated by a household, then it is a net fiscal burden or drain on remaining taxpayers (Rothman and Espenshade, 1992). Fiscal costs include transfer payments from means-tested entitlement programs, expenditures on elementary and secondary school education, and a range of government services that are provided to all residents regardless of age or need (for example, trash collection, public roads, and police and fire protection). Fiscal revenues include an assortment of tax payments, fees and licenses, and voluntary contributions made to governments by households. In recent years, knowledge of the fiscal impacts of immigrant households has taken on additional policy significance as numerous states have sued the federal government for the costs of services they are required by law to provide to resident illegal immigrants (Clark et al., 1994; U.S. General Accounting Office, 1994, 1995).[1]

Some studies of immigrants' fiscal impacts have been conducted by university researchers, but most have been prepared by analysts working for state or local governments.[2] Census data suggest that immigrants were slightly less likely than natives in 1970 to receive cash welfare payments (for example, Aid to Families with Dependent Children and Supplemental Security Income), but that by 1990 immigrant households were overrepresented among the welfare population (Borjas, 1994). In 1990 the fraction of immigrant households receiving welfare was 9.1 percent versus 7.4 percent among native households. Tracking immigrant cohorts reveals that immigrants "assimilate into welfare" the longer they are in the United States. Using data from the 1984, 1985, 1990, and 1991 panels of the Survey of Income and Program Participation, Borjas and Hilton (1996) found little difference between natives and immigrants in the probability of receiving cash welfare benefits, but a larger differential emerges when both cash and noncash means-tested programs are analyzed. For example, the fraction of immigrant households that receive some kind of public assistance is 21 percent compared with 14 percent among natives.

Part of the increase in the fraction of immigrant households receiving welfare is explained by growth in the refugee population. When refugees are excluded, Fix and Passel (1994) find that working-age migrants are less likely to receive welfare than their native-born counterparts, a conclusion that is consistent with Borjas's (1994) observation that households from Cambodia or Laos had a welfare participation rate in 1990 of almost 50 percent. Immigrants' legal status

---

[1]During 1994 Arizona, California, Florida, New Jersey, New York, and Texas filed suits in federal district courts to recover costs they claim they incurred because of the federal government's failure to enforce U.S. immigration policy, protect the nation's borders, and provide adequate resources for immigration emergencies (Dunlap and Morse, 1995). All six lawsuits sought compensation for the costs of imprisoning undocumented criminal aliens in state or local correctional facilities, and many included claims for public education, emergency health care, and other social services. The amounts involved ranged from $50 million in New Jersey for the 1993 costs of jailing 500 undocumented criminal felons and for future costs of new prison construction to more than $33 billion in the New York case which sought reimbursement of all state and county costs associated with illegal immigration between 1988 and 1993 (State and Local Coalition on Immigration, 1994). All six suits have been dismissed, but some states are appealing the decisions (Espenshade, 1996).

[2]For comprehensive reviews, see Rothman and Espenshade (1992) and Vernez and McCarthy (1995, 1996).

also matters in other ways. Current illegal immigrants pay less in taxes than former undocumented migrants who received amnesty under the terms of the 1986 Immigration Reform and Control Act, who in turn pay less than permanent resident aliens. Members of the native-born population pay the highest taxes, but the authors of these findings point out that the differentials reflect differences in average income rather than anything intrinsic to immigration status (Vernez and McCarthy, 1995).

There is only limited evidence bearing on the question of immigrants' net fiscal implications. Fix and Passel (1994) conclude that immigrant households on average are substantial fiscal benefits to other U.S. taxpayers when all levels of government are considered simultaneously. But these effects are not distributed uniformly. Only at the federal level do immigrants appear to contribute more than they receive (Vernez and McCarthy, 1995). Revenues and expenditures associated with immigrants appear to be more or less offsetting for state governments, whereas it is typically at the level of local governments where the fiscal impacts of immigrants are most negative (Rothman and Espenshade, 1992). Evidence from the 1980 census for New Jersey suggests that both immigrant and native families are fiscal burdens for local governments and that the negative impact is greater for immigrants (Espenshade and King, 1994).

Existing studies usually exhibit some combination of three problems. First, they look selectively at particular expenditure or revenue items associated with immigrants, which means that it is impossible to draw conclusions about immigrants' *net* fiscal impacts.[3] Second, only one previous study (Espenshade and King, 1994) makes use of available micro-level information about the demographic and economic circumstances of individual immigrant households that can be obtained routinely from decennial census data. Instead, researchers commonly employ a "top-down" or average cost strategy that amounts to allocating a simple pro rata share of government expenditures or revenues to each household. This approach ignores potentially important sources of household-level variation.[4] For example, Clark et al. (1994) assume the same per capita school expenditure for all students in a given state, even though these expenditures vary substantially by school district. Incorporating place of residence into estimates of elementary and secondary school expenditures could make a significant difference to the results. Third, researchers often emphasize the fiscal impacts of the immigrant population and ignore taxes paid and benefits received by native households. This approach may cast immigrants in a prejudicial light by overlooking the fact that both immigrants and natives can be fiscal drains on state and local government budgets (Espenshade and King, 1994). Results for immigrants should be interpreted in the context of natives' impacts.

In addition, one challenge for all fiscal impact studies is to cast the analysis

---

[3]See, for example, Borjas and Trejo (1991) and Clark et al. (1994).
[4]See Huddle (1993) and Clark et al. (1994) as examples.

in the context of a general equilibrium economic framework (Isbister, 1996). In contrast to simpler budgetary accounting approaches, general equilibrium models examine the lifetime interactions of natives and immigrants in the economy as workers, consumers, entrepreneurs, taxpayers, and recipients of government services. For example, educating immigrant children or providing them with sufficient health care to make learning possible may impose high short-run fiscal costs on local governments. However, as productive adults, these individuals are also potential net benefits to local governments as wage earners and as payers of sales and property taxes. Even in the short run, government expenditures flow as wages to teachers, health care workers, and other suppliers of goods or services to immigrant children. Moreover, if immigrants depress wage rates and reduce the employment opportunities of native workers, then there is an interaction between immigrants and the fiscal impacts of natives that is typically ignored in available research.

In this chapter we examine the fiscal impacts of immigrants from a micro perspective utilizing household-level information on New Jersey's population from the 1990 census. A comprehensive view is taken of state and local government revenues from and expenditures on noninstitutional households, which means that we are able to evaluate the net fiscal implications associated with immigrant families. Finally, we compare the budgetary consequences of households headed by native-born versus foreign-born individuals. Our results suggest that the typical New Jersey household, whether native or foreign born, uses more state and local government services than it pays for with taxes. Among nonelderly household heads, the negative fiscal impact of immigrant households exceeds that of native households by 46 percent at the state level and by 60 percent for county and municipal governments. In general, however, there is greater diversity within the foreign-born population, when stratified by region of origin, than there is between natives and immigrants.

CONCEPTUAL AND OTHER ISSUES

Attempts to estimate the fiscal impacts of immigrants encounter a variety of conceptual, methodological, and data issues. We do not claim to have resolved these issues definitively. Rather our purpose in this section is to describe the most critical ones as the basis for a subsequent discussion of the choices and assumptions we made in producing estimates for New Jersey.

Unit of Analysis

One issue involves the appropriate unit of analysis—whether it should be an individual, a family, or a household. There are reasons to prefer a household definition. First, many local government services such as fire and police protection are provided to households, and numerous taxes (such as property taxes) are paid by households. Second, a household comes closer to approximating a functioning socioeconomic unit of mutual exchange and support than a family. Using the "family" in the Census Bureau's sense of two or more individuals who are living together and who are related by blood, marriage, or adoption may be unnecessarily limiting for budgetary accounting purposes. Third, in most cases it makes little practical difference whether a family or household definition is used. In 1990 roughly 89 percent of the noninstitutional population in New Jersey lived in family households, approximately 8 percent lived alone, and just 3 percent lived in households with unrelated persons.

Households are usually labeled "immigrant" or "native" according to the householder's place of birth. But this practice encounters difficulty whenever some household members are foreign born and others are native born (Vernez and McCarthy, 1995). Immigrant-headed households may contain native-born children, and native-born householders may have a foreign-born spouse.

Marginal Versus Average Cost

Some services that governments provide have the characteristic of being pure or nearly pure public goods in the sense that consumption by one additional individual or household does not necessarily diminish the consumption of everyone else. National defense is the classic example at the federal level. Parks and other recreational facilities are illustrations of near-pure public goods at the state and local level. How should these expenditures be allocated to households? Some analysts argue that the appropriate cost to assign to an immigrant household for a public good is zero, because the marginal cost of servicing an additional household is negligible. There are two problems with this approach, however. One is the arbitrary manner of identifying the "last" household or households to benefit from the expenditure. A related difficulty pertains to threshold effects—that is, to assigning discrete jumps in marginal cost to particular households when population growth creates the need, for example, for a new school, road, or fire house.

An alternative perspective is that costs should be averaged over the general population if they cannot be earmarked to a well-defined subset of beneficiaries. This approach avoids the invidious comparisons inherent in marginal cost assignments, while recognizing that each household privately consumes a small portion of near-pure public goods. The issue is perhaps less important at the state level, because many services provided by the state arise from means-tested transfer programs in which recipient households are readily identifiable. At the county and municipal levels, however, a larger fraction of expenditures is not attributable directly to individual households. Net of education expenditures that benefit a student population, most of the goods provided by New Jersey's local governments are relatively public in nature (for example, parks and recreation, public health departments, public libraries, and judicial and legislative functions).

Top-Down Versus Bottom-Up

Two general and competing methodologies for assigning governmental expenditures and revenues are the top-down and bottom-up strategies—also known as macro and micro procedures, respectively. In the top-down approach one begins with a global sum, derived from governmental balance sheets, and then devises rules to distribute that total among beneficiary or taxpayer households. An alternative procedure is to build up to the aggregate total by inspecting the benefits received and the taxes paid by each individual household in the population and then cumulating the results. In principle, both methods should give the same or nearly the same answer, not only in the aggregate but also in the distribution of benefits and costs across households.[5] In actual practice, however, a macro or top-down approach minimizes variation across households because analysts frequently assign each household a prorated share of total tax revenue and public expenditure on goods and services. This approach will be inappropriate whenever the goods or services in question are not public goods or if households exhibit substantial variation by demographic or socioeconomic characteristics. Most studies of immigrants' fiscal impacts have used a macro perspective (Rothman and Espenshade, 1992). Recent exceptions include work reported by Borjas (1994) and Espenshade and King (1994).

Immigrants' Legal Status

Another practical difficulty is the common inability to distinguish among immigrants by their legal status. Decennial census data and the monthly Current Population Survey (since January 1994) contain questions on place of birth, year of immigration, and citizenship status for the foreign-born population. Roughly two-thirds of New Jersey's foreign-born household heads are naturalized U.S. citizens, but it is impossible to tell with census data whether noncitizen householders are permanent legal residents, temporary residents, refugees, or illegal migrants. Previous studies have suggested that different categories of immigrants have differential patterns of benefit receipt and tax payments (Rothman and Espenshade, 1992; Fix and Passel, 1994; Vernez and McCarthy, 1995, 1996). This problem is attenuated in studies that use a micro-level approach to calculate household benefit receipts and tax payments, because differences in average benefits received and taxes paid are permitted to fall out of the estimation and are not imposed by arbitrary rules that assign expenditures and revenues to house-

---

[5]There are obvious situations in which discrepancies would occur, however. Not all of the state sales tax collections come from New Jersey residents. Pennsylvania and New York residents who work or shop in New Jersey contribute to New Jersey's total sales tax revenues through their purchases. Moreover, out-of-state tourists visiting New Jersey contribute to sales tax receipts. A similar situation exists on the expenditure side. Public monies spent to build state roads provide benefits to out-of-state motorists as well as to New Jersey's residents.

holds. Simply prorating government expenditures and revenues across households blurs the distinctions between native- and foreign-born populations and
between naturalized citizens and resident aliens. The ability to distinguish the
legal status of immigrants is also relevant to policy, given recent changes to
welfare laws.

Who Benefits and Who Pays?

There are also questions regarding the proper attribution of tax revenues
received by state and local governments. First, the problem of tax incidence has
been largely ignored in the demographic literature. However tax incidence—that
is, who really bears the burden of a given tax levy—has generated considerable
research in public finance (Pechman, 1985; Fullerton and Rodgers, 1993; Metcalf,
1993). Previous studies of the fiscal impacts of immigrants have assumed that
the statutory payer of a tax bears the full incidence. Second, similar incidence
questions arise on the benefits side. Who are the beneficiaries of local public
school expenditures? The proximate beneficiaries of public education expenditures are the students, but an important rationale for public funding of elementary
and secondary schooling is that society as a whole is better off in the long run
with a more educated population. Third, the household sector is not the sole
beneficiary of state and local government expenditures. The corporate sector
benefits when, for example, an improved transportation or communication system permits a company to function more efficiently, or when a more educated
work force makes a business more productive. The fourth question concerns the
proper allocation of the costs of capital construction projects. Unlike a government's current expenditures on goods and services that are consumed in a single
period, capital investments (for example, roads, schools, water treatment plants)
generate a stream of services over time. For these items it is not obvious how to
identify the population of beneficiaries. Should it be the residents of a jurisdiction when construction is completed? Should it include residents when the debt
is retired? What about future residents who will enjoy the benefits years after the
initial capital outlays have been obligated? These could include as-yet-unborn
children and future in-migrants from other states or localities.

DATA

Numerous data sets from federal, state, and local sources were combined to
produce the estimates described in this chapter. The principal source of information is the 5 percent public use micro-data sample (PUMS) for New Jersey from
the 1990 Census of Population and Housing conducted by the Bureau of the
Census. This file contains detailed information on the demographic and socioeconomic characteristics (as of April 1, 1990) of approximately 145,000 randomly selected New Jersey households. We exclude from our analysis residents

of institutional and noninstitutional group quarters, who constitute less than 2 percent of New Jersey's total population. Income data for household members pertain to the 1989 calendar year.

Census data were extensively supplemented with state and local government budget information. The major source of additional information at the state level was the *State of New Jersey Budget: Fiscal Year 1991-1992* (State of New Jersey, 1991b). This document contains actual state program expenditures during the 1990 fiscal year (ending June 30, 1990) as well as explanations of program participation parameters and eligibility criteria. When these data were inadequate to identify the relevant beneficiary populations, we obtained additional information and program data from individual departments in the executive branch of the state government and from independent research organizations. For example, information about municipal aid distributions came from *State Aid Programs for Municipalities, 1989 and 1990* (Forsberg, 1995). Data on the state's share of school district expenditures were derived from the *1990 New Jersey Legislative District Data Book* (Rutgers, the State University of New Jersey, 1990). The principal supplementary sources of information at the local level were detailed municipal and county budget and tax data found in the *Fifty-Second Annual Report of the Division of Local Government Services, 1989* (State of New Jersey, 1990c). Clarifications of definitions for revenue and expenditure categories were frequently provided by representatives of the respective state and local agencies. A full listing of all data sources used together with a detailed description of the methodology used to arrive at our estimates of fiscal impacts are contained in the Appendix.

A demographic profile of our study population is shown in Table 3-1. It is constructed by multiplying unweighted PUMS data by 20. There were almost three million households in New Jersey in 1990. More than 85 percent of these are headed by someone born in the United States. Among foreign-born households, those headed by individuals born in Europe or Canada are the most numerous and comprise nearly one-half of the foreign-born total. Immigrant households are significantly larger than native households, although there is considerable diversity within the foreign population. Households with a head from Europe or Canada are somewhat smaller than the typical native household, whereas households headed by non-natives from other regions of the world have significantly more members.

There are also striking differences in age composition. The relative concentrations of children versus the elderly suggest that immigrant households are on average substantially younger than native households. Once again, however, there are sharp contrasts within the foreign population. Households headed by migrants from Europe or Canada are markedly older than their counterparts from other regions and have fewer minor children. On the other hand, households headed by Asian immigrants are the youngest on average, having the fewest elderly and the most children. Differences in the average age of household heads

TABLE 3-1 Demographic Profile of New Jersey Households, 1990

Characteristic (mean)	Total	Native Born	Foreign Born	Foreign-born Households by Region of Origin			
				Europe/ Canada	Asia	Latin America	Other
Number of Households	2,897,560	2,505,400	392,160	182,460	77,100	111,200	21,400
Persons in Household	2.74	2.68	3.10*	2.62*	3.59*	3.51*	3.16*
Children <18 in Household	0.66	0.63	0.81*	0.52*	1.14*	1.02*	0.99*
School-Age Children in Household[a]	0.43	0.41	0.54*	0.38*	0.76*	0.65*	0.59*
In Public School	0.34	0.33	0.42*	0.30*	0.60*	0.49*	0.45*
LEP Children <18 in Household[b]	0.03	0.01	0.11*	0.04*	0.19*	0.18*	0.10*
LEP Children in Bilingual Education[c]	0.02	<0.01	0.08*	0.03*	0.13*	0.12*	0.07*
Persons 65+ in Household	0.36	0.36	0.35	0.56*	0.15*	0.19*	0.19*
Age of Household Head	50.03	50.03	50.01	57.74*	42.06*	43.98*	44.06*
% Male Household Head	68.36%	67.45	74.14*	70.53*	85.40*	71.80*	76.54*

*Indicates native and foreign-born means are significantly different at the 5% level.

[a]School-age children are defined as those aged 6 to 17, inclusive.

[b]Limited English proficient children are defined as those who speak a language other than English at home and who speak English "well," "not well," or "not at all," as opposed to "very well."

[c]Defined as LEP children aged 6 to 17 inclusive, who are enrolled in public elementary and secondary schools.

confirm these conclusions. In short, the picture that emerges reflects a relatively large proportion of foreign households, nearly half of which are headed by European immigrants. These migrants tended to come to the United States earlier in the twentieth century and now head households that are both smaller and older than the average. Immigrants from Asia and Latin America predominate among more recent migrant cohorts, and they are now heads of households that are larger and more youthful than even native households.

The average number of children under age 18 who are enrolled in public school is significantly greater for immigrant households, with the exception of those from Canada and Europe. These differentials reflect differences in the number of minor children, not in the propensity of immigrant families to use public education services. Conditional on having school-age children, immigrant-headed households are no more likely to enroll their children in public school than native-headed households. Because local governments spend a large proportion of their budgets on public schools, these demographic differences across households have important fiscal consequences. Just slightly more than one-fourth (26 percent) of the average number of minor children in foreign-born households are themselves foreign born (0.21 out of 0.81). This proportion ranges between 15 percent in households headed by persons born in Europe or Canada to 32 percent in Asian-headed households. Of the 0.21 average number of foreign-born children in the typical foreign household, 84 percent are 6-17 years old. And of these, nearly 80 percent are enrolled in public elementary or secondary school. In other words, foreign- and native-born children have similar school attendance patterns, regardless of the nativity status of the native children's parents. Finally, there is remarkable uniformity in public school enrollment rates among foreign-born children when households are stratified by region of origin.

Socioeconomic variations by household type are shown in Table 3-2. Immigrant households from outside Europe and Canada have significantly above-average numbers of earners when compared with natives. This is partly a reflection of their greater size and youthfulness. Not only are households headed by Latin American immigrants significantly poorer than native households, they are also more likely to receive public assistance income than any other group of households. European and Asian immigrants are less likely to rely on public assistance than natives. On average, foreign-born households in 1989 had incomes that were about 6 percent below those for natives. However, income differences within the immigrant population are significantly greater than they are between natives and foreigners. Mean household income for Asian migrants, for example, is 56 percent higher than the average income for Latin American immigrants.

A simple measure of relative economic well-being can be obtained by calculating per capita income for each household and averaging across all households in a category. For the total population, per capita household income equals more than $20,900. It is approximately $21,500 for natives versus $17,600 for immi-

TABLE 3-2 Socioeconomic Profile of New Jersey Households, 1990

Characteristic	Total Born	Native Born	Foreign-born Households by Region of Origin				
			Foreign Canada	Europe/Asia	America	Latin Other	Other
Mean Number of Wage Earners in Household	1.39	1.37	1.51*	1.22*	1.76*	1.78*	1.54*
% of Households Receiving Public Assistance Income[a]	5.31%	5.24	5.79*	4.19*	4.46*	9.37*	5.70
% of Households Receiving SSI	1.66%	1.62	1.91	2.07*	0.96*	2.45*	1.21
% of Households Receiving AFDC	2.58%	2.57	2.63	1.01*	3.04	4.93*	2.99
Mean Public Assistance Income of Recipient Households, 1989	$4,428	4,459	4,250	4,502	4,163	4,135	3,905
Median Public Assistance Income of Recipient Households, 1989	$ 3,900	3,926	3,775	3,870	3,600	3,864	3,612
Mean Household Income, 1989	$50,684	51,085	48,122*	46,886*	62,836*	40,279*	46,404*
Per Capita[b]	$20,946	21,477	17,557*	19,335*	19,941*	13,144*	16,747*
Median Household Income, 1989	$41,929	42,110	39,000	37,200	54,180	34,000	37,000

*Indicates native and foreign-born means are significantly different at the 5% level.

[a]Public assistance income includes General Assistance, Supplemental Security Income, and Aid to Families with Dependent Children.

[b]Found by calculating per capita income for each household and averaging over all households in the category.

grants. But among foreign-born households, this measure ranges between $13,100 for Latinos to nearly $20,000 for households from Europe, Canada, and Asia. It is apparent that Latin American migrants are typically among the poorest of all immigrant households in New Jersey. As we will see below, this finding, too, has implications for fiscal impacts.

RESULTS

We present our results in terms of averages per household after stratifying households by type. Households are grouped according to characteristics of the household head, including age and sex, nativity status (that is, whether foreign or native born), and region of birth for immigrants. Using decennial census data, we are unable to identify legal administrative status among noncitizen immigrant households.

State Estimates

The main results at the state level are displayed in Table 3-3. The table's first panel shows state expenditures on households in FY 1989-1990. General state services and state aid along with costs for public elementary and secondary school education are the largest items in dollar terms. General state services are the same for all households because they are prorated using average cost principles. There are sharp differences in education expenditures according to the age of the householder, because there are relatively few school-age children in households headed by senior citizens.

Total estimated state expenditures are summed across the bottom row of the first panel. They show that the state spent an average of approximately $3,700 on each household with a head under age 65 and more than $2,300 on elderly households. This age difference is preserved among different types of households and primarily reflects the gap in educational expenditures between younger and older households. In general, immigrants are more costly to the state than natives. Immigrant households with younger heads received roughly $400 more benefits than natives in 1989-1990. Among older households, the immigrant advantage was closer to $200.

Differentials between immigrants and natives are small, however, in comparison with the variation in state expenditures among the foreign-born population. European households commanded relatively fewer state expenditures, whereas Asian, Latin American, and other immigrants received state benefits well in excess of the foreign-born average. Latin American households are especially costly to the state. They received public benefits almost $900 or 25 percent greater than amounts going to the typical younger New Jersey household. Elderly Latino households had more than an $1,800, or nearly 80 percent, advantage. Higher than usual expenditures on education and especially on Medicaid and welfare explain most of the

TABLE 3-3   Average State Expenditures, Revenues, and Net Fiscal Impact per Household, by Age and Nativity Status of Head, FY 1989-1990 (all figures in dollars)

State Expenditures[a]	Total		Native Born		Foreign Born	
	<65	65+	<65	65+	<65	65+
General State Services/ State Aid	1,119	1,119	1,119	1,119	1,119	1,119
Elementary & Secondary Education	1,523	124	1,489	127	1,733	101
Higher Education	382	74	365	70	490	103
Medicaid	289	410	288	394	297	521
AFDC/GA/SSI	79	70	79	67	78	86
PAAD	14	143	13	138	19	176
Municipal Aid Programs	84	85	76	82	137	107
Employment & Training Programs	25	15	26	15	20	12
Programs for Aged, Vets & Disabled	25	91	27	94	10	72
Property Tax Reimbursement	101	124	102	125	94	119
Other Allocable Expenditures	52	70	52	69	48	74
TOTAL	**3,693**	**2,324**	**3,636**	**2,300**	**4,044**	**2,489**
State Revenues						
Income Tax	1,375	411	1,389	410	1,291	417
Sales Tax	504	317	508	319	484	301
Auto/Fuels Tax	249	156	252	159	227	133
Alcohol/Tobacco Tax	121	102	119	101	134	105
Inheritance Tax	68	74	74	75	29	68
Business Property Tax	6	3	5	3	7	3
Realty Transfer Tax	41	7	40	7	48	9
TOTAL	**2,364**	**1,070**	**2,387**	**1,075**	**2,220**	**1,036**
Net Fiscal Impact[h]	−1,329	−1,254[b]	−1,249	−1,225	−1,824[c]	−1,453[g]

[a]See text for explanation of expenditure and revenue categories.

[b]Under 65 and 65+ mean deficits are significantly different at the 5% level.

[c]Native and foreign-born mean deficits differ significantly for household heads under 65.

[d]Native and foreign-born mean deficits differ significantly for household heads 65 and older.

[e]Foreign-born household heads under 65 from Europe and Canada have significantly smaller mean deficits than their counterparts from other regions.

[f]Foreign-born household heads 65 and older from Europe and Canada have significantly smaller mean deficits than those from Latin America.

[g]Both b and d, see above.

[h]Calculated as revenues minus expenditures.

Foreign-born Households by Region of Origin							
Europe/Canada		Asia		Latin America		Other	
<65	65+	<65	65+	<65	65+	<65	65+
1,119	1,119	1,119	1,119	1,119	1,119	1,119	1,119
1,466	46	1,808	295	1,971	416	1,767	78
410	88	622	200	481	180	504	90
180	365	245	733	468	1453	291	723
42	57	66	138	125	255	88	113
17	167	21	166	21	243	16	174
87	86	80	110	229	239	163	134
27	10	10	26	19	19	18	16
15	76	6	69	7	49	7	70
106	123	90	107	85	91	88	110
52	72	48	76	45	89	41	77
3,520	**2,208**	**4,115**	**3,037**	**4,569**	**4,153**	**4,102**	**2,705**
1,419	396	1,620	792	934	417	1,145	517
512	296	549	403	412	296	449	323
261	133	244	183	185	114	198	141
129	99	137	143	139	128	123	105
46	73	14	42	22	48	17	59
8	3	8	4	5	2	5	4
45	8	77	35	28	6	51	18
2,419	**1,008**	**2,648**	**1,602**	**1,725**	**1,011**	**1,988**	**1,166**
−1,101	−1,199	−1,467[e]	−1,435	−2,844[e]	−3,142[f]	−2,114[e]	−1,539

Latin American differential. As shown in Table 3-2, Latin American migrants' greater reliance on Medicaid and welfare is related to their poverty status. Education, including higher education, along with Medicaid costs help to explain the relatively higher amounts spent on Asian immigrants. Both education and Medicaid were comparatively less important for immigrants from Europe and Canada. Fewer school-age children largely accounts for lower educational expenditures on European and Canadian households.

Revenues that the state received from New Jersey households are shown in the lower panel of Table 3-3. The most important of these are income taxes, followed by sales and then automobile and gasoline taxes. Younger households paid a larger average amount in total taxes in FY 1989-1990 than senior households (roughly $2,400 versus $1,100), principally because labor force participation rates and income levels are higher for younger persons. Differences between immigrants and natives are once again small; total taxes paid by immigrant households averaged no more than 4-7 percent less than natives' tax contributions to the state. However, there is substantial diversity within the immigrant community. Compared with the statewide average for younger households, for example, total tax payments ranged between 12 percent above average for younger households headed by Asian immigrants to 27 percent below the statewide average for younger Latin American households. Much of the gap between younger Asians and Latinos is explained by differences in income taxes, which in turn reflect underlying differences in household income that were described in Table 3-2.

Households' net fiscal impacts are shown in the last row of Table 3-3. They are calculated by subtracting estimated per household state expenditures from state revenues. Our estimates suggest that every household type was a net burden on state government in FY 1989-1990, receiving more in state services than they paid for with state taxes. The typical budgetary deficit amounted to approximately $1,300 for each household in New Jersey. Some readers may wonder how this result is possible when the state's budget must balance every year. It arises because we have neglected other sources of revenue from corporations and the federal government that flow into the state's treasury and also because we have attributed as benefits to households some state expenditures that benefit the corporate sector.[6]

---

[6]An alternative approach that was used by Michael Clune in his California study is to assume that corporations (and tourists) receive public services equal in dollar value to the taxes they pay. With this added assumption, the net fiscal impact of the average household is *zero*. The typical household is neither a fiscal asset nor a fiscal burden. When this additional assumption is applied to the New Jersey results and the estimates are updated to reflect December 1996 prices, they suggest that the average native household generated an annual fiscal surplus of $232 (after combining local and state governments) and that the typical foreign household was a net burden of $1,484. By contrast, the corresponding estimates for California are an annual net surplus of $1,178 for natives and an annual net deficit of $3,463 for foreign households. Native and foreign households in New Jersey are more alike than they are in California in terms of family size, family composition, and household income. This fact helps to account for the smaller gap in New Jersey between the fiscal impacts of immigrant and native households (Smith and Edmonston, 1997:Tables 3-1 to 3-3).

There is a small difference in the general population between younger and older households' fiscal effects. Significantly larger gaps emerge between immigrants and natives. Among younger households, the fiscal burden associated with immigrants is $575 or 46 percent greater than for natives. Elderly foreign households generate a smaller discrepancy ($228) but one that is nevertheless 19 percent higher than the comparable figure for natives. Disparities in fiscal impacts are greater among immigrant groups than between immigrant and native-born households. European and Asian immigrant families engender fiscal consequences that are not much different from all families. On the other hand, immigrants from Latin America and from other places are least likely to be paying their way. The estimated net fiscal deficit for Latinos is well over twice as large as it is for the typical household in the state, and younger migrant families from other countries impose a fiscal burden 60 percent greater than all younger families combined. These results are consistent with findings from earlier studies (Espenshade and King, 1994).[7]

We used regression analysis to test whether differences in fiscal impacts result from something intrinsic to nativity status or simply reflect differences in socioeconomic and demographic characteristics between immigrants and natives. After controlling for age, education, marital status, English proficiency, place of residence, and number of children, we found that the difference in net fiscal impacts associated with nativity status was not statistically significant.[8] Our results suggest that it is not the fact of being foreign born per se, but rather the different configuration of immigrants' household characteristics that influences their net fiscal impacts on state government. Latin American and other immigrants, who are younger and have more children (and therefore incur greater state costs for elementary and secondary schooling), exert a larger fiscal imposition

---

[7]Using household-level information on the nativity status of children enrolled in public school, we can disaggregate state expenditures on public elementary and secondary school for immigrant-headed households into those for native- and foreign-born children (see the second row in the top panel of Table 3-3). The average household state expenditure on native-born children in households headed by migrants from Europe and Canada is $1,142 and $44 in younger versus older households, respectively. The corresponding figures are $1,043 and $182 in Asian households, $1,161 and $269 in Latino households, and $1,089 and $44 in other immigrant households. Recalculating net fiscal impacts of immigrant households by counting only educational expenditures on foreign-born children has a dramatic effect on the results in younger households. The deficit is reduced by 71 percent for Asian households, by 40 percent for Latin American households, and by slightly more than one-half for other immigrant households. For younger European and Canadian families, disregarding native-born children converts a per household fiscal deficit of $1,101 into a small surplus. However, focusing exclusively on foreign-born children in immigrant households encounters several problems. The native-born children are still someone's responsibility, and it can be argued that they are the responsibility of their immigrant parents. Moreover, disaggregating fiscal impacts at the level of individual children runs counter to our overall analysis which takes the household—not the individual—as the appropriate unit of analysis.

[8]However, when the immigrant-native differential is captured by modeling each region of origin separately, the coefficient on Latin America is still significant.

than their native-born counterparts. Asian immigrants also have large families, but their disproportionate use of state education benefits is largely offset by higher incomes and tax payments.

The household-level net fiscal deficits are cumulated up to the state level and shown separately for male- and female-headed households in Table 3-4. The household sector ran a combined $3.8 billion deficit in FY 1989-1990. Immigrant households contributed $683 million to this total. Even though immigrants comprised 13.5 percent of all New Jersey households, they accounted for 18 percent of the aggregate budget gap. Latino households were just 3.8 percent of all households in the state, but they contributed 8.4 percent of the aggregate deficit. Within the foreign-born population, Latinos made up 28 percent of all households, whereas they accounted for nearly half (47 percent) of the fiscal deficit attributable to migrants. The average net fiscal deficit associated with female-headed households is significantly larger than its male counterpart. The relative gap between the sexes is especially pronounced for younger households.

TABLE 3-4   Net Fiscal Impact of Households on State of New Jersey, by Age, Sex, and Nativity Status of Household Head, FY 1989-1990 (all figures in dollars)

Net Fiscal Impact	Total NJ Households		Native Born		Foreign Born	
	<65	65+	<65	65+	<65	65+
All Households						
State Total (millions)	−2,943	−856	−2,384	−732	−559	−124
Per Household	−1,329	−1,254	−1,249	−1,225	−1,824	−1,453
Per Capita[g]	−322	−874[a]	−302	−853[a]	−450	−1,022[a]
Male-Headed Households						
State Total (millions)	−1,421	−349	−1,035	−295	−386	−54
Per Household	−884[d]	−937[d]	−758[d]	−911[d]	−1,591[d]	−1,113[d]
Per Capita[g]	−132[d]	−504[d]	−97[d]	−488[d]	−330[d]	−608[d]
Female-Headed Households						
State Total (millions)	−1,522	−507	−1,348	−437	−174	−70
Per Household	−2,509	−1,635	−2,486	−1,599	−2,706	−1,897
Per Capita[g]	−827	−1,319	−818	−1,286	−902	−1,561

[a]Per capita mean deficit differs significantly (at 5% level) by age of household head.

[b]Foreign-born household heads under 65 from Europe and Canada have significantly different mean deficits from their counterparts in other regions.

[c]Foreign-born household heads 65 and older from Europe and Canada have significantly different mean deficits from their counterparts in other regions.

[d]Male-headed household mean deficit is significantly smaller than corresponding female-headed household mean deficit.

[e]Both b and d, see above.

[f]Both c and d, see above.

[g]Found by first calculating the net fiscal impact per capita for each household and then averaging over all households in the category.

This finding is hardly surprising. Women earn less than men on average and usually have custody of children that result from nonmarital births and parental divorces, making female-headed households eligible for AFDC and Medicaid.

Local Estimates

Table 3-5 contains estimates of local government expenditures on households and of household-level taxes that flow back to counties and municipalities. General county and municipal expenditures consist of such items as general government, judiciary, public safety, public works, health and welfare (excluding expenses for county welfare boards and for welfare/public assistance), recreation and conservation, nonschool education (for example, public libraries), public employee benefits and pension contributions, and debt service. These costs are apportioned evenly to all households in a given political jurisdiction. We assume that, if immigrant and native households are located in the same neighborhood,

Foreign-born Households by Region of Origin							
Europe/Canada		Asia		Latin America		Other	
<65	65+	<65	65+	<65	65+	<65	65+
−124	−83	−108	−5	−287	−33	−40	−4
−1,101	−1,199	−1,467	−1,435	−2,844	−3,142	−2,114	−1,539
−250	−908	−312[b]	−720	−752[b]	−1,842[c]	−574[b]	−1,176
−93	−34	−93	−3	−173	−15	−27	−1
−1,022[d]	−896[d]	−1,470[b]	−1,199	−2,361[e]	−2,386[f]	−1,772[e]	−993[d]
−166[d]	−542[d]	−295[e]	−507[d]	−546[e]	−1,042[f]	−410[e]	−584[d]
−32	−49	−15	−2	−113	−17	−13	−2
−1,421	−1,568	−1,450	−2,114	−4,132[b]	−4,393[c]	−3,412[b]	−2,246[c]
−586	−1,354	−415[b]	−1,333	−1,303[b]	−3,166[c]	−1,199[b]	−1,942[c]

TABLE 3-5   Average Local Expenditures, Revenues, and Net Fiscal Impact per Household, by Age and Nativity Status of Head, FY 1989-1990 (all figures in dollars)

	Total		Native Born		Foreign Born	
	<65	65+	<65	65+	<65	65+
Local Expenditures[a]						
General County	716	731	708	728	768	755
General Municipal	1,427	1,458	1,382	1,441	1,707	1,576
Elementary &						
Secondary Educ	2,134	154	2,034	154	2,754	156
County College	49	9	48	9	56	13
AFDC	17	4	17	4	16	4
TOTAL	4,344	2,356	4,190	2,335	5,302	2,503
Local Revenues						
Property Tax	2,472	2,162	2,448	2,150	2,619	2,247
Utility Tax	160	142	161	142	157	139
TOTAL	2,632	2,304	2,609	2,292	2,776	2,386
Net Fiscal Impact[h]	−1,712	−52[b]	−1,581	−43[b]	−2,526[c]	−117[g]

[a]See text for explanation of expenditure and revenue categories.

[b]Under 65 and 65+ mean deficits are significantly different at the 5% level.

[c]Native and foreign-born mean deficits differ significantly for household heads under 65.

[d]Native and foreign-born mean deficits differ significantly for household heads 65+.

[e]Foreign-born household heads under 65 from Europe and Canada have significantly lower mean deficits than their counterparts from other regions.

they receive the same level of government benefits from general county and municipal expenditures. Therefore, differences in these costs by household type in the first two rows of Table 3-5 reflect variations in the spatial distribution throughout New Jersey of the respective populations.

Households' estimated net fiscal impacts at the local level are shown in the last row of Table 3-5. The net fiscal cost is either negligible or very small for senior citizen households. Elderly immigrants from Europe and Canada even appear to generate a slight surplus for other taxpayers, although the amount ($63) is not statistically different from zero. The one exception is Latin American households. Elderly Latino immigrant households incurred a local deficit of almost $1,400 per household in FY 1989-1990, principally because they paid below-average amounts in property taxes and lived in urban areas in the northeastern part of New Jersey that spent relatively large sums on general municipal functions.

The typical nonelderly household received benefits from local government that exceeded taxes paid by more than $1,700. This amount is larger than the

| Foreign-born Households by Region of Origin | | | | | | | |
| Europe/Canada | | Asia | | Latin America | | Other | |
<65	65+	<65	65+	<65	65+	<65	65+
752	744	741	778	803	813	785	767
1,582	1,506	1,559	1,681	1,926	1,979	1,868	1,736
2,526	89	3,672	368	2,370	546	2,581	116
55	11	52	15	61	23	56	14
7	1	16	13	26	19	20	0
4,922	2,351	6,039	2,855	5,187	3,380	5,311	2,633
2,949	2,276	2,831	2,706	2,126	1,867	2,447	2,432
164	139	156	159	152	135	150	145
3,113	2,415	2,987	2,865	2,278	2,002	2,597	2,577
−1,809	63	−3,053[e]	10	−2,909[e]	−1,378[f]	−2,714[e]	−56

[f]Foreign-born household heads 65+ from Europe and Canada have a significantly lower mean deficit than those from Latin America.

[g]Both b and d, see above.

[h]Calculated as revenues minus expenditures.

fiscal burden these same households placed on state government in 1989-1990.[9] There is a substantial nativity differential at the local level. The deficit imposed by immigrant households exceeds the one for natives by nearly $1,000 per household, or by 60 percent. This comparison hides even larger variations when migrants are disaggregated by region of origin. European migrants have fiscal costs that are relatively close to those of natives. But the fiscal impacts associated with younger immigrants from outside Europe and Canada are between 72 and 93 percent greater than those for their native counterparts. Given our findings at the state level, budget gaps this large might be expected for Latin American and other immigrants. But the fiscal deficit for Asian households (nearly $3,100) requires comment. Asian families have the highest average number of

---

[9]A deficit of this magnitude arises because we have attributed general county and municipal expenditures entirely to the household sector and because we have neglected nonhousehold sources of revenue to local governments. The latter include real estate taxes paid on commercial and industrial property, public utility taxes paid by businesses, and federal revenue sharing.

school-age children, and they live in school districts that spend relatively large amounts per student. The disproportionately large public school expenditure on Asian children is only partially offset by the higher-than-average property taxes paid by younger Asian families. Parallel to findings at the state level, a regression analysis using a household's net fiscal impact as the dependent variable shows that nativity status is not a statistically significant predictor when household socioeconomic and demographic factors are controlled. Latin American immigrants again are the single exception.[10]

Table 3-6 shows that the combined household sector deficit at the local level was $3.83 billion in 1989-1990, approximately the same size as the aggregate deficit households imposed on state government. In contrast to the state picture, however, virtually all of the local fiscal deficit is attributable to younger households. Immigrant families are again responsible for a disproportionate share. Their fraction of the local deficit (20.5 percent) is half again as large as their portion of total households (13.5 percent). Among the immigrant population, European households' net use of local services is relatively small. Europeans and Canadians account for one-fourth of the aggregate local immigrant deficit but make up nearly half of all foreign households. Male-female differences are generally consistent with those at the state level in the sense that net fiscal deficits attributable to female-headed households are typically significantly greater than those for male-headed households. On the other hand, with the exception of Latinos, male-headed senior citizen households are net fiscal assets at the local level and might be expected to provide a small subsidy to other taxpayers.

CONCLUSIONS

This chapter uses data from 1990 census 5 percent PUMS files, supplemented extensively with information from state and municipal budgets, to estimate the state and local fiscal impacts of immigrant and native-born households in New Jersey. We take the household as the unit of analysis and pass each of the approximately 145,000 New Jersey households on the PUMS files under a microscope to estimate taxes paid to state and local governments and benefits received from the same jurisdictions. We do not claim that our methodology represents

---

[10]Once again, netting out public elementary and secondary school expenditures on native children in foreign-born households drastically reduces the implied fiscal deficit. The absolute amounts in question, on a per household basis, are $1,968 and $85 for younger and older, respectively, European and Canadian households; $2,119 and $227 for Asian households; $1,396 and $353 for Latin American households; and $1,591 and $65 in other immigrant families. In general, ignoring local educational expenditures on native children in foreign households has a stronger fiscal impact than a similar calculation at the state level.

"best" practice, but it is substantially better practice than many approaches taken in the past.

There are several new features of these estimates. First, they are based on a micro-level analysis instead of a top-down macro procedure that prorates government revenues and expenditures evenly across households on the basis of average cost assumptions. We attribute roughly two-thirds of FY 1989-1990 current state expenditures on the noninstitutionalized population to targeted households that actually benefit from the expenditure. Just one-third of state expenditures are allocated on a pro rata share basis, and these are typically costs for public goods. Second, we attach fiscal cost and benefit data to each household record, and these micro units can then be compared in different ways. We contrast the fiscal impacts of households headed by immigrants and natives. Differences by age and sex of household head and by region of origin for the foreign-born population are also featured in the analysis. Third, we view government expenditures on households and revenues provided by the household sector to the state and to municipalities in the broadest terms possible, which means that we are able to draw conclusions about the net fiscal impacts of different kinds of households.

We find that both immigrant and native households are net fiscal burdens on state and local government in New Jersey, receiving more in services than they pay in taxes. Part of the shortfall is made up from a variety of taxes paid by corporations and part by monies passed back from the federal government. There is typically greater variation in fiscal impacts within the foreign-born population than between immigrants and natives. Immigrant households on average have significantly larger fiscal deficits associated with them than native households at both the state and local level. Moreover, the relative burden imposed by immigrants is greater for county and municipal governments than for the state. This conclusion is consistent with research from other states showing that it is usually local governments that shoulder the most substantial burden in providing services to immigrant families (Rothman and Espenshade, 1992). It would be useful for comparative purposes to move beyond New Jersey and to apply these micro-analytic methodologies to data from other states with large immigrant populations. Because no state is necessarily representative of the entire United States, developing additional case studies would provide a richer and more comprehensive national picture of the state and local fiscal impacts of U.S. immigration.

Our study challenges future research in four ways. First, the nonhousehold sector needs to be brought into the analysis on both the revenue and expenditure side. We have ignored taxes paid by corporations and have interpreted most government expenditures as benefits to households, which helps to produce the conclusion that households on average receive more services than they pay for. Second, the methodology of fiscal accounting needs to move beyond single-period static analysis toward examining individuals' and households' use of public benefits and payment of taxes in a dynamic life-cycle context. Separating out

TABLE 3-6   Net Fiscal Impact of Households on Local Governments, by Age, Sex, and Nativity Status of Household Head, FY 1989-1990 (all figures in dollars)

Net Fiscal Impact	Total NJ Households		Native Born		Foreign Born	
	<65	65+	<65	65+	<65	65+
All Households						
State Total (millions)	−3,790	−36	−3,016	−26	−774	−10
Per Household	−1,712	−52	−1,581	−43	−2,526	−117
Per Capita[e]	−415	−79[a]	−383	−72[a]	−613	−133[a]
Male-Headed Households						
State Total (millions)	−2,585	87	−1,970	80	−614	7
Per Household	−1,607[d]	234[d]	−1,443[d]	247[d]	−2,535	146[d]
Per Capita[e]	−336[d]	108[d]	−293[d]	115[d]	−574[d]	62[d]
Female-Headed Households						
State Total (millions)	−1,206	−123	−1,045	−106	−160	−17
Per Household	−1,987	−396	−1,927	−387	−2,493	−459
Per Capita[e]	−625	−305	−608	−294	−761	−386

[a]Per capita mean deficit differs significantly (at 5% level) by age of household head.
[b]Foreign-born household heads under 65 from Europe and Canada have significantly different mean deficits from their counterparts in other regions.
[c]Foreign-born household heads 65+ from Europe and Canada have significantly different mean deficits from their counterparts in other regions.

age and cohort effects is impossible when the analysis is restricted to a single cross section. As a first step the methods we have developed in this chapter could be applied to successive cross sections. Age and cohort effects could then be deduced from the set of cross-sectional results. Third, second-round spillover and multiplier effects need to be accounted for in more complex, general equilibrium models. Immigrants' entrepreneurial activities may generate employment for other native and foreign workers. If immigrants have adverse labor market outcomes for native workers, these effects also need to be taken into account in computing fiscal impacts. Finally, estimating the fiscal impacts of immigrants is frequently a task assigned to in-house researchers working for state and local governments. These analysts are often laboring under tight budgetary and time constraints and may face incentives to reach a predetermined conclusion. An important challenge for future research is to engage the attention of academic economists, especially public finance specialists, in examining the fiscal implications of U.S. immigration.

APPENDIX

This methodological appendix provides a full listing of all data sources together with a detailed description of the methodology used in the simulation

| Foreign-born Households by Region of Origin | | | | | | | |
| Europe/Canada | | Asia | | Latin America | | Other | |
<65	65+	<65	65+	<65	65+	<65	65+
−204	4	−225	<0.1	−293	−14	−51	−0.1
−1,809	63	−3,053	10	−2,909	−1,378	−2,714	−56
−386	−48	−693[b]	61	−781[b]	−751[c]	−763[b]	−159
−176	13	−202	0.5	−198	−7	−38	0.9
−1,940[d]	340[d]	−3,186[d]	211	−2,699[d]	−1,129[d]	−2,568[d]	656[d]
−396	134[d]	−702	155	−661[d]	−468[d]	−681[d]	372[d]
−29	−9	−23	−0.5	−95	−7	−13	−1
−1,281	−273	−2,242	−567	−3,469	−1,790	−3,270	−980
−347	−271	−637	−209	−1,101	−1,220	−1,074	−848

[d]Male-headed household mean differs significantly from the corresponding female-headed household mean.

[e]Found by first calculating the net fiscal impact per capita for each household and then averaging over all households in the category.

program to produce the fiscal estimates described above. Its purpose is twofold. First, the reader interested in the assumptions underlying the model will have a clearer understanding of the sensitivity of our estimates to those assumptions. Second, the model is rendered reproducible, not only with 1989-1990 fiscal data for New Jersey, but also in its application to other states' census and state and local government budget information. In the descriptions given below, household and individual-level variables from the 1990 Public Use Microdata Sample A (PUMS) are denoted in upper-case letters. The reader will notice in some calculations that one-twentieth of an aggregate budget figure is used. This reflects the fact that the PUMS is a 5 percent sample of New Jersey households. The results presented in the chapter are rescaled by a factor of 20 to accurately reflect households' budgetary impact in the aggregate.

Methodological Approach

We concentrate our analysis on the household sector comprising the resident noninstitutional population in New Jersey, and we take the individual household as our principal unit of analysis. The central problem is then one of attributing to households the expenditures made and the revenues received by state and local governments during FY 1989-1990. To construct our estimates of fiscal impacts we adopt a micro-analytic perspective and examine each of the 145,000 households on the New Jersey PUMS file for 1990. We make four calculations for each household based on its demographic and socioeconomic makeup: (1) taxes paid to state government, (2) taxes paid to county and municipal governments, (2) benefits received from state government, and (4) benefits received from county and municipal governments. Each of these calculations is further disaggregated to reflect the composition of taxes paid and benefits received. These estimates are then appended to each household's record.

New Jersey's state budget for FY 1990 totaled $12.15 billion. Current expenditures made up $11.47 billion of this total. We exclude from consideration capital construction costs and the value of state bond redemptions because it is impossible to identify unambiguously the set of beneficiary households. Moreover, approximately $1.1 billion from current state expenditures was spent on goods and services that were not directly consumed by households. Roughly half of these costs are attributable to corrections and incarceration, whereas the remaining amounts were spent on the institutionalized disabled and handicapped population. We also exclude these expenditures on behalf of institutionalized populations, because we focus the analysis on the household sector. We are left with $10.38 billion in state expenditures to allocate to households.

We make simplifying assumptions about tax incidence that reflect the general consensus in the literature (Pechman, 1985; Rothman and Espenshade, 1992; Metcalf, 1993). We assume, for example, that the personal income tax is borne by the household paying the tax and that the sales and use tax is borne by consumers in proportion to their expected total expenditures. Purchasers of goods on which excise taxes are levied are presumed to bear the tax, and owners of personal business property and homeowners bear the burden of taxes assessed on these properties. Owners of residential rental properties, however, are assumed to pass local property taxes on to tenants. Equivalent assumptions are made about the incidence of public benefits; the proximate beneficiary is assumed to be the ultimate one. So, for example, we postulate that the benefits of public school expenditures lodge in households with school-age children who are enrolled in public schools and that there are no spillovers to the general population. Likewise, we neglect the possibility that government transfer payments or public expenditures on goods and services generate jobs and additional tax revenues when injected back into the economy. These multiplier effects could be accounted for in a general equilibrium model, but we do not consider them here.

Our study adopts a cross-sectional approach as a first step and implicitly ignores life-cycle costs and benefits of immigrants and natives. To our knowledge no fiscal impact analysis has been conducted with an explicit time dimension. Single-period accounting frameworks, although providing a useful guide to annual balance sheet impacts of immigrant and native households, cannot distinguish between cohort and aging effects. They cannot furnish evidence on how patterns of benefit receipt and tax payments vary with immigrant tenure in the United States, nor do they yield information on differential net fiscal impacts across immigrant cohorts. On the other hand, our household-level estimates would permit separating cohort and age effects if we applied the same methodology to two consecutive censuses.[11]

Another potential limitation of this study is our assumption that, apart from capital costs and institution-related expenditures, all governments' expenditures represent exclusive benefits to the household sector. But households are only one source of state revenues.[12] Corporations also pay taxes; the most important of these in New Jersey are the corporation income tax, real estate taxes on commercial property, and fees and profits taxes on banks and insurance companies operating in the state. Neglecting corporate-sector taxes causes us to underestimate state revenues by at least 25 percent. The potential revenue understatement for local property taxes is perhaps greater and varies across municipalities by the proportion of valued property owned by businesses. To anticipate some of our later findings, these omissions help to explain why both native- and immigrant-headed households are net fiscal drains at the state and local levels. They also suggest the use of caution in interpreting the results. It might be best if readers viewed the fiscal impact estimates in relative instead of absolute terms; that is, estimates for natives can be compared with immigrants at each level of government.

Illustrative Examples

Three different estimation strategies are used to produce our estimates of fiscal impacts. First, government expenditures on pure or near-pure public goods and on those in which it is otherwise difficult to identify an appropriate subset of beneficiaries are allocated to households on an *average* cost or prorated share basis.[13] For state expenditures the proration pertains to all households in New Jersey. For county and municipal expenditures the relevant geographic unit is the

---

[11]See Borjas (1985) for an example applied to immigrants' wage mobility between 1970 and 1980, and Garvey (1997), who applies the same methodology to New Jersey's immigrant and native population.

[12]Taxes paid by households constituted approximately 75 percent of total state tax revenue in FY 1990. The principal taxes included the gross income tax, sales and use tax, motor vehicle fees and the motor fuels tax, cigarette tax, the inheritance/estate transfer tax, business personal property tax, and the realty transfer tax.

[13]In calculations where we allocate general expenditures on the assumption of average use, we count all households, not just noninstitutional households, as the set of beneficiaries over which we prorate costs. Institutionalized persons include inmates of correctional institutions, nursing homes, and psychiatric hospitals, as well as persons in group quarters, such as residents of rooming houses, group homes, college dormitories, or homeless shelters (Bureau of the Census, 1993:B-9). This is a correct empirical approach, because general expenditures on near-pure public goods benefit all residents, regardless of institutional status.

Census Bureau's Public Use Microdata Area (PUMA), which is the smallest area that is identifiable with PUMS data. A PUMA is typically smaller than a county; New Jersey has 21 counties and 56 PUMAs. Populous counties usually have several PUMAs, with socioeconomically and geographically similar municipalities grouped together.[14] All households within a given PUMA are assumed to benefit equally from public goods expenditures made by local governments. Differences in local fiscal impacts between native and immigrant households may arise after aggregation to the state level to the extent that these populations exhibit dissimilar spatial distributions across New Jersey communities. State expenditures that are distributed using an average cost approach include general state services/state aid and municipal aid. At the local level, general county expenditures and general municipal expenditures are apportioned in the same fashion.

Second, numerous revenue and expenditure components are allocated using an average cost or benefit formula applied to the relevant population of "eligibles" (for example, individuals, households, or automobiles). Wherever possible we simulated public benefits to households as well as taxes paid by applying a knowledge of program rules and eligibility requirements to each household's income and demographic profile. The following aggregate expenditures were assigned using this methodology: administrative expenditures on elementary and secondary school education (both the state and local shares); higher education, including community colleges; Medicaid; general administrative expenses on Aid to Families with Dependent Children (AFDC), Supplemental Security Income (SSI), and General Assistance (GA); Pharmaceutical Assistance to the Aged and Disabled (PAAD); employment and training; programs for the aged, disabled, and veterans; property tax reimbursement; farm programs and agricultural extension services; Department of Motor Vehicles (DMV) administrative expenses; and gas and utility credits. Some revenue items are also estimated this way, including taxes on automobiles and gasoline, alcohol and tobacco, inheritances and estates, and business personal property.

Third, a micro-analytic approach is taken to build up estimates from the individual household level whenever the required information is included on the PUMS household record or when enough relevant data exist to approximate the benefit or tax payment with reasonable confidence. Items that are measured this way include AFDC benefits (from state and local government), per pupil expenditure on public elementary and secondary education, income taxes, state sales taxes, realty transfer taxes, property taxes, and utility taxes.

---

[14]Especially populous central cities are identified by the city alone. On the other hand, such sparsely settled counties as Salem, Cape May, Warren, and Sussex are not identified separately. With the exception of these four counties, PUMAs do not cross county boundaries, so it is a fairly straightforward task to assign the residents of each PUMA to a particular county.

Of the nearly $10.4 billion in current state expenditures that could reasonably be associated with households, we are able to assign nearly 70 percent on the basis of actual or probable use—that is, using either the second or third methodological approach mentioned above. The remaining 30 percent was for general state services. These comprise a number of general activities, including public safety and criminal justice, community development and environmental management, economic planning, transportation, and government administrative services (for example, legislature or governmental review). Government legislative and administrative functions account for nearly 40 percent of this total. These general costs were prorated among households. With the exception of education, most locally provided goods cannot be assigned to households on an actual-use basis. Most of these costs are truly general expenditures on indivisible public goods, and we allocate them using an average cost calculation. At the county level these items include general government expenditures, public safety, and public health.

Detailed Calculations

State Expenditures

Our discussion of the calculation of benefits received by New Jersey households from state government follows the order of their presentation in the tables accompanying this chapter. We first consider expenditures on general state services made on behalf of households and subsequently turn to expenditures on elementary, secondary, and higher education; Medicaid; means-tested income transfer programs; municipal aid; employment and training programs; programs for the aged and disabled; property tax reimbursements, and other allocable expenditures.

General State Services/State Aid. Expenditures on state-provided services and state aid programs include expenditures on near-pure public goods such as public safety and criminal justice; physical and mental health; educational, cultural, and intellectual development; community development and environmental management; economic planning, development, and security; transportation; and miscellaneous government administrative functions.[15] Because of their indivisibility, these expenditures cannot be allocated to households on an individual-cost basis. There are no studies to date that document differential consumption between immigrant- and native-headed households of general state services. Therefore, these expenditures are allocated to households on a per household average-use basis, regardless of the nativity status of the household head.

---

[15]Government administrative services include governmental review and oversight, legislative activities, financial administration, and general government services (State of New Jersey, 1991b:B12).

Expenditures on state-provided services and state aid programs that are not otherwise allocable to individual households are first identified in the state budget.[16] Total general expenditures are equal to the sum of expenditures on law enforcement, military activities, and the judiciary; general physical and mental health services; cultural and intellectual development services and supplemental education and training programs; community development and management of natural resources and recreational areas; economic planning and regulation and general social services programs; transportation programs, local and state highway facilities, and public transport; government direction and management and control functions; and special government services.[17] We take one-twentieth of reported state total general expenditures and divide by the total number of households, both institutional and noninstitutional, in the 1990 PUMS sample.[18] The resulting quotient of $1,119 is allocated equally to all New Jersey households, reflecting the assumption of average use by all households.

---

[16]General state services and state aid programs are funded under numerous subheadings and fund categories of the state budget. They may fall under the auspices of the Direct State Services, Grants-in-Aid, State Aid, or Debt Service subheadings of the General Fund, or they may be incurred as earmarked special expenditures or subsidies under the Property Tax Relief Fund, the Casino Control Fund, the Casino Revenue Fund, or the Gubernatorial Elections Fund. Because we are interested in allocating state expenditures to recipient households, not how the state labels these expenditures for accounting purposes, all current expenditures are considered in the model. See the Summary of Appropriations by Statewide Program in the General Information section of the State of New Jersey Budget (State of New Jersey, 1991b) for fund and subheading totals.

[17]A total of $3.4 billion was allocated as general expenditures on a prorated basis out of total state current expenditures of $11.47 billion for FY 1989-1990. General expenditures on law enforcement, military activities, and the judiciary equal the sum of three fund categories of expenditure under subheading (10) Public Safety and Criminal Justice. The first, under the Direct State Services and Grants-in-Aid subheadings of the General Fund, is net of expenditures on vehicular safety, detention/rehabilitation, and juvenile corrections. The second and third are expenditures on special law enforcement activities of the Casino Control Fund and the Gubernatorial Elections Fund, and comprise all the expenditures from these funds for FY 1989-1990. General physical and mental health expenditures include those under Program Classifications of the Department of Health, (20) Physical and Mental Health: (21) Health Services, (22) Health Planning and Evaluation, and (25) Health Administration, as well as expenditures on (23) Mental Health Services for Community Services, in the Direct State Services section of the budget (State of New Jersey, 1991b). They also include those under Program Classifications of the Department of Health: (21) Health Services, (22) Health Planning and Evaluation, and (23) Mental Health Services of the Grants-in-Aid section of the budget. Additional expenditures on the Department of Health: (21) Health Services—Family Health Services are also included from the State Aid subheading of the Casino Revenue Fund. General expenditures on educational, cultural, and intellectual development include those under Program Classifications of the Department of Human Services, (30) Educational, Cultural and Intellectual Development: (33) Supplemental Education and Training Programs—Commission for the Blind and Visually Impaired, under the Direct State Services and Grants-in-Aid sections of the budget. They also include expenditures under Program Classifications of the Department of Education: (37) Cultural and Intellectual

Development Services—library and museum support of the Direct State Services and State Aid sections of the budget. Additional general expenditures fall under Program Classifications of the Department of State: (37) Cultural and Intellectual Development Services—support of the arts of the Direct State Services, Grants-in-Aid, and State Aid sections of the budget. Finally, these expenditures also include, under Program Classifications of the Department of Human Services: (32) Operation and Support of Educational Institutions—Homemaker Adjustment Services in the Casino Revenue section of the budget. General expenditures on (40) Community Development and Environmental Management include expenditures under Program Classifications of the Department of Community Affairs: (41) Community Development Management—housing code, uniform construction code, and similar safety measures, of the Direct State Services, Grants-in-Aid, and State Aid sections of the budget. Also included are expenditures under the Program Classifications of the Department of Environmental Protection: (42) Natural Resource Management, (43) Environmental Quality, (44) Hazardous and Toxic Pollution Control, (45) Recreational Resource Management and (46) Environmental Planning and Administration under the Direct State Services, Grants-in-Aid, and State Aid sections of the budget. General expenditures on (50) Economic Planning, Development and Security include expenditures under Program Classifications of the Department of Commerce and Economic Development: (51) Economic Planning and Development—promoting business and tourism in the state, under the Direct State Services, Grants-in-Aid, and State Aid sections of the budget. Additional expenditures were incurred by the Department of Labor on (51) Economic Planning and Development—planning and program evaluation, under the Direct State Services section of the budget. Also included are expenditures on (52) Economic Regulation, given in the Direct State Services section of the General Fund in the Summary of Appropriations, by Statewide Program in the General Information Section of the budget, with the exception of expenditures on dairy industry regulation—market orders, as detailed in the Program Classifications of the Department of Agriculture: (52) Economic Regulation, under the Direct State Services section of the budget. The final component of these expenditures includes those on general (55) Social Services Programs—youth recreation, community resources, domestic and family/child abuse prevention/detection, as listed in the Direct State Services and Grants-in-Aid sections of the General Fund in the Summary of Appropriations, by Statewide Program in the General Information section of the budget. General expenditures on transportation programs include all expenditures on (60) Transportation Programs, as listed in the Direct State Services, Grants-in-Aid, and State Aid sections of the General Fund in the Summary of Appropriations, by Statewide Program, in the General Information section of the budget. Expenditures on government administrative functions include those classified under (70) Government Direction, Management and Control as detailed in footnote 5, in the Direct State Services, Grants-in-Aid, and State Aid sections of the General Fund in the Summary of Appropriations by Statewide Program, in the General Information section of the budget. Additional expenditures were incurred on (73) Financial Administration—casino gambling administration, of the Casino Control Fund, also given in the Summary of Appropriations by Statewide Program. Additional general government expenditures were incurred under Program Classifications of the Department of the Treasury: (75) State Subsidies and Financial Aid—general revenue sharing to municipalities, under the Property Tax Relief Fund (State Aid) section of the budget. General expenditures included (80) Special Government Services: (82) Protection of Citizens' Rights of the Direct State Services sections of the General and Casino Revenue Funds, as listed in the Summary of Appropriations by Statewide Program in the General Information section of the budget. Note as well that interest paid on publicly issued bonds was considered as a current general expenditure. These expenditures are detailed in the Debt Service section of the budget.

[18]Recall that, although we do not consider the institutional population in this household-level analysis, that population is still relevant for determining the population base across which general expenditures are allocated.

Elementary and Secondary Education. State expenditures on public elementary and secondary education equal the sum of the state's contribution to per pupil expenditures in a school district plus the average per pupil share of state costs on general education administration and support services.

In New Jersey, the state share of a locality's school district budget varies according to the resources available to the district.[19] In general, the fraction of per pupil expenditure paid by the state varies inversely with property wealth of the school district. Average per pupil expenditure for each PUMA is found by taking a weighted average of the per pupil expenditure of each school district[20] in the PUMA, using as weights the average daily enrollment (ADE) figures reported by school districts. The same weights are applied to the state's share of each school district's per pupil expenditures to compute a PUMA-wide average share of public schooling costs borne by the state.[21] The product of the PUMA's average per pupil expenditure and the average fraction for which the state is responsible yields a dollar figure for the state's elementary and secondary costs per pupil. This dollar figure is then allocated to every child who lives in the PUMA, is 6 to 17 years old, and for whom the variable ENROLL[22] indicates "in public school."

The state incurs additional costs for general education administration and management that are not part of a school district's per pupil expenditures.[23] Because there is no prior belief that immigrant- and native-born pupils consume

---

[19]In FY 1989-1990, the state contributed 39.8 percent, the federal government 3.8 percent, and local governments 56.4 percent on average to the per pupil cost of elementary and secondary education. The percentage breakdown is given in Evaluation Data of the Department of Education, (30) Educational, Cultural and Intellectual Development: (31) Direct Educational Services and Assistance in the Direct State Services section of the State of New Jersey Budget (State of New Jersey, 1991b). However, the state's share of school district expenditures varied dramatically by socioeconomic status of the school district, ranging from a low of 2.5 percent in Bay Head, Ocean County, to 78.2 percent in Woodlynne, Camden County (Rutgers, the State University of New Jersey, 1990).

[20]Per pupil expenditure data by district for the 1989-1990 school year were graciously supplied by Andrei Shidlowski of the New Jersey School Boards Association (1990).

[21]The ADE-weighted state share better reflects the true cost to the state of a public school pupil enrolled in a given PUMA than a simple average because it accounts for the fact that students are more likely to live in urban areas (with higher average state shares) than in suburban areas.

[22]ENROLL is the variable in the PUMS that indicates whether a person is currently enrolled in school, and conditional on enrollment, whether the school is public or private (Bureau of the Census, 1993:B-34).

[23]These general expenditures on elementary and secondary education are found in the Department of Education, (30) Educational, Cultural and Intellectual Development: (33) Supplemental Education and Training Programs—technical assistance and accreditation of local vocational education; (34) Educational Support Services—general academic education, curriculum development, and certification; and (35) Educational Administration and Management of the Direct State Services section of the budget. Additional general expenditures on (31) Direct Educational Services and Assistance— Teacher Recognition; (34) Educational Support Services and (35) Educational Support Services are

these general education expenditures differentially, such costs are allocated assuming average use by each public school pupil. Hence, we divide one-twentieth of general elementary and secondary education expenditures by the total number of public elementary and secondary school pupils in the state. The resulting average figure is then multiplied by the number of children ages 6 to 17 in the household who are enrolled in public school to arrive at state general elementary and secondary education expenditures for the household. The more children in a household who attend public schools, the higher is its utilization of state-funded school services.

Additional education costs are incurred by limited English proficient (LEP) students who are eligible for special education services such as remedial skills and bilingual education programs. Unfortunately, a direct estimate of these costs is not possible with the available data. The most detailed per pupil expenditure data available for the school year 1989-1990 do not separate bilingual education expenditures, but rather bundle them with expenditures on other state-sponsored education programs (New Jersey School Boards Association, 1990). There is no satisfactory way to break out bilingual education costs without making gross assumptions about relative school district participation in these state programs. Consequently, our methodology assigns the same per pupil expenditure to immigrant and native school children within a given PUMA, which is not entirely accurate because immigrants are more likely to utilize bilingual education programs. The problem is somewhat attenuated by the geographic concentration of immigrants in New Jersey in the large urban cores (Garvey, 1997). Per pupil expenditures are higher in the school districts serving these urban centers than in the surrounding school districts, partly reflecting the higher cost of education for LEP pupils.

Higher Education. The state of New Jersey supports 19 community colleges, 8 state colleges, 3 state universities (Rutgers, University of Medicine and Dentistry of New Jersey, and the New Jersey Institute of Technology), as well as private universities by providing scholarships and grants to eligible residents of the state who attend a private institution of higher learning in the state.

There are three important methodological issues involved in determining the costs to the state of a student enrolled in public higher education. First, the PUMS contains little information on receipt of higher education services. Although we can identify the type of institution attended with a reasonable degree

---

detailed in the Grants-in-Aid section of the budget. General education expenditures on (33) Supplemental Education and Training Programs—general vocational education, and (34) Educational Support Services—general academic education and teacher pension contributions are given in the State Aid section of the budget. Finally, general education expenditures are also found in (34) Educational Support Services—teacher's pension assistance under the Property Tax Relief Fund—State Aid section of the state budget (State of New Jersey, 1991b).

of confidence, we do not observe which college, technical college, or postgraduate school a household member attends, nor can we ascertain the program of study. A related empirical difficulty is determining the net cost to the state of a student's attendance at a state institution of higher learning, which is difficult to assess because of the unobserved variability in students' academic ability and receipt of financial aid. Finally, there is an ambiguity as to which households state expenditures on higher education should be attributed. The 1990 census questionnaire instructs respondents not to include their children who are away at college on the household roster (Bureau of the Census, 1990). Our household definition also excludes persons who live in group quarters. Hence, our measured cost to the state of higher education services is biased upward to the extent that students do not live at home or in noninstitutional settings within the state. On the other hand, a downward bias is imparted to estimates of average state expenditures on higher education insofar as students enrolled in New Jersey's institutions of higher learning are not residents of the state but temporarily form noninstitutional households within the state.

A partial resolution of the third problem is reasonably straightforward. In all the calculations, the population of interest across whom state higher education costs are to be attributed includes both households with students and students living in group quarters. The latter will pick up persons enrolled in public institutions of higher learning, but who live in dormitories or other group arrangements. Hence the denominator will reflect more correctly the universe of persons enrolled in public colleges and universities.[24]

Data supplied by the New Jersey Commission on Higher Education for fall 1994 (O'Connor, 1995) indicate that state residency is not an issue for most students enrolled in New Jersey institutions of higher education. Indeed, nearly 99 percent of full- and part-time undergraduates enrolled in community colleges were residents of the state, as were 90 percent of the full- and part-time undergraduates enrolled in New Jersey's public universities. Although over 95 percent of full-time undergraduates enrolled in the state colleges were residents of the state, only about 85 percent of their part-time counterparts were as well. However, the latter account for less than a fourth of undergraduate students enrolled part time in public institutions. A similar story is told even among undergraduates enrolled in private institutions in the state. Nearly 90 percent of part-time undergraduates enrolled in private institutions are New Jersey residents. Among full-time undergraduates enrolled in private institutions, the percent considered residents of the state is somewhat lower (70 percent), but again such enrollments account for less than 20 percent of full-time enrollments in all colleges and universities in the state. Hence, the bias caused by improperly estimating the size

---

[24]This solution does not assure a complete count of persons who attend New Jersey's institutions of higher education. Residents of a New Jersey household may attend school in another state, yet they will be considered as attendees of a New Jersey institution in our calculations.

of the recipient population of state expenditures on higher education services and state aid seems small.

The problem of estimating the net cost to the state of students enrolled in institutions of higher education is much thornier and cannot be fully addressed with census data. We assume that the net cost of educating a student enrolled in a particular type of institution is the same regardless of socioeconomic status, academic ability, or course of study. Although this is a questionable simplifying assumption, we find it preferable to the alternative of ignoring state expenditures on higher education altogether, or worse, assuming average per household use and allocating them in the same manner as general state expenditures.[25]

A person is coded as attending an institution of higher education if EN-ROLL indicates he or she "is enrolled in public or private school" and YEARSCH[26] indicates the person "is a high school graduate or holds a GED or diploma." One-twentieth of state general expenditure on higher education is divided by the total number of students enrolled in a postsecondary program to arrive at the per student figure. We then allocate to each enrolled student in the household this average per student general expenditure on higher education.[27] Clearly, the more students in a household who are enrolled in institutions of higher learning in the state, the greater the cost to the state of providing general education services to that household.[28]

State expenditures on different types of educational institutions are also allocated based on probable use in our model. A person is coded as attending a public institution of higher learning if ENROLL indicates the person is "enrolled in public school" and YEARSCH indicates he or she "is a high school graduate or holds a GED or diploma." One-twentieth of total state expenditure on public

---

[25]The PUMS does not contain enough detailed information on household assets, family income, and total family education expenditure and completely lacks data on student academic aptitude and program of study to permit accurate estimation of the value of student financial aid or the value of a particular state-provided or state-financed higher education.

[26]YEARSCH is the PUMS variable that describes educational attainment as the most recent grade completed at the time of the census (Bureau of the Census, 1993:B-4).

[27]General expenditures on higher education include expenditures on (30) Educational, Cultural and Intellectual Development: (36) Higher Educational Services, (5400) Office of the Chancellor—costs of educational grants, administration of student financial aid programs, in the Direct State Services and Grants-in-Aid sections of the state budget. They also include expenditures on (36) Higher Educational Services—interest on bonds for higher education facilities from the Debt Service section of the state budget (State of New Jersey, 1991b).

[28]Although our allocation algorithm considers all students enrolled in higher education as the population of "eligibles," we do not allocate higher education costs to students living in group quarters. This is consistent with adoption of the household as the unit of analysis.

[29]State expenditures on public higher education include expenditures on (30) Educational, Cultural and Intellectual Development: (36) Higher Educational Services, (5450+) State Colleges Programs—expenditures on state colleges and universities, in the Direct State Services section of the state budget (State of New Jersey, 1991b).

postsecondary institutions[29] is divided by the number of students enrolled in public institutions of higher learning to arrive at the average per student state expenditure on public higher education services. This average cost is allocated to each student in the household who is enrolled in a public institution of higher learning.

The state supports private institutions of higher learning in the state through grants to students and subsidies to institutions. A person is coded as attending a private postsecondary school if ENROLL indicates he or she is "enrolled in private school" and YEARSCH indicates the person "is a high school graduate or holds a GED or diploma." One-twentieth of total state expenditure on private postsecondary institutions[30] is divided by the number of students enrolled in private institutions to arrive at the average per student state expenditure on private higher education services. We then allocate to each student enrolled in a private institution the average state per student expenditure on private institutions.

Finally, the state provides support to county colleges through state aid programs that benefit students enrolled in community colleges. A person is coded as attending a community college if ENROLL indicates he or she is "enrolled in public school" and YEARSCH indicates the person "is a high school graduate or holds a GED or diploma" *and* who has attained no more than "an associate degree in college in an academic program."[31] One-twentieth of total state expenditure on community colleges[32] is divided by the number of students potentially enrolled in community colleges to arrive at the average per student cost of state aid to county colleges. Each student in the household who is potentially enrolled in a community college is then allocated the average state expenditure on assistance to community colleges.

Medicaid. The state of New Jersey provides assistance for the "diagnosis,

---

[30]State expenditures on support of private institutions include expenditures on (30) Educational, Cultural and Intellectual Development: (36) Higher Educational Services—expenditures on private colleges and universities, in the Grants-in-Aid section of the state budget (State of New Jersey, 1991b).

[31]The reader will notice the slight overlap in the definitions of persons enrolled in public and private institutions of higher education and those enrolled in community colleges. Census data do not provide detailed information on the type of institution where a student is enrolled. Rather, it must be inferred from the ENROLL and YEARSCH variables. Although students may be double counted as enrolled in both a community college and another public institution of higher learning, the degree of overlap is not critical to the nature of the analysis. State aid to community colleges, as described below, is distinct from and complementary to state support of public colleges and universities and general higher education expenditures.

[32]State expenditures on support of community colleges include expenditures on (30) Educational, Cultural and Intellectual Development: (36) Higher Educational Services—aid to county colleges, in the State Aid section of the state budget (State of New Jersey, 1991b).

treatment and correction" of medical problems for "New Jersey residents determined eligible for categorical assistance" under the auspices of its federally supported Medicaid program (State of New Jersey, 1991b:D-240). Those eligible for state Medicaid assistance include recipients of AFDC, SSI, medical assistance only, persons qualifying for the Special Supplemental Program for Women, Infants, and Children (WIC) and the state's medically needy programs, as well as foster children under the care of the Division of Youth and Family Services, and Cuban, Haitian, and Indo-Chinese refugees so certified under federal refugee programs.[33] Medicaid expenditures per household are allocated based on all eligible households, both institutional and noninstitutional.[34] Eligible households are those with a nonzero response to the census question on receipt of public assistance income (INCOME6), which includes SSI, AFDC, and GA payments (Bureau of the Census, 1993:B-17). We divide one-twentieth of total state expenditures on Medicaid payments and program costs by the number of households for which the variable INCOME6 is nonzero to arrive at the average state Medicaid cost per eligible household.[35] We then allocate this average state cost figure to households who received public assistance in 1989.

AFDC/GA/SSI. Three programs comprise AFDC: AFDC-C provides assistance to families with minor dependent children in which at least one parent is dead, disabled, or absent from the household; AFDC-F provides assistance to families in which the father is unemployed; and AFDC-N supports families in which the parents' income is below a predetermined level as a result of insufficient employment.[36] The first two programs were funded 50 percent by the

---

[33]Medicaid eligibility requirements are given in the objectives section of the Department of Human Services, (20) Physical and Mental Health Services: (24) Special Health Services, (7540) Division of Medical Assistance and Health Services in the Direct State Services section of the state budget (State of New Jersey, 1991b).

[34]Medicaid services are assumed to be consumed on an average per household use basis. This is a gross simplifying assumption, particularly as AFDC recipient households have different medical needs and resource utilization than disabled and elderly SSI recipients. Unfortunately, census data contain no information on health care expenditure or health care service use that would permit a better allocation of expenditures on an actual use basis.

[35]State expenditures on Medicaid payments and program costs are given in the Department of Human Services, (20) Physical and Mental Health: (24) Special Health Services—health services administration and management, in the Direct State Services section of the state budget. Expenditures are also given in the Department of Human Services, (20) Physical and Mental Health: (24) Special Health Services—general medical services of the Grants-in-Aid section of the state budget. Additional Medicaid expenditures are found in the Department of Human Services, (20) Physical and Mental Health: (24) Special Health Services—Medicaid expansion and Medical Assistance expenditures, in the Casino Revenue Fund (Grants-in-Aid) section of the state budget (State of New Jersey, 1991b).

[36]Eligibility requirements and payments for the three programs composing AFDC are detailed in the Introduction of the Department of Human Services, (50) Economic Planning, Development and Security: (53) Division of Economic Assistance and Security, (7550) Division of Economic Assistance in the State Aid section of the state budget (State of New Jersey, 1991b).

federal government, 37.5 percent by state government, and 12.5 percent by local governments in FY 1989-90. The third program was funded 75 percent by the state and 25 percent by local governments.[37] Because nearly 98 percent of state expenditures on AFDC payments are accounted for by AFDC-C and AFDC-F, we take 37.5 percent and 12.5 percent, respectively, as the state and local shares in AFDC payments in the analysis.[38]

The state share of AFDC payments received by households is calculated based on the household's response to the INCOME6 question. Households with children ages 17 and under, and where INCOME6 is reported as nonzero, are considered AFDC-eligible households; 37.5% of this reported income amount is allocated as the state's share in AFDC costs. There are also general administrative costs associated with AFDC program implementation that are not received by households as transfer payments.[39] These costs are assumed to be incurred equally by AFDC-eligible households. We divide one-twentieth of total state expenditures on AFDC program administration by the number of AFDC-eligible households to arrive at the average state AFDC administrative cost per eligible household. This figure is allocated equally among all AFDC-eligible households.

The federal Supplemental Security Income (SSI) program provides "direct federal income maintenance payments to aged, blind and disabled persons at a stipulated minimum level."[40] The state of New Jersey supplements the federal payment by guaranteeing a minimum income level in excess of the federal minimum. SSI-eligible households are determined based on a number of characteristics. Households with no children under 18 (to avoid confusion with AFDC-eligible households), who report nonzero public assistance income in 1989 (INCOME6 > 0), and whose head indicates either that he or she is prevented from working due to disability (DISABL2 = 1) or that he or she is over 65 years of age are considered SSI-eligible households. It is not possible to determine the fed-

---

[37]Federal, state, and local shares of AFDC expenditures for FY 1989-1990 are detailed in the Department of Human Services, (50) Economic Planning and Security: (53) Economic Assistance and Security, (7550) Division of Economic Assistance, in the State Aid section of the 1989-1990 budget (State of New Jersey, 1989).

[38]Expenditures by the state of New Jersey on AFDC-C and AFDC-F payments totaled $146,933,000 in FY 1989-1990, whereas expenditures on AFDC-N totaled only $3,268,000 (State of New Jersey, 1991b).

[39]State expenditures on AFDC administration are given in the Department of Human Services, (50) Economic Planning, Development and Security: (53) Economic Assistance, Division of Economic Assistance and Security—income maintenance program administration in the Direct State Services and Grants-in-Aid sections of the state budget (State of New Jersey, 1991b).

[40]Eligibility requirements and payments for SSI are detailed in the Introduction of the Department of Human Services, (50) Economic Planning, Development and Security: (53) Division of Economic Assistance and Security, (7550) Division of Economic Assistance in the State Aid section of the state budget (State of New Jersey, 1991b).

eral, and therefore, state share of SSI payments from census data because of a lack of detail on the source of transfer payments. Hence, average SSI receipt is assumed for each eligible household. For such households, the state share of SSI transfer payments is equal to one-twentieth of total state expenditure on SSI transfer payments, divided equally among SSI-eligible households.

GA consists of financial aid to "needy persons not otherwise provided for under the laws of New Jersey."[41] Households that indicate they received nonzero public assistance income in 1989 (INCOME6 > 0), that have no minor children (to avoid confounding AFDC and GA payments), and who are not eligible for SSI according to the above criteria are eligible households for GA. Because numerous programs with different eligibility requirements comprise GA, average receipt of state GA payments and administrative costs was assumed for all households. Hence, one-twentieth of total state expenditure on GA programs is divided equally among all potentially eligible households to allocate average state expenditure on GA programs to such households.

Pharmaceutical Assistance to the Aged and Disabled (PAAD). New Jersey funds a program that provides pharmaceutical assistance to the elderly and disabled. The state pays pharmacies the average wholesale price plus a dispensing fee for prescriptions required by low-income persons over 65.[42] A married person over 65 in a household with total household income less than $12,000, or a single person over 65 with personal income less than $9000, was potentially eligible for prescription assistance in FY 1989-1990. Because census data contain no information on health care utilization, we allocate expenditures on pharmaceutical assistance to the eligible elderly on a prorated share basis. We divide one-twentieth of total state expenditure on pharmaceutical assistance for the elderly by the number of potentially eligible persons in the state to arrive at average state expenditure per eligible elder. This dollar figure is then allocated to each elderly person in the household whom we identify as potentially eligible for pharmaceutical assistance.[43] The more impoverished elderly a household contains, the greater is its allocation of pharmaceutical assistance expenditures.

---

[41]Eligibility requirements and payments for GA are detailed in the Introduction of the Department of Human Services, (50) Economic Planning, Development and Security: (53) Division of Economic Assistance and Security, (7550) Division of Economic Assistance in the State Aid section of the state budget (State of New Jersey, 1991b).

[42]Eligibility requirements for PAA are given in the objectives section of the Department of Human Services, (20) Physical and Mental Health Services: (24) Special Health Services, (7540) Division of Medical Assistance and Health Services in the Direct State Services section of the state budget (State of New Jersey, 1991b).

[43]State expenditures on the pharmaceutical assistance program for the aged are detailed in the Department of Human Services, (20) Physical and Mental Health: (24) Special Health Services, (7540) Division of Medical Assistance and Health Services of the Direct State Services and Grants-in-Aid sections of General Fund, as well as in the Casino Revenue Fund (Grants-in-Aid) section of the state budget (State of New Jersey, 1991b).

Pharmaceutical assistance is also available for low-income persons under 65 who are disabled. State expenditures on pharmaceutical assistance for the disabled are allocated to persons who are potentially eligible to receive such benefits. A married person under 65 who is disabled (DISABL2 = 1) and has total household income less than $16,750, or a single disabled person with personal income less than $13,650, was potentially eligible for pharmaceutical assistance in FY 1989-1990. We allocate state expenditures on pharmaceutical assistance to the eligible disabled population in the same manner as the eligible elderly. We divide one-twentieth of total state expenditure on pharmaceutical assistance for the disabled by the number of potentially eligible persons in the state, which gives average state expenditure per person on pharmaceutical assistance for the disabled. This dollar figure is then allocated to each potentially eligible person in the household.[44]

Municipal Aid Programs. New Jersey's state government distributes aid to municipalities for various purposes.[45] Chief among these are Safe and Clean Neighborhoods, Municipal Revitalization, and Urban Aid. These expenditures are not randomly distributed across municipalities, but are targeted to depressed urban areas (Forsberg and Poethke, 1994; Forsberg, 1995). Because there is no evidence of differential consumption of state aid services by immigrant- and native-headed households within a municipality, state expenditures are assigned on an average use basis for each household. State expenditures on each municipal aid program are weighted by the population of each municipality in order to reflect the uneven distribution of households within a PUMA. For each municipal aid program, we take one-twentieth of weighted state expenditures on the program and divide by the number of households in the PUMA. The resulting figure is then allocated equally to each household in the PUMA.

Employment and Training Programs. State expenditures on employment

---

[44]State expenditures on pharmaceutical assistance for the disabled are detailed in the objectives section of the Department of Human Services, (20) Physical and Mental Health: (24) Special Health Services, (7540) Division of Medical Assistance and Health Services in the Casino Revenue Fund—Direct State Services and Grants-in-Aid sections of the state budget (State of New Jersey, 1991b).

[45]State expenditures on municipal aid programs are detailed in the Department of Community Affairs, (40) Community Development and Environmental Management: (41) Community Development and Management in the State Aid section of the state budget (State of New Jersey, 1991b).

[46]A detailed description of these employment and training programs can be found in the Program Classification of the Department of Labor (50) Economic Planning, Development and Security: (53) Economic Assistance and Security in the Direct State Services section of the state budget. Expenditures on unemployment insurance are given in this section, as well as in the Department of Labor (50) Economic Planning, Development and Security: (54) Manpower and Employment Services—UI job search, in the Grants-in-Aid section of the state budget (State of New Jersey, 1991b).

and training programs include expenditures on state unemployment insurance (UI), state disability/worker's compensation, vocational rehabilitation services, and general manpower and employment services expenditures. Administrative costs of these programs are allocated on an average per eligible worker basis.

The unemployment insurance system is a state-administered, federally funded system of unemployment insurance coverage for almost all nonagricultural workers in the state.[46] Persons are considered eligible for UI receipt if the variable INCOME8[47] is nonzero; YEARWK, which indicates the year the person last worked, is no earlier than 1989; and the person did not work a full 52 weeks in 1989 (1 <= WEEK89 < 52). One-twentieth of total state expenditure on UI administrative costs is divided by the number of potentially eligible UI recipients. The resulting average figure is then allocated to each eligible UI recipient in the household to arrive at the household's share of UI administrative costs.

Expenditures on state disability and workers' compensation administrative costs are also assigned on an average per eligible worker basis.[48] A person is deemed eligible for state disability/workers' compensation if INCOME7[49] is nonzero, he or she is between 16 and 65 years of age (to reduce the likelihood of counting retired persons and those not in the labor force), the person worked at some point in his or her life (YEARWK not equal to 7), and the person claims a disability that either limits (DISABL1 = 1) or prevents (DISABL2 = 1) work. We take one-twentieth of administrative expenditures on disability and workers' compensation programs and divide by the number of potentially eligible recipients to arrive at average administrative costs per eligible worker. Each potentially eligible person in a household is then assigned this average state expenditure on administration of worker disability and compensation programs.

Vocational rehabilitation services are provided to handicapped persons who are unable to work, with the goal of preparing them for gainful employment.[50] The state supports a wide variety of programs, which include sheltered workshop support, medical, and day training programs. A person is coded as

---

[47]INCOME8, other income, includes UI payments, veterans' administration payments, alimony and child support, as well as gambling winnings and other periodic income (Bureau of the Census, 1993:B-17).

[48]State administrative expenditures on workers' compensation and disability programs are given in the Department of Labor (50) Economic Planning, Development and Security: (53) Economic Assistance and Security in the Direct State Services section of the state budget (State of New Jersey, 1991b).

[49]INCOME7 includes retirement and disability income from federal, state, or private sources, as well as receipts from annuities and retirement plans (Bureau of the Census, 1993:B-17).

[50]Vocational rehabilitation services are detailed in the Program Classifications of the Department of Labor, (50) Economic Planning, Development and Security: (54) Manpower and Employment Services in the Direct State Services section of the state budget (State of New Jersey, 1991b).

eligible for vocational rehabilitation services if he or she is disabled in a way that prevents work (DISABL2 = 1) and the person is between the ages of 16 and 65.[51] Average use of vocational rehabilitation services is assumed for all eligible persons. Total state expenditure on vocational rehabilitation services is divided by the number of potentially eligible beneficiaries. This average state cost figure is then allocated equally to each eligible person in a household.[52]

State expenditures on manpower and employment services include expenditures on labor exchange services, employment development, and public- and private-sector labor relations.[53] These services are assumed to be enjoyed by all workers on an equal basis. Workers are defined as those persons in military or civilian jobs (RLABOR = 1, 2, 4, or 5). We take one-twentieth of state expenditures on manpower and employment services and divide by the number of workers in the PUMS, which gives us average state per worker expenditure on manpower and employment services. Each worker in a household is then allocated this average dollar figure.

Programs for the Aged, Disabled, and Veterans. Programs for the aged encompass a vast array of protective, transportation, and day care services for the elderly.[54] Allocation of these costs based on actual use is not possible due to limitations of census data. However, it is not unreasonable to allocate these expenditures on an average-use basis to all persons ages 65 and older. We divide one-twentieth of state expenditure on programs for the aged by the number of

---

[51]The eligibility criterion for use of vocational rehabilitation services certainly overestimates the potentially eligible population. In the absence of more detailed information on physical and mental impairment, however, it is the most precise eligibility definition possible.

[52]Expenditures on vocational rehabilitation services are given in the Department of Labor, (50) Economic Planning, Development and Security: (54) Manpower and Employment Services section of the Direct State Services and Grants-in-Aid sections of the General Fund in the state budget. Expenditures on these programs are also found under the same program heading of the Casino Revenue Fund, Grants-in-Aid section of the state budget (State of New Jersey, 1991b).

[53]Manpower and employment services expenditures are detailed in the Program Classifications of the Department of Labor, (50) Economic Planning, Development and Security: (54) Manpower and Employment Services—Employment Services, Employment Development, and Labor Relations of the Direct State Services section of the state budget (State of New Jersey, 1991b).

[54]Programs for the elderly are classified in many sections of the state budget. They include those in the Department of Community Affairs, (50) Economic Planning, Development and Security: (55) Social Services Programs—Programs for the Aging in the Direct State Services, General Fund section of the state budget. There are additional expenditures under the same program heading of the Casino Revenue Fund—Direct State Services and Grants-in-Aid sections. Other expenditures are given in the Department of Human Services, (50) Economic Planning, Development and Security: (55) Social Services Programs—Protective Services for the Elderly in the Casino Revenue Fund— Grants-in-Aid portion of the state budget. Additional expenditures are given in the Department of State, (70) Government Direction, Management and Control: (76) Management and Administration—respite care for elderly of the Casino Revenue Fund—Grants-in-Aid section of the state budget (State of New Jersey, 1991).

persons 65 and older in the PUMS to arrive at average state expenditure per elderly person. This figure is then allocated to each senior citizen in the household. Hence, the more elderly persons in a household, the higher is its utilization of state programs for the aged.

Many expenditures targeted to the disabled population have been allocated to the eligible population as described above within the context of specific program objectives (e.g., vocational rehabilitation services). There are additional state expenditures on improved access to public transportation facilities for disabled residents of New Jersey.[55] Because the census lacks information on public transportation use, we allocate a prorated share to eligible persons in each household. Eligible persons are defined as those who have a disability that either limits or prevents work (DISABL1 or DISABL2 = 1). We then divide one-twentieth of total state expenditure on transportation services for the disabled by the number of eligible disabled persons in the PUMS. This average state expenditure is then allocated to each eligible person in the household.

Programs for war veterans include various support programs and hospital services for veterans of U.S. military service.[56] In the absence of detailed utilization information in the census, average consumption of services is assumed for all veterans. The eligible population is defined as those for whom the variable MILITARY indicates past service in the military or national guard (MILITARY = 2 or 3). One-twentieth of total state expenditure on veterans' programs is divided by the number of veterans in the PUMS. This average state expenditure on veterans' programs is then allocated to each veteran in the household.

Property Tax Reimbursements. The state government reimburses municipalities for property tax revenues lost as a result of property tax exemptions for the elderly, disabled, and military veterans.[57] Householders who own or have a mortgage on their home (TENURE = 1 or 2) and who are either 65 or older, permanently disabled (DISABL2 = 1), or are military veterans are eligible for the tax exemption of $50. Households with such eligible household heads are then allocated the cost of the exemption.

---

[55]Expenditures on improved access to public transport are given in the Department of Transportation (60) Transportation Programs: (62) Public Transportation in the Casino Revenue Fund—State Aid section of the budget (State of New Jersey, 1991b).

[56]Expenditures on programs benefiting veterans are detailed in the Department of Military and Veterans' Affairs, (80) Special Government Services: (83) Services to Veterans in the Direct State Services and Grants-in-Aid sections of the state budget (State of New Jersey, 1991b).

[57]The property tax exemption program is detailed in the Program Classifications of the Department of the Treasury, (70) Government Direction, Management and Control: (75) State Subsidies and Financial Aid of the Direct State Services section of the state budget (State of New Jersey, 1991b, as well as in State of New Jersey, 1990d).

Other Allocable Expenditures. This category of expenditure includes expenditures on a few other state programs that are not classified elsewhere. Expenditures on agricultural programs that primarily benefit farmers comprise a part of these expenditures.[58] Farmers (defined as those for whom the OCCUP variable on the PUMS is between 473 and 476) are assumed to benefit equally from these expenditures. We divide one-twentieth of total state expenditure on farm programs by the number of farmers in the PUMS. We then allocate this average state expenditure on agricultural programs to each farmer in the household.

Department of Motor Vehicles (DMV) administrative costs are also included in this catchall category.[59] Total DMV administrative expenditures are divided by the number of registered vehicles in the state to arrive at average per vehicle administrative expenditure. Each AUTO in a household is then assigned the per vehicle average cost of DMV administrative services.

The final category of allocable state expenditure is the Lifeline Credit Program, which provides up to $225 in combined gas and electric utility credits for households eligible for pharmaceutical assistance, SSI, or Medicaid.[60] Households are deemed eligible for the Lifeline Credit Program if they are potentially eligible for AFDC/SSI/GA or pharmaceutical assistance as described under their respective program headings. Average use is assumed for eligible households. Thus, we divide one-twentieth of state expenditure on the Lifeline Credit Program by the number of potentially eligible households and then allocate this average state expenditure to each eligible household.[61]

---

[58]Expenditures on agricultural support programs are detailed in the Department of Agriculture (40) Community Development and Environmental Management: (42) Natural Resources Management—animal disease control, pest control, soil erosion programs, of the Direct State Services section of the state budget. Additional expenditures are classified under the Department of Agriculture, (50) Economic Planning, Development and Security: (51) Economic Planning and Development—marketing for New Jersey farm products and (52) Economic Regulation—market orders for dairy products, also in the Direct State Services section of the state budget (State of New Jersey, 1991b).

[59]Expenditures on DMV administrative services are given in the Department of Transportation, (10) Public Safety and Criminal Justice: (11) Vehicular Safety of the Direct State Services section of the state budget. The total number of registered vehicles in the state of New Jersey is given in the Federal Highway Administration's Highway Statistics 1990 (1991).

[60]Parameters of the Lifeline Credit Program are given in Program Classifications of the Department of Human Services, (50) Economic Planning, Development and Security: (53) Economic Assistance and Security, (7540) Division of Medical Assistance and Health Services in the Direct State Services section of the state budget (State of New Jersey, 1991b).

[61]Expenditures on the Lifeline Credit Program are detailed under the heading mentioned in the previous footnote, as well as in the Casino Revenue Fund—Direct State Services and Grants-in-Aid sections of the state budget (State of New Jersey, 1991b).

State Revenues

Revenues collected by the state that are paid directly by households include those from the gross income tax, sales and use tax, motor vehicle fees, motor vehicle taxes, alcoholic beverage tax, cigarette tax, inheritance/estate transfer tax, business personal property tax, and the realty transfer tax.[62] These sources accounted for nearly three-quarters of total state tax revenue in the fiscal year ending June 30, 1990 (State of New Jersey 1991a:4-5). We neglect corporate-sector taxes in our simulation, which causes us to underestimate state tax revenue by about 25 percent.

Gross Income Tax. The amount of income tax paid to the state is estimated using New Jersey state marginal tax rates and household income as reported by the household in the census. Gross income is first determined according to the procedures described in the 1989 New Jersey Gross Income Tax Resident Return form. Gross household income is calculated as the sum of wage and salary income (INCOME1); nonfarm self-employment income (INCOME2); farm self-employment income (INCOME3); and interest, dividend, and rental income (INCOME4) for all household members.[63] If gross income is less than $3,000, there is no tax liability in FY 1989-1990. We then subtract from gross income the dollar value of the household's total number of exemptions.[64] The resulting figure is New Jersey taxable income. The marginal tax rate on the first $20,000 of taxable income is 2 percent, the marginal tax rate on the next $30,000 of taxable income (up to $50,000) is 2.5 percent, and the marginal tax rate on income over $50,000 is 3.5 percent (State of New Jersey, 1990b). Persons with negative taxable income owe no tax, but do not receive a tax credit from the state.

Sales and Use Tax. We base our estimate of sales and use tax revenue on the guidelines developed by the Internal Revenue Service for itemizing sales tax deductions on the federal income tax form. As detailed in the Instructions for Preparing Form 1040, the approximation takes into account the sales tax rate

---

[62]The question of tax incidence, or who really bears the burden of a given tax, is discussed in the introduction to the appendix. Our assumptions about tax incidence, which reflect the general consensus in the public finance literature, enable us to attribute revenues to contributing households.

[63]There is a no-offset provision in the New Jersey tax code, which prohibits taxpayers from writing off gains in one income category against losses in another income category. Hence, losses in the INCOME2-INCOME4 categories are set to 0 prior to summation.

[64]Tax exemptions in 1989 were set as follows. Married persons deducted $2,000 from gross income, single payers, $1000, and there were additional $1,000 exemptions for each senior citizen and minor child under 18 in the household. There were additional exemptions in the tax code for blind taxpayers and for special classes of dependents and children attending college away from home. Such exemptions are not considered in our simulation because they are not observed in census data (State of New Jersey, 1990b).

[65]The sales tax rate effective in New Jersey from January 1983 to July 1, 1990 was 6 percent.

effective in the state at the time[65] and varies with household size and income. We use the PUMS variables HHINC and PERSONS to determine total household income and household size, respectively. We then approximate each household's contribution to state sales tax receipts by inflating the Optional Sales Tax Table values (in the Instructions for Preparing Form 1040, 1987) by the growth in the CPI-U from 1986 to 1989. [66]

Automobile and Fuel Taxes. Motor vehicle taxes and the motor fuels tax are levied on automobiles in the state of New Jersey. The first component of motor vehicle taxes is the per vehicle inspection fee, whereas the second consists of the registration fee, which varies with the weight of the automobile and its date of purchase. We took the average cost of registering an automobile as the per vehicle fee.[67] We then multiplied the number of automobiles owned by the household (AUTO) by the sum of the two motor vehicle taxes to arrive at the estimate of motor vehicle taxes paid by the household.

The motor fuels tax is levied on all motor vehicles in the state. The average per vehicle contribution to motor fuels tax revenue is estimated by dividing total revenues from the tax by the number of automobiles registered in the state.[68] This estimate slightly overstates the average per auto contribution to motor fuels tax revenue because the tax also applies to buses, trucks, and motorcycles. However, the number of cars registered in New Jersey far exceeds the number of other motor vehicles, and automobiles account for over 90 percent of the registered vehicles in the state in 1990. Furthermore, the bias induced by our estimation strategy affects immigrant and native-headed households approximately equivalently.[69]

Alcoholic Beverage and Cigarette Taxes. The calculations in our model take into account household composition in estimating each household's contribution to state revenue from alcoholic beverage and cigarette taxes. Average consump-

---

[66]The PUMS does not contain any information on household consumption expenditures, which renders a more precise estimate of household sales tax contributions impossible. The estimated sales tax payments in the Optional Sales Tax Tables are derived from estimates based on household consumption expenditures in the Consumer and Expenditure Survey (CEX). The CEX is a detailed survey of expenditures of a random sample of the U.S. population (U.S. Bureau of Labor Statistics, 1986). The estimates in the Optional Sales Tax are inflated by the CPI-U for the Northeast to reflect changes in the general price level in urban areas over the three-year period.

[67]The inspection fee was $2.50 per vehicle, and the average vehicle registration fee was $54.50 in FY 1989-1990 (Commerce Clearing House, 1990:930).

[68]State revenues from the Motor Fuels Tax for FY 1989-1990 are found in the Annual Report of the Division of Taxation State of New Jersey (1990a), while state automobile registrations are given in the Federal Highway Administration's Highway Statistics 1990 (1991).

[69]Foreign-born households possess 1.53 cars on average, whereas households with a native-born householder possess 1.70. Although this difference is statistically significant, it is negligible from the perspective of bias introduced by our estimation strategy.

tion is assumed for all persons of at least the legal purchase age for each taxed commodity.[70] Hence, we calculate an average contribution for each individual by dividing one-twentieth of the total revenue derived from each tax by the total number of persons eligible for that tax in the PUMS.[71] This figure is the average per person contribution for the given tax. Thus, a household's contribution to the state revenues derived from each of these taxes equals the product of the number of eligible persons in the household and the average per person contribution to the tax.

Transfer Inheritance and Estate Tax. The transfer inheritance and estate tax is most appropriately estimated on a per household basis. The likelihood that an immigrant-headed household must pay transfer inheritance taxes in a given year is less than a native-headed household of similar demographic and socioeconomic characteristics because immigrants are less likely to have friends or family members in the United States from whom they may inherit property.

In the absence of detailed inheritance data in the census, inheritance and estate taxes are allocated to eligible households on a prorated share basis. The number of households across whom revenue from the transfer inheritance and estate tax is to be attributed is taken as the number of native-headed households plus the number of immigrant-headed households whose head immigrated to the United States before 1970.[72] Twenty years serves as a conservative estimate of the length of time necessary to raise the probability of inheritance for an immigrant householder to that of a native-born householder in 1989. We take one-twentieth of total state revenue from the transfer inheritance and estate tax[73] and divide it by the number of potentially eligible households to arrive at a per eligible household figure. We then attribute this average contribution to households that potentially received an inheritance in 1989 to arrive at our estimate of inheritance taxes paid by each household.

Business Personal Property Tax. Revenues from the business personal property tax are allocated on a per eligible prorated share basis. Eligible persons are those for whom the variable CLASS[74] indicates that he or she is self-employed in

---

[70]The PUMS does not contain detailed information on consumption of goods and services. Although the CEX does provide such data, it is impossible to identify the state of residence from the survey.

[71]Eligible persons for the alcoholic beverage tax are those ages 21 and older, and for the cigarette tax, 18 and older. Revenues derived from the Alcoholic Beverage Tax and the Cigarette Tax are given in the Annual Report of the Division of Taxation (State of New Jersey, 1991a).

[72]Such immigrant heads have a value of 7 or greater for the IMMIGR variable on the PUMS, which indicates the period of arrival in the United States.

[73]State revenue from the Transfer Inheritance and Estate Tax is given in the Annual Report of the Division of Taxation (State of New Jersey, 1991a).

[74]CLASS indicates whether a worker is a private wage or salary worker; a local, state, or federal worker; a self-employed worker in an incorporated or unincorporated business; or an unpaid worker in a family business (Bureau of the Census, 1993:5-22).

an incorporated or unincorporated business. We then divide one-twentieth of the total state revenue from the business personal property tax[75] by the number of self-employed persons in the PUMS to arrive at the average contribution of each self-employed worker to the business personal property tax. Multiplying this average figure by the number of self-employed persons in the household gives our estimate of the business personal property tax paid by each household.

Realty Transfer Tax. The realty transfer tax is imposed on the recording of deeds and the transfer of titles to real property between individuals or institutions. We assume that statutory incidence of the tax is equivalent to economic incidence. Hence, the tax, which is paid by purchasers of homes at the time of closing, is allocated to potentially eligible households. Eligible households have householders for whom the variable TENURE[76] indicates the household owns its dwelling, and the variable YRMOVED[77] indicates the householder moved into the unit during 1989. For such households, revenues from the realty transfer tax[78] are calculated as $1.75 per $500 property VALUE[79] up to $150,000, and $2.50 per $500 property VALUE in excess of $150,000.

Local Expenditures

Local expenditures include those incurred by county and municipal governments. Our strategy involves prorating categories of local expenditure that do not permit allocation to specific households on an average-share basis. For municipal expenditures, the proration pertains to all households in the PUMA, which is typically smaller than a county. PUMAs are aggregated to the county level to prorate general county expenditures. Our discussion of the calculation of benefits received by New Jersey households from county and municipal government follows the order of their presentation in the tables describing the fiscal impact of households on local governments. We first consider expenditures on general county services made on behalf of households and subsequently turn to general municipal expenditures, expenditures on elementary and secondary public education services, county colleges, and transfer payments through AFDC.

---

[75]State revenue from the Business Personal Property Tax is given in the Annual Report of the Division of Taxation (State of New Jersey, 1991a).

[76]TENURE indicates whether a residential unit is owner or renter occupied (Bureau of the Census, 1993:5-11).

[77]YRMOVED indicates the year the householder moved into the dwelling (Bureau of the Census, 1993, p. B-50).

[78]The marginal tax rates of the realty transfer fee are given in the Annual Report of the Division of Taxation (State of New Jersey, 1991a).

[79]VALUE is the respondent's estimate of the sale price he or she would expect to obtain for the dwelling and its lot if it were put on the market (Bureau of the Census, 1993:B-49). Because VALUE is a categorical variable, midpoints of each category are used in the calculations.

General County Expenditures. Our model assumes average use of several types of services provided by county governments. Total general county expenditure includes general government operations, judicial functions (excluding correctional and penal expenditures), public safety, public works, general health and welfare (excluding expenditures for the county welfare board), recreation and conservation, nonschool education expenditures (i.e., libraries and other educational services), and interest payments on local debt.[80] We divide one-twentieth of total general county expenditures by the number of households in each county to arrive at average general county expenditures per household.[81] We then allocate average general county expenditures to each household residing in a particular county.

County expenditure on the local agricultural extension service is included under general county expenditures, although it is allocated to households on an actual-use basis. Although such services exist for the benefit of all households, they primarily benefit local farmers. Farmers (defined as those for whom the OCCUP variable is between 473 and 476) are assumed to benefit equally from these expenditures. Hence, we divide one-twentieth of county expenditures on the agricultural extension by the number of farmers in the county and allocate the resulting average figure to each farmer in the household.

General Municipal Expenditures. Our model also assumes average cost in allocating several types of municipal government expenditure to households. Total general municipal expenditures include those labeled General Government, Judiciary, Public Safety, Public Works, Health and Welfare (excluding expenditures on Welfare-Public Assistance), Recreation and Conservation, Education (excluding schools), Statutory Expenditures (includes costs of employee benefits, taxes, and pension contributions), and Debt Service (interest payments).[82] We sum these expenditures for all municipalities in a PUMA. We then take one-twentieth of this total general municipal expenditure and divide by the number of households in the PUMA to arrive at average general municipal expenditures per

---

[80]These expenditures are detailed by county in the Summary of 21 County Government Data Sheets in the County Government Fiscal Data section of the Fifty-Second Annual Report of the Division of Local Government Services, 1989: Statements of Financial Condition of Counties and Municipalities (State of New Jersey, 1990c).

[81]The PUMS does not permit separate identification of four counties. These include Sussex and Warren counties as well as Salem and Cape May counties (Bureau of the Census, 1993). For these two county groups, we determine average general county expenditure by summing one-twentieth of general county expenditures over the two counties and dividing by the number of households in both counties.

[82]Municipal government expenditures are given in the Municipal Fiscal Data section of the Fifty-Second Annual Report of the Division of Local Government Services, 1989: Statements of Financial Condition of Counties and Municipalities (State of New Jersey, 1990c).

household. The resulting average dollar figure is then allocated to each household in the PUMA.

Elementary and Secondary Education. There are three types of local government expenditure on education: general elementary and secondary education, the local share of per pupil expenditure on public elementary and secondary education, and county vocational schools. We allocate these expenditures to households on an actual-use basis.

General elementary and secondary education expenditures comprise county-level expenditures on the county superintendent of schools. As in the case of state expenditures on elementary and secondary education, we count all children enrolled in public school in the household. We aggregate this figure across all households in the county. We then take one-twentieth of the total expenditures on the county superintendent of schools, divide it by the number of public school pupils in the county, and allocate the resulting average to each public school pupil in a household. Summing across public school pupils in the household yields the household's contribution to general elementary and secondary education costs.

We discussed the calculation of average per pupil expenditure by PUMA in the section that describes the allocation of state elementary and secondary education expenditure. The fraction of average per pupil expenditure for which localities are responsible is calculated as one minus the average state share. Hence, each PUMA's local elementary and secondary school costs per pupil are simply the product of the PUMA's average per pupil expenditure and the average local share. Thus, for every child in the household ages 6 through 17 for whom the variable ENROLL indicates "in public school," the local share of the PUMA of residence's average per pupil expenditure is added to local expenditures on that household.

All counties, with the exception of Hunterdon, support county vocational schools that provide intensive preparation for students interested in technical occupations. Because these schools are highly specialized, they invest in costly equipment and enroll relatively few pupils. As a result, their per pupil expenditures are quite high, ranging from $8,000 to $23,000 per pupil in 1989.[83] We define persons who are potentially enrolled in county vocational education in the following way. Persons ages 18 through 21 who indicate they are ENROLLed in a public school, who have completed no less than 9th grade and no more than 12th grade, and do not have a diploma (6 <= YEARSCH <= 9) are considered potentially enrolled in a county vocational school.[84] We then take one-twentieth

---

[83]Figures provided by the New Jersey School Boards Association (1990).

[84]This definition, although as precise as possible with the available data, still overestimates by roughly a factor of three the number of persons enrolled in county vocational schools.

of the county's total expenditure on vocational schools and divide it by the number of potential vocational education students, which yields the county's average expenditure per potential vocational student. Multiplying this figure by the number of potential vocational education students in the household gives each household's contribution to the costs of county vocational education.

County College. Counties contribute to the support of their local community colleges. As described above under state expenditures, a person is coded as attending a community college if ENROLL indicates "enrolled in public school" and YEARSCH indicates "is a high school graduate or holds a GED or diploma" *and* if the person has attained no more than "an associate degree in college in an academic program." One-twentieth of the county's total expenditure on community colleges is divided by the number of students potentially enrolled in the county's community college to arrive at the per student cost. Each student potentially enrolled in a county college is then allocated the average county expenditure on the community college.

Aid to Families with Dependent Children. AFDC costs are allocated to households on an actual-use basis. For each eligible household,[85] local expenditures on AFDC are calculated as 12.5 percent of each household's reported public assistance income (INCOME6).

Local Revenues

Property Taxes. Property taxes are the most important taxes paid by households to local governments. To estimate property tax payments, we use actual property taxes paid by homeowners and impute property taxes paid by renters. Householders who own their own dwellings (TENURE = 1 or 2) were asked to report on their 1990 census questionnaire the amount of property tax they paid in 1989. Property taxes paid by such households are reported as ranges in the categorical variable RTAXAMT. We take the midpoint of the category as a point estimate of property tax paid in 1989. For homeowners who were in the highest category of RTAXAMT with no upper bound on property tax paid and for those who did not report paying real estate taxes, we use the estimated market VALUE of the residence and multiply this figure by the population-weighted equalized property tax rate for the PUMA of residence[86] to estimate property taxes paid.

---

[85]For a description of eligibility requirements for AFDC, state and local share of AFDC costs, and the determination of household AFDC receipt, see the discussion of the allocation of state AFDC expenditures.

[86]Equalized property tax rates correct for the fact that assessed value in New Jersey municipalities rarely equals the true market value of a residence. They are defined such that the product of the

To estimate property taxes paid by renters, we assume that taxes are capitalized in the value of rental property (Yinger, 1982) and that property taxes are passed on to renters by owners. If we conceptualize rent as payment for a stream of housing services, property taxes paid are equal to annual contract rent[87] multiplied by [t/(t+i)], where t is the local equalized property tax rate and i is a discount rate, assumed in our calculation to be the average 30-year mortgage rate over the 1985-1995 period or 8 percent.[88]

Public Utility Gross Receipts Tax. The public utility gross receipts tax is levied on water, sewer, gas, electric, and power utilities in the state. We calculate the taxes remitted by households on an actual-use basis. We sum the ELECCOST, GASCOST, WATRCOST, and FUELCOST payments of households to arrive at total utility payments.[89] We then apply the statutory tax rate, 7.5 percent to total utility payments to calculate the public utility tax paid by the household.

ACKNOWLEDGMENTS

This chapter is an expanded version of Deborah L. Garvey and Thomas J. Espenshade, "State and Local Fiscal Impacts of New Jersey's Immigrant and Native Households," in T.J. Espenshade, ed., *Keys to Successful Immigration: Implications of the New Jersey Experience* (Washington, D.C.: The Urban Insti-

---

equalized tax rate and the estimated market value of a residence equals the amount of property tax calculated by multiplying the statutory property tax rate by assessed value. Equalized property tax rates often vary widely across municipalities within a PUMA and tend to move inversely with the property wealth of a municipality. To account for this disparity in equalized rates and the fact that the population of a PUMA tends to be concentrated in the relatively high tax rate urban areas, we weight the equalized property tax rate by the fraction of the PUMA's population in the municipality to arrive at the equalized property tax rate of the PUMA.

[87]Annual contract rent is defined as 12 times monthly contract rent. Monthly rent is reported as ranges in the categorical variable RENT1 in the 1990 census. We take the midpoint of each category as an estimate of monthly rent paid (Bureau of the Census, 1993:B-41).

[88]We thank Robert Inman for suggesting the capitalized value approach to us. In earlier work, Espenshade and King (1994) used a different approach for estimating renters' property tax contributions. They based their calculations on New Jersey guidelines (State of New Jersey, 1990b; Public Law, 1990) and multiplied annual contract rent by 18 percent to approximate the fraction of rent payments that compensates owners for property taxes. This method and the capitalized value approach give identical results if the equalized tax rate is 1.76 percent and if the assumed discount rate is 8 percent.

[89]These variables give households' annual payments for electricity, gas service, water, and home heating fuel, respectively (Bureau of the Census, 1993:B-48). We assign the mean utility cost of same-sized households to those households who reported paying utilities as part of their rent (GASCOST or WATRCOST or ELECCOST or FUELCOST = 1). Approximately 1 percent of households reported no energy consumption whatsoever (WATRCOST = FUELCOST = ELECCOST = 2). These households were assigned the mean value of same-sized households' energy expenditures.

tute Press, 1997). Financial support for this research was provided by a grant from the Andrew W. Mellon Foundation. We are grateful to the following individuals for supplying information, data, and guidance about the operations of state and local government programs: Pat Austin, Maryann Belanger, Gerald Dowgin, Pamela Espenshade, Mary Forsberg, David Grimm, Evelyn Klingler, Robert Lupp, Linda O'Connor, Marc Pfeiffer, Deena Schorr, and Mel Wyns. Andrei Shidlowski, from the New Jersey School Boards Association, prepared the data on per pupil expenditure. Valuable comments were received from members of the National Research Council's Panel on the Demographic and Economic Impacts of Immigration at a workshop in Irvine, California, January 25-26, 1996. Melanie Adams and Maya Smith provided skillful technical and research assistance.

REFERENCES

Abowd, John M., and Richard B. Freeman, eds.
   1991   *Immigration, Trade, and the Labor Market*. Chicago: University of Chicago Press.
Borjas, George J.
   1985   "Assimilation, Changes in Cohort Quality, and the Earnings of Immigrants." *Journal of Labor Economics* 3(4):463-489.
Borjas, George J.
   1994   "The Economics of Immigration." *Journal of Economic Literature* 32(4):1667-1717.
Borjas, George J., and Richard B. Freeman, eds.
   1992   *Immigration and the Work Force: Economic Consequences for the United States and Source Areas*. Chicago: University of Chicago Press.
Borjas, George J., and Lynette Hilton
   1996   "Immigration and the Welfare State: Immigrant Participation in Means-Tested Entitlement Programs." *Quarterly Journal of Economics* 111(2):575-604.
Borjas, George J., and Stephen J. Trejo
   1991   "Immigrant Participation in the Welfare System." *Industrial and Labor Relations Review* 44(2):195-211.
Bureau of the Census
   1990   *Official 1990 U.S. Census Form*. Washington, D.C.: U.S. Department of Commerce.
Bureau of the Census
   1993   *Census of Population and Housing, 1990: Public Use Microdata Sample Technical Documentation*. Prepared by the Microdata Access Branch, Data User Services Division. Washington, D.C.: U.S. Department of Commerce.
Clark, Rebecca L., Jeffrey Passel, Wendy Zimmermann, and Michael Fix
   1994   *Fiscal Impacts of Undocumented Aliens: Selected Estimates for Seven States*. Report to the Office of Management and Budget and the Department of Justice, September. Washington, D.C.: The Urban Institute.
Commerce Clearing House
   1990   *State Tax Handbook as of October 1, 1990*. Chicago: Commerce Clearing House, Inc.
Dunlap, Jonathan C., and Ann Morse
   1995   "States Sue Feds to Recover Immigration Costs." *NCSL Legisbrief*, January, 3(1). Washington, D.C.: National Conference of State Legislatures.
Espenshade, Thomas J.
   1996   "Fiscal Impacts of Immigrants and the Shrinking Welfare State." Working Paper No. 96-1, Office of Population Research, Princeton University, Princeton, N.J.

Espenshade, Thomas J., and Vanessa E. King
    1994   "State and Local Fiscal Impacts of U.S. Immigrants: Evidence from New Jersey." *Population Research and Policy Review* 13:225-256.
Federal Highway Administration
    1991   *Highway Statistics 1990.* Thomas D. Larson, Federal Highway Administrator. Washington, D.C.: U.S. Department of Transportation.
Fix, Michael, and Jeffrey S. Passel
    1994   *Immigration and Immigrants: Setting the Record Straight.* Washington, D.C.: The Urban Institute.
Forsberg, Mary E.
    1995   *State Aid Programs for Municipalities, 1989 and 1990.* Trenton, N.J.: Office of Legislative Services; Revenue, Finance and Appropriations Section. Data File.
Forsberg, Mary E., and Martin Poethke
    1994   "Summary of State Aid Programs for Municipalities: Senate Bipartisan Task Force on Municipal Aid Reform." Office of Legislative Services, Trenton, N.J.
Friedberg, Rachel, and Jennifer Hunt
    1995a   "Immigration and the Receiving Economy." Paper prepared for the SSRC Conference on America Becoming/Becoming American, Sanibel Island, Florida, January 18-21, 1996.
Friedberg, Rachel, and Jennifer Hunt
    1995b   "The Impact of Immigrants on Host Country Wages, Employment and Growth." *Journal of Economic Perspectives* 9(2):23-44.
Fullerton, Donald, and Diane Lim Rodgers
    1993   *Who Bears the Lifetime Tax Burden?* Washington, D.C.: The Brookings Institution.
Garvey, Deborah L.
    1997   "Immigrants' Earnings and Labor Market Assimilation: A Case Study of New Jersey." Pp. 291-336 in *Keys to Successful Immigration: Implications of the New Jersey Experience*, T.J. Espenshade, ed. Washington, D.C.: The Urban Institute Press.
Huddle, Donald
    1993   *The Costs of Immigration.* Washington, D.C.: Carrying Capacity Network.
Isbister, John
    1996   *The Immigration Debate: Remaking America.* West Hartford, Conn.: Kumarian Press, Inc.
Metcalf, Gilbert E.
    1993   "The Lifetime Incidence of State and Local Taxes: Measuring Changes During the 1980s." NBER Working Paper No. 4252, Cambridge, Mass.
New Jersey School Boards Association
    1990   *1989-90 Cost of Education Index and Users' Guide.* Trenton, N.J.: NJSBA Information Systems. Computer File.
O'Connor, Linda
    1995   Enrollment of Undergraduates in New Jersey Colleges by County of Residence. State of New Jersey, Commission on Higher Education. FAX and personal communication, August 30.
Pechman, Joseph A.
    1985   *Who Paid the Taxes, 1966-85.* Washington, D.C.: The Brookings Institution.
Public Law
    1990   c.61, s.2 (New Jersey Statutes Annotated c.54:4-8.58).
Rothman, Eric S., and Thomas J. Espenshade
    1992   "Fiscal Impacts of Immigration to the United States." *Population Index* 58(3):381-415.
Rutgers, The State University of New Jersey
    1990   *1990 New Jersey Legislative District Data Book.* New Brunswick, N.J.: Bureau of Government Research and Department of Government Services.

Smith, James P., and Barry Edmonston, eds.
   1997   *The New Americans: Economic, Demographic, and Fiscal Effects of Immigration.* Washington, D.C.: National Academy Press.
State and Local Coalition on Immigration
   1994   "Three More States Sue Feds for Costs of Immigration." *Immigrant Policy News...The State-Local Report* 1(2), November 9 Washington, D.C.
State of New Jersey
   1989   *State of New Jersey Budget: Fiscal Year 1989-1990.* Trenton, N.J.:   Jim Florio, Governor
State of New Jersey
   1990a   *Annual Report of the Division of Taxation, Fiscal Year 1989.* Trenton, N.J.: Department of the Treasury, Division of Taxation.
State of New Jersey
   1990b   *Instructions for Preparing NJ Form 1040.* Trenton, N.J.: Department of the Treasury, Division of Taxation.
State of New Jersey
   1990c   *Fifty-Second Annual Report of the Division of Local Government Services, 1989.* Trenton, N.J.: Department of Community Affairs, Division of Local Government Services.
State of New Jersey
   1990d   *Owner Occupied Housing: Statistics from Homestead Rebate and Income Tax Data Match for 1988.* Trenton, N.J.:   Department of the Treasury, Division of Taxation, Office of Tax Analysis.
State of New Jersey
   1991a   *Annual Report of the Division of Taxation, Fiscal Year 1990.* Trenton, N.J.: Department of the Treasury, Division of Taxation.
State of New Jersey
   1991b   *State of New Jersey Budget: Fiscal Year 1991-1992.* Trenton, N.J.:   Jim Florio, Governor.
U.S. Bureau of Labor Statistics
   1986   *Consumer Expenditure Survey, 1984: Interview Survey and Diary.* Washington, D.C.: Bureau of Labor Statistics.
U.S. General Accounting Office
   1994   *Illegal Aliens: Assessing Estimates of Financial Burden on California.* GAO/HEHS-95-22. Washington, D.C.
U.S. General Accounting Office
   1995   *Illegal Aliens: National Net Cost Estimates Vary Widely.* GAO/HEHS-95-133. Washington, D.C.
U.S. Department of the Treasury
   1987   *Instructions for Preparing Form 1040.* Washington, D.C.:   U.S. Government Printing Office.
Vernez, Georges, and Kevin McCarthy
   1995   *The Fiscal Costs of Immigration: Analytical and Policy Issues.* DRU-958-1-IF. Center for Research on Immigration Policy. Santa Monica, Calif.: The RAND Corporation.
Vernez, Georges, and Kevin McCarthy
   1996   *The Costs of Immigration to Taxpayers: Analytical and Policy Issues.* Santa Monica, Calif.: The RAND Corporation.
Yinger, John
   1982   "Capitalization and the Theory of Local Public Finance." *Journal of Political Economy* 90(5):917-943.

4

The Fiscal Impacts of Immigrants: A California Case Study

Michael S. Clune

INTRODUCTION

Shifts in the settlement patterns of immigrants to the United States since 1965 have placed California at the forefront of any discussion of immigration issues. Along with sharp increases in the volume of immigration, a shift in the country of origin distribution away from flows from Europe to flows from Mexico, Central and South America, and Asia led a much larger share of immigrants to settle in California. Since 1976, California has been the top destination of choice for new legal immigrants to the United States, receiving 34.6 percent of immigrants in 1992. That year, 61.8 percent of Mexicans, 43.1 percent of Vietnamese, 44.0 percent of Filipinos, and 57.5 percent of Salvadorans admitted to the United States chose California as their state of intended residence. California receives a disproportionate share of immigrants from all entry categories. In 1992, 29 percent of admitted immigrants indicated California as the state of intended residence, and 32.7 percent of refugees and asylees granted permanent legal resident status in 1992 resided in California. In addition, the overwhelming majority of applicants for legalization under the Immigration Reform and Control Act of 1986 filed applications in California (U.S. Immigration and Naturalization Service, 1993).

As a result, California contains the largest population of immigrants, both as a proportion of total residents and in real numbers. By 1995, 7.7 million California residents were foreign born, 24.4 percent of the state population and 34.3 percent of all non-native U.S. residents. At that time, 34.0 percent of all California residents and 42.4 percent of children in California lived in a household headed by an immigrant. More than half of all immigrant-headed households in California were headed by an immigrant from Latin America and approximately one-fourth were headed by an Asian immigrant.

With the rise in the number of foreign-born residents, immigration issues have taken center stage on the California political scene. In 1994, Californians voted in favor of Proposition 187, which, had it not been blocked by the courts, would have eliminated public education and health services for undocumented aliens (Ayres, 1995). Decrying the costs of incarcerating and providing public education and other services to undocumented aliens, Governor Pete Wilson sued the federal government in 1994 for funds to cover the state's expenditures, claiming that California was adversely affected by failed federal policy (*New York Times*, 1994; Freedberg, 1997). In 1998, Californians will return to the polls to determine whether the state will continue to provide bilingual education in the public schools (Pyle, 1997).

The debate over the provision of services to immigrants and costs incurred has been fueled by extensive research into the fiscal impacts of immigration on government revenues and expenditures. Generally, these studies have found that both natives and immigrants make the largest tax contributions to the federal government, that immigrants make lower average tax contributions, and that immigrants are a greater burden on state and local governments (Vernez and McCarthy, 1996; Garvey and Espenshade, 1996). Three studies have examined fiscal impacts of immigrants in California. Los Angeles County (1992) found that recent legal immigrants, legalized aliens, and undocumented aliens and their children incurred costs to the county in excess of their share of the population. Although these immigrants and their families composed 25 percent of the county population, this group consumed 30.9 percent of total county services while paying only 8.7 percent of tax revenues, most of which flowed to the federal government. Two later studies (Romero et al., 1994; Urban Institute, 1994) found that the benefits and services consumed by undocumented aliens greatly exceeded their tax contributions. Rothman and Espenshade (1992) review immigrant fiscal impact studies completed through 1992; Vernez and McCarthy (1996) and MaCurdy et al. (in this volume) review more recent studies.

Several problems with these studies make the results difficult to compare and to fully assess the fiscal impacts of immigration. Among these problems, the earlier studies are limited in scope either because of their focus on undocumented aliens or a small geographic area. The studies do not provide estimates of the contributions of natives, preventing examination of the relative impacts of immigrants. Comparisons of subgroups of immigrants by age or region of origin are also not available. Finally, because the studies examine a limited number of benefits and taxes and fail to match estimates provided with administrative budget information, a full accounting of the relationship between immigrants and government budgets is not provided.

In this chapter I examine the fiscal impacts of native and foreign-born households in California on federal, state, and local governments. Five principles established by the Panel on Demographic and Economic Impacts of Immigration guide the research. First, the study seeks to identify the current annual impact of immigrants—the flows of government funds to and from Californian immigrants during the single fiscal year 1994-1995. Two questions summarize this focus. How much did the average immigrant pay in direct taxes and fees during 1994-1995, relative to the average native? How much did the average immigrant receive in government benefits during 1994-1995, relative to the average native? I do not consider the long-term fiscal effects of immigration, which may be different from current annual effects because of the age structure of the immigrant population.[1] Indirect effects of immigrants on government revenues or expenditures, which might occur through impacts on the wage rates of natives, prices of goods, or business income, are also not considered in this chapter. Thus, the analysis proposes a short-term partial equilibrium answer to the experimental question of how much an additional immigrant affects government budgets: what would happen to government revenues and expenditures if a single immigrant household entered the state at the beginning of the fiscal year *and* no adjustments were made in the structure of taxation or government spending per household *and* this arrival had no effect on other households, prices, or business income?

Second, the analysis considers the household as the unit of analysis, primarily because households or quasi-household units pay most taxes (e.g., income, property, sales, and excise taxes), and households or quasi-household units consume most government services (e.g., public assistance, police, and fire protection). Other taxes paid and benefits received by individuals (e.g., employment taxes, education benefits) can be aggregated to households with relative ease. Use of the household as the unit of analysis has one important effect on the results: native-born children, who receive high levels of education benefits while paying almost nothing in taxes, are counted as part of their parents' households. Thus, the household method appropriately assigns the costs of education for native-born children of immigrants to immigrant households. However, the native-born adult children of immigrants, who are no longer resident in their parents' households, are not counted as part of an immigrant household. The taxes paid and benefits received are counted as native contributions.[2]

Third, the analysis follows a micro-level "bottom-up" approach to assigning tax payments and benefit receipt to households. Sample households from survey data serve as the unit of analysis, and characteristics are identified that allow the estimation of each tax payment or benefit amount for each household. House-

---

[1]The lifetime fiscal impacts of immigrants and their descendants are considered in Chapter 7 of the panel's report (National Research Council, 1997) and by Lee and Miller (in this volume).

[2]This results in a seemingly unfair bias in the results, assigning the children of immigrants to the foreign-born impact during the childhood years in which they receive high levels of education benefits, but counting the taxes paid by these individuals during adulthood to the native impact. Lee and Miller (in this volume) consider the fiscal impacts of the adult children of immigrants.

holds are then organized into categories, such as by age, nativity, and region of origin of the householder, and the mean values of tax and benefit items are compared. Espenshade and King (1994) conducted the first application of this microdata approach to the study of immigrant fiscal impacts, examining the impact of immigrants in New Jersey using the 1980 Census. Garvey and Espenshade (1996) conducted a similar study for New Jersey using the 1990 Census. The methodology for this California study follows largely on the New Jersey studies. The alternative "top-down" approach, used in most other fiscal impact studies, involves making estimates of total taxes paid (or benefits received) by immigrant households as a group, which are then divided by the estimated number of immigrant households. One problem with this approach is that variation across households resulting from characteristics other than nativity is often ignored. As a result, the top-down method precludes comparisons of native and immigrant households by age of householder, region of origin, citizenship status, or household income. The microdata approach allows these comparisons.

Fourth, an attempt was made at comprehensive treatment of all tax and benefit items at the federal, state, and local government levels. In this study, 13 tax revenue items (67% of total government revenues) and 25 benefit and service items (100% of government expenditures, excluding federal debt interest payments) are allocated to households. The remaining 33 percent of government revenues, primarily taxes paid by corporations and tourists, are addressed later in the chapter.

Fifth, household tax and benefit estimates are reconciled to match administrative totals from government budgets. Allocations to households are made in such a way that the average revenue or expenditure allocated to each household multiplied by the total number of households equals the actual total revenue or expenditure in the government budget. In this way, the study provides a full accounting of the flows of revenues from and expenditures to native and immigrant households.

The following section describes the data and methodology used for this study. In the third section I review the structure of the federal, state, and local revenues and expenditures for fiscal year 1995. In the fourth section I provide an overview of the characteristics of California's native and immigrant households, providing the foundation for the tax and benefit estimates discussed in the fifth section. In the final section I summarize and discuss the results.

DATA AND ALLOCATION METHODOLOGY

The primary data source is the California sample of the Current Population Survey (CPS), March 1995, Annual Demographic File. The file contains data for 4,590 California households completing a detailed survey of income earned or received in 1994. The CPS universe encompasses the civilian noninstitutional population living in households and members of the Armed Forces living in civilian housing units on a military base or in households not on military bases. The CPS does not cover institutionalized persons, including residents of military barracks, rooming houses, mental hospitals, rest homes, and correctional institutions. The interviews contain questions about 20 types of cash income, and 9 types of noncash income, as well as participation in public housing programs. Among these are the major income transfer and noncash benefit programs provided by the federal government, the state of California, and local government agencies. The cash transfer income types identified are Social Security, federal retirement and disability benefits, welfare (AFDC and general assistance), Supplemental Security Income, unemployment compensation, workers' compensation, veterans' benefits, and educational assistance. The noncash income types identified are Medicare, Medi-Cal, food stamps, school lunch programs, public housing, rent subsidies, and energy assistance. The 1990 Census of Population and Housing Public Use Microdata Sample (PUMS) provides supplementary information.

Revenue and expenditure data for federal fiscal year 1995, which began October 1, 1994, and California budget year 1994-1995, which began July 1, 1994, are collected from a number of government sources. Federal revenue and expenditure data are estimates for 1995 reported in the 1996 federal budget (Office of Management and Budget, 1995). The Bureau of the Census (1996b) provides direct benefit and intergovernmental transfer amounts. Expenditure figures for the state of California reflect actual amounts of expenditures for 1994-1995 as reported in the 1996-1997 Governor's Budget (Department of Finance, 1996a). The 1994-1995 Governor's Budget provides state revenue estimates (Department of Finance 1995a); this information is supplemented by information on taxes collected from the Board of Equalization (1995). The California Office of the State Controller (1995, 1996a, 1996b, 1996c) compiles records of city, county, school district, and special district revenues and expenditures. The most recent reports provide information for fiscal year 1993-1994. The Governor's Budget provides supplementary information about transfers to local governments and local spending.

After estimation of taxes paid and benefits received, households are classed by the nativity and age of the householder. Native households are those in which the householder was born in the United States, Puerto Rico, or U.S. outlying areas, or born abroad of American parents. Third-generation households are those in which both parents of the householder were native born. Second-generation households are those in which at least one parent of the householder was foreign born. Immigrant households are those in which the householder was foreign born. Comparisons are made for each of these household types, as well as for households further classed by the age of the householder (15-39, 40-64, and 65+) and by the place of birth of the householder. These region-of-origin classes are Europe/Canada, Asia, Latin America (encompassing Mexico, Central and

South America, and the Caribbean), and other. Comparisons are also made for foreign-born households by citizenship status and native and foreign-born households by income level.

Tax Estimation Methodology

For each tax and benefit item, a combination of household demography, program participation, and income sources and amounts is used to estimate the contribution or cost to government. Estimates are developed for household payments of federal and California personal income taxes; federal and state employment taxes (Social Security, unemployment insurance, and state disability insurance); California and local sales taxes; local property taxes; federal and California tobacco, alcohol, gambling, and fuel taxes; California motor vehicle fees; and federal and California gift and estate taxes.

Federal and state personal income tax values imputed by the Bureau of the Census based on income, home ownership, and household size are adjusted proportionally to match budget or empirical figures.[3,4] Assuming that employer shares of employment taxes are passed on and borne by workers, Social Security, unemployment compensation, and state disability insurance taxes are calculated using earned income of household members employed in nonexempt sectors.[5] Sales taxes are calculated by estimating the amount of household income spent on taxable items, based on work by Sheffrin and Dresch (1995), and applying the average statewide tax rate of 8 percent. Property tax amounts are estimated for owner-occupied and rental properties using tax and rent payments reported in the 1990 Census by nativity and age of householder and adjusting these to 1995 levels. Taxes on rental properties are assumed to be passed on by property owners and fully borne by renters. Excise and other taxes are allocated based on estimates of household participation, such as the number of persons age 21 and older who are eligible to pay alcohol taxes, and assuming no differences in tax paid by participating households or individuals by nativity. The specific methods and assumptions made for each benefit item are included in Appendix A.

---

[3]The Bureau of the Census (1993a) used these variables to impute filing status, capital gains, itemized deductions, and exemptions and to calculate estimated tax payments.

[4]The total weighted sum of state personal income taxes imputed by the Census Bureau exceeds actual state receipts by $4 billion. In order to match the administrative total, household estimates are reduced proportionally by 16.95 percent. Similarly, federal income taxes imputed by the Census Bureau appear to underestimate federal receipts from California and these estimates are increased by 7.23 percent. With ideal data, the survey estimates would match administrative totals, and no adjustment would be necessary.

[5]My goal in this chapter is to provide a cross-sectional examination of tax and benefit flows. All taxes are treated as contributions to a general fund rather than to a trust fund from which the taxpayer may draw at a later date. Similarly, benefits are treated as monetary transfers from a general fund, rather than as a government-held retirement, disability, or health plan.

Corporations and out-of-state tourists pay less than 33 percent of taxes contributed in California. Although some share of corporate taxes is likely passed on to households through higher prices, these indirect taxes are not estimated in this chapter. Instead, an adjustment is made in the calculation of household fiscal impacts assuming that corporate and tourist taxes pay for services and benefits received by these entities, and the benefits received by households are reduced by the amounts of these taxes.

Benefit Estimation Methodology

For each budget item, the amount "paid" to California households by government entities is identified and, where possible, an estimate of administrative costs is added. The average household or individual benefit is estimated by dividing the total program expenditure amount by the CPS estimate of the number of participating households and individuals. Estimates of household benefits and services received are developed for all major federal, California, and local income transfer programs; health care; K-12 and higher education services; corrections costs; and other federal, California, and local expenditures.[6]

Three methods are used to allocate benefits. The first method identifies participating households and assumes no differences by nativity or age of householder in average benefits received by these households. Average household benefits are allocated to participating households for federal civilian and military benefits, railroad retirement benefits, veterans' benefits, unemployment compensation, workers' compensation, energy assistance, housing assistance, and general assistance. The second method identifies the number of benefit recipients in each participating household and assumes no differences by nativity or age of householder in average benefits received for each *individual* participant. Average recipient benefits are allocated to participating households based on the number of recipients for food stamps, educational assistance, Medicare, Medi-Cal, and school lunches, and the number of students participating in K-12 education[7] and higher education. The third method identifies participating households

---

[6]The multiple beneficiaries of government spending may not be reflected in this analysis. For example, education spending may benefit both those receiving educations resulting from government spending and indirect beneficiaries such as corporations that profit from a highly trained labor pool. In this case, the benefits of education spending are allocated to the students incurring the expenditure.

[7]The statewide average per pupil expenditure for K-12 education is allocated to each student. Two important issues arise here and in other studies of fiscal impacts. First, immigrants and their children may reside in school districts in which per pupil expenditures are different on average than those in which the children of natives are enrolled. This may not be a significant issue in California because the state attempts to equalize funding across school districts. In 1976, the California Supreme Court ruled in *Serrano* v. *Priest* that funding mechanisms which created disparities across school districts were unconstitutional. A study of California school financing found that by 1985-1986, 91 percent of public school students were enrolled in school districts with per pupil expenditures within $100 of

and assumes benefits depend on the nativity and age of the household head in proportion to benefit differentials observed in the 1990 Census. Average benefits for each householder nativity and age class are estimated for 1995 based on average benefits in 1990.[8] This method is used for allocation of Social Security, AFDC, and Supplemental Security Income (SSI).

Government expenditures on general government activities, national defense, environmental protection, transportation, public health, public safety, and criminal incarceration are assumed to benefit all households equally. Federal debt interest payments are not allocated. Average rather than marginal costs are allocated.[9] The specific methods and assumptions made for each benefit item are included in Appendix B.

Sources of Inaccuracy

Several sources of inaccuracy in the CPS data must be acknowledged. Sampling error may be large because the California sample is small (4,590 households) and is not a simple random sample. Census Bureau methods and parameters are used to calculate standard errors for household characteristics and program participation rates. These methods yield error estimates based on the size of the population for which the error is being calculated rather than the number of households or persons sampled. Adjustment parameters are included for specific characteristics and population subgroups and depend on the Bureau's assessment of the effect of the sampling method on the accuracy of the estimate.

Nonsampling error may result from inaccurate reporting of income sources and amounts. The Census Bureau reports an estimate of underreporting of 11 percent of all income in the 1987 survey, resulting both from underreporting of receipt and from underreporting of income amounts. Some income types are subject to greater underreporting than others, and 99.4 percent of wage and salary income is reported. Irregular income such as interest and unemployment com-

---

the statewide average expenditure (Silva and Sonstelie, 1995). A second issue is variation in the "true" benefit received by students, which may result from variation in the quality of education received across schools or school districts.

[8] For example, native recipient households in 1990 received higher average Social Security benefits compared with immigrant recipient households. Benefits allocated reflect this differential, after controlling for changes in the age and nativity distribution of recipients.

[9] Two areas where marginal costs are arguably important are K-12 education and incarceration costs. California's school districts spent approximately 10 percent of K-12 funds on building costs during 1993-1994 (Office of the State Controller, 1996b). Some of these funds were spent on new school buildings needed because of enrollment growth, whereas other funds were spent on retrofitting older school buildings for earthquake safety. For this reason, and because both immigrant and native households experienced increases in the number of school-age children since 1990, it is not clear to what extent capital outlay is attributable to enrollment growth due to immigrant households. Capital outlay was 1.2 percent of the $3.5 billion state corrections budget in 1994-1995 (Department of Finance, 1996a).

pensation is subject to particularly high underreporting (Bureau of the Census, 1993a). Underreporting of benefit receipt is corrected in this analysis by allocating total budget amounts to households reporting participation. This method has the effect of raising the average allocation to an individual participating household, but the average benefit across all households does not change. In other words, the underestimated participation rate is multiplied by an overestimated benefit amount. As mentioned above, ideally, survey data would reflect administrative totals, and these crude adjustments would not be necessary. However, if underreporting is proportional to the observed participation rate and not related to nativity or age, perfect reporting would not produce different results. Topcoding of income amounts will result in underestimates of income tax paid, particularly because of progressive taxation.

Furthermore, use of the March 1995 CPS data may underestimate income and overestimate program participation in 1995. Income levels and income transfer program participation rates in the data reflect household experiences during 1994, while the budget year examined includes part of 1994 and most of 1995. Improvement in California's economy likely led to lower participation in welfare programs and increased tax contributions. California payrolls grew 4.5 percent during the second quarter of 1995 and personal income rose 5.2 percent during the 1994-1995 budget year (Board of Equalization, 1995). The net effects of underreporting and economic shifts are likely to exacerbate underestimation of taxes contributed, but declines in program participation resulting from an improving economy should offset underreported participation. Underestimation of taxes is avoided by adjusting income tax amounts proportionally to match budget or empirical data.

GOVERNMENT REVENUES AND EXPENDITURES

Government Revenues

Revenues from California by government level are displayed in Table 4-1. Federal revenues from taxes and borrowed funds totaled $1,538 billion during fiscal year 1995. Personal income taxes constituted 39 percent of federal revenues, the largest single source of revenue. Social security and unemployment insurance contributions were the second largest revenue source (32%). Corporate taxes, excise taxes on alcohol, tobacco, and motor fuels, and miscellaneous receipts constituted another 18 percent of total revenues. Borrowed funds accounted for the remaining 11 percent (Office of Management and Budget, 1995).

Federal tax contributions in 1995 from California households and corporations are not directly available and must be estimated based on the percentage of federal revenues paid by California households and corporations during previous years. In 1993, 13.2 million California households and individuals filed federal income tax returns and paid $63.9 billion in federal personal in-

TABLE 4-1 Revenues by Level of Government, Fiscal Year 1995 (in thousands)

Revenue Item	Federal Government[a]	State of California	Local Governments	Total Government Revenues	Total Allocated to Households[b]
Individual Income Taxes	71,711,000	18,500,000		90,211,000	90,211,000
Social Security (OASDHI)	54,2311,750			54,311,750	54,311,750
Railroad Retirement	323,000			323,000	323,000
Unemployment Insurance	3,199,601			3,199,601	3,199,601
State Disability Insurance		1,967,827		1,967,827	1,967,827
Corporate Taxes	15,933,000	5,716,000		21,649,000	0
Sales Tax		16,283,000	7,130,000	23,413,000	10,540,019
Property Tax			19,300,000	19,300,000	11,287,156
Tobacco Tax	429,840	685,383		1,115,223	970,093
Alcohol Tax	990,486	269,056		1,259,542	1,094,743
Fuel Tax	2,913,429	2,752,005		5,665,434	3,206,937
Gambling Fees		649,829		649,829	649,829
Other Excise Taxes	1,685,756			1,685,756	0
Estate and Gift Taxes	2,335,283	599,000		2,934,283	2,934,283
Customs Duties	2,383,000			2,383,000	0
Vehicle Fees		4,700,000		4,700,000	1,944,968
Insurance Premiums		1,059,000		1,059,000	0
Current Services/Other Sources			27,705,000	27,705,000	0
Miscellaneous Receipts	2,428,000	1,689,344	4,680,000	8,797,344	0
Total Taxes and Fees	$158,644,145	$54,870,444	$58,815,000	$272,329,589	$182,641,206

[a] Federal amounts are estimates for taxes paid by California households and corporations based on Current Population Survey and historical data.

[b] Amounts in this column represent the revenues directly attributable to households. These amounts are allocated to households in later tables. The remaining revenues are revenues contributed primarily by corporations. Per-household shares of these "Unallocated Revenues" are included in Table 4-7.

Sources: Office of Management and Budget, 1994, 1995; Bureau of the Census, 1996b; Department of Finance, 1995a, 1996a; Office of the State Controller, 1995, 1996a, 1996b, 1996c.

come taxes, constituting 12.0 percent of federal personal income taxes collected (U.S. Internal Revenue Service, 1995b). In 1992, Californians contributed $44.94 billion to the OASDHI funds, 11.42 percent of the national total
(Social Security Administration, 1996). Railroad retirement contributions from
California were $323 million in 1994. The share of corporate taxes generated
from California is assumed to be proportional to California's share of total U.S.
households. Using these historical data, the estimated contributions of California households and corporations are approximately $72 billion in federal indi-
vidual income taxes, $54 billion in Social Security taxes, and $15.9 billion in
federal corporate taxes during fiscal year 1995. Based on state excise tax
revenues, sales of taxable items in California generated an estimated $2.9 bil-
lion in federal fuel taxes, $991 million in federal alcohol taxes, and $430
million in federal tobacco taxes (Board of Equalization, 1995). In 1994, 15.4
percent of federal estate taxes were paid in California (U.S. Internal Revenue
Service, 1995a). Based on this figure, the government generated an estimated
$2.3 billion in estate taxes from California in 1995. The total federal tax
contribution from California is estimated at $158.6 billion, 11.6 percent of total
federal receipts (excluding borrowed funds). California households' share of
borrowed funds equals $19.2 billion during fiscal year 1995.

The state of California collected $54.9 billion in taxes and other revenues
during 1994-1995. Personal income taxes are the largest source of revenue for
California: In 1994-1995, the state collected $18.5 billion in personal income
taxes, amounting to 33.8 percent of total state revenues. Sales taxes are the
second largest revenue source for the state, totaling $16.3 billion in 1994-1995.
Bank and corporation taxes constituted 10.5 percent of state revenues, and gasoline taxes and vehicle license fees were 13.4 percent of state revenues (Department of Finance, 1995a).

Local governments in California include 58 counties, 469 cities, 1,001 K-12
school districts, and more than 4,000 special districts. The primary source of
revenue for local governments is property tax revenue, totaling $19.3 billion
during 1994-1995. Of this revenue, 52 percent is allocated to K-14 schools, 19
percent to counties, 11 percent to cities, and 18 percent to redevelopment agencies and other special districts. Sales and use taxes contributed $7.13 billion to
local government coffers (Board of Equalization, 1995). Other taxes, including
utility users, business license, and transient occupancy taxes contribute $4.68
billion to local government revenues. Current services and other revenue sources
raised $27.7 billion[10] (Board of Equalization, 1995; Office of the State Control-
ler, 1995, 1996a, 1996b, 1996c).

---

[10]This figure was calculated as the total of other revenue sources for counties, cities, school
districts, and special districts as reported in the 1993-1994 series of reports from the Office of the
State Controller. The 1993-1994 values were carried over to 1994-1995.

Government Expenditures

Table 4-2 displays expenditures in California by government level. Federal spending during fiscal year 1995 totaled $1,538.9 billion. Benefits paid to individuals accounted for approximately 48 percent of spending. Social Security, federal retirement benefits, and Medicare amounted to 37.7 percent of the budget total. National defense and interest paid on the federal debt comprised 18 percent and 14 percent, respectively. Grants to states and localities were 15 percent of federal spending with the remaining 5 percent spent on other federal operations, including expenditures on scientific research, environmental protection, national parks, and public health services (Office of Management and Budget, 1995).

Federal spending on direct benefits to Californians totaled $75.8 billion in 1995. The largest components were Social Security benefits ($31.2 billion) and Medicare payments ($19.6 billion). In addition, the federal government transferred $26.9 billion to the state of California and local governments, and federal spending on poverty programs for Californians was more than $25 billion in direct payments and intergovernmental transfers. California's share of national defense, interest payments, and other expenditures equaled $61.4 billion. California's share of all federal spending totaled $170.5 billion (Bureau of the Census, 1996b).

State expenditures of state revenues totaled $53.9 billion in 1994-1995. Education comprises the largest share of expenditures: $16.4 billion was spent on K-12 education and $5.8 billion was spent on higher education; $10.9 billion was spent on the state shares of the three largest health and welfare programs for the poor: Medi-Cal, AFDC, and SSI. The state spent $3.6 billion on youth and adult corrections; and general government operations, including transportation, environmental protection, and legislative and judicial functions, totaled $8.2 billion. The remaining $9.2 billion was passed on to local governments (Department of Finance, 1996a).

California's 58 counties and 469 cities spent an estimated $45 billion in addition to welfare spending during fiscal year 1994-1995. Public protection, at one-third of total expenditures, is the single largest component of city and county spending. Additional county and city spending includes expenditures on public health, sanitation, recreation, culture, transportation, and public utilities. The state's 1,001 school districts spent $29 billion in 1994-1995, including $10.4 billion in local revenues (Office of the State Controller, 1995, 1996a, 1996b, 1996c). California's community colleges spent $1.3 billion in local property tax revenues. Additional local spending by special districts is not included (Department of Finance, 1995a).

CHARACTERISTICS OF CALIFORNIA HOUSEHOLDS

California was home to an estimated 31.7 million people living in noninstitutional housing in March 1995. Between 1990 and 1995, more than 1.2 million

TABLE 4-2   Expenditures by Level of Government, Fiscal Year 1995 (in thousands)

Expenditure Item	Federal Government	State of California	Local Governments	Total Government Expenditures
Social Security	31,243,608			31,243,608
Federal Retirement and Disability	3,823,317			3,823,317
Military Retirement and Disability	3,506,669			3,506,669
Railroad Retirement	480,925			480,925
Medicare	19,603,300			19,603,300
Unemployment Compensation	4,272,532			4,272,532
Workers' Compensation	291,882			291,882
Veterans' Benefits	1,505,386			1,505,386
Pell Grants	613,633			613,633
Medi-Cal	9,095,207	6,040,337		15,135,544
Aid to Families with Dependent Children	2,935,678	2,814,883		5,750,561
Supplemental Security Income	3,542,779	2,017,714		5,560,493
Housing Benefits	3,833,250			3,833,250
Food Stamps	2,723,221			2,723,221
School Lunches	899,757			899,757
General Assistance			450,000	450,000
Energy Assistance	66,796			66,796
Earned Income Tax Credit	2,405,545			2,405,545
K-12 Education	2,404,000	16,370,000	10,360,000	29,134,000
Higher Education	4,000,242	5,768,303	1,270,900	11,039,445
State Corrections	34,756	3,573,496		3,608,252
National Defense	30,799,440			31,234,000
Net Interest (less offsets)	21,867,149			22,175,680
Other Federal Operations	8,725,563			8,848,675
Other State Operations	7,815,697	8,155,559		15,971,256
Other Local Operations	3,962,351	9,164,556	46,734,100	59,861,007
Total Expenditures	$170,452,683	$53,904,848	$58,185,000	$283,172,531

SOURCES: Office of Management and Budget, 1994, 1995; Bureau of the Census, 1996b; Department of Finance, 1995a, 1996a; Office of the State Controller, 1995, 1996a, 1996b, 1996c.

international immigrants settled in California (Byerly and Deardoff, 1995; Bureau of the Census, 1996a). In March 1995, 7.7 million immigrants resided in California, 24.4 percent of the state's population, up from 21.6 percent in 1990. An additional 6.6 million Californians are second-generation Americans while 17.3 million Californians are third-generation natives. Of California's 11.2 million householders, 25.3 percent are foreign born, 14.0 percent are second-generation natives, and 60.7 percent are third-generation natives. More than half of foreign-born householders were born in Latin America. Latin American immigrant households constitute 14.1 percent of California households; Asian immigrant households make up 6.3 percent of the state total.

Household Size and Structure

Socioeconomic characteristics of households by nativity of householder are presented in Table 4-3a, 4-3b, and 4-3c. The average household contains 2.79 persons, including 0.83 children and 0.31 persons age 65 and older. Native households are slightly smaller on average, and second-generation households are slightly smaller than third-generation households. Immigrant households are larger, containing 3.72 persons on average, including 1.37 children. Among immigrant households, Latin American and Asian immigrant households are particularly large. Households headed by immigrants from Latin America contain 4.18 persons on average, including 1.70 children, but only 0.15 persons over age 64. Similarly, households headed by Asian immigrants contain 3.54 persons on average, including 1.15 children and 0.26 elderly persons. In contrast, European/Canadian immigrant households are the smallest, containing 2.18 persons on average. Immigrant households contain a higher average number of adult earners than natives, particularly Latin American immigrant households. Second-generation households contain fewer earners than third-generation households.

As a result of the larger average size of California's immigrant households, 34 percent of household residents live in a foreign-born household. While only 10.1 percent of children are immigrants themselves, 42.4 percent of children live in a household headed by an immigrant. The percentage of children who reside in the home of a Latin American immigrant householder is 30.4 percent. Of persons age 65 and older, 18.9 percent live in an immigrant household.

Characteristics of Householders

Foreign-born householders are younger than native householders on average, and second-generation householders are older than third-generation householders on average. Of immigrant householders, 47.5 percent are younger than age 40, and 87.6 percent are younger than age 65, compared with 77.1 percent of native householders. Only 12.4 percent of foreign-born householders are age 65 and older, compared with 22.9 percent of natives. Second-generation household-

TABLE 4-3a   Demographic and Economic Profile of California Households by
Nativity of Householder, 1995

	All Households	Native Born	Third Generation
Households	11,235,736	8,385,080	6,807,009
Persons	2.79	2.48	2.51
Children < Age 18	0.83	0.64	0.67
School-age Children	0.58	0.46	0.49
% LEP	16.8%	2.4%	2.2%
College Students (Age 16-24)	0.07	0.06	0.06
Persons age 65 and older	0.31	0.34	0.29
Adult Wage Earners	1.38	1.32	1.37
Householders			
Age 15-39	38.6%	35.6%	37.1%
Age 40-64	41.2%	41.5%	43.6%
Age 65+	20.2%	22.9%	19.3%
Mean Age	47.7	49.1	47.7
Male	60.9%	59.5%	60.3%
Spouse Present	53.4%	50.5%	50.9%
Immigrant Spouse | Spouse	32.2%	10.1%	7.5%
Educational Attainment			
< High School Diploma	19.4%	10.6%	8.7%
High School Diploma	24.1%	25.6%	25.5%
Some College	30.3%	35.1%	36.1%
Bachelor's Degree +	26.3%	28.7%	29.7%
Household Income, 1994			
Mean Household Income	$44,844	$47,884	$49,220
Per Capita[a]	$19,671	$22,241	$22,738
Median Household Income	$35,130	$39,184	$40,586
Per Capita[a]	$14,616	$17,122	$17,914
Mean Earned Income	$35,255	$37,208	$39,134
Below Poverty Level	14.8%	11.0%	10.7%
Income Above $50,000	35.4%	39.3%	41.1%
Homeowners	56.4%	61.8%	61.6%
n	4,590	3,058	2,379

*Indicates native and immigrant means (or third- and second-generation means) are significantly
different at the 5% level.

[a]Found by calculating per capita income for each household and averaging over all households in the
category.

SOURCE: Current Population Survey, March 1995.

		Foreign-born Households by Region of Origin			
Second Generation	Foreign Born	Europe/ Canada	Asia	Latin America	Other
1,578,070	2,850,656	345,234	698,952	1,592,190	214,280
2.36	3.72*	2.18	3.54*	4.18*	3.41*
0.52*	1.37*	0.42	1.15*	1.70*	1.22*
0.36*	0.93*	0.28	0.87*	1.10*	0.93*
2.0%	37.6%	9.3%	35.4%	40.4%	31.4%
0.07	0.10*	0.06	0.16*	0.09	0.10
0.53*	0.23*	0.45	0.26	0.15*	0.34
1.11*	1.56*	1.05	1.52	1.70*	1.42
29.4%	47.5%	21.6%	36.9%	58.3%	44.1%
32.4%	40.1%	44.0%	51.6%	33.9%	42.4%
38.1%	12.4%	34.4%	11.5%	7.8%	13.5%
54.9	43.7	56.0	45.2	40.0	45.8
56.1%	65.0%*	58.1%	66.2%	64.6%*	75.0%*
48.9%	61.8%*	46.7%	67.9%*	61.2%*	70.3%
21.5%	85.4%	57.8%	93.2%	87.7%	74.7%
18.7%*	45.3%*	21.8%*	19.7%*	65.6%*	15.8%
26.0%	19.6%*	21.3%*	20.3%	18.8%*	20.3%
30.8%*	16.0%*	24.6%*	23.8%*	10.4%*	18.3%*
24.5%*	19.1%*	32.4%	36.3%	5.1%*	45.6%*
$42,118	$35,903	$42,857	$45,589	$28,447	$48,499
$20,098	$12,114	$22,122	$15,135	$8,018	$16,572
$32,555	$26,193	$32,870	$37,800	$22,000	$38,634
$14,872	$7,805	$15,750	$12,076	$6,003	$14,825
$28,900	$29,513	$30,315	$38,007	$24,514	$37,656
12.1%	26.3%	17.6%	17.8%	33.1%	17.1%
31.6%	23.8%	35.6%	37.2%	13.5%	37.8%
62.4%	40.5%*	53.4%	42.8%*	34.4%*	56.6%*
679	1,532	131	335	977	88

TABLE 4-3b   Demographic and Economic Profile of California Households by Age and Nativity of Householder, 1995

| | Householders Age 15-39 | | | | | |
	All	Native Born	Third Gen.	Second Gen.	Foreign Born	All
Households	4,342,222	2,987,342	2,522,814	464,527	1,354,880	4,623,610
Persons	3.17	2.80	2.76	2.98	3.99	2.95
Children < Age 18	1.26	1.04	1.02	1.13	1.74	0.80
School-age Children	0.77	0.66	0.65	0.71	1.01	0.67
% LEP	19.0%	2.0%	2.0%	2.0%	43.4%	14.8%
College Students	0.06	0.06	0.06	0.08	0.05	0.12
Persons age 65+	0.02	0.01	0.01	0.02	0.04	0.06
Adult Wage Earners	1.56	1.54	1.55	1.51	1.59	1.69
Householders						
Mean Age	31.4	31.6	31.7	30.7	31.0	49.9
Male	60.8%	58.3%	58.7%	55.7%	66.4%	64.6%
Spouse Present	49.0%	43.8%	43.3%	47.0%	60.3%	61.9%
Immigrant Spouse I Spouse	42.2%	12.8%	9.0%	30.6%	89.4%	30.9%
Educational Attainment						
< High School Diploma	20.5%	8.2%	6.9%	15.7%	47.5%	14.8%
High School Diploma	24.0%	26.2%	27.1%	21.6%	19.1%	21.9%
Some College	32.4%	38.8%	39.0%	38.2%	18.3%	30.8%
Bachelor's Degree +	23.1%	26.7%	27.1%	24.5%	15.1%	32.5%
Household Income,1994						
Mean Household Income	$41,419	$45,877	$46,584	$42,039	$31,590	$54,610
Per Capita[a]	$17,012	$20,305	$20,723	$18,031	$9,751	$22,764
Median Household Income	$33,356	$39,919	$40,577	$36,700	$31,590	$47,025
Per Capita[a]	$12,020	$15,655	$15,952	$14,638	$6,370	$18,108
Mean Earned Income	$37,669	$42,061	$42,739	$38,380	$27,987	$46,643
Below Poverty Level	20.3%	14.4%	13.7%	17.8%	33.4%	11.6%
Income Above $50,000	31.7%	38.0%	38.8%	33.6%	17.7%	47.5%
Homeowners	34.5%	39.3%	39.3%	39.2%	24.0%	67.3%
n	1,862	1,109	890	219	753	1,866

*Indicates native and immigrant means (or third- and second-generation means) are significantly different at the 5% level.
[a]Found by calculating per capita income for each household and averaging over all households in the category.
SOURCE: Current Population Survey, March 1995.

ers are more likely to be age 65 or older (38.1%). European/Canadian householders are also older; Latin American householders are the youngest on average.

Foreign-born householders are more likely than natives to be male and more likely to reside with a spouse, particularly immigrant householders from Asia and Latin America. Among foreign-born householders with a spouse present, 85.4 percent are married to an immigrant, while married third-generation natives are unlikely to be married to an immigrant (7.5%). The nativity distribution of spouses of married second-generation householders more closely resembles that of the general population; 21.5 percent of spouses of second-generation householders are foreign born.

Householders Age 40-64					Householders Age 65+			
Native Born	Third Gen.	Second Gen.	Foreign Born	All	Native Born	Third Gen.	Second Gen.	Foreign Born
3,480,394	2,968,484	511,910	1,143,216	2,269,903	1,917,344	1,315,711	601,633	352,559
2.63	2.62	2.66	3.92	1.76	1.71	1.76	1.61	2.04
0.63	0.64	0.53	1.31	0.08	0.06	0.07	0.04	0.18
0.52	0.54	0.42	1.09	0.05	0.04	0.05	0.03	0.11
2.6%	2.7%	2.7%	31.7%	6.1%	0.0%	0.0%	0.0%	22.0%
0.09	0.09	0.12	0.19	0.01	0.01	0.01	0.01	0.04
0.05	0.04	0.08	0.11	1.36	1.36	1.39	1.31	1.36
1.63	1.64	1.63	1.85	0.43	0.42	0.45	0.36	0.47
50.2	49.7	52.9	49.0	74.5	74.4	73.9	75.3	75.1
63.7%	63.7%	63.6%	67.5%	53.7%	54.0%	55.8%	50.2%	51.5%
59.5%	59.1%	62.1%	69.2%	44.5%	44.6%	47.1%	39.2%	43.7%
9.6%	7.8%	20.0%	86.1%	14.8%	6.7%	3.8%	15.1%	59.7%
6.3%	5.1%	13.2%	40.4%	26.8%	22.0%	20.3%	25.8%	52.9%
22.3%	22.2%	22.7%	20.8%	28.6%	30.7%	30.0%	32.2%	17.2%
36.2%	36.7%	33.0%	14.4%	25.0%	27.3%	29.2%	23.2%	12.5%
35.2%	35.9%	31.2%	24.4%	19.5%	19.9%	20.4%	18.8%	17.5%
$58,214	$58,573	$56,130	$43,637	$31,503	$32,258	$33,173	$30,258	$27,397
$25,590	$25,821	$24,246	$14,163	$18,560	$19,179	$19,642	$18,165	$14,551
$51,390	$52,200	$50,360	$34,241	$20,373	$20,906	$21,078	$19,370	$14,929
$21,010	$21,346	$16,834	$9,350	$12,909	$13,649	$13,687	$13,593	$8,707
$49,595	$49,917	$47,727	$37,656	$7,441	$7,160	$7,892	$5,560	$8,972
8.5%	8.3%	9.3%	21.0%	11.1%	10.2%	10.3%	10.0%	15.9%
52.1%	52.3%	51.0%	33.4%	17.9%	18.2%	20.3%	13.6%	16.2%
71.3%	71.4%	70.3%	55.4%	75.8%	79.6%	82.2%	73.7%	55.1%
1,260	1,033	227	606	862	689	456	233	173

Foreign-born householders have lower educational attainment than natives, and wide variations exist across region-of-origin groups. Although nearly 90 percent of native householders have attained at least a high school diploma, only 54.7 percent of immigrant householders have completed high school. Approximately one-fifth of European/Canadian and Asian immigrant householders and two-thirds of Latin American immigrant householders did *not* complete high school. Of native householders, 28.7 percent have earned a bachelor's degree or higher, compared with 19.1 percent of immigrant householders. European/Canadian and Asian householders exhibit higher college attainment with 32.4 percent

TABLE 4-3c   Demographic and Economic Profile of California Households by Selected Household Characteristics, 1995

| | Foreign Born | | Income below Poverty | |
	Citizens	Non-citizens	Native Born	Foreign Born
Households	825,086	2,025,569	919,306	748,663
Persons	3.23	3.92	2.47	4.25
Children < Age 18	0.98	1.53	0.97	2.11
School-age Children	0.71	1.02	0.63	1.39
% LEP	34.2%	38.4%	2.1%	39.1%
College Students	0.12	0.10	0.08	0.06
Persons age 65 and older	0.38	0.17	0.26	0.15
Adult Wage Earners	1.57	1.55	0.55	0.99
Householders				
Age 15-39	24.9%	56.7%	46.7%	60.4%
Age 40-64	52.0%	35.3%	32.1%	32.1%
Age 65+	23.1%	8.0%	21.2%	7.5%
Mean Age	51.4	40.5	45.5	40.1
Male	64.7%	65.1%	37.8%	51.7%
Spouse Present	63.1%	61.3%	17.9%	52.4%
Immigrant Spouse I Spouse	74.6%	89.9%	17.9%	94.8%
Educational Attainment				
< High School Diploma	21.9%	54.9%	24.5%	68.2%
High School Diploma	20.5%	19.2%	36.4%	16.1%
Some College	24.4%	12.6%	29.7%	9.8%
Bachelor's Degree +	33.1%	13.4%	9.5%	5.9%
Household Income, 1994				
Mean Household Income	$50,854	$29,812	$8,115	$10,617
Per Capita[a]	$18,364	$9,568		
Median Household Income	$41,853	$22,743		
Per Capita[a]	$13,620	$6,428		
Mean Earned Income	$41,255	$24,730	$3,472	$7,125
Below Poverty Level	11.9%	32.1%		
Income Above $50,000	43.0%	16.0%		
Homeowners	65.4%	30.3%	32.5%	16.8%
n	394	1,138	357	425

* Indicates native and immigrant means (or third- and second-generation means) are significantly different at the 5% level.

a Found by calculating per capita income for each household and averaging over all households in the category.

SOURCE: Current Population Survey, March 1995.

Income above Poverty		Income below Median		Income above Median		Income above $50,000	
Native Born	Foreign Born	Native Born	Foreign Born	Native Born	Foreign Born	Native Born	Foreign Born
7,465,773	2,101,993	3,810,733	1,771,363	4,574,347	1,079,293	3,299,394	678,364
2.48	3.53	2.07	3.55	2.82	3.99	2.94	4.03
0.60	1.11	0.56	1.45	0.71	1.25	0.72	1.21
0.44	0.77	0.39	0.96	0.53	0.89	0.53	0.85
2.2%	36.6%	2.2%	38.7%	2.3%	35.4%	2.3%	33.7%
0.06	0.12	0.05	0.08	0.08	0.14	0.09	0.20
0.35	0.25	0.46	0.26	0.23	0.18	0.20	0.21
1.42	1.76	0.77	1.17	1.79	2.18	1.92	2.29
34.3%	42.9%	34.6%	51.7%	36.5%	40.6%	34.4%	35.3%
42.7%	42.9%	30.2%	33.0%	50.9%	51.8%	55.0%	56.3%
23.1%	14.1%	35.2%	15.3%	12.6%	7.6%	10.6%	8.4%
49.5	45.0	52.2	43.6	46.5	43.8	46.4	45.3
62.2%	69.7%	45.1%	59.4%	71.6%	74.1%	75.8%	77.8%
54.6%	65.1%	29.4%	55.0%	68.1%	72.9%	75.3%	76.8%
9.7%	82.8%	14.3%	90.0%	8.5%	79.7%	8.4%	76.7%
8.9%	37.2%	18.9%	58.8%	3.7%	23.2%	2.3%	17.2%
24.3%	20.8%	32.4%	19.2%	19.9%	20.2%	18.2%	14.8%
35.8%	18.2%	35.4%	11.7%	34.9%	23.1%	32.5%	25.4%
31.0%	23.8%	13.3%	10.3%	41.5%	33.5%	47.0%	42.6%
$52,781	$44,909	$17,598	$16,795	$73,114	$67,262	$85,159	$82,527
$41,362	$37,486	$9,613	$12,215	$60,197	$57,901	$70,925	$70,221
65.4%	48.9%	47.0%	26.4%	74.1%	63.6%	79.0%	69.9%
2701	1107	1645	544	1413	988	1179	330

of European/Canadian and 36.3 percent of Asian immigrant householders holding bachelor's degrees, while only 5.1 percent of Latin American immigrant householders have completed a bachelor's degree.

Income, Poverty, and Home Ownership

Median household income in 1994 was $35,130. Third-generation households had higher levels of total household and earned income than either second-generation or immigrant households in 1994. Median household income for third-generation households was $40,586, compared with $32,555 for second-generation households and $26,193 for immigrant households. Among foreign-born households, Asian immigrant households enjoyed the highest household income levels while Latin American households reported the lowest levels of income. Foreign-born households earned a greater share of their household income (82%) than did native households (77%). Foreign-born households are more likely to have household income below the poverty line. Of foreign-born households, 26.3 percent had incomes below the poverty line, compared with 14.8 percent of native households. Nearly one-third of Latin American immigrant households live below the poverty line.

In 1995 native householders were more likely than immigrant householders to own their residence. Of native householders, 61.8 percent were homeowners, compared with 40.5 percent of immigrant householders. No difference in home ownership is observed between third- and second-generation homeowners. European/Canadian householders were more likely than other immigrants to own, and Latin American householders are least likely to own.

Program Participation

Participation in income transfer, health care, and other assistance programs by nativity and age of householder is displayed in Table 4-4a. Generally, native households exhibit greater participation in nonpoverty programs than immigrant households while the reverse is true for poverty programs. Approximately 27 percent of native households received Social Security benefits in 1994 and a similar percentage included at least one person covered by Medicare, while 15.2 percent of immigrant households received Social Security and 16.2 percent contained at least one person covered by Medicare. Second-generation and European/Canadian households were more likely to receive benefits from these programs, reflecting higher average numbers of elderly in these households. Only 12 percent of Asian and Latin American households received benefits from Social Security and Medicare. Among households headed by someone age 65 or older, immigrant householders were less likely to receive Social Security benefits. Native households were also more likely to receive federal civilian and military retirement benefits and veterans' benefits but immigrant households were more likely to receive unemployment compensation, particularly Latin American immigrant households.

Participation in eight benefit programs for the poor are examined, and immigrant households exhibit greater participation in the six largest. Household participation rates for natives were 14.3 percent for Medicaid, 4.8 percent for AFDC, 4.2 percent for SSI, 3.5 percent for housing benefits, 5.9 percent for food stamps, and 5.6 percent for the school lunch program in 1994. Immigrant households are twice as likely as native households to participate in Medi-Cal, AFDC, SSI, housing programs, and food stamps, and more than four times as likely to participate in the school lunch program. For Medi-Cal, food stamps, and school lunches, participating immigrant households also report higher average numbers of participants. Participation in Medi-Cal, AFDC, food stamps, and school lunches was highest among Latin American immigrant households for all programs except SSI; Asian immigrant households were most likely to receive SSI. Of Latin American households, 36.3 percent report Medi-Cal coverage and 36.2 percent report participation in the school lunch program. These findings are consistent with the 1990 Census data and with other data sources (Borjas and Hilton, 1996; Bean et al., 1997). Among native households, second-generation households were more likely to receive SSI. Controlling for the age of the householder (Table 4-4b), immigrant households in all three age classes were more likely than natives to have Medi-Cal coverage. Immigrant households with heads age 15-39 and 40-64 exhibit statistically significant greater participation in food stamps and school lunch programs, and older immigrant households are more likely than natives to receive SSI and housing benefits. Among households with incomes below the poverty line (Table 4-4c), foreign-born households exhibit greater participation in Medi-Cal, food stamps, and the school lunch program and lower participation in AFDC, SSI, and housing benefits.

FISCAL IMPACTS OF CALIFORNIA HOUSEHOLDS

Tax Contributions of California Households

Table 4-5a displays average household tax contributions by nativity of household head. The average California household pays a total of $16,227 in taxes: approximately $8,000 in income taxes, $5,300 in employment taxes, $940 in sales tax, $1,000 in property tax, and $930 in miscellaneous other taxes. The federal government receives 73.7 percent of total contributions, 18.3 percent of taxes flow to the state of California, and 7.9 percent flow to local governments.

Native households pay higher average contributions than immigrant households for all taxes except unemployment insurance, state disability insurance, and excise taxes. The proportional differences between native and immigrant households are largest for federal and California personal income taxes. Native households pay an average tax of $7,224 in federal income tax and $1,862 in state

TABLE 4-4a   Household Participation in Income Transfer, Health Care, and
Assistance Programs by Nativity of Householder, 1994

	All Households	Native Born	Third Generation
Social Security	23.8%	26.7%	23.6%
Recipients[a]	0.322	0.363	0.324
1989 mean	$7,966	8,081	8,081
Medicare	23.5%	26.0%	22.7%
Recipients	0.317	0.35	0.307
Federal Benefits	2.1%	2.6%	2.3%
Military Benefits	2.1%	2.5%	2.6%
Railroad Benefits	0.9%	0.9%	0.8%
Unemployment Compensation	9.4%	8.8%	9.0%
Workers' Compensation	3.1%	3.2%	3.5%
Veterans' Benefits	2.3%	2.9%	3.0%
Pell Grants	4.7%	4.6%	4.8%
Recipients	0.052	0.048	0.05
Medi-Cal	18.3%	14.3%	13.7%
Recipients	0.463	0.308	0.305
AFDC	6.1%	4.8%	4.8%
Recipients	0.068	0.052	0.052
1989 mean	$7,315	6,902	6,902
SSI	5.0%	4.2%	3.8%
Recipients	0.056	0.045	0.041
1989 mean	$5,467	4,941	4,941
Housing Benefits	4.2%	3.5%	3.3%
Food Stamps	7.9%	5.9%	5.8%
Recipients	0.245	0.165	0.167
School Lunches	10.6%	5.6%	5.7%
Recipients	0.208	0.102	0.105
General Assistance	1.1%	0.8%	0.8%
Energy Assistance	2.9%	2.9%	3.0%

*Indicates native and immigrant means (or third- and second-generation means) are significantly
different at the 5% level.
[a]Average number of recipients per household.
SOURCE: Current Population Survey, March 1995; Census of Population and Housing, 1990.

income tax, compared with average taxes of $3,908 and $1,014 among immigrant
households; immigrant income tax averages are 54 percent of native averages.
The differential is due largely to higher adjusted gross incomes among native
households, but higher marginal tax rates among native households and larger
numbers of exemptions for household members among immigrant households
also play a role. To some extent, greater home ownership and itemization of
deductions among native households relative to immigrant households reduces
the differential. Third-generation households pay higher taxes than second-gen-

Second Generation	Foreign Born	Foreign-born Households by Region of Origin			
		Europe/ Canada	Asia	Latin America	Other
39.9%*	15.2%*	35.7%	12.0%*	11.9%*	16.9%*
0.531*	0.199*	0.449	0.161*	0.154*	0.255
8,081	7,297	8,370	6,574	6,307	6,780
40.4%*	16.2%*	34.2%	17.2%*	11.1%*	21.6%
0.533*	0.22*	0.435	0.269*	0.139*	0.32
3.8%	0.6%*	1.1%	0.8%	0.2%*	3.0%
2.4%	1.1%*	2.8%	1.5%	0.6%*	0.0%*
1.3%	0.8%	1.3%	0.4%	0.7%	1.4%
8.3%	10.9%	5.0%	5.8%	15.0%*	6.8%
2.2%	2.7%	2.1%	1.6%	3.2%	3.1%
2.3%	0.9%*	2.0%	1.5%	0.3%*	0.8%
4.0%	4.9%	2.8%	3.9%	5.3%	9.0%
0.041	0.063	0.04	0.051	0.066	0.124
16.8%	30.2%*	14.2%	27.1%*	36.3%*	21.4%
0.322	0.92*	0.307	0.85*	1.122*	0.643
5.0%	9.8%*	3.0%	8.8%*	12.5%*	4.7%
0.052	0.114*	0.041	0.121	0.131*	0.077
6,902	8,188	7,707	10,475	6,119	7,631
5.9%*	7.2%*	8.0%	10.0%*	5.9%	7.0%
0.062	0.087	0.107	0.128	0.064	0.097
4,941	6,721	5,555	8,073	5,483	5,420
4.3%	6.4%*	8.2%	6.5%	6.3%*	4.4%
6.0%	13.7%*	6.0%	12.2%*	16.7%*	8.9%
0.156	0.480*	0.130	0.480*	0.566*	0.408
4.9%	25.2%*	4.3%	14.1*%	36.2%*	13.4%
0.088	0.521*	0.054	0.332*	0.735*	0.3
1.1%	1.9%	2.6%	2.1%	1.5%	2.3%
2.4%	3.0%	6.3%	2.7%	2.8%	0.0%

eration households; among immigrant households, Latin American households pay the lowest taxes. Within age categories (Table 4-5b), the largest immigrant-native differential is observed for households in the 40 to 64-year-old group.

The immigrant-native difference for Social Security is somewhat smaller, and immigrant households actually pay higher unemployment insurance and state disability insurance taxes. The average Social Security tax for immigrant households is 81 percent of the average for native households. The smaller differential for Social Security and higher payments by foreign-born households are due in part to the tax structure; except for the hospital insurance portion of the tax, these taxes are flat up to a maximum taxable income amount. Unemployment insurance has the lowest maximum ($7,000). The higher tax contribution by immigrant households suggests that these households contain a higher average number of wage earners in nonexempt sectors who earn $7,000 or more. Because no deductions or exemptions are allowed for Social Security taxes, immigrant households pay an average Social Security tax higher than their average federal personal income tax. Employ-

TABLE 4-4b   Household Participation in Income Transfer, Health Care, and Assistance Programs by Age and Nativity of Householder, 1994

		Householders Age 15-39				
	All	Native Born	Third Gen.	Second Gen.	Foreign Born	All
Social Security	3.4%	3.6%	3.9%	2.2%	2.8%	11.2%
Recipients[a]	0.039	0.043	0.047	0.022	0.03	0.135
1989 mean	$5,366	5,522	5,522	5,522	4,937	6,419
Medicare	1.6%	1.7%	1.8%	1.4%	1.4%	8.4%
Recipients	0.021	0.021	0.023	0.014	0.019	0.101
Federal Benefits	0.3%	0.5%	0.4%	1.1%	0.0%	1.8%
Military Benefits	0.3%	0.3%	0.2%	0.8%	0.3%	2.3%
Railroad Benefits	0.8%	0.9%	0.8%	1.8%	0.5%	1.0%
Unemployment Compensation	10.5%	11.0%	10.9%	11.5%	9.5%	11.6%
Workers' Compensation	3.4%	3.9%	4.0%	3.2%	2.4%	3.7%
Veterans' Benefits	0.8%	0.9%	1.0%	0.0%	0.6%	2.4%
Pell Grants	7.3%	8.3%	8.2%	8.8%	5.2%*	4.1%
Recipients	0.078	0.085	0.084	0.091	0.062	0.049
Medi-Cal	21.4%	16.7%	16.3%	19.0%	31.8%*	15.8%
Recipients	0.648	0.461	0.448	0.532	1.06	0.399
AFDC	10.7%	9.7%	9.2%	12.3%	13.0%	4.3%
Recipients	0.116	0.104	0.099	0.13	0.141	0.05
1989 mean	$7,261	7,014	7,014	7,014	7,888	7,473
SSI	1.8%	1.5%	1.6%	0.8%	2.4%	5.4%
Recipients	0.02	0.015	0.016	0.008	0.031	0.06
1989 mean	$7,516	7,051	7,051	7,051	7,897	6,537
Housing Benefits	4.7%	4.7%	4.5%	6.2%	4.7%	2.9%
Food Stamps	12.2%	10.2%	9.6%	13.7%	16.4%*	6.7%
Recipients	0.394	0.304	0.288	0.39	0.593*	0.2
School Lunches	16.7%	10.0%	9.8%	11.0%	31.7%*	9.3%
Recipients	0.316	0.178	0.174	0.195	0.621*	0.2
General Assistance	1.2%	1.1%	1.0%	1.8%	1.5%	1.3%
Energy Assistance	2.6%	2.9%	3.0%	2.4%	2.0%	2.5%

*Indicates native and immigrant means (or third- and second-generation means) are significantly different at the 5% level.
[a]Average number of recipients per household.
SOURCE: Current Population Survey, March 1995; Census of Population and Housing, 1990.

ment tax contributions are lower than natives for immigrant households in the young and middle-age householder classes. Older immigrant households pay higher employment taxes than similar native households, but older households pay much lower employment taxes than younger households.

The average household contributes $938 in sales tax (Table 4-5a). Because sales tax is a flat tax on consumption, lower-income households pay a greater share of household income in sales tax. The average native household contribution is

| Householders Age 40-64 | | | | | Householders Age 65+ | | | |
Native Born	Third Gen.	Second Gen.	Foreign Born	All	Native Born	Third Gen.	Second Gen.	Foreign Born
11.5%	10.6%	16.5%*	10.4%	88.5%	90.3%	90.9%	88.9%	78.7%*
0.138	0.129	0.19	0.127	1.243	1.272	1.299	1.214	1.086
6,543	6,543	6,543	5,762	8,589	8,658	8,658	8,658	8,146
7.9%	7.7%	9.1%	9.8%	96.3%	96.9%	96.7%	97.2%	93.6%
0.09	0.087	0.108	0.133	1.324	1.333	1.35	1.294	1.275
2.1%	2.0%	2.8%	1.0%*	6.1%	6.8%	6.9%	6.7%	2.1%*
2.8%	2.9%	1.8%	1.1%*	5.2%	5.5%	6.1%	4.1%	3.6%
1.0%	0.7%	2.4%	1.3%	0.7%	0.8%	1.2%	0.0%	0.4%
10.4%	10.2%	11.6%	15.1%*	2.7%	2.7%	2.6%	2.9%	3.0%
3.7%	3.9%	2.7%	3.6%	1.2%	1.3%	1.5%	1.0%	0.5%
2.9%	3.0%	2.5%	0.6%*	5.3%	5.8%	6.7%	3.9%	2.5%
3.5%	3.5%	3.6%	6.0%*	0.8%	0.9%	1.1%	0.6%	0.4%
0.038	0.038	0.036	0.082	0.009	0.009	0.011	0.006	0.007
12.1%	11.4%	16.1%	26.9%*	17.7%	14.4%	13.9%	15.6%	35.2%
0.243	0.232	0.311	0.874*	0.242	0.188	0.196	0.17	0.537
2.9%	2.7%	3.9%	8.6%*	0.8%	0.7%	1.0%	0.2%	1.5%
0.031	0.03	0.039	0.109	0.011	0.008	0.011	0.002	0.024
6,809	6,809	6,809	8,526	6,926	6,214	6,214	6,214	8,422
4.5%	4.2%	6.3%	8.2%*	10.2%	7.9%	7.2%	9.5%	22.6%
0.049	0.046	0.063	0.092	0.117	0.085	0.077	0.102	0.29
6,013	6,013	6,013	7,376	6,000	4,523	4,523	4,523	6,062
2.2%	2.2%	2.3%	5.2%	5.8%	3.7%	3.4%	4.5%	17.2%
4.5%	4.4%	5.2%	13.2%	2.1%	1.6%	1.9%	0.8%	5.1%
0.114	0.113	0.115	0.465	0.049	0.041	0.055	0.01	0.097
4.5%	4.5%	4.3%	23.9%	1.4%	0.7%	0.7%	0.8%	4.9%
0.087	0.087	0.086	0.545	0.019	0.011	0.013	0.008	0.057
0.9%	1.0%	0.7%	2.5%	0.4%	0.3%	0.0%	0.9%	1.2%
2.4%	2.6%	1.4%	3.0%	4.3%	3.8%	4.1%	3.3%	6.7%

TABLE 4-4c   Household Participation in Income Transfer, Health Care, and
Assistance Programs by Selected Household Characteristics, 1994

	Foreign Born		Income below Poverty	
	Citizens	Non-citizens	Native Born	Foreign Born
Social Security	27.4%	10.3%	24.1%	9.9%
Recipients[a]	0.348	0.138	0.275	0.108
Medicare	27.6%	11.6%	28.5%	12.2%
Recipients	0.356	0.165	0.324	0.137
Federal Benefits	1.6%	0.3%	0.6%	0.0%
Military Benefits	1.9%	0.7%	0.6%	0.0%
Railroad Benefits	0.7%	0.8%	0.0%	0.0%
Unemployment Compensation	8.9%	11.7%	8.9%	8.8%
Workers' Compensation	2.1%	2.9%	1.7%	1.3%
Veterans' Benefits	2.0%	0.4%	2.2%	0.2%
Pell Grants	3.1%	5.7%	4.8%	4.4%
Recipients	0.047	0.07	0.053	0.052
Medi-Cal	17.6%	35.4%	47.2%	53.7%
Recipients	0.381	1.14	1.183	2.022
AFDC	2.5%	12.8%	25.2%	24.1%
Recipients	0.031	0.147	0.26	0.273
SSI	6.4%	7.6%	10.2%	8.0%
Recipients	0.076	0.092	0.11	0.087
Housing Benefits	3.8%	7.5%	13.1%	11.4%
Food Stamps	4.9%	17.3%	31.1%	36.4%
Recipients	0.144	0.617	0.882	1.344
School Lunches	9.6%	31.6%	20.0%	51.2%
Recipients	0.182	0.659	0.394	1.165
General Assistance	0.6%	2.4%	6.1%	3.3%
Energy Assistance	3.1%	2.9%	10.1%	6.5%

*Indicates native and immigrant means (or third- and second-generation means) are significantly
different at the 5% level.
[a]Average number of recipients per household.
SOURCE: Current Population Survey, March 1995; Census of Population and Housing, 1990.

$992 in sales tax, compared with $778 for the average immigrant household.[11]
These estimates are based on household income only and assume no differences in
expenditures on taxable items by nativity within income ranges. Immigrant households are larger on average, and may spend a greater share of income on food,

---

[11]These estimates of sales tax paid by households may underestimate actual taxes paid. Corporations pay a large share of sales tax and tourists from outside the state pay a small share of tax. A top-
down allocation based on assumptions that corporations pay 35 percent of sales tax and that out-of-
state tourists pay 8.5 percent of tax yields an average household contribution of $1,178, 26 percent
higher than allocated based on the bottom-up approach.

Income above Poverty		Income below Median		Income above Median		Income above $50,000	
Native Born	Foreign Born	Native Born	Foreign Born	Native Born	Foreign Born	Native Born	Foreign Born
27.0%	17.1%	38.7%	16.4%	16.7%	13.2%	14.4%	13.8%
0.374	0.232	0.494	0.209	0.255	0.182	0.224	0.197
25.7%	17.6%	38.7%	18.6%	15.5%	12.3%	13.2%	13.7%
0.353	0.25	0.49	0.252	0.233	0.168	0.204	0.188
2.9%	0.9%	1.9%	0.3%	3.2%	1.1%	3.8%	1.4%
2.8%	1.4%	1.8%	0.5%	3.1%	2.0%	3.3%	2.9%
1.0%	1.0%	1.0%	0.9%	0.9%	0.6%	0.8%	0.2%
8.8%	11.7%	8.3%	10.4%	9.3%	11.7%	8.3%	9.6%
3.4%	3.1%	2.6%	2.3%	3.8%	3.2%	3.5%	3.7%
2.9%	1.1%	2.4%	0.6%	3.3%	1.3%	3.4%	1.6%
4.6%	5.1%	4.8%	4.3%	4.5%	6.0%	4.6%	5.9%
0.047	0.067	0.049	0.055	0.047	0.078	0.048	0.075
10.2%	21.9%	24.4%	39.3%	5.9%	15.4%	4.9%	13.2%
0.2	0.528	0.543	1.244	0.112	0.389	0.085	0.335
2.3%	4.8%	9.3%	13.5%	1.1%	3.8%	0.4%	3.1%
0.026	0.057	0.097	0.159	0.014	0.039	0.004	0.031
3.5%	6.9%	7.9%	9.7%	1.1%	3.2%	1.1%	2.8%
0.037	0.088	0.086	0.12	0.011	0.034	0.011	0.028
2.3%	4.6%	7.4%	9.4%	0.1%	1.6%	0.2%	0.4%
2.8%	5.6%	12.0%	20.0%	0.8%	3.4%	0.3%	1.8%
0.076	0.172	0.334	0.705	0.024	0.112	0.013	0.063
3.8%	16.0%	10.2%	33.7%	1.7%	11.3%	1.2%	5.0%
0.066	0.292	0.185	0.704	0.032	0.221	0.018	0.099
0.2%	1.3%	1.8%	2.5%	0.0%	0.8%	0.0%	0.5%
2.0%	1.7%	6.4%	4.6%	0.0%	0.3%	0.0%	0.0%

which is nontaxable, than smaller native families at the same income level. Also, estimated remittances to the country of origin are not removed from household income before calculating the tax contribution.[12] As a result, the actual sales tax contributions of foreign-born households may be smaller.

The average property tax contribution is $1,004. Owner-occupied residences

---

[12]Recent estimates of remittances (see Vernez and McCarthy, 1996) suggest that sales tax paid by immigrant households would decline by $72 if all dollars remitted reduced spending on taxable goods.

TABLE 4-5a   Estimates of Household Taxes and Contributions Paid by Nativity of Householder, Fiscal Year 1995 (dollars)

	All Households	Native Born	Third Generation
Federal Individual Income	6,382	7,224	7,660
Social Security	4,834	5,073	5,324
Unemployment Insurance	285	271	282
California Personal Income	1,647	1,862	1,983
State Disability Insurance	175	171	178
Sales Tax	938	992	1,016
Property Tax	1,004	1,035	1,050
Tobacco Tax	86	81	81
Alcohol Tax	97	92	92
Fuel Tax	285	289	292
Motor Vehicle Fees	173	176	178
Gambling Taxes	58	55	55
Inheritance Tax	261	313	313
Federal Share	11,966	13,069	13,768
State Share	2,971	3,227	3,375
Local Share	1,290	1,337	1,360
Total Contributions	16,227	17,632	18,503

have higher assessed values and therefore owners incur higher average taxes. Because they are more likely to own their homes, native householders pay higher average property taxes than immigrant householders. However, because European/Canadian and Asian immigrant householders report higher average property taxes paid and higher average home values in 1990, higher estimates of property taxes result for these region-of-origin classes. Within the middle and older age classes, property tax differentials are small (Table 4-5b). Older householders pay lower average property taxes in part because they have owned their homes longer and have lower assessed values.

Among other taxes, immigrant households pay higher alcohol, tobacco, and gambling taxes because these households contain higher numbers of adults on average (Table 4-5a). Small differences in automobile ownership are observed in the 1990 Census, resulting in small differences in fuel taxes and vehicle registration fees paid. Only one-third of immigrant householders entered the United States before 1975, and therefore the estimate of inheritance tax paid by immigrant households is approximately one-third the tax paid by natives.

To summarize, foreign-born households contribute average total taxes that

| Second Generation | Foreign Born | Foreign-born Households by Region of Origin | | | |
		Europe/ Canada	Asia	Latin America	Other
5,340	3,908	5,832	5,875	2,234	6,831
3,990	4,131	4,146	5,262	3,494	5,151
226	325	204	322	361	265
1,340	1,014	1,468	1,550	586	1,712
143	186	135	204	191	171
889	778	904	949	645	1,004
967	915	1,059	1,174	736	1,169
81	103	78	105	109	96
91	113	90	117	117	107
274	275	266	301	268	259
167	167	162	183	163	157
54	67	53	70	70	64
313	109	199	77	105	105
10,050	8,721	10,576	11,808	6,444	12,586
2,588	2,219	2,683	2,918	1,702	3,032
1,237	1,152	1,335	1,463	933	1,474
13,875	12,092	14,594	16,189	9,078	17,092

are 68.6 percent of the average total tax paid by native households. Total taxes paid are highest for third-generation households in all age categories. These households pay more than $18,000 in tax. Second-generation households pay average taxes totaling $13,875, and immigrant households pay total taxes averaging $12,092. The differential between immigrant and native contributions is largest for Latin American immigrant households, which contribute $9,078 on average. Within age groups (Table 4-5b), the differential is slightly larger between native and immigrant households in the young and middle-age categories. The immigrant-native differential is small among older households, and older households pay average taxes one-third the level paid by middle-age households. Among households grouped by income level (Table 4-5c), foreign-born households with income below the poverty line pay more in total taxes than similar native households, and among households with incomes below California median income, the tax contribution of foreign-born households is just $100 below that of similar natives. These patterns are generally observed at all three levels of government, but the proportional difference in tax paid is smaller at the local level. At the federal and state levels, immigrant households make average contri-

butions that are approximately 67 percent the average contribution of native households; at the local level, the immigrant contribution is 86 percent of the native contribution.

Benefits Received by California Households

Table 4-6a displays estimates of benefits received by California households by nativity of the householder. The federal, state, and local governments spend $22,762 per household. Of household benefits, 56.7 percent are provided through federal funds, 20.2 percent from state funds, and 23 percent from local funds.

The largest single household benefit comes from Social Security benefits. Native households receive an average benefit of $3,334, compared with $1,638 among immigrant households. Benefits for immigrant households are also lower for federal, military, and railroad retirement benefits, Medicare, and veterans' benefits. Second-generation and European/Canadian households receive average benefits from these programs that are higher than those received by third-generation households. Among region-of-origin groups, Latin American immigrant

TABLE 4-5b   Estimates of Household Taxes and Contributions Paid by Age and Nativity of Householder, Fiscal Year 1995 (dollars)

		Householders Age 15-39				
	All	Native Born	Third Gen.	Second Gen.	Foreign Born	All
Federal Individual Income	5,517	6,509	6,772	5,080	3,328	8,829
Social Security	5,218	5,799	5,877	5,373	3,937	6,348
Unemployment Insurance	337	333	333	330	346	339
California Personal Income	1,422	1,653	1,724	1,264	912	2,304
State Disability Insurance	220	230	231	228	198	201
Sales Tax	883	966	979	896	700	1,112
Property Tax	978	1,051	1,051	1,050	816	1,165
Tobacco Tax	84	77	76	81	99	95
Alcohol Tax	95	88	88	89	111	105
Fuel Tax	273	281	281	281	256	333
Motor Vehicle Fees	166	170	170	170	156	202
Gambling Taxes	56	52	52	53	66	62
Inheritance Tax	228	313	313	313	40	273
Federal Share	11,500	13,133	13,474	11,277	7,900	16,023
State Share	2,729	3,044	3,124	2,606	2,035	3,841
Local Share	1,247	1,345	1,349	1,323	1,029	1,503
Total Contributions	15,475	17,522	17,948	15,206	10,964	21,367

households receive the lowest average benefits from these programs. These benefits flow largely to older households, and within this group, foreign-born households receive lower average benefits, but the differentials are smaller after controlling for the age of the householder.

Average household benefits are higher among immigrant households relative to natives for eight of nine poverty programs. Among these programs, the largest benefit received by immigrant households is the Medi-Cal benefit. The average immigrant household receives a benefit of $1,774, more than three times the average native household benefit. Average benefits from poverty programs total $5,067 for immigrant households, compared with $1,983 for native households. Second-generation households receive poverty program benefits that are higher on average than those received by third-generation households for five of the nine programs. Latin American and Asian households receive the highest average benefits among region-of-origin classes. Poverty program benefits are higher among immigrant households in all three age classes (Table 4-6b). Among households with incomes below the poverty level (Table 4-6c), foreign-born households receive higher benefits from Medi-Cal, food stamps, school lunches,

Householders Age 40-64					Householders Age 65+			
Native Born	Third Gen.	Second Gen.	Foreign Born	All	Native Born	Third Gen.	Second Gen.	Foreign Born
10,081	10,360	8,464	5,016	3,056	3,150	3,272	2,883	2,542
6,707	6,741	6,513	5,254	1,015	974	1,065	777	1,233
328	328	326	373	74	72	77	61	88
2,648	2,726	2,194	1,255	738	760	801	671	621
197	197	196	216	36	34	34	33	45
1,174	1,179	1,142	925	689	705	721	669	604
1,184	1,185	1,178	1,105	729	737	744	722	681
88	87	94	115	74	73	74	69	82
99	98	104	122	87	86	88	82	95
335	335	335	326	213	218	218	218	183
204	204	204	198	129	133	133	133	111
59	58	62	72	52	51	52	49	57
313	313	313	152	301	313	313	313	238
17,650	17,961	15,842	11,072	4,591	4,653	4,873	4,174	4,254
4,225	4,306	3,756	2,670	1,664	1,701	1,755	1,581	1,462
1,542	1,544	1,526	1,387	938	952	964	926	865
23,416	23,812	21,124	15,128	7,193	7,306	7,592	6,680	6,581

TABLE 4-5c   Estimates of Household Taxes and Contributions Paid by Selected Household Characteristics, Fiscal Year 1995 (dollars)

	Foreign Born		Income below Poverty	
	Citizens	Non-citizens	Native Born	Foreign Born
Federal Individual Income	7,049	2,629	223	166
Social Security	5,698	3,493	523	1,047
Unemployment Insurance	332	322	75	171
California Personal Income	1,848	673	53	24
State Disability Insurance	210	176	24	63
Sales Tax	1,044	670	221	278
Property Tax	1,167	813	838	721
Tobacco Tax	99	105	66	94
Alcohol Tax	110	114	73	102
Fuel Tax	278	274	285	271
Motor Vehicle Fees	169	166	173	165
Gambling Taxes	66	68	43	60
Inheritance Tax	193	75	313	67
Federal Share	13,501	6,774	1,299	1,693
State Share	3,278	1,787	706	730
Local Share	1,485	1,017	905	805
Total Contributions	18,264	9,578	2,910	3,228

and earned income tax credits. Among households with incomes above $50,000, foreign-born households receive higher benefits from eight of the programs, with large differences for Medi-Cal, AFDC, and SSI.

Foreign-born households contain higher average numbers of school-age children and college students, and therefore receive higher average educational benefits (Table 4-6a). The average immigrant household receives benefits of $4,209 for K-12 education and $1,391 for higher education, compared with native benefits of $2,044 for K-12 education and $844 for higher education. Second-generation and European/Canadian households receive lower average K-12 benefits, and Latin American households receive the highest average benefit. Asian immigrant households receive the highest average benefit from expenditures on higher education. Average household benefits from expenditures on state corrections and national defense are $321 and $2,741, respectively. General government expenditures total $6,251 per household, with the largest expenditure at the local government level.

Government expenditures per immigrant household are $2,904 higher than expenditures per native household. At the federal level, expenditures are lower for

Income above Poverty		Income below Median		Income above Median		Income above $50,000	
Native Born	Foreign Born	Native Born	Foreign Born	Native Born	Foreign Born	Native Born	Foreign Born
8,086	5,241	790	523	12,583	9,464	15,944	13,215
5,633	5,229	1,399	1,777	8,134	7,995	9,461	9,550
295	380	139	230	381	481	409	499
2,084	1,366	115	51	3,317	2,594	4,289	3,800
190	230	65	102	260	324	288	351
1,087	956	436	419	1,456	1,368	1,626	1,583
1,059	985	862	762	1,179	1,167	1,224	1,256
82	106	66	93	93	120	97	124
94	117	75	101	106	133	111	139
289	277	275	267	300	289	304	293
176	168	167	162	183	176	185	178
56	70	45	60	63	79	66	82
313	125	313	94	313	134	313	146
14,518	11,224	2,803	2,857	21,621	18,346	26,343	23,688
3,538	2,749	948	893	5,125	4,394	6,253	5,789
1,390	1,276	994	889	1,622	1,584	1,720	1,738
19,445	15,249	4,746	4,639	28,368	24,324	34,316	31,216

immigrant households by $283. Federal expenditures are highest for second-generation, European/Canadian immigrant, and native and foreign-born older households. The state and local governments spend $2,335 and $870 more, respectively, on immigrant households. Asian, Latin American, young, and middle-age immigrant households were particularly expensive for the state and local governments.

Net Costs to Government

Table 4-7a shows total contributions and benefits and the net costs to governments by level of government. Before an adjustment is made to offset unallocated revenues, the average household is a net burden on all three levels of government, receiving $6,535 more in services than paid in taxes. Unallocated taxes paid by corporations and tourists and local revenues for fees, fines, and services charges total $8,011 per household.[13] After reducing household benefits by this amount,

[13]The assumption is made that corporation and out-of-state tourists receive one dollar in benefits and services for each dollar paid in taxes. The further assumption is made that these benefits come largely from spending on national defense, environmental protection, public safety, and other general

TABLE 4-6a   Estimates of Benefits and Services Received by Nativity of Householder, Fiscal Year 1995 (dollars)

	All	Native Born	Third Generation	Second Generation
Federal Individual Income	6,382	7,224	7,660	5,340
Social Security	2,904	3,334	2,924	5,103
Federal Benefits	340	421	377	608
Military Benefits	312	366	371	343
Railroad Benefits	43	45	40	63
Medicare	1,618	1,785	1,569	2,719
Unemployment Compensation	380	359	364	336
Workers' Compensation	26	27	29	18
Veterans' Benefits	134	163	170	133
Pell Grants	55	51	52	43
Medi-Cal	893	594	587	621
AFDC	512	399	397	410
SSI	459	358	332	470
Housing Benefits	341	280	264	347
Food Stamps	242	163	165	154
School Lunches	80	39	40	34
General Assistance	40	31	29	39
Energy Assistance	6	6	6	5
Earned Income Tax Credit	192	113	116	101
K-12 Education	2,593	2,044	2,151	1,578
Higher Education	983	844	827	916
State Corrections	321	321	321	321
National Defense	2,741	2,741	2,741	2,741
Other Federal Operations	777	777	777	777
Other State Operations	1,421	1,421	1,421	1,421
Other Local Operations	5,328	5,328	5,328	5,328
Federal Share	12,921	12,993	12,313	15,928
State Share	4,606	4,014	4,052	3,847
Local Share	5,235	5,014	5,049	4,865
Total Benefits	22,762	22,021	21,414	24,639

the average California household becomes a net benefit to the federal government and the state and local governments break even.[14,15] Native households are a net benefit for all three levels of government, while foreign-born households are a net

expenditures. The average amount per household ($8,011) is subtracted from the benefits allocated to households.

[14] In Table 4-7a, column 1, the net fiscal impact at the federal level is $1,198 for the average household. This figure includes all federal taxes and expenditures, except debt interest payments, borrowed funds, and payments on behalf of institutionalized persons. The California share of debt

	Foreign-born Households by Region of Origin			
Foreign Born	Europe/ Canada	Asia	Latin America	Other
3,908	5,832	5,875	2,234	6,831
1,638	4,599	1,240	1,157	1,738
104	170	134	24	490
155	402	224	91	0
37	65	19	35	67
1,124	2,219	1,372	708	1,635
443	203	237	608	276
22	18	14	27	26
49	116	86	19	47
67	42	54	69	130
1,774	591	1,637	2,162	1,238
843	273	1,102	908	428
756	805	1,299	522	640
521	663	528	509	359
475	129	475	560	404
200	21	128	283	115
67	95	76	56	83
6	13	5	6	0
425	51	152	666	122
4,209	1,159	3,869	5,027	4,157
1,391	810	2,184	1,169	1,385
321	321	321	321	321
2,741	2,741	2,741	2,741	2,741
777	777	777	777	777
1,421	1,421	1,421	1,421	1,421
5,328	5,328	5,328	5,328	5,328
12,710	14,680	12,736	12,340	12,205
6,349	3,598	6,841	6,795	5,857
5,884	4,760	5,863	6,137	5,880
24,943	23,038	25,440	25,272	23,942

interest payments totals $21.9 billion, or $11,946 per household, based on California containing 11.34 percent of the nation's households. Adding federal interest payments as a benefit for households would make the average California household a net burden on the federal government. The California share of federal borrowing totals $19.2 billion, or $1,707 per household. Treating this amount as a current tax, the net federal fiscal impact of an average California household would be a surplus of $1,052. This surplus results from the exclusion of benefits for institutionalized persons and because California pays higher taxes and receives lower benefits relative to other states.

[15]The state share net fiscal impact is not zero because California had a small surplus at the end of the fiscal year and because state expenditures on Medi-Cal and SSI for institutionalized persons are not included.

TABLE 4-6b   Estimates of Benefits and Services Received by Age and
Nativity of Householder, Fiscal Year 1995 (dollars)

| | Householders Age 15-39 | | | | | |
	All	Native Born	Third Gen.	Second Gen.	Foreign Born	All
Social Security	274	308	330	190	198	1,091
Federal Benefits	54	78	61	170	0	297
Military Benefits	48	47	35	110	50	341
Railroad Benefits	38	45	37	87	23	51
Medicare	105	109	116	72	97	516
Unemployment Compensation	426	445	441	467	384	469
Workers' Compensation	29	33	34	27	20	31
Veterans' Benefits	45	49	58	0	35	135
Pell Grants	82	90	89	95	66	51
Medi-Cal	1,248	888	863	1,025	2,042	770
AFDC	883	811	771	1,027	1,041	380
SSI	197	161	175	84	277	534
Housing Benefits	382	384	363	503	378	238
Food Stamps	390	301	285	386	587	198
School Lunches	122	68	67	75	239	77
General Assistance	45	41	36	65	54	48
Energy Assistance	5	6	6	5	4	5
Earned Income Tax Credit	316	194	193	198	586	160
K-12 Education	3,435	2,941	2,903	3,148	4,523	2,946
Higher Education	810	864	822	1,090	692	1,542
State Corrections	321	321	321	321	321	321
National Defense	2,741	2,741	2,741	2,741	2,741	2,741
Other Federal Operations	777	777	777	777	777	777
Other State Operations	1,421	1,421	1,421	1,421	1,421	1,421
Other Local Operations	5,328	5,328	5,328	5,328	5,328	5,328
Federal Share	8,822	8,351	8,264	8,822	9,859	10,043
State Share	5,217	4,776	4,708	5,142	6,190	5,010
Local Share	5,519	5,345	5,323	5,470	5,902	5,432
Total Benefits	19,558	18,472	18,295	19,435	21,951	20,486

burden for all levels of governments. The average native household contributes
$2,229, $1,126, and $267 in surplus funds to the federal, state, and local govern-
ments, respectively, while the average foreign-born household receives net benefits of $1,835, $2,217, and $787, respectively.

Third-generation households are a net benefit for all three levels of government, but second-generation households are a burden on the federal government
and a smaller benefit than third-generation households to the state government.

| Householders Age 40-64 | | | | | Householders Age 65+ | | | |
Native Born	Third Gen.	Second Gen.	Foreign Born	All	Native Born	Third Gen.	Second Gen.	Foreign Born
1,156	1,069	1,660	893	11,627	12,002	12,082	11,825	9,589
343	324	450	157	977	1,096	1,104	1,079	331
400	425	256	163	758	800	892	597	529
47	36	115	61	36	39	57	0	19
462	446	553	681	6,755	6,801	6,891	6,605	6,506
422	414	472	612	111	109	105	119	122
31	33	23	30	10	11	12	8	5
168	172	145	36	303	332	381	224	144
40	40	38	86	9	9	11	6	8
469	447	599	1,684	466	362	377	328	1,034
236	222	318	819	70	54	72	13	159
417	387	590	889	807	557	507	665	2,166
178	175	190	421	473	304	277	361	1,395
112	112	114	460	49	40	54	9	96
33	33	33	210	7	4	5	3	22
34	36	24	91	15	10	0	31	43
5	5	3	6	9	8	8	7	14
94	89	127	360	20	21	29	4	14
2,271	2,349	1,818	5,000	265	232	264	163	440
1,229	1,159	1,635	2,495	172	113	88	169	493
321	321	321	321	321	321	321	321	321
2,741	2,741	2,741	2,741	2,741	2,741	2,741	2,741	2,741
777	777	777	777	777	777	777	777	777
1,421	1,421	1,421	1,421	1,421	1,421	1,421	1,421	1,421
5,328	5,328	5,328	5,328	5,328	5,328	5,328	5,328	5,328
9,369	9,191	10,400	12,096	26,627	26,805	27,119	26,117	25,659
4,235	4,216	4,347	7,370	2,614	2,425	2,427	2,421	3,644
5,142	5,164	5,018	6,315	4,288	4,265	4,264	4,268	4,416
18,746	18,571	19,764	25,782	33,529	33,495	33,810	32,805	33,718

This is partly the result of age structure; older households are a greater burden on the federal government and second-generation households are more likely to be older (Table 4-7b). Young and middle-age second-generation households are smaller net benefits than third-generation households on the federal and state governments.

Among immigrant households, European/Canadian households are a net burden on the federal government but provide surpluses for both the state and local

TABLE 4-6c   Estimates of Benefits and Services Received by Selected Household Characteristics, Fiscal Year 1995 (dollars)

	Foreign Born		Income below Poverty	
	Citizens	Non-citizens	Native Born	Foreign Born
Social Security	3,109	1,039	2,881	1,000
Federal Benefits	253	43	104	0
Military Benefits	277	105	86	0
Railroad Benefits	33	39	0	0
Medicare	1,817	841	1,655	701
Unemployment Compensation	363	476	360	359
Workers' Compensation	18	24	15	11
Veterans' Benefits	115	22	127	13
Pell Grants	49	74	56	55
Medi-Cal	735	2,197	2,279	3,897
AFDC	248	1,085	2,086	2,054
SSI	700	779	951	856
Housing Benefits	306	608	1,061	926
Food Stamps	142	611	873	1,331
School Lunches	70	254	152	448
General Assistance	21	86	222	121
Energy Assistance	6	6	20	13
Earned Income Tax Credit	202	516	299	854
K-12 Education	3,190	4,624	2,803	6,320
Higher Education	1,547	1,327	1,093	844
State Corrections	321	321	321	321
National Defense	2,741	2,741	2,741	2,741
Other Federal Operations	777	777	777	777
Other State Operations	1,421	1,421	1,421	1,421
Other Local Operations	5,328	5,328	5,328	5,328
Federal Share	13,187	12,516	15,957	15,136
State Share	5,132	6,844	6,284	8,726
Local Share	5,493	6,043	5,504	6,625
Total Benefits	23,813	25,403	27,744	30,487

governments. Asian immigrant households provide a net surplus at the federal level, albeit smaller than that of natives. These households are a net burden on the state and local governments. Latin American households are large burdens on all three levels of government. The average Latin American household receives $3,742 in net federal benefits, $3,181 in net state benefits, and $1,260 in net local benefits (Table 4-7a).

Among young and middle-age households (Table 4-7b), foreign-born households are a net burden to the state and local governments, while native house-

Income above Poverty		Income below Median		Income above Median		Income above $50,000	
Native Born	Foreign Born	Native Born	Foreign Born	Native Born	Foreign Born	Native Born	Foreign Born
3,390	1,866	4,900	1,818	2,029	1,343	1,722	1,430
460	141	301	55	520	184	605	221
400	210	262	72	452	291	473	425
50	51	47	41	43	31	39	8
1,802	1,274	2,498	1,285	1,192	859	1,044	961
359	473	336	423	378	476	335	389
29	27	22	20	32	27	30	31
167	62	135	33	186	76	196	92
50	71	52	57	49	82	51	79
386	1,017	1,046	2,397	217	750	163	645
192	411	768	1,167	92	310	34	260
285	720	667	999	100	356	97	322
184	377	603	761	11	128	15	32
76	171	331	697	24	111	13	62
25	112	71	271	12	85	7	38
7	49	67	90	1	31	0	17
4	4	13	9	0	1	0	0
90	272	202	591	39	153	31	77
1,950	3,457	1,725	4,338	2,309	3,996	2,339	3,785
813	1,585	626	1,060	1,025	1,934	1,204	2,665
321	321	321	321	321	321	321	321
2,741	2,741	2,741	2,741	2,741	2,741	2,741	2,741
777	777	777	777	777	777	777	777
1,421	1,421	1,421	1,421	1,421	1,421	1,421	1,421
5,328	5,328	5,328	5,328	5,328	5,328	5,328	5,328
12,628	11,846	16,177	14,181	10,341	10,296	9,936	10,425
3,734	5,502	4,195	6,745	3,863	5,699	3,922	5,883
4,954	5,620	4,912	5,914	5,099	5,834	5,130	5,829
21,316	22,968	25,284	26,840	19,303	21,829	18,989	22,137

holds provide surpluses to all three levels of government. The state government bears the largest burdens for these households. All older householders are a net burden on the federal government, and older foreign-born householders are a net burden on the state government. Among households with incomes below the poverty level (Table 4-7c), both native and foreign-born households are a burden on all three levels of government. These burdens are smaller, but still notable, among households with incomes below the state median. Foreign-born households with income above $50,000 are a small burden on local governments.

TABLE 4-7a   Net Fiscal Impacts by Nativity of Householder, Fiscal Year 1995 (dollars)

	All	Native Born	Third Generation	Second Generation
Total Contributions				
Federal Share	11,966	13,069	13,768	10,050
State Share	2,971	3,227	3,375	2,588
Local Share	1,290	1,337	1,360	1,237
Total Contributions	16,227	17,632	18,503	13,875
Total Benefits				
Federal Share	12,921	12,993	12,313	15,928
State Share	4,606	4,014	4,052	3,847
Local Share	5,235	5,014	5,049	4,865
Total Benefits	22,762	22,021	21,414	24,639
Net Costs				
Net Federal Share	−956	75	1,455	−5,878
Net State Share	−1,635	−787	−677	−1,258
Net Local Share	−3,945	−3,677	−3,689	−3,628
Net Total Cost	−6,535	−4,389	−2,911	−10,764
Unallocated Revenues				
Federal Share	2,154	2,154	2,154	2,154
State Share	1,912	1,912	1,912	1,912
Local Share	3,945	3,945	3,945	3,945
Net Fiscal Impacts				
Net Federal	1,198	2,229	3,610	−3,724
Net State	277	1,126	1,235	654
Net Local	0	267	256	317
Net Total	1,476	3,622	5,100	−2,753

Relative Contributions, Benefits, and Net Costs

Table 4-8 shows the tax contributions, benefit receipt, and fiscal impacts of foreign-born households relative to native households, for all households and household groups by age of householder and income level. Relative to native households, foreign-born households contribute lower average taxes to all three levels of government. This is true for all age groups and among most of the income groups. The notable exception is the tax contribution of households with incomes below poverty. Among these households, foreign-born households make tax contributions higher than those of natives to the federal and state governments. Relative benefit receipt is consistently higher for foreign-born households at the state and local government levels. Federal benefits are lower for foreign-

| Foreign Born | Foreign-born Households by Region of Origin | | | |
	Europe/ Canada	Asia	Latin America	Other
8,721	10,576	11,808	6,444	12,586
2,219	2,683	2,918	1,702	3,032
1,152	1,335	1,463	933	1,474
12,092	14,594	16,189	9,078	17,092
12,710	14,680	12,736	12,340	12,205
6,349	3,598	6,841	6,795	5,857
5,884	4,760	5,863	6,137	5,880
24,943	23,038	25,440	25,272	23,942
−3,989	−4,104	−928	−5,896	382
−4,130	−915	−3,923	−5,093	−2,826
−4,732	−3,426	−4,400	−5,204	−4,405
−12,850	−8,444	−9,251	−16,193	−6,849
2,154	2,154	2,154	2,154	2,154
1,912	1,912	1,912	1,912	1,912
3,945	3,945	3,945	3,945	3,945
−1,835	−1,950	1,226	−3,742	2,536
−2,217	997	−2,010	−3,181	−913
−787	519	−456	−1,260	−461
−4,839	−433	−1,240	−8,182	1,162

born households with householders over age 65 and in all income groups except households with incomes over $50,000.

The relative fiscal impact of foreign-born households is below zero for all households and for households classed by age and income. At the federal level, the relative deficit of $4,065 for the average foreign-born household derives entirely from lower relative tax contributions. In contrast, more than two-thirds of the relative deficits at the state and local levels are due to higher relative benefit receipt. Among the age groups, the greatest relative deficit exists between foreign-born and native households headed by persons age 40-64. In this group, the federal deficit results largely from lower relative tax contributions while the state and local deficits are due largely to higher relative benefit receipt.

Among households with incomes below poverty and households with incomes below the median, foreign-born households provide a relative surplus to the federal government, resulting primarily because of lower benefit receipt. The relative deficits at the state and local government levels are created almost entirely by higher relative benefit receipt of foreign-born households in these categories.

SUMMARY AND DISCUSSION

Several important differences between native and foreign-born households interact with fiscal policy to create different fiscal impacts. Among these differences, foreign-born households contain more students and have lower incomes

TABLE 4-7b   Net Fiscal Impacts by Age and Nativity of Householder, Fiscal Year 1995 (dollars)

		Householders Age 15-39				
	All	Native Born	Third Gen.	Second Gen.	Foreign Born	All
Total Contributions						
Federal Share	11,500	13,133	13,474	11,277	7,900	16,023
State Share	2,729	3,044	3,124	2,606	2,035	3,841
Local Share	1,247	1,345	1,349	1,323	1,029	1,503
Total Contributions	15,475	17,522	17,948	15,206	10,964	21,367
Total Benefits						
Federal Share	8,822	8,351	8,264	8,822	9,859	10,043
State Share	5,217	4,776	4,708	5,142	6,190	5,010
Local Share	5,519	5,345	5,323	5,470	5,902	5,432
Total Benefits	19,558	18,472	18,295	19,435	21,951	20,486
Net Costs						
Net Federal Share	2,678	4,781	5,210	2,455	−1,959	5,980
Net State Share	−2,488	−1,732	−1,584	−2,536	−4,155	−1,170
Net Local Share	−4,272	−4,000	−3,973	−4,147	−4,873	−3,929
Net Total Cost	−4,082	−951	−347	−4,229	−10,987	881
Unallocated Revenues						
Federal Share	2,154	2,154	2,154	2,154	2,154	2,154
State Share	1,912	1,912	1,912	1,912	1,912	1,912
Local Share	3,945	3,945	3,945	3,945	3,945	3,945
Net Fiscal Impacts						
Net Federal	4,832	6,935	7,364	4,609	195	8,134
Net State	−576	180	328	−624	−2,243	743
Net Local	−328	−56	−29	−202	−928	16
Net Total	3,929	7,060	7,664	3,783	−2,976	8,893

than native households, and foreign-born householders are younger and less likely to be homeowners than native-born householders. These differences persist after controlling for age of householder and household income ranges. Among region-of-origin groups, Latin American immigrant households contain the most K-12 students and have the lowest incomes. Households headed by naturalized citizens are more like native households than noncitizen households.

Foreign-born households are less likely than native households to receive benefits from Social Security, Medicare, and other nonpoverty income transfer programs, except unemployment compensation. In contrast, foreign-born households exhibit relatively high participation in poverty programs and contain more recipients in participating households than native households. These findings persist when households are grouped by the age of the householder and by in-

Householders Age 40-64					Householders Age 65+			
Native Born	Third Gen.	Second Gen.	Foreign Born	All	Native Born	Third Gen.	Second Gen.	Foreign Born
17,650	17,961	15,842	11,072	4,591	4,653	4,873	4,174	4,254
4,225	4,306	3,756	2,670	1,664	1,701	1,755	1,581	1,462
1,542	1,544	1,526	1,387	938	952	964	926	865
23,416	23,812	21,124	15,128	7,193	7,306	7,592	6,680	6,581
9,369	9,191	10,400	12,096	26,627	26,805	27,119	26,117	25,659
4,235	4,216	4,347	7,370	2,614	2,425	2,427	2,421	3,644
5,142	5,164	5,018	6,315	4,288	4,265	4,264	4,268	4,416
18,746	18,571	19,764	25,782	33,529	33,495	33,810	32,805	33,718
8,281	8,770	5,442	−1,024	−22,035	−22,151	−22,247	−21,943	−21,405
−10	90	−591	−4,701	−951	−724	−671	−840	−2,181
−3,601	−3,620	−3,492	−4,929	−3,350	−3,313	−3,300	−3,342	−3,551
4,670	5,241	1,360	−10,653	−26,336	−26,189	−26,218	−26,125	−27,137
2,154	2,154	2,154	2,154	2,154	2,154	2,154	2,154	2,154
1,912	1,912	1,912	1,912	1,912	1,912	1,912	1,912	1,912
3,945	3,945	3,945	3,945	3,945	3,945	3,945	3,945	3,945
10,435	10,924	7,596	1,130	−19,881	−19,997	−20,093	−19,789	−19,251
1,903	2,003	1,322	−2,788	962	1,188	1,241	1,072	−269
344	325	453	−984	595	632	645	602	394
12,681	13,252	9,371	−2,642	−18,325	−18,178	−18,207	−18,114	−19,126

TABLE 4-7c   Net Fiscal Impacts by Selected Household Characteristics, Fiscal
Year 1995 (dollars)

	Foreign Born		Income below Poverty	
	Citizens	Non-citizens	Native Born	Foreign Born
Total Contributions				
Federal Share	13,501	6,774	1,299	1,693
State Share	3,278	1,787	706	730
Local Share	1,485	1,017	905	805
Total Contributions	18,264	9,578	2,910	3,228
Total Benefits				
Federal Share	13,187	12,516	15,957	15,136
State Share	5,132	6,844	6,284	8,726
Local Share	5,493	6,043	5,504	6,625
Total Benefits	23,813	25,403	27,744	30,487
Net Costs				
Net Federal Share	314	−5,742	−14,658	−13,444
Net State Share	−1,854	−5,057	−5,578	−7,996
Net Local Share	−4,008	−5,026	−4,599	−5,820
Net Total Cost	−5,549	−15,825	−24,835	−27,259
Unallocated Revenues				
Federal Share	2,154	2,154	2,154	2,154
State Share	1,912	1,912	1,912	1,912
Local Share	3,945	3,945	3,945	3,945
Net Fiscal Impacts				
Net Federal	2,468	−3,588	−12,504	−11,289
Net State	58	−3,144	−3,666	−6,084
Net Local	−64	−1,082	−654	−1,875
Net Total	2,462	−7,814	−16,824	−19,248

come level, except for households below poverty. Among households below
poverty, foreign-born households are more likely than native households to participate in Medi-Cal, food stamps, and school lunches, but they are not more
likely to use AFDC, SSI, or housing benefits. Naturalized citizen households are
more likely than noncitizen households to participate in the nonpoverty transfer
programs and less likely to participate in poverty programs.

Compared with natives, foreign-born households pay lower federal and state
income, Social Security, and sales and property taxes. The differences between
native and foreign-born households are greatest for the progressive income taxes
and smaller for flatter and regressive taxes, such as Social Security and sales
taxes. Because of caps on taxable earned income and because foreign-born

Income above Poverty		Income below Median		Income above Median		Income above $50,000	
Native Born	Foreign Born	Native Born	Foreign Born	Native Born	Foreign Born	Native Born	Foreign Born
14,518	11,224	2,803	2,857	21,621	18,346	26,343	23,688
3,538	2,749	948	893	5,125	4,394	6,253	5,789
1,390	1,276	994	889	1,622	1,584	1,720	1,738
19,445	15,249	4,746	4,639	28,368	24,324	34,316	31,216
12,628	11,846	16,177	14,181	10,341	10,296	9,936	10,425
3,734	5,502	4,195	6,745	3,863	5,699	3,922	5,883
4,954	5,620	4,912	5,914	5,099	5,834	5,130	5,829
21,316	22,968	25,284	26,840	19,303	21,829	18,989	22,137
1,890	−622	−13,374	−11,324	11,280	8,050	16,407	13,263
−197	−2,753	−3,246	−5,851	1,262	−1,304	2,330	−93
−3,564	−4,344	−3,917	−5,025	−3,477	−4,250	−3,410	−4,091
−1,871	−7,719	−20,538	−22,201	9,065	2,495	15,327	9,079
2,154	2,154	2,154	2,154	2,154	2,154	2,154	2,154
1,912	1,912	1,912	1,912	1,912	1,912	1,912	1,912
3,945	3,945	3,945	3,945	3,945	3,945	3,945	3,945
4,044	1,532	−11,220	−9,170	13,434	10,204	18,561	15,417
1,716	−840	−1,334	−3,939	3,175	608	4,243	1,819
381	−400	27	−1,080	467	−305	534	−146
6,140	292	−12,527	−14,190	17,076	10,506	23,338	17,090

households contain more wage earners, foreign-born households actually pay higher unemployment and state disability insurance taxes. These differences persist for households in all age categories and in higher income brackets. Among households below poverty, foreign-born households pay higher total taxes and among households with incomes below the state median, native and foreign-born households pay almost equal total tax amounts. Naturalized citizen households pay higher total taxes than noncitizen households.

Native households receive higher average benefits from Social Security and Medicare, while foreign-born households receive higher benefits from all poverty programs, K-12 education, and higher education. These patterns generally persist within age groups and income classifications. Naturalized

TABLE 4-8 Fiscal Impacts of Foreign-Born Households Relative to Native Households, by Age of Householder and Income, Fiscal Year 1995 (dollars)

	All Households	Age of Householder			Household Income				
		18-39	40-64	65+	Below Poverty	Above Poverty	Below Median	Above Median	Above $50,000
Relative Tax Contribution									
Federal	-4,348	-5,233	-6,578	-400	394	-3,294	54	-3,275	-2,655
State	-1,008	-1,009	-1,555	-238	24	-788	-55	-731	-464
Local	-185	-316	-155	-87	-100	-114	-105	-38	19
Total	-5,540	-6,558	-8,288	-725	318	-4,196	-106	-4,044	-3,100
Relative Benefit Receipt									
Federal	-283	1,508	2,727	-1,146	-820	-782	-1,996	-45	489
State	2,335	1,414	3,136	1,219	2,442	1,768	2,550	1,836	1,960
Local	870	556	1,173	151	1,121	666	1,002	735	699
Total	2,921	3,479	7,035	223	2,742	1,652	1,556	2,525	3,148
Relative Fiscal Impact									
Federal	-4,064	-6,741	-9,305	747	1,214	-2,511	2,050	-3,230	-3,143
State	-3,343	-2,423	-4,691	-1,457	-2,418	-2,556	-2,605	-2,567	-2,424
Local	-1,054	-873	-1,328	-238	-1,221	-780	-1,108	-773	-681
Total	-8,462	-10,036	-15,323	-948	-2,424	-5,848	-1,663	-6,570	-6,248

citizen households are more like native households than noncitizen households.

After benefits are reduced to reflect those hypothetically received by corporations and tourists, California's native households provide net surpluses to all three levels of government while foreign-born households are a burden on the federal, state, and local governments. Among age groups, younger and middle-age foreign-born households provide a net surplus to the federal government. Among households in poverty, foreign-born households are a greater burden on the state and local governments than native households while the reverse is true at the federal level. Foreign-born households are a burden on local government even among households with incomes over $50,000.

Among all households, the negative relative federal impact of foreign-born households is created entirely by lower federal tax payments by foreign-born households, while the negative impacts at the state and local levels are dominated by higher benefit receipt of foreign-born households. The relative state, local, and total impacts of foreign-born households are negative in all categories, while foreign-born households in the age group 65 and older, below poverty, and below median income categories have a positive fiscal impact on the federal government.

Three interactions between immigrant characteristics and fiscal policy appear to be driving the fiscal impacts observed. First, working-age immigrant households have lower incomes, resulting in large differences between immigrant and native tax contributions. The higher numbers of dependents in foreign-born households, which result in lower income taxes, exacerbate these differences, but higher numbers of wage earners and regressive taxes on employment also offset the differences. Because the majority of income and employment taxes accrue to the federal government, the income differential creates the larger relative deficits at the federal level. Second, the lower incomes of immigrant households are related directly to greater participation in social service programs for the poor. This results in greater benefit receipt among foreign-born households. Again, the higher numbers of persons, particularly children, in foreign-born households exacerbate this difference, but it is offset by lower program participation by foreign-born households in poverty when compared with native households in poverty. Greater program participation has the largest impact at the state level. At the federal level, higher participation in poverty programs (particularly Medi-Cal and SSI) is offset by lower participation in Social Security and Medicare; in effect this trade-off shifts some of the cost of health care and income maintenance from the federal government to the state. Third, foreign-born households contain more children and therefore consume a greater share of state and local spending on both K-12 and higher education. This difference in education benefits accounts for nearly all of the relative deficit for foreign-born households at the local government level.

The fiscal impacts reported here are estimated entirely on the basis of reported household characteristics. Differences between native and foreign-born households are due to the interaction of fiscal policy with household characteristics such as income, income sources, household composition, and program participation. After controlling for these characteristics, no further differences in interaction between households and the government were assumed. As a result, these estimates ignore the possible effects of noncompliance with tax laws and remittances to the country of origin.

Three recent studies have provided analyses similar to those found in this chapter. Garvey and Espenshade (1996) examine the state and local government fiscal impacts of native and foreign-born households in New Jersey, using 1990 Census data. The methodologies of the New Jersey study and this study are very similar. Similar to the results reported here, the authors find that immigrants pay less in taxes and receive greater benefits than households headed by natives. However, the differences in fiscal impacts between natives and immigrants are somewhat smaller in New Jersey, largely because income differentials between natives and immigrants in income and the number of children per household are smaller in New Jersey than in California. Lee and Miller (1997) develop estimates of federal, state, and local impacts for the entire country, examining results under different methodological schemes. They compare current annual fiscal impact estimates generated by defining the immigrant unit in different ways: immigrants only, immigrant households (immigrants and their co-resident children), and immigrants and their concurrent descendants. Their "immigrant household" results are comparable to those reported in this study, except that their results apply to the entire country. The third group, "immigrants and their concurrent descendants," includes the tax contributions (and benefits received) by the adult children and grandchildren of still-living immigrants. They find that including the fiscal impacts of these concurrent descendants results in an overall positive impact of immigrants. In addition, Chapter 7 of the National Research Council report (1997) provides estimates of the long-term fiscal impacts of immigrants and their descendants. This research differs from the analysis presented here in several ways: individuals rather than households are considered the unit of analysis, the total U.S. population is considered, and the present value of future costs and benefits of both immigrants and their descendants are included along with current impacts. Similar to the Lee and Miller results, the lifetime impacts of immigrants and their descendants are found to be positive overall for the federal government.

APPENDIX A: TAX INFORMATION AND METHODOLOGY

Federal and State Income Taxes

The Census Bureau uses U.S. Internal Revenue Service data to estimate the federal and state income tax contributions paid by CPS households during 1994. Household structure determines filing status, and capital gains and itemized deductions are imputed based on home ownership and income level. The Bureau calculations produce an average federal tax contribution of $5,928 per household and a total contribution from California households of $66.9 billion (Bureau of the Census, 1993a). These figures underestimate total tax paid and are adjusted proportionally upward by 7.23 percent to coincide with empirical estimates. The state tax contributions imputed by the Census Bureau yield an overestimate of total tax contributions by $4 billion. These figures overestimate total tax paid and are adjusted proportionally downward by 16.95 percent to coincide with state budget figures.

The Bureau estimates ignore noncompliance with federal and state taxation laws. Well-documented evidence of tax compliance levels for immigrants and natives is not available. Cornelius et al. (1982) report results from several early studies of tax compliance among undocumented immigrants in which 87-100 percent of households had taxes deducted. The Los Angeles study used summary estimates that 83 percent of documented immigrants and 56 percent of undocumented immigrants have taxes withheld (Los Angeles County, 1992). Clark and Passel (1993) assumed 95 percent compliance with the federal income tax by natives and long-term immigrants and 74 percent compliance among recent immigrants.

Employment Taxes: Social Security, Unemployment, and State Disability

Earned income up to $60,000 is subject to a 12.4 percent tax contributed to the Old Age Survivors and Disability Insurance funds. A tax of 2.9 percent of earned income (no upper limit as of 1994) contributes to the Hospital Insurance fund. Wage and salary employees pay half of the contribution and employers pay the other half. The self-employed must pay the full 15.3 percent tax, but may deduct 7.65 percent from net earnings before calculating the Social Security contribution, making the effective tax paid 14.1 percent (Social Security Administration, 1996). In 1992, 15.9 million Californians had taxable earnings of $288.4 billion and contributed $44.9 billion to OASDI funds. In 1993, Social Security taxes covered 96 percent of all U.S. workers. The majority of workers not covered are federal, state, and local government employees. Beginning in 1983, federal employees were covered under the Medicare portion of the tax, and all federal employees hired after 1983 are covered under OASDI. In 1990, 67 percent of state and local government workers nationwide and 34 percent of California state and local government workers were covered by Social Security (Social Security Administration, 1996). Of working Californians, 95 percent are assumed to be employed in nonexempt sectors and are compliant with Social Security tax requirements.

The average unemployment insurance tax during 1994-1995 was 3.63 percent on the first $7,000 of wages for each worker (California Taxpayers Association, 1995b; California Legislature, 1995). Unemployment insurance contributions are paid by employers. Private employers in industry and commerce, agricultural employers with ten or more employees or a quarterly payroll exceeding $20,000, domestic employers paying wages of $1,000 or more per quarter, state and local government and nonprofit employers (except elected officials and nonprofit organizations employing fewer than four workers), and federal civilian and ex-service members of the Air Force are covered. Workers self-employed or employed by their families are excluded from coverage. Contributions are kept in separate funds for each state (Social Security Administration, 1996). In 1994-1995, contributions to the California fund totaled $3.08 billion (California Legislature, 1995). All wage and salary workers are assumed to pay unemployment compensation taxes.

The state disability insurance tax is 1 percent of the first $31,767 of wages. Exempt workers are those employed by public agencies, public schools, religious organizations, and the self-employed. Tax contributions totaled $2.67 billion in 1993-1994 (California Legislature, 1995). All employees of private firms are assumed to pay state disability insurance taxes. Both the employee and employer shares of taxes are allocated to workers.

Sales Tax

Sales and use taxes totaled $23.4 billion in 1994-1995: $16.3 billion in state revenues and $7.1 billion in local revenues. The state tax of 7.25 percent is supplemented by county-imposed additional taxes capped at 1.50 percent. The statewide average (weighted by sales volume) is 8 percent. Exemptions to the state sales tax are provided for essentials such as food for home consumption, prescription drugs, electricity and gas delivered through mains, and services including entertainment. Major components of the sales tax base are manufacturing and nonexempt services (20%), motor vehicles (14%), building (8%), and fuel (7%). The other category (51%) includes furniture, apparel, general merchandise, and eating and drinking establishments (Board of Equalization, 1995; Department of Finance, 1995a).

Remittances sent to the country of origin may reduce the contribution to sales and excise taxes by an immigrant household. This is important for studies in which these taxes are applied as a percentage of total household income. The Los Angeles County study (1992) reports average remittances of $1,087 per family in the Westat survey Los Angeles sample. Vernez and McCarthy (1996) report findings from a survey of Salvadoran and Filipino immigrants that 69-92 percent of households send remittances averaging between $900 and $1,400 each year. The study found that average remittances did not increase with income. If all of a $900 remittance would otherwise be spent on taxable items, the sales tax contribution for a remitting household would decrease by $72.

Sheffrin and Dresch (1995) report that 35 percent of sales and use taxes are levied on businesses. Other studies suggest the percentage of business-paid sales tax may be higher (DuBay, 1991). The California Division of Tourism (1995) estimates that tourism spending contributes $3.1 billion to state and local coffers, but that Californians themselves account for 82 percent of travel volume. Although international visitors outspend resident tourists overall, resident travelers outspend international visitors on food, shopping, entertainment, and lodging. International travelers spend $103 per day, compared with $69.3 per day by California resident leisure travelers and $78.1 per day by U.S. leisure travelers (Division of Tourism, 1995). Based on these figures, I estimate that 43.6 percent of taxes ($1.21 billion) contributed by tourists were actually paid by California households and businesses.

Studies of tax burdens find that sales taxes are generally regressive, but that California's sales tax is less regressive than other states because of the exemption for food consumed at home. Examining data from 1989, Sheffrin and Dresch (1995) find that taxable consumption as a percentage of income and taxable consumption as a percentage of expenditures both decline as income rises. As a result, the percentage of income paid in sales tax also declines with income (Sheffrin and Dresch, 1995). Similar findings are reported in previous studies (Citizens for Tax Justice, 1988; DuBay, 1991).

Data from the Sheffrin and Dresch study are used to estimate sales tax contributions. For each income level, the percentage of income spent on taxable goods and services (from Sheffrin and Dresch) is multiplied by household income to determine the amount of taxable spending per household. This estimate is then multiplied by the statewide average sales tax of 8 percent to determine the tax contribution. Remittances to the country of origin are ignored. This method yields a total sales tax contribution from households of $10.5 billion, 45 percent of sales taxes collected. This estimate of the household contribution of sales tax may be low; an alternative top-down approach and assuming businesses pay 35 percent of sales tax and out-of-state tourists pay 8.5 percent of sales taxes collected yields an estimate of household sales tax contributions totaling $13.24 billion.

Property Tax

The average property tax in California is 1.06 percent of assessed value. Assessed values are determined by the sale price of the property, and growth in assessed value is limited to 2 percent per year unless the property is sold or improved (Department of Finance, 1996a; Board of Equalization, 1995). As a result, two homeowners with equivalent property may pay very different amounts if one has owned the property for many years while the other purchased recently. A recent study determined that a new homeowner in Los Angeles County could pay up to five times the amount of annual tax paid by the long-term owner of a home of equal value (O'Sullivan et al., 1993). Property tax revenue in California totaled $19.3 billion in 1994-1995. For the 1995-1996 budget year, 41.5 percent of total tax collected was associated with commercial property. Owner-occupied housing with homeowners' exemption claims accounted for 37.3 percent of tax assessed, and other residential property made up the remaining 21.2 percent (Board of Equalization, 1995).[16]

Studies of property tax incidence assume that property taxes are borne by the owners of owner-occupied housing, but debate continues concerning the burden of taxes on rental property. For a review of perspectives and findings, see O'Sullivan et al. (1993), Carroll and Yinger (1994), and Wassmer (1993). Other studies of tax burden and immigrant fiscal impacts have generally allocated one-half of tax payments on rental property to renters (Los Angeles County, 1992; Clark et al., 1994; Sheffrin and Dresch, 1995). Estimates provided in this chapter are calculated using the assumption that the tax incidence falls on the renter.

CPS property tax amounts imputed by the Census Bureau are not used because the imputation method did not rely on length of tenure, which strongly affects tax amounts in California. Self-reported tax amounts in the 1990 Census show that among homeowners, immigrant households pay higher taxes than natives.[17] European and Asian immigrant homeowners report paying the highest average tax amounts while Latin American homeowners pay the lowest average taxes. The averages also decline with the age of the household head, but immigrants as a group report higher average taxes than natives in all three age groups. Higher tax contributions by immigrants may reflect more recent purchases, higher property values, or both. European and Asian immigrant homeowners also report property values and monthly mortgage payments higher than those of natives. Reported property values are highest for householders age 40-64 and lowest for homeowners age 65 and older. Effective tax rates, calculated as the reported tax paid divided by the reported property value, are slightly higher than for natives for all immigrant groups except European/Canadian homeowners. More notably, effective tax rates decline with the age of the homeowner. Young householders are taxed at 0.71 percent while householders age 40-64 are taxed at a rate of 0.56 percent and elderly householders are taxed at a rate of 0.41 percent.

State data prevent easy estimation of average property taxes paid by type of property because some owner-occupied properties are included in the category of rental property. In 1994-1995, the Board of Equalization reports that 5.09 million households took the homeowners' exemption of $7,000 of assessed value, while the CPS estimate of owner-occupied households exceeds 6.3 million, suggesting that 19.8 percent of owners failed to claim the exemption and/or did not

---

[16]In 1994-1995, the homeowners' exemption was claimed for only 5 million properties, while 6.3 million householders owned the property in which they lived. As a result, a sizable proportion of owner-occupied properties are classified as rental property by the Board of Equalization.

[17]Means for property taxes paid and property values are estimated by using the midpoint of each category on the census form.

pay taxes. Using the Board of Equalization figures, these 5.09 million owners paid average taxes of $1,415.62.

The following assumptions are made in estimating property taxes. First, the mean payment by homeowners is adjusted to reflect lower average payments by owners who failed to claim the homeowner's exemption. The 1.3 million owners who fail to claim the exemption and the 4.9 million renters paid total taxes of $4.09 billion and average taxes of $664.93. Adjusting the average owner-occupied tax paid to reflect lower tax payments by owners who did not take the exemption yields an average tax payment for owners of $1,267.14. Second, data from the 1990 PUMS are included to estimate differences in property taxes and rent paid by nativity and age. Proportional differences between natives and immigrants by region of origin and age were assumed to be the same in 1995. This adjustment lowers the average tax allocated to native owners and raises the average tax allocated to native renters.

Fuel Taxes

The state of California taxes motor vehicle fuel and diesel fuel at a rate of $0.18 per gallon. Additional taxes are levied on aircraft fuel, liquefied petroleum gas, liquid natural gas, alcohol fuel, and compressed natural gas (California Legislature, 1995). In 1994-1995, motor fuel sales in California generated $2.75 billion in state taxes (Board of Equalization, 1995). The federal government levies taxes of $0.183 per gallon of motor vehicle fuel and $0.244 per gallon on diesel fuel (California Legislature, 1995). Fuel consumption in California generated an estimated $2.9 billion in tax revenues to the federal government in 1994-1995, 12.4 percent of total federal fuel tax revenues. The shares of fuel taxes paid by businesses and tourists are estimated to be 35 percent and 8.5, percent, respectively, yielding an estimate of fuel taxes paid by California households of $3.21 billion. Fuel taxes are allocated to households on a per vehicle basis based on the average number of automobiles reported in the 1990 Census for age and nativity categories. The average household owned 1.78 automobiles in 1990. Using this average to estimate the number of vehicles per household in 1995, I calculate an average tax contribution of $161.02 per vehicle.

Liquor and Excise Taxes

California alcohol excise tax rates are $0.20 per gallon on beer, dry and sweet wine, and sparkling hard cider; $0.30 per gallon on sparkling wine; and $3.30-$6.60 per gallon on distilled spirits (California Legislature, 1995). Revenues for 1994-1995 totaled $269 million (Board of Equalization, 1995). Federal taxes on alcohol are $0.58 per gallon on beer, $1.07-$13.50 per gallon on wine depending on alcohol content, and $13.50 per gallon on distilled spirits (California Legislature, 1995). California alcohol sales accounted for an estimated $991 million in federal alcohol tax revenues in 1994-1995, 10.9 percent of total federal collections. Out-of-state tourists are assumed to contribute 8.5 percent of alcohol taxes paid in California. The remaining $1.1 billion is allocated to households based on the number of adults of legal drinking age per household. The average household contains 1.9 persons age 21 and older, and the estimated average tax contribution is $52.32 per adult.

Tobacco Taxes

The state of California levies tobacco taxes of $0.37 per package of cigarettes and, in 1994-1995, 31.20 percent of wholesale cost on tobacco-related products (California Legislature, 1995). State tobacco revenues in 1994-1995 were $685 million (Board of Equalization, 1995). The federal government levies tobacco taxes of $0.24 per package of cigarettes and additional taxes on other tobacco products (California Legislature, 1995). In 1994-1995, the federal government collected an estimated $430 million in tobacco taxes from sales in California (6.4% of revenues nationwide). Out-of-state tourists are assumed to pay 8.5 percent of tobacco taxes. The remaining $970 million is allocated to households based on the average number of adults age 18 and older per household. The average household contains 2.03 persons age 18 and older and the estimated average tax contribution is $43.95 per adult.

Motor Vehicle Fees

The state of California assesses annual operation fees of 2.0 percent of automobile market value, based on an 11-year depreciation period. The vehicle registration fee is $28 on motor vehicles, trailers, and other vehicles. License and registration fees generated $4.7 billion in revenue to the state of California in 1994-1995 (California Legislature, 1995). Assuming the average number of vehicles per household has remained constant since 1990, automobiles owned by households account for 35 percent of registered vehicles. The remaining 65 percent include automobiles owned by government and corporate entities and other vehicles such as trailers. Of vehicle license and registration fees, 35 percent is allocated to households based on the number of vehicles owned. For license fee allocation, all vehicles are assumed to have the same value. The average household contributes $97.86 in fees per vehicle annually.

Inheritance and Estate Taxes

California estate taxes range from 0.8 to 16 percent of the federal taxable estate, determined to pick up the maximum credit allowed against the federal tax rate. Federal tax rates range from 18 to 55 percent of the taxable estate (California Legislature, 1995). In 1994-1995, the state estimated total estate tax receipts at $599 million. Federal taxes collected on California estates totaled $2.335 billion in 1994-1995, 15.4 percent of total federal revenues (U.S. Internal Revenue Service, 1995a). Following the methodology of Garvey and Espenshade (1996), a household is considered eligible to pay inheritance taxes if the householder is a native or has been in the United States for more than 20 years. Taxes are allocated on an average per recipient household basis, assuming inheritance amounts are unrelated to recipient household income. This method is used to allocate federal and California estate taxes. The average eligible household contributes $312.73 in estate taxes.

APPENDIX B: BENEFIT INFORMATION AND METHODOLOGY

Social Security, Retirement, Health Care, and Poverty Programs

For the 17 programs listed in Table 4-B1, the government expenditure total was divided by the number of participating households or individuals identified in the CPS data. This average benefit was then allocated based on household participation or the number of recipients in the household. For most programs, the allocation is made with the assumption that no difference in recipient benefit levels exists by nativity. For Social Security, AFDC, and SSI, differentials in average recipient household benefits observed in the 1990 Census were incorporated. These average benefits were adjusted to reflect the total expenditure in 1995.

Earned Income Tax Credit

Earned income tax credits received by California households totaled $2.4 billion. CPS-imputed estimates of earned income tax credits are adjusted upward by 11.48 percent to reflect this figure.

K-12 Education

California households contained 6.19 million school-age children (children ages 5-17) in 1995, an average of 0.551. In 1990, 82.4 percent of children age 5-17 were enrolled in public schools, 9.7 percent were enrolled in private schools, and 7.8 percent were not enrolled in school.[18] Total expenditures for K-12 education were $29.14 billion in 1994-1995. Revenue sources were as follows: $16.37 billion of general and special fund state revenues, $2.40 billion in federal funds, $8.2 billion in local taxes, and $2.16 billion from miscellaneous local

---

[18]Application of this figure to the 1995 estimate of the school-age population yields an underestimate of enrollment in the public schools. Use of the 1990 figure yields an estimate of 0.454 public

TABLE 4-B1   Program Benefits, Expenditures, and Allocations

Program	Allocated Benefit	Allocated to
Social Security[a]		per recipient household
Federal Retirement	$16,074	per recipient household
Military Retirement	$14,534	per recipient household
Railroad Retirement	$4,836	per recipient household
Medicare	$5,104[b]	per recipient
Unemployment Benefits	$4,058	per recipient household
Workers' Compensation	$843	per recipient household
Veterans' Benefits	$5,713	per recipient household
Pell Grants[c]	$1,050	per recipient
Medicaid[d]	$1,927	per recipient
AFDC[a]		per recipient household
SSI[a]		per recipient household
Housing Assistance	$8,104	per recipient household
Food Stamps	$990	per recipient
School Lunches	$385	per recipient
General Assistance	$3,627	per recipient household
Energy Assistance	$203	per recipient household

[a]Benefit allocations for Social Security, AFDC, and SSI vary by nativity and age category of households. Benefit averages observed in the 1990 Census for each nativity and age category are inflated to reflect 1995 expenditures.

[b]Medicare allocations are reduced by the per-recipient annual premium of $493 for Supplemental Medical Insurance.

[c]Student loan interest subsidies for Californians totaled $120 million in 1995 (Bureau of the Census, 1996b). Because beneficiaries do not directly receive the subsidy, they are unlikely to report receipt in the CPS. These benefits are not allocated to households.

[d]The Medi-Cal allocation total was reduced by 33.7 percent, reflecting the share of costs paid for nursing facilities and intermediate care facilities for the mentally retarded.

sources (Department of Finance, 1996b). Schools report spending $2.8 billion of the budget on capital outlay (Office of the State Controller, 1995). The only funds designated explicitly for bilingual education are $91.97 million of federal funds (Bureau of the Census, 1996b).[19]

The number of children per household is multiplied by the estimate of the percentage of children attending public school by age and nativity of householder from the 1990 Census. The allocation of educational benefits to households is based on this estimated number of public school children per household; bilin-

---

school enrollees per household and a total enrollment of 5.10 million in 1995. This estimate is 200,000 students short of the budget estimate of 5.316 million students. According to the state budget, public school enrollment in 1994-1995 was projected to be 5.316 million, suggesting that 85.9 percent of school-age children attend public school.

[19]California school districts also receive $734.5 million in a fund called "Education for disadvantaged," but these are not dedicated specifically to educating the children of immigrants (Bureau of the Census, 1996b).

gual education funds are allocated based on the estimated average number of LEP students per household. The estimated average benefit per enrolled child is $5,362.74. The additional benefit per limited English proficiency (LEP) student is $101.39.

Higher Education

Total expenditures on public higher education (including state administrative offices) was $11.04 billion in 1994-1995. State, federal, and local shares of expenditures were 52.3 percent, 36.2 percent, and 11.5 percent, respectively. Of federal funds 85 percent went to the University of California (apparently research dollars). The CPS data only identify college students age 16-24. Surveyed households reported 882,975 college students age 16-24 either living at home or in college dormitories in 1995.[20] A higher education benefit of $13,428.62 is allocated to each identified college student.

The allocation of higher education benefits is made difficult by a number of problems. First, the CPS misses a large number of students, particularly those over age 24. However, those over 24 are much less likely to be full-time students (see Bureau of the Census, 1993b), and therefore students age 16-24 will incur most of the higher education costs. Differences in full-time and part-time status also exist across nativity categories, with students in native households more likely to attend full time in the 1990 Census. In 1990, college students in native households were also more likely than students in households from Latin American countries to attend private colleges, but they were less likely to attend private colleges than students in European/Canadian and Asian immigrant households. Finally, costs will vary across students due to differences in enrollment patterns. Nationally, Hispanic students are more likely than non-Hispanics to be enrolled at the community college level (Bureau of the Census, 1993b). In 1993 Asian-American students constituted a disproportionate share of new students at the University of California (Office of the President, 1995). Expenditures per full-time-equivalent student are much higher at the University of California than they are at California community colleges. Because data on the institutional attendance of college students by nativity of parents do not exist, average benefits are assumed for all students.

Incarceration Costs

The state of California spent $35 billion on youth and adult corrections

---

[20]The CPS questionnaire only asks about school enrollment for household members age 16-24. However, interviewees are asked to include information about family members living in college dormitories, so the CPS should provide a complete census of 16 to 24-year-old college students affiliated with California households. Some of these college students attend college out of state and some proportion attend private colleges.

during 1994-1995. Although incarceration costs are not directly attributable to households, the argument can be made that costs are linked to households as the former residences of the incarcerated population. To distribute costs to household classes, the nativity distribution of the prison population is needed.

Nativity data from the California Department of Corrections (CDC) is limited to undocumented persons. According to the Department of Finance, the CDC conducts a one-day census each year to estimate the number of deportable (undocumented) aliens in the prison population. In 1994-1995, 14.89 percent of the adult corrections population, 15.44 percent of the paroled population, and 10.9 percent of the youth corrections population were identified as deportable. Generally, 10 percent of those identified as deportable are determined not to be undocumented by the U.S. Immigration and Naturalization Service (Department of Finance, 1996b). These data appear inconsistent with the 1990 Census. In 1990, among all persons in institutions (primarily prisons and nursing homes), 15.5 percent were foreign born. PUMS coding does not allow direct estimates of the nativity of the incarcerated population, but among institutionalized persons with no income from public assistance, Social Security, or retirement, 16.6 percent were foreign born. It is unlikely that three-fifths of foreign-born inmates are undocumented. Because of the poor data, incarceration costs are allocated as a public protection benefit received by households, and each California household is allocated an average benefit.

ACKNOWLEDGMENTS

I gratefully acknowledge the research support, direction, and valuable comments of the Panel on Demographic and Economic Impacts of Immigration. Barry Edmonston and panel members Tom Espenshade, Ron Lee, Alan Auerbach, Bob Inman, and Jim Smith were particularly helpful in directing the research. Jim Smith also provided very helpful comments for editing the paper. Deborah Garvey and Tom Espenshade provided useful information about the methodological approach. I also thank the University of California Data Archive and Technical Assistance office and Tim Miller both for computing support and helpful comments.

REFERENCES

Ayres, B. Drummond, Jr.
    1995   "Federal Judge Voids Some Limits on California Services to Aliens." *New York Times* 145 (November 21):C18.
Bean, Frank D., Jennifer V.W. Van Hook, and Jennifer E. Glick
    1997   "Country-of-Origin, Type of Public Assistance and Patterns of Welfare Recipiency Among U.S. Immigrants and Natives." *Social Science Quarterly* 78(2):432-451.
Board of Equalization
    1995   *Annual Report.* Sacramento, Calif.

Borjas, George J.
  1994.   "Immigration and Welfare, 1970-1990." National Bureau of Economic Research Work-
           ing Paper No. 4872. Chicago: University of Chicago Press.
Borjas, George J., and Lynette Hilton
  1996   "Immigrants and the Welfare State: Immigrant Participation in Means-Tested Entitlement
           Programs." *Quarterly Journal of Economics* 111(2):575-604.
Bureau of the Census
  1993a *Measuring the Effect of Benefits and Taxes on Income and Poverty: 1992.* Current Popu-
           lation Reports, Series P-60, No. 186RD. Washington, D.C.: U.S. Government Printing
           Office.
Bureau of the Census
  1993b *School Enrollment—Social and Economic Characteristics of Students: October 1992.*
           Current Population Reports, Series P-20, No. 474. Washington, D.C.: U.S. Government
           Printing Office.
Bureau of the Census
  1993c *1990 Census of Population, Social and Economic Characteristics: California.* Washing-
           ton, D.C.: U.S. Government Printing Office.
Bureau of the Census
  1996a *Estimates of the Resident Population of States: July 1, 1990 to July 1, 1995.* Washington,
           D.C.: U.S. Government Printing Office.
Bureau of the Census
  1996b *Federal Expenditures by State for Fiscal Year 1995.* Washington, D.C.: U.S. Govern-
           ment Printing Office.
Byerly, Edwin, and Kevin Deardoff
  1995   *National and State Population Estimates: 1990 to 1994.* Current Population Reports P25-
           1127. Washington, D.C.: Bureau of the Census.
California Legislature.
  1995   *Revenue and Taxation Reference Book.* Sacramento: Assembly Publications Office.
California Taxpayers Association.
  1995a "Gasoline Taxes and Transportation Funding." *Cal-Tax News* 36(18).
California Taxpayers Association.
  1995b. "Automatic Boost: UI taxes go up $213 million in 1996." *Cal-Tax News* 36(23).
Carroll, Robert J., and John Yinger
  1994   "Is the Property Tax a Benefit Tax—The Case of Rental Housing." *National Tax Journal*
           47(2):295-316.
Census of Population and Housing
  1990   *Public Use Microdata Samples U.S.* (machine-readable data files) prepared by the Bureau
           of the Census (producer and distributor), 1992.
Census of Population and Housing
  1990   *Public Use Microdata Samples U.S. Technical Documentation.* 1992. Washington, D.C.:
           Bureau of the Census.
Citizens for Tax Justice
  1988   *Nickels and Dimes: How Sales and Excise Taxes Add up in the 50 States.* Washington,
           D.C.
Clark, Rebecca L., and Jeffrey S. Passel
  1993   "How Much Do Immigrants Pay in Taxes? Evidence from Los Angeles County." Wash-
           ington, D.C.: The Urban Institute.
Clark, Rebecca L., Jeffrey S. Passel, Wendy N. Zimmermann, and Michael E. Fix
  1994   "Fiscal Impacts of Undocumented Aliens: Selected Estimates for Seven States." Wash-
           ington, D.C.: The Urban Institute.

Clune, Michael S., and Cynthia T. Peete
  1995   "Levels of Public Assistance in Los Angeles County: Differentials by Immigration Sta-
          tus." Paper presented at the Population Association of America Meeting, April 7, 1995.
          Department of Demography, University of California, Berkeley
Committee on Ways and Means, U.S. House of Representatives
  1994   *Overview of Entitlement Programs, 1994 Green Book.* Washington, D.C.: U.S. Govern-
          ment Printing Office.
Cornelius, Wayne A., Leo R. Chavez, and Jorge G. Castro
  1982   *Mexican Immigrants and Southern California: A Summary of Current Knowledge.* La
          Jolla: Center for United States-Mexican Studies, University of California, San Diego.
Current Population Survey. March 1995. (machine-readable data file) conducted by the Bureau of
          the Census (producer and distributor), for the Bureau of Labor Statistics. 1995.
Current Population Survey. March 1995. Technical Documentation.
  1995   Washington, D.C.: Bureau of the Census
Department of Finance
  1995a   *Charting the Course for California's Future: Governor's Budget 1994-95.* Sacramento.
Department of Finance
  1995b   *Population Estimates for California Cities and Counties, January 1, 1995.* Report 95 E-
          1. Sacramento: Demographic Research Unit.
Department of Finance
  1996a   *Governor's Budget 1996-97.* Sacramento.
Department of Finance
  1996b   Telephone conversation with Louise Saucedo, July 16, 1996.
Division of Tourism
  1995   *Domestic Travel to California 1994.* Sacramento: California Trade and Commerce Agency.
Division of Tourism
  1996   *Highlights: California Travel Statistics.* Sacramento: California Trade and Commerce
          Agency.
DuBay, Ann
  1990   *California's Tax Burden: Who Pays? Part I, An Analysis of the California Personal
          Income Tax, Bank and Corporation Tax, Property Tax.* Sacramento: California Senate
          Office of Research.
DuBay, Ann
  1991   *California's Tax Burden: Who Pays? Part II, An Analysis of the California Sales and Use
          Tax, Alcoholic Beverages Taxes, Tobacco Taxes, Gas Tax.* Sacramento: California Sen-
          ate Office of Research.
Espenshade, Thomas J., and Vanessa E. King
  1994   "State and Local Fiscal Impacts of US Immigrants: Evidence from New Jersey." *Popula-
          tion Research and Policy Review* 13:225-256.
Freedberg, Louis
  1997   "Wilson's Immigrant Claim Rejected—Supreme Court Denies $3 Billion in Payments."
          San Francisco Chronicle (October 7):A1.
Garvey, Deborah L., and Thomas J. Espenshade
  1996   "State and Local Fiscal Impacts of New Jersey's Immigrant Population." Department of
          Economics, Princeton University, Princeton, N.J.
Hansen, Kristin A.
  1996   "Profile of the Foreign-born Population in 1995: What the CPS Nativity Data Tell Us."
          Paper presented at the annual meeting of the Population Association of American in New
          Orleans, La., May 9.
Keenan, Maureen, and Jeffrey B. Curry
  1995   "Individual Income Tax Returns, 1994: Early Tax Estimates." *Statistics of Income Bulle-
          tin* 15(2).

Lee, Ronald, and Timothy Miller
  1997   "The Current Fiscal Impact of Immigrants and Their Descendants: Beyond the Immigrant
          Household." Department of Demography, University of California, Berkeley.
Los Angeles County
  1992   *Impact of Undocumented Persons and Other Immigrants on Costs, Revenues and Ser-*
          vices in Los Angeles County. Los Angeles: Internal Services Division.
MaCurdy, Thomas, Thomas Nechyba, and Jay Bhattacharya
  1996   "An Economic Framework for Assessing the Fiscal Impacts of Immigration." Depart-
          ment of Economics, Stanford University.
National Research Council
  1997   *The New Americans: Economic, Demographic, and Fiscal Effects of Immigration.* Wash-
          ington, D.C.: National Academy Press.
New York Times
  1994   "California Sues U.S. Government Over Costs Tied to Illegal Aliens." (May 1):19.
Office of Management and Budget
  1994   *The Budget of the United States Government, Fiscal Year 1995.* Washington, D.C.: U.S.
          Government Printing Office.
Office of Management and Budget
  1995   *The Budget of the United States Government, Fiscal Year 1996.* Washington, D.C.: U.S.
          Government Printing Office.
Office of the President
  1995   "Anticipating Enrollment Growth: How Much? How Soon?" University of California,
          Oakland.
Office of the State Controller
  1995   *Annual Report of Financial Transactions Concerning Counties of California, Fiscal Year*
          1993-94. Sacramento.
Office of the State Controller
  1996a   *Annual Report of Financial Transactions Concerning Cities of California, Fiscal Year*
          1993-94. Sacramento.
Office of the State Controller
  1996b   *Annual Report of Financial Transactions Concerning School Districts of California, Fis-*
          cal Year 1993-94. Sacramento.
Office of the State Controller
  1996c   *Annual Report of Financial Transactions Concerning Special Districts of California,*
          Fiscal Year 1993-94. Sacramento.
O'Sullivan, Arthur, Terri A. Sexton, and Steven M. Sheffrin
  1993   *The Future of Proposition 13 in California.* Berkeley: California Policy Seminar.
Pyle, Amy
  1997   "Campaign Targets Bilingual Education." *Los Angeles Times* (July 9):B2.
Romero, Philip J., Andrew J. Chang, and Theresa Parker
  1994   *Shifting the Costs of a Failed Federal Policy: The Net Fiscal Impact of Illegal Immi-*
          grants in California. Sacramento: Governor's Office of Planning and Research.
Rothman, Eric S., and Thomas J. Espenshade
  1992   "Fiscal Impacts of Immigration to the United States." *Population Index* 58(3):381-415.
Social Security Administration
  1996   *Annual Statistical Supplement, 1995 to the Social Security Bulletin.* Washington, D.C.
Sheffrin, Steven M., and Marla Dresch
  1995   *Estimating the Tax Burden in California.* Berkeley: California Policy Seminar.
Silva, Fabio, and Jon Sonstelie
  1995   "Did Serrano Cause a Decline in School Spending?" *National Tax Journal* 48(2):199-
          215.

U.S. Immigration and Naturalization Service

  1993   *Statistical Yearbook of the U.S. Immigration and Naturalization Service, 1992.* Washing-
          ton, D.C.: U.S. Government Printing Office.

U.S. Internal Revenue Service

  1995a   *U.S. Internal Revenue Service Data Book 1993/1994.* Washington, D.C.: U.S. Govern-
          ment Printing Office.

U.S. Internal Revenue Service

  1995b   "Selected Historical and Other Data." *Statistics of Income Bulletin* 15(2).

Vernez, Georges, and Kevin McCarthy

  1996   *The Costs of Immigration to Taxpayers: Analytical and Policy Issues.* Santa Monica,
          Calif.: The RAND Corporation.

Wassmer, Robert W.

  1993   "Property Taxation, Property Base, and Property Value - An Empirical Test of the New
          View." *National Tax Journal* 46(2):135-159.

5

The Current Fiscal Impact of Immigrants and Their Descendants: Beyond the Immigrant Household

Ronald D. Lee and Timothy W. Miller

INTRODUCTION

Does immigration lead to higher taxes for state, local, and federal taxpayers? The question appears to be straightforward, but on closer consideration ambiguities emerge. Any answer must address a conceptual experiment in which the fiscal situations under two different immigration scenarios are compared. The result will depend on the particular experiment that is envisaged, or on the choice of scenarios to be compared. The possible experiments and scenarios differ along many dimensions, but in this chapter we focus on the demographic dimension: How is the immigrant study population defined?

One type of experiment takes the form: Suppose that the number of immigrants arriving during some time period were different. What would be the fiscal implications for the balance of the population? Because the fiscal impacts unfold over time, the question is intrinsically longitudinal. Fiscal impacts are distributed over the lifetime of the immigrants and the lifetimes of their descendants and can be summarized by taking a present value. All the consequences of the difference in the number of immigrants, including the change in the descendants of the immigrants, would have to be taken into account. Because the impacts would depend on changing historical and future economic contexts, these would have to be taken into account as well. We call this type of experiment, and the resulting calculations, longitudinal. The experiment could be historical: Suppose 10 percent fewer immigrants had arrived between 1905 and 1909, for example. Or it could hypothesize a different number of immigrants arriving today and trace the consequences into the future. We believe that these longitudinal conceptual experiments are the most appropriate guides for policy formation. Nonetheless, they are very seldom carried out. Lee and Miller (1997) and *The New Americans* (National Research Council,1997:Chap. 7) are the most comprehensive longitudinal calculations available.

Such calculations are complex and necessarily involve many assumptions and projections. Cross-sectional calculations are a simpler alternative to the longitudinal ones, but they are rarely justified by a clearly formulated conceptual experiment (see National Research Council, 1997, Chapter 6 for a discussion of these issues). One such experiment might be: How would the fiscal situation change if all the immigrants in the United States in some year were to vanish? We could attempt to answer this question by calculating the difference between all the taxes paid by immigrants and the marginal cost of all the benefits received by them. We would ignore any cumulative effect of the presence of the immigrants in the past, for example on government debt. Such a cumulative effect would be relevant in the longitudinal calculation, but not for this conceptual experiment.[1] We call this the "immigrant only" approach, because no U.S.-born descendants are included in the calculation. This approach is quite common in cross-sectional analyses of fiscal impacts.

Note, however, that this calculation takes no account of the costs and taxes for the U.S.-born children of immigrants, many of whom impose heavy public-sector costs by attending public schools and colleges. Although these children are U.S. citizens, and not immigrants, their presence is a direct consequence of their parents' immigration. For this reason, it appears appropriate to include their fiscal impact, which is typically done by analyzing the taxes and costs of benefits for all immigrant households or families. These are defined as households or families with an immigrant head or adult member. How would the fiscal situation differ in some year if all immigrant households (including U.S.-born members) were to vanish in that year? We call this the "immigrant household" formulation. This approach is also quite common in cross-sectional analyses of fiscal impacts.

However, there is a serious bias in this type of study, because it counts the U.S.-born children of immigrants only while they are young and living with their parents and while society is investing heavily in their education. As soon as they leave home and get jobs, they no longer live in immigrant households, and their contributions are lost from sight. But if the children are to be included while young and costly, they should also be included when they are older and paying taxes (as argued, for example, in MaCurdy et al., in this volume). Furthermore, these children may themselves have children, who also should be included. Thus, we propose a conceptual experiment in which all the immigrants vanish in some year, along with all the descendants of those immigrants,

---

[1]Taking into account the current effect of past fiscal impacts would be a complicated task because we do not know what the past fiscal impacts have been.

and the fiscal implications are assessed. Note that only the descendants of living immigrants are assumed to vanish along with the immigrants themselves. Descendants of deceased immigrants, comprising the vast majority of the U.S. population, would remain. We call this the "concurrent descendants" formulation. We believe that this is the first study to calculate fiscal impacts on this basis.

The primary reason for doing fiscal impact calculations is to inform current policy decisions about the number and characteristics of immigrants to admit to the United States. Cross-sectional approaches such as the three outlined above have serious problems in relation to this goal. The cross section includes immigrants who have arrived at different periods and have different characteristics (such as educational attainment or English language ability). In addition, the volume of immigration has changed dramatically over time. This means that the age distribution of immigrants in the population is very uneven. If there are relatively few immigrants of retirement age, then the cross-sectional analysis will reflect low immigrant costs of Social Security and Medicare benefits, even though we know that most immigrants will survive to collect these benefits in future years. Likewise, if there are relatively many children of immigrants, then the analysis will reflect high costs of education and low tax payments, even though we know that most of these children will grow up to pay taxes over a lifetime of work.

Furthermore, because taxes and benefits may vary over time as policy changes, their current levels may be misleading. For example, when the baby boom generation retires between 2010 and 2035, payroll taxes will have to be raised or Social Security benefits reduced. The cross-sectional calculation cannot take this into account. Finally, the cross-sectional results will depend on whether governments are running surpluses or deficits in the study year. In the longitudinal analysis, realistic constraints can be placed on the ability of governments to maintain unbalanced budgets in the long run; in the cross-sectional analysis, this cannot be done. For these reasons, the type of cross-sectional analysis reported here is inherently limited in its relevance for policy choices, and is certainly less useful for this purpose than the type of longitudinal analysis reported in Lee and Miller (1997) and National Research Council (1997:Chap. 7).

Almost all studies of which we are aware have taken the cross-sectional approach, other than Lee and Miller (1997) and National Research Council (1997:Chap. 7). Rothman and Espenshade (1992:411) survey the fiscal impact literature for the United States. Of the 17 studies they review, 9 take the immigrants-only approach, and the remaining 8 take the immigrant household (or family) approach. Vernez and McCarthy (1996:7-8) update this survey with a look at nine studies since 1992. Most of these are based on the immigrants-only approach, whereas a few are based on immigrant households or families. Two very recent studies reported in this volume (Garvey and Espenshade and Clune) are based on immigrant households. We are not aware of any previous study that takes the concurrent descendant approach. It is worthwhile, therefore, to consider how the calculated impact depends on the definition of the study population.[2]

In this chapter we carry out calculations pertaining to all three of the cross-sectional experiments, at the federal, state, and local levels, using the same data and many of the same assumptions. In this way, we can isolate the effects of the setup of each conceptual experiment on the outcome. The actual results depend very sensitively on the formulation chosen, in both sign and magnitude. Although we believe that the longitudinal formulation is most informative, the cross-sectional formulations have dominated the policy debate. Within this class, we argue that the concurrent descendant formulation is strongly preferable to the immigrant-only or the immigrant household formulations. In this chapter we focus on the concurrent descendant analysis, which we report in some detail. We also report comparative results for the other approaches.

DEFINING THE POPULATION OF IMMIGRANTS AND THEIR CONCURRENT DESCENDANTS

In our cross-sectional analysis, we assess the current impact of past immigration policies that have led to the presence of 22.8 million immigrants and their additional descendants in the United States in 1994-1995. We restrict our attention to the impact of these immigrants in that year. Our group of interest is all immigrants resident in the United States in 1994-1995 and the surviving U.S. resident children and grandchildren of these still-living immigrants. Once an immigrant dies, we no longer assess the impact of that immigrant's descendants. We also report results for the immigrant-only and the immigrant household formulations.

Our data sample is drawn from the March Current Population Survey (CPS) conducted in 1994 and 1995. The CPS is designed to represent the non-institutionalized population of the United States.[3] We define immigrants to be those reporting themselves as foreign born. The CPS estimate of this population in 1994-1995 is 22.8 million. This includes legal immigrants, undocumented immigrants, and the so-called nonimmigrant groups (students, businessmen, and temporary workers). About 31 percent of this group reported themselves as naturalized citizens.

---

[2]There are many variants on these basic methods. One can distinguish by country of origin and by time of arrival of the immigrant head of household. One can construct a quasi-longitudinal estimate by interpreting the fiscal impacts of householders at differing durations within the country as if they referred to the same immigrant householder over his or her life cycle (see Akbari, 1991). One can calculate fiscal impacts separately for first- and second-generation immigrants Clune (in this volume).

[3]We have simply combined years to form an aggregate sample. The CPS is a rotating sample such that one-half of the households interviewed in March of 1994 are reinterviewed in March 1995. One-fourth of our observations come from households interviewed only in 1994, one-fourth from those interviewed only in 1995, and one-half from households interviewed twice, once in each year.

Second-generation immigrants (U.S.-born children of immigrants) are defined primarily as those U.S.-born respondents who report that both parents were foreign-born. There remains a group of children with one parent foreign-born and one parent U.S-born, which we count as 50 percent second-generation immigrant and 50 percent third-plus-generation immigrant. We estimate that there are 21.1 million second-generation immigrants in the United States in 1994-1995. However, we count only the second-generation immigrants with surviving immigrant parents. To estimate the children of still-living immigrants, we assume that immigrants experienced the same mortality as the general population and that each parent (immigrant) is 30 years older than each child.[4] Of the 21.1 million U.S.-born children of immigrants, 65.5 percent have at least one parent alive by this calculation, which leads to our estimate of 13.8 million U.S.-born children of still-living immigrants. Of these, 5.6 million are the adult children of immigrants, who presumably are not members of immigrant households.

We estimate the grandchildren of still-living immigrants by estimating the number of children of the 5.6 million adult children of still-living immigrants. The June 1994 CPS provides the number of children ever born by age for the children of immigrants, which is very similar to the figures for the third and higher generations. We estimate that there are 3.9 million grandchildren of still-living immigrants.

Our group of interest is therefore composed of 40.4 million individuals: 22.8 million immigrants alive in 1994, their 13.8 million surviving U.S.-born children, and their 3.9 million grandchildren (born to U.S.-born children). How does the presence of these individuals affect federal, state, and local tax burdens? We turn now to estimation of the costs generated and the taxes paid by these individuals.

ESTIMATION OF THE COSTS GENERATED AND TAXES PAID

Immigrants, and indeed all people, affect the budget through four broad categories of government expenditures: public goods, servicing of public debt, congestible goods, and transfer programs (or assignable items). (See Table 5-1 for a breakdown of government budgets into these categories of expenditure.) We discuss each of these briefly here. A more detailed discussion can be found in Lee and Miller (1997) or National Research Council (1997:Chap. 7). MaCurdy et al. (in this volume) discuss the rationale for a categorization of this type.

---

[4]This assumed gap of 30 years between first and second generations is somewhat greater than the average age at which immigrants give birth to allow for the childbearing occurring at younger ages before arrival in the United States. We used cohort survival values taken from the Social Security Administration (1992) actuarial report to estimate immigrant survival. This probably underestimates the number of second-generation immigrants with a surviving immigrant parent because the survival rates for immigrants are somewhat higher than for nonimmigrants (Swallen, 1996).

TABLE 5-1   Government Expenditures by Category

Budget Category	Federal Budget	State and Local Budget
Public Goods	24%	0%
Congestible Goods	7	32
Transfers	55	53
Debt Servicing	14	15
Total	100	100

NOTE: Federal expenditures are for FY 1994; state and local are for FY 1994 and represent the total for all states and localities.

SOURCE: The detailed list of expenditures is taken from *1996 US Statistical Abstract, the Annual Survey of Government Finances, and Analytical Perspectives, Budget of the US Government, FY1996.* The table shows aggregates based on the principles discussed in the text and appendix.

Public Goods

By definition, the cost of providing a given level of public goods does not increase with population size. Public goods are not congestible. The presence of immigrants and their descendants, therefore, does not increase the cost of providing public goods.[5]   In our analysis, we treat the following as public goods: national defense; expenditures on veterans; and research on health, science, space, and technology. All of these are programs of the federal government. We do not treat any of the expenditures at the state and local levels as public goods. Immigrants certainly share in the benefits from public goods; and in an accounting of the value—rather than the cost—of the benefits they receive, services from public goods would be counted.

Servicing the Public Debt

Tax-paying immigrants help shoulder the costs of servicing the federal debt, which in 1994 came to about $4.6 trillion. In 1994 the cost of servicing the debt represented 14 percent of the federal budget. In a longitudinal historical formulation it would matter whether immigrants themselves were partially responsible for causing this debt to be larger or smaller through their fiscal impacts in the past. However, in the strictly current cost versions it does not matter whether immigrants contributed to the debt in the past. If the immigrants were to vanish today, all other taxpayers would have to make larger tax payments to service the debt, regardless of its origin. Somewhat similarly, we note that there is a vast

---

[5]However, the amount of public goods demanded may be influenced by population size. The larger the population, the cheaper the price per capita of providing the good and hence the greater the demand. The fact that the population of the United States was 260 million in 1994 means that public goods such as national defense, space exploration, and cancer research are relatively inexpensive.

federal debt in the form of unfunded obligations to pay pension and health benefits to future retirees through Social Security and Medicare. When the baby boom generation retires, it will not be possible for the federal government to meet these obligations without raising payroll tax rates or reducing benefits. Doing so will make the fiscal impact of immigrants more positive, which is taken into account in a longitudinal analysis. However, the current cross-sectional calculation is a snapshot for which neither the past nor the future matters.

In calculating the fiscal impacts of immigrants and their descendants, we always treat them as incremental population members with zero marginal costs for public goods. Many of the tables in this chapter show fiscal impacts for the balance of the population. These calculations also treat the balance of the population as incremental, and therefore with marginal costs of zero for public goods. We treat the debt servicing payments of immigrants and the balance of the population in a similar, symmetric way. These procedures make sense so long as we add or delete a modest proportional increment to the population. For these reasons, the presence of public goods and public debt tends to make the fiscal impact of any incremental member of the population less negative or more positive.

Congestible Goods

Unlike public goods, congestible goods have nonzero marginal costs. Included in this category are expenditures on roads, fire and police protection, libraries, airports, sewers, and so on. In assigning costs to immigrants and to the balance of the population, we assume that marginal costs equal average costs for these items. Capital expenditures are included in these outlays. We also experimented with a more direct method of imputing the capital costs of replicating the social infrastructure (school buildings, roads, sewers, etc.) for immigrants by calculating the annual user cost of capital from an estimate of the net capital stock per capita in 1994. We found that it yielded very similar cost estimates.

Transfer Programs

Here we include all government expenditures that can be assigned to specific individuals. Many cash and in-kind transfers such as Social Security, Medicare, Medicaid, AFDC, earned income tax credits, energy assistance, food stamps, public housing, school lunches, and unemployment benefits are included. Also included are public education at all levels and the costs of incarceration.

We draw on three types of information from the CPS for use in calculating transfers to and from immigrants and their families. The first type is responses to questions about amounts of benefits received. An example would be the amount of Social Security benefits received last year. In general, summing these responses over all individuals (appropriately weighted to reflect the noninstitutionalized population) will not equal the total costs of the program as reported in the budget. For example, summing all the Social Security benefits reported to have been received in our CPS sample yields an estimate of $265 billion in Social Security costs. Actual costs were $321 billion. The difference in these sums is due to the inclusion of administrative costs in the budget number, the exclusion of nonresident and institutionalized populations in the CPS, sampling variation in the CPS, and misreporting of benefits received. To account for these discrepancies, we simply adjust all responses upward by the same percentage so as to yield the aggregate budget numbers. For example, all interviewer responses on the amount of Social Security benefits received are multiplied by 1.2 (=321/265). This will create a bias in our estimates of aggregate benefits received by immigrants, their immediate descendants, and the general population to the extent that misreporting differs among these groups.[6]

The second type of information is response to interview questions about program participation. For example, the CPS tells us whether individuals reported that they participated in the Medicare program. We assume that all program participants generate the same amount in costs, so we equally divide the total program costs among all program participants. This will distort our estimates to the extent that misreporting and/or program usage per participant differ between the general population and immigrants and their descendants.

The third type of information is for items such as federal income tax and property taxes, which are constructed by CPS based on reported income and other household characteristics.

Although the majority of variables were drawn directly from the CPS, we needed to construct several ourselves. The federal tax incidence of corporate and business taxes is assumed to be shifted to individuals who own the business capital. Therefore, we assign these taxes to individuals based on their income from dividends and interest as reported in the CPS. At the state and local levels, we assume that the mobility of businesses means that income, sales, and property taxes paid by businesses are payments for business services provided by the state and local governments. If states or localities attempted to collect more in taxes than the service they provided, businesses would simply move to a new locality. The tax incidences of payroll taxes and sales taxes are assumed to be shifted to the individuals who receive the wage or purchase the goods. We allocated all the payroll taxes (FICA) paid by both employee and employer to the employee. Sales taxes were estimated based on household income and immigrant status (immigrant households are assumed to remit $1,000 in income and hence pay lower sales taxes than nonimmigrant households) using an algorithm estimated

---

[6]In the case of Social Security benefits, we observed a higher frequency of "zero" responses among immigrants and lower reported benefits among those who did respond. However, these responses are consistent with the shorter work histories of recently arrived immigrants and lower incomes of immigrants. We do not interpret this as a sign of higher misreporting among immigrants.

by Sheffrin and Dresch (1995). Owners of rental units are assumed to shift the majority of the property tax burden to their renters. Property taxes paid by renters were estimated by assuming that 70 percent of the tax on rental properties was borne by renters and this aggregate amount was equally divided among all renters. (For a full discussion of the issue of tax incidence, see National Research Council, 1997:Chap. 6.)

Medicaid costs and incarceration costs were assigned based on institutionalization rates by age and immigrant status, taken from the 1990 Census. Medicaid institutionalized costs (for nursing home care) were divided equally among the institutional population over age 65 (a smaller portion of the elderly immigrant population than of natives was found to be institutionalized, however). Incarceration costs were divided equally among the institutional population below age 65. Refugee costs were divided equally among all immigrants.

In assessing the educational costs of immigrant and second-generation children, we took into account the state-to-state variations in per student costs and the distribution of immigrant children across states. We also took into account the special costs of bilingual (limited English proficiency; LEP) education. These special costs were based on a study of Florida schools that showed that LEP students were 1.44 times more costly than other students. Immigrant children (51%) and, to a lesser extent, second-generation children (37%) are likely to be classified as LEP and hence are significantly more costly than other students.[7] We estimate bilingual education costs to all states and localities to be $6.559 billion.

These estimates suffer from several limitations. First, they are based on a Florida estimate of bilingual costs that may not be representative of the experience of immigrants in other states. The Florida courts have intervened in school financing on behalf of bilingual students. Second, this method ignores the possibility that immigrant children live in poorer (or richer) school districts and thus generate higher (or lower) than average costs to the federal and state governments and lower (or higher) than average costs to local school districts. Third, the method assumes that the same proportions of first-generation school children are LEP across states, and similarly for second-generation children.

---

[7]Clark (1994:Table A.5 "State Costs of Bilingual Education") reports the extra cost of bilingual education in Florida in 1990-1991 as $2,334 per bilingual student. This is 44 percent of average student costs in Florida ($5,276). Furthermore, she estimates 51 percent of foreign-born children are LEP. Weighting by the probability of having LEP foreign-born children of immigrants is estimated to be 1.22 times as expensive as other children in their state (0.51*1.44 + 0.49*1.00). Clark estimates 3.68 percent of U.S.-born children are LEP. We assume that all U.S.-born children defined as LEP are children of immigrants. Our CPS sample shows one in ten U.S.-born children are children of immigrants. Therefore, the proportion of LEP students among the U.S.-born children of immigrants is estimated to be 36.8 percent. U.S.-born children of immigrants are estimated as being 1.16 times as expensive as other students in their state (0.368*1.44 + 0.632*1.00). We apply these ratios to each state, allowing state-to-state differences in educational spending to influence immigrant costs. That is, we assume that the relative costs of educating an immigrant child do not vary between the states, but the absolute costs do.

Other Considerations

This is at best a partial equilibrium analysis. We do not try to calculate all the indirect fiscal consequences arising from the ways in which immigrants affect the economy in general. For example, immigration might affect housing prices, wages, unemployment rates, prices of other goods and services, profits on capital, rents on land, the geographic location of the nonimmigrant population, international trade flows, and so on (National Research Council, 1997). It is our view that it would be hazardous to single out one or two of these indirect effects for attention while ignoring others. In particular, some studies have estimated an indirect fiscal impact arising from the displacement of other workers, who then may claim unemployment insurance, swell the welfare rolls, and pay lower taxes than otherwise.

The National Research Council report (1997) finds that immigration probably raised or had little effect on the wages of most workers, but that it may have considerably depressed the earnings of the least educated workers such as high school dropouts. Clearly these are important issues. It is important to keep in mind, however, that immigration also probably raised the earnings of nonlabor factors. On net, the National Research Council (1997) report concluded that the aggregate income of nonimmigrants was probably raised by $1 billion to $10 billion. Such a net increase in income would have engendered a corresponding increase in taxes at all levels of government, in addition to the tax payments by immigrants that we have explicitly included. Whether immigration may also have raised various types of welfare payments significantly by worsening the economic situation of less educated nonimmigrant workers, and whether any such effect would outweigh the positive effect on tax payments, are questions for further research.

Because of the presence of public goods, public debt, and current deficit spending, there can be substantial differences between total tax revenues and total costs of nonpublic goods. Public goods and public debt make fiscal impacts more positive or less negative, whereas current deficit spending tends to make fiscal impacts less positive or more negative. Calculations for FY 1994 show that federal tax revenues exceeded costs for nonpublic goods by $345 billion, whereas state and local taxes exceeded total costs by $17 billion. Therefore, our calculations of net fiscal impacts presented in the next section sum to these positive values, not zero. Further details on the treatment of federal, state, and local budgets are described in the Appendix.

RESULTS

Examining the Fiscal Impacts Among Governments

In Tables 5-2, 5-3, and 5-4 we examine fiscal impacts under the "immigrant and concurrent descendants" approach. Results for all state and local governments combined are presented in Table 5-2. The presence of immigrants and their concurrent descendants generated $89 billion in costs to states and localities across the United States. This group paid an estimated

TABLE 5-2   Fiscal Impact on State and Local Governments
(1994 in 1994 dollars)

| | Aggregate (in $ billions) | | Per capita ($) | | | |
	Immigrants & Concurrent Descendants	All Others	Immigrants & Concurrent Descendants	All Others	Ratio	Diff
Taxes						
Income Tax	15.7	113.1	387	513	0.75	−126
Property Tax, Homeowners	10.4	76.1	257	345	0.74	−88
Property Tax, Renters	5.2	23.6	130	107	1.21	23
Sales Tax	17.6	127.8	435	579	0.75	−144
Unemployment & Workers Comp. Contributions	4.3	27.1	106	123	0.86	−17
Other Taxes	8.3	60.1	206	273	0.76	−67
Total Taxes	61.5	427.9	1,520	1,941	0.78	−421
Costs of Benefits						
Medicaid, Institutional	1.1	14.3	27	65	0.42	−38
Medicaid, Non-institutional + Other Medical Welfare	12.3	49.8	305	226	1.35	79
SSI	0.7	3.1	17	14	1.22	3
AFDC + Other Welfare	7.7	28.1	190	127	1.49	63
Food Stamps	0.3	1.5	8	7	1.19	1
Unemployment Compensation	3.3	18.3	81	83	0.97	−2
Worker's Compensation	1.2	9.3	30	42	0.71	−12
Bilingual Education	6.2	0.0	154	0	n.a.	154
Elementary and High School	42.2	191.6	1,043	869	1.20	174
Public College	7.5	29.1	186	132	1.41	54
Incarceration Costs	4.2	28.1	103	127	0.81	−24
Congestible Goods	2.1	11.4	52	52	1.01	0
Total Costs	88.8	384.5	2,197	1,744	1.26	453
Total:						
(Taxes − Costs)	−27.4	43.4	−677	197	−3.44	−874

$62 billion in taxes, for a net burden of $27 billion. Other taxpayers in the states and localities in which these immigrants resided shouldered this burden through increased taxes.

The average immigrant and concurrent descendant had a net fiscal impact at the state and local levels of about –$680, in contrast to a positive net impact of about $200 for the rest of the population. The difference is nearly $900 per person. This difference reflects per capita costs that are 26 percent higher for immigrants than for the rest of the population. Particularly expensive are general public education, bilingual education programs, and noninstitutional Medicaid and other medical welfare costs. But just as important, per capita tax payments for immigrants and their concurrent descendants are 22 percent below those of the rest of the population, reflecting the lower incomes of immigrants and their families.

Table 5-3 presents the federal fiscal impact. Here we see a net positive fiscal impact with immigrants and their concurrent descendants paying nearly $51 billion more in taxes than they generate in costs. This served to reduce the tax burden borne by taxpayers throughout the nation, not just in states with immigrants. Particularly important were transfers from immigrants and their descendants of about $28 billion to the rest of the nation through the Social Security system (OASDHI), reflecting the young age distribution of this group. Although there are many elderly members of the second generation, they are far less likely to have surviving immigrant parents than are the younger members of the second generation, and so they are less likely to enter our calculations. Of course, working-age immigrants are going to become old themselves in the future and receive costly benefits that are not reflected in this calculation. That is a general problem with the cross-sectional approach. Longitudinal calculations fully reflect such future costs.

In per capita terms, immigrants and their concurrent descendants contributed about $700 more in payroll taxes than they received in OASDHI benefits each year, whereas the balance of the population just broke even. For the remainder of the federal budget, immigrants and their concurrent descendants paid $500 or $600 more in taxes than they cost in benefits, and in total they had a positive federal fiscal impact of about $1,260, exceeding their net cost at the state and local levels. The balance of the population had a very similar positive fiscal impact of $1,340 (when each person's impact is assessed at the margin, with zero costs for public goods and national debt).

Table 5-4 reports the incremental tax burden on the residual population that is due to the presence of immigrants and their concurrent descendants.[8] Results are reported separately for residual residents in the high-immigration states (Cali-

---

[8]That is, the aggregate fiscal impacts of immigrants and concurrent descendants, reported in Tables 5-2 and 5-3, are divided by the size of the population that is neither immigrant nor descended from a living immigrant.

TABLE 5-3 Fiscal Impact on the Federal Government (1994 in 1994 dollars)

	Aggregate (in $ billions)		Per capita (in dollars)			
	Immigrants	Others	Immigrants	Others	Ratio	Diff
Taxes						
Income Tax	15.7	113.1	387	513	0.75	−126
Income Tax	65.5	477.6	1619	2166	0.75	−547
Corporate Tax	13.3	126.7	329	575	0.57	−246
Excise Tax	5.2	49.8	129	226	0.57	−97
FICA	62.7	398.8	1551	1809	0.86	−258
SMI contribution	1.0	10.0	24	45	0.53	−21
Other Taxes	5.7	41.4	140	188	0.75	−48
Total Taxes	153.3	1,104.3	3793	5008	0.76	−1215
Costs of Benefits						
OASDI	24.7	296.4	612	1344	0.46	−732
HI	9.8	102.6	243	465	0.52	−222
SMI	5.4	55.9	132	254	0.52	−122
Medicaid, Institutional	1.5	19.0	36	86	0.42	−50
Medicaid, Non-institutional	12.2	49.1	301	223	1.35	78
SSI	5.0	22.5	123	102	1.20	21
AFDC + Other Welfare	6.6	24.1	163	109	1.49	54
EITC Refund	2.4	8.5	60	39	1.56	21
School Lunch	1.7	5.8	41	27	1.55	14
Food Stamps	5.4	25.9	134	117	1.14	17
Energy Assistance	0.2	1.6	4	7	0.56	−3
Rent Subsidy	2.2	12.2	55	55	0.99	0
Public Housing	0.8	5.4	19	25	0.77	−6
Unemployment Compensation	1.1	6.1	27	28	0.98	−1
Refugee Aid	0.4	0.0	9	0	n.a.	9
Bilingual Education	0.2	0.0	5	0	n.a.	5
Elementary and High School	2.4	10.7	58	49	1.19	9
Public College	0.3	1.2	8	5	1.49	3
Federal Student Aid	1.6	8.0	39	36	1.07	3
Incarceration costs	0.3	2.0	7	9	0.77	−2
Federal Retirement	1.3	35.6	32	162	0.20	−130
Military Retirement	1.2	25.6	29	116	0.25	−87
Railroad Retirement	0.2	4.4	5	20	0.25	−15
Congestible Goods	15.8	86.1	391	391	1.00	0
Total Costs	102.5	808.7	2535	3668	0.69	−1133
OASDHI: Taxes − Costs	28.2	−0.2	696	−1	n.a.	697
All Other: Taxes − Costs	22.7	295.7	562	1341	n.a.	−779
Total: Taxes − Costs	50.9	295.5	1258	1340	n.a.	−82

TABLE 5-4   Per Capita Fiscal Impact in High- and Low-Immigration States
(Immigrants and Concurrent Descendants)

A. Change in per capita tax burden

	All taxes	Federal	State and Local
The Nation	$107	$231	−$124
High immigration states	−$49	$231	−$280
All other states	$182	$231	−$49

B. Population (millions)

	Total	Immigrants and Concurrent Descendants	All Others
The Nation	260.9	40.4	220.5
High immigration states	101.6	29.7	71.9
All other states	159.3	10.7	148.6

NOTE: Per capita is calculated by dividing aggregate totals from Tables 5-2 and 5-3 by the residual
population figures given in Panel B of the table. (This table gives fiscal impacts in 1994 measured in
1994 dollars.)

fornia, Texas, New York, Florida, Illinois, and New Jersey) and those in the rest
of the nation.   The calculations assume that immigrants and their concurrent
descendants live in the same states. If immigrants and their concurrent descendants were to have vanished in 1994, the average member of the remaining
population would have had to pay $107 more in taxes, or suffer a comparable
reduction in benefits. This figure can be translated into the tax increase per
residual household by multiplying by the average household size of 2.6 members,
to arrive at $278.   The population figures in Table 5-4, Panel B, can be used to re-
express these figures relative to the total national population instead of the residual population, if so desired.

However, this national average masks important interstate differences. Per
capita taxes in high-immigration states would have been $49 lower had there
been no immigrants or descendants, whereas per capita taxes in low-immigration
states would have been $182 higher. Within the group of high-immigrant states,
presumably some states had higher burdens and others had lower burdens because of interstate differences in the characteristics of the immigrants and state
fiscal policies.   The same methods employed here could be used to make estimates of the net costs of immigration for individual states.   But these calculations
would be correct only under the strong assumption that immigrants resided in the
same state as their concurrent descendants.   The high rate of geographic mobility
in the United States undermines any state-specific methods that include descendants of immigrants who have left their parental home.

Taxpayers in high-immigration states bear the full increased burden of providing state and local government services to immigrants who reside in their

state, whereas they share the federal fiscal benefits of immigration with taxpayers throughout the nation. This substantial discrepancy arises in large part because states and localities fund education and other youth services, whereas the federal government funds Social Security, Medicare, and other services for the elderly. (See Goldstein, 1995, for a discussion of interstate transfers arising from differences in age distribution and the funding of education and social security.)

It is sometimes suggested that the federal government should address these interstate discrepancies through a national policy of compensation to state and local governments. According to these calculations, the federal government realized a net fiscal gain of about $51 billion in 1994 from the presence of immigrants and their concurrent descendants. At the same time, there were net fiscal costs of $27 billion per year incurred in total by a subset of state and local governments. The federal government could compensate states and localities for the $27 billion net cost, leaving the remaining $24 billion of federal net gain as a benefit to be shared equally among all U.S. taxpayers.[9] There are many complicated issues regarding such a policy of federal compensation. The presence of immigrants and their descendants may confer nonfiscal economic net gains to the residents of states and local areas, for example through cheaper goods and services or through higher wages of skilled workers and higher returns to nonlabor factors. The federal government does not generally compensate states for other discrepancies; what is special about the case of immigration? We do not consider these and other issues here.

Comparison of Results for Immigrants Only, Immigrant Households, and Concurrent Descendants

Table 5-5 shows comparable measures of fiscal impact for the different demographic formulations of the cross-sectional conceptual experiment. In the most restrictive definition, only immigrants themselves are counted. Here we find that immigrants pay about $32 billion more in taxes overall than they generate in costs. This positive balance reflects the age distribution of the immigrant population: There are relatively many working-age people and relatively few children and elderly.

---

[9]Two other levels of compensation are possible, but neither is immigrant neutral. In one alternative, taxpayers in high-immigration states could be compensated so that they are not bearing any net increased fiscal burden of immigration. That is, state and local costs would just offset their reduction in national taxes ($4 billion annually to high-immigration states). In this scenario, states would compete to discourage immigration. Under another alternative, taxpayers would receive a share of the national benefits of immigration ($51 billion) in direct proportion to the number of immigrants in their state. Under this scenario, states would compete for immigrants. States are indifferent to immigrants only in the basic compensation scenario in which states are compensated for the full state and local costs of immigrants, and the remaining national benefits are shared equally among all states.

TABLE 5-5   How the Aggregate Fiscal Impact Depends on the Definition of the Study Population (1994 in 1994 $ billions)

A. Aggregate Fiscal Impact			
Study Population:	Overall	Federal	State and Local
1. Immigrants Only	32.4	28.2	4.2
2. Immigrant Households	−13.3	16.0	−29.3
3. Immigrants and Concurrent Children	29.5	48.9	−19.3
4. Immigrants and Concurrent Descendants (Children and Grandchildren)	23.5	50.9	−27.4

B. Population Subtotals		
Study Population:	Number	Cumulative Total
1. First Generation	22,766,711	22,766,711
2. Second Generation under age 20	8,201,368	30,968,079
3. Concurrent Second Generation age 20 and over	5,597,759	36,565,838
4. Concurrent Third Generation	3,862,610	40,428,448

Immigrant households include nearly all immigrants, plus nearly all U.S.-born children of immigrants up to the age of 20 or so, because such children will co-reside with their immigrant parents. Expanding the definition to include immigrants plus their U.S.-born children under the age of 20, the estimated fiscal impact flips from $32 billion to −$13 billion. The biggest change is at the state and local levels, where the impact shifts from $4 billion to −$29 billion. Evidently it makes a decisive difference which of the two most common demographic formulations of the problem is used. Measured impacts are strongly positive for immigrants only and strongly negative overall for immigrant households.

The bias from excluding the adult U.S.-born children of immigrants, together with their children, becomes apparent when we recompute and take them into account. When we count all the relevant descendants of still-living immigrants we find a net positive fiscal impact of about $24 billion. There is a very large positive fiscal impact of $51 billion at the federal level, partially offset by a large negative fiscal impact of −$27 billion at the state and local levels. Looking separately at the federal, state, and local components, we find that at the state and local levels, the results including all descendants are little different from the immigrant household results: –$27 billion versus –$29 billion. The impacts of the two missing groups (adult children of immigrants and grandchildren of immigrants) offset each other. This is not true at the federal level, where the discrepancy is severe. Including all concurrent descendants of immigrants triples the federal surplus!

Comparison with a Longitudinal Study

In a separate study, we analyzed the fiscal impact of immigrants in a forward-looking longitudinal model. For each age at arrival and education level, we calculated the impact of the immigrant and all future descendants by projecting their survival, fertility, return migration, educational attainment, taxes, and benefits (see Lee and Miller, 1997; National Research Council, 1997:Chap. 7). In that analysis, we also calculated the average impact of immigrants, weighting by the age and educational composition of recently arrived immigrants. The average present value (over a 300-year horizon and expressed in 1996 dollars) of the stream of net fiscal impacts of an immigrant arriving in 1994 to state and local governments combined is –$25,000, to the federal government $105,000, and overall is $80,000 per immigrant admitted. For the purpose of comparison, we can multiply these present values by the interest rate (3%) to convert to annual flows: –$750 at the state and local levels, $3,150 at the federal level, and a combined annualized fiscal impact of $2,400 per immigrant. The concurrent descendant cross-sectional approach yielded estimates of –$1,200 at the state and local levels, $2,230 at the federal level, and a combined annual fiscal impact of $1,030 per immigrant (in 1994 dollars).

There is no reason to expect a close agreement for these two very different methods, except perhaps under certain hypothetical steady-state conditions. The cross-sectional method is affected by the historical trends in the volume and composition of immigration streams and in vital rates, because these shape the current age and educational distribution of immigrants and descendants. These do not enter into the longitudinal calculation. At the same time, the cross-sectional method does not take into account projected trends in taxes, benefits, educational attainment, and vital rates, unlike the longitudinal method. The longitudinal calculation refers to an immigrant arriving in 1994, whereas the cross-sectional calculation is based on immigrants arriving at various times in the twentieth century.

CONCLUSIONS

We have argued that the longitudinal approach is the preferred method of assessing the fiscal impact of immigrants for most purposes. Yet because this method is forward looking, it must inevitably rely on projections far into the future and make many assumptions. Some people, therefore, may prefer the down-to-earth cross-sectional estimates of the fiscal impact of immigrants in a particular year, which appear to be more straightforward and to involve fewer assumptions. Indeed, almost all published estimates of fiscal impact are of this cross-sectional type. Many of these are limited in scope because they include only a subset of tax payments and benefits received. The estimates in this chapter reflect a broad coverage, including 28 types of transfers (assignable benefits), both in cash and in-kind; public goods; servicing the government debt; and the costs of congestible goods and services. All benefits and taxes included in government budgets are counted in one way or another in our calculations. Our main point in this chapter, however, is to investigate the effects of formulating the conceptual experiment in terms of differing subpopulations.

All the analyses reviewed by Rothman and Espenshade (1992) or Vernez and McCarthy (1996), and the more recent studies of which we are aware, take either the immigrant-only approach or the immigrant household approach. The first is flawed for most purposes because it ignores all U.S.-born descendants of the immigrants and thus underestimates the costs caused by the immigrants. The second approach is flawed because it includes the U.S.-born descendants only while they are young, costly, and reside in their immigrant parents' homes. In this way, the U.S.-born children of immigrants are counted only during the ages in which society is investing heavily in their education, not when they in turn grow up to become taxpayers themselves. This tends to make the estimated fiscal impact be more negative, or less positive.

Our calculations indicate that definition of the study population is critical to the outcome. If limited to immigrants themselves, the overall fiscal impact is $1,400 (taxes paid less costs generated) per immigrant. If limited to immigrants plus their U.S.-born children under the age of 20, corresponding to the immigrant household formulation, the average fiscal impact is about –$600 per immigrant (or –$400 per immigrant and young child). If extended to all descendants of living immigrants, the average fiscal impact is $1,000 expressed per immigrant, or $600 expressed per immigrant and descendants.[10] Therefore, the most widely used method based on the immigrant household is the only one that returns a negative value.

We argue that if the U.S.-born children are to be included in the calculation (and we believe they should be), then they should be included at all ages and not just while they represent heavy costs to society. Therefore, we believe that the calculation inclusive of all concurrent descendants is most appropriate within the category of cross-sectional calculations. However, all cross-sectional calculations give the wrong answer. The longitudinal calculation remains the method of choice.

In the longitudinal formulation, the appropriate demographic specifica-

---

[10]These per capita numbers are calculated from the numbers given in Table 5-5.

tion follows closely from the question posed. An incremental immigrant arrives, and a long chain of consequences follows, continuing after the immigrant's death through all of the descendants. In the cross-sectional approach, the appropriate demographic formulation has been less clear. We hope to have shown, however, that whatever the general weaknesses of the cross-sectional approach, the failure to include the effects of all concurrent descendants biases the outcome. In practice, the resulting distortions are very large and cannot be ignored.

APPENDIX: DETAILED ASSUMPTIONS FOR FEDERAL, STATE, AND LOCAL CALCULATIONS

Why Do Taxes Exceed Costs?

By definition, federal, state, and local budgets must meet the basic accounting identity: total revenue equals total expenditures. Therefore, one might expect that taxes could not exceed costs in our calculations. However, for purposes of examining the fiscal impact of an incremental member of the population, we exclude from consideration (a) expenditures on public goods, payments for debt interest or principal, and purchase of financial assets; and (b) revenues from interest on assets, the sale of assets, and new debt issued. We assume that adding or subtracting an incremental member of the population will not have any impact on these types of expenditures and revenues in the current period. It is certainly true that immigration will affect public assets and public debt in the long run. This impact is considered in longitudinal studies, but cannot be incorporated into cross-sectional studies.

At the federal level, we excluded (a) $346 billion in expenditures on public goods, (b) $203 billion in expenditures for debt repayment, and (c) $203 billion in revenue from net new borrowing. Therefore, federal tax revenues exceed federal expenditures by $345 billion. The fact that debt repayment equaled net new borrowing in FY 1994 is purely coincidental. For example, in FY 1996 federal debt repayment exceeded net new borrowing by $96 billion. The larger debt payments and smaller deficit in FY 1996 would make the federal fiscal impact of immigrants significantly more positive in 1996 relative to 1994.

At the state and local levels, we excluded (a) $65 billion in expenditures for debt interest, (b) $167 billion in expenditures for debt repaid, (c) an estimated $46 billion in expenditures for financial assets or funds otherwise not accounted for, (d) $49 billion in revenue from interest earnings and the sale of assets, and (e) $211 billion in new debt issued. Therefore, state and local tax revenues exceed expenditures by $17 billion. This represents 1.2 percent of total revenues and could be considered as a measurement error due to difficulties in estimation as a result of the statistical nature of the data and misreporting.

Notes on the Federal Budget

1. Federal budget expenditure program totals for FY 1994 are taken from *Budget of the United States Government, FY 1996, Analytical* Perspectives (Executive Office of the President, 1996). The following lists the programs and budget item codes taken from this source: OASDI [650], HI [570], SMI [570], SSI [609], AFDC + other welfare [609 and 506], earned income tax credit [item code 609], school lunch [605], food stamps [605], energy assistance [609], rent subsidy and public housing [604], unemployment compensation [603], refugee aid [609], K-12 expenditures [501], public college [501], direct student aid [502], federal retirement [602], military retirement [602], and railroad retirement [601].

2. Federal public assistance is broadly defined to include (a) $4.7 billion for child and family services programs [code 506]; (b) $3.0 billion for payments to states for foster care and adoption assistance [code 506]; (c) $3.8 billion for social services block grants [code 506]; (d) $2.3 billion for rehabilitation services [code 506]; and (e) $16.8 billion for family support payments [code 609].

3. Federal public goods totaling $346 billion are defined to include (a) $282 billion for national defense [codes 051-054]; (b) $16 billion for general science, space, and technology [codes 251-232]; (c) $11 billion for health research and training [code 552]; and (d) $38 billion for veterans benefits and services [codes 701-705].

4. The reported outlay of $20.6 billion for public housing and rental subsidies [code 604] is allocated to public housing (30%) and rental subsidies (70%) according to the proportions observed in Table 577, *1996 US Statistical Abstract of the United States: 1996* (Bureau of the Census, 1996).

5. Program expenditures for federal incarceration costs were taken from Table 517, *Statistical Abstract of the United States: 1996* (Bureau of the Census, 1996).

6. Program expenditures for the federal and state Medicaid programs were taken from *Medicaid National Summary Statistics* (Table 1). About 25 percent of Medicaid expenditures are for the institutionalized population (Table 170, *Statistical Abstract of the United States: 1996*. Bureau of the Census, 1996).

7. Federal congestible goods were defined as a residual. Starting with total federal outlays of $1,461 billion, we subtracted (a) $203 billion in interest payments, (b) $346 billion in public goods, and (c) $809 billion in transfers (assignable costs). [Table 515, *Statistical Abstract of the United States: 1996* (Bureau of the Census, 1996)].

8. Federal tax receipts consisted of (a) FICA payroll tax, (b) income taxes, (c) corporate taxes, (d) excise taxes, (e) supplementary medical insurance (Medi-

care, Part B) contributions, and (f) other taxes. The CPS includes estimates of FICA payroll tax and federal income tax. Corporate taxes and excise taxes were assigned to individuals according to their earnings from dividends and interest as reported in the CPS. Supplementary Medical Insurance (SMI) contributions were assigned to individuals based on their participation in Medicare. Other taxes were assigned to individuals according to their federal income tax payments.

Notes on State and Local Budgets

1. We assume that revenues from corporations (income tax and estimated property and sales taxes) and revenues from charges/fees/special assessments are exactly matched by state and local government expenditures on congestibles and in-kind transfers. These revenues and the congestible goods and in-kind transfers they purchase are removed from consideration.

2. Nationally, corporations were assumed to pay 41.5 percent of total property taxes based on estimates from California (California Board of Equalization, 1995). Corporations were assumed to pay 35 percent of sales taxes based on estimates from California (Sheffrin and Dresch, 1995).

3. Transfers and congestibles purchased with federal tax dollars are also removed from the analysis of state and local budgets to avoid double counting, because we counted these expenditures as part of the federal budget.

4. We do not consider revenue nor expenditures for public employee retirement trusts.

5. State and local budget expenditure totals for FY 1993-1994 are taken from the *Annual Survey of Government Finances, 1993-94* collected by the Bureau of the Census (1997). The following lists the programs and their budget item codes taken from this source: other medical welfare [EFG32-36,74 less Medicaid expenditures]; other welfare [EFG67-79 less Medicaid expenditures]; K-12 education [EFG9-13]; public college [EFG16-21]; incarceration costs [EFG4-5]; unemployment compensation [Y05-06]; worker's compensation [Y14-15]; income taxes [T40]; property taxes [T01]; general and selective sales taxes [T09-19]; unemployment compensation contributions [Y01]; worker's compensation contributions [Y14-15]; and other taxes that include fines and forfeits [U30], rents [U40], royalties [U41], donations [U50], lottery [U95], miscellaneous general revenues [U99], death and gift taxes [T50], documentary and stock transfer taxes [T51], severance [T53], and miscellaneous taxes [T99].

6. Total expenditure data for Medicaid, SSI, AFDC, general assistance, and food stamps were taken from Table 577, *Statistical Abstract of the United States: 1996* (Bureau of the Census, 1996).

7. Of the total property taxes collected from individuals, we assumed that 64 percent was collected from homes and 36 percent from rental properties based on California data (California State Board of Equalization, 1995). Furthermore, we

assumed that 70 percent of the tax on rental properties was borne by renters, so that renters paid an estimated 25 percent of total property taxes collected from individuals.

8. The CPS had estimated taxes for income tax, property taxes, and payroll taxes. We used these estimates to assign the aggregate totals for state income tax, property tax paid by homeowners, and contributions for worker's compensation and unemployment insurance.

9. We needed to estimate taxes for property tax paid by renters, sales tax, and other taxes. We assigned property tax paid by renters by equal shares among all renters. We assigned sales tax based on household income and immigrant status using an algorithm derived by Sheffrin and Dresch (1995). We assigned other taxes in proportion to state income tax paid.

ACKNOWLEDGMENTS

We are grateful to the members and staff of the Panel on Demographic and Economic Impacts of Immigration, Michael Clune, James Smith, and an anonymous referee for helpful comments. Research for this chapter was funded by a grant from the National Institute on Aging, AG11761.

REFERENCES

Akbari, Ather H.
  1991   "The Public Finance Impact of Immigrant Population on Host Nations: Some Canadian Evidence." *Social Science Quarterly* 72(2):334-346.
Bureau of the Census
  1997   *Annual Survey of Government Finances, 1993-94.* The 1994 Finance Estimate Detail Data. Ascii file: fin94est.txt.
Bureau of the Census
  1996   *Statistical Abstract of the United States: 1996.* Washington, D.C.: U.S. Government Printing Office.
California State Board of Equalization
  1995   *Annual Report.* Sacramento.
Clark, Rebecca
  1994   "The Costs of Providing Public Assistance and Education to Immigrants." PRIP-UI-34 Program for Research on Immigration Policy, The Urban Institute, Washington, D.C.
Executive Office of the President
  1996   *Budget of the United States Government. FY1996. Analytical Perspectives.* Washington, D.C.: U.S. Government Printing Office.
Goldstein, Joshua
  1995   "From California to Florida: Interstate Wealth Flows in a Pay-as-you-go Social Security System." Paper presented at the 1995 annual meeting of the Population Association of America, San Francisco.
Health Care Financing Administration
  1997   "Medicaid National Summary Statistics." Internet site, http://www.hcfa.gov/medicaid/ 195.htm (accessed 11/17/97).

Lee, Ronald, and Timothy Miller
1997   "The Future Fiscal Impacts of Current Immigrants." Working paper of the project on Intergenerational Transfers, Department of Demography, University of California, Berkeley.
National Research Council
1997   *The New Americans: Economic, Demographic, and Fiscal Effects of Immigration.* Panel on the Demographic and Economic Impacts of Immigration. James P. Smith and Barry Edmonston, eds. Washington, D.C.: National Academy Press.
Rothman, Eric S., and Thomas J. Espenshade
1992   "Fiscal Impacts of Immigration to the United States." *Population Index* 58(3):381-415.
Sheffrin, Steven M., and Marla Dresch
1995   *Estimating the Tax Burden in California.* Berkeley: California Policy Seminar.
Social Security Administration, Office of the Actuary
1992   *Life Tables for the United States Social Security Area, 1900-2080.* Actuarial Study No. 107. (August).
Swallen, Karen Caperton
1996   "Morbidity, Mortality, and Nativity: The Influence of Early-age Effects and Health Selection on Health at Old Age." Ph.D. dissertation, Department of Demography, University of California, Berkeley.
Vernez, Georges, and Kevin F. McCarthy
1996   *The Costs of Immigration to Taxpayers: Analytical and Policy Issues.* Santa Monica, Calif.: The RAND Corporation.

6

Immigrants and Natives in General Equilibrium Trade Models

Daniel Trefler

Nothing captures the links between trade and migration better than the discussions about whether migration belonged on the North American Free Trade Agreement (NAFTA) bargaining table. On the one hand, the free flow of goods was viewed by the U.S. Commission for the Study of International Migration and Cooperative Economic Development (1990) as the single most important remedy for stemming illegal immigration. On the other hand, as was the case for U.S. citrus producers threatened by NAFTA, expanded quotas for seasonal migrants were advanced as an alternative to the free flow of goods. Stated crudely but accurately, NAFTA was often seen in terms of a trade-off between expanded imports of Mexican goods and expanded "imports" of Mexican people, legal and illegal.

Interest in trade and migration stems from the enormous disparity between U.S. and Mexican wages. For example, Samsung recently moved its picture tube production facilities from New Jersey where it paid workers $9 an hour to Tijuana where it now pays workers $1.10 an hour (*New York Times*, May 23, 1996). It would seem that even the most misguided of U.S. managers should long ago have recommended a move south. If so, *why are there any jobs left in the United States?* The Mexicans play the flip side of this sad song. If wages are so high in the United States, why are there any Mexicans left in Mexico? The answer, of course, is the focus of the NRC Panel on the Demographic and Economic Impacts of Immigration.

There are tangible concerns about the impact of trade and immigration on a U.S. labor force that is reeling from three decades of rising wage inequality. As is well known, U.S. average wages have stagnated, and the spread in wages between the highest- and lowest-paid workers has grown by 40 percent (Murphy and Welch, 1993). This has naturally led to a suspicion that competition from unskilled foreign workers is at the heart of the trend. The sense is that U.S. workers are getting the short end of the globalization stick and are victims of a U.S. immigration policy that is out of control.

This chapter is divided into two parts. The first two sections outline the incentives to migrate and the impact of immigration on native welfare and income distribution. I show how immigration changes the allocation of industry outputs and changes the terms of trade in ways that significantly alter Borjas's (1995) conclusions about the costs and benefits of immigration. There are two major lacunae in this chapter. The first deals with income redistribution through the tax system. As I document in what follows, the impact of immigrants is felt unevenly by the native population. This means that the tax system can and should be used to redistribute income from native losers to native winners. How this is best done is discussed by Wildasin (1991, 1994). The second lacuna is that all the models presented here have predictions that hinge critically on the full employment assumption. However, models of immigration and trade with unemployment are developed extensively in Razin and Sadka (1996). Their survey also deals with the fiscal burden of immigrants. In the third section I offer new empirical results about trends in earnings convergence across 75 countries and hence about the supply of immigrants to the United States. In the final section I present a new factor content study whose results significantly differ from those of previous research and point to a large negative impact of changing trade flows on America's least skilled workers. I then offer some caveats about how the lack of a well-defined policy experiment underlying the existing trade-and-wages empirical work has often led to the misinterpretation of that work.

THE IMMIGRATION SURPLUS IN A TWO-GOODS ECONOMY

Borjas (1995) made the important point that we focus on those who lose from immigration despite the fact that there are also those who benefit. In a stylish exposition, Borjas then showed that even in simple situations it is possible that the benefits created by immigration outweigh the losses. This is the "immigration surplus." Before assessing how the global environment might influence this conclusion, I present Borjas's idea. His original exposition was in terms of a single good, but because international trade requires at least two goods (exports and imports) I need an extension of his results. I do this using the specific factors model of international trade (Mayer, 1974; Mussa, 1974).

Let x and y be two industries. Each has a stock of an industry-specific factor (K_x and K_y) that has no value except when employed in its own industry. It may be capital, the industry-specific portion of a worker's human capital, union rents, etc. The other factor is labor. Labor is mobile between industries and earns wage w in both industries. The economy-wide labor supply is L of which L_x is employed in industry x and L_y in industry y. Let MP_x (K_x, L_x) be the marginal product of labor in industry x. Labor demand in industry x is calculated from the value of the marginal product of labor, $p_x MP_x (K_x, L_x)$. Panel (a) of Figure 6-1 illustrates labor demand functions for industries x and y. Industry x (y) demand is read from the left (right) origin and the length of the figure's base is the supply of labor in the economy. At wage w, labor supply (L) equals the sum of the industry labor demands $(L_x + L_y)$. The income generated by industry x is the area bounded by $O_x L_x MN$ of which $O_x L_x Mw$ goes to labor and wMN goes to the specific factor. Industry y's income of $O_y L_x MP$ is similarly divided between labor and the specific factor.

The impact of migration on native welfare depends on whether a specific factor or labor is migrating. The case of migrating labor is shown in panel (b) of Figure 6-1 as an increase in the base of the graph. Δ immigrants arrive. Industry y labor demand shifts right by Δ from $p_y MP_y$ to $p_y MP_y'$ so that it is unchanged relative to its new origin O_y'. Δ_x immigrants find employment in industry x and $\Delta - \Delta_x$ find employment in industry y. Competition between native labor and immigrants drives down the wage to w', thus transferring income $(w - w')L$ from native labor to the specific factors. Native labor loses at the expense of capital. Against this is an efficiency gain. Because immigrants complement the specific factors, immigration increases the specific factors' incomes. Net of the transfer from labor, the increases are given by the two shaded areas in Figure 6-1(b), one for industry x and one for industry y. These triangles are Borjas's "immigration surplus" generalized to two industries. Immigration of an industry-specific factor also creates an immigration surplus. In fact, that analysis is very similar to Borjas's analysis of immigrant externalities.[1] *Immigration in this setting thus appears unambiguously beneficial.*

GENERAL EQUILIBRIUM MODELS OF INTERNATIONAL TRADE

Many of the gains from immigration can be expected over the very long periods it takes for immigrants to assimilate. One would therefore need to know whether the immigration surplus exists in long-run models. Unfortunately, the specific factors model deals with the short run. It allows industry-specific factors to earn rents that are neither equalized across industries nor dissipated over time. Restated, the model does not impose the long-run equilibrium condition of zero profits. In this section I present three long-run general equilibrium models of international trade: the Heckscher-Ohlin model with its factor price equalization theorem, the Ricardian model, and a model of increasing returns to scale.

---

[1]The relevant diagram for immigration of K_x appears as Appendix Figure 6-A1. When immigrants are mobile factors and convey a positive externality, the analysis is just a mix of Figures 6-1(b) and 6-A1. The immigrants convey a surplus by complementing existing capital [Figure 6-1(b)]. In addition, the externality raises native labor productivity and so leads to the Figure 6-A1 analysis, but with both shaded areas contributing to the immigration surplus.

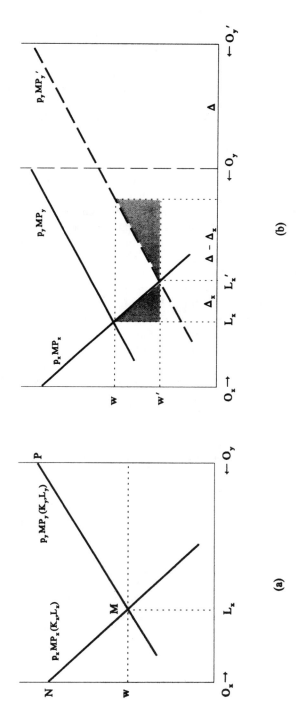

FIGURE 6-1 Immigration surplus with mobile factor migration.

Factor Price Equalization

As the short-run specificity of K_x and K_y dissolve so that capital is mobile between industries, one ends up with the long-run Heckscher-Ohlin model. In this model international trade is a source of product market competition that drives profits to zero. Zero profits in turn impose wage discipline on producers. The model makes a set of strong assumptions aimed at isolating the wage-disciplining effects of trade from all other factors. Consider a perfectly competitive world with constant returns to scale in which countries are identical in every respect except in their endowment of the two factors. In this section I call them skilled labor (S) and unskilled labor (U). Let w_S and w_U be wages for these two types. There are two goods (x and y) with prices p_x and p_y and constant returns to scale production functions $f_x(S,U)$ and $f_y(S,U)$. Figure 6-2(a) plots the unit-value isocost line giving pairs of skilled and unskilled labor costing one dollar. The figure also plots unit-value isoquants, that is, pairs of skilled and unskilled labor yielding one dollar of output. If product price p_x is high it takes very little labor to produce a dollar of output [see Figure 6-2(a)]. This leads to positive profits and industry expansion that drive down the price; conversely for low prices. The zero-profit equilibrium is illustrated by the tangency of the two curves in Figure 6-2(a). General equilibrium is illustrated in Figure 6-2(b) where industries x and y both have zero profits. As drawn, industry x is the capital-intensive industry. Because prices of goods and production functions are the same in all countries, the unit-value isoquants are the same in all countries. Because only one isocost can be tangent to both isoquants, unit-value isocosts are the same in all countries. Reading off the isocost intercepts, it follows that w_S and w_U are the same in every country. This is the factor price equalization theorem. It states that a worker earns the same in all countries. *Factor price equalization therefore implies that there are no incentives to migrate.*

Obviously, the prediction of this theorem is false. But this is the wrong criterion for evaluating it. Like all good theories, factor price equalization uses extreme assumptions to isolate just one of several determinants of international wage differences, namely, the tendency for trade with developing countries to place downward pressure on U.S. wages. The popular press terms this "leveling down." More flamboyantly, Ross Perot calls it the "giant sucking sound." Figure 6-3 explains why the theory is so compelling in a way that abstracts from mathematical detail. International trade forces producers to charge a common price for their goods. With zero profits, this means that they must all have the same production costs. This cost discipline implies, under certain restrictions, that wages will be the same in all countries. Figure 6-3 also points out other determinants of international wage differences that disguise the tendency toward factor price equalization. I do not discuss these, as the main points are either familiar, obvious, or overly technical.

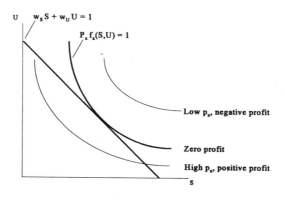

(a)

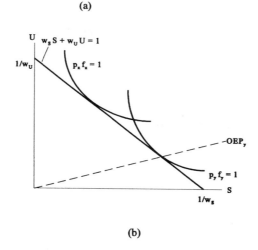

(b)

FIGURE 6-2 Factor price equalization theorem.

The Heckscher-Ohlin Model

If workers' wages are the same across countries then there is no incentive for migration. In the jargon of international trade economists, trade is a substitute for migration (see Markusen, 1983). However, it remains possible that immigration is beneficial to natives. Figure 6-2(b) illustrates an output expansion path giving the combination of skilled and unskilled worker pairs that minimize costs at wages w_S and w_U. With constant returns to scale, an output expansion path is a ray through the origin whose slope depends only on the ratio of factor prices w_S/w_U. Figure 6-4 plots the x and y output expansion paths for the United States.

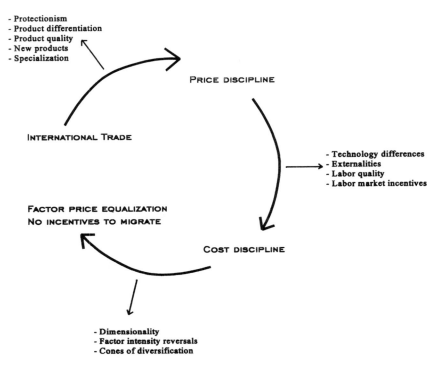

FIGURE 6-3 Factor price equalization.

Point E_0 illustrates the U.S. endowment of skilled and unskilled labor. In a full employment equilibrium all these workers must be employed. This occurs only if industry x employs the combination of skilled and unskilled workers given by x_0 and industry y employs the combination of workers given by $E_0 - x_0$. Suppose the United States allows immigration of unskilled Mexican labor so that E_0 moves to E_1 and x_0 moves to x_1. Figure 6-4 illustrates what happens in Mexico. Assume initially that factor price equalization holds so that the Mexican and U.S. expansion paths are identical. Because Mexican emigrants are U.S. immigrants, $E_1 - E_0$ equals $E_0^* - E_1^*$. Assume momentarily that the migration leaves wages and hence expansion paths unaltered. Then $x_0 + x_0^*$ must equal $x_1 + x_1^*$; likewise in the y industry.[2] That is, total inputs into each industry are unaltered. Consequently, so are total outputs. Because earnings are the same, product markets clear at the old product prices. But if product prices do not change, then factor prices do not change [see proof of factor price equalization in Figure 6-2(b)]. Migration is consistent with unchanged product and factor prices. *Thus,*

---

[2]For the y industry $(E_0 - x_0) + (E_0^* - x_0^*)$ must equal $(E_1 - x_1) + (E_1^* - x_1^*)$.

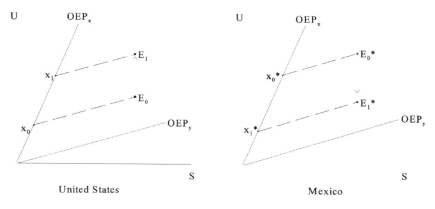

FIGURE 6-4 Migration in a Heckscher-Ohlin model.

in this model, immigration has zero welfare implications for both natives and immigrants. The immigration surplus is zero.

Modified Factor Price Equalization and the Heckscher-Ohlin Model

The previous model can be modified to allow for international differences in factor quality and technology. Let π_c be a measure of productivity in country c and let $\pi_c f_g(S,U)$ be country c's production function for good g (g = x, y). Unlike the Heckscher-Ohlin model, there are international technology differences as indicated by the π_c.[3] With constant returns to scale, $\pi_c f_g(S,U) = f_g(\pi_c S, \pi_c U)$. Thus, another interpretation of the π_c is that they capture international differences in input quality (e.g., better labor market incentives or higher school quality). Let S_c be the national endowment. $S_c^* \equiv \pi_c S_c$ is the national endowment measured in internationally comparable or productivity-adjusted units. One unit of S_c^* is equivalent to $1/\pi_c$ units of S_c (i.e., $S_c = S_c^*/\pi_c$). Because one unit of S_c earns w_{Sc}, it follows that one unit of S_c^* earns w_{Sc}/π_c; likewise for $U_c^* \equiv \pi_c U_c$ and w_{Uc}/π_c.

The amended model is exactly the same as the original Heckscher-Ohlin model but with (S_c^*, U_c^*) replacing (S_c, U_c) and (w_{Sc}/π_c, w_{Uc}/π_c) replacing (w_{Sc}, w_{Uc}).[4] Thus, factor price equalization holds for productivity-adjusted wages:

$$w_{Sc}/\pi_c = w_{S,US}/\pi_{US} \quad \text{for all c.} \tag{1}$$

---

[3]In Trefler (1993b, 1995) I considered the more general model $f_g(\pi_{Sc} S, \pi_{Uc}U)$. This allows for *Hicks non-neutral* factor-augmenting international technology differences.

[4]For example, Figure 6-2 has unit-value isoquants $p_x f_x(S^*,U^*) = 1$ and unit-value isocost line $(w_{Sc}/\pi_c)S^* + (w_{Uc}/\pi_c)U^* = 1$. It follows that (w_{Sc}/π_c) and (w_{Uc}/π_c) are equalized across countries.

To understand this, if country c labor were half as productive as U.S. labor (π_c / π_{US} = $^1/_2$), then one would expect country c wages to be half the U.S. wage (w_{Sc} = $w_{S,US}\, \pi_c/\pi_{US}$). Also, the Heckscher-Ohlin prediction about location of production and patterns of trade holds, but again with (S_c ,U_c) replaced by (S_c^*,U_c^*).

This amendment is important empirically. Factor price equalization and the Heckscher-Ohlin predictions do not work well empirically (Trefler, 1995). On the other hand, the above modification does work well. Specifically, in Trefler (1993b) I calculated the unique π_c /π_{US} that make the Heckscher-Ohlin prediction work perfectly for aggregate labor. I then showed that equation (1) holds almost exactly when the calculated π_c /π_{US} are plugged in. Figure 6-5 plots relative wages w_c /w_{US} against π_c /π_{US}. Modified factor price equalization [equation (1)]

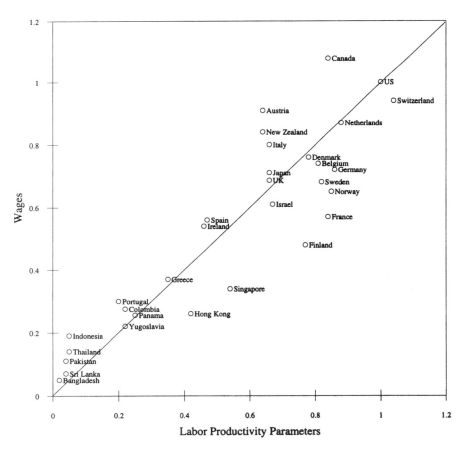

FIGURE 6-5 Modified factor price equalization.

implies that all the data should lie along the 45° line as is in fact the case. This kills two birds with one stone: both the factor price equalization and the Heckscher-Ohlin model work well empirically after a slight amendment that accounts for international technology or input quality differences.

Such a model may lead to predictions about the impact of immigration that are very different from those of the textbook Heckscher-Ohlin model. Consider a skilled worker deciding whether or not to migrate from his or her low-productivity country to the United States. If π_c is an attribute of the worker (e.g., a poor education) then a migrant will have low productivity no matter which country he or she works in and so will not earn more in the United States. There will be no incentive to migrate and no labor market impacts of migration. On the other hand, if productivity is an attribute of the country (e.g., poor labor market incentives) then the worker will earn more in the United States and so will have an incentive to migrate. Suppose skilled workers migrate to the United States and become more productive. This is equivalent to increasing the world supply of skilled workers relative to that of unskilled workers. This expands world production of good x relative to good y (the Rybczynski effect). As a result, p_x/p_y falls. This reduces real wages of skilled natives and raises real wages of unskilled natives (the Stolper-Samuelson theorem). Once again, general equilibrium models of migration yield impact channels very different from those outlined by Borjas (1995). In this case, migration changes migrants' productivity and thus affects the terms of trade.

The Ricardian Model

To focus more clearly on the terms-of-trade effect, consider a long-run, zero-profit economy in which labor is the only productive input. Let g index goods. One unit of output is produced using a_g units of labor. Restated, $1/a_g$ is both labor productivity as well as the marginal product of labor. I use an asterisk to denote foreign country values (e.g., a_g^*). Following Dornbusch et al. (1977), I order the goods index g so that

$$a_1/a_1^* < \ ... \ < a_{g'}/a_{g'}^* < \ ... \ < a_G/a_G^* . \qquad (2)$$

For some g', the home country is said to have a comparative advantage in goods $g \leq g'$. This implies that the home country exports goods $g \leq g'$ and imports goods $g > g'$. Let w and w^* be wages in the two countries.

For long-run zero profits the price of good g (p_g) must equal the cost of producing one unit of good g (wa_g or $w^* a_g^*$). I write $w/p_g > 1/a_g$ to denote zero profits and $w/p_g > 1/a_g$ to denote losses. For almost all parameter values each good will be produced in only one country. This production specialization result is very different from what was assumed in the Heckscher-Ohlin model and frees the model from the factor-price-equalization straightjacket. If $w/p_g = 1/a_g$ then the home country produces good g, not the foreign country. If $w/p_g > 1/a_g$ then the foreign country produces good g, not the home country. For simplicity, assume that there are three goods and that initially the home country produces only good 1.

Consider the effect of immigration.[5] The immigrants are employed producing good 1, thus creating excess supply of the good at prevailing prices. The resulting home trade deficit drives down the home wage until $w/p_2 = 1/a_2$. At that point the home country produces good 2. Likewise, in the foreign country w* rises until industry 2 shuts down. What has happened to real wages and per capita native utility? It is simple enough to show that there is a fall in w/p_2 and w/p_3 and no change in w/p_1.[6] Thus, w has fallen relative to any basket of consumer prices. The first conclusion is that migration lowers per capita native welfare. That is, Borjas's immigration "surplus" is negative. *To be crystal clear, the negative immigration "surplus" is driven by the fact that immigration adversely affects the home country's terms of trade.* Because immigrant and native labor compete for the same jobs at the same wages, the home country can only absorb the immigrants in low-productivity industries that spring up in response to immigration. One should think of these industries as garments or citrus fruit industries that would disappear in the absence of migrant workers. There are no downward-sloping labor demand functions as in Borjas's analysis, only general equilibrium industrial reallocations between countries in response to changes in the terms of trade.[7]

External Increasing Returns to Scale

Increasing returns to scale potentially generate an immigration surplus. One sees this in the opening up of prairie agriculture: without mass immigration there would not have been large enough grain production to warrant investment in transportation infrastructure. In this subsection I examine the immigration surplus in a long-run increasing returns to scale model. In particular, I consider Helpman's (1984) general equilibrium model in which perfect competition is preserved by assuming that returns to scale are external to the firm.

---

[5]The analysis that follows is informal. A strict statement of results, and one that holds for a continuum of goods rather than three goods, can be found in Dornbusch et al. (1977). The importance of Cobb-Douglas preferences is clearly explained in that paper. I therefore do not deal with the issue here.

[6]The proof is as follows. Because home always produces good 1, $w/p_1 = 1/a_1$ is unchanged by migration. w/p_2 has fallen to $1/a_2$. Because w* has risen and $w*/p_3 = 1/a_3^*$ is unchanged, p_3 has risen. Hence, w/p_3 has fallen.

[7]There is a second conclusion, this one regarding the incentives to migrate and hence the pool of potential migrants. Assume that migration is from poor to rich countries (w > w*). Migration causes w and per capita native utility to fall. Symmetrically, it causes w* and per capita foreign utility to rise. Hence, migration unambiguously leads to international convergence of wages and per capita utility. This is particularly surprising in view of the fact that increased trade flows need not lead to increased convergence of wages or utility (Dixit and Norman, 1980).

Labor is the only factor and national labor supply is denoted L in the United States and L* in the foreign country. There are two goods, x and y. One unit of y is produced with one unit of labor. Let L_j be the amount of labor employed by firm j, let x_j be firms j's output, and let $x = \Sigma_j x_j$ be industry output. Firm j's production function is $x_j = x^{1/2} L_j$. The term $x^{1/2}$ captures increasing returns to scale. Scale returns are external to the firm in the sense that each firm treats $x^{1/2}$ as if it were exogenous. Demand is given by a representative consumer with Cobb-Douglas preferences.

There are many equilibria in this model including ones that display factor price equalization and the Heckscher-Ohlin result that immigration has no impact on native welfare (see Appendix Table 6-A1 for a description of such an equilibrium). An equilibrium with a Ricardian terms-of-trade flavor is one in which the United States produces only x and the foreign country produces only y. Immigration has two impacts. First, immigration increases native productivity. To see this sum, $x_j = x^{1/2} L_j$ across firms, I use $\Sigma_j L_j = L$ to obtain $x = x^{1/2} L$, or $x = L^2$, or finally $x/L = L$. That is, U.S. productivity x/L rises with the size of the labor force L. It follows that immigration improves native productivity and hence welfare by increasing the labor force. Second, immigration expands output of x. This leads to a fall in the price of x because output expansion leads to lower units costs that zero-profit firms pass on to consumers and because consumers need lower prices as an inducement to purchase more. The fall in the price of x is a negative terms-of-trade shift that reduces native welfare. It follows that there is a trade-off between the terms-of-trade effect and the productivity effect. A diminishing marginal rate of substitution in consumption implies that the negative terms-of-trade effect grows faster than the positive productivity effect. This leads to an optimal level of immigration (possibly zero) beyond which new immigrants reduce native welfare. This is illustrated in Figure 6-6, which plots per capita native utility against the ratio of immigrants to natives. The dashed curve involves a scenario with high demand for x relative to population size. Immigration improves native welfare at low levels of immigration, but worsens it beyond the socially optimal level of 35 immigrants per 100 natives. The solid curve involves a scenario with low demand for x relative to population size.[8] With a large native work force, the socially optimal level of immigration is zero. The conclusion to be drawn is that immigration policy should target immigrants who, perhaps because of rare skills, are likely to establish new industries that interact synergistically with existing ones. Being a new industry, the terms-of-trade effect will be negligible. A good example is Russian emigrés to Israel who set up the Israeli software industry.

---

[8]See Appendix Table 6-A1 for an algebraic expression for per capita native utility. In both scenarios, L + L* = 1. In the dashed curve scenario, L = 0.4 and the Cobb-Douglas consumption share for x is 0.8. In the solid curve scenario, L = 0.67 and the consumption share for x is 0.75. The solid line terminates early on because beyond a certain level of immigration the foreign country does not have enough workers to meet world demand for y, and the specialization equilibrium disappears.

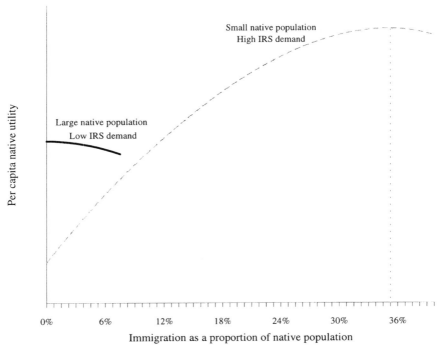

FIGURE 6-6 Effect of immigration with increasing returns to scale (IRS).

Demand-Side Models

Much of the analysis of this section has used the assumption that immigrants and natives consume the same bundle of goods. This assumption of consumption similarity is central to general equilibrium trade models for a simple reason. A country's industrial output is either consumed domestically or exported. Most trade theories begin by predicting a country's structure of industrial output. Predictions about industrial structure are then translated into predictions about trade flows by assuming that countries have similar consumption. This point is the main focus of Trefler (1996). There is, however, empirical evidence that immigrants affect trade patterns in ways that violate the assumption of consumption similarity. For example, immigrants' consumption patterns differ from those of natives so that immigrants demand more foreign goods. Also, immigrants import more from their countries of origin because of immigrant social networks (see Baker and Benjamin, 1996).

Conclusions

We tend to focus on those who lose from immigration and ignore those who gain. Borjas (1995) showed that in simple situations the gainers outweigh the losers and there is an immigration surplus. Although the insight holds in at least one short-run general equilibrium model of international trade (the specific factors model), it need not hold in long-run, zero-profit models. In models displaying factor price equalization, zero profits pin down wages so that immigration has no effects. This radically differs from Borjas's (1995) conclusion. The intense product market competition and ensuing wage discipline associated with factor price equalization are most common in low- and mid-level manufactures. One should therefore not expect much from an immigration policy that merely provides excess labor supply for these industries. In the Ricardian model, immigration adversely affects the home country's terms of trade, which unambiguously reduces native welfare while at the same time "ghettoizing" immigrants in low-productivity industries such as garments and citrus picking. These industries would otherwise disappear in the absence of immigrant labor. I doubt that the terms-of-trade effects are large enough to seriously reduce native welfare. Evidence from studies of trade liberalization indicates that the U.S. terms of trade are driven by the dynamics of new product introduction, not immigration. I find ghettoization to be a more significant problem. Finally, with increasing returns to scale the adverse Ricardian terms-of-trade effect is partially mitigated by an immigrant externality. Provided that immigrants bring skills that enhance the productivity of natives, immigration can improve native welfare.

CHANGING INCENTIVES FOR MIGRATION: EVIDENCE ON FACTOR PRICE CONVERGENCE

Given the central role of factor price equalization in determining whether there is an immigration surplus, it is worth reviewing the extent to which wages differ across countries and whether there is any tendency for wages or skill prices to converge over time. We do not know exactly how unequal the wages are because we do not have comprehensive data on international wage differences purged of human capital and other effects. However, international wage differences seem too large to be accounted for solely by such effects. For example, Filipino migrant bricklayers earn three times more in Singapore than in Manilla and eight times more in Japan (see Appendix Table 6-A2 for details). By implication, there are large incentives to migrate and select the best host country.

Evidence on cross-country wage convergence can be garnered from the UNIDO INDSTAT database. The data are based on manufacturing surveys of payroll and employment to which UNIDO introduced a degree of international comparability. I cleaned this data set, applied purchasing power party corrections, and subjected it to internal and external validation. The data consist of 75

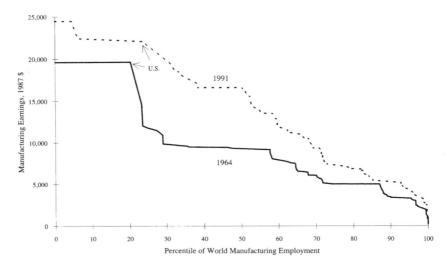

FIGURE 6-7 Lorenz curve (Leamer's waterfalls).

countries over the period 1963-1992. They are informative about broad differences in the earnings of widely divergent economies. Details for any individual country should be treated with caution. Full data documentation will appear in a separate paper. The data have been smoothed by a three-year moving average. In what follows, years refer to the midpoint of the three-year average.

Figure 6-7 reports a variant of a Lorenz curve or Leamer (1992) "waterfall" for the years 1964 and 1991. Each "kink" in the curve represents a data point for one of the 75 countries. For example, in 1964 U.S. average manufacturing earnings were $19,600, and the United States accounted for 25 percent of world manufacturing employment. In contrast, Japanese earnings averaged $5,000, and Japan accounted for 13 percent of world manufacturing employment. The 1964 data document substantial international earnings differences. Leamer encourages us to see the 1964 curve as a waterfall seeking a flat level, that is, seeking earnings equalization in manufacturing. The impression is that equalization would require U.S. wages to fall sharply but developing country earnings to rise only slightly. The 1991 curve shows no such pattern. If so, then pressures for migration to the United States remain similar to what they were 30 years ago. Unfortunately, this evidence regarding failure of earnings convergence is not persuasive. Convergence may have been disguised by opposing movements in unobservables such as capital accumulation, human capital accumulation, other sources of worker heterogeneity, anomalies in global integration, and transition dynamics. In the next two subsections I attempt to control for some, though not all, of these potentially offsetting factors.

Worker Sorting

Industry of affiliation conveys two pieces of information about the sources of earnings dispersion. First, workers sort across industries based on unobservable characteristics such as education. Second, certain industry characteristics such as capital intensity are likely to be common across countries. Thus, industry of affiliation offers an ad hoc control for unobserved worker and industry characteristics. To exploit this I consider a within-industry variance decomposition of earnings. Let g index industries, c index countries, and t index time. Let e_{gct} be employment and let w_{gct} be log earnings where the italics denote logs. Let $e_{ct} = \Sigma_g e_{gct}$, $e_{gt} = \Sigma_c e_{gct}$, $e_t = \Sigma_{c,g} e_{gct}$, $w_{ct} = \Sigma_g w_{gct} e_{gct}/e_{ct}$, $w_{gt} = \Sigma_c w_{gct} e_{gct}/e_{gt}$, and $w_t = \Sigma_{c,g} w_{gct} e_{gct}/e_t$. The variance of log earnings between countries is

$$\sigma_t^2 = \Sigma_c (w_{ct} - w_t)^2 e_{ct}/e_t. \qquad (3)$$

Within-industry variance is defined as

$$\sigma^2_{Wt} = \Sigma_g \{\Sigma_c (w_{gct} - w_{gt})^2 e_{gct}/e_t\}. \qquad (4)$$

The term in braces is like σ_t^2 except that in equation (4) one centers around a single industry rather than around the average across industries. σ_t^2 and σ^2_{Wt} are reported in Table 6-1. In 1964 the standard error of log earnings across the 75 countries was 62 log points. This is comparable in size with the 70-30 log wage differential in the United States (Murphy and Welch, 1993). More important, there is no tendency toward earnings equalization for either between-country or within-industry standard errors.

In searching for convergence, the Heckscher-Ohlin model predicts that trade liberalization and factor accumulation will lead to changing industrial composition. This implies that variation in the employment weights of equations (3) and

TABLE 6-1 Standard Error of Log Earnings

	1964	1991	1991-1964
TIME-VARYING EMPLOYMENT WEIGHTS			
Between-country (σ_t)	0.62	0.65	0.03
Within-industry (σ_{Wt})	0.60	0.60	−0.01
Within-HK-K ($\sigma_{\omega t}$)	0.35	0.37	0.02
FIXED (1991) EMPLOYMENT WEIGHTS			
Between-country (σ_{Ft})	0.74	0.65	−0.09
Within-industry (σ_{WFt})	0.76	0.60	−0.16
Within-HK-K ($\sigma_{\omega Ft}$)	0.40	0.37	−0.03

NOTES: σ_t and σ_{Wt} are defined in equations (3) and (4), respectively. $\sigma_{\omega t}$ uses equation (3), but replaces w_{ct} with human and physical capital adjusted earnings i.e., with the estimated country fixed effects from equation (6). For $\sigma_{\omega t}$ and $\sigma_{\omega Ft}$, 1964 refers to the period 1963-72 and 1991 refers to the period 1983-92.

(4) is economically meaningful. To control for this I consider an Oaxaca or fixed-weight decomposition based on $\sigma^2_{W91} - \sigma^2_{Wt}$ and report only the fixed-weight variance:

$$\sigma^2_{WFt} = \Sigma_g \{\Sigma_c (w_{gct} - w_{gt})^2 \, e_{gc1991}/e_{1991}\} . \tag{5}$$

σ_{WFt} is reported in Table 6-1. The striking feature is that during 1964-1991 the standard error of log earnings fell from 0.75 to 0.60 or 16 log points. Why fixing weights is so important is a question that Joe Hotz and I are actively pursuing. At any rate, this is the only evidence I have presented so far of earnings convergence.

Human and Physical Capital Formation

In the absence of labor force surveys of worker characteristics and manufacturing surveys of capital and other nonlabor inputs, it is impossible to adequately purge the earnings data of the human and physical capital effects that contribute to international earnings differences. As a second-best alternative, I control for human and physical capital by regressing the UNIDO manufacturing earnings data on the economy-wide stocks of education (Barro and Lee, 1993) and capital (Summers and Heston, 1991). In country c in year t let E_{ict} be the population 25 years and older with education level i. There are four schooling categories: no education, primary education (usually grades 1-6), secondary education (usually grades 7-12), and some tertiary or college education (usually years 13+). Let K_{ct} and L_{ct} be the capital stock and population aged at least 25, respectively. I consider the regression

$$w_{ct} = \Sigma_i \beta_i (E_{ict}/L_{ct}) + \Sigma_i \beta_{Ki}(E_{ict}/L_{ct})(K_{ct}/L_{ct}) + \beta_K(K_{ct}/L_{ct}) + \omega_c + \varepsilon_{ct} \tag{6}$$

where w_{ct} is log wages and ω_c is a country fixed effect to be estimated. ω_c captures a variety of errors in the specification of equation (6). However, I heroically interpret it as the country average log wage after netting out international differences in human and physical capital. Thus, I refer to ω_c as the adjusted log wage. Our method here is similar to the way in which labor economists construct indicators for local labor markets (see Card and Krueger, 1992). In these studies the authors usually include quadratic and even cubic terms of the education variables. We have not tried this. Table 6-1 reports the variance decomposition for ω_c when estimated separately for the periods 1963-1972 and 1983-1992. By construction, the estimated ω_c must have a smaller standard error than the w_{ct} (after averaging across years). In fact, the standard error is almost half, suggesting that human and physical capital explain about half of the observed earnings dispersion. More important though, there is no strong evidence of convergence over time even when using fixed 1991 employment weights.

Conclusions

Given the rapid pace of globalization I am surprised that evidence of manufacturing earnings convergence is so difficult to find. It thus appears that supply pressures for migration to the United States remain strong and show little or no tendency to diminish over time.

TRADE, IMMIGRATION, AND WAGES

The debate about the extent to which trade and immigration have led to rising wage inequality in the United States has been one of the most fruitful empirical debates in international trade. In this section I briefly review the debate, present some new evidence, itemize differences in the way trade and immigration are expected to impact on native wages, and offer some methodological observations about constructing an econometric experiment that captures the impact of proposed trade and immigration policies.

Sources of Rising Wage Inequality

There are four contenders for the privileged position of having "immiserized" unskilled U.S. labor. The first is *immigration*. Borjas (1987) showed that immigrant cohorts have been increasingly unskilled. In addition, immigration levels tripled between 1988 and 1991. The second is *international trade*. There is a coincidence of globalization, the U.S. trade deficit, and rising U.S. wage inequality (e.g., Borjas and Ramey, 1993). The third is *technology-induced skill upgrading,* which has raised the demand for skilled workers relative to unskilled workers (e.g., Berman et al., 1994; Krueger, 1993; and Katz and Murphy, 1992). The fourth is capital deepening associated with a *falling price of physical capital.* To the extent that capital complements skilled labor and substitutes for unskilled labor (Goldin and Katz, 1996), capital deepening displaces unskilled labor and increases demand for skilled labor. The mainstream view among economists of the sources of rising wage inequality is that skill upgrading was far more important than immigration, which in turn was somewhat more important than international trade. The capital deepening hypothesis has not yet been investigated adequately.

Trade and Wages

Among the many arguments that have been advanced about the role of international trade, let me single out a few that support the mainstream view that trade is unimportant. *(1) The timing is wrong for trade arguments.* Juhn et al. (1993) used a variance decomposition to show that the rise in inequality is largely due to factors other than education and experience and that this residual component of inequality began rising long before the major trade events of the late 1970s. *(2) Trade is too small a component of the U.S. economy to explain major changes in the domestic economy.* Krugman and Lawrence (1994) pointed out that the sector of the U.S. economy directly exposed to trade employs only about 20 percent of the work force. They argued that this 20 percent tail cannot wag the dog. Although persuasive, this argument suffers from a lack of theoretical support. It is easy to construct theoretical models in which the tail does wag the dog. For example, the Stolper-Samuelson impact of changing import prices on wage inequality can be made arbitrarily large simply by making the ratio of skilled to unskilled labor arbitrarily similar across industries. Even when countries do not produce the same range of goods so that the Stolper-Samuelson theorem no longer holds, wages are determined at the margin, and what may matter is how substitutable the marginal U.S. worker is with foreign workers (Leamer, 1996). *(3) Rising wage inequality and skill upgrading have occurred within industries, not between industries* (Davis and Haltiwanger, 1991). In the Heckscher-Ohlin model a fall in the price of the unskilled-intensive good drives down the unskilled wage. This leads firms to (a) hire unskilled workers and fire skilled workers and (b) expand output of skill-intensive industries to fully employ laid-off skilled workers. Both predictions are wrong empirically.[9] An implication of this argument is that *Stolper-Samuelson effects must have been small.* Indeed, a number of studies have shown that product price movements have not been strong enough to entail large Stolper-Samuelson effects (e.g., Sachs and Shatz, 1994), though in view of data problems this empirical result may be misleading. To summarize, there are a number of persuasive arguments, none of them knockouts, that trade has not contributed significantly to rising wage inequality.

It is perhaps worth noting that changes in protection and exchange rates cannot readily explain average wage changes. Gaston and Trefler (1994, 1995) argued that U.S. levels of protection have been too small to explain average wage developments. This is true in spite of Trefler's (1993a) finding that the import-reducing effects of protection are much greater than previously thought. Revenga (1992) finds some evidence that the run-up of the dollar in the first half of the 1980s depressed U.S. wages.

Trade and Wages: A New Factor Content Study

The view that the tail cannot wag the dog has been confirmed in a number of factor content studies (e.g., Borjas et al., 1992). In this subsection I explain what a factor content study is and offer a challenge to existing studies. Let g index

---

[9]Again, this is not entirely persuasive. Feenstra and Hanson (1996) considered the following model. Every industry includes both unskilled processes (assembly) and skilled processes (design). Offshore sourcing sends the low-skill processes abroad. This raises the average skill level of processes that remain in the United States and exposes unskilled U.S. workers to greater foreign competition (i.e., offshore sourcing explains within-industry skill upgrading and rising wage inequality).

industries, t index time, and i index the level of education. Let $a_{gt}^d(i)$ be the amount of type i labor needed to produce one unit of good g in year t. Following the convention among labor economists, $a_{gt}^d(i)$ is defined as the amount of type i labor employed in industry g divided by industry output. In input-output terminology this is the "direct" input coefficient, hence the d superscript. The factor content of trade is the derived demand for labor induced by observed trade flows. Let $L_t(i)$ be employment of type i labor in year t and let M_{gt} and T_{gt} be imports and net imports, respectively. Then expressed as a proportion of employment, the factor content of imports and net imports is calculated as

$$FM_t^d(i) = \Sigma_g\, a_{gt}^d(i)\, M_{gt}\, /L_t(i) \quad \text{and} \quad FT_t^d(i) = \Sigma_g a_{gt}^d(i)\, T_{gt}\, /L_t(i). \qquad (7)$$

$FT_{92}^d(i) - FT_{72}^d(i)$ is the change in demand for type i labor associated with the changing pattern of trade flows over the period 1972-1992. This interpretation is subject to a number of caveats that I will return to.

To calculate the factor content of trade, I use data for 103 trading partners accounting for well over 95 percent of U.S. trade. Trade data are from Statistic Canada's World Trade Data Base. The input coefficients are from the U.S. input-output benchmark tables, the U.S. Department of Commerce's Employment and Earnings series, and the Current Population Survey. In each case 1972 and 1992 data were used. Nominal data were double deflated as is required for input-output analysis.

Table 6-2 reports new calculations of the factor content of net imports and imports in 1992, and the change during 1972-1992. These appear in the four "direct" columns. The key column is that associated with "net imports, 1992-1972." For example, the all-labor factor content of net imports rose by 0.2 percentage points between 1972 and 1992, indicating that changing trade patterns have augmented the U.S. labor force by 0.2 percentage points. The numbers are uniformly small for all types of labor indicating that *trade has had little impact.* This would have been the conclusion of Borjas et al. (1992) had they continued their analysis to 1992 instead of ending in 1986, a year with a large trade deficit.

A problem with this factor content calculation is that it uses direct or partial equilibrium employment output ratios. This ignores Leontief's general equilibrium interactions in the economy. For example, producing steel requires inputs of transportation equipment which in turn requires more steel. Input-output analysis sums the direct and indirect effects to obtain "total" or general equilibrium effects. Let $a_{gt}^t(i)$ be this total labor demand induced by producing one unit of output for final demand. Factor content calculations based on $a_{gt}^t(i)$ are reported in the four "total" columns of Table 6-2. Using total requirements, the 1972-1992 change in trade patterns led to no change in the factor content of net imports (0.0%) despite a large increase in the factor content of imports (6.2%).

Wood (1994) initiated an interesting challenge to the factor content literature. He argued that both $a_{gt}^d(i)$ and $a_{gt}^t(i)$ are applied inappropriately. Although there are several elements to the argument, the one I find most intriguing is that a

TABLE 6-2 The Factor Content of Net Imports and Imports

Net Imports

Education	1992 - 1972				1992			
	employment (1000s)	direct %	total %	adjusted %	employment (1000s)	direct %	total %	adjusted %
None	−236	−6.3	−7.7	168.6	921	1.3	1.5	343.6
Primary	−12,198	0.7	0.4	37.0	8,674	1.6	1.8	37.7
Secondary (entered)	5,430	0.7	0.5	4.7	25,947	1.0	1.3	4.8
Secondary (complete)	17,588	0.4	0.3	−5.6	45,005	0.6	0.7	−9.4
College	22,909	0.1	0.0	−3.7	44,655	0.1	0.2	−5.6
All Labor	33,492	0.2	0.0	0.0	125,201	0.5	0.6	0.6

Imports

Education	1992 - 1972				1992			
	employment (1000s)	direct %	total %	adjusted %	employment (1000s)	direct %	total %	adjusted %
None	−236	−5.8	−5.6	170.8	921	6.2	12.3	354.3
Primary	−12,198	4.9	9.1	45.7	8,674	8.2	15.7	51.6
Secondary (entered)	5,430	3.1	6.8	10.9	25,947	5.7	12.4	16.0
Secondary (complete)	17,588	3.6	7.6	1.7	45,005	5.9	12.9	2.7
College	22,909	2.4	5.7	2.1	44,655	4.0	9.4	3.6
All Labor	33,492	2.8	6.2	6.2	125,201	5.0	11.2	11.2

NOTES: See equation (7).

job performed by a high school dropout in the United States is probably performed by a primary school dropout in India. Feenstra and Hanson (1996) offered a complementary argument. Every industry includes both unskilled processes such as assembly and skilled processes such as design. Offshore sourcing sends the low-skill processes abroad so that imports are produced with much less skilled labor than are exports. For trade with developing countries, the factor content of trade is thus biased up for skilled labor and biased down for unskilled labor.

To implement this line of reasoning consider panel A of Table 6-3. I made up the numbers so as to simplify the presentation. In India, 25 percent of the population aged 25 or more has no education. In the United States, 25 percent of the population aged 25 or more has a secondary (entered) education or less (25% = 0% + 10% + 15%). I assume that what matters is one's position in the education distribution, not one's absolute level of education. For example, a job done by a U.S. worker with a secondary (entered) education or less is done by an Indian worker with no education. Panel A in Table 6-3 also gives a hypothetical example for the textiles industry. Suppose that production of one dollar of textiles in the United States requires 0.12 (= 0.00 + 0.02 + 0.10) workers with a secondary (entered) education or less. I assume that production of one dollar of textiles in India requires 0.12 workers with no education. Likewise, college U.S. jobs are assumed to be secondary (entered) Indian jobs. In practice, these adjustments were done for groups of countries and appear in Panel B in Table 6-3. For example, a job done by a U.S. worker with a secondary (completed) education is done in a high-income country by a worker with a secondary (entered) education and done in a middle-income country by a worker with a primary education. It is surprising how the education distribution of the U.S. is so "right-shifted" compared with other countries—U.S. education levels are high. This leads me to the conclusion that the adjustments may be exaggerated. To investigate further, consider in Panel B in Table 6-3 the "Import Shares" columns. Sixty-five percent of U.S. imports come from high-income countries and face almost no adjustment. Moreover, this number has changed only a little since 1972. Low-income countries have only a small share of imports, and oil exporters produce very capital-intensive goods so that the adjustments can only have a limited effect. If the adjustments are to matter, it is for middle-income countries. But even here the change in import share is only 10 percent which in turn is only a small fraction of U.S. gross domestic product. Thus, it is by no means obvious that the adjustment will matter.

There is a basic asymmetry between imports and exports. Consider industry g. We observe $a_{gt}^t(i)$, the amount of type i labor used in observed U.S. production. Imports use less of educated labor and more of uneducated labor than is given by $a_{gt}^t(i)$. This is because the United States imports unskilled processes. I therefore use the adjustment in Panel B in Table 6-3 to calculate the type i factor content of imports from country c. On the other hand, exports probably use

TABLE 6-3 Method for Adjusting Labor Input Requirements

A. Hypothetical Example

	None	Primary	Secondary – Entered	Secondary – Complete	College – Complete	College
Educational Attainment in Population 25+						
United States[a]	0%	10%	15%	35%	40%	
India[a]	25%	35%	40%	0%	0%	
Educational Attainment in Textiles ($a^t_{gt}(i)$)						
United States[b]	.00	.02	.10	.05		.03
India[b]	.12	.05	.03	.00		.00

B. Actual Adjustments

Country[c]	Import Shares 1992	Import Shares 1972	None (N)	Primary (P)	Secondary Entered (SE)	Secondary Complete (SC)	College Entered (CE)	College Completed (CC)
Above Example			N	N	N	P	SE	SE
High Income	65%	72%	N	N	P	SE	SC	CE
Middle Income	16%	6%	N	N	N	P	P	SE
Low Income	10%	13%	N	N	N	N	P	P
Oil and CME	9%	9%	N	N	N	P	P	P

a) Data are percent so that each row sums to 100%.
b) Data are in numbers of workers per dollar of textile output.
c) The World Bank country classifications are followed closely, but not exactly.

somewhat more of educated labor and somewhat less of uneducated labor than is given by $a_{gt}^t(i)$, because exports consist of skilled processes. To weaken my argument I nevertheless use $a_{gt}^t(i)$ to calculate the type i factor content of exports. By construction, the modification makes no difference to "all labor."

Factor contents calculated in this way are reported in the four Table 6-2 "adjusted" columns. *It is remarkable that the no-education labor content of U.S. net imports grew an enormous 168.6 percentage points.* It was 343.6 percent of the no-education labor force in 1992, up from 175 percent in 1972 (not reported). For primary education the increase was 37.0 percentage points. Surprisingly, there are even interesting results for skilled labor. The college labor content of net imports fell by 3.7 percentage points. The results are the same when oil producers and nonmarket economies are omitted. I do not think that this exercise is rigged to obtain big impacts. I therefore find the conclusions startling.

Can these trade-induced supply changes account for wage trends in the United States? Like a bull in a china shop, let me push forward while deferring discussion of the myriad of caveats. We know the horizontal shift in demand induced by setting the factor content of trade back to its 1972 level [$-\Delta FT(i)$ from Table 6-2]. We also know 1992 employment levels [$L_{92}(i)$ from Table 6-2] and have estimates of the elasticities of labor demand $\varepsilon_D(i)$ and supply $\varepsilon_S(i)$. The percentage change in wages induced by changes in the factor content of trade is thus [10]

$$\Delta w(i) \equiv [w_{92}(i) - w_{72}(i)]/w_{92}(i) = [-\Delta FT(i)/L_{92}(i)]/[\varepsilon_D(i) + \varepsilon_S(i)]. \quad (8)$$

Table 6-4 reports the values of $\Delta w(i)$ for the adjusted factor content calculations, i.e., for the $\Delta FT(i)$ given by the Table 6-2 column labeled "net imports, 1992-1972, adjusted." Because elasticities are not known with certainty, I report results for different estimates. The first and third rows are extreme combinations of estimates and provide upper and lower bounds on the wage movements. The middle row elasticity estimates of 0.75 for labor demand and 0.5 for labor supply are more common. In the middle row experiment, changing trade patterns reduce wages of primary education workers by 30 percent and raise wages of college graduates by 5 percent. This 35 percent spread is of the same order of magnitude

TABLE 6-4   Wage Effects of Changing U.S. Trade Patterns

Elasticities		Secondary					
Demand	Supply	None (%)	Primary (%)	Entered (%)	Complete (%)	College (%)	All (%)
0.50	0.10	−573	−63	−8	16	9	−1.9
0.75	0.50	−275	−30	−4	8	5	−0.9
1.00	1.00	−172	−19	−2	5	3	−0.6
Percentile			0.7	7.7	29.8	68.1	100

NOTE: The table reports $100(w_{92} - w_{72})/w_{92}$ induced by the 1972-92 changes in the *adjusted* factor content of net imports. See equation (8).

as that actually experienced by the U.S. economy.[11] For reasons discussed below, I do not want to push too hard on this point except to say that it is surprisingly easy to use factor content calculations to partially mimic observed wage changes.[12] On the other hand, what I find completely persuasive is the wage effects at the bottom of the education distribution. *For the 0.7 percent of the labor force with no education, imports have augmented their supply by almost 170 percentage points and reduced their wage by 275 percent. Imports are devastating the small portion of the work force with little education.*

There are a number of issues omitted in this simplistic study. I have not introduced elasticities of substitution between types of labor. Adding this effect diminishes the wage impacts. Nor have I considered labor-capital substitution possibilities. Because net imports of capital have increased by only 0.1 percentage points over the period, trade has not led directly to capital deepening. If capital is a substitute for unskilled labor and a complement for skilled labor, my implicit assumption of zero elasticities leads to overstated wage impacts. Finally, and arguably most important, I ignored the participation decision. As is apparent from the tables, the biggest effect is on those workers who are most likely to be fluidly moving in and out of the labor force. By forcing workers out of the labor force, trade is likely to have significant effects on poverty that are not apparent from wage data.

Trade Versus Immigration as an Explanation of Wage Trends

Borjas et al. (1992) raised the question of whether trade or immigration has been more important in explaining wage trends. Factor content analyses gloss over several facts that are difficult to quantify.

Immigration is a stock whereas trade is a flow. That is, an immigrant arrival increases the stock of immigrants not only in the year of arrival, but also in subsequent years. Trade, or at least nondurable trade, has an impact only in the year it arrives. For example, in 1992 immigration and the labor content of net imports were of comparable magnitudes: 1.0 million immigrants and 1.4 million workers embodied in trade. This is a flow calculation. The stock calculation for

---

[10]To see this let $D_{92}(w_{72})$ be the 1992 labor demand schedule evaluated at 1972 wages and shift this demand curve out from the 1992 equilibrium by an amount $-\Delta FT = D_{92}(w_{72}) - L_{72}$ that can be calculated from Table 6-2. To obtain equation (8), start with $\varepsilon_D = -[L_{92} - D_{92}(w_{72})] / [L_{92} \Delta w]$, substitute out $D_{92}(w_{72})$ using the expression for $-\Delta FT$, and substitute out L_{72} using $\varepsilon_S = [L_{92} - L_{72}] / [L_{92} \Delta w]$.

[11]This requires an obvious caveat. The bottom of the table reports that the education groups map poorly into percentiles of the U.S. labor force.

[12]For the unadjusted factor content calculations (i.e., when $\Delta FT(i)$ is taken from the Table 6-2 column labeled "net imports, 1992-1972, total"), $\Delta w(i)$ is tiny for all types of labor except no-education labor where it ranges between 5-17 percent for the Table 6-4 choice of elasticities. Thus, it is the factor content adjustment rather than the elasticities that drives the wage result.

the period 1972-1992 yields 30 million immigrants compared with a 0.5-million worker change in the labor content of net imports. Thus, immigration would appear to have much greater labor market consequences. Against this must be balanced the fact of assimilation. Over sufficiently long horizons one might want to treat past immigrants as natives.

Immigration has income effects, but without the price-reducing benefits of trade. Import competition has two offsetting effects. It drives down consumer prices (a benefit), and it drives down the incomes of at least some natives (a cost). However, at the point where import competition totally displaces the domestic industry, increased imports have no further negative impact on native incomes. The only effect is beneficial lower consumer prices. This safety valve of comparative advantage specialization is not a feature of immigration. As long as immigrants have skills comparable to those of natives and as long as labor markets are not perfectly segmented along immigrant-native lines, immigrants will compete for native jobs and incomes. When a Mexican arrives in the United States, the impact is felt in every sector where the immigrant is potentially employable. The comparative advantage safety valve suggests that immigration has a more adverse consequence than trade.

Import levels are not indicative of all the potentially harmful labor market consequences of trade. For example, there are cases of foreign firms that do not compete in the U.S. market even though they would if the U.S. product price rose by a small amount. In such contestable markets the *possibility* of imports constrains the behavior of U.S. firms as tangibly as do realized imports (see also Brander and Spencer, 1981, for a limit-pricing model of trade). None of this is captured by the existing empirical literature, but such a study would lead one to raise the importance of trade relative to migration.

On the other hand, *trade has positive welfare implications not captured by the existing empirical work surrounding the trade and wages debate.* These are the benefits associated with comparative advantage, specialization, procompetitive effects, dynamic efficiency gains, etc. None of these enter into existing empirical work. The same could be said of the immigration benefits of reunifying families, sheltering refugees, etc., as well as the long-run growth facilitated by immigration. My predilection as a trade economist is to argue that *at the margin* the unmeasured gains from trade far exceed the unmeasured benefits of migration.

What Is the Experiment?

As Leamer (1993) notes, a problem with analysis of the type considered so far is that it is not built around a well-defined policy experiment. Questions about whether immigration is good or trade is bad tend to be overly vague, too grand in conception, and irrelevant to what we care about, namely policy interventions. Like the water and diamond paradox, this leads to confusion between the total consumer surplus from trade and the marginal consumer surplus created or destroyed by current policy proposals. Total consumer surplus from trade is enormous (imagine a U.S. economy that had not imported journals documenting the British discovery of DNA) but irrelevant to policy. This subsection illustrates the importance of building empirical studies around well-defined policy interventions.

Immigration has a clear policy handle. The level of immigration is controlled through quotas, and the type of immigrant is selected through such criteria as the need for specific skills. Although policy does not fully control immigrant quality and even less so illegal immigration (Hanson and Spilimbergo, 1996), at least there is some possibility for designing policies to affect these outcomes.

In contrast, trade levels are endogenous equilibrium outcomes only partially amenable to policy interventions. *The level and composition of trade is less a policy instrument than a vehicle through which policies are transmitted.* For example, the run-up of the merchandise trade deficit during the 1980s was not a policy. To the contrary, U.S. trade policy was increasingly protectionist at that time. The deficit at least partly reflected President Reagan's fiscal policies that were totally unrelated to trade (Krugman, 1994). For another example, immigrants promote trade with their country of origin (Baker and Benjamin, 1996) so that trade patterns are to some degree driven by immigration policies!

This raises doubts about the meaning of, among other things, factor content studies. Suppose a trade deficit develops not because of policy interventions but because of falling transport costs and other components of globalization. Because the impact of globalization is not simply a changed U.S. trade pattern, one wonders what the above factor content calculation captures. Consider an assessment of the factor content of trade that explicitly recognizes the multicountry general equilibrium changes associated with globalization. Let L_c and L_w denote the supplies of labor in country c and the world, respectively. Let gdp_c and gdp_w denote gross domestic product in country c and the world, respectively. Under the assumption of consumption similarity, each country indirectly consumes a fraction $s_c = gdp_c/gdp_w$ of the world labor supply. $L_c - s_c L_w$ is the difference between country c's supply of labor and consumption of labor. By definition, this is the factor content of trade. How would one calculate this using input-output tables and trade flow data? Let a^t_{gc} be the total (in an input-output sense) amount of labor needed to produce one unit of good g in country c. Let X_{gc} be country c's exports of good g and let $M_{gc,US}$ be U.S. imports from country c of good g. All the interesting action is with intermediate goods (the bulk of trade flows), so assume that all trade is in intermediate goods. It is tempting to think that

$$L_{US} - s_{US} L_w = \Sigma_g \{a^t_{g,US} X_{g,US} - \Sigma_c a^t_{gc} M_{gc,US}\}, \qquad (9)$$

where one uses country c technology a^t_{gc} when assessing the factor content of goods produced in country c. However, this turns out to be incorrect because it ignores the impact of globalization on the rest of the world.

As shown in Trefler (1996), the correct equation is

$$L_{US} - s_{US} L_w = \Sigma_g \{ a^t_{g,US} (X_{g,US} - M_{g,US}) - s_{US} \Sigma_c a^t_{gc} (X_{gc} - M_{gc}) \}, \quad (10)$$

where M_{gc} is country c imports of good g from the rest of the world. From the perspective of the United States alone, national income accounting rules dictate that net exports of intermediate goods are a component of final demand. This explains the equation (10) term $\Sigma_g a^t_{g,US} (X_{g,US} - M_{g,US})$ which is just the usual definition of the U.S. factor content of trade. However, from the perspective of the world as a whole, an intermediate good does not magically become a final good simply by crossing a national boundary. Restated, for the United States alone, net exports are exogenous whereas for the world as a whole net exports are endogenous. The second term on the right-hand side of equation (10) is a correction that accounts for the endogeneity of trade. The choice between equations (9) and (10) depends on whether one wants to treat changes in U.S. trade flows as an exogenous shock or whether one wants to look for a more fundamental international shock that drives U.S. trade flows. For policy analysis, clearly the latter is what matters, and factor content studies based on equation (9) are flawed. In short, one can be seriously misled by failing to clearly articulate the policy environment, including the exogenous shock and the policy instrument.

CONCLUSIONS

We tend to focus on those who lose from immigration to the exclusion of those who benefit. Borjas (1995) used this observation to show that in the short run immigration may yield a net social benefit. Unfortunately, the argument unravels when imbedded in long-run models of international trade. Borjas's immigration "surplus" is zero in the Heckscher-Ohlin model with its factor price equalization theorem. The immigration surplus is negative in the Ricardian model with its negative terms-of-trade effect and industrial "ghettoization" of immigrant labor. To obtain an immigration surplus, an additional kick from immigration is needed as in the increasing returns to scale model with its immigrant externality.

The second half of this chapter had an empirical focus. In light of the dramatic growth in globalization pressures, there is surprisingly little evidence of earnings convergence across countries. This implies that the supply pressures for migration to the United States remain as strong as they were 30 years ago. This appears to hold true even after disaggregating by the level of education of different types of potential immigrants. Another empirical surprise comes from my new factor content study. It indicates that changes in U.S. trade patterns almost certainly battered wages of those at the very bottom of the skill ladder. It also hints at the possibility that, contrary to conclusions of previous research, the changing composition of international trade can explain a large proportion of rising U.S. wage inequality. If so, then trade may be at least as important as immigration in explaining recent labor market trends in the United States. However, I offered a number of caveats to this last interpretation. Finally, much of the research in this area treats observed changes in equilibrium trade flows as equivalent to the changes one might expect from altering international trade policies. This has led researchers to overstate the importance of trade policy. In contrast, immigration policy is more efficacious in application and should therefore play center stage in policy discussions.

ACKNOWLEDGMENTS

I am indebted to my students at the Harris School for pursuing many of the ideas in this chapter as term papers, to Edgard Rodriguez for data on Filipino migrants, to Huiwen Lai for his research assistance, to Chris Thornberg for data from the 1972 Current Population Survey, and to Michael Baker and Alysious Siow for helpful comments. The third section of this chapter borrows from work in progress with Joe Hotz. George Borjas and Richard Freeman helped frame the questions, and Danny Rodrik helped bring the answers into focus.

REFERENCES

Baker, Michael, and Dwayne Benjamin
   1996   "Asia-Pacific Immigration and the Canadian Economy." Pp. 303-347 in *The Asia-Pacific Region in the Global Economy: A Canadian Perspective*, Richard G. Harris, ed. Calgary: University of Calgary.
Barro, Robert J., and Jong-Wha Lee
   1993   "International Comparisons of Educational Attainment." NBER Working Paper 4349. Cambridge Mass.: National Bureau of Economic Research.
Berman, Eli, John Bound, and Zvi Griliches
   1994   "Changes in the Demand for Skilled Labor Within U.S. Manufacturing Industries: Evidence from the Annual Survey of Manufacturing." *Quarterly Journal of Economics* 109(March):367-397.
Borjas, George J.
   1987   "Self-Selection and the Earnings of Immigrants." *American Economic Review* 77 (September):531-553.
Borjas, George J.
   1995   "The Economic Benefits from Immigration." *Journal of Economic Perspectives* 9 (Spring):1-22.
Borjas, George J., and Valarie A. Ramey
   1993   "Foreign Competition, Market Power, and Wage Inequality: Theory and Evidence." NBER Working Paper 4556. Cambridge Mass.: National Bureau of Economic Research.
Borjas, George J., Richard Freeman, and Lawrence F. Katz
   1992   "On the Labor Market Effects of Immigration and Trade." In *Immigration and the Workforce*, George J. Borjas and Richard Freeman, eds. Chicago: University of Chicago Press.
Brander, James A., and Barbara J. Spencer
   1981   "Tariffs and the Extraction of Foreign Monopoly Rents under Potential Entry." *Canadian Journal of Economics* 14:371-389.
Card, David, and Alan B. Krueger
   1992   "Does School Quality Matter? Returns to Education and the Characteristics of Public Schools in the United States." *Journal of Political Economy* 100 (February):1-40.

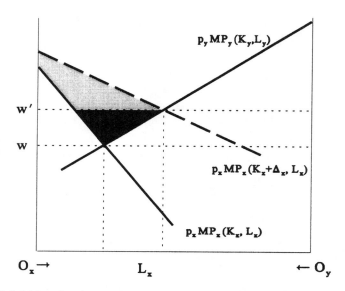

FIGURE 6-A1 Immigration surplus with industry-specific migration.

Notes: The figure illustrates the impact of an immigration-induced rise in the industry x specific factor K_x by an amount Δ_x. A discussion of why industry x labor demand shifts as drawn appears in Dixit and Norman (1980:Figure 2.6). There is one analytic difficulty. Because specific factor rents are not set competitively, it is not clear what portion of industry rents accrue to native rather than immigrant K_x. A sensible assumption is that the division is proportional to the size of the labor demand shift. Then the shaded area is rents that accrue to immigrant Δ_x. Only the darkly shaded triangle is the immigration surplus. It is positive.

TABLE 6-A1   External Returns to Scale Equilibria

Equilibrium	Diversification Equilibrium[a]		Specialization Equilibrium[a]	
IRS price (p_x)	$1/[\alpha(L+L^*)]$		$\beta L^*/L^2$	
CRS price (p_y)	1		1	
	U.S.	Foreign	U.S.	Foreign
wages (w)	1	1	$\beta L^*/L > 1$[c]	1
Per capita welfare[b]	$\alpha^\alpha (L+L^*)^\alpha$	$\alpha^\alpha(L+L^*)^\alpha$	$\beta^{1-\alpha}(L^*/L)^{1-\alpha} L^\alpha$	$\beta^{-\alpha}(L^*/L)^{-\alpha} L^\alpha$

a) In the U.S. diversification equilibrium, the U.S. produces both goods and the foreign country produces only the constant returns (CRS) good. In the U.S. specialization equilibrium, the U.S. produces the increasing returns (IRS) good and the foreign country produces only the CRS good.

b) $\beta = \alpha/(1 - \alpha)$.

c) The specialization equilibrium only exists when demand for x is too large to be supplied by a single unspecialized country. See Helpman (1984). Mathematically, the equilibrium only exists for $\alpha > L/(L+L^*)$ or, equivalently, $\beta L^*/L > 1$.

TABLE 6-A2 Monthly Wage Differentials for Filipinos Across Selected Countries

Occupation	Males					Females				
	US$ Philippines	Philippines = 1				US$ Philippines	Philippines = 1			
		Japan	Hong Kong	Singapore	Saudi Arabia		Japan	Hong Kong	Singapore	Saudi Arabia
Technical Salesmen & related	140	4.7	7.0	6.5	3.3	103	7.6	2.9		3.4
Transport Equipment Operators	134	2.6	2.9	3.0	2.8	80	13.9	3.4	8.5	4.1
Housekeeping & related	117	4.7	2.9	2.7	3.7					
Bricklayers, Carpenters & other construction workers	111	8.1	7.9	2.9	3.3					
Sales Supervisors & Buyers	108	6.4	7.6	9.5	6.1					
Chemical Processors & related	104	5.2	4.3	6.0	4.8					
Blacksmiths, Toolmakers, Machine-Tool Operators	100	5.9	6.5	6.6	4.7					
Machinery Fitters, Assemblers, Precision Instr. Makers	99	4.1	4.3	5.3	4.4					
Protective Service Workers	97	2.6	4.9	4.2	4.2					
Printers & related	91	4.3	3.7	3.6	3.6					
Plumbers, Welders, Sheet-metal & Structural Metal Prep.	86	4.2	5.1	4.9	4.6					
Tailors, Dressmakers, Sewers, Upholsterers & related	82	10.0	6.9	6.7	4.9	61	8.8	4.3		6.3
Cooks, Waiters, Bartenders & related	75	6.3	6.0	5.6	4.3	38	16.9		9.1	10.0
Building Caretakers, Cleaners & related	69		3.5	3.4	4.1					
Transport Conductors	53	5.5	8.5	9.9	7.8					
Launderers, Dry-cleaners & Pressers	52	7.8	7.6		7.0					
Fishermen	38	6.9	13.7	8.5	11.0					

SOURCE: Data were prepared by Edgard Rodriguez. For host countries data are from the Philippines Overseas Employment Agency and date from the period April-July, 1993. For the Philippines data are from the October 1991 Labor Force Survey. Data were converted to current U.S. dollars using spot exchange rates i.e., there is no PPP correction. The data do not include in-kind transfers such as accommodation.

Davis, Steven J., and John Haltiwanger
  1991   "Wage Dispersion between and within U.S. Manufacturing Plants, 1963-1986."
          Brookings Papers on Economic Activity: Microeconomics 115-180.
Dixit, Avinash K., and Victor Norman
  1980   *Theory of International Trade: A Dual, General Equilibrium Approach.* Cambridge:
          Cambridge University Press.
Dornbusch, Rudiger, Stanley Fischer, and Paul A. Samuelson
  1977   "Comparative Advantage, Trade and Payments in a Ricardian Model with a Continuum
          of Goods." *American Economic Review* 67 (December):823-839.
Feenstra, Robert C., and Gordon H. Hanson
  1996   "Globalization, Outsourcing, and Wage Inequality." *American Economic Review Papers
          and Proceedings* 86 (May):240-245.
Gaston, Noel, and Daniel Trefler
  1994   "Protection, Trade, and Wages: Evidence for U.S. Manufacturing." *Industrial and Labor
          Relations Review* 47 (July):574-593.
Gaston, Noel, and Daniel Trefler
  1995   "Union Wage Sensitivity to Trade and Protection." *Journal of International Economics*
          39 (August):1-25.
Goldin, Claudia, and Lawrence F. Katz
  1996   "Technology, Skill, and the Wage Structure: Insights from the Past." *American Economic
          Review Papers and Procedings* 86 (May):252-257.
Hanson, Gordon, and Antonio Spilimbergo
  1996   "Illegal Immigration, Border Enforcement, and Relative Wages: Evidence from Appre-
          hensions at the U.S.-Mexico Border." NBER Working Paper 5592. Cambridge, Mass.:
          National Bureau of Economic Research.
Helpman, Elhanan
  1984   "Increasing Returns, Imperfect Markets, and Trade Theory." In *Handbook of Interna-
          tional Economics,* Vol. I, Ronald W. Jones and Peter B. Kenen, eds. Amsterdam: North-
          Holland.
Juhn, Chinhui, Kevin M. Murphy, and Brooks Pierce
  1993   "Wage Inequality and the Rise in Returns to Skill." *Journal of Political Economy* 101
          (May):410-442.
Katz, Lawrence F., and Kevin M. Murphy
  1992   "Changes in Relative Wages, 1963-1987: Supply and Demand Factors." *Quarterly Jour-
          nal of Economics* 107 (February):35-78.
Krueger, Alan B.
  1993   "How Computers Have Changed the Wage Structure: Evidence from Microdata, 1984-
          1989." *Quarterly Journal of Economics* 1 (February):33-60.
Krugman, Paul
  1994   *The Aged of Diminished Expectations: U.S. Economic Policy in the 1990s,* revised and
          updated edition. Cambridge, Mass.: MIT Press.
Krugman, Paul, and Robert Z. Lawrence
  1994   "Trade, Jobs and Wages." *Scientific American* (April):44-49.
Leamer, Edward E.
  1992   "Wage Effects of a U.S.-Mexican Free Trade Agreement." NBER Working Paper 3991.
          Cambridge, Mass.: National Bureau of Economic Research.
Leamer, Edward E.
  1993   "Factor-Supply Differences as a Source of Comparative Advantage." *American Eco-
          nomic Review Papers and Proceedings* 83 (May):436-439.
Leamer, Edward E.
  1996   "What's the Use of Factor Contents?" NBER Working Paper 5448. Cambridge, Mass.:
          National Bureau of Economic Research.

Markusen, James
  1983   "Factor Movements and Commodity Trade as Complements." *Journal of International Economics* 14 (May):341-356.
Mayer, Wolfgang
  1974   "Short-Run and Long-Run Equilibrium for a Small Open Economy." *Journal of Political Economy* 82:955-967.
Murphy, Kevin M., and Finis Welch
  1993   "Inequality and Relative Wages." *American Economic Review Papers and Proceedings* 83 (May):104-109.
Mussa, Michael
  1974   "Tariffs and the Distribution of Income: The Importance of Factor Specificity, Substitutability, and Intensity in the Short and Long Run." *Journal of Political Economy* 82:1191-1203.
Razin, Assaf, and Efraim Sadka
  1996   "International Migration and International Trade." In *Handbook of Population and Family Economics*, Mark R. Rosenzweig and Oded Stark, eds. Amsterdam: North-Holland.
Revenga, Ana L.
  1992   "Exporting Jobs? The Impact of Import Competition on Employment and Wages in U.S. Manufacturing." *Quarterly Journal of Economics* 107 (February):255-282.
Sachs, Jeffrey D., and Howard J. Shatz
  1994   "Trade and Jobs in U.S. Manufacturing." *Brooking Papers on Economic Activity: Microeconomics* 1:1-84.
Summers, Robert, and Alan Heston
  1991   "The Penn World Table (Mark 5): An Expanded Set of International Comparisons, 1950-1988." *Quarterly Journal of Economics* 106:327-368.
Trefler, Daniel
  1993a   "Trade Liberalization and the Theory of Endogenous Protection: An Econometric Study of U.S. Import Policy." *Journal of Political Economy* 101 (February):138-160.
Trefler, Daniel
  1993b   "International Factor Price Differences: Leontief was Right!" *Journal of Political Economy* 101 (December):961-987.
Trefler, Daniel
  1995   "The Case of the Missing Trade and Other Mysteries." *American Economic Review* 85 (December):1029-1046.
Trefler, Daniel
  1996   "The Structure of Factor Content Predictions." Unpublished document, University of Toronto.
U.S. Commission for the Study of International Migration and Cooperative Economic Development
  1990   *Unauthorized Migration: An Economic Development Response.* Washington, D.C.
Wildasin, David E.
  1991   "Income Redistribution in a Common Labor Market." *American Economic Review* 81 (September):757-774.
Wildasin, David E.
  1994   "Income Redistribution and Migration." *Canadian Journal of Economics* 27 (August):637-654.
Wood, Adrian
  1994   *North-South Trade Employment and Inequality: Changing Fortunes in a Skill-Driven World.* Oxford: Clarendon Press.

7

Labor Market Outcomes of Female Immigrants in the United States

Edward Funkhouser and Stephen J. Trejo

INTRODUCTION

In recent years, the increased volume and changing national origins of immigration to the United States have reopened public debate over immigration policy. During the postwar period, the share of immigrants originating in Europe and Canada fell sharply, with the slack taken up by surging immigration from Asia and Latin America. A growing body of empirical research indicates that more recent immigrant arrival cohorts are less skilled and have been less successful in the labor market than earlier cohorts, and that there are important links between the shifts in national origins and declining immigrant skills (Borjas, 1994).[1] Contrary to the traditional view that immigrants rapidly assimilate into the economic mainstream of American society, the revisionist studies predict that most foreign-born workers who entered the United States during the past two decades will throughout their lifetimes earn substantially less than native workers (Borjas, 1995).

These conclusions, however, are based almost entirely on analyses of immigrant *men*. Few studies of foreign-born women have attempted to estimate the effects of arrival cohort and assimilation on outcomes in the manner that has revolutionized research on male immigrants.[2] Using microdata from the 1980

---

[1]In particular, immigrant earnings in the United States are strongly correlated with per capita gross national product in the source country (Jasso and Rosenzweig, 1986; Borjas, 1987), presumably because workers from industrialized countries are better trained than workers from developing countries and their skills transfer more readily to the U.S. labor market.

[2]We know of three studies that analyze immigrant women to the United States using this approach, and two of these are somewhat limited in scope. Blau's (1992) research on fertility includes only

and 1990 U.S. censuses, we perform such an analysis of two key labor market outcomes for immigrant women: employment and hourly earnings. The availability of census data at more than one point in time allows us to track changes for arrival cohorts as they gain experience in the United States, and it also lets us compare outcomes across cohorts.

The chapter proceeds as follows. In the next two sections we describe the census data and some of the basic patterns evident in these data. In the fourth section we discuss the regression framework we use to estimate the effects of arrival cohort and assimilation on immigrant outcomes. In the fifth and sixth sections we present our regression analyses of the employment and hourly earnings of foreign-born women. For comparison purposes, in these sections we also report similar employment and wage regressions for men. In the concluding section we summarize our results.

DATA

We analyze microdata from the 1980 and 1990 U.S. censuses. We started with the 5 percent samples of the population available in each census, but to lighten the computational burden we randomly sampled U.S.-born individuals while retaining all foreign-born individuals so as to end up with 1 percent samples of natives and 5 percent samples of immigrants.[3] All of the estimates reported here are weighted to reflect both our differential sampling of natives and immigrants and the sampling weights that accompany the 1990 Census microdata.[4]

Persons born abroad of American parents were excluded from study because the distinction between immigrant and native is ambiguous for such individuals. For persons born in outlying areas of the United States (e.g., Puerto Rico), information on year of arrival in the United States is available in the 1990 Census but not in the 1980 Census, and therefore we group these persons separately from other immigrants for whom we can track arrival cohorts across censuses.

We restrict attention to persons aged 25-59. For each woman in the sample, we searched all other records in the same household to ascertain the number and

---

immigrants from high-fertility regions (the Middle East, Asia, Latin America, and the Caribbean), and Reimer's (1996) wage analysis focuses on Mexican immigrants living in California and Texas. In work done independently of but concurrently with our research, Schoeni (1996b) estimates female employment regressions broadly similar to those we report below, and in general his results are similar to ours. Recently, we have received the paper by Baker and Benjamin (1997)— which finds different patterns than ours for employment—for Canada.

[3]In this chapter, we use the term "immigrant" as synonymous with foreign-born individuals not born of U.S. parents, in contrast to the official terminology used by the U.S. Immigration and Naturalization Service in which immigrants are legal permanent residents, and other foreigners such as tourists, business travelers, and recent refugee arrivals are "nonimmigrant aliens." The census data analyzed here cannot make such distinctions among foreign-born individuals.

[4]The 1980 census microdata are self-weighting.

ages of her children under age 18 who were living with her.[5] In the 1990 (but not 1980) Census data, the Census Bureau provides its own imputation of this type of information, and our imputation matches the Census Bureau's quite closely.

Our calculation of an hourly wage measure requires a bit of explanation. We compute average hourly earnings for each worker as the ratio of annual earnings to annual hours of work in the calendar year preceding the census, where annual earnings are the sum of wage and salary income and self-employment income, and annual hours of work are the product of weeks worked and usual weekly hours of work. Only individuals with positive earnings and hours were included in the wage analyses. Because the top codes and bottom codes applied to the income variables differ between the 1980 and 1990 censuses, we imposed top and bottom codes that were the same (in real dollars) across years.[6] In addition, observations in the 1980 Census data with computed hourly wages below $1 or above $200 are considered outliers and excluded. In the 1990 Census data, corresponding wage thresholds of $1.66 and $332 are applied so as to be consistent in real terms.

BASIC PATTERNS

Before turning to the regression analysis, we describe the characteristics of immigrant and native women in our census samples. In the first part of this section, we examine the cross-sectional patterns of immigrant cohorts using the 1990 Census. In the second part of the section, we follow synthetic arrival cohorts of immigrants and natives between the 1980 and 1990 censuses. To examine the potential importance of household decisions in labor market outcomes, we distinguish between two age groups of women: those most likely to bear children during the 1980s (women age 25-39 in 1980) and those beyond the main childbearing years (women age 40-49 in 1980).

Characteristics by Arrival Cohort in the 1990 Census

One of the important aspects of analysis of immigrants is the changing country composition of immigration as immigration laws, economic conditions, and political conditions have changed. Changes in the region of origin of immigrant females

---

[5]In census data, it is often impossible to distinguish stepchildren from biological children when matching mothers with their children, and so our counts of children do not make this distinction.

[6]For example, wage and salary income is top coded at $75,000 in the 1980 Census and at $140,000 in the 1990 Census. According to the gross national product deflator for personal consumption expenditure, the price level rose by 66 percent between 1979 and 1989. Therefore, we lowered the ceiling on wage and salary income in the 1990 Census data to $124,500 ($75,000 inflated from 1979 to 1989 dollars), so as to impose top codes that are equivalent in real terms. In a similar fashion, we reconciled across years the top and bottom codes for farm and nonfarm self-employment incomes.

TABLE 7-1   Region of Origin (1990 Census)

	Before 1950 (1)	1950-1959 (2)	1960-1969 (3)	1970-1979 (4)	1980-1984 (5)	1985-1989 (6)	Total (7)
North America	0.139	0.098	0.105	0.019	0.016	0.019	0.036
Western Europe	0.393	0.469	0.259	0.097	0.060	0.078	0.157
Eastern Europe	0.050	0.159	0.042	0.035	0.034	0.053	0.045
Mexico	0.163	0.130	0.163	0.241	0.183	0.169	0.189
Latin America	0.071	0.087	0.269	0.225	0.285	0.230	0.231
Asia	0.063	0.096	0.163	0.322	0.351	0.379	0.281
Other	0.047	0.039	0.046	0.061	0.071	0.072	0.060
Share of Total	0.018	0.089	0.202	0.301	0.194	0.195	1.000

NOTE: For Rows 1 to 7, entries are percent of each immigrant cohort from the indicated region. Other includes country not specified. Sample size is 824,501.

reported in the 1990 Census are shown in Table 7-1. Overall, over 70 percent of all female immigrants reported Mexico, Latin America, or Asia as their country of birth and only 19.3 percent reported North America or Western Europe.

These total percentages reflect the change in source country of immigration from those of Europe to the developing countries of Asia and Latin America. Female immigrants from North America and Western Europe were over half of the immigrant cohorts that arrived prior to 1960. The proportion of immigrants from these countries fell significantly, especially during the 1960s and 1970s, to less than 10 percent of the arrival cohorts of the 1980s.

Over the arrival cohorts in which the share from North America and Western Europe declined, the share of immigrants from Latin America and Asia increased from less than one-third of the pre-1960 arrival cohorts to over three-fourths of the total of the arrival cohorts of the 1970s and 1980s. This increase occurred in two stages, with the proportion of immigrants from Latin America increasing to one-fourth of the total during the 1960s and the increase in the proportion of immigrants from Asia to over one-third of the total occurring in the cohorts of the 1970s and 1980s.[7]

Mean characteristics calculated from the 1990 Census for each immigrant cohort, persons born in outlying areas of the United States, and natives are shown in Table 7-2.[8] In columns (1) through (6), values for each immigrant arrival cohort are shown, grouping the 1960s arrivals and 1970s arrivals into one column for each decade. In columns (7), (8), and (9), the values for all immigrants, persons from outlying areas of the United States, and natives are shown, respectively.

---

[7]Passel and Edmonston (1994) have noted the importance of the changes in country composition of immigration on the ethnic composition of the U.S. population.

[8]The patterns are similar when regressions controlling for age are estimated.

The first rows of Table 7-2 report mean values of several human capital variables—age, education, and English ability. These data show the bimodality in educational attainment that has also been observed for males. Overall, immigrants are disproportionately in the high and low categories of educational attainment—they are much more likely than natives not to have graduated from high school (30.6 to 12.2 percent) and they are nearly as likely to have graduated from college (20.2 to 21.3 percent). The declining trend in education levels over the cohorts from the 1960s through the first half of the 1980s is reversed slightly with the cohort of the second half of the 1980s.

The difference in English ability between immigrants and natives is substantial. In the 1980 and 1990 censuses, all respondents were asked whether they "speak a language other than English at home," and only those who answered affirmatively were asked how well they speak English, with possible responses of "very well," "well," "not well," or "not at all." Only 52.1 percent of all immigrants speak English at least "very well" (speak only English or speak English very well), compared with 98.7 percent for natives. In contrast to improvement in educational attainment among the cohorts that arrived during the late 1980s, the English ability of the most recent immigrant cohorts (39.9 percent of the 1970-74 cohort and 35.3 percent of the 1975-79 cohort) is lower than that of all previous arrivals.

In the next rows of the table, labor market outcomes—percent employed, weeks worked, hours worked, log hourly earnings, and annual earnings—are shown. The main finding from these rows is the low employment rate, low number of weeks worked, and lower earnings of the two most recent immigrant cohorts (1980-1984 and 1985-1989) compared both with earlier immigrants and with natives.

Overall, immigrant women have lower employment rates than natives (67.3 percent for immigrants compared with 77.3 percent for natives). These rates are extremely low for immigrant arrivals in the 1985-1989 cohort, who had an employment rate of only 54.5 percent. The deficit diminishes with increases in time spent in the United States. The cohort of arrivals with six to ten years of experience, the 1980-1984 cohort, has employment rates only 4 to 6 percentage points below those of the immigrant cohorts that arrived in the 1960s and 1970s (67.3 percent for the 1980-1984 cohort relative to 71 to 73 percent for the earlier ones). Among employed females, the most recent immigrants also worked fewer weeks during the previous calendar year of 1989 (38.8 weeks compared with 42.6 weeks for the 1980-1984 cohort and 44.1 weeks for natives). Usual hours worked per week for those who report positive hours are very similar across both nativity and arrival cohort, including the most recent arrivals.

On average, immigrant females who report positive earnings have lower log hourly earnings (2.122 compared with 2.167 for natives). The pattern in these data are similar to the pattern of "catch-up" in earnings that has been documented in cross-sectional data for males. Recent immigrants earn significantly

TABLE 7-2 Mean Characteristics Females 25-59 in 1990

	Before 1950 (1)	1950-1959 (2)	1960-1969 (3)	1970-1979 (4)	1980-1984 (5)	1985-1989 (6)	Total (7)	Outlying Areas (8)	Natives (9)
Age	50.93 (0.245)	48.15 (0.111)	43.42 (0.074)	39.08 (0.061)	36.09 (0.075)	35.02 (0.075)	39.61 (0.034)	40.48 (0.122)	39.55 (0.011)
Less than High School	0.215 (0.009)	0.210 (0.004)	0.247 (0.003)	0.347 (0.002)	0.356 (0.003)	0.306 (0.003)	0.306 (0.001)	0.423 (0.004)	0.122 (0.000)
High School Graduate	0.323 (0.012)	0.360 (0.006)	0.310 (0.004)	0.252 (0.003)	0.260 (0.004)	0.259 (0.004)	0.278 (0.002)	0.300 (0.006)	0.365 (0.001)
Some College	0.237 (0.012)	0.261 (0.005)	0.256 (0.004)	0.204 (0.003)	0.194 (0.004)	0.186 (0.004)	0.215 (0.002)	0.179 (0.006)	0.300 (0.001)
College Graduate	0.226 (0.010)	0.168 (0.005)	0.188 (0.003)	0.196 (0.003)	0.190 (0.003)	0.249 (0.003)	0.202 (0.001)	0.098 (0.005)	0.213 (0.001)
English Very Well	0.845 (0.005)	0.809 (0.002)	0.678 (0.001)	0.497 (0.001)	0.399 (0.002)	0.353 (0.001)	0.521 (0.001)	0.518 (0.002)	0.987 (0.000)
Percent Employed	0.687 (0.011)	0.692 (0.005)	0.727 (0.003)	0.712 (0.003)	0.673 (0.003)	0.545 (0.003)	0.673 (0.001)	0.534 (0.005)	0.773 (0.001)
Weeks Worked	44.71 (0.43)	44.68 (0.19)	44.57 (0.12)	43.55 (0.10)	42.57 (0.13)	38.78 (0.15)	42.95 (0.06)	42.67 (0.24)	44.09 (0.02)

Hours Worked	36.57 (0.37)	36.60 (0.17)	37.90 (0.11)	38.48 (0.09)	38.37 (0.11)	37.78 (0.13)	38.01 (0.05)	37.28 (0.21)	37.12 (0.02)
Log Hourly Earnings	2.321 (0.020)	2.249 (0.009)	2.236 (0.006)	2.147 (0.005)	2.017 (0.006)	1.943 (0.007)	2.122 (0.003)	2.129 (0.011)	2.167 (0.001)
Annual Earnings	13,961 (364)	12,950 (165)	13,774 (109)	12,276 (90)	9,663 (112)	6,565 (111)	11,047 (49)	8,311 (181)	13,243 (16)
Poverty Rate	0.083 (0.008)	0.068 (0.004)	0.090 (0.002)	0.144 (0.002)	0.195 (0.002)	0.266 (0.002)	0.159 (0.001)	0.314 (0.004)	0.102 (0.000)
Percent Married	0.696 (0.012)	0.735 (0.005)	0.709 (0.004)	0.739 (0.003)	0.708 (0.004)	0.702 (0.004)	0.718 (0.002)	0.503 (0.006)	0.667 (0.001)
Children Ever Born	2.722 (0.013)	2.425 (0.019)	2.143 (0.013)	2.282 (0.011)	2.081 (0.013)	1.786 (0.013)	2.139 (0.006)	2.650 (0.021)	1.967 (0.002)
Any Children	0.868 (0.011)	0.853 (0.005)	0.814 (0.003)	0.830 (0.003)	0.790 (0.003)	0.698 (0.003)	.796 (.001)	0.871 (0.005)	0.776 (0.001)

Note: Employment status, weeks worked, usual hours worked, logarithm of hourly income, and annual income are for 1989 calendar year. Means for weeks worked, usual hours worked, and logarithm of hourly income are calculated for those with positive values. Sample sizes are 824,501 for age, education, English ability, and percent employed; 602,530 for weeks worked and usual hours; 586,490 for logarithm of hourly wage; 824,501 for annual earnings; 822,099 for poverty status; 824,501 for marital status and fertility.

below natives (1.943), but the cohorts that arrived 10-20 years prior to the census have log hourly earnings similar to natives (2.147 for the 1970-1979 arrivals). And immigrants who arrived more than 20 years prior to the 1990 Census earn significantly above natives (2.236 for the 1960-1969 cohort). The combination of lower employment rates, fewer weeks worked, and lower hourly wages result in lower annual earnings for immigrants ($11,047) compared with those of than natives ($13,243).

In this table, we include poverty levels as a measure of household economic status. The pattern is similar to that for earnings except that the increase across successive earlier cohorts is more gradual, with even the 1970-1979 cohort having significantly higher poverty rates than natives. Only for immigrants who arrived prior to 1970 are poverty rates similar to or lower than those of natives.

In the final rows of the table, marriage and fertility characteristics are shown. Overall, immigrants are more likely to be married with spouse present than are natives (71.8 to 66.7 percent). In contrast to the patterns in the other variables in the table, the two most recent cohorts have marriage rates that are similar to the average for all immigrants (70.2 percent for the 1985-1989 cohort and 70.8 percent for the 1980-1984 cohort).[9] In these data, the cohort that arrived between 1970 and 1979 has the highest marriage rate (73.9 percent). Even from these summary data, it can be seen that the role for changes in marital status to explain labor market behavior during the first years of entry to the United States is low.

There are significant fertility differences between immigrants and natives. In the next row, it can be seen that immigrants have had more children than natives (2.139 to 1.967) and that earlier arrivals (who are, on average, older) have had more children than more recent arrivals. The lower total number of children of the most recent cohort (1.786 compared with 1.967 for natives), reflects a lower number of woman who have had any children (69.8 to 77.6 percent), while the number of children per woman who has had children is similar to that of natives.

Although not the primary focus of our study, the patterns for immigrants from outlying areas, 90 percent of whom are from Puerto Rico, are an interesting comparison because of their unique legal status. The characteristics of immigrants from these areas are shown in column (8). These immigrants have out-

---

[9]An issue of interest is the effect of the Immigration and Reform Control Act (IRCA) on the household composition of immigrants. Because 56 percent of the population legalized under the provisions of IRCA are male and 84 percent are from Mexico and Central America, initial projections were that other family members entered the United States to reside with the recently legalized, predominantly male immigrants. In addition, the Legalized Population Survey followed households that legalized under the provisions of IRCA. The average household size of the legalized population decreased from 4.7 members to 4.5 members, while the size of the immediate family increased from 2.9 to 3.4 members. The main shifts in the composition of the immediate family include an increase in the proportion with spouses from 51 to 63 percent and an increase in the mean number of children from 1.4 to 1.7 members.

comes in the labor market that are similar to those of the most recent immigrant arrivals. In fact, this group has employment rates that are lower and poverty rates that are higher than those of the 1985-1989 immigrant cohort. Their household characteristics are quite different, however, from the most recent immigrant arrival cohorts. Women from these areas have the lowest marriage rates and have high fertility.

The patterns in this table show that more recent immigrants have lower employment and lower earnings than both earlier arrivals and natives. Among the observable characteristics we have examined, these immigrants have lower mean age, a higher proportion with less than high school education, and worse English ability than other groups, characteristics that may explain some of the differences in labor market outcomes.

Assimilation and Changes Across Cohorts Without Controls

Although interesting, the mean characteristics provide only partial information on the role of the U.S. experience on immigrant outcomes. The comparison of the performance of an earlier immigrant cohort (the 1975-1979 cohort with 11-15 years of experience in the United States at the time of the 1990 Census, for example) with the performance of a more recent cohort (the 1985-1989 cohort with 0-5 years of experience in the United States, for example) does not provide all the information necessary to infer how the more recent cohort will perform as it gains more experience in the United States. Two things are changing when we compare immigrant arrival groups using one cross-section of data. The first is the number of years in the United States (going from 0-5 years of experience to 11-15 years of experience in the example). The second change is the population that is being observed (the 1975-1979 arrival cohort versus the 1985-1989 arrival cohort). Because of changes in country composition or changes in the self-selection within the pool of immigrants from a particular country, immigrants are not drawn from the same population over time. An earlier cohort may perform better because it has had more time to integrate into the labor market or because it arrived in the United States with better observable or unobservable skills than more recent cohorts. We refer to differences in how different immigrant cohorts may perform at all levels of experience in the United States as cohort effects and the changes related to additional time in the United States as assimilation effects.[10]

To examine how immigrant characteristics change with additional time in the United States, it is necessary to follow immigrant cohorts between the data

---

[10]It is not surprising, for example, that more recent immigrant cohorts do not speak English as well as do earlier arrivals since they are more likely to come from non-English-speaking countries. Similarly, it may not be surprising that more recent immigrant cohorts that arrived after U.S. immigration policy placed greater emphasis on family reunification and less emphasis on labor market skills do not perform as well in the labor market.

provided in the censuses. For each initial level of experience (0-5 years of U.S. experience for the 1975-1979 cohort in 1980, for example), the change in an outcome between the census years provides a measure of the effect of an additional ten years in the United States. To examine how more recent immigrant cohorts compare with earlier ones (how the 1985-1989 cohort compares with the 1975-1979 cohort), it is necessary to compare groups at times in which they have the same amount of experience in the United States. It is important to note that factors other than an immigrant's assimilation may be changing between the two census years. For each of the two types of comparisons, natives provide a baseline to capture these other factors that change between census dates.

Given our initial sample, we follow arrival cohorts separately for two age groups—those aged 25-39 in 1980 (and 35-49 in 1990) and those aged 40-49 in 1980 (50-59 in 1990).[11] Changes in labor market behavior related to fertility are most likely to affect females aged 25-39. In contrast, as will be seen in Table 7-6, most of the females aged 40-49 in 1980 had completed their fertility (though not child care) and did not experience changes between 1980 and 1990. The older group is a natural control group to examine changes in labor market behavior related to fertility, although not necessarily for the presence of children.

Tables 7-3 to 7-6—employment, logarithm of hourly earnings, marital status, and fertility, respectively—include a column for 1980, a column for 1990, and a column for the difference between the two years. To control for general economic conditions, each entry in columns (1) and (2) for the immigrant groups is the difference calculated relative to natives. The comparison of changes between the two years in column (3) then indicates the extent to which immigrant groups are catching up to or falling behind natives.

For the two outcome variables that we examine in more detail with regression analysis in the next section—employment rates and the logarithm of hourly earnings—and a third potentially important outcome—fertility—we include two additional columns so we can calculate cohort effects. The cleanest comparison of outcomes across cohorts compares immigrants of the same age and same amount of experience in the United States, but from different arrival cohorts. We make these comparisons in columns (4) and (5). In column (4), cohort means are calculated for 1990 that use the same age restrictions as those used in 1980. In column (5), we calculate the mean difference between each cohort and the cohort that arrived ten years prior.[12] An important note about all of these tables is that,

---

[11]For groups for which emigration and death are not large, these samples are drawn from the same population in the two years. For most groups, attrition does not appear to be a large issue. The exception is the immigrant cohort that arrived prior to 1950. To a lesser extent there is also attrition from the 1950-1959 cohort.

[12]In the tables for education, English ability, and marital status, in which we are most interested in assimilation between the two census dates, we do not provide calculations of the cohort effects at the same point in the life cycle for most immigrant groups. In the bottom rows of these tables, we calculate cohort effects for the arrival cohorts of the 1980s relative to those of the 1970s.

by following narrow age groups over time, year of arrival is also an indicator of age at arrival. For example, within the 25-39 age group observed in the 1990 Census, those who arrived between 1970 and 1974 were between the ages of 5 and 23 at arrival, while those who arrived between 1980 and 1984 were between the ages of 15 and 33 at arrival.

Labor Market Assimilation

We begin with the measures that have been most studied for males—employment rates and the logarithm of hourly earnings, shown in Tables 7-3 and 7-4, respectively. To see how these tables are organized, consider employment rates in Table 7-3. In 1980, employment rates of native females were 70.7 percent for those

TABLE 7-3, Panel A   Employment in Previous Year in 1980 and 1990

	Age 25 to 39 in 1980	Age 35 to 49 in 1990	Age 25 to 39 in 1990		
	Percent Employed		Actual Changes	Percent Employed	Cohort
	1980	1990	1980-1990	1990	Change
	(1)	(2)	(3)	(4)	(5)
Natives	0.707	0.797	0.090	0.801	
	(0.001)	(0.001)	(0.001)	(0.001)	
Relative to Natives:					
Outlying	−0.267	−0.222	0.045	−0.242	
Areas	(0.009)	(0.007)	(0.011)	(0.008)	
Immigrants:					
Pre-1950	−0.054	−0.021	0.033		
	(0.016)	(0.016)	(0.023)		
1950-1959	−0.025	−0.023	0.002	−0.022	
	(0.008)	(0.007)	(0.011)	(0.011)	
1960-1964	−0.045	−0.046	−0.001	−0.020	
	(0.008)	(0.007)	(0.011)	(0.009)	
1965-1969	−0.052	−0.057	−0.005	−0.038	
	(0.006)	(0.006)	(0.008)	(0.007)	
1970-1974	−0.069	−0.076	−0.007	−0.077	−0.032
	(0.006)	(0.005)	(0.008)	(0.006)	(0.010)
1975-1979	−0.157	−0.068	0.089	−0.094	−0.042
	(0.005)	(0.005)	(0.007)	(0.005)	(0.008)
1980-1984				−0.125	−0.056
				(0.004)	(0.007)
1985-1989				−0.247	−0.090
				(0.004)	(0.006)

NOTE: Entries are the proportion of each group that report being employed during the previous calendar year. Sample sizes are 343,713 in Column 1, 331,543 in Column 2, and 430,836 in Column 4.

aged 25-39 in 1980 (shown in Panel A of Table 7-3) and 66.7 percent for those aged 40-49 in 1980 (shown in Panel B of Table 7-3). In 1990, this proportion had increased to 79.7 percent for the younger group and declined to 66.2 percent for the older group. The changes of 9.0 percent (in Panel A) and –0.5 percent (in Panel B) are shown in the third column of the first row in each panel.

Similar calculations relative to natives are shown for each immigrant cohort. For example, the employment rate of persons aged 25-39 who arrived between 1950 and 1959 was 68.2 percent, or 2.5 percentage points below natives (–0.025 in the fourth row and first column of Table 7-3, Panel A) in 1980. In 1990, the employment rate of this group increased to 77.4 percent. But because the employment rate of natives grew as well, the gain on natives was only 0.2 percentage points to a deficit in 1990 of 2.3 percentage points.

TABLE 7-3, Panel B   Employment in Previous Year in 1980 and 1990

	Age 40 to 49 in 1980	Age 50 to 59 in 1990	Age 40 to 49 in 1990		
	Percent Employed		Actual Changes	Percent Employed	Cohort
	1980	1990	1980-1990	1990	Change
	(1)	(2)	(3)	(4)	(5)
Natives	0.667	0.662	–0.005	0.795	
	(0.001)	(0.001)	(0.001)	(0.001)	
Relative to Natives:					
Outlying	–0.247	–0.242	0.005	–.225	
Areas	(0.013)	(0.013)	(0.018)	(0.009)	
Immigrants:					
Pre-1950	–0.038	–0.037	0.001	–0.020	
	(0.014)	(0.016)	(0.021)	(0.016)	
1950-1959	–0.049	–0.044	0.005	–0.027	
	(0.007)	(0.007)	(0.010)	(0.009)	
1960-1964	–0.029	–0.008	0.021	–0.052	
	(0.009)	(0.009)	(0.013)	(0.008)	
1965-1969	0.003	0.007	0.004	–0.054	
	(0.010)	(0.010)	(0.014)	(0.007)	
1970-1974	0.019	–0.004	–0.023	–0.063	–0.034
	(0.011)	(0.011)	(0.016)	(0.006)	(0.011)
1975-1979	–0.136	–0.026	0.110	–0.058	–0.061
	(0.012)	(0.012)	(0.017)	(0.007)	(0.012)
1980-1984				–0.092	–0.111
				(0.007)	(0.013)
1985-1989				–0.221	–0.085
				(0.008)	(0.014)

NOTE: Entries are the proportion of each group that report being employed during the previous calendar year. Sample sizes are 159,595 in Column 1, 154,365 in Column 2, and 229,102 in Column 4.

For persons aged 25-39 in 1980, there is a large increase in employment rates for all groups. The increases for immigrants who arrived prior to 1974 are insignificantly different from the increases for natives. The most recent arrival cohort in 1980 (those who arrived in 1975-1979), however, experienced an increase in employment rates of 17.8 percent, or 8.6 percentage points above the gain for natives.

In contrast to the increase in employment rates for all younger females, for persons aged 40-49 in 1980, there is little change in employment rates between 1980 and 1990 for any group except the most recent arrivals (1975-1979) in 1980. This older group of recent arrivals also had a large deficit in the employment rate relative to natives in 1980 (13.6 percentage points) and gained considerably between 1980 and 1990 (11.0 percentage point gain relative to natives). For both age groups, however, there is some "catching up" for the most recent arrivals; employment rates of immigrant females do not overtake those of native females of similar ages.

In columns (4) and (5) of Table 7-3, the changes across immigrant cohorts with the same amount of U.S. experience, or cohort effects, are shown. Column (4) reports means for the same age group as that reported in column (1). In column (5), the difference between the value in column (4) and the value in column (1) for the cohort that arrived 10 years earlier is calculated. For example, the 1975-1979 cohort in 1990 and the 1965-1969 cohort in 1980 each had 11-15 years of U.S. experience at the time of the census. In Panel A, persons aged 25-39 in the 1975-1979 cohort in 1990 had employment rates 9.4 percentage points below natives (column 4). Persons aged 25-39 in the 1965-1969 cohort in 1980 (at the same level of U.S. experience) had employment rates 5.2 percentage points below the comparison group of natives (column 1). In column (5), we calculate the employment rate of the 1975-1979 cohort to be 4.2 percentage points lower than that of the 1965-1969 cohort at the same level of U.S. experience.

Similarly, the employment rate for immigrants aged 25-39 in the 1985-1989 cohort at 0-5 years of U.S. experience in column (4) is 24.7 percentage points below the rate of natives in 1990. The corresponding deficit for the 1975-1979 cohort in 1980 of the same age group is 15.7 percentage points in column (1). Thus, even though the employment rate of the 1985-1989 cohort during the first five years in the United States was the same as that of the 1975-1979 cohort, this cohort performed 9 percentage points worse relative to natives, and we conclude that there was a decline across these cohorts.

Calculations of changes across cohorts in employment rates in column (5) of Panels A and B show that more recent cohorts perform worse relative to earlier ones. Each of the arrival cohorts over the 1970s and 1980s have significantly lower employment rates relative to natives than the cohort that arrived ten years earlier, ranging from 3 to 9 percentage points.[13]

---

[13]These patterns contrast with those found by Baker and Benjamin (1997) for Canada. Using samples of married couples for 1986 and 1991, they find that immigrant women work more than comparable natives and the difference erodes over time.

Table 7-4 provides similar calculations for the logarithm of real hourly earnings (deflated by the consumer price index) for the two age groups. Between 1980 and 1990, native earnings grew by 0.102 log points for the 25 to 39-year age group (Panel A) and 0.064 log points for the 40 to 49-year age group (Panel B). Hourly earnings of most immigrant cohorts grew more rapidly than that of natives, although the differences are not statistically significant. The most recent immigrants are again an exception, with rapid earnings growth in both age groups. Among those 25-39, hourly earnings of the 1975-1979 arrivals grew by 0.049 log points more than the growth in earnings of natives between 1980 and 1990 (column 3, Panel B). For those aged 40-49 in 1980, the growth was 0.074 log points relative to natives.

TABLE 7-4, Panel A   Log Hourly Earnings in Previous Year in 1980 and 1990

	Age 25 to 39 in 1980	Age 35 to 49 in 1990	Age 25 to 39 in 1990		
	Log Hourly Earnings		Actual Changes	Log Hourly Earnings	Cohort
	1980	1990	1980-1990	1990	Change
	(1)	(2)	(3)	(4)	(5)
Natives	2.110	2.212	0.102	2.139	
	(0.001)	(0.001)	(0.001)	(0.001)	
Relative to Natives:					
Outlying	−0.029	−0.059	−0.029	−0.021	
Areas	(0.018)	(0.016)	(0.024)	(0.016)	
Immigrants:					
Pre-1950	0.086	0.145	0.059		
	(0.027)	(0.029)	(0.040)		
1950-1959	0.052	0.087	0.035	0.154	
	(0.013)	(0.013)	(0.018)	(0.019)	
1960-1964	0.031	0.053	0.022	0.154	
	(0.014)	(0.014)	(0.020)	(0.015)	
1965-1969	0.038	0.027	−0.009	0.088	
	(0.011)	(0.011)	(0.016)	(0.013)	
1970-1974	−0.033	−0.013	0.020	0.023	−0.008
	(0.009)	(0.009)	(0.012)	(0.010)	(0.017)
1975-1979	−0.120	−0.054	0.074	−0.028	−0.066
	(0.010)	(0.010)	(0.014)	(0.008)	(0.019)
1980-1984				−0.112	−0.079
				(0.007)	(0.017)
1985-1989				−0.182	−0.062
				(0.008)	(0.018)

NOTE: Entries are the mean of the logarithm of hourly earnings for each group, calculated for those with positive values. Sample sizes are 223,924 in Column 1; 249,879 in Column 2; and 315,208 in Column 4.

TABLE 7-4, Panel B   Log Hourly Earnings in Previous Year in 1980 and 1990

	Age 40 to 49 in 1980	Age 50 to 59 in 1990	Age 40 to 49 in 1990		
	Log Hourly Earnings		Actual Changes	Percent Employed	Cohort
	1980	1990	1980-1990	1990	Change
	(1)	(2)	(3)	(4)	(5)
Natives	2.107	2.171	0.064	2.218	
	(0.002)	(0.002)	(0.003)	(.002)	
Relative to Natives:					
Outlying	−0.056	−0.052	−0.004	−.069	
Areas	(0.028)	(0.028)	(0.040)	(.020)	
Immigrants:					
Pre-1950	0.055	0.117	0.062	.139	
	(0.024)	(0.028)	(0.037)	(.029)	
1950-1959	0.008	0.025	0.017	.078	
	(0.013)	(0.014)	(0.019)	(.016)	
1960-1964	0.020	0.039	0.019	.019	
	(0.015)	(0.016)	(0.022)	(.016)	
1965-1969	0.020	0.021	0.001	.029	
	(0.016)	(0.017)	(0.023)	(.012)	
1970-1974	−0.064	−0.031	0.033	.005	−0.015
	(0.018)	(0.019)	(0.026)	(.011)	(0.019)
1975-1979	−0.161	−0.113	0.049	−.074	−0.094
	(0.021)	(0.021)	(0.030)	(.013)	(0.021)
1980-1984				−.205	−0.141
				(.014)	(0.023)
1985-1989				−.293	−0.131
				(.017)	(0.027)

NOTE: Entries are the mean of the logarithm of hourly earnings for each group, calculated for those with positive values. Sample sizes are 99,271 in Column 1; 96,630 in Column 2; and 169,727 in Column 4.

As in Table 7-3, cohort effects are calculated for those aged 25-39 in each census year in Panel A and for those aged 40-49 in Panel B. Comparison of immigrant arrival cohorts at similar levels of U.S. experience, shown in column (5), suggests that the labor market quality of immigrant cohorts has fallen continuously since the 1970s. The 1970-1974 cohort performs similarly, relative to natives, to the 1960-1964 cohort ten years earlier. After this cohort, however, each successive cohort earns less than the arrival cohort ten years earlier. For the younger age group, these differences range from 6-8 percentage points. For the older age group, these differences are larger, reaching 9-14 percentage points.

Educational Attainment and English Ability

As was seen in the overall means with the 1990 Census data, there are differences among natives, earlier immigrant cohorts, and later immigrant cohorts in educational attainment and English ability. Changes in these characteristics over time may explain some of the observed differences in labor market outcomes. Although we do not report the results here in a table format, we conducted comparisons of cohorts over time for educational attainment and English ability similar to those reported for employment and hourly earnings.

To summarize changes in educational attainment between 1980 and 1990, the proportion of each cohort with less than a high school degree and the proportion with a college degree were calculated. The main finding is that there is relatively little difference between natives and immigrant cohorts in the accumulation of education after arrival in the United States. For all immigrant and native groups—including those age 40 and above in 1980, there was a reduction in the proportion without a high school diploma between 1980 and 1990, but this difference is between 0.06 and 0.08 points for all groups (including those over age 40 in 1980) except the younger group of recent arrivals (age 25-39 in 1980, who arrived in 1975-1979). These drops are slightly greater for earlier immigrant cohorts.

For college completion, there is a difference by age group. For persons aged 25- 39 in 1980, immigrants who arrived in the 1960s are were less likely to have completed college than natives in 1980, while the most recent arrival cohort (1975-1979) was more likely to have completed college. Between 1980 and 1990, the 1960s arrival cohorts continued college at rates similar to natives, while the college completion rate of subsequent cohorts declined relative to natives. For the older age group, there is very little difference relative to natives in the change in college completion for any of the arrival cohorts.

For both age groups there has been a drop in the proportion that has completed high school across arrival cohorts that leveled off with the most recent arrival cohort of 1985-1989. At the high end of educational attainment, there has been an increase in the college completion rate across successive cohorts for the younger age group and a decline for the older age group.

We summarize English ability by grouping those who only speak English or speak English very well and grouping all other abilities to speak English. Because there was no change in the English ability of natives in either age group, all changes relative to natives between 1980 and 1990 reflect changes in immigrant English ability. Over this period, all immigrant groups improved English ability, with more rapid gains for more recent immigrant groups (that were also younger at the time of arrival). The gains were largest for immigrants aged 25-39 who arrived in the United States between 1975 and 1979—an improvement of 9.1 percentage points between the two census years. Comparison of the cohorts at the same level of U.S. experience shows a continuous decline in English ability across cohorts through the cohort that arrived in the first half of the 1980s (1980-1984). For the cohort of the late 1980s (1985-1989), this trend levels off and there is a slight improvement relative to the cohort that arrived in 1975-1979.

Marital Status and Fertility

The potential role of household behavior in explaining differences between labor market outcomes of native and immigrant females is seen in Tables 7-5 and 7-6. For each age group, percent married and children ever born relative to natives are shown for each arrival cohort in 1980 and 1990. There are two patterns to note before turning to the comparison of immigrants and natives. First, when followed over time, fewer women in each nativity age group were married in 1990 than in 1980 (Table 7-5). This pattern is more pronounced for those aged 40-49 in 1980, but is statistically significant for many of the younger female groups as well. Second, women age 40 and over in 1980 had completed their fertility (Table 7-6, Panel B). For no nativity group is there a statistically significant increase in the number of children ever born between 1980 and 1990 for those over age 40.

In the comparison of immigrant and native marriage rates for the group aged 25-39 in 1980 (columns 1 and 2 of Table 7-5), all of the immigrant arrival cohorts have higher marriage rates than natives. The changes in the marriage rates are quite similar for immigrants and natives, however, and only for the 1965-1969 cohort is the decline in percent marriage statistically different from that of natives. Again, the one exception to the pattern of decline in marriage rates is the most recent immigrant cohort that arrived between 1975 and 1979. After ten years in the United States (in 1990), the marriage rate of this cohort increases significantly relative to natives.[14]

In Table 7-5, we present the cohort changes only for the most recent two five-year cohorts in the final rows of the table. These rows compare the marriage rates of immigrants relative to natives using the same age group in both 1980 and 1990. It can be seen that the arrival cohorts of the 1980s are more likely to be married in 1990 than earlier cohorts at the point in which they had the same amount of experience in the United States.

Changes in fertility for immigrants and natives are presented in the two panels of Table 7-6. Between 1980 and 1990, native women aged 25-39 in 1980 had an additional one-third of a child, on average (column 3). Immigrant females in this age group who arrived prior to 1970 had higher levels of fertility than natives in 1980 (by 0.2 to 0.3 children per women in column 1), but changes in

---

[14]Unfortunately, because we do not know the marital status at the time of entry to the United States, we cannot determine changes in marital status within the first five years after arrival in the United States.

TABLE 7-5 Marital Status in 1980 and 1990

	Age 25 to 39 in 1980 (35 to 49 in 1990)			Age 40 to 49 in 1980 (50 to 59 in 1990)		
	Percent Married		Actual Changes	Percent Married		Actual Change
	1980 (1)	1990 (2)	(3)	1980 (4)	1990 (5)	(6)
Natives	0.707	0.697	–0.01	0.767	0.698	–0.069
	(0.001)	(0.001)	(0.001)	(0.001)	(0.001)	(0.001)
Relative to Natives:						
Outlying	–0.154	–0.175	–0.021	–0.164	–0.197	–0.033
Areas	(0.009)	(0.008)	(0.012)	(0.012)	(0.013)	(0.018)
Immigrants:						
Pre-1950	0.028	0.001	–0.027	–0.021	–0.004	0.017
	(0.015)	(0.018)	(0.027)	(0.013)	(0.015)	(0.020)
1950-1959	0.013	0.032	0.019	0.046	0.050	0.004
	(0.008)	(0.008)	(0.011)	(0.007)	(0.007)	(0.010)
1960-1964	0.049	0.031	–0.018	0.036	0.021	–0.015
	(0.008)	(0.008)	(0.011)	(0.008)	(0.009)	(0.012)
1965-1969	0.073	0.056	–0.017	0.001	0.003	0.002
	(0.006)	(0.006)	(0.008)	(0.009)	(0.009)	(0.013)
1970-1974	0.090	0.083	–0.007	0.013	0.003	–0.010
	(0.006)	(0.005)	(0.008)	(0.010)	(0.011)	(0.015)
1975-1979	0.059	0.078	0.019	0.012	–0.001	–0.013
	(0.005)	(0.006)	(0.008)	(0.010)	(0.012)	(0.016)
Aged 25 to 39 Relative to Natives 25 to 39 (40 to 49):						
1980-1984		0.074			0.018	
		(0.004)			(0.008)	
1985-1989		0.061			0.035	
		(0.005)			(0.009)	

NOTE: Entries are percent of group that were married at time of census. Sample sizes are 343,713 in Column 1; 331,543 in Column 2; 159,595 in Column 4; and 154,365 for Column 5, not including the 1980s cohorts. The sample sizes in the regressions used to estimate the coefficients for the 1980s cohorts are 430,836 in Column 2 and 229,102 in Column 5.

fertility between 1980 and 1990 for most immigrant arrival cohorts are statistically similar to those of natives (column 3).

Once again, the exception to this pattern is the most recent immigrant arrival group—in this case, those who arrived between 1970 and 1979. The two five-year arrival cohorts in this group had much higher changes in fertility between 1980 and 1990 than did either natives or earlier immigrant cohorts.. The immigrant cohort that arrived between 1970 and 1974 had an initial mean number of 0.13 children more than natives in 1980, which increased to 0.35 more than natives in 1990. This represents a gain of 0.21 children relative to natives (col-

TABLE 7-6, Panel A Children Ever Born in 1980 and 1990, Women 25 to 39 in 1980

	Age 25 to 39 in 1980	Age 35 to 49 in 1990	Age 25 to 39 in 1990		
	Children Ever Born		Actual Changes	Children Ever Born	Cohort
	1980 (1)	1990 (2)	1980-1990 (3)	1990 (4)	Change (5)
Natives	1.723 (0.003)	2.058 (0.003)	0.335 (0.004)	1.475 (0.002)	
Relative to Natives:					
Outlying	0.734	0.670	−0.064	0.602	
Areas	(0.028)	(0.028)	(0.040)	(0.025)	
Immigrants:					
Pre-1950	0.460 (0.050)	0.269 (0.060)	−0.191 (0.078)		
1950-1959	0.008 (0.026)	0.062 (0.027)	0.054 (0.037)	0.292 (0.036)	
1960-1964	0.303 (0.027)	0.225 (0.027)	−0.078 (0.038)	0.046 (0.029)	
1965-1969	0.212 (0.021)	0.259 (0.021)	0.047 (0.030)	0.157 (0.024)	
1970-1974	0.136 (0.018)	0.349 (0.018)	0.213 (0.025)	0.517 (0.019)	0.214 (0.033)
1975-1979	−0.153 (0.018)	0.374 (0.018)	0.527 (0.025)	0.517 (0.015)	0.305 (0.026)
1980-1984				0.250 (0.013)	0.114 (0.022)
1985-1989				−0.139 (.013)	0.014 (0.022)

NOTE: Entries are number of children ever born. Sample sizes are 343,713 in Column 1; 331,543 in Column 2; and 430,836 in Column 4.

umn 3). For the 1975-1979 cohort, the change is even more dramatic. This cohort had fertility less than that of natives in 1980 and, after having nearly one additional child per women between 1980 and 1990, had fertility levels significantly more than native females in 1990. This cohort gained 0.53 children relative to natives between 1980 and 1990.

The comparisons of cohort changes in columns (4) and (5) are calculated similarly to those shown above for employment rates and hourly earnings. These calculations show a steadily increasing number of children ever born across immigrant cohorts through the 1980-1984 cohort. For women 25-39, the 1970-1974 and 1975-1979 cohorts had 0.2 to 0.3 more children, on average, than the 1960s cohorts at the same level of U.S. experience. In the 1980s, these two

TABLE 7-6, Panel B   Children Ever Born in 1980 and 1990, Women 40 to 49 in 1980

| | Age 25 to 39 in 1980 | Age 35 to 49 in 1990 | Age 25 to 39 in 1990 | | |
| | Children Ever Born | | Actual Changes | Children Ever Born | Cohort |
	1980 (1)	1990 (2)	1980-1990 (3)	1990 (4)	Change (5)
Natives	3.029 (0.005)	3.010 (0.005)	−0.019 (0.007)	2.202 (0.003)	
Relative to Natives:					
Outlying	0.542	0.576	0.034	.704	
Areas	(0.058)	(0.056)	(0.081)	(.035)	
Immigrants:					
Pre-1950	−0.060	−0.006	0.054	.125	
	(0.062)	(0.067)	(0.091)	(.062)	
1950-1959	−0.189	−0.247	−0.058	.056	
	(0.032)	(0.032)	(0.045)	(.034)	
1960-1964	−0.551	−0.560	−0.009	.211	
	(0.039)	(0.038)	(0.054)	(.032)	
1965-1969	−0.500	−0.502	−0.002	.124	
	(0.041)	(0.041)	(0.058)	(.025)	
1970-1974	−0.216	−0.196	0.020	.202	0.355
	(0.048)	(0.046)	(0.066)	(.023)	(0.045)
1975-1979	0.125	0.231	0.106	.380	0.731
	(0.050)	(0.051)	(0.071)	(.027)	(0.049)
1980-1984				.410	0.194
				(.028)	(0.057)
1985-1989				.420	0.295
				(.030)	(0.058)

NOTE: Entries are number of children ever born. Sample sizes are 159,595 in Column 1; 154,365 in Column 2; and 229,102 in Column 4.

cohort effects are smaller, with the difference between the 1975-1979 and 1985-1989 cohort being statistically insignificant. For females 40-49, the differences in number of children ever born across immigrant arrival cohorts are larger, ranging from 0.2 to 0.7 additional children, and continue through the 1985-1989 cohort.

ESTIMATION APPROACH

We now turn to a multivariate analysis of employment and wages. We adopt the regression framework developed by Borjas (1985, 1995) for estimating the effects of year of arrival and duration of U.S. residence on immigrant outcomes.

This framework exploits the availability of comparable cross-sectional data from two different points in time, and the resulting regression analysis is very similar in spirit to that in Tables 7-3 through 7-6 in the previous section. Without strong restrictions, cross-sectional regressions cannot distinguish immigrant cohort and assimilation effects because, at any given point in time, variation across immigrants in years of U.S. residence arises only from differences in year of entry to the United States. With repeated cross sections, however, outcomes for immigrant arrival cohorts can be tracked over time, and the trick then becomes to isolate changes that are due to assimilation from changes that are caused by different economic conditions in the survey years being compared (i.e., period effects). The most popular solution to this problem, and the one adopted here, is to estimate period effects from the outcome changes experienced by an appropriate group of native workers. After netting out these estimates of the period effects, remaining changes for immigrant cohorts are attributed to assimilation.[15]

To be explicit, let y_j^g represent the outcome for worker j, where the superscript g takes on the values I for immigrants and N for natives. Pooling data from the 1980 and 1990 censuses, immigrant outcomes are determined by the equation

$$y_j^I = C_j\lambda^I + A_j\delta^I + \pi T_j + (1-T_j)X_j\beta_{80}^I + T_jX_j\beta_{90}^I + \varepsilon_j^I, \qquad (1)$$

where the vector C is a set of mutually exclusive dummy variables identifying immigrant arrival cohorts, the vector A is a set of mutually exclusive dummy variables indicating duration of U.S. residence, T is a dummy variable marking observations from the 1990 Census, the vector X contains other determinants of outcomes, ε is a random error term, and the remaining parameters are the objects of estimation. This specification gives each immigrant arrival cohort its own intercept, and differences in these intercepts represent permanent outcome differentials between cohorts. The coefficients of the duration of U.S. residence dummies measure the effects of immigrant assimilation on the outcome variable. In addition, the coefficients of the variables in X are allowed to vary across census years, with the subscripts 80 and 90 indicating the survey year of a particular parameter vector.

The corresponding equation for natives is

$$y_j^N = \alpha^N + \pi T_j + (1-T_j)X_j\beta_{80}^N + T_jX_j\beta_{90}^N + \varepsilon_j^N, \qquad (2)$$

where α^N is the intercept for natives, and the immigrant arrival cohort and duration of U.S. residence variables are excluded from this equation because they are not relevant for U.S.-born workers.

To see the identification problem in equation (1), it is easiest to think of C, A, and T as being scalar variables denoting, respectively, year of entry to the United

---

[15] A key assumption of this approach is that compositional changes in the subsample of an immigrant cohort observed in the U.S. labor market—such as those caused by emigration, mortality, and labor force entry and exit—do not bias measured outcome changes.

States, years since entry, and survey year. In this case, $C + A = T$, which implies that we cannot estimate the separate effects of these variables without imposing some restriction. An analysis of immigrant outcomes must confront the classic problem of identifying cohort, age, and period effects. The identifying restriction imposed in equations (1) and (2) is that the period effect π is the same for immigrants and natives, as indicated by the absence of a superscript on this parameter. In essence, the period effect is estimated from U.S.-born individuals, and this information is used to identify cohort and assimilation effects for the foreign born. To estimate the parameters of equations (1) and (2), we pool observations on immigrants and natives from both the 1980 and the 1990 censuses into a single regression, and then impose the restrictions implicit in these equations by introducing the appropriate interaction terms between nativity, the 1990 Census dummy, and the other explanatory variables.

EMPLOYMENT REGRESSIONS

The first characteristic of female immigrants that we analyze in detail is their attachment to the labor market. Tables 7-7 and 7-8 present estimates of equations (1) and (2) in which the dependent variable is a dummy identifying women who worked at any time during the calendar year preceding the census.[16] The coefficients were estimated by least squares, with sampling weights used in the regressions.[17] Standard errors are shown in parentheses. These regressions, and all further regressions reported in this chapter, exclude immigrants who arrived prior to 1950, both because of the ambiguity as to when these immigrants arrived, and also because this is the only cohort to show signs of substantial attrition between the 1980 and 1990 censuses. To avoid complications that arise with immigrants who arrived as children, we also exclude all foreign-born individuals whose age and arrival cohort imply any possibility that they entered the United States prior to age 15.[18]

Table 7-7 reports the immigrant cohort and assimilation effects, as well as the period effects, from employment regressions that successively add control

---

[16]We experimented with indicators of labor market attachment other than employment last year, including weeks worked last year and employment or labor force participation during the census survey week. Similar patterns emerged using these alternative measures.

[17]Given our very large sample, we employ least squares here with a dichotomous dependent variable for the sake of computational convenience. Probit estimates produced similar results.

[18]Immigrants who arrive as children, and who therefore acquire much of their education and all of their work experience in the United States and who are more likely to speak English fluently, experience greater economic success than immigrants who come as adults (Kossoudji, 1989; Friedberg, 1991; Smith, 1991). Given the age and other restrictions typically used to construct analysis samples, the average age at arrival within the extracted subsample of a cohort falls with duration of residence in the United States, because as an immigrant arrival cohort ages, its youngest members enter the sample and its oldest members leave the sample. These factors combine to produce a spurious correlation between immigrant outcomes and duration of U.S. residence.

variables.[19] In column (1), the only controls are for geographic location (dummy variables identifying census division and whether the individual lives in a metropolitan area) and age (dummy variables representing five-year age groups). Column (2) adds controls for racial-ethnic affiliation (Mexican, Puerto Rican, other Hispanic, non-Hispanic black, non-Hispanic Asian, non-Hispanics who report some other nonwhite race, and the reference category of non-Hispanic white). Column (3) also includes indicators of educational attainment, English language proficiency, marital status, and whether the woman is the mother of any children under age 18 who currently live with her. The coefficients of the geographic controls are restricted to be the same for immigrants and natives, but these coefficients can differ in 1980 and 1990.[20] The coefficients of all other control variables are allowed to vary both by nativity and by census year.

In column (1) of Table 7-7, the estimated coefficients of the immigrant cohort dummies represent differences in the employment rates of U.S.-born women aged 25-29 and foreign-born women the same age who are members of a particular immigrant arrival cohort and who have lived in the United States for five years or less. The negative coefficients indicate that, on arrival, young immigrant women from all cohorts are much less likely to work than young native women, with this employment gap ranging from 13 to 28 percentage points across arrival cohorts. In addition, the estimates imply that employment rates are similar for immigrant cohorts arriving before 1970, but jobholding has declined steadily among later cohorts. For example, 1970-1974 arrivals have an employment rate about 5 percentage points below that of the 1965-1969 cohort, and the most recent immigrants in our data (1985-1989 arrivals) are in turn 10 percentage points less likely to work than the 1970-1974 cohort.

Continuing down the first column of estimates in Table 7-7, the pattern of coefficients for the duration of U.S. residence dummies suggests that migration may initially disrupt the labor market activities of women. Employment rates for female immigrants jump 9 percentage points between their first five years in the United States and their second five years, and then employment declines somewhat with further exposure to America. In his analysis of microdata from the 1970-1990 censuses, Schoeni (1996b) finds a similar pattern of labor force assimilation for female immigrants from most national origin groups.

When ethnicity is controlled for in column (2) of Table 7-7, employment differences between immigrant arrival cohorts shrink somewhat, with the largest intercohort differential now reaching 9 percentage points, as compared with the maximum differential of 15 percentage points in column (1). This result provides

---

[19]To ease computing requirements, these regressions use a 30 percent random sample of the larger data set described in the second section. The resulting data set provides a 1.5 percent sample of the relevant immigrant population and a 0.3 percent sample of the native population.

[20]The geographic variables are included to control for regional variation in the cost of living and economic conditions, factors which may impact immigrants and natives to a similar extent.

TABLE 7-7   Female Employment Regressions, Immigrant Cohort and
Assimilation Effects and Period Effects

Regressor	(1)	(2)	(3)
Immigrant Cohort:			
1985-89 Arrivals	−.281	−.277	−.203
	(.009)	(.011)	(.015)
1980-84 Arrivals	−.241	−.248	−.195
	(.030)	(.031)	(.031)
1975-79 Arrivals	−.199	−.224	−.165
	(.011)	(.013)	(.019)
1970-74 Arrivals	−.177	−.208	−.171
	(.028)	(.029)	(.032)
1965-69 Arrivals	−.132	−.195	−.158
	(.023)	(.030)	(.040)
1960-64 Arrivals	−.131	−.187	−.168
	(.029)	(.035)	(.043)
1950-59 Arrivals	−.144	−.220	−.192
	(.038)	(.048)	(.062)
Born in Outlying Area of U.S.	−.290	−.179	−.144
	(.010)	(.024)	(.025)
Duration of U.S. Residence:			
0-5 Years (reference group)			
6-10 Years	.089	.099	.131
	(.028)	(.028)	(.027)
11-15 Years	.071	.111	.123
	(.015)	(.019)	(.024)
16-20 Years	.051	.098	.111
	(.028)	(.030)	(.033)
21-30 Years	.031	.107	.102
	(.029)	(.037)	(.048)
31-40 Years	.051	.148	.126
	(.047)	(.058)	(.072)
1990 Census Dummy	.065	.074	−.030
	(.006)	(.006)	(.007)
R^2	.043	.045	.128

a rough indication that changes in the national origin composition of immigrant
flows to the United States account for perhaps a third of the employment decline
observed between pre-1970 and post-1980 cohorts of female immigrants. To
determine whether more detailed controls for immigrant source countries can
explain a larger portion of this employment decline, we re-estimated the specification in column (2) after replacing the ethnicity dummies for immigrants with an
alternative set of dummies identifying 17 different world regions of birth.[21] This

---

[21]As was the case with the immigrant ethnicity dummies, the coefficients of the immigrant birthplace dummies are allowed to differ across census years. These birthplace dummies identify the
following regions: Africa, North America, Mexico, South America, Central America, the Caribbean,

TABLE 7-7   continued

Regressor	(1)	(2)	(3)
Other Controls:			
Census Division and			
Metropolitan Status	Yes	Yes	Yes
Age	Yes	Yes	Yes
Ethnicity	No	Yes	Yes
Educational Attainment	No	No	Yes
English Proficiency	No	No	Yes
Marital Status and Presence			
of Children	No	No	Yes

NOTE: The dependent variable is a dummy indicating whether the individual worked at any time during the calendar year preceding the Census. The coefficients were estimated by least squares, with standard errors shown in parentheses. Sampling weights were used in the regressions. Data are from the 1980 and 1990 Censuses. The sample includes women aged 25-59. Excluded are any immigrants who may have been younger than age 15 when they first arrived in the United States. The total sample size is 413,943 observations: 117,697 immigrants and 296,246 natives. The effects of Census division and metropolitan status are restricted to be the same for immigrants and natives, but these effects can differ in 1980 and 1990. The effects of all other control variables are allowed to vary both by nativity and Census year.

alternative specification produced similar estimates of immigrant cohort and assimilation effects, and the less aggregated information on national origins did not further attenuate the estimated employment differentials between arrival cohorts.

In column (2) we once again observe a steep rise in employment as foreign-born women move from 0-5 to 6-10 years in the United States. Unlike the column (1) estimates, however, employment rates do not decline with further time spent in the United States.

The final column in Table 7-7 adds controls for education, English proficiency, marital status, and children. Educational attainment is represented by a set of dummy variables identifying the following categories for completed years of schooling: 0-8 years, 9-11 years, 12 years (the omitted dummy), 13-15 years, and 16 or more years.[22] For immigrants, we measure English proficiency with a set of dummy variables identifying each of the five possible responses, with the omitted group representing English monolinguals. Because few U.S.-born individuals report speaking English "not well" or "not at all," for natives we collapse

---

East Asia, Southwest Asia, Southeast Asia, the Middle East, Northern Europe, Western Europe, Southern Europe, Eastern Europe, the former USSR, Oceania, and a final category for immigrants whose specific birthplace is not reported.

[22]We follow Jaeger's (1997) recommendations for how to maximize consistency between the different education questions asked in the 1980 and 1990 censuses.

the three lowest categories of English proficiency into a single dummy variable identifying bilinguals who speak English worse than "very well." Marital status is represented by a set of dummies assigning women to three categories: never married (the omitted group); currently married, excluding those who are separated; and widowed, divorced, or separated. Finally, dummy variables signal the presence of any own children living in the household who fall into the following age groups: 0-2, 3-6, and 7-17 years old.

After conditioning on the extensive control variables included in the column (3) specification, remaining employment differences between immigrant cohorts are small, with the most noticeable distinction being that 1950s and 1980s arrivals have employment rates 2-4 percentage points below those of other immigrants. With these controls for observable characteristics, the jump in immigrant employment occurring after the initial five years in the United States increases to 13 percentage points, and the subsequent employment changes that are due to assimilation are small.

Recall that the employment regressions include a vector of dummy variables identifying five-year age groups whose coefficients are allowed to vary by nativity and census year. In all three specifications and in both survey years, these age coefficients (not reported) imply that employment rates fall with age more sharply for natives than immigrants. According to our estimates, predicted employment differences between immigrants and natives vary with age, partly because of the differential age effects, and also because assimilation can influence the employment of foreign-born women as they age in the United States.

Figure 7-1 displays representative employment profiles for immigrant and native women that illustrate the combined impact of age and assimilation on immigrant-native employment differentials. The top panel of Figure 7-1 derives from the estimates of specification (1) in Table 7-7. In addition to immigrant cohort and assimilation effects, age effects, and period effects, this specification includes controls for census division and metropolitan status. The predicted employment rates pictured in the top panel of Figure 7-1 are for women in 1990 who live in a metropolitan area in the Pacific division. For natives, we use their 1990 age coefficients to calculate how employment rates vary across five-year age groups. For immigrants, we perform a similar calculation using both their 1990 age coefficients and the appropriate duration of U.S. residence coefficients from column (1) of Table 7-7, under the assumption that immigrants arrive in the United States at age 25. Employment differences between immigrant cohorts are calculated from the cohort coefficients in column (1) of Table 7-7, with simple averages of the relevant coefficients used to aggregate up to ten-year arrival cohorts.

The bottom panel of Figure 7-1 presents analogous predictions from specification (3) in Table 7-7 that include a more extensive set of control variables. As before, the calculations represent women in 1990 who live in a metropolitan area

A. Limited Controls

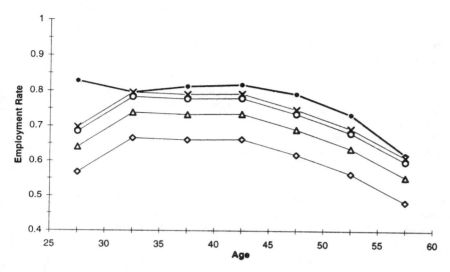

B. Extensive Controls

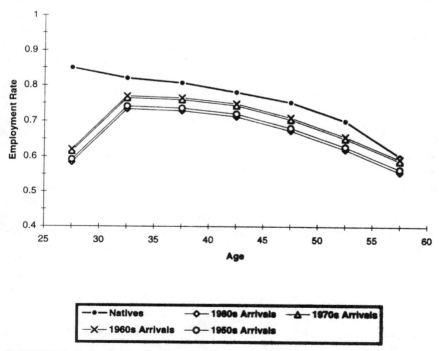

FIGURE 7-1 Estimated employment profiles for immigrant and native women.

in the Pacific division, but we now also specify that these are white, married women with 12 years of schooling who speak only English and have no children.

Figure 7-1 nicely illustrates the main features of employment differentials both between U.S.-born and foreign-born women and across immigrant arrival cohorts. Considering first the top panel with limited control variables, we see that the predicted employment rate of female immigrants rises sharply between the 25-29 and 30-34 age groups, even as the employment rate of native women falls between these same age groups. This pattern arises because of the jump in immigrant employment that takes place after five years of U.S. residence. After this initial adjustment period, the employment rate of foreign-born women varies with age in much the same manner as the employment rate of U.S.-born women, and immigrants who arrived before 1970 are only slightly less likely to work than natives. The figure also highlights the decreased labor market activity of more recent cohorts of female immigrants, with the 1970s arrivals having an employment rate about 6 percentage points below that of earlier arrivals, and the employment rate falling an additional 7 percentage points for 1980s arrivals.

The bottom panel of Figure 7-1 shows that qualitatively similar patterns emerge after controlling extensively for observable characteristics. In this case, however, the rise in immigrant employment after five years in the United States is even more dramatic, and employment differences across immigrant cohorts are greatly reduced. Indeed, observable variables can account for essentially all of the employment differential between the 1970s arrivals and earlier cohorts, and these same variables explain most of the employment deficit for the 1980 arrivals.

A word of caution is in order regarding the employment profiles depicted in Figure 7-1. Because the age coefficients in our model are identified by cross-sectional variation,[23] they undoubtedly confound birth cohort effects with true age effects. This issue is particularly relevant in the current context, because the dramatic growth in female labor force participation witnessed during this century was in large part driven by the changing behavior of birth cohorts (Smith and Ward, 1985; Goldin, 1990:Chap. 2). For this reason, Figure 7-1 and similar figures presented below are only intended to illustrate how comparisons between immigrants and natives vary with age, rather than to portray life-cycle changes.

Table 7-8 presents the estimated coefficients of selected control variables from the most extensive specification. These coefficients are from the same employment regression reported in column (3) of Table 7-7. For both immigrants and natives, the positive relationship between education and employment strengthened over the 1980s, and there is also some indication that during this decade English language deficiencies became a bigger obstacle to holding a job,

---

[23]Although we pool data from the 1980 and 1990 censuses, the intertemporal variation is used to identify period effects and distinguish for immigrants the separate effects of arrival cohort and assimilation.

TABLE 7-8   Female Employment Regressions, Selected Coefficients, by Nativity and Census Year

Regressor	Natives		Immigrants	
	1980	1990	1980	1990
Education:				
0-8 Years	−.205	−.289	−.029	−.058
	(.004)	(.006)	(.011)	(.009)
9-11 Years	−.100	−.156	−.023	−.059
	(.003)	(.004)	(.013)	(.012)
12 Years (reference group)				
13-15 Years	.055	.083	.038	.062
	(.003)	(.002)	(.012)	(.009)
16 or More Years	.114	.132	.087	.111
	(.003)	(.003)	(.013)	(.009)
English Proficiency:				
Speaks Only English (reference group)				
Speaks English Very Well	.033	−.013	.008	.0003
	(.006)	(.005)	(.012)	(.010)
Speaks English Well	−.006	−.034	−.025	−.029
	(.009)	(.009)	(.013)	(.011)
Speaks English Not Well			−.066	−.100
			(.015)	(.012)
Speaks English Not at All			−.133	−.169
			(.018)	(.015)
Marital Status:				
Never Married (reference group)				
Married	−.056	.015	−.102	−.052
	(.004)	(.003)	(.014)	(.010)
Widowed, Divorced,	.084	.083	−.005	.014
or Separated	(.004)	(.004)	(.016)	(.012)
Presence of Own Children in Household:				
Age 0-2	−.204	−.131	−.159	−.124
	(.004)	(.003)	(.012)	(.010)
Age 3-6	−.176	−.133	−.126	−.110
	(.003)	(.003)	(.011)	(.009)
Age 7-17	−.052	−.039	−.061	−.035
	(.002)	(.002)	(.009)	(.007)

NOTE: These coefficients are from the same employment regression reported in column (3) of Table 7-7; see the note to that table for more information. Standard errors are shown in parentheses. For natives, the English proficiency categories representing bilinguals who speak English "well," "not well," or "not at all" have been collapsed into a single dummy variable.

TABLE 7-9   Male Employment Regressions, Immigrant Cohort and Assimilation Effects and Period Effects

Regressor	(1)	(2)	(3)
Immigrant Cohort:			
1985-89 Arrivals	−.127	−.124	−.070
	(.005)	(.007)	(.009)
1980-84 Arrivals	−.168	−.162	−.102
	(.020)	(.020)	(.021)
1975-79 Arrivals	−.146	−.161	−.092
	(.007)	(.008)	(.012)
1970-74 Arrivals	−.163	−.177	−.110
	(.019)	(.019)	(.021)
1965-69 Arrivals	−.162	−.197	−.116
	(.015)	(.019)	(.025)
1960-64 Arrivals	−.169	−.205	−.131
	(.019)	(.022)	(.027)
1950-59 Arrivals	−.165	−.227	−.137
	(.024)	(.030)	(.039)
Born in Outlying Area of U.S.	−.152	−.104	−.066
	(.007)	(.014)	(.014)
Duration of U.S. Residence:			
0-5 Years (reference group)			
6-10 Years	.135	.135	.121
	(.019)	(.019)	(.019)
11-15 Years	.133	.152	.119
	(.009)	(.012)	(.015)
16-20 Years	.150	.169	.133
	(.018)	(.020)	(.022)
21-30 Years	.161	.201	.144
	(.018)	(.023)	(.029)
31-40 Years	.143	.202	.128
	(.031)	(.037)	(.045)
1990 Census Dummy	−.019	−.016	−.0001
	(.004)	(.004)	(.004)
R^2	.021	.040	.095

especially for immigrants who speak little or no English. These findings are consistent with other well-documented signs that the demand for skilled workers was rising over this period (Bound and Johnson, 1992; Murphy and Welch, 1992; Juhn et al., 1993). In addition, the employment differential between married and never-married women shrank during the 1980s, disappearing altogether for natives. Similarly, children were less of a deterrent to work in 1990 than they were a decade earlier.

Turning now to immigrant-native comparisons, Table 7-8 indicates that employment differences by education level are wider for natives than for immigrants, particularly when comparing high school dropouts with high school gradu-

TABLE 7-9   continued

Regressor	(1)	(2)	(3)
Other Controls:			
Census Division and			
Metropolitan Status	Yes	Yes	Yes
Age	Yes	Yes	Yes
Ethnicity	No	Yes	Yes
Educational Attainment	No	No	Yes
English Proficiency	No	No	Yes
Marital Status	No	No	Yes

Note: The dependent variable is a dummy indicating whether the individual worked at any time during the calendar year preceding the Census. The coefficients were estimated by least squares, with standard errors shown in parentheses. Sampling weights were used in the regressions. Data are from the 1980 and 1990 Censuses. The sample includes men aged 25-59. Excluded are any immigrants who may have been younger than age 15 when they first arrived in the United States. The total sample size is 391,537 observations: 109,174 immigrants and 282,363 natives. The effects of Census division and metropolitan status are restricted to be the same for immigrants and natives, but these effects can differ in 1980 and 1990. The effects of all other control variables are allowed to vary both by nativity and Census year.

ates. This result suggests that the U.S. labor market values an additional increment of U.S. schooling by more than it values an additional increment of foreign schooling, which is the interpretation often used to explain the finding that the returns to education—in terms of earnings—are higher for natives than for immigrants (Chiswick, 1978). Table 7-8 also implies that the relationship between marital status and employment is different for immigrants and natives. Using never-married women as the reference group, marriage reduces employment more for immigrants than for natives, and losing a husband (through either death or divorce) does not raise employment for immigrants the way it does for natives.

For purposes of comparison, we estimated similar employment regressions for men; Tables 7-9 and 7-10 and Figure 7-2 report these results.[24] In contrast to the strong pattern for female immigrants of lower employment rates for more recent arrival cohorts, employment differences between cohorts of male immigrants are negligible, particularly in the column (1) regression that employs a minimal set of control variables. Indeed, when ethnicity and other controls are

---

[24]The specifications of the male and female employment regressions are identical except that the dummy variables indicating the presence of own children in the household are never included in the male regressions.

TABLE 7-10   Male Employment Regressions, Selected Coefficients, by
Nativity and Census Year

	Natives		Immigrants	
Regressor	1980	1990	1980	1990
Education:				
0-8 Years	−.115	−.199	−.038	−.051
	(.002)	(.003)	(.008)	(.006)
9-11 Years	−.045	−.080	−.023	−.033
	(.002)	(.002)	(.010)	(.007)
12 Years (reference group)				
13-15 Years	.008	.031	−.033	.013
	(.002)	(.002)	(.009)	(.006)
16 or More Years	.030	.052	−.007	.022
	(.002)	(.002)	(.008)	(.006)
English Proficiency:				
Speaks Only English (reference group)				
Speaks English Very Well	−.005	−.011	−.019	−.016
	(.004)	(.003)	(.008)	(.007)
Speaks English Well	−.020	−.025	−.035	−.031
	(.006)	(.005)	(.009)	(.007)
Speaks English Not Well			−.075	−.061
			(.010)	(.008)
Speaks English Not at All			−.126	−.122
			(.013)	(.010)
Marital Status:				
Never Married (reference group)				
Married	.119	.106	.105	.073
	(.002)	(.002)	(.008)	(.005)
Widowed, Divorced,	.045	.042	.057	.022
or Separated	(.003)	(.002)	(.011)	(.008)

Note: These coefficients are from the same employment regression reported in column (3) of Table
7-9; see the note to that table for more information. Standard errors are shown in parentheses. For
natives, the English proficiency categories representing bilinguals who speak English "well," "not
well," or "not at all" have been collapsed into a single dummy variable.

added in columns (2) and (3), the estimates indicate that the most recent cohorts
of immigrant men have slightly higher employment rates than earlier cohorts.[25]

The impact of assimilation on immigrant employment, however, is strikingly
similar for men and women. Male employment rates shoot up 13 percentage

_____

[25]Other analyses of the labor force activity of male immigrants have found a different pattern of
cohort effects (Borjas, 1992; Fry, 1996a, 1996b, 1996c). Using various indicators, ranging from
census week employment or labor force participation to Fry's definition of long-term idleness (not
currently enrolled in school and jobless for at least the past 15 months), these studies report lower

points after five years of U.S. residence and change relatively little thereafter. Figure 7-2 displays predicted employment profiles for immigrant men that strongly resemble those for immigrant women. After an initial period of adjustment, immigrant employment rates follow the same age path as native employment rates.

To investigate employment differences across national origin groups in a broad yet informative fashion, we repeated this analysis separately for immigrants from five major racial-ethnic categories: non-Hispanic white, non-Hispanic black, non-Hispanic Asian, Mexican, and other Hispanic.[26] The regressions for particular immigrant groups are much less precisely estimated than the previous regressions for all immigrants combined. As a result, many of the differences across arrival cohorts or duration of U.S. residence intervals are no longer statistically significant. Nonetheless, the basic patterns within and across ethnic groups are of some interest, and we briefly describe these results below.

In general, the patterns noted above for all immigrants combined are also evident within ethnic groups. For example, women and men of every immigrant group experience a sizable burst in labor market activity following the initial five years of U.S. residence. In addition, all groups of female immigrants exhibit employment declines for more recent arrival cohorts, although the usual ordering of employment rates across cohorts is reversed for blacks and Asians when extensive control variables are introduced.

In Figures 7-3 and 7-4, we present the patterns for immigrants from the most important country of origin, Mexico, for females and males. The organization of the figures is the same as for Figures 7-1 and 7-2—we use the specification with limited controls in the top panel and the specification with extensive controls in the bottom panel. The lower employment rates during the first five years in the United States is evident for females, although there is a predicted drop in employment rates as age increases above 40. The lower employment rates of more recent cohorts for females have been especially large for Mexican and other Hispanic immigrants. The employment rates of the 1950s arrivals exceed those of the 1980s arrivals at the same point in the U.S. experience profile by as much as 20 percentage points. The comparison of these two panels for females reveals that much of this difference is due to differences across arrival cohorts in observable characteristics.

---

activity among more recent cohorts. Nevertheless, the estimated differences across cohorts of male immigrants are quite small, especially when compared with the much larger employment differences across cohorts of female immigrants that we report here.

[26]So that it is easy to compare results across these groups, the same native sample—non-Hispanic whites—was used in all regressions. We now employ the full 5 percent sample for each of the immigrant groups, and we use a 0.1 percent sample of non-Hispanic white natives. Because the 1980 Census does not report when they arrived in this country, immigrants born in outlying areas of the United States (including Puerto Rico) are excluded.

A. Limited Controls

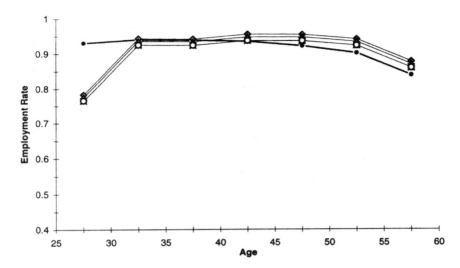

B. Extensive Controls

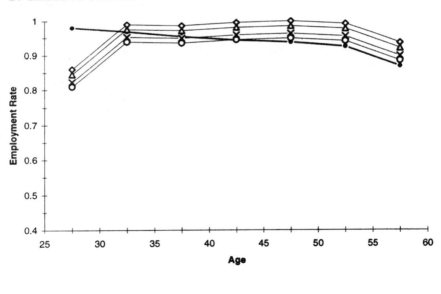

FIGURE 7-2 Estimated employment profiles for immigrant and native men.

A. Limited Controls

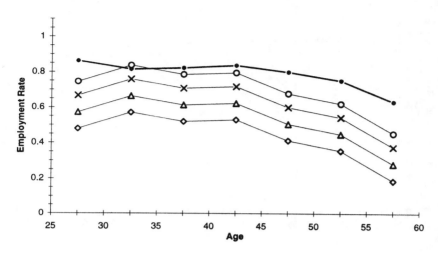

B. Extensive Controls

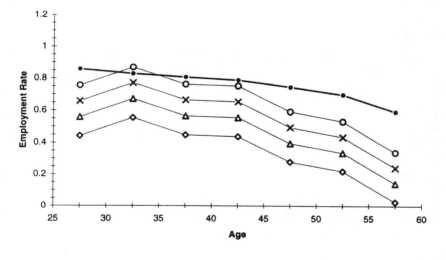

FIGURE 7-3 Estimated employment profiles for women: Mexican immigrants and white natives.

A. Limited Controls

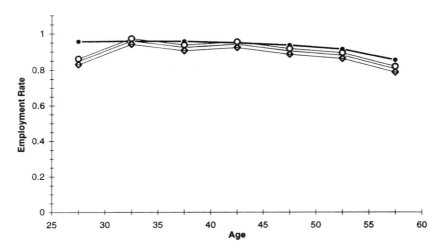

B. Extensive Controls

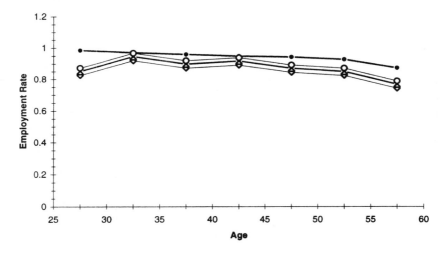

FIGURE 7-4 Estimated employment profiles for men: Mexican immigrants and white natives.

For immigrant men, intercohort employment differences are small among Asians, Mexicans, and other Hispanics, whereas recent cohorts of white and black immigrants are more likely to work than their predecessors. The patterns for Mexicans, shown in Figure 7-4, show significantly lower employment rates during the first five years of U.S. experience. These assimilation patterns are very similar for the lines representing each arrival cohort. In contrast to the patterns for females, there is not much difference in the cohort effects between the two panels.

HOURLY EARNING REGRESSIONS

We now analyze the hourly wages of female immigrants using the same approach that guided the employment analysis in the preceding section. The dependent variable is the natural logarithm of average hourly earnings in the calendar year preceding the census. Only women with positive earnings are included in the sample.

Tables 7-11 and 7-12 present log wage regressions with the same independent variables as the female employment regressions, except that specification (3) no longer includes the children dummies as control variables. Once again, the coefficients were estimated by least squares, with sampling weights used in the regressions.[27] These regressions pool immigrants from all ethnic groups, using the same sampling proportions as before (see footnote 19).

The predicted wage profiles in Figure 7-5 summarize the regression results. The top panel of the figure, in which the only controls are for census division and metropolitan status (i.e., specification (1) in Table 7-11), shows lower wages for female immigrants arriving in the 1970s and 1980s. The coefficients on the duration of U.S. residence dummies suggest that wage growth that is due to assimilation emerges after ten years of U.S. experience, and subsequent wage growth of this kind allows foreign-born women to erase some of their initial wage disadvantage relative to U.S.-born women. Nonetheless, even at the end of their careers immigrant women from all arrival cohorts are estimated to earn less than native women, with final wage gaps ranging from about 8 percent for pre-1970 arrivals to 20 percent for 1980s arrivals. Column (1) of Table 7-11 indicates that the wage deficit is particularly large for the most recent immigrants, the 1985-1989 arrivals.

The bottom panel of Figure 7-5 shows that the additional variables included in specification (3) of Table 7-11—ethnicity, education, English proficiency, and marital status—explain why foreign-born women earn less than U.S.-born

---

[27]Selective labor force participation can bias least-squares estimates of wage equations for women. To correct for this sample selection problem, we employed the two-step procedure developed by Heckman (1979). In implementing Heckman's procedure, we assumed that the presence of children influences the employment decision but does not affect wages conditional on employment. The pattern of immigrant cohort and assimilation effects estimated with the selection correction is similar to what we get using least squares, so only the least-squares estimates are reported here.

TABLE 7-11   Female Wage Regressions, Immigrant Cohort and Assimilation Effects and Period Effects

Regressor	(1)	(2)	(3)
Immigrant Cohort:			
1985-89 Arrivals	−.256	−.127	−.063
	(.017)	(.020)	(.026)
1980-84 Arrivals	−.190	−.056	−.007
	(.052)	(.053)	(.053)
1975-79 Arrivals	−.189	−.138	−.051
	(.021)	(.025)	(.032)
1970-74 Arrivals	−.117`	−.059	−.005
	(.049)	(.051)	(.053)
1965-69 Arrivals	−.113	−.141	−.050
	(.044)	(.054)	(.068)
1960-64 Arrivals	−.095	−.129	−.054
	(.052)	(.062)	(.073)
1950-59 Arrivals	−.106	−.234	−.116
	(.071)	(.086)	(.107)
Born in Outlying Area of U.S.	−.082	.094	.113
	(.020)	(.042)	(.042)
Duration of U.S. Residence:			
0-5 Years (reference group)			
6-10 Years	.006	.022	.041
	(.049)	(.049)	(.047)
11-15 Years	.091	.188	.151
	(.028)	(.035)	(.042)
16-20 Years	.079	.184	.148
	(.048)	(.053)	(.057)
21-30 Years	.162	.335	.239
	(.054)	(.067)	(.081)
31-40 Years	.190	.414	.275

women. After controlling for these variables, wage differences among post-1960 immigrant cohorts shrink dramatically, and immigrants from these cohorts earn about as much as natives during their initial ten years in the United States and more than natives after labor market assimilation takes place. Female immigrants who arrived during the 1950s stand out as having the lowest wages of any cohort.[28]

---

[28]The low unobserved skills of the 1950-1959 cohort compared with the 1960s arrivals may explain why Long's (1980) cross-sectional analysis of 1970 Census data led him to conclude that the earnings of married female immigrants *decrease* rather than increase with duration of U.S. residence. Because over the relevant time period immigrant wages were rising across arrival cohorts, cross-sectional estimates of the impact of U.S. experience would be biased downward by the omitted cohort effects. Log wage equations for immigrant women estimated on the 1980 and 1990 Census cross-sections show the more familiar pattern of higher wages for earlier cohorts, which is consistent with the switch to wage declines across cohorts that took place for immigrants arriving after 1960.

TABLE 7-11   continued

Regressor	(1)	(2)	(3)
	(.088)	(.105)	(.124)
1990 Census Dummy	.451	.456	.387
	(.010)	(.010)	(.011)
R^2	.203	.208	.299
Other Controls:			
Census Division and			
Metropolitan Status	Yes	Yes	Yes
Age	Yes	Yes	Yes
Ethnicity	No	Yes	Yes
Educational Attainment	No	No	Yes
English Proficiency	No	No	Yes
Marital Status	No	No	Yes

Note: The dependent variable is the natural logarithm of average hourly earnings in the calendar year preceding the Census. The coefficients were estimated by least squares, with standard errors shown in parentheses. Sampling weights were used in the regressions. Data are from the 1980 and 1990 Censuses. The sample includes women aged 25-59 with positive earnings in the calendar year preceding the Census. Excluded are any immigrants who may have been younger than age 15 when they first arrived in the United States. The total sample size is 276,776 observations: 70,632 immigrants and 206,144 natives. The effects of Census division and metropolitan status are restricted to be the same for immigrants and natives, but these effects can differ in 1980 and 1990. The effects of all other control variables are allowed to vary both by nativity and Census year.

Comparing the cohort coefficients in columns (1) and (2) of Table 7-11, we see that controlling for immigrant ethnicity shakes up the pattern of wage differences across arrival cohorts, but overall these wage differences do not narrow substantially. Similar results were obtained using the more detailed birthplace dummies (described previously in footnote 21) in place of the immigrant ethnicity dummies. It is adding the controls for education, English proficiency, and marital status in column (3) that compresses wage differences among immigrant cohorts arriving after 1960.

Table 7-12 reports the estimated coefficients of the additional variables included in the third specification. For both immigrants and natives, the returns to education and English proficiency increased during the 1980s. Over the same decade, the marriage penalty vanished for foreign-born women and came close to doing so for U.S.-born women. Finally, the returns to education are lower for immigrants than for natives. These findings for wages echo the patterns described above for employment, and the explanations proposed for employment are likely to apply here as well.

Tables 7-13 and 7-14 present the coefficients from comparable wage regressions for men, and Figure 7-6 displays predicted wage profiles from these regressions. The estimates reported in column (1) of Table 7-13 and graphed in the top panel of Figure 7-6 reproduce the familiar earnings decline for successive cohorts

TABLE 7-12   Female Wage Regressions, Selected Coefficients, by Nativity and Census Year

Regressor	Natives		Immigrants	
	1980	1990	1980	1990
Education:				
0-8 Years	−.184	−.184	−.083	−.080
	(.008)	(.012)	(.021)	(.017)
9-11 Years	−.121	−.174	−.063	−.075
	(.006)	(.006)	(.025)	(.021)
12 Years (reference group)				
13-15 Years	.127	.181	.131	.160
	(.005)	(.004)	(.021)	(.015)
16 or More Years	.425	.519	.360	.434
	(.005)	(.004)	(.022)	(.015)
English Proficiency:				
Speaks Only English (reference group)				
Speaks English Very Well	.010	.002	.013	−.005
	(.010)	(.008)	(.022)	(.016)
Speaks English Well	.009	−.031	−.039	−.092
	(.017)	(.015)	(.023)	(.018)
Speaks English Not Well			−.097	−.175
			(.027)	(.021)
Speaks English Not at All			−.131	−.216
			(.036)	(.028)
Marital Status:				
Never Married (reference group)				
Married	−.068	−.029	−.068	.001
	(.006)	(.004)	(.022)	(.016)
Widowed, Divorced,	−.026	.002	−.042	−.006
or Separated	(.006)	(.005)	(.026)	(.019)

Note: These coefficients are from the same hourly earnings regression reported in column (3) of Table 7-11; see the note to that table for more information. Standard errors are shown in parentheses. For natives, the English proficiency categories representing bilinguals who speak English "well," "not well," or "not at all" have been collapsed into a single dummy variable.

of male immigrants (Borjas, 1994, 1995). Note that the magnitude of the earnings decline is broadly similar for women and men: the estimates in column (1) of Table 7-11 indicate that the relative wages of immigrant women fell 15 percent between the 1950-1959 and 1985-1989 arrival cohorts, whereas in Table 7-13 the corresponding wage decline for immigrant men is 18 percent. Controlling for ethnicity reverses the direction of the cohort wage effects for men, a finding which attests to the powerful link between immigrant skill changes and the dramatic shifts in the national origin composition of U.S. immigration flows that have occurred during the postwar period (Borjas, 1992; LaLonde and Topel, 1992).

A. Limited Controls

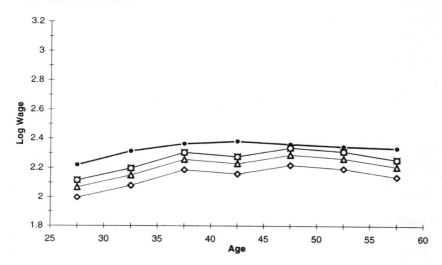

B. Extensive Controls

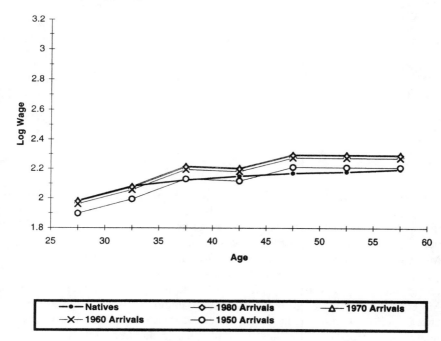

FIGURE 7-5 Estimated wage profiles for immigrant and native women.

TABLE 7-13   Male Wage Regressions, Immigrant Cohort and Assimilation Effects and Period Effects

Regressor	(1)	(2)	(3)
Immigrant Cohort:			
1985-89 Arrival	−.286	−.007	.105
	(.014)	(.017)	(.021)
1980-84 Arrivals	−.272	.019	.155
	(.047)	(.048)	(.048)
1975-79 Arrivals	−.256	−.118	.034
	(.017)	(.021)	(.028)
1970-74 Arrivals	−.195	−.033	.112
	(.045)	(.046)	(.049)
1965-69 Arrivals	−.182	−.212	−.031
	(.037)	(.046)	(.059)
1960-64 Arrivals	−.084	−.126	.025
	(.046)	(.054)	(.065)
1950-59 Arrivals	−.102	−.351	−.151
	(.060)	(.073)	(.093)
Born in Outlying Area of U.S.	−.210	.095	.195
	(.016)	(.035)	(.035)
Duration of U.S. Residence:			
0-5 Years (reference group)			
6-10 Years	.035	.052	.037
	(.045)	(.045)	(.043)
11-15 Years	.124	.312	.247
	(.023)	(.029)	(.035)
16-20 Years	.135	.329	.251
	(.044)	(.047)	(.051)
21-30 Years	.220	.574	.440
	(.045)	(.057)	(.070)
31-40 Years	.243	.753	.582
	(.077)	(.091)	(.109)
1990 Census Dummy	.358	.369	.390
	(.009)	(.009)	(.010)

Finally, we briefly discuss results from wage regressions estimated separately for immigrants from the major racial-ethnic groups. For both women and men, white and Asian immigrants have wage profiles similar to those of U.S.-born workers. As in the case of employment, we present a separate figure for Mexican wage profiles in Figures 7-7 and 7-8. In contrast to some other groups, Mexicans stand out with a very pronounced pattern of lower wages for more recent immigrant cohorts, even after controlling for observable characteristics. Moreover, wages do not grow for Mexican immigrants as they acquire experience living and working in the United States, which results in huge wage deficits relative to natives for Mexicans from all age and duration of U.S. residence groups. Previous studies have documented these patterns for Mexican men (Smith, 1991; Borjas, 1995; Schoeni, 1996a), and our analyses indicate that labor market outcomes are similar for Mexican women.

TABLE 7-13   continued

Regressor	(1)	(2)	(3)
R^2	.190	.206	.286
Other Controls:			
Census Division and			
Metropolitan Status	Yes	Yes	Yes
Age	Yes	Yes	Yes
Ethnicity	No	Yes	Yes
Educational Attainment	No	No	Yes
English Proficiency	No	No	Yes
Marital Status	No	No	Yes

Note: The dependent variable is the natural logarithm of average hourly earnings in the calendar year preceding the Census. The coefficients were estimated by least squares, with standard errors shown in parentheses. Sampling weights were used in the regressions. Data are from the 1980 and 1990 Censuses. The sample includes men aged 25-59 with positive earnings in the calendar year preceding the Census. Excluded are any immigrants who may have been younger than age 15 when they first arrived in the United States. The total sample size is 350,074 observations: 94,792 immigrants and 255,282 natives. The effects of Census division and metropolitan status are restricted to be the same for immigrants and natives, but these effects can differ in 1980 and 1990. The effects of all other control variables are allowed to vary both by nativity and Census year.

CONCLUSION

In this concluding section, we summarize our findings about the employment and wages of female immigrants and place these findings in the context of other studies that compare labor market outcomes across immigrant arrival cohorts and track changes experienced by cohorts as they adapt to life in the United States. Existing empirical research of this type focuses almost exclusively on male immigrants.

Broadly speaking, the employment and wages of foreign-born women exhibit the same pattern of decline across arrival cohorts that has been uncovered for immigrant men, but some important differences emerge. For women, the pattern of cohort decline is particularly strong for employment, with steady reductions in the employment rate of successive immigrant cohorts arriving after 1970. This basic trend shows up for female immigrants from every ethnic group that we examine, and the drop in labor market activity is particularly severe for women from Mexico. Shifts in the national origin composition of immigrant flows to the United States account for roughly a third of the employment decline between pre-1970 and post-1980 cohorts of female immigrants, and remaining cohort differences are largely explained by variables such as education, English proficiency, marital status, and fertility. Even with extensive control variables, however, the employment rate of the 1980s arrivals remains well below that of earlier immigrants. Finally, after an initial period of adjustment to the United States, female immigrants who arrived before 1970 are only slightly less likely to

TABLE 7-14 Male Wage Regressions, Selected Coefficients, by Nativity and Census Year

Regressor	Natives		Immigrants	
	1980	1990	1980	1990
Education:				
0-8 Years	−.226	−.221	−.082	−.122
	(.006)	(.008)	(.019)	(.014)
9-11 Years	−.102	−.151	−.040	−.076
	(.005)	(.005)	(.023)	(.018)
12 Years (reference group)				
13-15 Years	.069	.114	.071	.095
	(.004)	(.003)	(.020)	(.014)
16 or More Years	.277	.407	.363	.400
	(.004)	(.004)	(.019)	(.014)
English Proficiency:				
Speaks Only English (reference group)				
Speaks English Very Well	−.041	−.025	−.063	−.080
	(.008)	(.008)	(.019)	(.015)
Speaks English Well	−.079	−.043	−.136	−.144
	(.014)	(.013)	(.020)	(.016)
Speaks English Not Well			−.238	−.250
			(.024)	(.018)
Speaks English Not at All			−.333	−.326
			(.033)	(.024)
Marital Status:				
Never Married (reference group)				
Married	.255	.237	.161	.148
	(.005)	(.004)	(.019)	(.013)
Widowed, Divorced,	.140	.080	.081	.030
or Separated	(.006)	(.005)	(.028)	(.019)

Note: These coefficients are from the same hourly earnings regression reported in column (3) of Table 7-13; see the note to that table for more information. Standard errors are shown in parentheses. For natives, the English proficiency categories representing bilinguals who speak English "well," "not well," or "not at all" have been collapsed into a single dummy variable.

work than native women, whereas more recent immigrants display much lower levels of labor market attachment.

For immigrant men, studies by Borjas (1992) and Fry (1996a, 1996b, 1996c) use census data to analyze differences in labor force activity across arrival cohorts, and these authors report a tendency for lower activity among more recent cohorts. The estimated differences across cohorts of male immigrants are quite small, however, especially when compared with the much larger employment differences observed across cohorts of female immigrants. Indeed, the employment regressions for men that we report here imply negligible cohort differen-

A. Limited Controls

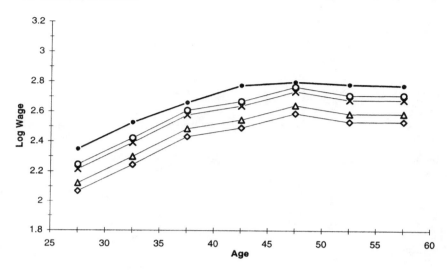

B. Extensive Controls

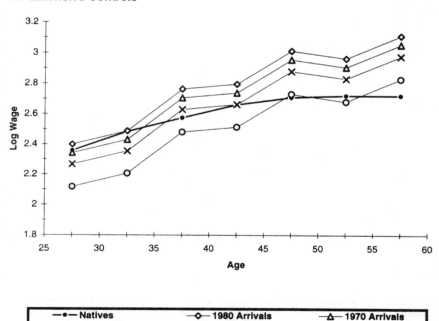

FIGURE 7-6 Estimated wage profiles for immigrant and native men.

A. Limited Controls

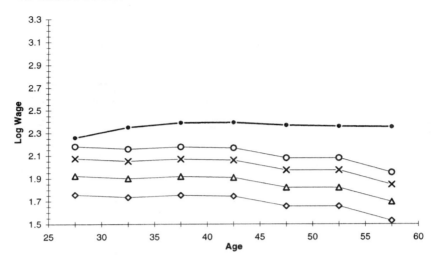

B. Extensive Controls

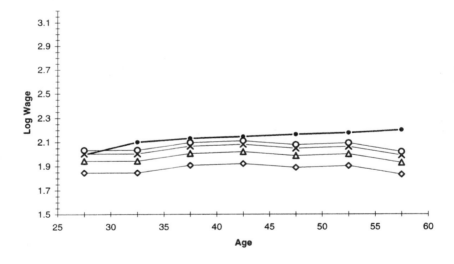

FIGURE 7-7 Estimated wage profiles for women: Mexican immigrants and white natives.

A. Limited Controls

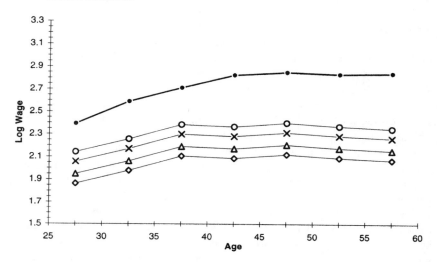

B. Extensive Controls

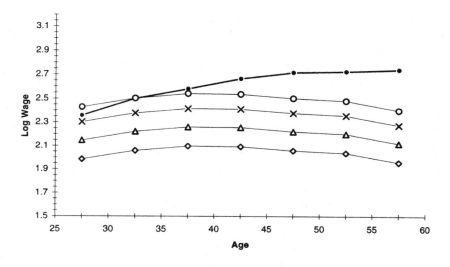

FIGURE 7-8 Estimated wage profiles for men: Mexican immigrants and white natives.

tials. Our reading of the available evidence is that a strong pattern of lower employment rates for more recent immigrant arrival cohorts exists only for women and not for men.

The impact of assimilation on immigrant employment, however, is strikingly similar for men and women. Regardless of gender, employment rates rise sharply—on the order of 10 percentage points—as the foreign born pass from their initial five years of U.S. residence to the next five years, and thereafter employment rates change relatively little with further exposure to America.[29] Except during this period of adjustment, immigrant employment rates follow a similar age path as native employment rates.

A growing body of evidence indicates that recent cohorts of foreign-born men have lower wage profiles than earlier cohorts.[30] Our analysis of hourly earnings reveals a similar pattern of cohort decline for the wages of immigrant women. The magnitude of this wage decline does not appear to differ much by gender, with our own estimates indicating that the hourly earnings of immigrants (relative to natives) fell by 15 percent for women and 18 percent for men between the 1950-1959 and 1985-1989 arrival cohorts. For Mexican immigrants, in particular, the same story describes male and female earnings: sharply declining wages across arrival cohorts, large wage deficits relative to native workers, and little indication that immigrants erase much of this wage gap over their lifetimes. Previous studies have documented these patterns for Mexican men (Smith, 1991; Borjas, 1995; Schoeni, 1996a), and we find similar patterns for Mexican women.

The source of the wage decline across immigrant arrival cohorts, however, may differ for men and women. Specifically, shifts in the national origins of U.S. immigration flows can account for the diminished earning capacity of more recent male immigrant cohorts, whereas these shifts play a relatively minor role in explaining the earnings changes observed for female immigrant cohorts. Instead, wage differences across arrival cohorts of foreign-born women are more closely related to human capital variables such as education, English proficiency, and martial status. After controlling for these variables, wage differences among post-1960 cohorts of female immigrants shrink dramatically, and these immigrants earn about as much as native women during their initial ten years in the United States and more than natives after labor market assimilation takes place.

Overall, our analysis indicates that the empirical techniques that have revolutionized research on the labor market outcomes of foreign-born men can also provide insight into the experiences of female immigrants to the United States. Many of the same patterns arise for men and women, along with some interesting

---

[29]Schoeni (1996b), for women, and Chiswick et al. (1997), for men, report patterns of immigrant labor force assimilation consistent with what we find.

[30]Borjas (1994) surveys this literature.

differences, and both the similarities and the differences invite further study. In particular, theoretical and empirical models that emphasize the family context of migration decisions (Mincer, 1978; Borjas and Bronars, 1991) have the potential to advance our understanding of immigrant selectivity and adaptation.

REFERENCES

Baker, Michael, and Dwayne Benjamin
    1997   "The Role of Family in Immigrants' Labor Market Activity: An Evaluation of Alternative Explanations." *American Economic Review* 87(4):705-727.

Blau, Francine D.
    1992   "The Fertility of Immigrant Women: Evidence from High-Fertility Source Countries." Pp. 93-133 in *Immigration and the Work Force: Economic Consequences for the United States and Source Areas*, George J. Borjas and Richard B. Freeman, eds. Chicago: University of Chicago Press.

Borjas, George J.
    1985   "Assimilation, Changes in Cohort Quality, and the Earnings of Immigrants." *Journal of Labor Economics* 3(4):463-489.

Borjas, George J.
    1987   "Self-Selection and the Earnings of Immigrants." *American Economic Review* 77 (4):531-553.

Borjas, George J.
    1992   "National Origin and the Skills of Immigrants in the Postwar Period" Pp. 17-47 in *Immigration and the Work Force: Economic Consequences for the United States and Source Areas*, George J. Borjas and Richard B. Freeman, eds. Chicago: University of Chicago Press.

Borjas, George J.
    1994   "The Economics of Immigration." *Journal of Economic Literature* 32(4):1667-1717.

Borjas, George J.
    1995   "Assimilation and Changes in Cohort Quality Revisited: What Happened to Immigrant Earnings in the 1980s?" *Journal of Labor Economics* 13(2):201-245.

Borjas, George J., and Stephen G. Bronars
    1991   "Immigration and the Family." *Journal of Labor Economics* 9(2):123-248.

Bound, John, and George Johnson
    1992   "Changes in the Structure of Wages in the 1980's: An Evaluation of Alternative Explanations." *American Economic Review* 82(3):371-392.

Chiswick, Barry R.
    1978   "The Effect of Americanization on the Earnings of Foreign-Born Men." *Journal of Political Economy* 86(5):897-921.

Chiswick, Barry R., Yinon Cohen, and Tzippi Zach
    1997   "The Labor Market Status of Immigrants: Effects of the Unemployment Rate at Arrival and Duration of Residence." *Industrial and Labor Relations Review* 50(2):289-303.

Friedberg, Rachel M.
    1991   *"The Labor Market Assimilation of Immigrants in the United States: The Role of Age at Arrival."* Boston: Massachusetts Institute of Technology.

Fry, Richard
    1996a "Has the Quality of Immigrants Declined? Evidence from the Labor Market Attachment of Immigrants." *Contemporary Economic Policy* 14(3):53-70.

Fry, Richard
    1996b *What Explains the Decline in the Relative Employment of Immigrants?* Washington, D.C.: U.S. Department of Labor.

Fry, Richard
  1996c   *The Increase in Idleness of Immigrant Arrivals: The Role of Age at Arrival, Refugees, and Country of Origin.* Washington, D.C.: U.S. Department of Labor.
Goldin, Claudia
  1990   *Understanding the Gender Gap: An Economic History of American Women.* New York: Oxford University Press.
Heckman, James J.
  1979   "Sample Selection Bias as a Specification Error." *Econometrica* 47(1):153-261.
Jaeger, David A.
  1997   "Reconciling the Old and New Census Bureau Education Questions: Recommendations for Researchers." *Journal of Business and Economics Statistics* 15(3).
Jasso, Guillermina, and Mark R. Rosenzweig
  1986   "What's in a Name? Country-of-Origin Influences on the Earnings of Immigrants in the United States." Pp. 75-106 in *Research in Human Capital and Development*, Vol. 4, Oded Stark, ed. Greenwich, Conn.: JAI Press.
Juhn, Chinhui, Kevin M. Murphy, and Brooks Pierce
  1993   "Wage Inequality and the Rise in Returns to Skill." *Journal of Political Economy* 101(3):410-442.
Kossoudji, Sherrie A.
  1989   "Immigrant Worker Assimilation: Is It a Labor Market Phenomenon?" *Journal of Human Resources* 24(3):494-527.
LaLonde, Robert J., and Robert H. Topel
  1992   "The Assimilation of Immigrants in the U.S. Labor Market." Pp. 67-92 in *Immigration and the Work Force: Economic Consequences for the United States and Source Areas*, George J. Borjas and Richard B. Freeman, eds. Chicago: University of Chicago Press.
Long, James E.
  1980   "The Effect of Americanization on Earnings: Some Evidence for Women." *Journal of Political Economy* 88(3):620-629.
Mincer, Jacob
  1978   "Family Migration Decisions." *Journal of Political Economy* 86(5):749-773.
Murphy, Kevin M., and Finis Welch
  1992   "The Structure of Wages." *Quarterly Journal of Economics* 107(1):285-326.
Passel, Jeffrey S., and Barry Edmonston
  1994   "Immigration and Race: Recent Trends in Immigration to the United States." Pp. 31-71 in Barry Edmonston and Jeffrey S. Passell, eds., *Immigration and Ethnicity: The Integration of America's Newest Arrivals*. Washington, D.C.: The Urban Institute Press.
Reimers, Cordelia W.
  1996   "The Progress of Mexican and White Non-Hispanic Immigrants in California and Texas, 1980 to 1990." Unpublished manuscript, Hunter College, New York.
Schoeni, Robert F.
  1996a   "New Evidence on the Economic Progress of Immigrant Men in the 1970s and 1980s." Unpublished manuscript, The RAND Corporation, Santa Monica, Calif.
Schoeni, Robert F.
  1996b   "Labor Market Assimilation of Immigrant Women." Unpublished manuscript, The RAND Corporation, Santa Monica, Calif.
Smith, James P.
  1991   "Hispanics and the American Dream: An Analysis of Hispanic Male Labor Market Wages 1940-1980." Manuscript, The RAND Corporation, Santa Monica, Calif.
Smith, James P., and Michael P. Ward
  1985   "Time-Series Growth in the Female Labor Force." *Journal of Labor Economics* 3(1, pt. 2):S59-S90.

8

Historical Background to Current Immigration Issues

Susan B. Carter and Richard Sutch

Immigration has had a long history in the United States. For the most part, however, it was seldom treated dispassionately even when an attempt was made only to ascertain the pertinent facts and their reliability. Books and innumerable articles were written to "prove" that immigration did not contribute to the population growth of this country because immigration depressed the fertility rate of the native population: that immigration, if it continued, would result in race suicide of the Nordic element; that immigration was a threat to "American" institutions, etc. For this reason much of the literature on the subject is almost worthless.

Simon Kuznets and Ernest Rubin (1954:87)

INTRODUCTION

As background for the work of the Panel on Demographic and Economic Impacts of Immigration, we present a broad overview of the scholarly literature on the impacts of immigration on American life in the late nineteenth and early twentieth centuries.

We emphasize at the outset that this is a formidable undertaking. There is an enormous literature on the subject ranging over every conceivable genre. These include nineteenth-century political broadsides, serious and masterfully written histories, the 42 volume report of the first Immigration Commission appointed in 1907, focused cliometric studies appearing in scholarly journals, autobiographies that witness the era of high immigration, two forthcoming economic histories of pre-World War I immigration (Ferrie, 1997; Hatton and Williamson, 1998), obscure statistical compendia, and theoretical analyses some of which are highly abstract and mathematically intricate.

The subject is also emotional and controversial. In the past, as today, immigration policy arouses strong feelings and in some cases these have colored the analysis offered. As Kuznets and Rubin suggested, dispassionate inquiry is hard to find. Many authors express their conclusions with a degree of certitude that is difficult to justify from the evidence they offer. Writers on opposite sides often have failed to take account of the evidence and arguments of their opponents. On many aspects of the question a modern consensus of scholarly opinion cannot be found.

The economic impact of immigration is a complex issue and one that simple models of supply and demand do not address very well. Indeed, even predictions derived from elaborate general equilibrium models are only as good as the assumed linkages across disparate sectors of the economy. Because of the complexity of the social science, it has become easy for partisans in the debate to ignore scholarly work altogether or to pick and choose studies compatible with their preconceptions from the wide array of findings reported in the literature.

Nevertheless, we believe that it is possible to survey the literature and extract a list of tentative conclusions. These identify rather dramatic differences in the immigrant flows and in immigration's probable impacts between the earlier era of mass immigration and immigration today.

Not everyone will agree with our distillation nor welcome our attempt to cover such an intractable subject with the guise of apparent order. Our "findings" might be better read as provocation for further research. Nevertheless, the process of writing this chapter has convinced us, at least, that this entire area is ripe with important and researchable topics. To encourage debate, we begin by summarizing our findings regarding four interrelated topics.

FINDINGS

The Magnitude and Character of Immigrant Flows

• Immigrant flows were larger in the past. This is true whether the flows are measured relative to the size of the resident population or to its growth rate.

• Immigration around the turn of the century was dominated by single males of young working ages. Today's flows include many more women and children.

• Many of the immigrants during the period of high immigration were sojourner workers who came to the United States to work for a few years and then return to their home country. Today's immigrants are far more likely to be reuniting with family members in this country or to be refugees. Far more than was ever true in the past, today's immigrants come to stay.

• In the past, immigrant flows were highly responsive to economic conditions in the United States. The numbers swelled when the U.S. economy was booming, wages were rising, and unemployment was low. They ebbed when the economy was depressed. Emigration, the return flow, was highest during American depressions and was reduced during booms. Today the ebbs and flows over time are related to political—not economic—conditions. In particular, some of the largest annual flows in recent years occurred during periods of economic recession in the United States.

• In the past, America selected people with above-average skills and backgrounds from their countries of origin. Today this pattern still holds for some sending countries, but is less clear for some others.

• In the past, immigrants took jobs that were concentrated near the middle of the American occupational distribution. There were significant numbers of native-born American workers both below and above the strata occupied by the foreign-born labor force. Today the occupational distribution of immigrants is bimodal, with one group displaying much higher and the other much lower skills than the resident American work force.

Immigration and Economic Growth

Immigration's impact on American economic growth has been the major focus of the scholarship on the previous episode of high immigration. This work suggests that immigration caused the size of the American economy to grow more rapidly than would have been the case in the absence of immigration. The key mechanisms emphasized in the literature are

• the high labor force participation rate of immigrants;
• immigration-induced capital flows from abroad, particularly from immigrants' countries of origin;
• high immigrant saving rates; much of this saving was invested in residential structures and in the capital necessary to operate self-owned businesses;
• the role of immigration in stimulating inventive activity;
• the role of immigration in allowing the economy to take advantage of economies of scale; and
• immigrants' importation of significant stocks of human capital into the United States.

Immigration and the American Income Distribution

Immigration's impact on American income distribution has been much less emphasized in the scholarship on turn-of-the-century immigration. Income inequality appears to have grown over the period of mass immigration, but it is not clear what role immigration played in this development. Key conclusions in the literature are

• There is no evidence that immigrants permanently lowered the real wage of resident workers overall in the nineteenth and early twentieth centuries.
• There is no evidence that international immigrants increased the rate of unemployment, took jobs from residents, or crowded resident workers into less attractive jobs.
• There is no evidence that the early twentieth-century immigrant community placed a disproportionate burden on public charitable agencies or private philanthropies.
• The turn-of-the-century educational system does not appear to have been

an important arena for transferring resources between the foreign- and native-born populations.

• There is some evidence that immigration may have reduced regional differences in income inequality.

On the other hand, there is no consensus regarding the impact of immigration on racial wage differentials. A number of scholars argue that the flow of European-born workers into the rapidly growing industrial cities of the North may have helped to delay the migration of blacks from the South to the North. If it delayed black migration, then immigration from abroad also would have delayed the convergence of black and white incomes.

Immigration and the Character and Quality of American Life

• There is a broad consensus that immigration did not depress the fertility of the native-born population.

• The children of nineteenth- and early twentieth-century immigrants appear to have assimilated rather quickly into the mainstream of American life.

THE MAGNITUDE AND CHARACTER OF IMMIGRANT FLOWS

Immigration to the United States has increased steadily in the post-World War II period.[1] In 1995, the latest year for which data are available, the number of immigrants admitted into the United States was three times the annual flow between 1951 and 1960 and nearly double that of the 1970s.[2] Figure 8-1 displays

---

[1]"Immigrants" are aliens who have been admitted into the United States for legal, permanent residence. In the post-World War II period, immigrants account for only a small fraction of the total number of aliens who arrive in the United States each year (Bureau of the Census, 1996:Table 7, p.11). In recent years the number of nonimmigrant aliens exceeds the number of immigrants by approximately twentyfold. Note that the data on nonimmigrants count arrivals rather than individuals so a person making multiple visits would be counted once for every visit. The overwhelming majority of these nonimmigrants are tourists, business travelers, and people in transit. Students are another important category of alien nonimmigrants. The number of alien nonimmigrant student arrivals each year is about half as great as the total number of people admitted as immigrants. Over the past ten years the number of temporary workers and trainees has grown very rapidly to become another important category of alien nonimmigrants. In 1995, the latest year for which data are available, the number of temporary workers admitted was almost as great as the number of students. Illegal border crossers, crewmen, and "insular travelers" are a third category of aliens who enter the country. They are not included in any of the totals reported here.

[2]The number of immigrants admitted in 1993 was 880,000 exclusive of those admitted under the legalization adjustments permitted by the IRCA. The number of immigrants admitted during the years 1951-1960 was 2.5 million and between 1971 and 1980 it was 4.5 million (Bureau of the Census, 1996: Tables 5 and 6, p.10).

[3]These are the "official" numbers as published by the U.S. Immigration and Naturalization Service in its annual *Statistical Yearbook* (1997:Table 1, p. 27). Also see Bureau of the Census (1975/ 1997, series C89; 1996:Tables 5 and 6).

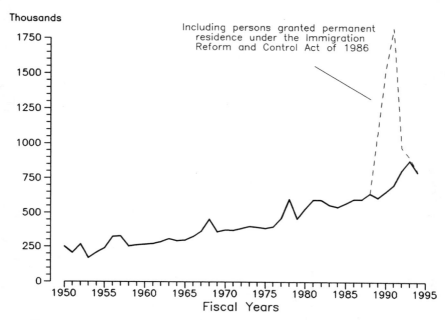

FIGURE 8-1 Immigrants to the United States, 1950-1995.

the number of legal immigrants arriving in the United States annually between 1950 and 1995.[3] The spike in the graph for the years 1989 through 1992, shown by the dashed line, includes persons granted permanent residence under the legalization program of the Immigration Reform and Control Act (IRCA) of 1986. Even excluding these "special" immigrants, the figure shows a pronounced upward trend in immigration over the last third of the century. Moreover, if the response to the IRCA can be interpreted as some measure of the "excess supply" of potential immigrants, then the pressure on American borders may have grown much faster than the numbers plotted in Figure 8-1 would suggest.

As a direct consequence of the recent increase in immigration, the fraction of the American population that is foreign born has risen dramatically. Figure 8-2 charts this change for the post-World War II period.[4] In the 1950s and 1960s, the small number of immigrants, together with the high fertility of the native population, meant that the fraction of the population that was foreign born actually declined. In 1950 the foreign born comprised 6.9 percent of the population; by 1970 their share had dropped to only 4.8 percent. The increasing numbers of immigrants after 1970 led to a reversal of this downward trend. By 1990 the foreign born had surpassed their 1950 share, accounting for 7.9 percent of the

---

[4]Bureau of the Census (1975/1997, series A91; 1990:Table 253; 1993:Table 1).

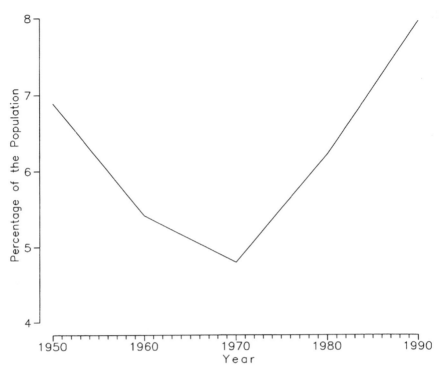

FIGURE 8-2 Foreign born as a percentage of the U.S. population, 1950-1990.

population. A recent news release by the Census Bureau puts the 1996 share at 9 percent.

Because immigrants tend to be young adults, the recent increase in immigration has had a disproportionate impact on the population in the age range of 20 to 40 years. This is shown in Figure 8-3, which plots the fraction of the foreign-born population by age at three post-World War II census dates.[5] In 1950, and even more so in 1970, the foreign born tended to be older than the average American. These people had migrated to the United States in the early decades of the century when *they* were in their late teens and early twenties. By the post-World War II period, they had aged, but the long period of reduced immigration beginning in the 1920s and lasting through 1970 meant that there were far fewer new recruits at the lower end of the age spectrum. The resumption of heavier immigration in the 1980s and 1990s substantially altered the age structure of the foreign-born population. Because the new immigrants were disproportionately

---

[5]Bureau of the Census (1975/1997, series A119-A134; 1984:Table 253; 1993:Table 1).

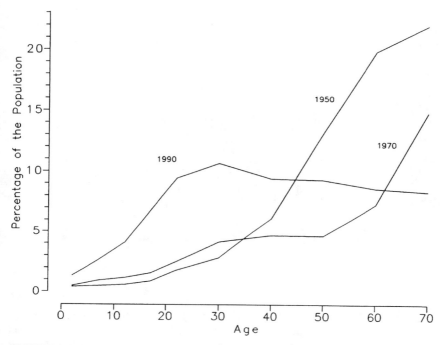

FIGURE 8-3 Foreign born as a percentage of the U.S. population, 1950, 1970, and 1990.

young adults, their arrival increased the foreign-born fraction of the population in the economically active age groups. It is no wonder that the current policy debate over immigration centers on labor market and employment impacts (Borjas, 1995).

Current Flows in Historical Perspective

The level of immigration in the 1980s and 1990s is certainly high in the context of the immediate post-World War II decades—and, indeed, in the experience of almost all of the native-born population of the United States today. Yet it is relatively modest from the perspective of the experience in the period 1880-1914, the era of "mass immigration." Figure 8-4 displays the numbers of immigrants admitted into the United States over the period 1820-1995. This is the same series as the one displayed in Figure 8-1; Figure 8-4 presents this series over

---

[6]These are the "official statistics" of immigration which are the result of the Passenger Act of March 2, 1819, that required the captain of each vessel arriving from abroad to deliver a manifest of all passengers taken on board in a foreign port, with their sex, age, occupation, country of origin, and whether or not they intended to become inhabitants of the United States. These reports were col-

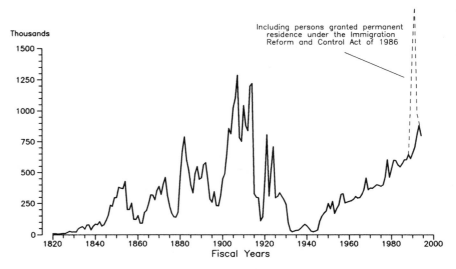

FIGURE 8-4 Immigrants to the United States, 1820-1995.

a longer period of time.[6] Although the spike of 1991, reflecting the response to the IRCA, still stands out, the chart reveals that the number of immigrants admitted through normal channels in the recent period is decidedly smaller than the number admitted in the first decade of the twentieth century.

Moreover, the United States was a much smaller country early in the century. To put the current immigration flows into proper perspective, we deflate the *numbers* of immigrants by the number of people resident in the United States at

lected and abstracted for the period 1820-1855 by Bromwell (1856/1969), for the period 1820-1874 by the Secretary of State, for the period 1867-1895 by the Treasury Department's Bureau of Statistics, and since 1892 by the Office or Bureau of Immigration which is now part of the U.S. Immigration and Naturalization Service (1997). The statistics for the period 1820-1910 were compiled by the U.S. Immigration Commission (1911:Volume 1, Table 1, p. 56). The defects of the official series are well known (Bureau of the Census, *Historical Statistics of the United States*, 1975/1997:97-98, series C89; Jerome, 1926:29-33; Kuznets and Rubin, 1954:55-64; Hutchinson, 1958; Thomas, 1954/ 1973:42-50; McClelland and Zeckhauser, 1983:32-35; and Schaefer, 1994:55-59). The chief biases are the following: (1) the figures apparently exclude first-class passengers for the early decades, (2) they may include some passengers who died en route, (3) before 1906 they exclude immigrants arriving by land from British North America (Canada) and Mexico, (4) immigrants arriving at Pacific ports before 1849 and at Confederate ports during the Civil War are excluded, and (5) the data measure gross rather than net immigration. Despite these imperfections the official series is thought to measure gross flows reasonably well.

[7]The data in Figure 8-5 have been extended back to 1790, and the data before the Civil War have been corrected for the undercounts noted in footnote 6. The figures for 1790-1799 are from Bromwell (1856/1969:13-14) and should be considered as nothing more than educated guesses by contemporaries Blodget (1806/1964) and Seybert (1818). The data for 1800-1849 are estimates made by

Per 1,000

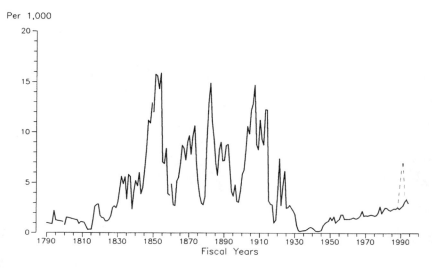

Fiscal Years

FIGURE 8-5 Immigrants to the United States, 1790-1990 (per thousand of resident population).

the time of the immigrants' arrival and display the result in Figure 8-5.[7] Our calculations reveal that, in proportionate terms, the current inflow of immigrants is rather modest. If we look only at the "regular" immigrants—that is, exclusive of those admitted under the IRCA—then the current inflows approximate those in the very *slowest* years from the period between 1840 and the onset of World War I. Before the imposition of a literary test for admission in 1917 (overriding President Wilson's veto) and the passage of the Emergency Quota Act in May 1921, only the disruptions of World War I pushed the flow of immigrants relative to the native population to levels below the relatively low levels that we experience today.[8]

Immigration as a Source of Population Change

As a consequence of the large and persistent immigrant flows in the 1845-1914 period, the foreign born came to comprise a rather large fraction of the total population. Figure 8-6 shows that, in the years between 1860 and 1920, the number of resident Americans born abroad ranged between 13 and 15 percent of the total population (Bureau of the Census, 1975/1997, series A91). The foreign-

McClelland and Zeckhauser (1983:Table A-24, p. 113). Those for 1850-1859 are estimates by Schaefer (1994:Table 3.1, p. 56). Thereafter the official statistics from the U.S. Immigration and Naturalization Service are used (1997:Table 1, p. 27). The resident population is taken from Bureau of the Census (1975/1997, series A7; 1996:Table 2, p. 8).

[8]Goldin (1994) discusses the legislative and political history of immigration restriction.

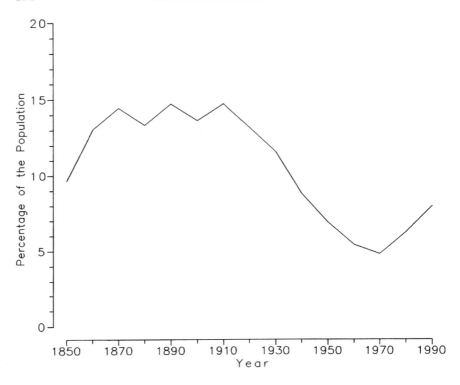

FIGURE 8-6 Foreign born as a percentage of the U.S. population, 1850-1990.

born fraction of the population in that period was approximately three times the level recorded in 1970 and over one and one-half times as high as it is today.

The historical record thus reveals that the numerical impact of immigration flows were once substantially larger than what we have now and were also larger than the levels we are likely to experience in the foreseeable future. Thus we are tempted to suggest that the economic and demographic consequences of immigration in the 1845-1914 period are likely to have been greater than the impact of immigration flows today.

Yet any comparative analysis should explicitly incorporate at least three ways in which the situation today is different from that of the era of mass immigration. First, the structure of the economy and labor market have changed. Some would say the structure is both more complex and less flexible and that labor markets are more segmented. Second, the government is a much larger entity both in terms of the resources it consumes and the fraction of national income it reallocates through tax and transfer mechanisms. Third, immigration is now regulated. We return to these points later in this chapter.

Percent

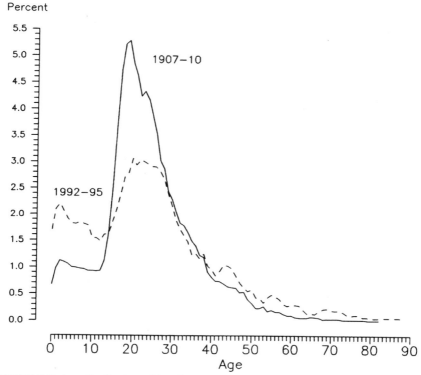

FIGURE 8-7 Age distribution of immigrants to the United States, 1907-1910 compared with 1992-1995.

Age and Gender of Immigrants

The overwhelming proportion of immigrants are young adults. This is true today and it was so in the early years of the twentieth century as well. Figure 8-7 contrasts the age distribution of immigrants in 1907-1910 with that for immigrants in 1992-1995.[9] Clearly, the propensity to immigrate is strongest from

---

[9]The data for 1909-1910 are based on the Public Use Microdata Sample from the enumerator's manuscripts for the 1910 population census. We use the version of this sample that was prepared in a way that improves their comparability with census samples from other years. This file is known as the Integrated Public Use Microdata Sample or IPUMS (see Ruggles and Sobek, 1995). All immigrants (both males and females) who reported arriving in the United States in 1907 or after were included (n = 7658). This census was taken on April 15, 1910. The sample thus includes all 1907-1909 immigrants and slightly more than one-fourth of the 1910 arrivals. The 1992-1995 data are based on the March Current Population Surveys, or CPS, of the Bureau of Labor Statistics for 1994 and 1995. They include all immigrants who reported a permanent move to the United States during or after 1992. All migrants residing in the United States in 1994 or 1995 who immigrated in 1992-1994 and the first few months of 1995 are included (n = 3841).

ages 18 to 30 in both periods. One change that is visible is that modern immigrants are more likely to be accompanied with young children than was true in 1907-1910. This finding is understandable in terms of the reduced costs of migration but it also reflects a sharp change in the gender composition of immigrants. In the late nineteenth and early twentieth centuries men were far more likely to come to America than women. This gender imbalance was particularly pronounced among the young adults who constituted the bulk of all immigrants.

Figure 8-8 contrasts the data on gender composition of immigrants by age from the 1907-1910 period with the most recent data available on gender composition. The proportion male was well over 70 percent in the age range 18-40 in 1907-1910. This represents a male-female ratio of more than two to one. For those in their late twenties, the ratio is greater than three to one. The data from the beginning of the century, when the age of independence was younger than today, show a modest imbalance in favor of young women aged 12-16, undoubtedly produced by the earlier maturation of girls than boys. Yet the startling

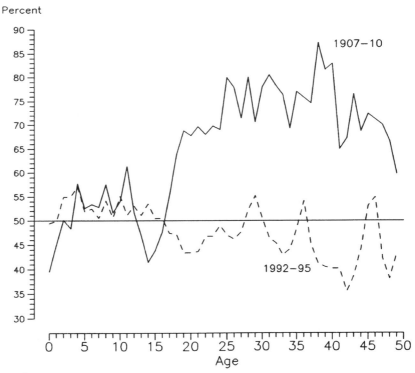

FIGURE 8-8 Proportion of immigrants to the United States who are male, 1907-1910 compared with 1992-1995.

Percent

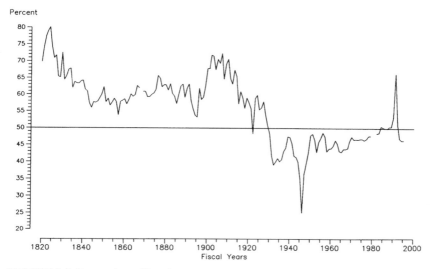

FIGURE 8-9 Proportion of immigrants to the United States who are male, 1810-1990.

finding revealed by Figure 8-8 is the relative gender equality in immigration in the modern data. Today women actually predominate in the prime migration age cohorts.

The data on the gender of immigrants are available beginning in 1820.[10] The long time series of the proportion male is plotted in Figure 8-9. The predominance of males is clearly a phenomenon of the entire period of uncontrolled immigration but it disappears within a decade following the imposition of limitations in 1921. The spike in 1991 shows the impact of the IRCA, which facilitated the transition to immigrant status of certain illegal alien residents.

The age selectivity of migration and the size of the annual flows affect the age composition of the foreign-born population. Figure 8-10, which displays the fraction of the foreign-born population by age for selected census years beginning in 1870 (Bureau of the Census, 1975/1997, series A119-134), shows that persons resident in the United States at the turn of the century were in the prime working age groups. Although the overall fraction of the foreign-born population in the earlier period was about twice the percentage for 1990 (Figure 8-6), the fraction in the prime working ages was close to three times as great as today. It is no wonder that the first U.S. Immigration Commission (1911) concentrated its attention on the impact of immigration on the labor market and employment.

---

[10]Census Bureau (1975/1997, series C138-C139); U.S. Immigration and Naturalization Service (1979:Table 10, p. 27; 1990:Table 11, p. 24; 1997:Table 12, p. 54). Official data on gender are not available for 1868, 1980, or 1981.

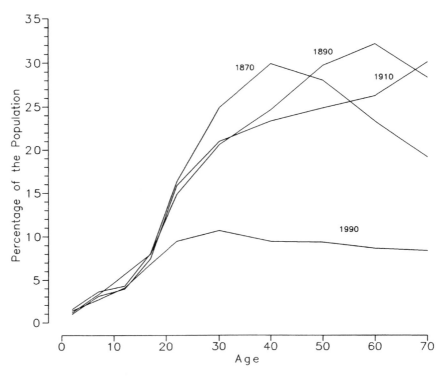

FIGURE 8-10 Foreign born as a percentage of the U.S. population, selected census years.

Return Flows: Sojourners or Permanent Residents?

The literature on the mass migrations in the early part of this century emphasizes the role of sojourners who moved to the United States for a temporary
period to earn income, accumulate assets, and then returned to their home countries (Baines, 1985, 1991; Wyman, 1993). These temporary migrants in the
earlier era bear some similarities with the "guest workers" in today's Europe or
the Braceros of the southwestern United States during the early postwar era.[11]
Quite possibly, recent illegal immigrants to the United States should be thought
of more like these early twentieth-century sojourners than as individuals intend-
ing to settle permanently—albeit illegally—in this country (Warren and Kraly,
1985).

---

[11]The Braceros program was established during World War II to relieve wartime shortages in the
agricultural labor markets of Southern California and Texas. These migrant workers were allowed to
remain in the United States for up to 18 months. The program was extended after the war and was
not ended until 1965 (Feliciano, 1996).

Percent

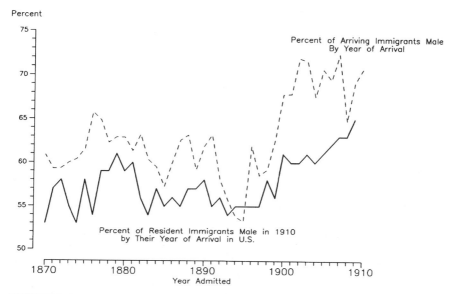

FIGURE 8-11 Proportion of the foreign born in 1910 who were male according to year of arrival compared with proportion of foreign born who were male at various arrival years.

The magnitude of the actual return flows are difficult to measure with precision, yet all of the evidence we have been able to assemble suggests that the return flows were quite large. For example, we think it is interesting to note that, while the age composition of the immigrants had a strong impact on the age distribution of the subsequent foreign-born population, the proportion of males among the foreign-born population recorded at the various censuses from 1880-1910, although greater than 50 percent, was not heavily imbalanced. In Figure 8-11 we make use of the 1910 IPUMS (Ruggles and Sobek, 1995) to calculate the proportion of foreign-born males in 1910 according to their year of arrival in the United States. These numbers are compared with the proportion of immigrants arriving in each year who were male (dashed line).[12] The farther the distance back in time from 1910, the smaller the male share among those who arrived in the year and who remained in the United States as compared with the male share among arrivals in that year. Clearly many more male then female immigrants returned to their homelands with just a brief stay in the United States.

Another clue regarding the relative importance of sojourners in the earlier immigrant flows is contained in the time series displayed in Figure 8-9. There,

---

[12]The immigration data are the same as displayed in Figure 8-9 except that calendar year flows are estimated by averaging the fiscal year data. That is, calendar year 1905 is an average of fiscal year 1905 (which ends June 30, 1905) and fiscal year 1906.

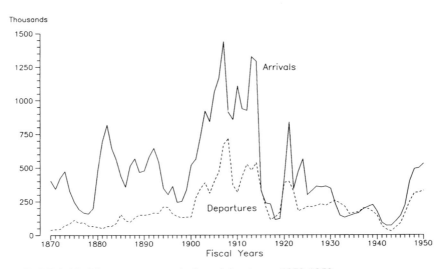

FIGURE 8-12 Alien passenger arrivals and departures 1870-1950.

the predominance of males among new immigrants declines during periods in which the economy was depressed—1857, 1874-1876, 1894-1895, 1920-1921— precisely the same periods when the number of immigrants declined. This cyclical pattern to the male share is consistent with the hypothesis that male immigrants were primarily sojourners whose migration decisions were quite sensitive to economic conditions in the United States.

Certainly it is plausible that a depressed economy would discourage sojourners. But in fact little is known about the phenomenon in the era of mass migration. Before 1908 the official statistics count only arrivals. They do not distinguish between permanent settlers and temporary guest workers, nor is there any comprehensive count of returning immigrants during this period. Kuznets and Rubin (1954:Table B-1, pp. 95-96) have estimated return migration for the period 1870-1908 based on official reports of passenger departures and several assumptions about the mix of American citizens and returning immigrants in the departure data, the mortality of foreign born in the United States, and the mortality of Americans when visiting abroad.[13] The Kuznets and Rubin estimates are displayed in Figure 8-12 together with the official departure data from 1908 onward. We have also reproduced the official figures on arrivals in Figure 8-12. This is the same series as the one displayed in Figure 8-4. Figure 8-13 displays what we call the "immigrant return rate." It is the number of departures each year expressed as a percentage of arrivals.

---

[13]These data from Kuznets and Rubin have been accepted by Hatton and Williamson (1998), who use them for calculating annual estimates of *net* migration.

Percent

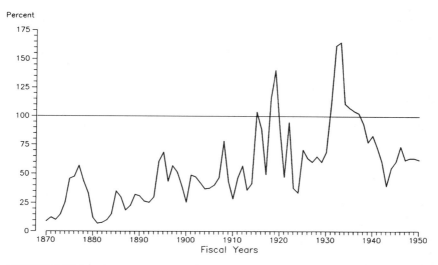

FIGURE 8-13 Immigrant return rate (departures as a percent of arrivals).

Figure 8-13 shows that the return rate rose from less than 10 percent in 1870 and 1881 to over 70 percent just before World War I. This increasing propensity of the United States to attract sojourners makes sense given the declining cost of transatlantic passage due to the continual technological improvement of the steamship following the introduction of scheduled service on the North Atlantic in the 1860s (Baines, 1991:40-42).

Immigration and the American Business Cycle

If we return to Figure 8-4, we find that it reveals another striking difference between the data for the recent and the distant past. In the recent past, immigration flows have increased in almost every year, showing little sensitivity to year-to-year changes in macroeconomic conditions. This is because immigration is today closely regulated and because more wish to migrate than the number of visa slots available. Most successful immigrants have been waiting for admission for several years. Today, year-to-year changes in the number of immigrants reflect policy changes, particularly regarding the admission of refugees and asylees, not changes in demand for admission. In the early period, by contrast, immigration was extremely sensitive to economic conditions in the United States. Between 1891 and 1895, for example, when the unemployment rate almost doubled from 4.5 to 8.5 percent, the number of immigrants fell by more than half, from 560,000 to 259,000. Even more dramatic is the almost 40 percent reduction in the number of immigrants in a single year, from 1.3 million 1907 to 783,00 in 1908 in response to a sharp jump in the unemployment rate from 3.1 to 7.5 percent between those same years (Bureau of the Census, 1975/1997, series C89; Weir, 1992:341). Jerome (1926:208) concluded that the lag between economic activity and immigration in this period was only one to five months.

The relationship between the American business cycle and the flow of immigrants has been examined extensively (Jerome, 1926; Thomas, 1954/1973; Abramovitz, 1961; Williamson, 1964; Easterlin, 1968). The consensus is that the pull forces of American opportunities dominated the push forces of European poverty, land scarcity, and military conscription (Easterlin, 1968:35-36; Cohn, 1995). Thomas (1954/1973) has developed an elegant model of the "Atlantic economy" as an integrated economic unit with flows of immigrants, goods, and capital moving in a rhythm of self-reinforcing and inversely related long-swing Kuznets cycles.[14]   This raises the possibility that immigration acted as a "governor" for the economy, slowing down the booms and cushioning the depressions. Early writers on the business cycle such as Mitchell did not believe that immigration was likely to have been a major factor in moderating the cycle (1913:225-228). Jerome on balance thought immigration may have exacerbated depressions, but his conclusion drew a strong rejoinder from Rorty.[15]   More recent work on the business cycle tends to ignore the role of immigration, perhaps for the obvious reason that the cyclical nature of the immigration flows ended with the Quota Act. However, Thomas (1954/1973) and Hickman (1973) have both suggested that the reduction in immigration was responsible for the decline in demand for housing that preceded and may have contributed to the Great Depression.

It was not just the inflow of immigrants that responded to economic conditions in this country; the outflow of emigrants also responded to the rate of unemployment. Figure 8-13 shows large increases in the rate of departure during the business downturns after 1873, in 1885, after 1893, and in 1908. Throughout the period preceding World War I, the inward and outward movements of immigrants show a negative correlation.[16]   In 1910 and 1913, when arrivals are up, departures are down. In 1912, when arrivals are down, departures are up. The relationship changes with the onset of the war. Both arrivals *and* departures are down during the war years and up during the immediate postwar period.

---

[14]Fishlow (1965:200-203) has expressed doubts about the Thomas model.

[15]Jerome (1926:120-122) was impressed by the fact that net immigration was positive even during times of depression (he was writing before the Great Depression). Rorty, who as a Director of the National Bureau of Economic Research (NBER) by appointment of the American Statistical Association, had the right to attach a dissenting footnote to Jerome's NBER Occasional Paper, correctly, we think, pointed out that the cause of the growth rate in the population should be irrelevant to population growth's impact on the business cycle. Because immigration flows slowed during business downturns, the cyclical movement of immigration can only have helped reduce the magnitude of the unemployment problem.

[16]However, a glance at Figure 8-12 reveals that the magnitude of changes in departures is much smaller than that for arrivals.

Kindleberger (1967), commenting on the European economy in the post-World War II period, has emphasized the potentially important role that sojourners might play in moderating the business cycle. In the upturns an elastic labor supply from abroad might relieve bottlenecks, moderate wage increases, and thereby extend an expansion. In downturns an elastic labor supply can reduce downward pressure on the wage rates earned by the resident population and reduce the drain on public coffers for support of the unemployed. Recently, Hatton and Williamson (1998) have revived the issue of the role of sojourners in moderating the consequences of economic fluctuations in the United States. They compare the actual course of the business cycle of the 1890s with a "no-guest-worker counterfactual" and conclude that the impact of guest workers on moderating the business cycle was "surprisingly small." This assessment is based on their finding that "free migration muted the rise in unemployment during the biggest pre-World War I depression, 1892 to 1896, by only a quarter." Size, of course, is in the eye of the beholder. Some would judge this effect as gratifyingly large. Clearly, an important area for further research would be to improve our understanding of the impact of the sojourner on the American economy at the turn of the century, especially in light of the possibility that illegal migrants might be playing a similar role in the American economy today.

The Question of Immigrant "Quality"

Although it is probably an unfortunate term, the historical literature has given considerable attention to the issue of immigrant "quality." Simply put, the question is whether the United States attracted the more-highly skilled, the more entrepreneurial, and the more adventurous from abroad, or whether it received the "tired, . . . poor, your huddled masses," the unlucky, the least educated, and the least able?[17] Presumably, "high-quality" immigrants would accelerate economic growth, vitalize and enrich the society, and more quickly assimilate into the American "melting pot." "Low-quality" immigrants would, it has often been charged, be more likely to become a burden on the economy, exacerbate inequality, and prove to be a disruptive social force.

In 1891 Francis Walker, the first President of the American Economic Association and former Superintendent of the U.S. Census, expressed his opinion on the matter with little generosity:

> [N]o one can surely be enough of an optimist to contemplate without dread the fast rising flood of immigration now setting in upon our shores. . . . [T]he

---

[17]Recall the poem by Emma Lazarus inscribed at the base of the Statute of Liberty:
> Give me your tired, your poor,
> Your huddled masses yearning to breathe free,
> The wretched refuse of your teeming shore.
> Send these, the homeless, tempest tossed to me:
> I lift my lamp beside the golden door.

immigration of the present time . . . is tending to bring to us no longer the more alert and enterprising members of their respective communities, but rather the unlucky, the thriftless, the worthless. . . . There is no reason why every stagnant pool of European population, representing the utterest failures of civilization, the worst defeats in the struggle for existence, the lowest degradation of human nature, should not be completely drained off into the United States. So long as any difference of economic conditions remains in our favor, so long as the least reason appears for the miserable, the broken, the corrupt, the abject, to think that they might be better off here than there, if not in the workshop, then in the workhouse, these Huns, and Poles, and Bohemians, and Russian Jews, and South Italians will continue to come, and to come by millions (Walker, 1891, as quoted in Handlin, 1959:73-74).

Treatment of immigrant "quality" is intimately bound up with the pull versus push debate about the motives underlying immigration. If immigrants were pushed out of their home country by increasing immizeration, lack of jobs, or shortage of land, the presumption is that immigration would tend to select individuals from the lower tail of the skill and resourcefulness distributions of their country of origin. On the other hand, if immigrants were pulled to the United States by the attractiveness of American opportunities, they are more likely to come from the upper tail of the home country distribution.[18]

Did Migration Select the Best from Europe?

Whether looked at from the point of view of the attributes of the arrivals or the push versus pull controversy, the consensus among economic historians is that, before World War I, America selected immigrants from the upper tail of the

---

[18]Historical studies of immigration debate the relative importance of these "push" and "pull" forces. We note that the differential selectivity of push and pull forces is not a certainty. The push view is based on a threshold model in which low incomes in the origin country depress incomes in the lower tail of the income distribution below some intolerable poverty line. This is thought to compel the migration of the most wretched. Those more fortunately situated are thought to want to remain. Those critical of the push view note that the very poor do not have the resources to afford long-distance migration. This emphasis moderates or even reverses the conclusion that push works to select the least able and least skilled. The pull model assumes that those with the highest ability and the most education will have the most to gain by transferring their skills to a country with a higher capital-labor ratio and a stronger growth-induced excess demand for skilled workers. This conclusion is not a certainty, either. Perhaps the highly skilled can earn more at home in a poor country or perhaps their relative income position matters most to them. If so, they would prefer to be a big fish even if they have to live in a small pond. The recent literature on the selectivity of immigration in the modern period makes heavy use of a different model of selectivity developed by Roy (1951). For an application to modern immigration patterns see Borjas (1987, 1994). The Roy model focuses on differences between countries in the variance of their earnings distributions as well as in the mean. Countries with a large variance in earnings tend to select immigrants from the upper tail of the earnings distribution in sending countries; the reverse is true for countries with small earnings variance.

skill distribution in their countries of origin (Easterlin, 1971; Dunlevy and Gemery, 1983). Mokyr (1983:247-252), for example, has studied the occupations of Irish immigrants before 1850 and concluded that immigration selected from the upper tail of the occupational distribution of Ireland, although the magnitude of the difference between the occupational mix of immigrants and that of the resident population of Ireland was small.[19]   Authors who emphasize the pull of American opportunities suggest that these forces would select the higher-skilled, better-situated members of European society. Even Thomas (1954/1973: 56-62), one of the relatively few writers who sees a strong role for push factors in motivating immigration, agrees that migrants to the United States tended to come from the upper strata of their own societies.

How Did Immigrants Compare with Native-Born Workers?

Whether these select workers from Europe's perspective appeared as high-skilled and advantaged competitors in the American labor market is more controversial. It could be true that immigrants selected from the upper tail of their home country's distribution of skills and other endowments nevertheless fell below the median of native-born American workers. It has also been asserted that the quality of immigrants fell as mass migration continued. A popular textbook in economic history states that "It is probably true that immigrants after 1880 were less skilled and educated than earlier immigrants."[20]

Historians have sometimes asserted or assumed that the bulk of immigrants were unskilled.[21] Handlin (1951/1973:58, 60) in the classic history of immigration to America, *The Uprooted*, described immigrants as "peasants," people who lacked training for merchandising and the skills to pursue a craft. This view also appears in some surveys of American history. The textbook by Nash et al. (1986:604), for example, reports that "most immigrants" after the Civil War "had

---

[19]Others who have reached similar conclusions include Baines (1985:51-52), Erikson (1972, 1981, 1989, 1990), and Van Vugt (1988a, 1988b). Cohn (1992, 1995) has criticized this work for using biased samples that underestimated the numbers of laborers and farmers in the years before the Civil War. The issue is how to treat the "questionable" passenger lists. These are lists on which *every* passenger is recorded as a laborer (or farmer) usually by the use of ditto marks down the occupation column. Most researchers have excluded such lists from their samples. Cohn disagrees. When Cohen includes the questionable lists in his sample, he finds more laborers and farmers among immigrants from England and Scotland and more laborers and servants from Ireland than in the occupational distributions of the countries of origin. In the case of Germany, on the other hand, Cohn's work supports the select immigrant hypothesis.

[20]Walton and Rockoff (1994:402). This exact sentence has passed down to this edition of the textbook from Robertson (1973:387) through Walton and Robertson (1983:444). None of these texts offers a citation or evidence.

[21]The proposition advanced in this literature is that the immigrants arrived without skills acquired in their home country. This is somewhat different from asserting that immigrants took unskilled jobs in this country regardless of their ability to perform skilled work.

few skills." Cliometric investigation suggests a quite different story. Available evidence implies that skill differences between native- and foreign-born workers throughout the period of mass immigration were small or nonexistent and that the relative quality of immigrants did not fall over time.

Occupations of Arriving Immigrants

One source of evidence on the relative skills of newly arriving immigrants are the ship manifests giving the occupation of arriving passengers, recorded since the United States began the formal collection of immigration statistics in 1819. These data have been compiled by broad occupational grouping in *Historical Statistics of the United States* (Bureau of the Census, 1975/1997, series C120-137) and by more detailed occupations for 1819-1855 in Bromwell (1856/1969). Table 8-1 displays the occupational distribution of immigrants who reported an occupation at the time of their arrival into the United States according to broad occupational categories. Figures are presented as decadal averages for the 50-year period 1861-1910. The high proportion of immigrants describing themselves as unskilled laborers in the passenger lists (40-50 percent before 1900) seems to suggest that the skill content of immigration during this period was low. At the same time, farmers and agricultural workers are not particularly evident. They are certainly proportionately less evident in the immigrant flows than in the resident American labor force.

Table 8-2 compares Lebergott's (1964) estimates of the percentage of the resident labor force in the agricultural sector over the 50-year period beginning in 1861 with comparable data on the occupations of arriving immigrants presented

TABLE 8-1   Occupation Upon Arrival to the United States for Immigrants Reporting an Occupation, 1861-1910

Decade	Total	Agri-culture	Skilled Labor	Unskilled Labor	Domestic Service	Pro-fessional	All other Occu-pations
1861-1870	100.0	17.6	24.0	42.4	7.2	0.8	8.0
1871-1880	100.0	18.2	23.1	41.9	7.7	1.4	7.7
1881-1890	100.0	14.0	20.4	50.2	4.9	1.1	9.4
1891-1900	100.0	11.4	20.1	47.0	5.5	0.9	15.1
1901-1910	100.0	24.3	20.2	34.8	5.1	1.5	14.1

NOTE: The category "All Other" consists primarily of managers, sales and clerical workers, and self-employed proprietors and merchants.
SOURCE: Ernest Rubin. "Immigration and the Economic Growth of the U.S.: 1790-1914." *Conference on Income and Wealth.* New York: National Bureau of Economic Research, 1957: 8. As reported in Elizabeth W. Gilboy and Edgar M. Hoover. "Population and Immigration." In Seymour E. Harris, ed., *American Economic History.* New York: McGraw-Hill, 1961, table 7: 269. An obvious error in the Domestic Service column for the last three decades has been corrected.

TABLE 8-2   Agricultural Occupations as a Percentage of All Occupations in
U.S. Work Force and the Percentage of Immigrants Reporting an Agricultural
Occupation Upon Arrival, 1860-1910

Decade	Agriculture Occupations as a Percentage of United States Work Force	Percentage of Immigrants Reporting an Agricultural Occupation Upon Arrival
1861-1870	52.7	17.6
1871-1880	51.8	18.2
1881-1890	46.4	14.0
1891-1900	41.3	11.4
1901-1910	35.2	24.3

NOTE: The figures on agricultural occupations as a percentage of the resident U.S. workforce are averages of data for the two census years that span each decade. That is, the figure for 1861-1870 averages the data for 1860 and 1870.
SOURCES: Occupations of the U.S. workforce: Stanley Lebergott. Manpower in Economic Growth: The American Record Since 1800. New York: McGraw-Hill, 1964, table A-1: 510. Occupations of arriving immigrants: Ernest Rubin. "Immigration and the Economic Growth of the U.S.: 1790-1914." Conference on Income and Wealth. New York: National Bureau of Economic Research, 1957: 8. As reported in Elizabeth W. Gilboy and Edgar M. Hoover. "Population and Immigration." In Seymour E. Harris, ed., American Economic History. New York: McGraw-Hill, 1961, TABLE 7: 269]. An obvious error in the Domestic Service column for the last three decades has been corrected.

from Table 8-1.[22]   In no decade is the proportion of agricultural workers in the immigrant flow over 25 percent; in no decade is the proportion of agricultural workers in the American labor force less than 35 percent. Because farmer and agricultural occupations are generally classified as unskilled, this evidence implies that a large fraction of the American labor force was also unskilled in the nineteenth century. The high proportion of laborer occupations among the arriving immigrants cannot support the suggestion that new immigrants were less skilled than the average resident worker.

Also, immigrants do not appear to have been particularly deficient in skills as compared with the nonagricultural labor force in the United States. Table 8-3 makes the comparison for the first decade of the twentieth century, the first decade for which the required data are available. Taking the usual definition of skilled workers—craftsmen, foremen, and kindred workers—Table 8-3 reveals a higher proportion of skilled workers among the immigrants, 26.7 percent, than

[22]Because the populations of the primarily European origin countries were more heavily agricultural than the American population and because by most accounts the agricultural labor force in Europe ("peasants") were the least skilled and least educated of European workers, these data provide further support to the conclusion stated above that the immigrants tended to come from the higher strata of European society.

TABLE 8-3   Occupational Distribution of Nonagricultural Workers in the
U.S. Work Force in 1910 and Occupations Reported by Immigrants Upon
Their Arrival During the Decade 1900-1910

Occupation Classification	U.S. Work Force	Immigrants
Skilled	16.8	26.7
Unskilled	39.3	46.0
Domestic Service	14.1	6.7
Professional	6.8	2.0
All Other	23.0	18.6

NOTE: For the U.S. labor force the occupational classification for skilled corresponds to "crafts-men, foremen and kindred workers," unskilled are "operative and kindred workers and laborers except farm and mine" domestic service include "private household workers and [other] service workers," and professional include "professional, technical, and kindred workers."

SOURCES: *U.S. Workforce*: David L. Kaplan and M. Claire Casey. *Occupational Trends in the United States, 1900-1950.* U.S. Bureau of the Census Working Paper No. 5. Washington: U.S. Government Printing Office, 1958. As reported in United States Bureau of the Census. *Historical Statistics of the United States, Colonial Times to 1970, Bicentennial Edition.* Two volumes. Washington: U.S. Government Printing Office, 1975. Electronic edition edited by Susan B. Carter, Scott S. Gartner, Michael R. Haines, Alan L. Olmstead, Richard Sutch, and Gavin Wright. [machine-readable data file]. New York: Cambridge University Press, 1997, Series D182 -198. *Occupations of arriving immigrants*: Ernest Rubin. "Immigration and the Economic Growth of the U.S.: 1790-1914." *Conference on Income and Wealth.* New York: National Bureau of Economic Research, 1957: 8. As reported in Elizabeth W. Gilboy and Edgar M. Hoover. "Population and Immigration." In Seymour E. Harris, ed., *American Economic History.* New York: McGraw-Hill, 1961, table 7: 269. An obvious error in Domestic Services has been corrected.

among the resident American labor force, 16.8 percent. Table 8-3 also reveals a relatively lower proportion of domestic servants among arriving immigrants.

Yet as we have noted, at the same time, immigrants were relatively more likely to report "unskilled" occupations than were American workers, which complicates the interpretation of the data. Moreover, and not surprisingly given the young ages of immigrants, professionals were also not well represented among the new arrivals. In an effort to help clarify the picture, we have grouped the skilled, the professional, and "all other" occupations into a single category and contrast the share of these relatively high-status occupations with the share of the unskilled and domestic service occupations. This exercise reveals that 47.3 percent of the nonagricultural immigrants reported relatively high-status occupations while 52.7 percent were unskilled or in domestic service. In this sense, immigrants were (slightly) more likely to be unskilled than skilled. Yet this distribution is nearly exactly the split within the resident American nonagricul-tural labor force: 46.6 percent in relatively high-status occupations and 53.4 percent in either unskilled or domestic service occupations. We might even say that the newly arriving immigrant nonagricultural work force in this decade was (slightly) *more skilled* than the resident American labor force.

The data on the occupations of arriving immigrants, shown in Table 8-1, reveal very little in the way of a trend over time. The high-status occupations accounted for a stable 40 percent of immigrants reporting nonagricultural occupations between 1860 and 1900 and then *rose* to 47 percent in the final decade before World War I. This evidence contradicts the frequently made claim—put forth without evidence—that the skills of immigrants were falling in this period.

Of course, there is good reason to be cautious about data on immigrant skills. The occupations were self-reported and recorded by ship captains who may have imposed prejudices of their own. Presumably the new arrivals reported the occupation they had followed in the old country, but perhaps young immigrants reported their father's occupation or perhaps some reported their intended occupation in America. In any case, there is strong evidence that many of the new arrivals took jobs other than those they reported on entry. Farming, in particular, was difficult to enter because of the cost of purchasing and equipping a farm and the evident fact that a year's worth of provisions or credit would be required before the first crops came in. Differences in technologies, the quality of the final product, and the organization of trades may have reduced the value of European-acquired skills (Eichengreen and Gemery, 1986). For this reason many researchers have examined, not the occupations immigrants reported on arrival, but the occupations actually taken up by immigrants in their new home.[23]

Occupations of the Foreign Born in the United States

The federal census provides data on the occupations of the labor force by the nativity of the worker. Hill (1975) categorized these occupations as either "skilled," "semiskilled," or "unskilled," using the classification devised by Edwards (1943). The results of this exercise led Hill to conclude that "the native and foreign born were of relatively comparable economic status" during the period of mass immigration (Hill, 1975:59). Although the foreign born were slightly less likely to have been employed in skilled positions and slightly more likely to have been employed in unskilled positions, they were *much more* likely to have held semiskilled jobs. Their share of the semiskilled jobs is disproportionately large enough to bring them close to occupational parity with the native

---

[23]Occupations actually taken up by immigrants will not adequately indicate their skills either if immigrants face discrimination in their entry into occupations. A number of scholars have argued that immigrants did in fact face occupation-based discrimination during the era of mass migration (Azuma, 1994; Barth, 1964; Brown and Philips, 1986; Cloud and Galenson, 1987; Daniels, 1962; Hannon, 1982a, 1982b; Higgs, 1978; LaCroix and Fishback, 1989; Liu, 1988; Murayama, 1984; and Saxton, 1971). But see Chiswick (1978a, 1978b, 1991a, 1991b, 1992, 1994) for an analysis that emphasizes the role of human capital in immigrant occupational attainment. The consensus in the literature is that within occupations immigrants were paid roughly equal pay for equal work (Blau, 1980; Ginger, 1954; Higgs, 1971a; McGouldrick and Tannen, 1977).

born despite their disadvantage at the upper and lower ends of the occupational spectrum.[24]

WAS IMMIGRATION GOOD FOR GROWTH?

Mass immigration occurred during a period of very rapid economic growth and America's ascendancy to international industrial leadership (Wright, 1990; Abramovitz, 1993). Most of the historians and economic historians who have studied immigration have tried to assess its relationship to these positive economic developments. To do so they relied, explicitly or implicitly, on a model of economic growth and of factor mobility. For those unfamiliar with this literature, it will be helpful to begin with some key definitions and a simple version of the model.

Defining Growth

There is little doubt that immigration caused the American population and the American labor force to grow more rapidly than it would have in its absence.[25] Figure 8-14 shows the contribution of net immigration to American population growth. During the period of mass immigration preceding World War I, immigration accounted for somewhere between a third and a half of U.S. population growth.[26]

More workers meant more output. Population, after all, is fundamental to production, not only because people supply the labor required, but because the consumption of the population is the raison d'être of the production system. Thus the size of the economy, measured, say, by real gross domestic product (GDP), grew more rapidly than it would have without immigration. This is, we think,

---

[24]The semiskilled class is largely made up of factory operatives, a class of occupations that is classified as "unskilled" in Table 8-1.

[25]Because net immigration was positive throughout the entire history of the country before World War I, this would be a tautology except for the possibility that the flow of immigrants somehow might have induced a decline in the natural rate of increase of the native-born population sufficiently large to numerically cancel the inflow. This possibility was actually suggested by Walker (1891, 1896). Although it is true that both the fertility rate and the rate of net population growth from natural increase fell over the nineteenth and first third of the twentieth centuries, most demographic studies of population dynamics lend little or no support to the Walker hypothesis. We summarize this literature in the section of this chapter on population dynamics.

[26]It is interesting to note that net immigration also accounts for about a third of the growth in the U.S. population today. This is true despite the fact that the numbers of arriving immigrants are smaller and the base population is larger today than it was in the decades immediately preceding World War I. The reason for the relatively large contribution of immigration to American population growth today is that the rate of natural increase is so low. Data on net immigration come from McClelland and Zechhauser (1983) for 1820-1860, Kuznets and Rubin (1954) for 1870-1940, and the Bureau of the Census (1990, 1993) for the recent period.

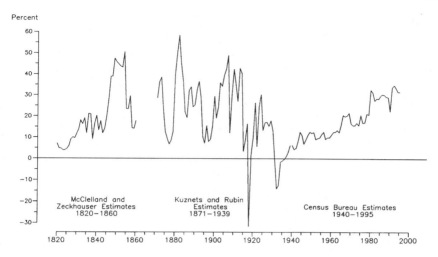

FIGURE 8-14 Net immigration's contribution to national population growth.

what historian Maldwyn Allen Jones had in mind when he wrote in his classic book, *American Immigration*:

> The realization of America's vast economic potential has . . . been due in signif-
> icant measure to the efforts of immigrants. They supplied much of the labor
> and technical skill needed to tap the underdeveloped resources of a virgin conti-
> nent. This was most obviously true during the colonial period . . . . But immi-
> grants were just as indispensable in the nineteenth century, when they contrib-
> uted to the rapid settlement of the West and the transformation of the United
> States into a leading industrial power (Jones, 1992/1960:309-310).

But this concept of growth, sometimes called "extensive growth," is not what economists usually mean by the phrase "economic growth." Instead, the growth of labor productivity, or the growth of per capita output, or the growth in the standard of living—"intensive growth"—is usually of greater interest. Labor productivity for the economy as a whole is measured by dividing GDP by the number of workers. Thus, if productivity is to grow, GDP must grow faster than the employed labor force. If per capita output is to grow, GDP must grow faster than the population. So the question becomes: Does immigration increase or reduce labor productivity? If workers are paid a wage that reflects their produc-tivity, we can ask the same question as: Does immigration increase or reduce the real wage?[27]

---

[27]There are other influences on the real wage than productivity. Of particular importance in this context would be discrimination (presumably against immigrants and in favor of native-born work-ers) and unionization (presumably weakened by heavy immigration).

The statistical record is clear: Intensive economic growth did take place during the era of mass immigration. Per capita GDP grew in real terms (Balke and Gordon, 1986), so did labor productivity. Real wages rose (Long, 1960; Rees, 1960). Nonetheless, this evidence is not adequate to rule out a harmful role for immigration. During the late nineteenth century, and, indeed for most of U.S. history, output per worker was growing.[28] Thus, the real question is whether immigration retarded or accelerated the *rate* of intensive growth.

At first glance it would appear that there is no clear consensus among economic historians about the impact of turn-of-the-century immigration on the rate of intensive growth. The most careful of the several reviews of the historical literature, that by Atack and Passell (1994:236-237), concludes that there was a large, positive, and "profound" effect of immigration on the rate of growth measured in per capita terms. On the other hand, Williamson asserts without qualification that

> The issue in American historiography, however, has never been whether immigration tended to suppress the rise in the real wage . . . . Surely, in the absence of mass migrations, the real wage would have risen faster . . . (Williamson, 1982:254).

Hatton and Williamson test this proposition in their recent book, *The Age of Mass Migration: An Economic Analysis*.[29] They conclude that late nineteenth- and early twentieth-century immigration "significantly retarded the growth of real wages and living standards economy-wide" (Hatton and Williamson, 1998:Chap. 8).

It seems to us that there are three factors that underlie the apparent divergence of opinion about the impact of immigration: definitions of the population of interest, composition effects, and model specification.

Defining the Population of Interest

Which is the population for whom the effects of immigration are to be measured? Is it the entire population, including the newly arrived immigrants? Is it the population resident in the United States at the time of the immigrants'

---

[28]Annual additions to per capita output averaged 1.7 percent per year in the early era of mass immigration between 1901 and 1913 (two business-cycle peaks). (This calculation is based on figures reported in Bureau of the Census (1975/1997, F4). This sustained growth meant that over that 12-year period, average per capita income increased nearly 25 percent. This calculation includes the newly arrived immigrants in the base population.

Changes in the standard of living over a lifetime are very sensitive to small changes in the annual rate of growth. For example, with an annual rate of growth of only 1 percent, output increases 63 percent over a 50-year period. With a 2 percent growth rate the improvement is 164 percent, and with a 5 percent growth rate (much slower, by the way, than the rate of growth of per capita output in China today) the standard of living increases 100-fold.

[29]This book is scheduled to be published in 1998. Hatton and Williamson graciously provided us with a manuscript copy at the time we were writing this chapter.

arrival? Perhaps it is the native born, or even the native born of native parentage. Are workers alone to be considered, or the workers and their dependents? Just workers and their families, or capitalists and landowners as well? Any of these populations may be a legitimate focus of attention. The appropriate definition depends on the question being asked. One source of confusion in the literature stems from the fact that scholars have not always been explicit about the definition they have chosen.[30]

Composition Effects

To measure the impact of immigration on the wages of natives and of past immigrants, one needs to partition the population between the resident population and the new immigrants and consider changes in the welfare of the resident population alone. For the most part, however, long-term historical data on wages, income, and wealth are available only for the population as a whole. Scholars are forced to deduce the impact of immigration on the welfare of the resident population (or the native born or the native born of native parents) from data on the entire population.

Such a project is, of course, fraught with hazards. An aggregate time series on wage rates (or living standards) may rise slowly or even fall at the same time that the wages of *both* the resident population and the newly arrived immigrants are rising rapidly. This would occur if, say, the newly arrived immigrant share of the population were rising rapidly and the wages of the newly arrived immigrants were below those of the resident workers.

Model Specification

To assess the impact of immigration on intensive economic growth, economic historians have implicitly or explicitly relied on a theoretical construct known as the "aggregate production function." This approach asserts that the aggregate output produced by an economy (its gross national product) is determined by the quantities and qualities of its "factors of production": capital, labor, and land. Technological progress plays a role too, either because better machines and tools are used ("embodied" technical change) or because existing machines and tools are organized in better ways ("disembodied" technical change).

Capital includes machinery and buildings and other structures—all of the

---

[30]Thus, it becomes clear only after a careful reading that Lebergott (1964:163) is interested in the impact of immigration on the wage rates of the entire population of workers, including the wages of the newly arrived immigrants. Hatton and Williamson (1998:Chap. 8), however, cite Lebergott in support of their contention that immigration slowed the growth rate of wages of *natives* and of *past immigrants* in the early decades of this century.

manufactured physical inputs into the production process that contribute to the level of output. Labor includes number of persons involved in the production process, their hours of work per day, their days of work per year, the intensity of their work effort, and their level of skill. Land includes improvements to land, natural resources, and raw materials. A key feature of this theoretical construct is that it focuses attention on the productivity of factors of production and on the possibility of *substitution* among capital, labor, and land. Thus, for example, an increase in labor (perhaps from immigration) would be supposed to raise the productivity of capital and thus would create an incentive to invest and further expand the capital stock.

The aggregate production function approach is used to compare the historical record with an explicit counterfactual; a comparison between the historical record and an explicit counterfactual; a comparison of "what was" with "what might have been" had immigration flows been absent or reduced. To assess the impact of immigration on growth, the investigator must specify a general equilibrium model of both the labor and capital markets and of the production and distribution of output.[31]

The counterfactual method has a long history in cliometric work.[32] By now it is clear that the outcome of such an exercise is quite sensitive to the specification of the formal theoretical model that describes the workings of the counterfactual universe. The aggregate production function must be specified mathematically and assigned numerical parameters. Is the production function Cobb-Douglas, or constant elasticity of substitution (CES), or Leontief? Are there economies of scale? Is the growth of the capital stock constrained by the flow of savings or by available investment opportunities? Is the model static or dynamic? The results also depend upon the assumptions built into the model about the distribution of wealth, income, and employment. Are workers paid their marginal product? Are governments redistributive? Do immigrants import or export capital? Do immigrants and native born have different savings propensities? Is the macro economy Keynesian or neoclassical? Because the conclusions reached through counterfactual modeling are so sensitive to the model's structure, the persuasiveness of any such exercise depends crucially upon the plausibility of the model specification.

Given this state of affairs, the most helpful thing we can do is to describe some of the prominent arguments about relevant aspects of the economy that appear in the literature. The reader will note that many of these issues are difficult to resolve with the available data and that the literature itself has given insufficient attention to the data that are available. In the absence of more

---

[31]For an early and influential example of the counterfactual method that uses a computable general equilibrium model to examine the immigration question with late nineteenth-century data, see Williamson (1974a). Williamson concludes, "An America without immigrants indeed would have grown very differently from how she actually did in the late nineteenth century" (p. 387).

[32]For a discussion see Fogel (1967).

empirical work, the conclusion readers reach will depend in large part on their tastes for various theoretical constructs. In the process of constructing our catalog, we reveal our own priors.

Labor Force Participation of Immigrants

Most economic historians noted that early twentieth-century immigration caused the labor force to grow more rapidly than the population (Kuznets, 1952:196-204). Immigrants in that period were disproportionately young males and more likely than their native-born counterparts to be labor force participants. Most economic historians place great weight on the fact that immigrants who arrived in the last era of mass migration were far more likely to participate in the labor force than the average American at the time. This pattern is shown in Table 8-4, which displays the share of the native- and foreign-born populations engaged in the work force for the decennial census years 1870 through 1940. The participation rate for the foreign born is 50 percent or more from 1880 onward, with the rate rising with the rising tide of immigration. The participation rate of the native born is only about two-thirds of this level. Kuznets explained the high labor force participation of immigrants in this way:

> Because the immigrants were predominantly males, because by far the preponderant proportion of them (over 80 percent) were over 14 or 15 and in the prime working ages, and because their participation in the labor force tended to be higher than that of the native population even for the same age and sex classes, the share of foreign born among the gainfully occupied was, throughout the period, markedly greater than their share in total population (Kuznets, 1952, 1971b).

We have already examined data demonstrating the predominance of males of young working ages in the turn-of-the-century immigrant streams. If these foreign-born workers were as productive as the native born and if their arrival did not depress the capital-labor ratio (that it *did not* is commonly supposed in the historical literature), then immigration would cause per capita income of the resident population to rise more rapidly than it would have in the absence of immigration (Gallman, 1977:30).[33]

The first element of the argument—that *overall* per capita incomes tend to rise because of the immigration-induced increase in the labor force participation rate—is well established. The balance of the argument—that immigration had at least a short-term positive impact on the economic well-being of the *resident* population—depends on two assumptions that are less well supported by empirical work. One

---

[33]As already mentioned, in the short run the influx of new labor is likely to depress the capital-labor ratio before it is restored through new investment. If the capital stock is disproportionately owned by native-born residents, as was surely the case in the late nineteenth and early twentieth centuries, then native-born owners of capital will benefit temporarily from higher returns to capital. Indeed, it is this higher return to capital that (in part) is thought to induce an increased volume of investment that ultimately restores the capital-labor ratio to its preimmigration level.

TABLE 8-4   Labor Force Participation Rate, Native and Foreign-Born, 1870-1940

Year	Native Born	Foreign Born
1870	29.7	48.5
1880	32.0	52.2
1890	33.1	55.1
1900	35.5	55.5
1910	37.7	57.8
1920	37.8	55.7
1930	38.1	52.2
1940	39.1	50.5

NOTE: "Labor force participation rate" is defined here as the share of the total population of a given nativity that is engaged in the workforce.
SOURCE: Calculations are based on Kuznets (1971b).

point has to do with the nativity differences in worker productivity (or immigrant "quality") discussed above. The consensus is that any differences in the average productivity of the native- and foreign-born work force were small. The second key point—the impact of immigration on capital formation—has been left largely to assumption and speculation. Very little empirical work with historical data has been reported in the literature. There are really two questions. One is, was the growth of capital constrained by saving (at a given interest rate) or was it constrained by the growth of investment opportunities? A second question is to what extent did immigrants either import physical capital or save heavily?

Immigration and the Capital-Labor Ratio

In the short run at least, an influx of immigrants who do not bring capital with them will have the effect of "diluting" the capital stock, that is, reducing the economy-wide capital-labor ratio. If capital and labor are substitutes, this reduction in the capital-labor ratio will raise the rate of return to capital and lower the real wage of workers. The overall impact of this dilution of capital on the initial resident population is predicted by theory to be positive. Capital owners—all of whom are posited to be native born—will gain and workers will lose, but the gains of the capital (and land) owners should exceed the losses of the resident laborers. This is because the labor and capital owned by residents can produce more output after the arrival of the immigrants than before. Immigrants will increase output by more than they will take home in wages.[34]

---

[34]Denison (1962:177) suggests that immigrants will take home only 77.3 percent of the increase (labor's share in national income); the rest goes to the resident owners of capital and land. Other scholars estimate an even lower share for labor—closer to 60 percent (Abramovitz, 1993; Taylor and Williamson, 1997).

In his discussion of the probable magnitudes of the redistribution affected by this mechanism in the modern era, Borjas estimates that immigration effects a loss to native workers of about 1.9 percent of GDP and a gain to native capital owners of approximately 2 percent of GDP. Borjas suggests that this relatively small net surplus, especially compared with the larger wealth transfers from labor to capital, "probably explains why the debate over immigration policy has usually focused on the potentially harmful labor market impacts rather than on the overall increase in native income" (Borjas, 1995:8-9).

When considering the relevance of this redistribution for the period of rapid immigration in the early part of this century, we note first that many of the resident workers were also capital owners.[35] Lebergott (1964:512-513) estimates that, as late as 1900, about one-third of the labor force were at the same time owners of land and capital. They were self-employed farm owners and the owners and operators of small retail shops and manufacturing plants. Others were providers of professional and personal services (Carter and Sutch, 1996). Also we note that a substantial fraction of American household heads and workers owned their own homes. Haines and Goodman (1995) put the level at over one-third near the turn of the century. To the degree that the arrival of new immigrants increased the demand for housing, owners of the existing stock of housing would enjoy capital gains.[36]

Second, a substantial fraction of the turn-of-the-century working-class population owned capital assets indirectly through the agency of insurance companies. Ransom and Sutch (1987:386) estimate that in 1905 there were approximately 9 million tontine insurance policies outstanding at a time when there were only about 18 million households. Tontine policies were, in effect, self-financed pension funds invested in assets and equities whose value rose (or fell) with the return to capital.[37]

In any case, the widespread ownership of capital by resident workers at the turn of the century meant that any immigration-initiated redistribution of income among *individuals* was far more muted than the redistribution between labor and capital as *factors of production*. Although we know of no empirical work on this

---

[35]This is true today, as well. Many workers own shares of pension and mutual funds that give them a direct and obvious owners' share in the nation's capital stock.

[36]For evidence on the strong positive impact of immigration on the relative price of housing in New York City during the period 1830-1860, see Margo (1996).

[37]A tontine insurance policy combined a term life insurance policy with a saving fund that pooled the contributions of policyholders, invested them, and then divided the principal and accumulated returns at the expiration of the policy among the surviving policyholders. Thus, if the purchaser died prematurely, his or her heirs would receive a death benefit from the insurance portion of the policy. But if the policyholder should live out the term of the contract (typically 25 or 30 years), he or she would receive a share of the savings fund that had been augmented by the contributions of policyholders who had died or defaulted on their premium payments. Tontine insurance was declared illegal and such policies were ultimately phased out after a corruption scandal in the insurance industry. On these issues, see Ransom and Sutch (1987).

topic, the fact of widespread worker ownership of assets suggests that workers may not have been harmed significantly by immigration even if there was a depressing effect on their real wages in the short run.

Third, to the extent to which the immigrants brought sufficient capital with them, capital dilution and the resulting redistributional effect would not even be present. Available evidence on the relation between capital and labor flows in the early part of this century suggests that immigrants brought some capital with them, although the per capita value of these stocks was generally smaller than the capital-labor ratio in the United States at the time of their arrival (North, 1960; Simon, 1960).

Another point to note in connection with the capital-dilution argument is that, whatever its effects on the returns to capital, asset values, and real wages, the effects are likely to have been transitory. Higher returns to capital should, in a dynamic economy, increase the demand for capital, that is shift the demand for investment outward. If the supply of savings is elastic or if the supply of savings shifted outward as a consequence of immigration, then the capital stock would increase, the capital-labor ratio would rise, real wages would rise, and the return to capital would fall. We return to these possibilities shortly.

Immigration and Physical Capital Formation

Kuznets (1961) has argued that American economic growth was constrained by an inelastic supply of savings. Abramovitz and David (1973, 1996) and David (1977) prefer a model in which expanding opportunities for investment (in turn driven by the flow of technological innovation) play the chief dynamic role, pushing out along a responsive and elastic supply of funds. The debate has not been settled.[398] What we know is that the capital stock did grow and grew fast enough to prevent any decline in the capital-labor ratio. Abramovitz and David report that the capital-labor ratio grew 0.6 percent annually between 1800 and 1855, 1.5 percent between 1855 and 1890, and 1.34 percent between 1890 and 1927 (Abramovitz, 1993:Table 1; p. 223). What was the mechanism behind this relative increase in the capital stock? What was the likely role played by immigration?

Suppose, first, that savings is the constraint to capital formation. In this case,

---

[38]We lean heavily toward the side of the debate that argues that savings was an active constraint on capital formation. First, our view rests on our belief in the historical applicability of the life-cycle model of savings (due to Modigliani, 1966 and 1986), and the implication of that model that the supply of domestic savings is not likely to be interest elastic. Second, we are impressed with the evidence that the flow of capital from abroad in this period was relatively small in magnitude (North, 1960; Simon, 1960; Davis and Gallman, 1973; and Davis and Cull, 1994) and not very interest sensitive (Ransom and Sutch, 1984). Second, we are impressed by a variety of historical studies that seem to us to support Kuznets' version of the mechanism behind capital formation (see Williamson, 1974a, 1974b; David and Scadding, 1974; and Ransom and Sutch, 1988).

immigration would have to increase the rate of capital formation either by increasing the importation of capital from abroad or by increasing the flow of domestically generated saving. Importation of capital may have been tied to the volume of immigration through two possible mechanisms. There is the possibility that immigrants may have imported substantial amounts of capital with them when they moved. Although little empirical work has been done on this question, it is generally supposed that the amount of immigrant-supplied capital was trivial and, indeed, that any such inward flows were partially offset by an outward flow of "remittances" from immigrants to friends and relatives in the old country.[39] Another possibility is that the foreign born were able to attract foreign investment to the American economy by alerting prospective investors in their country of origin of investment opportunities and by acting as principals or intermediaries connecting the foreign investor with an American borrower. A third possibility is that the higher rates of return to capital produced by the capital-dilution effect attracted more capital from abroad.

We know of no systematic study of such induced investment flows from abroad, although Thomas (1954/1973) has incorporated such a mechanism in his model of the Atlantic economy. We note the fact that much of the flow of British investment abroad was directed to economies with a high proportion of English settlers: the United States, Canada, and Australia (Edelstein, 1974; Davis and Gallman, 1973; Davis and Cull, 1994). Because England was the primary source of international capital flows during the late nineteenth and early twentieth centuries, this gave the United States an important advantage (Cairncross, 1953).[40]

Another mechanism that linked immigration to capital formation is the behavior of the immigrants themselves who appear to have been unusually heavy savers and investors in the American economy. This possibility was briefly discussed by Ransom and Sutch (1984:49-51) in the context of a life-cycle model of saving. They make two points. First, because the bulk of turn-of-the-century immigrants arrived as young adults, they entered the country at a life-cycle stage when saving is typically heavy. Second, on arrival, most immigrants owned very little in the way of marketable, tangible wealth, particularly so in relation to their earning power in their new home country. Partly this was because the immi-

---

[39]North (1960:612-617) estimates the average amount of capital per immigrant at $75 in the period 1815-1840 and a varying sum according to nationality (per capita sums of $100 for Germans but only $25 for the Irish) for the period 1840-1860. For comparison, free farm laborers are estimated to have averaged $8.50 to $13.70 per month (including board) over the same period (Lebergott, 1960:462). Thus, the imported capital is less than a year's wages. In the latter part of the nineteenth century, capital imports by immigrants appear to have been smaller still (Simon, 1960:672).

[40]Argentina and India also received significant flows of capital from England, reflecting the substantial presence of English-born settlers in these two countries. Indeed, a key factor in directing and controlling the foreign investments appears to be community connections with the capital-sending countries. Even today there is a close connection between flows of capital from Asia to the United States and the presence of Asian-American communities in several American cities.

grants had consumed much of their wealth in financing their passage to the United States; partly this was because they were poor by American standards before they left their country of origin. When they began receiving the new, higher American income stream, they found themselves in an "asset-income disequilibrium"; that is, their stock of assets was too low relative to their permanent income. Under these circumstances they would attempt to restore themselves to equilibrium by saving heavily.

What evidence is there that immigrants were particularly heavy savers? There has not been much research on the question. One bit of evidence consistent with higher saving rates among the foreign born is their differentially high rates of self-employment. These nativity-based differentials were just as evident in the past as they are today (Higgs, 1976; Light, 1984; Light and Bonacich, 1988; Borjas, 1986; Borjas and Bronars, 1989; Aldrich and Waldinger, 1990; Aronson, 1991; Carter and Sutch, 1992). Because entry into self-employment requires physical and human capital acquisition, these data suggest differentially high saving rates among the foreign born. The 1910 Public Use Microdata Sample allows us to give a particularly vivid demonstration of the probable role of financial (and human) capital acquisition on the part of immigrants *after their entry into the United States*. In Figure 8-15 we show the fraction of the foreign-born self-employed among cohorts of men in their twenties, thirties, forties, and fifties in 1910, arrayed by the number of years they have been living in the United States. The shorter the line, the younger the cohort in 1910. This figure suggests

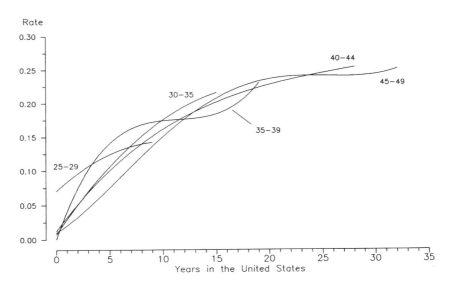

FIGURE 8-15 Self-employment rates for foreign born, five age cohorts defined by age in 1910, male foreign-born nonfarm labor force.

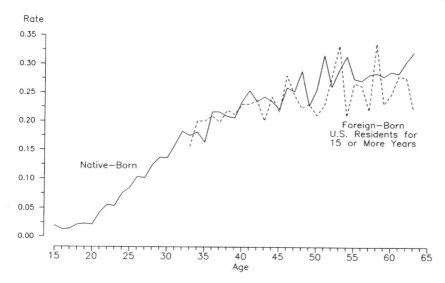

FIGURE 8-16 Self-employment rates by age, native-born and foreign-born male non-farm labor force, 1910.

that newly arrived immigrants, whatever their age, began their American employment careers as wage workers and then moved into self-employment as their tenure in the United States increased. The similarity of the upward movement for men arriving at different ages suggests heavy saving rates in the years following their arrival into the United States.[41]

The saving rates of immigrants may have been higher than those of the native born. Figure 8-16 displays self-employment rates by age for both the native- and foreign-born males nonfarm work forces in 1910. We restrict the foreign-born population to those who had been resident in the United States for 15 years or more and were at least 33 years of age. This restriction eliminates the sojourners and also those who arrived in the United States as children. Figure 8-16 shows that the self-employment rates at each age of these two groups are quite similar. Both groups show movement at about the same rate into self-employment between their early thirties and mid-forties. If we imagine that some of the movement of the native (but not the foreign) born at these ages was facilitated by the receipt of an inheritance, then the similarity of their rates of movement into self-employment suggests *heavier* saving on the part of immigrants.

---

[41]The upward slope to the self-employment rate line may also reflect possible differences in the self-employment rates of sojourners and those who intended to settle permanently in the United States. The available cross-sectional data do not allow us to assess the relative importance of this selection factor.

A second piece of evidence of differentially high rates of saving among the foreign born is Haines and Goodman's finding of relatively larger differences in the rates of home ownership between young and older adults for the foreign born in several samples they investigate from the turn of the century (Haines and Goodman, 1995:Table 7.3, pp. 220-221).

There exists an extensive collection of budget studies from the turn of the century that surveyed both foreign- and native-born American workers (Carter et al., 1991). Often a question was included to ask the length of time an immigrant had been in the United States. These surveys, if handled carefully, might be used to estimate the differential savings propensities of immigrants and native-born workers. This work has yet to be done.

Whether the additional "boom in saving" triggered by immigration, hypothesized by Ransom and Sutch, was strong enough by itself to offset the initial capital dilution remains an open question. What is clear is that aggregate American saving rates were very high during this period. Gross saving as a fraction of GDP exceeded 20 percent (Davis and Gallman, 1973; Ransom and Sutch, 1984). What is also clear is that the capital-labor ratio did not fall during this period—it rose! Whether it would have risen even higher had immigration been less strong remains a question for further research.

Kuznets (1958:34) argued that immigration was likely to shift the demand for investment outward, primarily by stimulating the demand for housing, urban infrastructure, and other "population-sensitive capital formation."[42] This is undoubtedly true. However, if saving were inelastic in supply and if there had been no immigration-induced shift of the supply of saving, then the increased demand for investment would have simply pushed up the rate of interest rather than increased the capital stock. Yet in fact real interest rates were low and falling during the last half of the nineteenth century, and the rise in real rates during the early decades of the twentieth century was modest (Temin, 1971:70-74; Williamson, 1974a:656). We conclude that immigration actually helped stimulate the increase in the capital stock and in the capital-labor ratio.[443]

Immigration and Inventive Activity

America became a world leader in many technologies over the late nineteenth and early twentieth centuries (Mokyr, 1990:268; Wright, 1990). Rapid immigration may have contributed to this ascendancy by the simple fact that the

---

[42]This effect is one of the supposed underlying causes of the strong association between immigration and the "long swings" in economic activity, known as Kuznets' cycles (Thomas, 1954/1973).

[43]Gallman (1977:30) points out that, insofar as the new capital put in place as a consequence of immigration catered exclusively to immigrant demands for goods and services, the welfare effect on the resident worker need not have been positive, although again capitalists and landowners would have gained.

foreigners enlarged the size of the economy. A larger economy means that more is being produced at any one time. A greater volume of production meant more opportunities to discover better ways of doing things. Historians of technology have demonstrated the quantitative importance of this "learning by doing" in stimulating technological advance. Small incremental improvements, repeated many times, appear to have contributed more than well-known breakthroughs to advances in design and to reductions in the costs of production (Rosenberg, 1982, 1981/1995; David, 1975). By promoting extensive economic growth, immigration gave the country's inventors and tinkerers more to do, thereby offering them more opportunities to learn.[44]

The immigration-induced increase in the size of the economy may have also been good for inventiveness (Kelley, 1972). Adam Smith thought that invention was accelerated by the division of labor which in turn was limited by the size of the market (Smith, 1776:11). Higgs (1971b) found a link between patenting activity and urbanization in the United States during the period 1870-1920. Simon and Sullivan (1989) show a connection between population size and the invention of new agricultural techniques. Because the foreign born enlarge the population, tend to reside in urban areas, and expand the size of the market, we suggest that here too is an indirect impact of immigration on inventive activity.

Immigrants may have played a more direct role in this development as well. Some scattered evidence suggests that immigrants accounted for more than their share of the major inventive breakthroughs in this era. A list of names of the "great" American inventors suggests a disproportionate share of immigrants. Why might this be a systematic aspect of the invention process rather than a coincidence or the result of a flawed sampling procedure? A good answer, we think, is that America was the leading laboratory for invention in the world at the time, with the most advanced industries and one of the highest rates of capital formation. Thus, it would be a magnet for would-be inventors, scientists, and innovators who would benefit from the working conditions, resources, and venture capital not available in their home country.

Immigration and Technological Innovation

Invention will have no impact on economic performance unless the new ideas diffuse, are adapted to existing conditions, and transform the capital stock. Immigration helped to speed the diffusion of new technologies because it enhanced the rate of growth of the population and the GDP of the economy, thereby stimulating a rapid growth in the capital stock. In the process of undertaking the new investment required, the latest and most productive technology was adopted. By providing an incentive for new investment, rapid extensive growth of the

---

[44]For some empirical evidence connecting manufacturing and patenting activity, see Higgs (1971b), Sokoloff (1988), Sokoloff and Khan (1990), and Khan and Sokoloff (1993).

economy lowered the average age of capital, bringing more of the advanced techniques into the production process (Nelson, 1964).

Most new technologies are embodied in new designs of capital machinery and factory structures. The new, mass-production techniques introduced in the era of mass immigration required new machines and the redesign of the factory itself. Effective use of refrigeration technology required new railroad cars; use of the electric motor to drive machines required the redesign of factories. So too with continuous flow technology, department store merchandising, and nearly all of the other important innovations of this era. Given the high costs of transatlantic shipping and other barriers to international trade, U.S. firms were heavily dependent on the domestic market. Had the country not welcomed the new immigrants to its shores, aggregate demand would have grown more slowly, there would have been less new investment, and the diffusion of new technologies would have been delayed.[45]

Immigration and the Exploitation of Economies of Scale

To the extent that there were and are large unexploited economies of scale in various industries (external to the firm), then the extensive growth of the economy by itself would expand per capita output. To the extent to which international trade was limited, growth of the domestic economy would be required for the realization of this opportunity.

Chenery (1960), in a study of the productivity of manufacturing workers across 63 countries, found that, other things being equal, a doubling of a country's size would increase the productivity of its workers by 20 percent. The models of growth most often invoked do not envision such an effect as a possibility, however (Denison, 1962). They begin with the view that the various sources of and contributions to economic growth may be calculated separately and independently and then added up without consideration of economy-wide increasing returns. But if the research begins with a model that includes the possibility of economies of scale, then one is certain to come to the conclusion, independent of the data collected and the historical research undertaken, that no single measurable source of growth is by itself very important (Abramovitz, 1993). Recently Romer (1986b, 1996) has urged a reconsideration of the use of such models for addressing broad-scope, long-run questions such as the one at hand.

As far as we are aware, no one has explicitly tried to examine turn-of-the-century immigration as a possible accelerator of endogenous growth using the "new growth theory" advocated by Romer.[46] There is some evidence that has

---

[56]Rosenberg (1982:249) has also noted the role played by immigrants in accelerating the diffusion of technology from the country of their origin in the United States.

[46]For several applications of an endogenous approach to growth modeling in an historical context see Johnston (1990), De Long (1995), and Romer (1986b).

been put forward, however, to lend support to the notion of increasing returns that work at the level of the national economy (Cain and Patterson, 1986). Johnston (1990) has attempted to model these effects by suggesting that the productivity-enhancing effect of scale is proportional to the total stock of capital and he suggests a specific parameterization. Based on his study of increasing returns in the mid-nineteenth century, he suggests that the rate of growth of output might be increased by a factor equal to 5 percent of the increase in the capital stock on account of economies of scale and quite apart from the direct contribution of capital stock growth to economic growth. De Long (1995) suggests that the true factor might be as high as 10 percent.

What would such parameters mean for the impact of immigration? If the flow of new immigrants increased the labor force by 4-8 percent over a decade (compare these numbers with those in Table 8-1) and (eventually) increased the capital stock by the same proportion, then output would be increased by 0.2-0.8 percentage points more than the direct effects of the increase in labor and capital would suggest. This translates to a 5-10 percent increase in productivity. This extra supplement to growth, although proportional to the increase in capital, is not entirely captured in an increase in business profits. Instead the entire economy is made more productive, and both labor and capital share in the "disembodied" increase in efficiency.

So far, empirical modeling with the new growth theory is in its infancy. The profession is far from persuaded that the economies-of-scale effects are or were significant, and the parameterization of such effects is little advanced from educated speculation.[47] Yet in the hands of a skillful economic historian the notion of economies of scale can be made to sound plausible and in good theoretical company as well. Consider Abramovitz's account:

> In the nineteenth century . . . capital's share [in national income] rose substantially—by 19 percent during the first half and by another 19 percent during the second half, a 41 percent increase overall. It is this result that creates, as I say, at least a presumption that technology was advancing, not in the neutral fashion that the growth accounts assume, but in a capital-using fashion. A series of powerful forces, each manifestly connected with technological progress, worked in this direction. First, the great expansion in the total size of the domestic market and its increasingly unified character encouraged production on a larger scale and heavier investment in the application of steam power and in more specialized capital equipment. This, indeed, is the message of all the great economists of the nineteenth and early twentieth centuries, in a line stemming from Adam Smith, running through Böhm-Bawerk, Sidgwick, and Taussig, and stretching to Allyn Young. But these men did not see the economies of scale as a source of growth separate from technological progress itself. Rather, they

---

[47]This state of affairs is surprising in light of the fact that the effects of scale and size on productive efficiency are "one of the oldest and most widely acknowledged sources of economic growth" (Kelley, 1972:36).

thought of the advances they saw with their own eyes as an emerging technology that was both capital and scale intensive. It was increasingly specialized and roundabout in its organization; required increasing amounts of capital per worker to employ it; and therefore demanded larger-scale operations in its plants and in the aggregate to make the heavier use of capital economical.

[Second, the] rise of cities, itself a requirement of scale-intensive production, was another capital-intensive development. It required heavy investment in structures for housing, trade, finance, government, and schools and, especially in its early stages, for streets, water supplies, sewage disposal, and urban transport.

[Third, the] westward movement . . . by attracting immigrants, enlarged the effective aggregate scale of the economy. . . (Abramovitz, 1993:225-226).

Immigration and the Supply of Human Capital

Kuznets made an argument for a positive impact of immigration on the native born that suggests a very large effect coming from the importation of human capital.

Considering the magnitude and duration of [the immigration flow], it is difficult to exaggerate its importance as a factor in the economic growth of the United States. Since immigration brought in a large labor force, the cost of whose rearing and training was borne elsewhere, it clearly represented an enormous capital investment that dwarfed any capital inflows of the more orthodox type (Kuznets, 1952:197).

Neal and Uselding elaborated on this point (Neal and Uselding, 1972; Uselding 1971). They begin by noting that most immigrants came to the United States as young adults and entered the labor force, thus producing output, earning wages, and consuming almost immediately on their arrival. Their income can be thought of as the return to the "human capital" they imported when they moved to this country. Yet that human capital—manifest both in its potential for purely physical labor and in the skills and learned abilities of immigrants—was created in another country. The American economy (and a new American) earned the returns from the human capital that had been transferred from—and without payment to—the economy that spent its resources on raising the individual to young adulthood and endowing him or her with education and other valuable skills. Freed of having to pay for this importation of human capital, the American economy was able to invest the equivalent resources in physical or human capital produced at home. Neal and Uselding calculate the contribution to the U.S. capital stock of these gifts by compounding the flows at a rate of 6 percent. They suggest that immigration might have contributed as much as 9 percent of the capital stock by 1850, 18 percent by 1880, and 42 percent by 1912.[48] With this

---

[48]Gallman (1977) suggests that these figures are too high for two reasons: first, because they are built on wage and work-year data, and, second, because Uselding's (1971) estimates are based on the

larger capital stock—larger than the same immigrants' contribution to the labor force—the national capital-labor ratio was higher than it would have been otherwise. Thus, labor productivity was higher than it would have been without immigration.[49]

Immigration and the Real Wage

We come to the final argument in our list of possible links between immigration and economic growth. This is the one that is most often used to suggest a negative impact of immigration. Throughout the period of open immigration, contemporary observers, and especially spokesmen for labor, charged that the inflow of immigrants depressed the real wage of labor. The "more the supply of labor the lower must certainly become its price," said Henry Carey a prominent economist of the time in 1873 (cited in Lebergott, 1964:161). His reasoning, as we deconstruct it today, would appear to rest on a static, partial equilibrium model of the supply and demand for all labor, analogous to the familiar supply and demand for a single, homogeneous commodity such as wheat. If this analysis is meant to apply to all labor it is—of course—naive. The supply and demand analysis of labor markets makes sense only when applied to the market for a specific type of labor (say bricklayers). The macroeconomic view of the labor market is quite different. An increase in the quantity of labor employed would immediately change the demand for labor. Because the new labor would earn and then spend income, increased employment would increase aggregate demand and thus the demand for labor.[50] Whether the immigration-induced increased demand for labor fully offsets the increased supply is an empirical question. It is certainly not a foregone conclusion.

Nonetheless, some distinguished economic historians have suggested without much qualification that the real wages of all Americans were depressed by immigration. They have also pointed to evidence that they claim buttresses this

---

occupations that immigrants reported on arrival rather than the occupations that they actually pursued in the United States. Gallman believes that some immigrants were forced to pursue occupations beneath their skill level because of discrimination and their lower level of literacy in English.

[49]Gallman (1977) is critical of this argument because he feels it implicitly assumes an extreme version of the Walker effect which Gallman rejects. To Gallman it appears that the saving that Neal and Uselding calculate would only be present if, in the absence of immigration, Americans chose to increase the native birth rate enough to fill the labor force gap left by the absent immigrants. In that case, America would have had to invest in the child rearing and education for this shadow cohort. We suggest that Gallman's line of attack introduces an unnecessary confusion into the analysis. Kuznets' original insight was to see that immigrants not only import labor, they import human capital as well. Thus, America gained a valuable productive resource and the origin countries lost one every time a young adult chose to immigrate.

[50]The effect of a new immigrant on aggregate demand may appear even before he or she takes a job in this country. The immigrant will have to spend and consume during the transition period between disembarkation and the receipt of the first paycheck.

view.   Lebergott looked at the increase in wages following the restriction of immigration:[51]

> When the immigration flow was cut off in 1914 (first by German submarines, then by legislation) wages rose markedly, as shown in Table 26.3. In the 15 years after 1914, workers' incomes rose as much as they had over the prior half-century. No speedup in entrepreneurial ingenuity or productive energies of workers was occurring at that dramatic rate. Congress, by shutting off the flow of workers from Europe, had helped push up workers' wages.

Average Earnings of Nonfarm Workers
(In 1914 Dollars)

1860	$457
1914	696
1929	898

Source: Computed from Lebergott (1964:428,524).

There are, of course, many reasons why real wages might have risen during World War I and the Roaring Twenties. Lebergott's evidence is consistent with his thesis, but it is certainly not a rigorous test.[52]

Hatton and Williamson (1998:Chap. 8) have estimated that the immigration between 1890 and 1913 augmented the labor force in 1910 by 11.8 percent and reduced the real wage in 1913 by between 4.5 and 5.6 percent. Their calculation was made using a Phillips curve model of the aggregate labor market rather than a micro-economic supply and demand model. Nonetheless, their theoretical apparatus dictates their finding of a negative impact of immigration. The Phillips curve is an inverse relationship between the rate of wage inflation and the unemployment rate (Phillips, 1958). Hatton and Williamson argue that by "altering labor supply and unemployment in the short run, immigration should drive down the wage along some long run Phillips curve." We question the applicability of the Phillips curve in this context. During the 1900-1913 period, immigration was *negatively* correlated with unemployment and *positively* correlated with wage growth.[53]

---

[51]Lebergott (1984:34, who in turn cites Lebergott, 1964:163).

[52]In looking at the rate of change of real wages before and after the reduction in immigration, Lebergott was echoing an older argument of Douglas (1930), who estimated a very low rate of increase of real wages (0.3 percent annually) in the period of greatest immigration, 1890 and 1914. Douglas's estimates for the period of mass immigration were especially slow compared to the rates of growth of real wages in the period immediately preceding and following this period. Douglas's real wages estimates have been superseded by those of Rees (1961), which show a reasonably rapid growth of wages (1.4 percent) during the era of high immigration.

[53]The unemployment rate by any measure was relatively low (4.7 to 4.9 percent) for the period 1900-1913 (Lebergott, 1964; Romer, 1986a; Weir, 1992). The earlier decade of the 1890s was a period of industrial depression and high unemployment, but during that decade immigration was greatly reduced. As the depression ended and unemployment rates dropped, immigration flows increased and ran at high levels throughout the booming period between 1900 and 1913.

Hatton and Williamson get around this seeming contradiction by combining the Phillips relationship with an aggregate demand for labor function derived from a CES production function (no economies of scale). By substitution they are able to eliminate the unemployment rate from their estimating equation. Their formulation reduces the Phillips curve to a positive relationship between the real wage and output per worker. They then use data from the period to estimate a positive relationship between real wages and aggregate labor productivity. They *assert* that immigration must have had a negative impact on real wages by claiming that immigration would lower productivity. They estimate the magnitude of this presumed negative impact of immigration on productivity by reference to labor's share of output in the long run (0.6, they say). For them, "the long run impact of labor force growth on output is simply the labor share times labor force growth."

Hatton and Williamson's calculation, then, is simply an empirical estimation of the capital-dilution argument discussed above. Because, by assumption, Hatton and Williamson deny any impact of immigration on the capital stock and abstract away from labor market dynamics over the business cycle, they exclude all of the dynamic effects that are hypothesized to generate a positive effect of immigration on real wages and the rate of economic growth. They have not ruled out these positive effects by an examination of the data, the historical record, nor the logic of the arguments.[54]

At this point it is worth pointing out two facts that are not in dispute. The first is that, whatever the effect of immigration, real wages of labor rose throughout the period between the Civil War and World War I. Figure 8-17 displays data on the real wage in manufacturing (Long, 1960; Rees, 1961). There is no striking slowdown of real wage growth during the period of most rapid immigration between 1900 and 1914. The second point is that the waves of immigrants ebbed and flowed in synchronization with the economy. When immigration rates were high, unemployment was low and real wages rose rapidly; when immigration was less, the economy was depressed. We are not, of course, suggesting that immigration caused an improvement in real wages. Rather, we side with Easterlin (1968:30-33), who interpreted these patterns as evidence that immigration responded to increases in the demand for labor in the United States and that the shifts in demand were larger than the shifts in supply.

There is no evidence that immigration slowed growth or lowered living standards of the resident population. There are good reasons to think that immigration increased the pace of economic growth and the relative welfare of the resident population in the 50 years following the end of the Civil War. Indeed, the impact of immigration on economic growth and on

---

[54]Hatton and Williamson (1998) also use their computable general equilibrium model to assess the impact of immigration on wages. Their exercise also excludes the possibility of dynamic or short-run effects or the possibility of economies of scale.

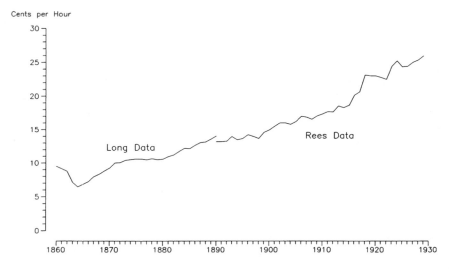

FIGURE 8-17 Real hourly wages in manufacturing, 1899 prices.

the economic welfare of the resident population appears to have been pro-
foundly positive.

IMMIGRATION AND THE AMERICAN INCOME DISTRIBUTION

Potential impacts of immigration on the American income distribution are at
the heart of much of the debate over current immigration policy. In the words of
Borjas:

> The debate over immigration policy is not over whether the entire country is
> made better off by immigration—it is over how the economic pie is sliced up
> (Borjas, 1996:77).

The current debate has centered on both the labor market and the public sector as
arenas in which resources may be redistributed away from poor Americans and
toward the foreign born.

The facts are that income inequality in the United States has risen as immigration flows have surged. A number of scholars have argued that the two
developments are linked (see Levy and Murnane, 1992).

In the scholarship on the economic impacts of the earlier mass immigration
to the United States the focus is on growth. The potential impacts of immigration
on the American income distribution have received much less attention, at least
until very recently. Why is this and what do we know?

Trends in Income Inequality During the Earlier Era
of Mass Immigration

Williamson and Lindert (1980) developed what has become the standard measure of long-term trends in American income inequality during the earlier era of mass immigration to the United States. It is the ratio of the real wage rates of urban skilled workers to those of urban unskilled workers. The larger the ratio, the greater the gap between rich and poor. We reproduce their series in Figure 8-18.

The inequality measure displayed in Figure 8-18 has a strong, positive correlation with the series on the annual number of immigrants displayed in Figure 8-4. There is a noticeable increase in American income inequality during the 15 years preceding World War I when the inflows of immigrants from abroad reached their highest levels in American history. Inequality abated during World War I, when immigration was curtailed, and then rebounded after the war with the resurgence of immigration. During the 1920s, inequality was roughly stable and then plunged in the 1930s with the onset of the Great Depression and the virtual cessation of immigration.

Correlation does not imply causation, of course. Williamson and Lindert consider immigration as one of a number of possible explanations for the trends in inequality. Ultimately they choose to downplay its role. They write:

> While the high tide of immigration of low-skilled workers from southern and
> eastern Europe may have accelerated labor quantity growth and decelerated

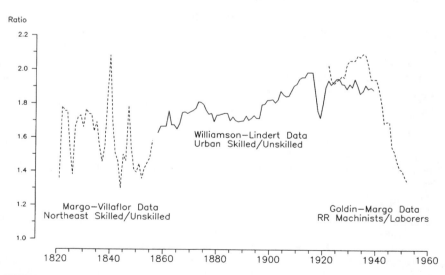

FIGURE 8-18 Williamson-Lindert index of wage inequality ratio of skilled to unskilled wages, urban workers.

labor "quality" growth . . . these labor supply forces were apparently offset by acceleration in indigenous skills growth. The farmland frontier began to close up sharply in this period, but the model again assigns almost no importance to this change in explaining wage inequality trends. What we know about factor supply growth turns out to play a minor role in explaining the resurgence of wage rate inequality at the start of this century.

The model clearly points to changes in the pattern of technological progress as the explanation of the resurgence. . . . [T]his acceleration of productivity in the skill-intensive tertiary sector explains why teachers, mechanics, carpenters, and other skilled groups enjoyed rising wage advantages in the first decade of this century (Williamson and Lindert, 1980:236).

In his more recent work with Hatton, Williamson reconsiders this conclusion. Hatton and Williamson establish the plausibility of the view that immigration increased wage inequality not only in the United States, but in all countries experiencing rapid immigration. They do this by asserting that immigrants tended to be unskilled.

Since the migrants tended to be unskilled and increasingly so as the late nineteenth century unfolded (much like the late twentieth century), they served to flood the immigrant country labor markets at the bottom, thus lowering the unskilled wage relative to skilled wages, white collar incomes and rents. Immigration implied rising inequality in rich countries (Hatton and Williamson, 1998:Chap. 11).

Hatton and Williamson test their proposition by examining trends in inequality across countries. They find that in countries where immigration flows were large relative to the size of the labor force, inequality rose more rapidly than otherwise; "when countries had to accommodate heavy immigration, inegalitarian trends were strong."

Goldin (1994b:12) also suggests that immigration increased American income inequality in the early years of this century. Citing Coombs's (1926) data on the trend in the real wages of unskilled laborers, she emphasizes their downward movement after 1907 and their rise during World War I.[55] She speculates

---

[55]We have serious reservations about Coombs' data, which are a pastiche of observations drawn from a variety of sources. Coombs used one primary source for the period between 1890 and 1907 and another for the period 1908-1914. The decline in real wages cited by Goldin is largely a matter of a change at the break in sources. There was a sharp recession in 1908 (unemployment jumped from 3.1 to 7.5 percent), and there was an across the board decline in wages as a response. There was also a large decline in gross immigration (from 1.3 to 0.8 million between FY 1907 and 1908) and an increase in departures (Bureau of the Census, 1975/1997, C89, and Weir, 1992:341). Net immigration fell from 767,000 to only 210,000 (Kuznets and Rubin, 1954:95). In fact, 1907 was the peak year for immigration. Moreover, the adjustment to hourly wages for the second segment of Coombs is made by a different procedure than that used for the first segment (David and Solar, 1977:63-64). Data for the 1920s are from yet a third source, the National Industrial Conference Board. Those data were collected by mail questionnaires and left the definition of "unskilled" production workers to the responding firms. The National Industrial Conference Board (NICB) data

that the influx of immigrant labor and then the wartime cutoff might have been the cause of this fall and subsequent rise.

We find both the Hatton and Williamson and the Goldin arguments unconvincing. Both simply point to a correlation between immigration and various measures of wage inequality, relying on assertions about immigrants' relative skills to make plausible a cause and effect relationship. Yet it looks to us as though immigrant skills belonged in about the *middle* of the American skill distribution. If this is correct, then we believe that there is no reason to expect that immigration would increase wage inequality. In our view this issue is currently unresolved and would benefit from further research.

The historical literature has focused on two additional dimensions of wage inequality. These are wage differentials based on race and on geography.

Immigration and Racial Wage Differentials

There is another large literature that focuses on the impact of foreign immigration on the geographic mobility and relative wages of black Americans. For the early period, Thomas (1954/1973) suggested that the mass immigration from Europe in the decades before World War I kept African Americans "bottled up" in the agricultural South. There is no doubt that their wages in the low-productivity, stagnant, and oppressive South were lower than they would have been in the dynamic and prosperous North in the 50 years between Emancipation and World War I. Their failure to migrate in any significant numbers is one of the mysteries of late nineteenth-century American economic history. There is no shortage of explanations in the literature, but other than Thomas' speculations, no one emphasizes the role of immigration. Ransom and Sutch (1975, 1977) emphasized the institutional structure of the crop-lien, tenant-farming system of post-Civil War agriculture in which blacks were "locked in" by a form of "debt peonage." Wright (1986) discussed the role of the peculiar and controlling labor markets of the South. Margo (1990) stressed the inadequate Southern schooling system that left most blacks ill-prepared to compete for urban jobs. Tolnay and Beck (1995) explored the role of extra-legal coercion. Whether the hypothetical absence of competition from European immigrants in this era would have induced blacks to overcome these oppressive forces and begin their "great migration" before the 1920s is an important and unanswered historical question.

Immigration and Regional Wage Differentials

Regional wage differentials have been a persistent feature of American labor markets, at least since 1840 (Easterlin, 1960; Williamson, 1964; Rosenbloom,

---

begin in 1921 but there is also a retrospectively reported prewar wage collected in 1922. It is these retrospectively reported data that are used by Coombs to link the NICB data to the middle segment of the series. It is difficult to know how to compare them with the prewar data.

1996). One question is whether immigration acted to exacerbate or to ameliorate these differentials.

Immigrants tend to concentrate geographically in a small number of "magnet" destinations.[56] This is true today and it was also true during the earlier wave of mass immigration preceding World War I. There are two principal hypotheses in the literature regarding the forces that create these magnets. One is that these destinations are regions of high opportunity and high wages that attract in-migration of the foreign born and residents alike. Another view is that immigrants are attracted to cities that already have thriving immigrant communities with well-developed ethnic support networks and they flock to them without reference to their relative economic prosperity.

If the first view is correct, then immigration would serve to accelerate economic growth by removing allocative inefficiencies and relieving bottlenecks. It would also tend to reduce wage inequality by expanding the labor supply in high-wage markets. The second view, by contrast, suggests that immigrants would soon overcrowd local labor markets and the ethnic neighborhoods that originally attracted them. Their geographic concentration would likely harm the native-born workers in these areas, exacerbate income inequality, slow cultural and linguistic assimilation, and retard the economic advancement of the immigrants themselves.

One recent study that bears on the relative importance of these two hypotheses was conducted by Goldin (1994a), who was interested in the impacts of immigration on intercity differences in wage rates during the turn of the century. In the cross section, Goldin finds a strong *positive* relationship between the fraction of a city's population that was foreign born and the city's average wage. In other words, cities with a large fraction of immigrants had the highest wages. We are persuaded by Goldin's (1994a:247) conjecture that "immigrants sought out labor markets with high wages." Goldin also finds that the arrival of immigrants caused wage rates to rise more slowly than they might have, had the immigrants not come. More precisely, "in general, a 1-percentage-point increase in the population share that was foreign born depressed wages by about 1 to 1.5 percent" relative to cities with fewer foreign born (Goldin, 1994a:250). In other words, without the influx of immigrants, wages in high-wage cities would have been higher still. Because of their propensity to move to high-wage cities, immigrants helped to equalize intercity wage rate differences by alleviating labor shortages. Had there been no immigration, native-born workers would have moved to fill these positions and the negative wage impact would have still been felt by the native-born residents of boom cities (though the movement toward equalization of wages across regions would have proceeded more slowly). To

---

[56]For analyses of immigrant settlement patterns in the period prior to World War I, see Lee (1957); Galloway and Vedder (1971, 1972); Galloway et al. (1974); Dunlevy and Gemery (1977a, 1977b, 1978); Dunlevy (1980, 1983); and Dunlevy and Saba (1992).

blame the immigrants for the adjustment back to equilibrium is simple scapegoatism.[57]

The key point that emerges from this literature is that regional wage inequality was *reduced* by immigration. The reason for this is that immigrants tended to locate in high-wage regions.

Income Redistribution Through Social Spending

One source of the modern opposition to immigration stems from a perception that resources may be transferred from the native to the foreign born through government social spending programs. Borjas and Trejo (1991) developed one influential estimate of the possible magnitude of such transfers and their trend over time. They noted that in 1990 immigrants were more likely than the native born to participate in cash-benefit government welfare programs and that the gap between immigrant and native welfare participation has been growing steadily since 1970. Because they believe that immigrants' disproportionately high welfare participation is not offset by disproportionately high income and (presumably) tax payments, Borjas and Trejo conclude that immigrants in modern America do not "pay their way" (summarized in Borjas, 1994:1704-1708).[58]

Here we examine the evidence on possible redistribution from natives to the foreign born through social spending programs in the early part of this century. Of course, government programs were tiny in this era. In that era, private charities and self-help organizations took the lead in the provision of social insurance, educational services, old-age security, disaster relief, and income redistribution. In this sense, it would be impossible to identify a quantitatively important role for government in income redistribution. For this reason we take a broad view of redistributive schemes and their proportionate impacts on the native and foreign born. We focus on three services that account for the bulk of public expenditures in our own era: poverty relief, old-age relief, and educational services. We also assemble some evidence on immigrants' contributions to the support of these services.

---

[57]Goldin's estimates were made to help understand the reasons for a political sentiment to restrict immigration. In a sense it was the "scapegoat factor" that she was attempting to measure.

[58]These conclusions are highly controversial. For example, Borjas and Trejo limit their discussion of social transfers to means-tested entitlement programs such as food stamps, Medicaid, low-income housing assistance, and Head Start. In doing so, they ignore the substantial social redistribution from income earners to retirees through the Social Security system and from single young adults to families through the educational system. Because recent immigrants are disproportionately single, young adults, and labor force participants, they are less likely than the native born to use educational services, especially the more expensive higher education services. They are certainly net contributors to the Social Security system.

In their discussion of immigrants' contributions to the governments' income, Borjas and Trejo simply assert that "immigrants do not receive a disproportionately high share of income; they also do

Poverty Relief in the Gilded Age

Before the New Deal legislation of the 1930s, publicly funded welfare programs were small in scale, limited in geographic scope, and were under local control. Throughout the century preceding the Great Depression, there was stiff public opposition to government-sponsored poor relief (Almy, 1899-1900; Mohl, 1983; Hannon, 1984, 1985; Ziliak, 1996). In the view of many contemporary observers, the root of the problem facing public poverty relief was the massive increase in immigration. "The increase of pauperism amongst us" is due to "the increase of our foreign population," according to a writer quoted by Katz (1986:17). In the view of the publicly funded Philadelphia Board of Guardians of the Poor in 1827:

> One of the greatest burthens that falls upon this corporation, is the maintenance of the host of worthless foreigners, disgorged upon our shores (cited in Katz, 1986:17).

In 1900, Joseph Lee, a national leader of the movement for urban playgrounds, suggested that

> (T)he problems with which American philanthropy has at present to deal have been largely imported along with the greatly increased volume of immigration that has come during the last fifty or sixty years (quoted in Patterson, 1981:22).

We know of no scholarship that has systematically explored the relative propensity of the foreign born to seek public charity relief in this era. Some statistical information on this matter, however, was collected by the first Immigration Commission, appointed by Congress in 1907 to make a "full inquiry" into "all aspects" of immigration. The Commission was eager to explore these controversial allegations, especially because it noted that, in earlier times,

> It is recorded that in some cases a considerable part of the immigrants arriving on a ship would be so destitute of means of support that it was necessary to transport them immediately to almshouses, and the earlier poorhouse records show that there were constantly being cared for large numbers of newly arrived foreign-born (U.S. Immigration Commission, 1911:Volume I, p.35).

To uncover the extent of the problem at the turn of the century, the Commission conducted its own investigation of "Immigrants as Charity Seekers." It went to "organized city (i.e., public) charity societies" in 43 different cities and collected evidence on "cases," that is, individuals or families requesting assistance at some time during the six-month period, December 1908 through May 1909.

---

not pay a disproportionately high share of taxes" (summarized in Borjas, 1994:1705). This statement is probably true if the reference group is the employed only. But because immigrants are so much more likely than the native born to be concentrated in the wage-earning age groups and to be both labor force participants and income tax payers, it is not clear that immigrants pay a disproportionately low share of taxes compared with the population as a whole. The population as a whole forms the denominator in calculations about relative welfare use, thus the population as a whole is the appropriate reference for evaluating the fiscal contributions of immigrants.

The Commission itself was unable to calculate the relative propensity of the foreign born to seek charity because it did not at the same time survey the population, but instead anticipated the results of the 1910 federal census of population. Nonetheless, the notable absence of recent immigrants from the public charity rolls was striking enough that the Commission concluded that at least this group of immigrants could not have been a burden.

> The number of those admitted [into the country] who receive assistance from organized charity in cities is relatively small. In the commission's investigation, which covered the activities of the associated charities in 43 cities, including practically all the larger immigrant centers except New York, it was found that a small percentage of the cases represented immigrants who had been in the United States three years or under, while nearly half of all the foreign-born cases were those who had been in the United States twenty years or more. This investigation was conducted during the winter of 1908-9 before industrial activities had been fully resumed following the financial depression of 1907-8, and this inquiry showed that the recent immigrants, even in cities in times of relative industrial inactivity, did not seek charitable assistance in any considerable numbers. Undoubtedly conditions would have been otherwise had it not been for the large outward movement of recent immigrants following the depression, but however that may be, it is certain that those who remained were for the most part self-supporting (U.S. Immigration Commission, 1911:Volume I, p. 36).

The charity seeking of *all* immigrants was more difficult to characterize given the absence of nativity-specific population figures, and thus the Commission avoided any judgment on the issue. Unlike the Commission, we have access to an electronic version of the 1910 population census, and thus we were able to explore the relative charity-seeking propensities of immigrants overall. The results are presented in the scatter diagram displayed in Figure 8-19. In the scatter diagram, each point plotted represents one of the 43 cities included in the Immigration Commission study. Along the horizontal axis we map the proportion of household heads who were foreign born, calculated from the IPUMS from the 1910 Census. Along the vertical axis we show the proportion of charity "cases" who were foreign born. The majority of points fall below the 45-degree line, indicating that in most cities, the foreign born disproportionately eschewed public charity. The unweighted average of the ratio of foreign-born charity seekers to foreign-born household heads across cities is 0.84, whereas the average ratio weighted by city size is 0.92. Because the overwhelming proportion of all immigrants as well as all charity seekers were city dwellers, these results suggest that turn-of-the-century immigrants were not disproportionately heavy users of public welfare agencies.[59]

---

[59]Although the ratio of foreign-born charity seekers to foreign-born household heads averages less than one for the sample of cities as a whole, the data in Figure 8-19 show a disproportionately large share of foreign-born charity seekers in cities with large foreign-born population shares. We

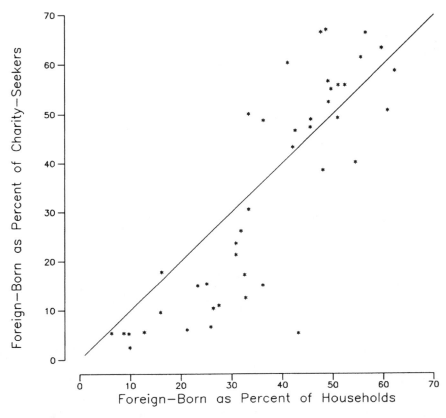

FIGURE 8-19 Foreign born as a percentage of charity seekers and of households, 43 cities, 1909-1910.

One explanation for this pattern is the one the Commission itself suggested: A large fraction of immigrants came as sojourners to this country to work; when work was unavailable, they returned to their native lands. Another reason for the relative absence of immigrants from the rolls of city charities was the importance of immigrants' own efforts to help themselves and one another. These immigrant self-help organizations were noted at the time. A Massachusetts commission commented:

> The societies which are organized and maintained by the members of the differ-
> ent nationalities, and which flourish in some form in every community where
> there are large groups of immigrants, are a factor in helping the immigrant

are tempted to speculate that local government in such cities may have been unusually responsive to the needs of these communities. For the moment, however, this remains an area for further research.

through the trials of immigration and the difficulties of adjustment to new conditions. The chief reason among all nationalities for the formation of these societies is insurance against sickness and death, but most of them combine with this some other objects. Nearly all of them outline an educational and civic program. They may lack the means to carry this out, yet the statement of these purposes has an influence upon the members (Massachusetts Commission of Immigration, 1914:202, quoted in Handlin, 1959:84).

Thus, private, ethnic charity organized through fraternal societies, labor unions, and churches played an important part in the poverty relief system of the time.

Katz (1986:45) estimates that roughly half of the income of all charitable institutions in New York State in 1900 came from private sources. He calls particular attention to the role of Catholics, a numerically important segment of the new immigrant community at that time.

Catholics gave exceptionally large amounts for relief. Indeed, many of the nonpublic institutions were affiliated with the Catholic church. It is difficult to quantify the proportion of institutional, nonpublic relief provided by Catholic facilities in Buffalo, but it is unlikely that it was less than 50 percent. Given the relative poverty of the Catholic community, these efforts made on behalf of the needy are truly impressive (Katz, 1986:46).

Immigrants also purchased insurance to protect themselves and their families against the many contingencies that might put them at financial risk. For example, Pittsburgh's local of the Brotherhood of Railroad Brakemen earmarked a portion of dues to compensate union members' families in case of a work-related death or disability (Kleinberg, 1989:273). More systematic evidence of immigrants' participation in such "beneficial societies" is contained in Table 8-5 that summarizes data collected by the labor bureaus in key industrial states in the late nineteenth century. The table displays the fraction of surveyed workers belonging to beneficial societies by nativity. Although the numbers vary from survey to survey, overall we find about a fourth of all workmen belonging to such societies, with the membership rates generally a little higher for the foreign than the native born.

These benefit societies and the many labor and ethnic organizations from the period also promoted informal acts of charity. Kleinberg describes some such activities in Pittsburgh:

There were spontaneous collections in the mill or at the gates on almost every payday. The workers and their families shared what they had, aware that they, too, might suffer a similar tragedy. The collective culture enshrined generosity and reinforced it through appeals in the labor press "to do the handsome thing" for disabled comrades. It was the trade unionists' duty to do everything in their power to make philanthropic gestures "a grand success financially" (Kleinberg, 1989:273).

Although the early twentieth-century immigrant community may have been disproportionately needy, we have found no evidence that it placed a disproportionate burden on public charitable agencies or on private philanthropies.

TABLE 8-5   Membership in Beneficiary Societies by Nativity, Various
Surveys of Male Workers, 1884-1894

Year	State	Survey of	Percent Belonging to Beneficiary Society	
			Native-Born	Foreign-Born
1844	Iowa	Teachers	16.8%	35.7%
1884-1887	Kansas	Wage Earners	26.5	25.9
1888	Michigan	Stone Workers	5.4	10.7
1889	Michigan	Furniture Workers	21.9	25.5
1890	Michigan	Detroit Iron Workers	21.6	33.8
1890	Michigan	Iron Workers outside of Detroit	21.2	26.4
1890	Maine	Wage Earners	51.3	39.9
1892	Missouri	Wage Earners	48.3	58.8
1892	California	Wage Earners	47.8	60.2
1894	Michigan	Farm Laborers	14.7	14.7

SOURCES: Susan B. Carter, Roger L. Ransom, Richard Sutch, and Hongcheng Zhao. *Codebook and User's Manual: Survey of 3,493 Wage-Earners in California, 1892; Reported in the Fifth Biennial Report of the California Bureau of Labor Statistics.* Berkeley: Institute of Business and Economic Research, 1993; Susan B. Carter, Roger L. Ransom, Richard Sutch, and Hongcheng Zhao. *Codebook and User's Manual: Survey of 347 Teachers in Iowa, 1884; Reported in the First Biennial Report of the Iowa Bureau of Labor Statistics.* Berkeley: Institute of Business and Economic Research, 1993; Susan B. Carter, Roger L. Ransom, Richard Sutch, and Hongcheng Zhao. *Codebook and User's Manual: A Survey of 1,165 Workers in Kansas, 1884-1887; Reported in the First, Second, and Third Annual Reports of the Kansas Bureau of Labor and Industrial Statistics.* Berkeley: Institute of Business and Economic Research, 1993; Susan B. Carter, Roger L. Ransom, Richard Sutch, and Hongcheng Zhao. *Codebook and User's Manual: A Survey of 1,084 Workers in Maine, 1890; Reported in the Fifth Annual Report of the Maine Bureau of Industrial and Labor Statistics.* Berkeley: Institute of Business and Economic Research, 1993; Susan B. Carter, Roger L. Ransom, Richard Sutch, and Hongcheng Zhao. *Codebook and User's Manual: A Survey of 719 Stone Workers in Michigan, 1888; Reported in the Sixth Annual Report of the Michigan Bureau of Labor and Industrial Statistics.* Berkeley: Institute of Business and Economic Research, 1993; Susan B. Carter, Roger L. Ransom, Richard Sutch, and Hongcheng Zhao. *Codebook and User's Manual: A Survey of 5,419 Workers in the Furniture Industry of Michigan, 1889; Reported in the Seventh Annual Report of the Michigan Bureau of Labor and Industrial Statistics.* Berkeley: Institute of Business and Economic Research, 1993; Susan B. Carter, Roger L. Ransom, Richard Sutch, and Hongcheng Zhao. *Codebook and User's Manual: A Survey of 3,920 Workers in the Ironworking Industry of Detroit, 1890; Reported in the Eighth Annual Report of the Michigan Bureau of Labor and Industrial Statistics.* Berkeley: Institute of Business and Economic Research, 1993; Susan B. Carter, Roger L. Ransom, Richard Sutch, and Hongcheng Zhao. *Codebook and User's Manual: A Survey of 4,918 Agricultural Implement and Ironworkers in Michigan Outside of Detroit, 1890; Reported in the Eighth Annual Report of the Michigan Bureau of Labor and Industrial Statistics.* Berkeley: Institute of Business and Economic Research, 1993; Susan B. Carter, Roger L. Ransom, Richard Sutch, and Hongcheng Zhao. *Codebook and User's Manual: A Survey of 5,600 Farm Laborers in Michigan, 1894; Reported in the Twelfth Annual Report of the Michigan Bureau of Labor and Industrial Statistics.* Berkeley: Institute of Business and Economic Research, 1993; Susan B. Carter, Roger L. Ransom, Richard Sutch, and Hongcheng Zhao. *Codebook and User's Manual: A Survey of 259 Wage-Workers in Missouri, 1891; Reported in the Fourteenth Annual Report of the Missouri Bureau of Labor Statistics and Inspection.* Berkeley: Institute of Business and Economic Research, 1993.

Old-Age Support

During the age of mass immigration about the turn of the century, the only significant public program of old-age support was a federal pension system providing benefits for Union Army veterans of the Civil War.[60] By 1907 every male over the age of 62 who had served in the Union Army was eligible to receive a pension. Close to 20 percent of all males over age 60 actually received pensions. In monetary terms these pensions amounted to approximately 30 percent of the average annual nonfarm income of males (Ransom et al., 1996). Because the pension was limited to those who served in the armed forces of the United States during the Civil War, it did not provide support for the bulk of immigrants, most of whom arrived in the United States after that war's end.[61] Up to 1935, then, the government-run pension system redistributed income from the foreign born to the native born.[62]

The first comprehensive public program of old-age support was established by the Social Security Act of 1935 that initiated a pay-as-you-go system in which the elderly are supported by the tax payments of those currently in the labor force.[63] Redistribution between the native and foreign born can take place within such a system if the relative proportions of each group in the wage-earning and retirement age groups differ.[64]

In Figure 8-20 we plot the percentage of the foreign-born population by age at 20-year intervals beginning in 1930, shortly before the Social Security Act was

---

[60]For descriptions of the establishment and evolution of this system see Oliver (1917), Glasson (1902, 1918), and McMurray (1922).

[61]For analyses of the politics of this legislation see Quadagno (1988), Skocpol (1992), Orloff (1993), and Ransom et al. (1996).

[62]Tontine and other private insurance would have redistributed resources from the foreign to the native born if, as seems likely, the foreign born had higher mortality and default rates.

[63]The original 1935 Act creating old-age "insurance" inaugurated a payroll tax (contributed to equally by the employee and the employer) but deferred all benefits until 1942 and based them on total lifetime earnings. These tax receipts were to be accumulated in a reserve fund; however, no attempt was made to fund the proposed benefits on an actuarial basis, and the benefit formulas had a progressive bias in favor of low-income earners. Amendments made in 1939 moved the system even more explicitly to pay as you go. Benefits would begin in 1940, they would be based on earnings over a set period and would not be tied to lifetime contributions, benefits would be paid by current tax contributions, and the reserve fund would buffer the system against recessions (see Dulles, 1939; Pechman et al., 1968:31-34; and Achenbaum, 1986:18-37).

[64]Borjas argues against the notion that the Social Security system redistributes resources to the native born by focusing on an age difference between the native and foreign born in their point of entry into the system: "It is important to realize that the median age of immigration is 30, so that many immigrants pay into the Social Security system for a much shorter time span than natives, yet collect roughly the same benefits" (Borjas, 1994:1707-1708). This rate of return consideration is irrelevant. Our pay-as-you-go system transfers resources to the group with proportionately more contributors than recipients. At the present time, the foreign born are the disproportionate contributors. Only if immigration were cut off or reduced considerably would the Social Security system transfer resources from the native to the foreign born in coming decades.

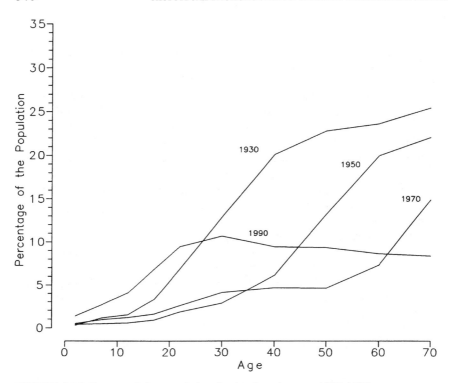

FIGURE 8-20 Percent of the population foreign born by age, 1930-1990.

passed, and ending in 1990, the date of the latest federal census. The figure shows that, in 1930, and increasingly so up to 1970, the foreign-born fraction of the population in the retirement age group was larger than the fraction in the wage-earning age groups. This is because the Quotas Act, the Great Depression, and World War II dramatically reduced the inflow of immigrants beginning in the early 1920s to a level well below that which had prevailed up until that time. The radical reduction in the immigrant flows led to a parallel reduction in the foreign-born fraction of the young adult population. As time passed without any new inflows, the foreign-born population aged, until by 1970 it was comprised overwhelmingly of older persons who had migrated prior to the 1920s.

Under these conditions, the Social Security system effected a substantial transfer of resources from the native to the foreign born. Yet as the age distribution of the foreign born in 1990 reveals, the resumption of immigration in the 1980s reversed the direction of the flow of old-age benefits by raising the relative proportion of foreign born in the working-age groups. Today the Social Security system works to redistribute resources from the foreign born to the native born.

Were the admission of immigrants to increase, the magnitude of the redistribution would be greater still.

Educational Services

In the period of massive immigration near the turn of the century, America had the most extensive and best-funded public education system in the world.[65] Financed through the property tax with attendance rates influenced by compulsory schooling and child labor laws, this system educated an increasing fraction of all youths over an increasing fraction of their lives. Did the immigrants pay their share of these public education expenditures? To the best of our knowledge, this question has never been posed in the historical literature. Indeed, the concern of contemporary observers and of historians of the period has been the opposite one. The Immigration Commission, for example, sought to determine "to what extent children of the various races of immigrants *are availing themselves* of educational facilities and what progress they make in school work" (U.S. Immigration Commission, 1911:Volume 2, p. 5, emphasis added). The native born of this period *encouraged* school attendance for the children of immigrants. According to Handlin:

> Toward mid-(nineteenth) century, an explosive fusion of conversion and reform transformed the mission of the schools in the view of many influential Americans. The schools, they argued, were less important as media for the transmittal of specific bodies of knowledge or skills--Latin, grammar, writing, and the like. They were rather instruments for molding the thoughts and behavior of the next generation and thereby reshaping society (Handlin, 1982:7).

Schools were the primary institution for "Americanizing" the children of immigrants. For many immigrant parents, on the other hand, schools were, "at best, institutions apart. . . . At worst, the school had been the representative of the state, which imposed on youth a set of values foreign to the parents" (Handlin, 1982:6).

Overall, the children of immigrants were less likely than the children of the native born to be in attendance. Although the differences were not very large among elementary school-age children, at older ages and higher (and more expensive) levels of schooling, the children of immigrants were far less likely to be in school. Licht (1992:22), for example, found that 71 percent of 13-year-old sons of native white Americans were in school in Philadelphia in 1900. That rate compared with 60 and 55 percent for sons of the Irish and Russians, respectively. The daughters of immigrants fared even worse. Licht accounts for these ethnic differences in terms of the lower socioeconomic status of foreign-born parents. However, Perlmann, in a study of Providence, Rhode Island, found that large ethnic differences remained even after controlling for background factors. In

---

[65]For some international comparisons of school enrollment and literacy rates in the late nineteenth century, see O'Rourke and Williamson (1995).

1880 the son of a Yankee was 5.8 times more likely than the son of an Irishman to begin high school and still 1.8 times more likely after controlling for father's occupation, family property value, number of siblings, and whether or not both parents were present. Of the specific ethnic groups Perlmann studied, only the children of Russian Jews (in 1915) faced better educational prospects than the children of the native born (Perlmann, 1988:204-205).

Yet another reason to doubt that immigrants received positive transfers through the education system was that many immigrants sent their children to private, church-affiliated schools. In 1890, the first year for which national statistics are available, approximately 12 percent of all elementary and secondary school students were enrolled in private schools (Bureau of the Census, 1975/1997, series H418 and H426). Virtually all of these pupils were in Catholic schools which served predominantly immigrant communities.

Finally, as we noted above, immigrants tended to be homeowners at greater rates than the native born. Because the financing of the schools was based on the local property tax, the high foreign-born home ownership rate suggests that immigrants may have contributed a disproportionate share to school finances.[66] On the other hand, immigrant families tended to be larger and to have more school-age children than the average native-born household head and homeowner.

In an effort to gauge the direction of the net flow of public education services we examined school attendance and home ownership patterns in large urban areas in the United States, using the 1910 IPUMS. We restricted our search to large urban areas in an effort to control for school costs. Schools in rural areas spent far less per pupil, yet these were far more likely to enroll children of the native born. We counted the number of school children (through age 19) according to the nativity of their fathers.[67] We then compared this count with the number of homeowners by nativity. We found a higher ratio of school children to home-owning household heads among the foreign born—4.7 school children per property taxpayer for the foreign born as compared with a ratio of 3.7 for the native born. These calculations suggest that there may have been a net transfer of resources from the native to the foreign born through the public school system. However, the case is far from clear. For example, if 20 percent of these urban children of foreign-born (and none of the children of native-born) fathers attended Catholic schools *or* if the cost differential between an elementary and a high school education was large enough, then the imputed direction of the redistribution would be from immigrant to native born.

We conclude by noting that, although there is clearly room for further research on this topic, our overview suggests that the education system does not appear to have been an important arena for transferring resources from the native

---

[66]Alternatively, renters might be thought to pay the school tax indirectly through higher rents. The issue of the incidence of the property tax is not resolved by empirical work in public finance.

[67]Unfortunately, the federal census, from which the IPUMS sample was drawn, did not collect information on the nature of the institutions in which students were enrolled.

to the foreign born during this period. It is certainly clear that the native born were not as concerned about the possibility of such transfers in the way they are today.

IMMIGRATION AND THE CHARACTER AND QUALITY OF AMERICAN LIFE

Immigration and Population Growth: The Question of Race Suicide

One concern in the previous era of immigration was that immigrants and their children would overwhelm the native stock in the country's population.

> Foreign immigration into this country has . . . amounted not to a reenforcement of our population, but to a replacement of native by foreign stock. . . . If the foreigners had not come, the native element would long have filled the places the foreigners usurped (Walker, 1899:422-425).

In speaking thus, Francis Amasa Walker, President of the American Economic Association, spoke for many of his contemporaries. There were two fears. If the foreign born had a relatively higher rate of natural increase, then they would dominate in the population sooner or later. Moreover, the presence of foreigners may have somehow discouraged the native born from procreating. The rapid influx of immigrants, in other words, actually *depressed* the rate of natural increase among the native born.

King and Ruggles (1990) report that fears about the differentially high fertility of the foreign born were expressed as early as 1867. In the words of John Todd, a Congregrational minister:

> while our foreign population has large families, our own native American families are running out, and, at this rate, must and will entirely run out. The statistics presented to our legislators on this subject are fearful (Todd, 1867, quoted in King and Ruggles, 1990:348).

King and Ruggles explored this first of the so-called Walker effects using data from the Public Use Microdata Sample from the federal census of 1900. Contrary to the beliefs of contemporary observers, their analysis of the data showed no tendency for the "ethnics," as King and Ruggles refer to them, to have higher levels of fertility than those of the native-born population. Although the foreign born themselves had higher levels of fertility than the native born, the *children* of the foreign born had strikingly lower levels of fertility. Overall, these "ethnics" had *lower* rates of natural increase than the native born. The explanation offered by King and Ruggles focuses on the geographic distribution of the native and foreign groups. The foreign born and their children tended to live in urban sections of the Northeast where the fertility for *all* residents were the lowest in the nation. Whatever were the conditions depressing the fertility in these sections of the country, they affected the immigrants and the native stock to a similar degree.

The weight of scholarship leans heavily against the second of the alleged Walker effects, as well, that is, the purported depressing effect of immigration on the fertility of the native born. Although fertility fell dramatically during the period of high immigration, scholars emphasize the roles of the decline in child mortality and developments such as the spread of universal schooling, urbanization, increased employment opportunities for women, and the introduction of new goods. All of these developments raise the cost of children and thereby reduce parents' demand for them (Easterlin, 1996:111; Thomas, 1961).

The Economic Mobility of Immigrants

Ferrie (1997) has made an extensive study of immigrants who arrived in the 1840s. By matching the names of immigrants on the passenger manifests submitted by ship captains to immigration officials with individuals located in the manuscript censuses of population for 1850 and 1860, Ferrie was able to obtain an estimate of the skills, wealth, and economic mobility of recently arrived immigrants in those two years. He finds that immigrants rapidly accumulated wealth and human capital, exhibited substantial upward occupational mobility, and fared best if they entered with some skills than without. Compared with the rapid assimilation and improvement in status of modern immigrants, however, the pre-Civil War immigrants fared less well.

The upward mobility of immigrants and their children is illustrated by data from the 1910 Census assembled by Hutchinson (1956). He created an index of occupational concentration. Setting the proportion of foreign born in the labor force at the scale of 100, he then calculated the relative proportion of foreign-born workers in each industry. An industry in which the foreign born were underrepresented has an index number below 100, one with a more than proportionate share of foreign-born workers receives an index number greater than 100. The exercise is then repeated for the native-born workers of foreign parentage. A sample of results is displayed in Table 8-6. The foreign born appear to be concentrated in the lower-skilled and lower-status occupations listed at the bottom of the table. By the second generation, however, the prestigious professional occupations of accountant, engineer, and lawyer are at or above parity, and the concentration of immigrants in the low-status occupations has all but disappeared.

CONCLUSIONS

The assigned task for this chapter was to review, synthesize, and assess the scholarly literature on the economic and demographic impacts of the last great mass migration to the United States in the early part of this century. Our objec-

TABLE 8-6   Occupational Concentration Index for the Foreign-Born and Foreign-Stock Work Forces by Occupation, 1910 ("All Occupations" equal 100)

	Foreign-Born	Foreign-Stock
All Occupations	100	100
Accountants	62	131
Engineers	47	104
Lawyers	25	102
Physicians and dentists	45	86
Teachers	39	75
Domestics	173	87
Charwomen, porters	208	104
Janitors	168	102
Construction laborers	169	84
Transport laborers	224	58

SOURCE: Edward P. Hutchinson, *Immigrants and Their Children, 1850-1950*. New York: John Wiley, 1956, table 39: 204-206. As reproduced in Stanley Lebergott. *The Americans: An Economic Record*. New York: W.W. Norton, 1984, table 26.4: 344.

tive was to do this in a way that would lend further understanding of the consequences of current migration flows. While we have carried out our assignment as well as we were able, we must conclude that there are no simple lessons that emerge for the current set of policy concerns. This is true for at least four different reasons, which we have noted in more detail in the body of this report.

- *First*, the immigrants are different. Another way of saying this is that the level, character, and dynamics of the immigrant flows in the two periods are very different. Largely open borders appear to engender different flows than the highly regulated entry policy we have today.
- *Second*, the economy is different. Today, education is a key ingredient in the economic success of individuals. The U.S. economy now operates in a more open world economy than was true at the beginning of the century. For that reason, the size of the U.S. market may be a less important constraint on the ability of U.S. industries to take advantage of economies of scale. Communication and transportation within the United States are faster, easier, and cheaper than before. For that reason, the pace of invention and innovation may be less dependent upon the geographic proximity of interrelated activities.
- *Third*, the scale and role of government are different. Today, government plays a much larger role in the provision of services and in redistribution among members of the population than was true at the turn of the century.
- *Fourth*, the theoretical approach taken by scholars who analyzed the impacts of the mass migrations in the two decades preceding World War I was

different from the approach taken by scholars analyzing the current immigrant flows today. Broadly speaking, the scholarly literature analyzing the earlier flows was couched in terms of the "aggregate production function" and emphasized the long-run consequences of immigration on economic growth, advancing technology, productivity, and changes in factor proportions. The various elements of the economy at the beginning of this century were seen as diverse, complex, and interdependent. The propensity in the current literature is to concentrate only on the first-round impacts of immigration. Judging from the current literature, it must be easy to show that these first-round consequences tend to be harmful to resident workers who come into direct competition with new immigrants. Economic historians writing about the earlier period of high immigration went beyond the first-round effects. Taking a long-run perspective, they identified many aspects of the mass immigration that were beneficial from the point of view of the resident population.

Although there is no simple, single "lesson" from our review of the effects of the earlier immigration for policy makers today, there is one constancy that emerges. It is that, although different, the American economy is probably no less complex and interdependent than it was at the turn of the century. This fact suggests that scholars might profitably take a longer view and shift at least some of their attention away from redistributive issues and toward the impact of immigration on productivity, growth, and economic development. The picture that will emerge is likely to be less worrisome and to offer a wider range of policy options than is widely recognized today.

ACKNOWLEDGMENTS

We would like to thank Ron Lee, James Smith, and Gavin Wright for their detailed comments and suggestions. We also received valuable advice from James Dunlevy, Claudia Goldin, Christopher Hanes, Peter Lindert, and Simone Wegge. The students of the Universidad de San Andres, Buenos Aires, gave us an invaluable international perspective when we presented an early draft of the paper at their seminar in April 1997. Joseph Ferrie and Jeffrey Williamson made available manuscripts of their forthcoming books on the economic history of immigration. Organizations that provided data used in this paper include the Historical Labor Statistics Project at the University of California, the Social History Research Laboratory at the University of Minnesota, and the Inter-university Consortium for Political and Social Research at the University of Michigan. We have also received assistance from Robert Barde, Tiffany Lee, and Chris Meissner. We are grateful to all these individuals and institutions.

REFERENCES

Abramovitz, Moses
 1961 "The Nature and Significance of Kuznets Cycles." *Economic Development and Cultural Change* 9:225-248.

Abramovitz, Moses
 1993 "The Search for Sources of Growth: Areas of Ignorance, Old and New." *Journal of Economic History* 53:217-243.

Abramovitz, Moses, and Paul A. David
 1973 "Reinterpreting Economic Growth: Parables and Realities." *American Economic Review* 63:428-439.

Abramovitz, Moses, and Paul A. David
 1996 "Convergence and Deferred Catch-up: Productivity Leadership and the Waning of American Exceptionalism." Pp. 21-62 in *The Mosaic of Economic Growth*, Ralph Landau, Timothy Taylor, and Gavin Wright, eds. Stanford, Calif.: Stanford University Press.

Achenbaum, W. Andrew
 1986 *Social Security: Visions and Revisions.* New York: Cambridge University Press.

Aldrich, Howard, and Roger Waldinger
 1990 "Ethnicity and Entrepreneurship." *Annual Review of Sociology* 16:111-135.

Almy, Frederic
 1899- "The Relation between Private and Public Outdoor Relief-1." *The Charities Review*
 1900 (March-February):22-33.

Aronson, Robert L.
 1991 *Self-Employment: A Labor Market Perspective.* Cornell Studies in Industrial and Labor Relations, No. 24. Ithaca, N.Y.: ILR Press.

Atack, Jermy, and Peter Passell
 1994 *A New Economic View of American History*, 2nd ed. New York: W.W. Norton.

Azuma, Eiichiro
 1994 "Japanese Immigrant Farmers and California Alien Land Laws: A Study of the Walnut Grove Japanese." *California History* 73(1):14-29.

Baines, Dudley
 1985 *Migration in a Mature Economy.* Cambridge: Cambridge University Press.

Baines, Dudley
 1991 *Emigration from Europe, 1815-1930.* Houndmills, Basingstoke, Hampshire: Macmillan.

Balke, Nathan S., and Robert J. Gordan
 1986 "Historical Data." In *The American Business Cycle: Continuity and Change,* Robert J. Gordon, ed. Chicago: University of Chicago Press and the National Bureau of Economic Research.

Barth, Bunther
 1964 *Bitter Strength: A History of the Chinese in the United States, 1850-1870.* Cambridge: Harvard University Press.

Blau, Francine D.
 1980 "Immigration and Labor Earnings in Early Twentieth Century America." Pp. 21-41 in *Research in Population Economic,* Julian L. Simon and Julie DaVanzo, eds. Greenwich, Conn.: JAI Press.

Blodget, Samuel
 1806/ *Economica: A Statistical Manual for the United States of America.* City of Washington:
 1964 Printed for the Author, 1806. Reprint edition, Augustus M. Kelley, New York, 1964.

Borjas, George
 1986 "The Self-Employment Experience of Immigrants." *Journal of Human Resources* 21:(Fall)485-506.

Borjas, George
  1987   "Self-Selection and the Earnings of Immigrants." *American Economic Review* 77(Sep-
          tember):531-553.
Borjas, George
  1994   "The Economics of Immigration." *Journal of Economic Literature* 32(4):1667-1717.
Borjas, George J.
  1995   "The Economic Benefits from Immigration." *Journal of Economic Perspectives* 9(2):3-22.
Borjas, George J.
  1996   "The New Economics of Immigration: Affluent Americans Gain; Poor Americans Lose."
          The Atlantic Monthly 278(5):72-80.
Borjas, George, and Stephen G. Bronars
  1989   "Consumer Discrimination and Self-Employment." *Journal of Political Economy* 97:581-
          605.
Borjas, George, and Stephen J. Trejo
  1991   "Immigrant Participation in the Welfare System." *Industrial and Labor Relations Review*
          44(2):195-211.
Bromwell, William J.
  1856/   *History of Immigration to the United States 1819-1855.* New York: Redfield, 1856.
  1969   Reprint edition Augustus M. Kelley, New York, 1969.
Brown, Martin, and Peter Philips
  1986   "Competition, Racism, and Hiring Practices Among California Manufacturers, 1860-
          1882." *Industrial and Labor Relations Review* 40(1):61-74.
Bureau of the Census
  1975/   *Historical Statistics of the United States, Colonial Times to 1970, Bicentennial Edition.*
  1997   Two volumes. Washington, D.C.: U.S. Government Printing Office, 1975. Electronic
          edition edited by Susan B. Carter, Scott S. Gartner, Michael R. Haines, Alan L. Olmstead,
          Richard Sutch, and Gavin Wright (machine-readable data file). New York: Cambridge
          University Press, 1997.
Bureau of the Census
  1990   *United States Population Estimates, by Age, Sex, Race, and Hispanic Origin: 1980 to
          1988,* by Frederick W. Hollmannn. Current Population Reports, Population Estimates and
          Projections, Series P-25, No. 1045. Washington, D.C.: U.S. Government Printing Office.
Bureau of the Census
  1993   *United States Bureau of the Census. U.S. Population Estimates, by Age, Sex, Race, and
          Hispanic Origin: 1980 to 1991,* by Frederick W. Hollmannn. Current Population Re-
          ports, Population Estimates and Projections, Series P-25, No. 1095. Washington, D.C.:
          U.S. Government Printing Office.
Bureau of the Census
  1996   *Statistical Abstract of the United States,* 1996 (116th ed.). Washington, D.C.:
          U.S.Government Printing Office.
Cain, Louis P., and Donald G. Patterson
  1986   "Biased Technical Change, Scale, and Factor Substitution in American Industry." *Journal
          of Economic History* 46(1):153-164.
Cairncross, A.K.
  1953   *Home and Foreign Investment 1870-1913.* Cambridge: Cambridge University Press.
Carter, Susan B., and Richard Sutch
  1992   "Self-Employment in the Age of Big Business: Disguised Unemployment, Hidden Re-
          tirement, and the Decline of an American Labor Market Institution." *Working Papers on
          the History of Retirement No. 7.* History of Retirement Project, University of California,
          Berkeley.

Carter, Susan B., and Richard Sutch
  1996   "Myth of the Industrial Scrap Heap: A Revisionist View of Turn-of-the-Century Ameri-
          can Retirement." *Journal of Economic History* 56(1):5-38.
Carter, Susan B., Roger L. Ransom, and Richard Sutch
  1991   "The Historical Labor Statistics Project at the University of California." *Historical Meth-
          ods* 24(2):52-65.
Chenery, Hollis B.
  1960   "Patterns of Industrial Growth." *American Economic Review* 50(4):624-654.
Chiswick, Barry R.
  1978a   "The Effects of Americanization on the Earnings of Foreign-Born Men." *Journal of Po-
          litical Economy* 86:897-921.
Chiswick, Barry R.
  1978b   "A Longitudinal Analysis of the Occupational Mobility of Immigrants." In *Proceedings
          of the Industrial Relations Research Association,* Dennis Barbara, ed. Madison, Wisc.:
          Industrial Relations Research Association.
Chiswick, Barry R.
  1991a   "Jewish Immigrant Skill and Occupational Attainment at the Turn of the Century." *Explo-
          rations in Economic History* 28:64-86.
Chiswick, Barry R.
  1991b   "Speaking, Reading, and Earnings Among Low-Skilled Immigrants." *Journal of Labor
          Economics* April:149-170.
Chiswick, Barry R.
  1992   "Jewish Immigrant Wages in America in 1909: An Analysis of the Dillingham Commis-
          sion Data." *Explorations in Economic History* 29:274-289.
Chiswick, Barry R.
  1994   "The Performance of Immigrants in the United States Labor Market." In *Economic As-
          pects of International Migration,* Herbert Giersch, ed. Berlin: Springer-Verlag.
Cloud, Patricia, and David W. Galenson
  1987   "Chinese Immigration and Contract Labor in the Late Nineteenth Century." *Explorations
          in Economic History* 24:22-42.
Cohn, Raymond L.
  1992   "The Occupations of English Immigrants to the U.S., 1836-1853." *Journal of Economic
          History* 52(2):377-388.
Cohn, Raymond L.
  1995   "Occupational Evidence on the Causes of Immigration to the United States, 1836-1853."
          Explorations in Economic History 32(3):383-408.
Coombs, Whitney
  1926   *The Wages of Unskilled Labor in the Manufacturing Industries in the United States,
          1890-1924.* New York: Columbia University Press.
Daniels, Roger
  1962   *The Politics of Prejudice: The Anti-Japanese Movement in California and the Struggle
          for Exclusion.* Berkeley: University of California Press.
David, Paul A.
  1975   *Technical Choice, Innovation and Economic Growth.* Cambridge: Cambridge University
          Press.
David, Paul A.
  1977   "Invention and Accumulation in America's Economic Growth: A Nineteenth Century
          Parable." *Journal of Monetary Economics* 6(Suppl.):179-240.
David, Paul A., and John L. Scadding
  1974   "Private Savings: Ultrarationality, Aggregation, and 'Denison's Law'." *Journal of Politi-
          cal Economy* 82(2, Part I):225-250.

David, Paul A., and Peter Solar
    1977   "A Bicentenary Contribution to the History of the Cost of Living in America." *Research in Economic History* 2:1-80.
Davis, Lance E., and Robert J. Cull
    1994   *International Capital Markets and American Economic Growth, 1820-1914.* Cambridge: Cambridge University Press.
Davis, Lance E., and Robert Gallman
    1973   "The Share of Savings and Investment in Gross National Product During the 19th Century in the U.S.A." Pp. 437-466 in *Fourth International Conference of Economic History, Bloomington, 1968.* Mouton La Haye.
De Long, J. Bradford
    1995   "Late Nineteenth-Century Tariffs and American Economic Growth." Paper presented at the meetings of the Economic History Association, Chicago, September.
Denison, Edward F.
    1962   *The Sources of Economic Growth in the United States and the Alternatives Before Us.* Washington, D.C: Committee for Economic Development.
Douglas, Paul H.
    1919   "Is the New Immigration More Unskilled Than the Old?" *Journal of the American Statistical Association* June:393-403.
Douglas, Paul H.
    1930   *Real Wages in the United States, 1890-1926.* New York: Houghton Mifflin.
Dulles, Eleanor Lansing
    1939   "Financing Old-Age Insurance." *Annals of the American Academy of Political and Social Science* 202:176-183.
Dunlevy, James
    1980   "Nineteenth-Century European Immigration to the United States: Intended versus Lifetime Settlement Patterns." *Economic Development and Cultural Change* 29:77-90.
Dunlevy, James
    1983   "Regional Preferences and Immigrant Settlement." *Research in Economic History* 8:217-251.
Dunlevy, James A., and Henry A. Germery
    1977a   "British-Irish Settlement Patterns inthe U.S.: The Role of Family and Friends." *Scottish Journal of Political Economy* 24(3):257-263.
Dunlevy, James A., and Henry A. Germery
    1977b   "The Role of Migrant Stock and Lagged Migration in the Settlement Patterns of Nineteenth Century Immigrants." *The Review of Economics and Statistics* 59:137-144.
Dunlevy, James A., and Henry A. Germery
    1978   "Economic Opportunity and the Responses of 'Old' and 'New' Migrants to the United States." *Journal of Economic History* 38:901-917.
Dunlevy, James, and Henry Gemery
    1983   "Economic Opportunity and the Responses of 'Old' and 'New' Migrants to the United States." *Journal of Economic History* 43:901-917.
Dunlevy, James A., and Richard P. Saba
    1992   "The Role of Nationality-Specific Characteristics on the Settlement Patterns of Late Nineteenth Century European Immigrants." *Explorations in Economic History* 29(2):228-249.
Easterlin, Richard A.
    1968   *Population, Labor Force, and Long Swings in Economic Growth: The American Experience.* New York: National Bureau of Economic Research.
Easterlin, Richard A.
    1971   "Influences in European Emigration Before World War I." Pp. 384-395 in *The Reinterpretation of American Economic History*, Robert Fogel and Stanley Engerman, eds. New York: Harper & Row.

Easterlin, Richard A.
1996   *Growth Triumphant: The Twenty-first Century in Historical Perspective.* Ann Arbor: University of Michigan Press.
Easterlin, Richard A.
1960   "Regional Growth of Income: Long Term Tendencies." Pp. 141-204 in *Population Redistribution and Long Term Growth: United States, 1870-1950,* Vol. 2. Philadelphia, Pa.
Edelstein, Michael
1974   "The Determinants of U.K. Investment Abroad, 1870-1913: The U.S. Case." *Journal of Economic History* 34:980-1007.
Edwards, Alba M.
1943   Comparative Occupation Statistics for the United States, 1870 to 1940. In U.S. Department of Commerce, Bureau of the Census, *Sixteenth Census of the United States: 1940. Population* Washington, D.C.: U.S. Government Printing Office.
Ehrenberg, Ronald G., and Robert S. Smith
1994   *Modern Labor Economics: Theory and Public Policy,* 5th ed. New York: HarperCollins.
Eichengreen, Barry, and Henry Gemery
1986   "The Earnings of Skilled and Unskilled Immigrants at the End of the Nineteenth Century." *Journal of Economic History* 46(2):441-454.
Erikson, Charlotte J.
1972   "Who Were the English and Scots Emigrants to the United States in the Late Nineteenth Century?" Pp. 347-381 in *Population Studies,* D.V. Glass and R. Revelle, eds. New York.
Erikson, Charlotte J.
1981   "Emigration from the British Isles to the U.S.A. in 1831." *Population Studies* 25:175-197.
Erikson, Charlotte J.
1989   "Emigration from the British Isles to the U.S.A. in 1841: Part I. Emigration from the British Isles." *Population Studies* 43:347-367.
Erikson, Charlotte J.
1990   "Emigration from the British Isles to the U.S.A. in 1841: Part II. Who Were the English Emigrants?" *Population Studies* 44:21-40.
Feliciano, Zadia M.
1996   "Mexican Immigrants to the United States: Evidence on Selection and Economic Performance from 1910 to 1990." Paper presented at the Meetings of the Economic History Association, Berkeley, Calif., September.
Ferrie, Joseph P.
1997   *"Yankeys Now" Immigrants in the Antebellum U.S., 1840-60.* New York: Oxford University Press.
Fishlow, Albert
1965   *American Railroads and the Transformation of the Ante-Bellum Economy.* Cambridge: Harvard University Press.
Fogel, Robert W.
1967   "The Specification Problem in Economic History." *Journal of Economic History* 27(3):283-308.
Gallman, Robert E.
1977   "Human Capital in the First 80 Years of the Republic: How Much Did America Owe the Rest of the World?" *American Economic Review* 67(1):27-31.
Galloway, Lowell E., and Richard K. Vedder
1971   "Mobility of Native Americans." *Journal of Economic History* 31:613-649.

Galloway, Lowell E., and Richard K. Vedder
  1972   "Geographic Distribution of British and Irish Emigrants to the United States after 1800."
          Scottish Journal of Political Economy 19:19-36.
Galloway, Lowell E., Richard K. Vedder, and Vishwa Shukla
  1974   "The Distribution of the Immigrant Population in the United States: An Economic
          Analysis." *Explorations in Economic History* 11:213-226.
Gilboy, Elizabeth W., and Edgar M. Hoover
  1961   "Population and Immigration." In Seymour E. Harris, ed., *American Economic History*.
          New York: McGraw-Hill.
Ginger, Ray
  1954   "Labor in a Massachusetts Cotton Mill, 1853-60." *Business History Review* 28(1):67-91.
Glasson, William H.
  1902   "The National Pension System as Applied to the Civil War and the War with Spain."
          Annals of the American Academy of Political and Social Science 19:204-226.
Glasson, William H.
  1918   *Federal Military Pensions in the United States.* London: Oxford University Press.
Goldin, Claudia
  1994a   "The Political Economy of Immigration Restriction." In *The Regulated Economy: A
          Historical Approach to Political Economy*, Claudia Goldin and Gary D. Libecap, eds.
          Chicago: University of Chicago Press.
Goldin, Claudia
  1994b   "Labor Markets in the Twentieth Century." National Bureau of Economic Research:
          Working Paper Series on Historical Factors in Long Run Growth. Historical Paper No.
          58.
Haines, Michael R., and Allen C. Goodman
  1995   "A Home of One's Own: Aging and Homeownership in the United States in the Late
          Nineteenth and Early Twentieth Centuries." Pp. 203-228 in *Aging in the Past: Demogra-
          phy, Society, and Old Age*, David I. Kertzer and Peter Laslett, eds. Berkeley: University
          of California Press.
Handlin, Oscar
  1951/   *The Uprooted.* New York: Grosset and Dunlap, 1951. Second Enlarged Edition, Little,
  1973   Brown and Company, Boston, 1973.
Handlin, Oscar, ed.
  1959   *Immigration as a Factor in American History.* Englewood Cliffs, N.J.: Prentice-Hall.
Handlin, Oscar
  1982   "Education and the European Immigrant, 1820-1920." Pp. 3-16 in *American Education
          and the European Immigrant 1840-1940*, Bernard J. Weiss, ed. Chicago: University of
          Chicago Press.
Hannon, Joan Underhill
  1982a   "Ethnic Discrimination in a 19th-Century Mining District: Michigan Copper Mines,
          1888." *Explorations in Economic History* 19(1):28-50.
Hannon, Joan Underhill
  1982b   "City Size and Ethnic Discrimination: Michigan Agricultural Implements and Iron Work-
          ing Industries, 1890." *Journal of Economic History* 42(4):825-846.
Hannon, Joan Underhill
  1984   "Poverty in the Antebellum Northeast: The View from New York State's Poor Relief
          Rolls." *Journal of Economic History* 44(4):1007-1032.
Hannon, Joan Underhill
  1985   "Poor Relief Policy in Antebellum New York State: The Rise and Decline of the Poor-
          house." *Explorations in Economic History* 22:233-256.

Hatton, Timothy, and Jeffrey G. Williamson
  1998   *The Age of Mass Migration: An Economic Analysis.* New York: Oxford University
          Press (forthcoming).
Hickman, Bert G.
  1973   "What Became of the Building Cycle?" In *Nations and Households in Economic Growth:
          Essays in Honor of Moses Abramovitz,* Paul David and Melvin Reder, eds. New York:
          Academic Press.
Higgs, Robert
  1971a   "Race, Skills and Earnings: American Immigrants in 1909." *Journal of Economic History*
          (June):420-428.
Higgs, Robert
  1971b   "American Inventiveness, 1870-1920." *Journal of Political Economy* 79(3):661-667.
Higgs, Robert
  1976   "Participation of Blacks and Immigrants in the American Merchant Class, 1890-1910:
          Some Demographic Relations." *Explorations in Economic History* 13:153-164.
Higgs, Robert
  1978   "Landless by Law: the Japanese Immigrants in California Agriculture to 1941." *Journal
          of Economic History* 38(1): 205-251.
Hill, Peter J.
  1975   "Relative Skill and Income Levels of Native and Foreign-Born Workers in the United
          States." *Explorations in Economic History* 12(1):47-60.
Hutchinson, Edward P.
  1956   *Immigrants and Their Children, 1850-1950.* New York: John Wiley.
Hutchinson, Edward P.
  1958   "Notes on Immigration Statistics of the United States." *Journal of the American Statisti-
          cal Association* 53:963-1025.
Jerome, Harry
  1926   *Migration and Business Cycles.* New York: National Bureau of Economic Research.
Johnston, Louis
  1990   "Endogenous Growth and the American Economy." Ph.D. dissertation, University of
          California, Berkeley.
Jones, Maldwyn Allen
  1960/   *American Immigration.* Chicago: University of Chicago Press, 1960; Second Edition,
  1992   1992.
Khan, Zorina B., and Kenneth L. Sokoloff
  1993   "Schemes of Practical Utility": Entrepreneurship and Innovation among 'Great Inventors'
          in the United States, 1790-1865." *Journal of Economic History* 53(2):289-307.
Kamphoefner, Walter D.
  1987   *The Westfalians: From Germany to Missouri.* Princeton, N.J.: Princeton University Press.
Kaplan, David L., and M. Claire Casey
  1958   *Occupational Trends in the United States, 1900-1950.* Bureau of the Census Working
          Paper No. 5. Washington, D.C.: U.S. Government Printing Office.
Katz, Michael
  1986   *In the Shadow of the Poorhouse: A Social History of Welfare in America.* New York:
          Basic Books.
Kelley, Allen
  1972   "Scale Economies, Inventive Activity, and the Economics of American Population
          Growth." *Explorations in Economic History* 10(1):35-52.
Kindleberger, Charles P.
  1967   *Europe's Postwar Growth: The Role of Labor Supply.* Cambridge: Harvard University
          Press.

King, Miriam, and Steven Ruggles
  1990   "American Immigration, Fertility Differentials, and the Ideology of Race Suicide at the
          Turn of the Century." *Journal of Interdisciplinary History* 20(3):347-369.
Kleinberg, S.J.
  1989   *The Shadow of the Mills: Working Class Families in Pittsburgh, 1870-1907.* Pittsburgh,
          Pa.: University of Pittsburgh Press.
Kuznets, Simon
  1952   "Long-Term Changes in the National Income of the United States of America Since
          1870." In *Income and Wealth of the United States: Trends and Structure.* International
          Association for Research in Income and Wealth.
Kuznets, Simon
  1958   "Long Swings in the Growth of Population and in Related Economic Variables." *Pro-
          ceedings of the American Philosophical Society* 102:31-36.
Kuznets, Simon, assisted by Elizabeth Jenks
  1961   *Capital in the American Economy: Its Formation and Financing.* National Bureau of
          Economic Research. Princeton, N.J.: Princeton University Press.
Kuznets, Simon
  1971a   "The Contribution of Immigration to the Growth of the Labor Force." In *The Reinterpre-
          tation of American Economic History,* Robert William Fogel and Stanley L. Engerman,
          eds. New York: Harper & Row.
Kuznets, Simon
  1971b   "Long-Term Changes in the National Income of the United States of America Since
          1870." Pp. 196-204 in *Income and Wealth of the United States: Trends and Structure.*
          International Association for Research in Income and Wealth. Reprinted as "The Contri-
          bution of Immigration to the Growth of the Labor Force." In *The Reinterpretation of
          American Economic History,* Robert William Fogel and Stanley L. Engerman, eds. New
          York: Harper & Row.
Kuznets, Simon, and Ernest Rubin
  1954   *Immigration and the Foreign Born.* Occasional Paper 46, National Bureau of Economic
          Research, New York.
LaCroix, Sumner J., and Price Fishback
  1989   "Firm-Specific Evidence on Racial Wage Differentials and Workforce Segregation in
          Hawaii's Sugar Industry." *Explorations in Economic History* 26(4):403-423.
Lebergott, Stanley
  1960   "Wage Trends, 1800-1900." Pp. 449-498 in *Trends in the American Economy in the
          Nineteenth Century,* William N. Parker, ed. National Bureau of Economic Research,
          Studies in Income and Wealth, Vol. 24. Princeton, N.J.: Princeton University Press.
Lebergott, Stanley
  1964   *Manpower in Economic Growth: The American Record Since 1800.* New York: McGraw-
          Hill.
Lebergott, Stanley
  1984   *The Americans: An Economic Record.* New York: W.W. Norton.
Lee, Everett S., Ann Ratner Miller, Carol P. Brainerd, and Richard A. Easterlin
  1957   *Population Redistribution and Economic Growth, United States,* 1870-1950, Vol. I, *Meth-
          odological Considerations and Reference Tables.* Philadelphia, Pa: The American Philo-
          sophical Society.
Levy, Frank, and Richard J. Murnane
  1992   "U.S. Earnings Levels and Earnings Inequality: A Review of Recent Trends and Pro-
          posed Explanations." *Journal of Economic Literature* 30(3):1333-1381.
Licht, Walter
  1992   *Getting Work: Philadelphia, 1840-1950.* Cambridge: Harvard University Press.

Light, Ivan
   1984   "Immigrant and Ethnic Enterprise in North America." *Ethnic and Racial Studies* 7:195-216.
Light, Ivan, and Edna Bonacich
   1988   *Immigrant Entrepreneurship: Koreans in Los Angeles, 1965-1982.* Berkeley: University of California Press.
Liu, Kwang-Ching
   1988   "Chinese Merchant Guilds: An Historical Inquiry." *Pacific Historical Review* 57:1-23.
Long, Charlene D.
   1958   *The Labor Force under Changing Income and Employment.* Cambridge, Mass.: National Bureau of Economic Research.
Long, Clarence D.
   1960   *Wages and Earnings in the United States 1860-1890.* National Bureau of Economic Research. Princeton, N.J.: Princeton University Press.
Margo, Robert A.
   1990   *Race and Schooling in the South, 1880-1950.* Chicago: University of Chicago Press.
Margo, Robert A.
   1996   "The Rental Price of Housing in New York City, 1830-1860." *Journal of Economic History* 56(3):605-625.
McClelland, Peter, and Richard Zeckhauser
   1983   *Demographic Dimensions of the New Republic: American Interregional Migration, Vital Statistics, and Manumissions, 1800-1860.* Cambridge: Cambridge University Press.
McGouldrick, Paul F., and Michael B. Tannen
   1977   "Did American Manufacturers Discriminate Against Immigrants Before 1914?" *Journal of Economic History* 37:723-746.
McMurray, Donald L.
   1922   "The Political Significance of the Pension Question, 1885-1897." *The Mississippi Historical Review* 9:19-36.
Mitchell, Wesley Clair
   1913   *Business Cycles.* Berkeley: University of California.
Modigliani, Franco
   1966   "The Life Cycle Hypothesis of Saving, the Demand for Wealth and the Supply of Capital." *Social Research* 33:160-217.
Modigliani, Franco
   1986   "Life Cycle, Individual Thrift, and the Wealth of Nations." *American Economic Review* 76:297-313.
Mohl, Raymond A.
   1983   "The Abolition of Public Outdoor Relief, 1870-1900." Pp. 35-50 in *Social Welfare or Social Control?,* Walter I. Trattner, ed. Knoxville, Tenn.: University of Tennessee Press.
Mokyr, Joel
   1983   *Why Ireland Starved: A Quantitative and Analytical History of the Irish Economy, 1780-1850.* London.
Mokyr, Joel
   1990   *The Lever of Riches: Technological Creativity and Economic Progress.* New York: Oxford University Press.
Murayama, Y.
   1984   "Contractors, Collusion, and Competition: Japanese Immigrant Railroad Laborers in the Pacific Northwest, 1898-1911." *Explorations in Economic History* 21:290-305.
Nash, Gary B., Julie Roy Jeffrey, John R. Howe, Peter J. Frederick, Allen F. Davis, and Allan M. Winkler
   1986   *The American People: Creating a Nation and a Society.* New York: Harper & Row.

Neal, Larry, and Paul Uselding
    1972   "Immigration: A Neglected Source of American Economic Growth, 1790 to 1912." *Oxford Economic Papers* 24:68-88.
Nelson, Richard R.
    1964   "Aggregate Production Functions and Medium Range Growth Projections." *American Economic Review* 54:575-606.
North, Douglass C.
    1960   "The United States Balance of Payments, 1790-1860." Pp. 573-628 in *Trends in the American Economy in the Nineteenth Century*, William N. Parker, ed. National Bureau of Economic Research, Studies in Income and Wealth, Vol. 24. Princeton, N.J.: Princeton University Press.
Oliver, John William
    1917   "History of the Civil War Military Pensions, 1861-1885." *Bulletin of the University Wisconsin*, Number 844, History Series, Number 1:1-120.
Orloff, Ann Shola
    1993   *The Politics of Pensions: A Comparative Analysis of Britain, Canada, and the United States, 1880-1940.* Madison: University of Wisconsin .
O'Rourke, Kevin H., and Jeffrey G. Williamson
    1995   "Around the European Periphery 1870-1913: Globalization, Schooling and Growth." NBER Working Paper 5392. Cambridge, Mass.: National Bureau of Economic Research.
Patterson, James T.
    1981   *American's Struggle Against Poverty 1900-1980.* Cambridge: Harvard University Press.
Pechman, Joseph A., Henry J. Aaron, and Michael K. Taussig
    1968   *Social Security: Perspectives for Reform.* Washington, D.C.: The Brookings Institution.
Perlmann, Joel
    1988   *Ethnic Differences: Schooling and Social Structure among the Irish, Italians, Jews & Blacks in an American City, 1880-1935.* Cambridge: Cambridge University Press.
Phillips, A.W.
    1958   "The Relation Between Unemployment and the Rate of Change of Money Wages in the United Kingdom 1861-1957." *Economica* 25:283-299.
Quadagno, Jill
    1988   *The Transformation of Old Age Security: Class and Politics in the American Welfare State.* Chicago: University of Chicago Press.
Ransom, Roger L., and Richard Sutch
    1975   "The 'Lock-In' Mechanism and Overproduction of Cotton in the Post-Bellum South." *Agricultural History* 49:405-425.
Ransom, Roger L., and Richard Sutch
    1977   *One Kind of Freedom: The Economic Consequences of Emancipation.* New York: Cambridge University Press.
Ransom, Roger L., and Richard Sutch
    1984   "Domestic Saving as an Active Constraint on Capital Formation in the American Economy, 1839-1928: A Provisional Theory." *Working Papers on the History of Saving* No. 1. Institute for Business and Economic Research, University of California, Berkeley.
Ransom, Roger L., and Richard Sutch
    1987   "Tontine Insurance and the Armstrong Commission: A Case of Stifled Innovation in the American Life Insurance Industry." *Journal of Economic History* 47(2):379-390.
Ransom, Roger L., and Richard Sutch
    1988   "Capitalists Without Capital: The Burden of Slavery and the Impact of Emancipation." *Agricultural History* 62:133-160.

Ransom, Roger L., Richard Sutch, and Samuel H. Williamson
  1996   "Protecting Soldiers and Republicans: Civil War Pensions, and the Failure of the Social
          Insurance Movement in the Progressive Era." *Working Papers on the History of Retire-
          ment*. History of Retirement Project, University of California, Berkeley.
Rees, Albert
  1960   "New Measures of Wage Earner Compensation in Manufacturing 1914-57." Occasional
          Paper 75. New York: National Bureau of Economic Research.
Rees, Albert
  1961   *Real Wages in Manufacturing 1890-1914*. Princeton, N.J.: Princeton University Press.
Robertson, Ross M.
  1973   *History of the American Economy*, 3rd ed. New York: Harcourt Brace Jovanovich.
Romer, Christina
  1986a   "Spurious Volatility in Historical Unemployment Data." *Journal of Political Economy*
          94(1):1-37.
Romer, Paul M.
  1986b   "Increasing Returns and Long-Run Growth." *Journal of Political Economy* 94(3):1002-
          1037.
Romer, Paul M.
  1996   "Why, Indeed, in America? Theory, History, and the Origins of Modern Economic
          Growth." *American Economic Review* 86(2):202-206.
Rosenberg, Nathan
  1982   *Inside the Black Box: Technology and Economics*. New York: Cambridge University
          Press.
Rosenberg, Nathan
  1981/   "Why in America?" In *Yankee Enterprise, The Rise of the American System of Manufac-
  1995   tures*, Otto Mayr and Robert C. Post, eds. Washington, D.C.: Smithsonian Institution Press,
          1981. Reprinted in *Exploring the Black Box*, Cambridge University Press, Cambridge.
Rosenbloom, Joshua L.
  1996   "Was There a National Labor Market at the End of the Nineteenth Century? New Evi-
          dence on Earnings in Manufacturing." *Journal of Economic History* 56(3):626-656.
Roy, Andrew D.
  1951   "Some Thoughts on the Distribution of Earnings." *Oxford Economic Papers, New Series*
          3:135-146.
Rubin, Ernest
  1957   "Immigration and the Economic Growth of the U.S.: 1790-1914." *Conference on Income
          and Wealth*. New York: National Bureau of Economic Research.
Ruggles, Steven R., and Matthew Sobek
  1995   *Integrated Public Use Microdata Series: Version 1.0*. Minneapolis: Social History Re-
          search Laboratory, University of Minnesota.
Sawada, Mitzko
  1991   "Culprits and Gentlemen: Meiji Japan's Restrictions on Emigrants to the United States,
          1891-1909." *Pacific Historical Review* 60(3):339-359.
Saxton, Alexander
  1971   *The Indispensable Enemy: Labor and the Anti-Chinese Movement in California*. Berke-
          ley: University of California Press.
Schaefer, Donald
  1994   "U.S. Migration, 1850-59." Pp. 53-69 in *American Economic Development in Historical
          Perspective*, Thomas Weiss and Donald Schaefer, eds. Stanford, Calif: Stanford Univer-
          sity Press.

Seybert, Adam
    1818   *Statistical Annals: Embracing Views of the Population, Commerce, Navigation, Fisher-
            ies, Public Lands, Post-Office Establishment, Revenues, Mint, Military and Naval Estab-
            lishments, Expenditures, Public Debt.* Philadelphia, Pa.: Thomas Dobson.
Simon, Mathew
    1960   "The United States Balance of Payments, 1861-1900." Pp. 629-711 in *Trends in the
            American Economy in the Nineteenth Century*, William N. Parker, ed. National Bureau
            of Economic Research, Studies in Income and Wealth, Vol. 24. Princeton, N.J.: Princeton
            University Press.
Simon, Julian L., and Richard J. Sullivan
    1989   "Population Size, Knowledge Stock, and Other Determinants of Agricultural Publication
            and Patenting: England, 1541-1850." *Explorations in Economic History* 21(1):21-44.
Skocpol, Theda
    1992   *Protecting Soldiers and Mothers: The Political Origins of Social Policy in the United
            States.* Cambridge, Mass.: Belknap Press of Harvard University Press.
Smith, Adam
    1776   *An Inquiry into the Nature and Causes of the Wealth of Nations.* London: W. Strahan and
            T. Cadell, in the Strand.
Sobek, Matthew
    1996   "Work, Status, and Income: Men in the American Occupational Structure since the Late
            Nineteenth Century." *Social Science History* 20(2):169-207.
Sokoloff, Kenneth L.
    1988   "Inventive Activity in Early Industrial America: Evidence from Patent Records." *Journal
            of Economic History* 48(4):813-850.
Sokoloff, Kenneth L., and Zorina B. Khan
    1990   "The Democratization of Invention during Early Industrialization: Evidence from the
            United States, 1790-1846." *Journal of Economic History* 50(2):363-378.
Taylor, Philip
    1960   *The Distant Magnet: European Immigration to the U.S.A.* New York: Harper & Row.
Taylor, Alan M., and Jeffrey G. Williamson
    1997   "Convergence in the Age of Mass Migration." *European Review of Economic History*
            (forthcoming).
Temin, Peter
    1971   "General Equilibrium Models in Economic History." *Journal of Economic History*
            31(1):58-75.
Thomas, Brinley
    1954/   *Migration and Economic Growth.* Cambridge, England: Cambridge University Press, 1954;
    1973   second edition, 1973.
Thomas, Brinley
    1961   "The Rhythm of Growth in the Atlantic Economy." Pp. 39-48 in *Money, Growth, and
            Methodology: And Other Essays in Economics in Honor of Johan Akerman*, Hugo
            Hegeland, ed. Lund: Gleerup.
Thomas, Brinley
    1972   *Migration and Urban Development: A Reappraisal of British and American Long Cycles.*
            London: Methuen & Co. Ltd.
Tolnay, Stewart E., and E. M. Beck
    1995   *A Festival of Violence: An Analysis of Southern Lynchings, 1882-1930.* Urbana: Univer-
            sity of Illinois Press.
Turner, Frederick Jackson
    1920   *The Frontier in American History.* New York: H. Holt.

U.S. Immigration Commission
  1911 *Report on Immigrants in Industries*, 23 vols., 61st Congress, 2nd session. Washington, D.C.: U.S. Government Printing Office.
U.S. Immigration and Naturalization Service
  1979 *Statistical Yearbook of the Immigration and Naturalization Service, 1979.* Washington, D.C.: U.S. Government Printing Office.
U.S. Immigration and Naturalization Service
  1990 *Statistical Yearbook of the Immigration and Naturalization Service, 1989.* Washington, D.C.: U.S. Government Printing Office.
U.S. Immigration and Naturalization Service
  1997 *Statistical Yearbook of the Immigration and Naturalization Service, 1995.* Washington, D.C.: U.S. Government Printing Office.
Uselding, Paul
  1971 "Conjectural Estimates of Gross Human Capital Inflows to the American Economy: 1790-1860." *Explorations in Economic History* 9(1):49-62.
Van Vugt, William E.
  1988a "Prosperity and Industrial Emigration from Britain during the Early 1850s." *Journal of Social History* 5:390-405.
Van Vugt, William E.
  1988b "Running from Ruin? The Emigration of British Farmers to the U.S.A. in the Wake of the Repeal of the Corn Laws." *Economic History Review* 41:411-428.
Walker, Francis Amasa
  1891 "Immigration and Degradation." *Forum* (August):634-644.
Walker, Francis Amasa
  1896 "Restriction on Immigration." *Atlantic Monthly* (June):822-829.
Walker, Francis A.
  1899 "Our Domestic Service." In *Discussions in Economics and Statistics*, Davis R. Dewey, ed. New York.
Walton, Gary M., and Ross M. Robertson
  1983 *History of the American Economy*, 5th ed. New York: Harcourt Brace Jovanovich.
Walton, Gary M., and Hugh Rockoff
  1994 *History of the American Economy*, 7th ed. Fort Worth, Texas: The Dryden Press.
Warren, Robert, and Ellen Percy Kraly
  1985 *The Elusive Exodus: Emigration from the United States.* Washington, D.C.: Population Reference Bureau, Policy Trends and Public Policy Series, No. 8, March 1985.
Weir, David
  1992 "A Century of U.S. Unemployment, 1890-1990: Revised Estimates and Evidence for Stabilization." *Research in Economic History* 14:301-346.
Weiss, Bernard J.
  1982 *American Education and the European Immigrant 1840-1940.* Chicago: University of Chicago Press.
Weiss, Thomas
  1990 "Farm Gross Product, Labor Force, and Output per Worker in the United States, 1800 to 1900." Lawrence, Kansas: University of Kansas. Manuscript.
Williamson, Jeffrey G.
  1964 *American Growth and the Balance of Payments, 1820-1913: A Study of the Long Swing.* Chapel Hill, North Carolina: University of North Carolina Press.
Williamson, Jeffrey G.
  1974a "Watersheds and Turning Points: Conjectures on the Long-Term Impact of Civil War Financing." *Journal of Economic History* 34:636-661.

Williamson, Jeffrey G.
    1974b   "Migration to the New World: Long Term Influences and Impact." *Explorations in Eco-
            nomic History* 11:357-89.
Williamson, Jeffrey G.
    1982   "Immigrant-Inequality Trade-Offs in the Promised Land: Income Distribution and Ab-
            sorptive Capacity Prior to the Quotas." In *The Gateway: U.S. Immigration Issues and
            Policies,* Barry R. Chiswick, ed. Washington: American Enterprise Institute.
Williamson, Jeffrey G.
    1995   "The Evolution of Global Labor Markets since 1830: Background Evidence and Hypoth-
            eses." *Explorations in Economic History* 32(2):141-196.
Williamson, Jeffrey G., and Peter H. Lindert
    1980   *American Inequality: A Macroeconomic History.* New York: Academic Press.
Whitney, Coombs
    1926   The Wages of Unskilled Labor in the Manufacturing Industries in the United States,
            1890-1924. New York: Columbia University Press.
Williamson, Jeffrey
    1995   "The Evolution of Global Labor Markets since 1830: Background Evidence and Hypoth-
            eses." *Explorations in Economic History* 32(2):141-196.
Wright, Gavin
    1986   *Old South, New South: Revolutions in the Southern Economy since the Civil War.* New
            York: Basic Books.
Wright, Gavin
    1990   "The Origins of American Industrial Success, 1879-1940." *American Economic Review*
            80(4):651-68.
Wyman, Mark
    1993   *Round-Trip to America: The Immigrants Return to Europe, 1880-1930.* Ithaca, NY:
            Cornell University Press.
Ziliak, Stephen
    1996   "The End of Welfare and the Contradiction of Compassion." *The Independent Review*
            11:55-74.

9

Immigration and Crime in the United States

John Hagan and Alberto Palloni

INTRODUCTION

There is increasing concern about the presence of immigrants in the criminal justice system of the United States, especially about the number of legal and illegal immigrants in prisons. In this chapter we include estimates that from 4 to 7 percent of the more than 1.5 million persons held in American jails and prisons are noncitizens. At an average annual cost of more than $30,000 per inmate, the financial source of public and policy concern is obvious. This concern is increasing as state and federal governments become better informed about the immigrant status of offenders in their custody. The public and its politicians understandably are eager to find ways to reduce or shift this expense, while responding as well to concerns about public safety. One response involves efforts by states to shift expenses to the federal government by demanding compensation for the expense of incarcerating immigrants; another response is to press for the deportation of immigrants who are convicted of crimes; and a third response is to lobby for limitations on immigration and for stricter control of illegal immigration (see Cornelius et al., 1994). Our purpose in this chapter is not to assess directly the wisdom of these various policies, but instead to provide information and perspective on the relationship between immigration and crime. This information is relevant but not determinative with regard to selecting among the various policy options that arise from linkages between immigration and crime.

The United States has experienced at least four major waves of immigration over the past two centuries. Concerns about crime have been salient in conjunction with the two most recent waves, which occurred at the turn of this century and again toward this century's end. We focus on issues of immigration and crime during these third and fourth waves. These periods are sufficiently different and far apart in time that it is necessary to relearn and rethink much of what was once taken for granted about this topic. This task is made more difficult by the fact that, in between the last two periods of concern about immigration and crime, many criminal justice agencies stopped recording information about the presumed immigration and citizenship status of offenders. It is therefore necessary to piece together information about our topic from a patchwork of sources. As we note, the depth and detail of the data sources we must draw from are uneven and uncertain. The results of our work suggest that some of the public concern about immigration and crime may be overdrawn; however, the nature of the data problems also limits the certainty with which conclusions can be drawn in this field.

Undoubtedly the most salient questions involve the issue of whether immigration increases crime. Of course, in an absolute sense, it probably does. Immigration brings more people into the country, and unless this process is counterbalanced by emigration, the absolute volume of crime will very likely increase. In addition, immigrants are often disproportionately male and at early ages of labor market entry and advancement. Because young males are disproportionately likely to be involved in crime in all parts of the world that we know about (Hirschi and Gottfredson, 1983), this may also contribute to increases in crime. If our concern is solely to reduce crime, it simply does not make sense to encourage young males to immigrate in large numbers. However, because we also value the labor of young male immigrants, and indeed often rely on this labor in the context of shortages of particular kinds of workers, questions about contributions of immigration to crime are more likely to be relative than absolute. In this sense we will probably want to know whether immigrants who enter the country contribute to crime beyond what we could otherwise expect of citizens of similar numbers, ages, gender, and so on.

A further complication in assessing the involvement of immigrants in crime is that immigrants may not be treated the same as citizens in the criminal justice system. If immigrants are more or less vulnerable than citizens to arrest, detention, conviction, and imprisonment, their representation in official crime statistics may be correspondingly biased. This problem as well must be addressed in assessing the relationship between immigration and crime. These difficulties help to explain why questions about immigration and crime have recurred over the past century in the United States. We first review the historical background of these concerns and then turn to contemporary developments in reaching tentative conclusions about immigration and crime.

IMMIGRATION AND CRIME IN AN EARLIER ERA

The close of the Past century brought concerns about immigration and crime that persisted for several decades. These concerns were associated with a third wave of immigration depicted in Figure 9-1; the persistence of these concerns ultimately helped to justify a closing off of this wave of immigration. A bill passed by Congress in 1891 barred immigrant carriers of contagious diseases and "immoral" people. Later, public perceptions of immigrant alcohol use and public drunkenness in association with fears of crime facilitated the passage of Prohibition. Congressional acts in 1921 and 1924 substantially reduced the numbers of immigrants admitted to the United States. Special attention was directed toward southern and eastern Europeans during this time, although statistical analyses usually compared native-born whites with the foreign born more generally.

Aside from highly questionable writings associated with the eugenics movement, the research of this earlier era provided little evidence of a causal association between immigration and crime. Homicide rates from this period in New York City, presented in Figure 9-1, reveal no systematic relationship, and McCord's (1995) assessment of the research literature from this period indicates that immigrants were not, as was often alleged, particularly prone to drunkenness or crime (Abbott, 1915; Powell, 1966; Taft, 1936; van Vechten, 1941; compare

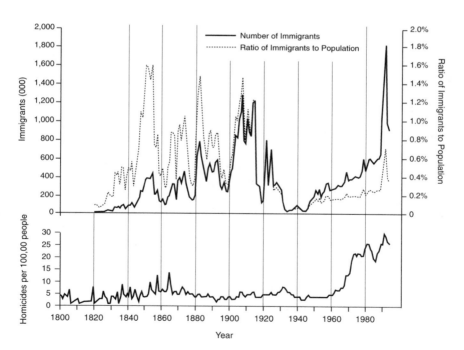

FIGURE 9-1 Number and ratio of immigrants to population in the United States, 1820-1993 and New York City homicide rates, 1800-1993. Source: Isbister (1996:34) and Butterfield (1994).

with O'Kane, 1992). Although McCord noted that immigrants accounted for a disproportionate amount of crime in Boston in 1914, in Chicago native-born residents were more likely to be criminal (Gault, 1932). Meanwhile, increasing immigration did not bring higher crime rates to Philadelphia (Hobbs, 1943), and homicide rates in this city were lower among almost all foreign-born groups than among the native born (Lane, 1979).

Where causality was seen to operate, its direction often was in the opposite direction expected. A report by the United States Immigration Commission found higher crime rates among the children of native-born parents and among children of immigrants than among immigrants themselves (Park et al., 1925/1967). Such findings provided early support for the view that it was the acculturation of immigrants into American life that most notably increased their likelihood of involvement in crime.

In the first part of this century prominent criminologists, such as Edwin Sutherland and Thorsten Sellin, wrote extensively about immigration and crime (see Hawkins, 1995). Sutherland and Sellin were critical of both the data and commentary of this early period, especially when it purported to show higher rates of crime among foreign-born immigrants than among the native born (see United States Immigration Commission, 1911; National Commission on Law Observance and Enforcement, 1931). In several early editions of the most influential textbook on crime of this century, Sutherland (1924, 1934) advanced the view that acculturation rather than immigration was associated with crime. He reported evidence that second-generation immigrants had higher rates of crime than first-generation immigrants, and that immigrants to America had higher rates of serious crime than their counterparts in their native countries (citing Taft, 1933). Sutherland (1934) and Sellin (1938) both noted that immigrants who came to America as children were imprisoned at a higher rate than immigrants who came as adults.

Sutherland and Sellin further argued that official crime statistics were dubious resources for reaching conclusions about immigration and crime. Sutherland (1924) observed that comparisons of crime among the foreign and native born were not meaningful unless differences in ages, rural-urban, and sex distributions were taken into account. Sellin (1938) added that the official data sources were often crude and mistaken in their attributions of national origins to assumed offenders. Researchers were increasingly concerned about ethnic and racial biases that resulted from the discretion involved in policing and prosecution of crime (see Brown and Warner, 1995).

Still, Sutherland and others reserved room in their thinking for the possibility that in some circumstances some national groups might bring increased risks for particular kinds of crime. Similarly, they noted that no single nationality grouping displayed the same level of involvement across *all* types of crime. Sutherland and Cressey (1978:149) reasoned as late as the 1978 edition of their text that certain crimes or groups of crimes are characteristic of certain national groups. These same types of crime are, usually, characteristic of the home countries also. The Italian and Turkish immigrants residing in Germany in 1965 had high rates of conviction for murder and assault; Italy and Turkey also have high murder and assault rates. Italians in America have a low rate of arrest for drunkenness, and drunkenness is comparatively rare in Italy. The traditions of the home country are transplanted to the host country and determine the relative positions of the immigrant groups to the types of crime.

In apparent contrast with this view, Shaw and McKay (1942:152-154) argued that, although immigrants came to North America with differing national propensities to crime, the disorganizing forces of poverty in the centers of American cities where immigrants most often settled tended to produce a convergence in their involvements in crime. So that where, ". . . the older immigrant nationalities as well as the recent arrivals range in their rates of delinquency from the very highest to the lowest," nonetheless, "within the same type of social area, the foreign-born and the natives, recent immigrant nationalities, and older immigrants produce very similar rates of delinquency." These contrasting views emerging out of the early twentieth century American experience with immigration and crime are not necessarily contradictory, a point we return to later.

Meanwhile, during the middle third of this century concern about immigration and crime declined and nearly disappeared. A reflection of this is that the lengthy discussion of immigration and crime that had been an important part of the earlier versions of Sutherland's classic text was eliminated completely between the tenth and eleventh editions. Official statistics on crime no longer regularly included reports of the foreign nationalities of offenders. With the exception of occasional panics about Italian-American involvement in organized crime (Cressey, 1969) and scholarly speculation about the successive involvement of the Irish, Jews, and Italians in organized crime (Ianni, 1972; see also O'Kane, 1992), fears about immigration and crime gradually faded into the background of public and criminological concerns. Earlier waves of European immigrants assimilated into American society and became citizens, while immigration and crime both declined through the 1950s, and public fears subsided.

IMMIGRATION AND CRIME IN A NEW ERA

As a fourth wave of immigration emerged in the last third of this century, earlier concerns took on renewed life. As indicated in Figure 9-1, the increase in immigration during this latter period was more notable in absolute volume than in relation to population. Nonetheless, the renewed fear was that "under current immigration laws and procedures, frighteningly large numbers of newcomers see crime as their avenue to the American dream" (Tanton and Lutton, 1993:217). The new circumstances were, however, somewhat different than those at the beginning of the century. Whereas concerns linking immigration to crime in the first half of this century coincided with historically low crime rates, from the later 1960s until relatively recently, violent crime increased in the United States. So that while between 1960 and 1990 the annual migration rate per 1,000 population in the United States increased from 1.7 to 3.0, during this same period the U.S. homicide rate increased from 4.8 to 8.3 per 100,000 population. This recent increase in homicide, and even more recent decline, is further reflected in the homicide rates for New York City displayed in the bottom panel in Figure 9-1.

With the data available to us we were able to trace time trends in the rate of arrests, rates of incarceration, and rates of immigration. Estimated rates of immigration were obtained by adding together figures for legal immigrants and estimated illegal immigrants. The latter were determined by distributing over time estimated numbers of individuals who entered the country between 1975 and 1990.

Our preliminary analyses indicated that trends in arrest rates and immigration rates were only weakly if at all related; however, there was a modest association between the latter and trends in the arrest rates. This association is attributable mostly to a sharp upturn in both trends that occurred particularly after 1985. So increases in violent and other forms of crime may be mixed in the perceptions of the American public with the renewed growth in immigration.

As was the case at the turn of the century, concerns at this century's end are prominently focused around the presence of inmates in American prisons who are not citizens. Indeed, the most comprehensive national statistics we now have on immigration and crime come from prison and correctional department data. Most police and court agencies do not systematically collect information on the citizenship and national origins of persons arrested and prosecuted, probably because it is now better recognized that the attributions involved would often be mistaken. Unfortunately, the pictures provided by prison statistics may also be distorted, not only by mistaken attributions of citizenship and national origin, but also because only a small proportion of criminal offenders ultimately are incarcerated and because bias may be introduced by the long sievelike process that leads to incarceration. This sievelike progression includes selection processes that result in both the exclusion and the inclusion of immigrants from the ultimate risk of incarceration. For example, although it is the case that police are often assumed to concentrate attention on immigrants along with other minorities, it is also the case that immigrants are sometimes simply deported rather than charged with crimes. Research is needed to establish whether these early sources of selection in the criminal justice system simply counterbalance one another or lead to systematic over- or underrepresenation of immigrants in prison.

Meanwhile, even our knowledge of prisoners is limited by the absence of comprehensive national data. Our knowledge of incarcerated offenders is based largely on a survey of state prison inmates conducted in 1991 (U.S. Department of Justice, 1993) and on a survey of state and federal departments of corrections conducted in 1995 (Wunder, 1995). The former study is documented in greater detail, with a reported response rate by surveyed inmates of about 94 percent, but is susceptible to the failings of the subjects' self-reporting, including problems of memory and deceit. The latter survey of correctional agencies reached high levels of coverage on some matters, but encountered bureaucratic problems on others, as illustrated by the California Department of Corrections, the largest prison system in the United States, which reported national origins of "immigrants" based on data collected on citizens as well as noncitizens. We are as careful as possible in this chapter to use the term immigrant only to refer to noncitizens and to use the term noncitizen instead of immigrant when the original sources do so; but there may be some cases in which the original sources we rely on have included foreign-born citizens among immigrants without indicating they are doing so.

By 1980 the percentage of the U.S. population formed by noncitizens was estimated to be between 4 and 5 percent (see Isbister, 1996:37). The Survey of State Prisons reported that more than 4 percent, or 31,300 state prison inmates, were not U.S. citizens. The Department of Corrections survey indicated that more than 7 percent, or 71,294 state and federal prison inmates, were not U.S. citizens. The latter figure is larger in part because it includes federal prisoners and also because the survey was conducted two years later during a growth spurt in prison populations. However, there is still a disparity between these two sources that underscores the difficulties of assembling information on immigration and crime in the United States. This point is further underscored by a recent Bureau of Justice Statistics report (Scalia, 1996) that indicates that there were less than 19,000 noncitizens in federal prisons in 1994, more than 7,000 fewer noncitizens than indicated in the *Corrections Compendium* report from one year earlier referenced above (Wunder, 1995). Scalia's report indicates in its first figure (1996:1) that about 14,000 noncitizens were serving a sentence of imprisonment in a federal prison in 1991, whereas the last table in this report (1996:10) indicates that 9,916 noncitizens were inmates in federal prisons in 1991.

We are left with a range of estimates that between 4 and 7 percent of prison inmates in the United States are noncitizens, compared with estimates that legal immigrants constitute between 4 and 5 percent of the U.S. population, with perhaps as much as 1 percent more of the U.S. population being illegal immigrants (Passel and Woodrow, 1984). Of course, this tells us nothing about whether specific immigrant groups are over- or underrepresented in prisons. The most systematic and comprehensive published data on the national origins of noncitizens in prisons are found in the 1991 Survey of State Prisons. Nearly half of the immigrants in state prisons (47%) came from Mexico, whereas nearly another fourth (26%) were from Latin and Caribbean countries. Together, these figures indicate that a large majority of immigrant inmates in U.S. state prisons, perhaps between 70 and 80 percent, are of Hispanic origin. This distribution of the national origins of immigrants in state prisons is quite similar to that found among immigrants convicted of an offense in the U.S. district courts in 1994 (see

Scalia, 1996:Table 2). About 45 percent of the legal immigrants to the United States are Hispanic in origin (Heer, 1996:Table 5.4). Of course this grouping is itself quite heterogeneous, including immigrants from Mexico, Cuba, the Dominican Republic, Colombia, El Salvador, Guatemala, and other countries in Central and South America and the Caribbean islands.

The heterogeneity of immigrant groups is an important source of complication in the relationship between immigration and crime. Not only is there social and cultural variation, for example, among Hispanic immigrants, there may be further significant variation in self-selection to participate in particular kinds of crime, as well as in legal documentation, with regard to vulnerability to statutory mandatory sentences and further group-linked variations in age and gender. Of course, such sources of variation also plague studies of other general correlates of crime, such as poverty and family breakdown, and crime itself is a heterogeneous entity. These problems do not stop research on these topics, but they do constitute reasons for caution in reaching policy-related conclusions. We attempt to address some of these concerns below.

Calculated on the basis of the Survey of State Prisons, the imprisonment rate for U.S. citizens is about 3.5 per 1,000 population. This rate is used as the base for calculating ratios presented in the first column of Table 9-1 for the most frequently imprisoned immigrant groups in U.S. state prisons. These figures indicate that immigrants from Cuba and the Dominican Republic are incarcerated at rates between four and five times those of citizens, that immigrants from Mexico, Jamaica and Colombia are incarcerated at rates from two to two and one-a half times those of citizens, and that immigrants from Guatemala and El Salva-

TABLE 9-1   Rates of Incarceration in U.S. State Prisons Per 1,000 Population

National Origin	Number of Persons who entered U.S. between 1980 and 1990 (in thousands)	Inmates in State Prisons	State Imprisonment Rate	State Imprisonment Rate for Males 15-34***
Mexico	2,145	14,711	6.858	47.61
Cuba	188	3,130	16.649	131.78
United Kingdom	154	313	2.032	19.34
Vietnam	336	313	1.073	6.81
El Salvador	350	1,252	3.577	26.48
Dominican Republic	185	2,817	15.227	126.98
Jamaica	155	1,252	8.077	69.52
Colombia	146	1,252	8.575	78.242
Guatemala	154	626	4.065	73.33
State Citizens	217,182*	751,200**	3.459	45.51

*U.S. Population less foreign-born noncitizens
**Inmates who are U.S. citizens
***Rate based on adjusting base for country-specific immigrant sex ratio and overall immigrant age distribution

dor are incarcerated at about the same rate as citizens. Recall that the circumstances of immigration from Cuba and the Dominican Republic have been shaped quite uniquely by political forces that have led many individuals with backgrounds in crime to migrate to the United States: for example, when Castro allowed over 100,000 people, including many prison inmates, to leave Cuba in 1980. A result is that there is considerable variability in Hispanic rates of imprisonment, and it is therefore a mistake to assume that these rates are uniformly high or that there is an undifferentiated relationship between immigration and crime.

Rates of immigrant imprisonment are complicated further by the fact, noted at the outset of this chapter, that immigrants are younger and more often male than are citizens. Because young men are at much greater risk than others for involvement in crime and imprisonment, the base used in calculating an imprisonment rate for immigrants is probably most usefully adjusted for sex and age. In the last column of Table 9-1 we have calculated imprisonment ratios using denominators for the compared rates that estimate the male populations of immigrants between 15 and 34 years of age from the various countries. The resulting ratios reveal a greater similarity between immigrants and citizens than was previously apparent.

The adjusted male rate for Mexican immigrants between ages 15 and 34 (47.61) is particularly notable because it is quite similar to the U.S. citizen rate (45.51). By this measure, the image of Mexican immigrants as more criminal than citizens is somewhat misleading. The imprisonment rates for some of the remaining countries are still substantially higher than the citizen rate. The Jamaican (69.52), Guatemalan (73.33), and Colombian (78.24) rates cluster at an intermediate level, whereas the Dominican (126.98) and Cuban (131.78) rates cluster at a higher level. However, even the latter rates are now less than three times, whereas they were previously more than four times, the citizen rate. It is important to keep in mind that, although the Cuban and Dominican *rates* are relatively high, in absolute terms these are rather small immigrant population groups, and therefore their contributions to prison populations are limited. Mexicans (14,711) form by a multiple of more than four (compared with 3,130 Cubans) the largest group of state prison inmates, even though their age-adjusted male state imprisonment rate is similar to that for citizens. This brings us back to a point made above, that if crime reduction is the sole and absolute priority, there is reason for concern.

However, there is also the further consideration that imprisonment rates inevitably are a result of several factors: involvement and apprehension for criminal behavior and decisions made about the prosecution and punishment of this behavior. As we further document below, there is reason to believe that Mexican and other immigrants may experience some unique risks of imprisonment for their crimes. These risks may result from differences in initial and predisposition custody decisions for illegal aliens. Detention prior to trial and sentencing is commonly found to increase the likelihood of conviction and ultimate incarceration (see Hagan and Bumiller, 1983). It may also be the case that immigrant drug offenders are sentenced with greater severity than others.

The most detailed recent study of criminal justice processing decisions involving immigrants was undertaken in El Paso and San Diego by Pennell et al. (1989). This study found in both cities that illegal aliens made up the largest proportion of immigrants prosecuted, and that these illegal aliens were much less likely than others to be released from jail prior to trial. For example, in El Paso only 14 percent of illegal immigrants compared with over 50 percent of all others were able to "bailout" prior to trial. This difference may be associated with the fact that the Immigration and Naturalization Service can place "holds" on illegal immigrants, that illegal aliens are financially less able to post bail, and that illegal immigrants are less likely to have the community ties that often are required for early release. When accused persons are unable to obtain release they may have greater difficulty generating resources to defend themselves in court, leaving them more vulnerable to conviction, and ultimately to imprisonment.

To assess the above possibilities we reanalyzed the Pennell et al. data that were collected in El Paso and San Diego. The results are presented in Table 9-2. These results confirm that immigrants in general in El Paso and San Diego are more likely to be detained prior to trial, and that, in turn, detention before trial increases the risks of conviction and imprisonment. That is, immigrants are at greater risk of conviction and imprisonment because they are more vulnerable to pretrial detention. In addition, immigrants in El Paso and San Diego who are charged with drug offenses are more likely than others to be sentenced to prison. These differences cannot be the result of immigrants having more extensive criminal histories, because Scalia (1996:Table 4) demonstrates that noncitizens are much less likely to have a prior known criminal history. A likely implication of these findings is that processing differences result in immigrants being overrepresented in prison populations. It will be important for further research to examine counterbalancing decisions, for example involving deportation, but the current findings suggest the likelihood that immigrants are overrepresented in prison as a result of justice system decision making.

An additional source of misperceptions about immigration and crime that may result from the uncritical reliance on prison statistics involves ways in which these figures are often used in characterizing immigrant criminality. The 1991 Survey of State Prison Inmates reported that nearly half of all alien inmates were incarcerated for drug offenses, that about 40 percent of these alien inmates used drugs during the month prior to their arrest, and that about 20 percent were under the influence of drugs at the time of their current offense. The 1991 survey reports that very high proportions of alien inmates from Colombia (87 percent) and the Dominican Republic (67 percent) were incarcerated for drug offenses.

Although it is the case that just over 20 percent of all inmates were incarcerated for drug offenses in 1991, about half of all inmates said they had been using

TABLE 9- 2   Logit Models for Being Detained, Convicted, and Imprisoned in El Paso and San Diego

Variables	A. El Paso		
	Pre-Trial Detention (n=2253)	Conviction (n=2253)	Incarceration (n=885)
Immigrant	1.35(.13)*	−.08(.19)	−.52(.40)
Male	.63(.19)*	.48(.19)*	.90(.39)*
Less than 20	−.67(.11)*	.34(.11)*	−1.13(.19)*
Violence	−.49(.13)*	−.68(.13)*	.43(.25)+
Drugs	−.70(.14)*	.06(.14)	.08(.24)
Violence*Immigrant	−1.10(.26)*	−.09(.29)	.36(.53)
Drugs*Immigrant	−.82(.39)*	−.20(.30)	1.17(.51)*
Detained		.44(.11)*	1.74(.19)*
Detained*Immigrant		.33(.21)	−.61(.42)
Log Likelihood	−1420	−1449	−506

Variables	B. San Diego		
	Pre-Trial Detention (n=2253)	Conviction (n=2253)	Incarceration (n=885)
Immigrant	1.26(.17)*	−.59(.20)*	−.16(.40)
Male	1.42(.37)*	−.12(.21)	−.16(.40)
Less than 20	−.05(.17)	.15(.18)	−.32(.25)
Violence	−.17(.22)	−.33(.21)	.18(.70)
Drugs	−1.46(.37)*	−.37(.22)+	−2.96(1.02)*
Violence*Immigrant	.05(.30)	−.29(.38)	.71(.41)+
Drugs*Immigrant	−.07(.44)	.57(.33)+	2.16(1.13)+
Detained		2.29(.33)*	2.29(.29)*
Detained*Immigrant		.79(.42)+	−1.15(.43)*
Log Likelihood	−730	−683	−372

* p<.05, two-tailed.
+ p<.10, two-tailed.

drugs in the month before their current offense, and more than 30 percent of all inmates said that they had been under the influence of drugs at the time of their current offense. So although there may be a concentration in drug offenses among imprisoned Hispanic offenders, especially from Colombia and the Dominican Republic, levels of drug use among Hispanic offenders in general seem to be about the same or lower than in the broader population of inmates. Scalia (1996:7) also reports that noncitizen offenders tend more often than citizens to be involved in "minor" and "low-level" drug offenses. This adds to the uncertainty as to whether and to what extent the imprisonment of Hispanic defendants from particular countries for drug offenses may be a product of their concentration in this type of crime as contrasted with the courts selecting this type of crime among immigrants from Colombia and the Dominican Republic.

There is further reason to question the impression left by prison statistics that Hispanic offenders are heavily involved with drugs. The research literature indicates that Hispanics compared with other Americans have lower rates of crack cocaine smoking (Wagner-Echeagary et al., 1994) and of drug-related deaths (Hayes-Bautista et al., 1994). These findings are part of a larger pattern indicating that recently arrived Hispanic immigrants are healthier on a variety of measures than other Americans, and that over time these differences diminish, with Hispanic Americans becoming more like other Americans in their health problems (Scribner, 1996).

Nonetheless, the perception remains that immigrants are a significant cause of American crime problems. The 1994 U.S. Commission on Immigration Reform set out to assess perceived and actual links between immigration policy and crime in El Paso. The Commission found that the El Paso crime rate was perceived as escalating dramatically in recent years in spite of efforts of local law enforcement agencies. This escalating crime problem was seen as resulting from El Paso's rapid urban growth, which in turn was fed by migration from Mexico, including a large illegal population. The Commission reported that ". . . many people believe that undocumented aliens are the source of the increase in serious crime in El Paso and that the increasing number of undocumented aliens is due to the U.S. Government's inability to control the border" (1994:18).

The Commission sought to assess the basis of these perceptions in several ways, including a comparison of El Paso with other cities of similar size and a regression analysis focusing on the effects of proximity to the Mexican border on crime rates in El Paso and elsewhere. The initial comparison with similarly sized cities was revealing. El Paso's total 1992 crime rate ranked 30th among 40 U.S. cities of comparable size. El Paso ranked above the mean for the 40 cities only on larceny-theft, for which it ranked 13th and was within 10 percent of the mean for all cities. This concentration in minor forms of property crime is consistent with the El Paso and San Diego study cited above (Pennell et al. 1989), which finds that about two-thirds of the illegal immigrants in each of these cities were arrested for property crimes, with only 9 to 15 percent arrested for drug crimes. Meanwhile, the 1994 Commission report indicates that the El Paso murder rate was little more than one-third of that for all the cities and was 12 percent lower than the national average. The murder rate for El Paso is also comparable to its border city Juarez. So in spite of its much higher rate of poverty, Juarez too has a relatively low homicide rate as least as compared with U.S. cities. Although, like other cities, El Paso saw increases in violent crime in the 1980s, it still remains at the lower end of the spectrum for cities of comparable size.

As a further means of assessing the possible effects of Hispanic immigration on crime, the Commission also reported the results of regression analyses on violent and property crime for 244 metropolitan statistical areas (MSAs) in the United States. In addition to including conventional measures of urban and economic conditions in these MSAs, the regression equations also included variables representing location within 100 miles of the U.S.-Mexican border or in Texas (if not on the border) or in another border state (Arizona, California, or New Mexico). The results of these regression analyses revealed that the border effects were all negative for violent crime and largely so for property crime. The conclusion from this analysis is that "if the data suggest anything about the border's impact on crime, it is that crime is lower on average in border areas than in other U.S. cities when the characteristics of the urban population are held constant" (1994:20). Nevertheless, the Commission concedes that a more direct test of the effects of immigration, especially illegal immigration, requires more specific measures.

We undertook a more direct test of immigration effects at the level of standard metropolitan statistical areas (SMSAs) by joining measures of legal and illegal immigration, developed by Bean et al. (1988) and based on a methodology used previously for the nation and states by Warren and Passel (1987), with Uniform Crime Report data collected by the Federal Bureau of Investigation. The estimate of the legally resident noncitizen population was generated using alien registration data for 1980 from the Immigration and Naturalization Service and data on legally admitted aliens for January-March 1980 for SMSAs. This number was then subtracted from the figure for aliens counted in the 1980 census (corrected for nonreporting of country of birth, misreporting of citizenship, and misreporting of nativity) to obtain an estimate for undocumented aliens. Application of these procedures also yielded an estimate of legal noncitizens. The corrections and adjustments used in developing these estimates are described in greater detail by Warren and Passel (1987) and Passel and Woodrow (1984). Although these estimates of illegal immigrants are dependent on the numbers of undocumented immigrants included in the 1980 census, not the number actually present, Bean et al. (1988:39) indicate that "it is likely that the distribution . . . of the undocumented population not included in the 1980 Census might be similar to the distribution of those included."

We began our analysis with the 47 SMSAs considered by Bean et al. (1988) that are located in the five southwestern states of Arizona, California, Colorado, New Mexico, and Texas, with four border SMSAs in Texas deleted because they include substantial areas and populations in Mexico. Thirteen of these SMSAs were not represented in the Uniform Crime Report data, so 34 SMSAs were ultimately available for our analysis. The three outcome measures of crime included violent crime rates, property crime rates, and total crime rates. Results are presented in Table 9-3.

We initially regressed logged arrest rates on the proportions of the population age 15 and over who were estimated in the 34 SMSAs to be illegal immigrants or noncitizens, black, and living in poverty. The illegal immigrant and noncitizen measures were introduced separately in equations to avoid collinearity problems. Box-Cox transformations were applied in this analysis and we selected the variant that produced the highest R^2, which involved taking the logs of

TABLE 9-3   Linear Models of Crime Rates in Selected Southwestern SMSAs (n=34)[a]

Total Variables[b]	Linear Models for Logged Arrest Rates		
	Violence Arrests	Property Arrests	Arrests
A. Illegal Immigrant Equations			
Illegal Immigrants	.07	.23	−.04
	(.12)	(.12)	(.10)
Black	−.07	−.03	−.11
	(.08)	(.08)	(.07)
Poverty	−.30	−.64	−.50
	(.30)	(.43)	(.37)
R^2/L	.03	.14	.10
B. Noncitizen Equations			
Noncitizens	.19(.14)	.43(.12)[*]	.12(.12)
Black	−.05(.08)	.02(.07)	−.10(.07)
Poverty	−.45(.45)	−.92(.40)[*]	−.59(.78)
R^2/L	.08	.25	.12

[a] Standard errors in parentheses

[b] Independent variables in linear models are proportions of population age 15 and above.

[*] $p < .05$

the independent and dependent variables. In no case was the measure of percent illegal immigrants significantly correlated with any of the three outcome crime measures, and the noncitizen measure was significant in only one case. As a further test of potential influence, we created dummy variables, with the SMSAs in the highest quartile on each variable coded as a dummy variable in poisson models of arrest counts. This operationalization was an attempt to capture the effects of more extreme concentrations of effected groups, with, for example, the dummy variable for proportion of illegal immigrants indicating SMSAs with more than 1 percent of the population in this group. This coding yielded more statistically significant but nonetheless inconsistent results, and so we do not present them. There is no consistent or compelling evidence at the SMSA level that immigration causes crime.

DISCUSSION AND CONCLUSIONS

We have suggested that an overreliance on prison statistics is a problematic basis for developing our understanding of immigration and crime. It is of further concern, in the political and economic context of cost reduction and shifting described at the outset of this chapter, that the prisons that collect these crime statistics may have an understandable interest in attracting attention to them, for purposes of offsetting high per inmate costs of incarceration. These statistics often are used to make the point that the numbers of immigrants in prison are substantial, and that a large proportion of immigrants who are in prison for drug charges are from Mexico. However, it is also the case that increasing numbers of immigrants have been coming to the United States from Mexico to work for employers who are eager to have them as employees (Calavita, 1994). These immigrants are disproportionately young and male, and therefore of an age and gender for whom crime is a relatively common and frequently transient experience, regardless of citizenship. So a first concern is to take into account not only the increased immigration that is occurring from Mexico, but also the age and sex distribution of these immigrants in considering their numbers in prison. When we do this we find that Mexican immigrants are found in state prisons at an adjusted rate that is not strikingly different from U.S. citizens. Of course, this does not mean we should be unconcerned about the growing numbers of Mexican immigrants in prison. The costs of this imprisonment are high and a concern with the absolute volume of crime involved is understandable. The adjustments for gender and age that we have introduced are intended to provide a context for understanding the numbers and costs involved.

At the same time, it is also important to take into account that immigrants from Mexico and elsewhere may be subject to differential treatment in the criminal justice system. For example, we have demonstrated that immigrants in El Paso and San Diego are at greater risk of being detained prior to trial, and that this results in their increased likelihood of being convicted and imprisoned. Also, we have shown that immigrants in these cities who are charged with drug offenses are at an elevated risk of being sentenced to prison. The overall implications of these findings will not be certain, however, until more is learned about potentially offsetting practices that result from diverting immigrants from the criminal justice system and deporting them from the country.

Another source of public concern is that immigrants, and especially illegal immigrants, are a source of drug problems in the United States. However, arrest records in cities such as El Paso and San Diego suggest that illegal immigrants are less likely than citizens to be involved in drug crime, and instead that they are most distinctively involved in property crime. This kind of petty property offense activity is consistent with the picture of offending that Freeman (1996) has suggested in his foraging model of crime. That is, young male illegal immigrants may be most likely to become involved in petty property crime as they attempt to satisfy basic subsistence needs while moving through the early stages of seeking, finding, losing, and regaining employment.

Overall, we did not find consistent evidence in macro- or micro-level data that immigrants are much more likely than citizens of similar ages and gender to be involved in crime. In particular, we have found that the image presented in prison statistics of the largest group of current immigrants to the United States, from Mexico, is potentially misleading. Our data suggest that Mexican immigrants are more like their age and gender peers than is commonly assumed. This finding helps to resolve a paradox in the picture of Mexican immigration to the United States, because by other measures of health and well-being—including smoking, drug use, and the birthweight of babies—Mexican immigrants are generally found to do as well or better than U.S. citizens. One argument is that this is because of the strength of extended and nuclear families and religion in Mexican families. Insofar as this is the case, we may wish to place the priority on finding ways to preserve, protect, and promote the social and cultural capital that Mexican immigrants bring to their experience in the United States, rather than overemphasize issues of crime and punishment.

One especially important way in which Mexican and other immigrants to this country might benefit from better protection involves the risks to which they are exposed as victims of crime. In this chapter we have not considered the criminal victimization of immigrants largely because we could find no available source of data on this topic (but see Sorenson and Shen, 1996). The U.S. government invests large sums in public surveys of crime victimization, but these surveys do not include significant numbers of immigrants, and no special surveys of immigrants have been undertaken for this purpose. This task deserves special priority.

Also, and notwithstanding the potentially misleading picture we have found with regard to issues of immigration and crime, especially in the Mexican context, further work should be attentive to at least two poorly understood issues. The first involves the important task of making projections into the future that take into account interrelations among immigration, differential fertility, and social behavior. As we discuss in the Appendix to this chapter, higher rates of fertility among immigrant groups, either alone or in combination with other factors, such as criminal justice system bias, could result in immigrants forming larger proportions of prison populations in the future, even if their group propensities to crime remain constant. These processes are in need of further study.

Second, it is also likely the case that specific groups of immigrants, much like specific groups of citizens, do have a heightened propensity that leads them to be disproportionately involved in crime. This typically involves countries with relatively few immigrants to the United States. In these cases in which immigration is rather limited, there may be unique social networks and selection processes that explain the higher rates of crime involvement. If legal immigration from these countries was greater, it is plausible that rates of crime associated with these immigrant groups in the United States would be less striking, if only because the effects of these selection processes and social networks would be diluted. We know too little about these special cases to say much more, but enough to recognize that it is likely misleading to extrapolate from such cases to the experience of immigrants more generally.

APPENDIX: PROJECTIONS INTO THE FUTURE: INTERRELATIONS BETWEEN IMMIGRATION, DIFFERENTIAL FERTILITY, AND SOCIAL BEHAVIOR

A natural issue to address is the extent to which recent immigration trends will influence future trends of criminal behavior. The fact that we found little compelling evidence suggesting that those who enter the United States, either illegally or legally, have higher propensities to become involved in illegal activities does not necessarily imply that the relation will be absent in the future. The following are several hypotheses that deserve further consideration when data and resources become available.

Differential Fertility of Recent Immigrants Makes a Difference

Assume for the sake of simplicity that the immigration flow is stopped now and that those who have already gained entrance into the United States continue to behave as they have so far, that is, that their propensity to become involved in criminal activities remains constant and roughly the same as that of citizens. To the extent that current immigrants do indeed experience higher fertility than citizens—as some evidence seems to verify—the population exposed to become involved in crime 10-15 years from now will be disproportionately drawn from among recent immigrant groups. Several regularities will follow. First, the contribution of the immigrant population (also including the second generation) to the total crime rate will increase, as will their share among those who are incarcerated. This is not an effect of higher involvement in crime or of higher level of seriousness of offenses, but a simple result of the influence of differential fertility on the distribution of populations exposed to criminal activity. The larger than proportional contribution of immigrants to the population convicted and incarcerated will also persist if, as the data available to us seem to indicate, immigrants involved in crime are more likely to be convicted and incarcerated than comparable counterparts among citizens.

The relative contribution of immigrant groups will, of course, be higher if immigration trends continue and if their risk of becoming involved in criminal activities exceeds that of citizens. This is addressed below.

Success, Adaptation, and Increase in Criminal Behavior

As argued in the text of this chapter, a small subset of those who enter legally or illegally into the United States have higher propensities to commit crimes because their entrance into the United States is associated with ties to networks and organizations that employ them as cheap labor for organized criminal activities. The majority of immigrants, however, do not differ initially from other citizens of comparable socioeconomic status in their immediate involvement in crime. Indeed, it can be argued that they may have even less propensity to become involved in criminal activities, if only as a way of protecting their legal residence status or of averting outright repatriation.

However, as adaptation and acculturation proceed, there are a number of scenarios that could take place. First, if adaptation to U.S. society proceeds seamlessly, the immigrant will be exposed to roughly similar conditions as the population of citizens, and consequently their involvement in crime will be comparable to that of citizens, and their response to change in economic well-being (employment and real wages) will be roughly similar to the population as a whole. If so, the overall crime rates will be affected hardly at all. As suggested above, however, if differential fertility persists for a generation or so, the result will be a higher contribution of first- and second-generation immigrants to the total pool of criminal activities and criminals apprehended.

Second, if the integration of the immigrant population is more arduous and difficult due to obstacles ranging from those associated with their human capital limitations to inflexibilities in the social system, their propensity to be involved in crime could be higher than that found in the rest of the population. This will raise the overall crime rate unless there are comparable reductions among citizens. Furthermore, to the extent that the second generation experiences even worse adaptation difficulties—as has been informally documented in the literature in other areas—the rate of criminal activity will increase and therefore will enhance the contribution to crime associated with a particular migration flow.

The second scenario suggests the possibility that first- and second-generation immigrants will be involved more permanently in criminal activities, rather than participating in them intermittently, as a foraging model would suggest. A counterargument is that shadow wages are lower among immigrants in both the first and second generation and that this should slow down or prevent altogether their involvement in crime.

Differential Fertility and Differential Adaptation

Adaptation under conditions of scarcity, poverty, and lack of access to education and training may turn out to be difficult for both the first generation of immigrants and their descendants. Insofar as higher fertility adds to the stress to which they are exposed upon arrival, one should expect a direct relation among relatively high fertility, conditions of poverty, and exposure to the risk of involvement in crime. This mechanism will ensure that subgroups of immigrants— those with higher fertility—will manifest higher propensities to become involved in crime than those among immigrants with lower fertility and than among citizens with lower comparable levels of fertility.

If all three processes described above do in fact operate, the results should be (a) an increase in the overall rate of crime and (b) an increase in the contribution to criminal activities associated with immigrants. If, in addition, apprehension of immigrants and the subsequent judicial processes contain biases similar to those illustrated in this chapter, then (c) a disproportionate share of the population of detained and incarcerated individuals as well as an unequal share of the corresponding costs will be associated with first- or second-generation immigrants.

A simple tool to study the trajectory of the identified process is the projection of populations of citizens and immigrants by classes of age, poverty status, propensity to crime, and rates of detention and incarceration. A year-by-year accounting of the populations in the various classes can be achieved with information on fertility, mortality, and social mobility across classes. Information on propensity to criminal activity, changes in the propensity over time, and the various risks associated with the unfolding of the judicial process could be obtained from surveys eliciting self-reported criminal activity from various ethnic or national groups and from time series of arrests and incarceration, where the latter also include information on national origins.

ACKNOWLEDGMENTS

We acknowledge the helpful assistance of Frank Bean, Jeffrey Passel, Patricia Parker, Elizabeth Arias, Handamala Rafalimanana, and Elaine Sieff.

REFERENCES

Abbott, G.
   1915   "Immigration and Crime." *Journal of Criminal Law and Criminology* 6(4):522-32.
Bean, Frank D., B. Lindsay Lowell, and Lowell J. Taylor
   1988   "Undocumented Mexican Immigrants and the Earnings of Other Workers in the United States." *Demography* 25:35-49.
Brown, M. Craig, and Barbara D. Warner
   1995   "The Political Threat of Immigrant Groups and Police Aggressiveness in 1900." Pp. 82-98 in *Ethnicity, Race, and Crime,* Darnell F. Hawkins, ed. Albany: State University of New York Press.
Butterfield, F.
   1994   "A History of Homicide Surprises the Experts." *New York Times,* October 23:10.
Calavita, Kitty
   1994   "U.S. Immigration and Policy Responses: The Limits of Legislation." Pp. 52-82 in *Controlling Immigration,* Wayne A. Cornelius, Philip L. Martin, and James F. Hollifield, eds. Stanford, Calif.: Stanford University Press.
Cornelius, Wayne A., Philip L. Martin, and James F. Hollifield, eds.
   1994   *Controlling Immigration.* Stanford, Calif.: Stanford University Press.
Cressey, Donald
   1969   *Theft of the Nation.* New York: Harper & Row.
Freeman, Richard
   1996   "The Supply of Youths to Crime." Pp. 81-102 in *Exploring the Underground Economy,* Susan Pozo, ed. Kalazmazoo, Mich.: W.E. Upjohn Institute for Employment Research.
Gault, R.H.
   1932   *Criminology.* Boston: D.C. Heath.

Hagan, John, and K. Bumiller
    1983   In *Research on Sentencing: The Search for Reform*, Vol. II, A. Blumstein, J. Cohen, S.E.
            Martin, and M.H. Tonry, eds. Washington, D.C.: National Academy Press.
Hawkins, Darnell F.
    1995   "Ethnicity, Race and Crime: A Review of Selected Studies. Pp. 11-45 in *Ethnicity, Race,
            and Crime*, Darnell F. Hawkins, ed. Albany: State University of New York Press.
Hayes-Bautista, D.E., L. Beazconde-Garbanati, W.O. Schink, and M. Hayes-Bautista
    1994   "Latino Health in California, 1985-1990: Implications for Family Practice." *Family
            Medicine* 9:556-562.
Heer, D.
    1996   *Immigration in America's Future*. Boulder, Colo: Westview Press.
Hirschi, Travis, and Michael Gottfredson
    1983   "Age and the Explanation of Crime." *American Journal of Sociology* 89:552-584.
Hobbs, A.H.
    1943   "Criminality in Philadelphia: 1790-1810 Compared with 1937." *American Sociological
            Review* 8:198-202.
Ianni, Francis
    1972   *A Family Business*. New York: Russell Sage.
Isbister, John
    1996   *Immigration Debate*. West Hartford, Conn.: Kumarian Press.
Lane, R.
    1979   *Violent Death in the City*. Cambridge, Mass.: Harvard University Press.
McCord, Joan
    1995   "Ethnicity, Acculturation, and Opportunities: A Study of Two Generations." Pp. 69-81 in
            Ethnicity, Race and Crime, Darnell F. Hawkins, ed. Albany: State University of New
            York Press.
National Commission on Law Observance and Enforcement
    1931   *Report on Crime and the Foreign-Born*. Washington, D.C.: U.S. Government Printing
            Office.
O'Kane, James M.
    1992   *The Crooked Ladder*. New Brunswick, N.J.: Transaction Books.
Park, R.E., E.W. Burgess, and R.D. McKenzie
    1925/   *The City*. Chicago: University of Chicago Press.
    1967
Passel, J.S., and K.A. Woodrow
    1984   "Geographic Distribution of Undocumented Immigrants: Estimates of Undocumented
            Aliens Counted in the 1980 Census by State." *International Migration Review* 18:642-
            671.
Pennell, Susan, Christine Curtis, and Jeff Tayman
    1989   *The Impact of Illegal Immigration on the Criminal Justice System*. San Diego: San
            Diego Association of Governments.
Powell, E.H.
    1966   "Crime as a Function of Anomie." *Journal of Criminal Law, Criminology and Police
            Science* 57:161-171.
Scalia, John
    1996   *Noncitizens in the Federal Criminal Justice System, 1984-94*. Washington, D.C.: U.S.
            Department of Justice, Bureau of Justice Statistics.
Scribner, R.
    1996   "Paradox as Paradigm - The Health Outcomes of Mexican Americans." (editorial) *Ameri-
            can Journal of Public Health* 3:303-305.

Sellin, Thorsten
    1938   *Culture Conflict and Crime.* New York: Social Science Research Council.
Shaw, Clifford R., and Henry D. McKay
    1942   *Juvenile Delinquency and Urban Areas: A Study of Rates of Delinquents in Relation to Differential Characteristics of Local Communities in American Cities.* Chicago: University of Chicago Press.
Sorenson, S.B., and H. Shen
    1996   "Homicide Risk among Immigrants in California, 1970 through 1992." *American Journal of Public Health* 86(1):97-100.
Sutherland, E, and D. Cressey
    1978   *Criminology.* Philadelphia: Lippincott.
Sutherland, Edwin H.
    1924   *Criminology.* Philadelphia: Lippincott.
Sutherland, Edwin H.
    1934   *Principles of Criminology.* Chicago: Lippincott.
Taft, Donald R.
    1933   "Does Immigration Increase Crime?" *Social Forces* 12:69-77.
Taft, Donald R.
    1936   "Nationality and Crime." *American Sociological Review* 1:724-736.
Tanton, John, and Wayne Lutton
    1993   "Immigration and Criminality." *Journal of Social, Political and Economic Studies* 18(2):217-234.
U.S. Commission on Immigration Reform
    1994   *U.S. Immigration Policy: Restoring Credibility.* Washington, D.C.: U.S. Commission on Immigration Reform.
U.S. Department of Justice
    1993   *Survey of State Prison Inmates, 1991.* Washington, D.C.: Bureau of Justice Statistics.
United States Immigration Commission
    1911   *Immigration and Crime* Vol. 36. Washington, D.C.: U.S. Government Printing Office.
van Vechten, C.C.
    1941   "Criminality of the Foreign-Born." *Journal of Criminal Law and Criminology* 32:139-147.
Wagner-Echeagary, F.A., C.G. Schutz, H.D. Chilcoat, and J.C. Anthony
    1994   "Degree of acculturation and the risk of crack cocaine smoking among Hispanic Americans." *American Journal of Public Health* 84(11):1825-1827.
Warren, R., and J.S. Passel
    1987   "A Count of the Uncountable: Estimates of Undocumented Aliens Counted in the 1980 United States Census." *Demography* 24:375-393.
Wunder, Amanda
    1995   "Foreign Inmates in U.S. Prisons: An Unknown Population." *Corrections Compendium* 20(4):4-18.

10

The Impact of Recent Immigration on Population Redistribution Within the United States

William H. Frey and Kao-Lee Liaw

INTRODUCTION

In this chapter we examine how recent immigration affects population redistribution within the United States, both directly and indirectly, by promoting a secondary domestic migration among native-born residents. Although this impact has been given less prominence in public and academic forums than recent immigration's impact on the nation as a whole, the redistributional aspects of immigration hold important local consequences for the labor force, public service costs, and minority-majority relations. Even from a national perspective, the concentrated distribution of the recent foreign-born immigrant population in comparison with the longer-term resident native-born portends widening demographic disparities across broad regions of the country with respect to race-ethnic composition, race-class structures, and age profiles.

Our research to date on these issues suggests that these kinds of divisions may be emerging from the following: (1) most recent immigrants still locate in a small number of traditional port-of-entry states and metropolitan areas; (2) greatest domestic native-born migrant gains occur in different areas than those attracting recent immigrants; and (3) evidence of a unique, accentuated out-migration of less-skilled domestic migrants away from high-immigration areas.

Though there were hints of these patterns already at the end of the 1970s (Frey and Speare, 1988; Filer, 1992; White and Imai, 1994; Long and Nucci, 1995), these patterns are especially evident in the two five-year periods for which the most recent data are available: 1985-1990 and 1990-1995. Of the three redistribution patterns noted above, it is the latter which holds the greatest potential significance as an immigration impact. The apparent demographic displacement of domestic migrants by immigrants at the low-skilled end of the spectrum implies that a more bifurcated race-class structure may emerge in areas of high immigration if this process persists. Moreover, if the mechanism for this displacement is a labor substitution, this may explain why many earlier studies, that do not take domestic migration into explicit account, show only modest or negligible impacts of immigration on a local area's unemployment rate or wage level (see review in Borjas, 1994).

In this chapter we review evidence for the 1985-1990 and 1990-1995 periods and relevant findings from our own and others' work to assess the impacts of immigration on internal redistribution patterns in the United States. Particular attention is given to the apparent demographic displacement of less-skilled domestic migrants by new immigrants in high-immigration areas where we estimate the nature of this displacement under assumed increases or decreases in current immigration levels. In the sections that follow we provide an overview of immigration and internal migration processes over the 1985-1995 period, review findings that document the nature of selective demographic displacement in metropolitan areas and states, and present findings from a model that estimates the impact of changing immigration levels on this displacement. In the concluding section we discuss some implications of these redistributional impacts of immigration.

IMMIGRATION AND INTERNAL MIGRATION-RELATED POPULATION SHIFTS

The clustering of immigrants into areas that are not attractive destinations for domestic migrants can be illustrated by recent census statistics and estimates. Between 1985 and 1995, approximately two-thirds of all immigrant growth accrued to just ten metropolitan areas. These areas housed only 30 percent of the total U.S. 1995 population and an estimated 19 percent of the native-born non-Hispanic white population. Moreover, nine of the ten areas registered a net out-migration of internal migrants for at least some part of the 1985-1995 period. In the aggregate, these areas lost 4.5 million internal migrants, while they gained 5.3 million immigrants over the 10-year period (Frey, 1996).

Concentration of Immigrants

The concentration of immigrants in a few familiar port-of-entry areas is consistent with the nation's immigration preference statutes that favor family reunification and with earlier research that indicates that kinship ties give rise to chain migration that links family members and friends to common destinations (Massey et al., 1994; Pedraza and Rumbaut, 1996). Yet post-1965 shifts in the origin countries of U.S. immigrants toward Latin America and Asia (Immigration and Naturalization Service, 1996) and toward widening disparities between immigrant and native skill levels (Borjas, 1994) may have increased the importance of kinship ties and, hence, the geographic concentration of immigrants. This is an implication of our analysis of 1985-1990 young adult (aged 20-34) immigrants to the United States (Liaw and Frey, 1998). We found that race-specific immigrant destination choices were most concentrated for Hispanics and least concentrated for whites, with blacks and Asians lying in between. Furthermore, within each race, demographic concentration was greatest for those with less than a high school education and tended to decrease monotonically with higher education levels. For example, 81 percent of Hispanics with less than a high school education resided in the top five states with highest concentrations, compared with 68 percent of Hispanics with college degrees. This pattern of findings is consistent with Bartel's (1989) analysis of immigrant destinations in the 1970s.

In the same paper (Liaw and Frey, 1998), we also conducted a multivariate analysis of these immigrants' destination choices. Using the destination state's racial composition similarity (to the immigrant) as a proxy for the influence of "friends and relatives," we found this factor to be more important than conventional labor market attributes in these immigrants' destination selections. This was especially the case for Hispanics and blacks and for those with a high school education or less. This finding reinforces the inference that the immigration country-of-origin patterns and skill-level profiles of recent immigrants are associated with their high geographic concentration within select destination areas.

A related issue involves the degree to which new foreign-born immigrants eventually disperse from these high-immigration states and metropolitan areas. Earlier studies suggest that the internal migration patterns of Hispanics and Asians are highly channelized, following same-race and ethnic networks and social ties (Bean and Tienda, 1987; McHugh, 1989; Pedraza and Rumbaut, 1996). Specific research on the internal migration of foreign-born or new immigrants from the 1980 Census (Bartel and Koch, 1991) or 1990 Census (Nogle, 1996) indicates that broader dispersal did not occur, especially among those with lower levels of education. This and other evidence for legalized aliens from administrative records (Newman and Tienda, 1994) suggest that the overall impact of internal migration toward reducing the concentration of recent foreign-born immigrants has been small.

Figure 10-1 provides data from the 1995 Current Population Survey (CPS) that confirms this continued concentration of recent immigrant cohorts. Displayed here are the concentration of the native-born and of specific foreign-born cohorts in the ten high-immigration metropolitan areas (listed in Table 10-1). These data show that post-1965 foreign-born immigrants are more concentrated than either the native born or pre-1965 immigrants. Moreover, among Latinos, 1965-1985 arrivals are no more dispersed than those who arrived in the past decade. Asians who arrived between 1975-1985 are no more dispersed than more recent immigrants. Both these Hispanic and Asian contrasts hold, as well, when

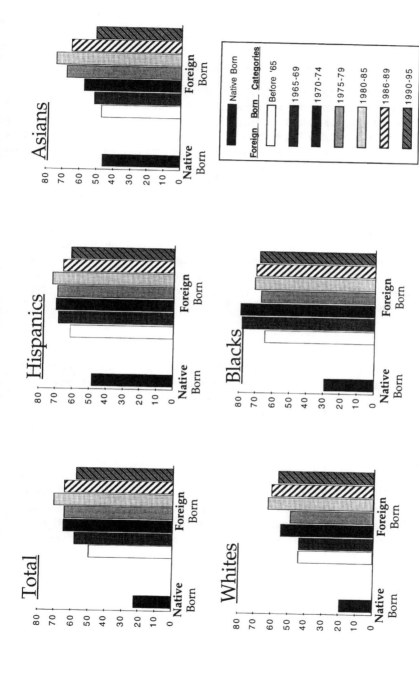

FIGURE 10-1 Percent resident in ten high-immigration metropolitan areas, 1995, by nativity, foreign-born year of arrival, and race and ethnicity.

controls are included for education attainment, family income, and age (Frey, 1996). These statistics, along with the previously cited studies, suggest a continuing concentration of the recent foreign born in selected areas.

Dispersed Internal Migration

Unlike recent immigrants who are often dependent on their families and friends to integrate them into job networks in traditional port-of-entry areas, internal migrants tend to be less constrained in their destinations and are more apt to respond to labor market forces, as well as other amenities, that occasionally shift in response to economic cycles and global economic forces (Long, 1988; Gober, 1993). For most of this century, the port-of-entry areas for immigrants were also attractive employment centers for internal migrants so that these areas grew from both sources of migration. However, this was not the case in the past decade. In addition, for a variety of reasons (discussed in later sections), there is a possible immigrant push effect to consider that may be precipitating the selective out-migration of native-born less-skilled workers in high-immigration areas.

The sections below make plain that internal migrants are relocating to different states, metropolitan areas, and regions of the country than recent immigrants. These are reviewed in the context of the changing economic and amenity attractions for those geographic units.

States

During the 1985-1995 period, internal migrants were attracted to different primary destinations than the traditional port-of-entry states of immigrants. It is, in fact, possible to classify states into "high-immigration states" and "high internal migration states." The former represents states that receive the largest number of immigrants but where immigration is not overwhelmed by internal migration. The latter represents states that receive the greatest number of internal migrants and where internal migration substantially dominates immigration as a component of change.

Table 10-1 presents the high-immigration states and high internal migration states as defined by the migration patterns of the 1990-1995 and 1985-1990 periods.[1] High-immigration states are the same for both periods and include the port-of-entry states: California, New York, Texas, Illinois, New Jersey, and

---

[1]In this chapter, we use the term "internal migration" to denote all within-U.S. migration and the term "domestic migration" to denote within-U.S. migration of the native-born population only. It is the latter that is of primary interest in this chapter. However, in some cases it is not possible to identify separately the native-born migrants from all internal migrants. This is the case in the analysis of 1985-1990 and 1990-1995 trends shown in this section of the chapter. In reality, most internal migration is domestic migration, so we interpret internal migration patterns as a proxy for domestic migration patterns.

TABLE 10-1 A Migration Classification of U.S. States for the Periods 1990-1995 and 1985-1990

Rank	State	Contribution to 1990-95 Change		Rank	State	Contribution to 1985-90 Change	
		Immigration	Net Internal Migration			Immigration	Net Internal Migration
HIGH IMMIGRATION STATES —1990-95*				*HIGH MIGRATION STATES* —1985-90*			
1	California	1,314,792	-1,531,979	1	California	1,356,920	173,586
2	New York	546,713	-1,001,379	2	New York	550,846	-820,886
3	Texas	355,295	318,840	3	Texas	268,498	-331,369
4	Illinois	221,926	-283,043	4	New Jersey	186,510	-193,533
5	New Jersey	184,887	-220,131	5	Illinois	173,548	-342,144
6	Massachusetts	78,527	-181,117	6	Massachusetts	133,897	-96,732
*HIGH INTERNAL MIGRATION STATES** —1990-95*				*HIGH INTERNAL MIGRATION STATES** —1985-90*			
1	Florida	245,482	615,670	1	Florida	314,039	1,071,682
2	Georgia	39,792	344,574	2	Georgia	51,419	302,597
3	Arizona	48,302	291,661	3	North Carolina	32,059	280,882
4	North Carolina	22,359	269,440	4	Virginia	90,133	227,872
5	Washington	61,032	257,234	5	Washington	67,145	216,270
6	Colorado	27,889	244,969	6	Arizona	56,518	216,177
7	Nevada	18,447	227,145				
8	Tennessee	13,241	217,044				

SOURCE: Compiled by the authors from Special 1990 US Census migration tabulations and US Census postcensusal estimates.

*States with largest immigration (excepting Florida, where internal migration substantially dominates)

**States with largest net internal migration and substantially exceeds immigration.

Massachusetts. The high internal migration states that attract more than 200,000 net internal migrants differ over the two five-year periods, however. (Note: Florida is included in this group because its internal migration contribution substantially exceeds its immigration contribution.)

Florida and Georgia appear at the top of this list for both periods. It is clear that the states in the South Atlantic division and Mountain and Pacific divisions are attractive to internal migrants during each period. Some Mountain states, such as Colorado, sustained declines in the late 1980s but rebounded in the early 1990s (Miller, 1994). In fact, the western states, in general, were more prominent in attracting internal migrants in the early 1990s (Spiers, 1995).

What is important from these classification schemes is that most of the high-immigration states show net out-movement for internal migrants during both periods, suggesting that employment or amenity attractions for them lie else-where—along with the possible "immigration push." (Migration rates for these states are depicted in Figure 10-2.) Favorable economic conditions can also *attract* internal migrants to these states, which was the case for California in the late 1980s and Texas in the early 1990s. In some respects, these states are mirror images of each other for these two periods. For Texas, hard times in the oil and gas industries during the late 1980s rebounded as the economy diversified in the early 1990s (Jennings, 1994). California's economy stumbled badly during the 1989-1992 recession and the early 1990s defense cutbacks (Bolton, 1993; Gabriel et al., 1995). Yet evidence discussed below suggests that some of this out-migration may also be attributed to immigration.

Metropolitan Areas

As with states, there is a fairly clear distinction between the prime destinations for recent immigrants to the United States, and those that attract internal migrants (see Table 10-2). Furthermore, the high-immigration metros constitute the same set of places for both periods of analysis, whereas the high-internal migration metros—following the patterns for states—change in accordance with geographic fluctuations in the economy.

Another parallel with the state-level analysis is that most of these high-immigration metros sustain negligible or negative net internal migration over both periods. The shift to a metropolitan-level analysis makes plain that Miami should be treated differently from the rest of Florida as its population gains are plainly dominated by immigration. Still, the net domestic migration levels tended to fluctuate across most of these areas between the late 1980s and early 1990s, in part, reflecting changing economic circumstances.

The shifts are again most dramatic for metropolitan areas in California and Texas. Los Angeles was especially hard hit during the early 1990s through a combination of recessions, defense cutbacks, and a variety of natural disasters (Center for the New West, 1996). Already losing net migrants in the late 1980s,

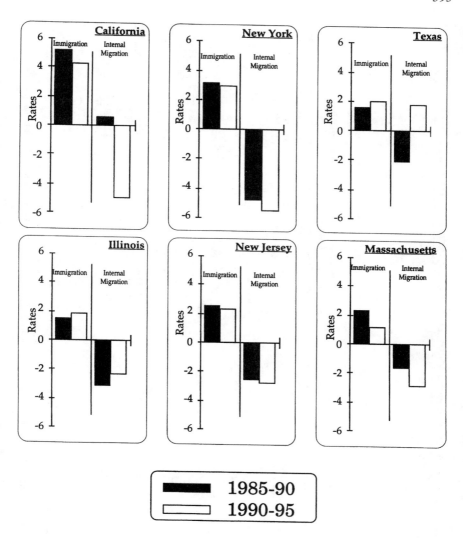

FIGURE 10-2 Immigration and internal migration rates for high-immigration states, 1985-1990 and 1990-1995.

TABLE 10-2 High-Immigration Metros and High Internal Migration Metros for Periods 1990-95 and 1985-90

	Contribution to 1990-95 Change			Contribution to 1985-90 Change	
Metro Area*	Immigration	Net Internal Migration	Metro Area*	Net Internal Immigration	Migration
HIGH IMMIGRATION METROS —1990-95			*HIGH IMMIGRATION METROS* —1985-90		
Los Angeles CMSA	792,712	-1,095,455	Los Angeles CMSA	842,675	-174,673
New York CMSA	705,939	-1,113,924	New York CMSA	714,346	-1,058,078
San Francisco CMSA	262,519	-260,961	San Francisco CMSA	262,185	-103,498
Chicago CMSA	216,309	-279,763	Miami CMSA	194,491	45,287
Miami CMSA	157,059	-4,631	Washington DC CMSA	163,696	103,616
Washington DC CMSA	125,479	-91,643	Chicago CMSA	160,760	-285,204
Houston CMSA	110,323	45,017	Boston NECMA	123,958	-75,331
San Diego CMSA	85,025	-140,591	San Diego MSA	96,350	126,855
Boston CMSA	74,316	-165,822	Houston CMSA	82,964	-142,562
Dallas CMSA	72,246	75,978	Dallas CMSA	63,289	37,925
*HIGH INTERNAL MIGRATION METROS** —1990-95			*HIGH INTERNAL MIGRATION METROS** —1985-90		
Atlanta MSA	32,391	259,094	Atlanta MSA	31,799	205,010
Las Vegas MSA	12,501	211,536	Seattle CMSA	46,886	183,820
Phoenix MSA	27,516	165,760	Tampa MSA	23,905	159,112
Portland MSA	22,618	128,878	Orlando MSA	27,842	154,520
Denver MSA	22,360	118,696	Las Vegas MSA	14,979	152,197
Seattle MSA	42,617	89,347	Phoenix MSA	33,789	145,226
Austin MSA	10,253	86,696	Sacramento CMSA	28,366	117,732
Raleigh MSA	6,175	86,016	West Palm Beach MSA	17,993	107,940
Orlando MSA	16,675	80,685	Portland CMSA	22,939	73,294
Tampa MSA	18,297	77,650	Raleigh MSA	9,824	72,390
West Palm Beach MSA	18,899	74,903	Charlotte MSA	5,859	66,961
Charlotte MSA	6,214	69,198	Daytona Beach MSA	4,088	66,773
Nashville MSA	5,096	63,592	Norfolk MSA	12,868	60,704

SOURCE: Compiled by the authors from Special 1990 US Census migration tabulations and US Census postcensusal estimates.
*The metropolitan area definitions are consistent with Office of Management and Budget definitions of CMSAs, MSAs and NECMA counterparts of June 30, 1995. Official names are abbreviated.

this pattern accelerated during the 1992-1995 period (see Figure 10-3). San Diego, the single high-immigration metro that grew substantially from internal migration over the late 1980s, was affected by substantial employment losses, leading to a sharp reversal in its domestic migration. San Francisco was somewhat less affected than the Southern California metros but still exhibited higher domestic migration losses in the early 1990s.

Of the two Texas high-immigration metros, Houston displayed the greatest domestic migration reversal. Partially affected by the petroleum-related declines of the late 1980s, its economy rebounded in the early 1990s, leading to domestic migration gains over the first three years of the decade (see Figure 10-3). Dallas, which receives the lowest number of immigrants of the high-immigration metros, showed more consistent domestic migration gains over the late 1980s and early 1990s. Its more diversified economic base was able to weather the late 1980s economic downturns which more severely affected Houston.

All of the other high-immigration metros showed a negative domestic net migration over the early 1990s. New York and Chicago, the two largest non-California ports of entry, showed consistently high net out-migration levels over the 1985-1995 period. Miami's modest domestic gains of the late 1980s turned to losses for part of the early 1990s, whereas Washington, D.C. sustained more consistent although modest losses over the 1990-1995 period. Finally, Boston's domestic net out-migration was most pronounced in the first years of the 1990s, reflecting the area's declines in employment opportunities.

Although it is clear that the trends in domestic migration for the high-immigration metros are shaped by changing economic circumstances imposed by recessions and industry-specific growth patterns, the most dominant of these areas (Los Angeles, New York, San Francisco, Chicago) show a consistent net out-migration compared with other parts of the United States over the 1985-1995 period; and the rest (with the exception of San Diego prior to the 1990s defense cutbacks) display fluctuating levels of either declines or modest gains. These patterns suggest the possibility that immigration itself may exert some impact on domestic migration patterns, regardless of the current economic conditions.

Consistent with the late 1980s to early 1990s regional fluctuations discussed above, most of the high internal migration metros differ across each of these periods. (These are defined as metros with greatest numerical net internal migration gains over the period, where internal migration substantially dominates immigration as a component of population growth.)[2] The ascendancy of the non-California Pacific and Mountain division metros is apparent from the improved rankings of Las Vegas, Phoenix, and Portland, as well as the new inclusion of

---

[2] Although there are very few cases in which metro areas are gaining large numbers from both net internal migration and immigration, this is the case for San Diego in 1985-1990 and for Dallas in 1990-1995. They both are classed as high-immigration metros because net internal migration does not substantially dominate the immigration component.

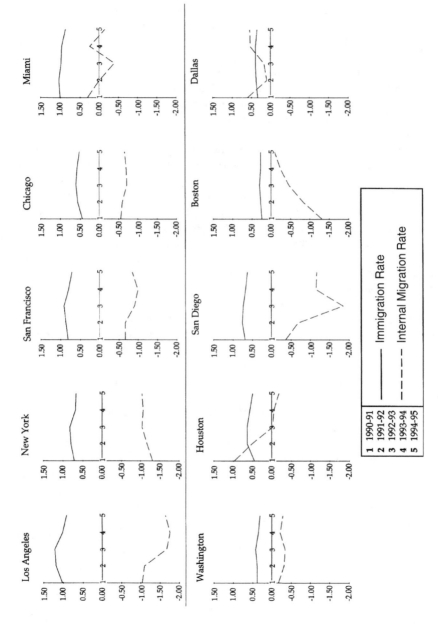

FIGURE 10-3 Annual immigration and internal migration rates, high-immigration metros, 1990-1995.

Denver on the 1990-1995 list (Table 10-2). This, in part, reflects the re-emergence of this region due to the wider dissemination of industries involved with computers, telecommunications, and entertainment/recreation (Labich, 1994). It also explains the inclusion of Austin as the single Texas area classed as a high internal migration metro. Despite the resurgence of these Western and Southwestern areas, South Atlantic division metros continue to attract internal migrants from other parts of the country. Atlanta continues to gain the largest number of internal migrants of any metro in the United States. Similarly, the metros in North Carolina (Raleigh and Charlotte), Florida (Orlando, Tampa, and West Palm Beach), and Tennessee (Nashville) continue to attract large numbers of domestic migrants. Corporate relocations to more pro-business environments, the growth of new knowledge-based industries around universities, and the attraction of these warmer states for northern retirees are all attributed to the growth of these areas for domestic migrants (Labich, 1994; Longino, 1995).

Regional and Nonmetro Patterns

Another perspective can be gained by focusing on how the two types of migration differ in their broad regional destinations, and across the metropolitan and nonmetropolitan continuum. Historically, immigrants have been prone to focus primarily on large metropolitan areas and, as discussed above, this is the case through the early 1990s. However, since the early 1970s the overall population of the United States has gone through various stages of disbursement—both regionally away from the Northeast and Midwest census regions toward the Sun Belt—and toward smaller-sized and even nonmetropolitan areas (Frey and Speare, 1988; Long and Nucci, 1995). Although over three-fourths of Americans reside in metropolitan areas, and half live in metros with more than one million population (mostly in the suburbs), early 1990s statistics suggest a continuation of population dispersal, first observed in the 1970s (Johnson and Beale, 1995). This dispersal across regions and toward smaller areas is largely a product of internal migration.

Evidence from the early 1990s shows that nonmetropolitan employment growth has gained on that in the metropolitan part of the country (Fuguitt and Beale, 1995), lending support for some dispersal. The migration data shown in Table 10-3 confirm that there is a dispersal toward smaller and nonmetropolitan areas in the first half of the 1990s and that it is dominated by internal migrants. Moreover, those parts of the country that exhibit the highest internal migration gains exhibit some of the lowest gains through immigration. These include nonmetropolitan territory in the West, as well as smaller metropolitan areas and nonmetropolitan territory in the South. Among geographic divisions, the Mountain census division in the West shows the highest rate of growth and counterbalances the sharp decline in the Pacific division. Clearly, there is a redistribution away from the larger metropolitan areas in California that is rippling out into the smaller, nonmetropolitan territory in other parts of the West.

TABLE 10-3   Rates of Immigration and Net Internal Migration for U.S. Geographic Divisions and Metropolitan-Non metropolitan Categories

Geographic Category	Immigration Rates		Net Internal Migration Rates	
	1985-90	1990-95	1985-90	1990-95
Geographic Divisions				
NORTHEAST				
New Englands	1.9	1.0	–0.2	–2.9
Mid-Atlantic	2.3	2.1	–3.1	–3.4
MIDWEST				
East North Central	0.8	0.8	–1.7	–0.8
West North Central	0.5	0.4	–1.2	0.6
SOUTH				
South Atlantic	1.6	1.1	5.3	2.9
East South Central	0.3	0.2	0.9	2.5
West South Central	1.2	1.4	–2.8	1.4
WEST				
Mountain	1.2	1.0	1.1	7.6
Pacific	4.4	3.7	1.2	–2.9
Metro-Non Metro Categories				
NORTHEAST				
Large Metro*	2.8	2.4	–3.9	–4.3
Other Metro	0.9	0.5	1.1	–1.3
Non-Metro	0.5	0.2	2.1	0.2
MIDWEST				
Large Metro*	1.1	1.2	–1.8	–1.5
Other Metro	0.6	0.3	–0.5	–0.1
Non-Metro	0.3	0.1	–2.0	1.4
SOUTH				
Large Metro*	2.2	1.7	2.3	1.8
Other Metro*	0.9	0.7	2.8	2.8
Non-Metro	0.3	0.3	0.1	2.6
WEST				
Large Metro*	4.5	3.6	1.4	–2.1
Other Metro	2.3	2.0	1.9	2.0
Non-Metro	1.0	0.9	–1.0	6.2
TOTAL US				
Large Metro*	2.7	2.3	–0.5	–1.6
Other Metro	1.1	0.8	1.6	1.4
Non-Metro	0.4	0.3	–0.6	2.5

SOURCE: Compiled by the authors from Special 1990 U.S. Census migration tabulations and U.S. Census and U.S. Census postcensusal estimates.
*Large Metro pertains to areas with 1995 populations greater than 1,000,000 people.

The above review makes plain that the state, metropolitan area, regional, and nonmetropolitan destinations of internal migrants differ sharply from those of recent immigrants. The identification of different sets of state and metropolitan-area "magnets" for each group, as well as renewed internal migration dispersal to smaller-sized places and less-developed regions, are further evidence that these two migration processes are somewhat distinct.

SELECTIVE OUT-MIGRATION FROM HIGH-IMMIGRATION AREAS

The different destinations of immigrants and internal migrants may reflect different motivations. The former are influenced by social ties and informal networks, whereas the latter are more responsive to labor market fluctuations (Liaw and Frey, 1996, 1998). Yet a body of research and empirical evidence suggests that immigration may provide the impetus for at least some of the domestic out-movement from high-immigration states and high-immigration metro areas. This possible "immigrant push"[3] was suggested in areas that were doing relatively well economically and were *attracting* domestic migrants among demographic groups that were less negatively affected by immigrants (e.g., college graduates who moved into California during the state's relatively prosperous 1985-1990 period, while less-educated domestic migrants were moving out).

It is, in fact, the uniqueness of the population groups that move away from high-immigration states and metros that suggests that immigration may be exerting a selective impact on domestic out-migration. Unlike more conventional migration that tends to overly select college graduates to areas with the most well-paying or fast-growing employment opportunities (Lansing and Mueller, 1967; Long, 1988; Liaw and Frey, 1996), there was a unique and fairly consistent pattern of out-migration among high school graduates, high school dropouts, and lower-income residents away from most high-immigration metropolitan areas (Frey, 1995b) and high-immigration states (Frey, 1994, 1995a, 1997a) for the 1985-1990 period. A similar "downwardly selective" out-migration pattern from such areas was evident for the 1975-1980 period as well (Walker et al., 1992; Filer, 1992).

The unique selectivity of domestic out-migration is illustrated for selected high-immigration metros in Table 10-4. Shown are foreign immigration and native-born internal migration rates specific to education attainment for the 25-to 64-year-old age groups over the 1985-1990 period. In almost all cases, rates of internal net out-migration are highest for persons with a high school education or less. Moreover, numerically and in terms of rates, these statistics make plain that

---

[3] The use of the term "immigrant push" is simply a descriptive device consistent with the convention in migration studies to identify various sets of origin "pushes" and destination "pulls" (Lee, 1966; Long, 1988).

TABLE 10-4 Foreign Immigration and Native-Born Internal Migration Components, by Education and Selected High-Immigration Metro Areas

Metro Areas	1985-90 Migration Components (Ages 25-64)		Rates per 1990 Population* (Ages 25-64)		Native Born Net Internal Migration Rates per 1990 Population (Ages 25-64)		
	Foreign Immigration from Abroad	Native Born Internal Migration	Foreign Immigration from Abroad	Native Born Internal Migration	Total	Whites	Blacks
LOS ANGELES							
Less than High School	190,460	−29,681	28.3	−4.4	−4.7	−7.5	−3.9
High School Graduates	66,193	−43,233	5.7	−3.7	−3.3	−4.3	−2.2
Some College	65,595	−49,494	3.5	−2.7	−1.6	−2.0	0.1
College Graduates	84,484	40,753	6.4	3.1	10.2	11.0	12.0
NEW YORK							
Less than High School	132,564	−60,803	14.6	−6.7	−8.5	−9.2	−8.2
High School Graduates	92,991	−132,081	4.6	−6.5	−7.3	−7.4	−7.1
Some College	71,527	−127,952	4.2	−7.5	−7.5	−7.4	−8.0
College Graduates	118,599	−85,173	5.3	−3.8	−1.2	−1.1	−1.4
SAN FRANCISCO							
Less than High School	44,989	−18,338	18.4	−7.5	−7.9	−9.2	−6.5
High School Graduates	23,891	−32,794	4.4	−6.1	−5.7	−7.0	−1.9

Some College	29,957	−33,090	3.2	−3.6	−2.0	−2.1	−0.9
College Graduates	47,694	32,283	5.2	3.5	13.0	14.5	8.9
CHICAGO						
Less than High School	28,829	−28,568	5.6	−5.6	−6.5	−5.7	−8.4
High School Graduates	17,488	−38,252	1.7	−3.8	−3.2	−2.6	−5.6
Some College	15,060	−32,557	1.4	−3.1	−1.9	−1.1	−5.0
College Graduates	27,147	9,768	2.8	1.0	7.2	8.0	0.8
MIAMI						
Less than High School	41,491	−4,056	27.5	−2.7	−4.3	−7.1	−3.6
High School Graduates	24,407	−3,146	9.4	−1.2	−2.3	−3.9	−2.1
Some College	23,076	−3,049	8.2	−1.1	−1.1	−2.1	−0.7
College Graduates	21,037	8,691	9.1	3.8	10.3	11.5	3.7
HOUSTON						
Less than High School	16,129	−14,500	5.7	−5.1	−5.7	−11.6	−2.6
High School Graduates	5,948	−23,639	1.4	−5.4	−5.6	−9.3	0.6
Some College	6,999	−22,865	1.4	−4.5	−3.6	−5.6	0.2
College Graduates	12,649	−4,629	2.0	−1.1	5.8	5.9	3.3

*Per 1990 Native Born Population

there is a demographic displacement of foreign immigrants for native-born migrants that is especially imbalanced toward the former among persons with less than a high school education in Los Angeles, New York, San Francisco, Miami and, to a lesser extent, in Chicago and Houston. The education-selective out-migration is also apparent among populations restricted to young adult movers aged 25-34 and among whites as well as blacks. What is also apparent from this table is the "dual economy" nature of some of these areas, suggested by the net in-migration of college graduates to Los Angeles, San Francisco, Chicago, and Miami. This is consistent with arguments that suggest that high levels of immigration tend to benefit the kinds of professional and advanced service jobs that attract college graduates (Walker et al., 1992; White and Hunter, 1993).

These distinct education-related patterns are also shown in Map 10-1, which depicts education-specific net domestic migration patterns for states in 1985-1990. Among 25-34 year olds, high-immigration states accounted for four of the five greatest losing states for those with at most a high school education. At the other extreme, college graduates were most apt to relocate away from the economically declining Northeast, farm belt, and oil patch states toward coastal areas (including California, Florida, and states surrounding Washington, D.C.) with high levels of immigration.

Explanations

The connection between immigration and the unique out-migration selectivity of the less skilled is consistent with a number of explanations. First, relatively low-skilled immigrants compete with less well-educated, long-term, and native-born residents for jobs and, therefore, they serve to bid down their wages and take away employment opportunities (Borjas, 1994; Borjas et al., 1996). Second, longer-term residents may hold the perception, correctly or not, that the new immigrants contribute to a variety of social costs including higher crime rates, reduced services, or increased taxes which imply greater out-of-pocket expenses for lower- and middle-class residents. Patterns of public support for California's 1994 statewide referendum on Proposition 187, which would restrict *illegal* immigrants' access to a variety of state services (Martin, 1995), show that the perceived immigrant burden is fairly widespread. Espenshade and Calhoun's (1993) analysis of California's public opinion data show antimigrant sentiment to be strong among residents who view immigrants as such a burden. Third, there is the possible race and ethnic prejudice factor, which has long been known to affect local moves across neighborhoods and between cities and suburbs when earlier immigrant waves entered cities (Lieberson, 1963; White, 1987). It is conceivable that the increased multiethnic presence that now encompasses entire metropolitan areas, and most neighborhoods within them (Denton and Massey, 1991), could precipitate some of the metropolitan-wide out-migration in high-immigration areas.

MAP 10-1 1985-1990 native-born net migration for states (ages 25-34 by education).

High School Grad

College Grad

Less Than High School

Some College

■ 5 Greatest Gaining   □ 5 Greatest Losing

▨ Other Gaining   ▨ Other Losing

Previous findings consistent with these explanations include a series of multivariate analyses of 1985-1990 net internal migration for metropolitan areas (Frey, 1995b) and for states (Frey, 1995c). These studies show that, when other relevant economic and amenity variables are added to the analysis, immigration exerts a significant independent effect on net domestic out-migration that is strongest for persons in poverty and for persons with less than a college education (in the metropolitan area analysis). These latter studies were followed up with more rigorous analyses of the migration process that separated the explanation of migration departures from a state from the explanation of migrants' destination choices (Frey et al., 1996; Liaw and Frey, 1996). These studies provide evidence that immigration's impact on the interstate migration process is more pronounced in affecting departure from a state (i.e., the decision to move) than in affecting the migrants' destination selection. It lends support to the view that immigration is more likely to serve as a "push" rather than as a reduced "pull" for domestic migration to high-immigration states.

Studies using similar and other multivariate techniques for migration over the late 1970s (Walker et al., 1992; Filer, 1992; White and Hunter, 1993; White and Imai, 1994) and for the 1980s (White and Liang, 1994) show general but not uniformly consistent support for an immigration effect on the internal out-migration of less-skilled residents. One study, conducted by Barff et al. (1995), shows general support for this effect in the late 1970s but inconsistent results for the late 1980s.

1990s Evidence

We now examine available evidence for the first half of the 1990s to see if the unique selectivity pattern of domestic net out-migration from high-immigration states persists for this period. It is not possible to undertake the detailed analysis of demographic subgroups for areas (states or metropolitan areas) that was conducted for the 1985-1990 (Frey, 1995b, 1995c) with decennial census migration data. However, it is possible to compile reasonably comparable rates over the first four years of the 1990s using the "migration one-year ago" question from the Census Bureau's Annual CPS. The rates for the 1990-1994 period can be compiled by adding the net migration components for each year and computing a rate based on the average mid-year population over the period. These rates, along with comparable rates for the 1985-1990 period (from the census) appear in Table 10-5.

The unique out-migration patterns shown for high-immigration states are generally apparent for both the late 1980s and early 1990s. In most cases, there is a higher rate of net out-migration for persons with "less select" demographic attributes—those with less than a college education and those with incomes below poverty. Also, consistent with findings from the earlier period, selectivity is more pronounced for the white populations of these states than for the overall populations. (Sample sizes preclude our conducting analyses specific to blacks or providing overall measures for Hispanics and Asians.)

The rates shown for the state of New Jersey provide an example. Here, persons in poverty are most apt to leave the state. For example, in the early 1990s, New Jersey's poverty population showed a net out-migration of –8.3 percent versus only –2.6 percent for the nonpoverty population. Similar results were obtained when comparing the migration of persons with only high school educations or less than high school educations with those who are college graduates (e.g., white persons with less than high school educations left New Jersey at a rate of –3.3 percent over the early 1990s compared with less than a 1 percent net out-movement among college graduates).

It is useful to compare the selectivity patterns of California with those of Texas because, as mentioned above, these states underwent somewhat divergent economic circumstances between the late 1980s and early 1990s. That is, during the first period, California's economy was still relatively robust, while Texas was undergoing severe employment declines—conditions which reversed for the early 1990s. Nonetheless, over both periods, each state's migrant selectivity patterns displayed an accentuated net out-migration for their poverty populations and either accentuated net out-migration or reduced net in-migration for persons with less education. (A more extensive analysis of this phenomenon for California can be found in Johnson and Lovelady, 1995.) Indeed, during the "good" periods for each state (1985-1990 in California and 1990-1994 in Texas) college graduates and nonpoverty persons were moving in while poverty persons were moving out. This is consistent with the view that the poverty and unskilled segments of the population may be less responsive to the current cyclical conditions of the overall economy than they are to the labor competition and other out-migration-inducing pressures of immigrants to these states (Frey, 1995a).

The general pattern of net out-migration shown in Table 10-5 is unlike the "circulation of elites" characterization that is typically applied to interstate or intermetropolitan migration (Frey, 1979, 1995b). Usually, states that are losing migrants because they are undergoing economic downturns lose them disproportionately among their college graduate or more well-off segments of the younger population. In a like manner, states that are gaining internal migrants gain them disproportionately from these groups. The unique pattern of selective out-migration shown for most of these states during both the late 1980s and early 1990s is consistent with explanations discussed above that link immigration to domestic out-migration.

IMPACT ANALYSIS OF SELECTIVE OUT-MIGRATION

Although the previous descriptive statistics along with earlier analytic studies show a statistical relationship between immigration and the selective net out-migration of less-skilled native-born residents, no previous research has esti-

TABLE 10-5   Net Internal Migration Rates for Selected Social and Demographic
Categories, 1985-1990 and 1990-1994 High-Immigration States

| | NET INTERNAL MIGRATION RATES | | | |
| | CALIFORNIA | | NEW YORK | |
Categories	1985-90	1990-94	1985-90	1990-94
RACE				
Total	0.7	−2.3	−4.8	−5.0
Whites*	0.7	−4.2	−4.4	−4.1
Blacks	1.1	4.6	−5.7	−7.8
EDUCATION**				
Less than HS	−0.8	−2.1	−3.7	−6.7
HS Grad	−1.0	−4.5	−4.5	−3.8
College Grad	3.4	−2.3	−5.9	−3.7
POVERTY STATUS				
Poverty	−1.7	−1.5	−4.7	−6.8
NonPoverty	0.8	−2.5	−4.8	−4.7
WHITES-EDUCATION**				
Less than HS	−1.9	−3.9	−3.4	−5.4
HS Grad	−1.4	−7.2	−4.2	−2.9
College Grad	3.5	−3.0	−5.7	−3.8
WHITES-POVERTY STATUS				
Poverty	−4.0	−6.0	−4.2	−8.0
NonPoverty	0.8	−4.0	−4.4	−3.7

SOURCE: Compiled by author from Special 1990 US Census migration tabulations (1985-90), and
from single year migration tabulations (1990-91, 1991-92, 1992-92, 1993-94 US Census Bureau
Current Population Surveys.

mated the impact of immigration in terms of the numbers of domestic migrants
that are affected by this relationship. In this section, we present the results of
such an impact analysis for states (48 contiguous states and the District of Columbia). Because the most recent detailed data, available for such an analysis,
are based on the 1990 Census for migration over the 1985-1990 period (based on
the "residence 5-years ago" census question), we focus on this period. Our
analysis is restricted to examining the impact of different immigration levels on
the domestic migration for persons with a high school education and less and who
were aged 25-64 at the end of the migration period (in 1990). The focus on this
education attainment group is consistent with earlier research indicating that the
unique selective out-migration response to immigration is largely confined to this
group. The focus on the age group 25-64 is for persons of labor force age who,
for the most part, have completed their formal educations.

| TEXAS | | ILLINOIS | | NEW JERSEY | | MASSACHUSETTS | |
1985-90	1990-94	1985-90	1990-94	1985-90	1990-94	1985-90	1990-94
-2.1	0.9	-3.2	-0.3	-2.7	-3.2	-1.7	-2.2
-2.6	1.3	-3.1	0.1	-3.4	-3.1	-2.3	-1.9
0.5	-1.6	-3.8	0.6	-1.1	-3.8	1.0	3.4
-1.9	0.5	-2.5	-0.3	-2.1	-4.6	-1.7	-3.7
-2.6	1.8	-2.7	-0.1	-2.6	-1.7	-2.8	-1.1
-1.8	3.3	-2.6	-1.8	0.8	-0.6	-2.1	-1.7
-2.3	-2.1	-5.2	1.5	-10.1	-8.3	-0.4	-3.3
-2.1	1.5	-2.6	-0.6	-1.5	-2.6	-2.2	-2.0
-2.6	0.5	-2.5	-0.2	-2.4	-3.3	-2.4	-2.7
-3.3	2.5	-2.6	-0.8	-3.0	-2.4	-3.0	-0.9
-1.8	2.9	-2.4	-1.3	-0.3	-0.6	-2.2	-1.7
-4.8	-0.7	-5.2	-1.5	-15.4	-8.1	-3.3	-4.1
-2.4	1.5	-2.6	0.2	-2.1	-2.8	-2.5	-1.7

*   Non-Latino Whites
** Ages 25 and above

In examining the impact of immigration on domestic migration, we focus on the changing levels of immigrants who are also less skilled (high school education or less). This focus is consistent with the thesis that immigrants represent labor substitutes for domestic migrants with similar skill levels—an often-held explanation for the observed negative impact between immigration and domestic migration. As such, our impact analyses will address two questions:

(1) How would a 50 percent increase or a 50 percent decrease in current immigration of less-skilled labor-force-aged immigrants affect domestic migration patterns of less-skilled native-born Americans?

(2) How would a similar increase or decrease in less-skilled *immigrants to California only* affect domestic migration patterns between California and other states?

The answer to the first question would indicate the impacts of policies that would change the overall levels of immigration (proportionately across skill levels, *or* those that would change the preference system in a way that would alter the numbers of less-skilled immigrants). The answers to the second question are relevant to research findings that show that the domestic out-migration from California among less-skilled and poverty residents disproportionately relocates them to the nearby states of Washington, Oregon, Nevada, and Arizona (Frey, 1995a). From the perspective of those states, domestic in-migration from California accounts for a large share of their overall in-migrating populations who have a high school education or less and incomes below poverty. This impact analysis will be able to assess the magnitude of California's domestic migration exchanges with these states which are affected by California's immigration levels.

Methodological Approach

Methodological details for both components of this impact analysis are specified in Appendices A and B, respectively. Our approach can be summarized in terms of two separate components. The first involves estimating the effects of low-skilled immigration on the migration process for native-born interstate migrants using the nested logit model that permits a separate estimation of residents' departures and migrants' destination choices as part of the overall migration stream process. This specific technique is one that has been developed by Liaw and his associates to examine migration processes in a number of contexts (Liaw and Ledent, 1987; Liaw, 1990; Liaw and Otomo, 1991; Liaw and Frey, 1996). This analysis evaluates the effects on a state's domestic migration of low-skilled immigration to the state compared with other well-known migration determinants associated with the state's labor force, social and environmental amenities, and geographic contiguity.

The second component of the impact analysis uses the results of the nested logit model to generate estimated changes in migration rates, associated with assumed alternative low-skilled immigration levels, and applying these rates to appropriate populations at risk to generate various alternative interstate domestic migration outcomes that would be consistent with the assumed alternative immigration levels. Both components of this methodology are first estimated in separate age-disaggregated analyses for the broad age groups 25-29, 30-44, and 45-64 because these different age groups are subject to somewhat different mixes of migration determinants. The results of these age-specific impact analyses are then aggregated to produce results for the entire 25- to 64-year-old age group for our population of interest (i.e., native-born residents with a high school education or less).

Because the results of the nested logit model provide the basis for estimating the effect of low-skilled immigration on the domestic migration process, we summarize the results of these models here. (Relevant equations for the departure rates submodel can be found in appendix tables 10-A1, 10-A2, and 10-A3 for the age groups 25-29, 30-44, and 45-64, respectively. The results for the destination choice submodel appear in appendix tables 10-A4, 10-A5, and 10-A6, for these respective age groups.) We note that our estimate of low-skilled immigration included in these models is based on 1985-1990 immigrants reported in the 1990 census, and, therefore, is likely to understate, to some degree, the number of illegal immigrants in this group.[4] Common state attribute variables that are included in both submodels are the low-skilled immigration rate, labor market variables (per capita income, unemployment rate, civilian employment growth, service employment growth), state AFDC and food stamp benefits, a racial similarity measure (specific to whites, blacks, Asians, American Indians, and Hispanics), measures of extreme hot or cold climate, and the state's violent crime rate. (State variations in the cost of living, incorporating state variations in housing costs, are used to adjust the per capita income measure.) In addition to these, the destination choice model includes measures of distance and contiguity between origin and potential destination states. (Definitions of all variables are listed in Appendix A.)

Within each age-specific (25-29, 30-44, 45-64) analysis, it is possible to interact the above state-level attributes with personal attributes including detailed age (five-year age groups), race (white, black, Asian, American Indian, Hispanic), education attainment (below high school, high school graduate), poverty status (below poverty, above poverty), and gender (male, female). This is because our analysis makes use of a detailed migration matrix that disaggregates 1985-1990 interstate moves by a cross classification of the demographic variables just described. This matrix was drawn from a special tabulation of the full "long form" 16.7 percent sample of the 1990 U.S. census and weighted up to approximate the total population. In estimating the final departure and destination choice models presented in Appendix A tables, a series of preliminary analyses were conducted to identify statistically significant interactions between state

---

[4] The measure of immigration used in this analysis identified all 1990 state residents with at most a high school education who reported a residence abroad in 1985. Although it would be preferable to employ a net immigration estimate (comparable to the net internal migration estimate), neither the U.S. Census nor any other U.S. statistical agency collects reliable estimates of emigrants from the United States. This use of the census "residence abroad" question is also consistent with previous research. However, we note that this estimate does not necessarily overstate total net immigration to the United States, despite its omission of the emigration component. This is because migration from abroad, as reported in the census, substantially understates the illegal immigrant population.

It is estimated that, during a given year, there is an emigration of between 150,000 and 200,000 residents (of all education levels). However, it is also estimated that there is a net annual immigration of 300,000 illegal immigrants, many of whom are not counted by the census (Martin and Midgley, 1994). Thus, the figures we use tend to overstate legal immigration but understate illegal immigration for the 1985-1990 period. Because the latter is likely to be disproportionately comprised of those with lower education levels, our estimates of low-skilled immigration are understated.

area attributes and personal characteristics that were consistent with reasonable expectations about migration behavior.

Most of the effects in the final age-disaggregated nested logit models were consistent with expectations and can be found in Appendix A tables. Our main interest is in the impact of the low-skilled immigration rate on the departure rates of residents, destination choices of migrants, and interactions with personal characteristics, when other relevant attributes are controlled. The low-skilled foreign immigration rate is defined on the basis of working-aged (15- to 64-year-old) immigrants with high school educations or less[5] divided by the corresponding beginning-of-period state population. Our analysis indicates that the primary impact of low-skilled immigration on native-born migration operates through the departure from high-immigration states, rather than as a reduced tendency to choose such states as destinations. This is because the contribution to total explanation, associated with low-skilled immigration, is much stronger in the departure models than it is in the destination choice models. In fact, low-skilled immigration has an almost similar effect in the departure models as do the combined effects of the labor market variables. Its contribution to explanation is stronger than the combined labor market variables for persons in the 45-64 age group, suggesting that many of these pre-retirees are influenced as much by factors associated with states with high immigration levels as by standard income, unemployment rate, and employment growth attributes.

Equally noteworthy as the strong impact that low-skilled immigration exerts on the departure of low-skilled domestic residents is its interaction with specific subgroups. Strong interactions are shown for whites and especially whites below the poverty line. This is consistent with descriptive analyses that indicate, when controlled for education, that poverty residents are most likely to leave high-immigration states (Frey, 1995c; Frey et al., 1996). Other significant interactions with low-skilled immigration are shown for blacks, poor blacks, and poor Hispanics (see appendix tables 10-A1, 10-A2, and 10-A3).

Although low-skilled immigration is not an important explanatory factor in the destination choices of migrants, it is noteworthy that the racial similarity of a destination state shows as much explanatory power as the conventional labor market variables (see appendix tables 10-A4, 10-A5, and 10-A6). This is especially the case for blacks, Hispanics, and Asians as well as Hispanics with less than a high school education and consistent with earlier observations that longer-term residents and native-born members of the new immigrant minority groups are likely to locate in areas with large numbers of same-nationality residents.

---

[5] In assessing alternative immigration levels for impact analysis, we have chosen to focus on the age groups 15-64 because alternative immigration policies are likely to affect the entire labor- force-aged population. Hence, although the focus of our domestic migration impact estimations are persons aged 25-64 (for reasons discussed in the text), we assume that their migration patterns will be affected by changes in low-skilled immigrant levels at all labor force ages.

In sum, the nested logit model analyses confirm the results of earlier research, indicating that states with high levels of immigration of persons who might be labor substitutes for resident workers will show an accentuated out-migration of lower-skilled native residents when other state attributes are controlled. This effect operates more strongly through the departure part of the migration process than through the destination choice. Our results also confirm earlier findings suggesting that the effect is most prominent among lower-income native-born residents of these high-immigration states. The results of these models are incorporated into the impact analysis discussed in Appendix B.

Impact of Nationwide Immigration Changes

Our first set of impact analyses makes two alternative assumptions. The first assumption is that the observed level of immigration for working-aged immigrants with at most a high school education is decreased by 957,000 over the 1985-1990 period. The second assumption is that the current level is increased by a similar amount over the 1985-1990 period. These numbers approximate 50 percent increases, or 50 percent decreases, of such immigration compared with the observed levels in the census. These increases and decreases occur proportionately to each state with respect to their actual immigration levels. (For convenience, we refer to these assumptions as 50 percent increases in immigration and 50 percent decreases in immigration.) The analyses below present the estimated impacts that these assumptions imply for net domestic migration of states' native-born residents, aged 25-64, with high school educations or less.

The results of these scenarios for each state are shown in Table 10-6. These data make plain that when immigration is decreased, it is the high-immigration states that tend to retain more of their native-born domestic low-skilled migrants who might otherwise have relocated to a low-immigration state. Similarly, when immigration is increased, high-immigration states are the most prone to lose domestic native-born low-skilled migrants to other states. This is depicted in Map 10-2 which shows the estimated change in net domestic migration for states on the assumption that there is a 50 percent increase in U.S. immigration levels. Under this scenario, only ten states (including the District of Columbia) would show increased net domestic out-migration or (in the case of Florida) reduced net domestic in-migration with at most a high school education. These changes would accrue to California (−189,312), New York (−61,671), Florida (−20,313), Texas (−19,702), and Illinois (−15,810). The states gaining most from these net domestic migration shifts would be Arizona (36,863), Georgia (22,950), Pennsylvania (22,768), and Nevada (22,764). Clearly, the states surrounding California, and those in the South Atlantic region—presumably attracting migrants from New York, New Jersey, Massachusetts, Illinois, and Florida—would gain larger numbers of less-skilled domestic migrants under this scenario of higher immigration.

TABLE 10-6 Estimated 1985-1990 Net Domestic Migration Assuming a 50 percent Increase or Decrease in U.S. Immigration Levels, Ages 25-64 with High School or Less Education

| State | Scenario I: Assuming Decrease in Immigration | | | Scenario II: Assuming Increase in Immigration | | |
| | Expected Net Migration | | | Expected Net Migration | | |
	Before Change	After Change	Impact	Before Change	After Change	Impact
ALABAMA	27,927	17,250	-10,677	27,927	42,510	14,583
ARIZONA	69,662	48,444	-21,218	69,662	106,525	36,863
ARKANSAS	20,104	13,799	-6,305	20,104	28,731	8,627
CALIFORNIA	-59,914	44,654	104,568	-59,914	-249,226	-189,312
COLORADO	-72,935	-69,459	3,476	-72,935	-75,805	-2,870
CONNECTICUT	7,560	5,210	-2,350	7,560	11,598	4,038
DELAWARE	19,780	16,168	-3,612	19,780	24,566	4,786
DC	-8,304	-6,100	2,204	-8,304	-10,822	-2,518
FLORIDA	135,673	151,330	15,657	135,673	115,360	-20,313
GEORGIA	79,338	63,248	-16,090	79,338	102,288	22,950
IDAHO	-14,596	-14,421	175	-14,596	-14,140	456
ILLINOIS	-68,465	-54,242	14,223	-68,465	-84,275	-15,810
INDIANA	6,115	-1,430	-7,545	6,115	16,411	10,296
IOWA	11,400	7,106	-4,294	11,400	17,418	6,018
KANSAS	-1,444	-3,696	-2,252	-1,444	2,330	3,774
KENTUCKY	16,897	9,459	-7,438	16,897	27,028	10,131
LOUISIANA	-56,689	-60,181	-3,492	-56,689	-51,239	5,450
MAINE	9,816	6,785	-3,031	9,816	14,033	4,217
MARYLAND	21,312	18,265	-3,047	21,312	26,544	5,232
MASSACHUSETTS	-6,745	-3,471	3,274	-6,745	-10,019	-3,274
MICHIGAN	-25,574	-29,914	-4,340	-25,574	-18,943	6,631

MINNESOTA	-18,220	-19,333	-1,113	-18,220	-15,969	2,251
MISSISSIPPI	10,482	5,413	-5,069	10,482	17,400	6,918
MISSOURI	-3,843	-10,081	-6,238	-3,843	4,952	8,795
MONTANA	-16,879	-17,110	-231	-16,879	-16,356	523
NEBRASKA	-5,774	-7,362	-1,588	-5,774	-3,359	2,415
NEVADA	38,133	25,486	-12,647	38,133	60,897	22,764
N. HAMPSHIRE	22,528	17,546	-4,982	22,528	29,293	6,765
NEW JERSEY	-9,977	-3,671	6,306	-9,977	-16,746	-6,769
NEW MEXICO	-14,011	-14,542	-531	-14,011	-12,820	1,191
NEW YORK	-91,374	-48,050	43,324	-91,374	-153,045	-61,671
N. CAROLINA	59,163	45,906	-13,257	59,163	77,229	18,066
N. DAKOTA	-13,791	-13,861	-70	-13,791	-13,575	216
OHIO	-30,077	-37,725	-7,648	-30,077	-18,985	11,092
OKLAHOMA	-52,622	-54,210	-1,588	-52,622	-49,620	3,002
OREGON	22,392	13,203	-9,189	22,392	38,013	15,621
PENN	19,278	3,441	-15,837	19,278	42,046	22,768
RHODE ISLAND	2,605	2,903	298	2,605	2,411	-194
S. CAROLINA	37,368	28,100	-9,268	37,368	50,030	12,662
S. DAKOTA	-8,109	-8,623	-514	-8,109	-7,318	791
TENNESSEE	36,746	26,776	-9,970	36,746	50,429	13,683
TEXAS	-92,168	-73,001	19,167	-92,168	-111,870	-19,702
UTAH	1,544	-1,045	-2,589	1,544	5,753	4,209
VERMONT	7,791	5,205	-2,586	7,791	11,348	3,557
VIRGINIA	11,275	9,889	-1,386	11,275	15,373	4,098
WASHINGTON	6,233	3,511	-2,722	6,233	11,983	5,750
W. VIRGINIA	-4,812	-9,072	-4,260	-4,812	829	5,641
WISCONSIN	-4,038	-7,801	-3,763	-4,038	1,469	5,507
WYOMING	-20,758	-20,697	61	-20,758	-20,665	93

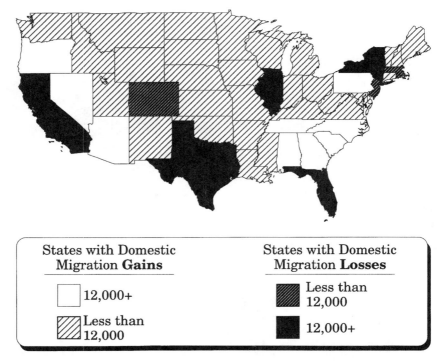

States with Domestic Migration **Gains**	States with Domestic Migration **Losses**
☐ 12,000+	▨ Less than 12,000
▨ Less than 12,000	■ 12,000+

MAP 10-2 Estimated five-year change in net domestic migration for states assuming 50 percent increase in U.S. immigration levels (ages 25-64 with high school or less education).

Figure 10-4 shows how the two different assumptions about immigration would impact the net domestic migration for four high-immigration states: California, New York, Texas, and Illinois. California would show the greatest disparities in the net domestic migration of their less-educated population. Given the observed level of immigration over the 1985-1990 period, California shows an expected domestic out-migration of 59,914 low-skilled residents. However, if immigration were reduced by 50 percent, the state would show a gain of 44,654 low-skilled persons, while under a 50 percent increase immigration scenario, it would lose 249,226 such persons. The other three states show net domestic out-migration under each scenario with New York showing the widest fluctuation of these three.

Another way to assess the impact of these different immigration scenarios is to examine how many low-skilled domestic migrants a state would gain for every 100 low-skilled immigrants who did not come in (under a reduced immigration scenario); or to estimate how many low-skilled domestic migrants it would lose

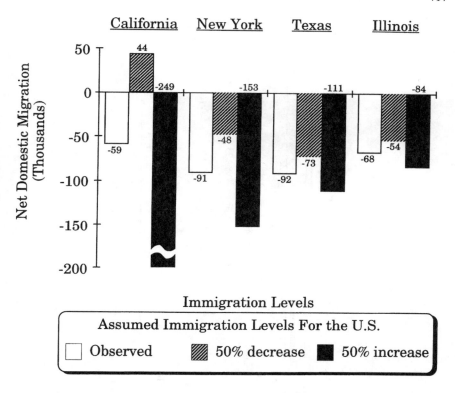

FIGURE 10-4 Estimated 1985-1990 net domestic migration for states assuming a 50 percent decrease/increase in U.S. immigration levels (ages 25-64 with high school or less education).

for every 100 additional low-skilled immigrants arriving (under an increased immigration scenario). These figures are shown for states with greatest immigration in Table 10-7, where the changes are calculated on the basis of immigrants and domestic migrants aged 15-64. Results show that there are not similar levels of exchange under both the decreased immigration and the increased immigration scenarios. For example, under a decreased immigration scenario, California would gain 27 low-skilled domestic migrants for every 100 such immigrants who did not come into the state. Yet under an increased immigration scenario, California would lose 51 low-skilled domestic migrants for every 100 additional such immigrants that came into the state. Migrant exchanges under the increased immigration scenario are the most dramatic: The exchange of low-skilled immigrants for low-skilled domestic migrants is 2 to 1 in California. It is just as strong in New York and Illinois, and about 5 to 2 in Texas.

TABLE 10-7 Estimated 1985-1990 Change in State's Net Domestic Migration per 100 Changes in its Immigration Levels,* Ages 15-64 with High School or Less Education

	Scenario I: Assuming 50 Percent Decrease in Immigration			Scenario II: Assuming 50 Percent Increase in Immigration		
	Change in Immigration	Change in Net Domestic Migration	Domestic Increases Per 100 Immigrant Decreases	Change in Immigration	Change in Net Domestic Migration	Domestic Decreases Per 100 Immigrant Increases
CALIFORNIA	-369,882	100,970	27	369,882	-188,123	-51
NEW YORK	-133,012	53,150	40	133,012	-74,508	-56
FLORIDA	-74,444	8,820	12	74,444	-12,279	-16
TEXAS	-67,956	24,774	36	67,956	-26,419	-39
NEW JERSEY	-41,096	4,447	11	41,096	-4,505	-11
ILLINOIS	-41,007	20,735	51	41,007	-23,445	-57
MASSACHUSETTS	-28,312	4,067	14	28,312	-4,266	-15

SOURCE: Liaw, Lin and Frey, 1996

*Changes in both Immigration and Net Domestic Migration pertain to persons ages 15-64 with High School or less education.

Because our impact analysis permitted a disaggregation by race-ethnicity, poverty status, and detailed age, it is possible to examine the impact of immigration changes for different demographic groups of a state's population. Figure 10-5 presents an analysis for California, based on our simulation, that shows the domestic net migration rates specific to different groups under the assumptions (a) that actual immigration levels occurred over the 1985-1990 period, and (b) that a 50 percent reduction in immigration took place over the 1985-1990 period. As in the above analysis, these results pertain to persons with a high school or less education and also are restricted to the ages 25-64. The results show that under the conditions of actual immigration levels, rates of net out-migration are somewhat higher for low-skilled whites than for the low-skilled population overall. The out-migration rates are substantially larger among the low-skilled poverty population, and especially the white low-skilled poverty population.

When a 50 percent reduction in national immigration levels is assumed, these patterns change noticeably. Under the latter scenario, the net migration

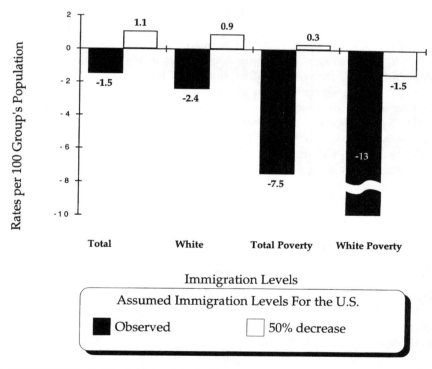

FIGURE 10-5 California, impact on groups, estimated 1985-1990 net domestic migration rates assuming actual/50 percent decrease in U.S. immigration levels (ages 25-64 with high school or less education).

rates for three of the four low-skilled groups shown (total, whites, total poverty) change from negative to positive. However, the most dramatic changes occur with the two poverty groups. The rate for the total low-skilled poverty population changes from –7.5 (when actual immigration is assumed) to 0.3 (when a 50 percent reduction in immigration is assumed). Even more significantly, the rate for the white low-skilled poverty population changes from –13 to –1.5. These results indicate that the impact of immigration on the net domestic out-migration of California's low-skilled population is somewhat more accentuated among whites but that it is especially important in accounting for the net out-migration of the low-skilled poverty population. These results also hold up when the analysis is confined to specific age groups so that they do not reflect patterns of only the younger or older populations within the state. Moreover, similar simulations with other high- immigration states show that, as with California, immigration disproportionately affects their low-skilled white and poverty populations (see Liaw et al., 1996).

These impact analyses have shown that reduced or increased levels of low-skilled immigration show considerable effects on the redistribution of less-skilled domestic migrants for high-immigration states. The fact that, under an increased immigration scenario, 100 new low-skilled immigrants to California will precipitate a net out-migration of 51 low-skilled native migrants from California suggests that there is a substantial demographic displacement occurring in this high-immigration state. Another important finding of this analysis is the "spillover effects" that changing immigration levels impose indirectly on low-immigration states as a result of increased or decreased domestic migration out of high-immigration states. Under the scenario of a 50 percent increase in immigration nationwide, 39 states would register increased net domestic migration gains on low-skilled native-born residents. Alternatively, most of these states would lose low-skilled domestic migrants to the high-immigration states under a scenario of a 50 percent reduction in immigration to the United States.

Impact of California Immigration Changes

Following this discussion of "spillover effects" of immigration, we now focus on an impact analysis that assumes that only California experiences a 50 percent decrease or 50 percent increase in its low-skilled immigration levels. The purpose of this, as indicated above, is to assess the indirect impacts of these changes on California's domestic migration exchanges with nearby states: Washington, Oregon, Nevada, and Arizona. From a numeric standpoint, we are assuming under a "decreased immigration scenario" that California's 1985-1990 immigration of low-skilled labor-force-aged persons is reduced by 400,000. Similarly, under the "increased immigration" scenario, we assume that an additional 400,000 such immigrants move into the state. The "spillover" impact of these assumed reductions and increases in California's immigration can be seen in Figure 10-6.

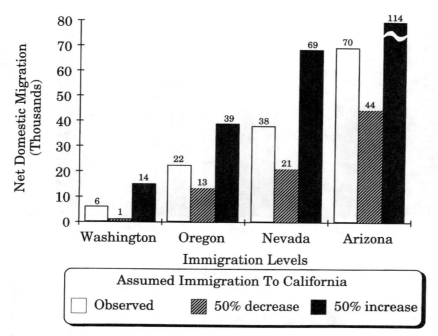

FIGURE 10-6 Estimated 1985-1990 net domestic migration for states assuming a 50 percent decrease/increase in California immigration levels (ages 25-64 with high school or less education).

Shown here are the net domestic gains of low-skilled native-born migrants for the States of Washington, Oregon, Nevada, and Arizona under three different California immigration scenarios. It is clear from these statistics that Arizona and Nevada show the greatest changes as a result of these different scenarios. If immigration to California were reduced by 50 percent, Arizona's net domestic gains of 69,662 low-skilled migrants would become reduced to 44,317. If California's immigration level were to increase by 50 percent, Nevada's net domestic gains of low-skilled migrants would be raised from 38,133 to 68,524. Smaller, but similar, fluctuations are observed for Oregon and Washington.

The "spillover effects" of immigration to California on surrounding states are selective on different demographic groups within the low-skilled populations just discussed. To illustrate this, we present results from our simulations for Nevada and Arizona that compare their net domestic migration patterns under the conditions in which (a) California received its actual immigration levels over the 1985-1990 period, and (b) California's immigration levels were reduced by 50 percent over the 1985-1990 period. The comparison for Nevada is shown in Figure 10-7 and indicates that when California's immigration levels are not re-

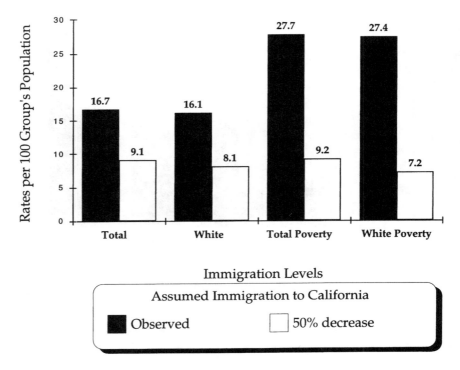

FIGURE 10-7 Nevada, impact on groups, estimated 1985-1990 net domestic migration rates assuming actual/50 percent decrease in California immigration levels (ages 25-64 with high school or less education).

duced, Nevada's net domestic in-migration rates are substantially higher for its low-skilled poverty populations than for its low-skilled nonpoverty populations. However, when California's immigration is reduced, it has the spillover effect of reducing, disproportionately, domestic net migration of the low-skilled poverty population to Nevada. The latter scenario has the effect of reducing Nevada's domestic migration gains for all of the groups shown in Figure 10-7, but the impact is especially large on Nevada's poverty population.

A similar impact is also shown for Arizona in Figure 10-8. Here, a reduction in California's immigration levels has a disproportionate effect on Arizona's net domestic migration levels for both its poverty population and its white poverty population. Under the assumption of actual immigration to California, Arizona's low-skilled domestic migration gains are somewhat higher for whites than overall, but are substantially higher for low-skilled whites in poverty. Under the assumption of reduced immigration to California, Arizona's low-skilled poverty migration rates are dramatically lowered, such that for poor whites, the domestic

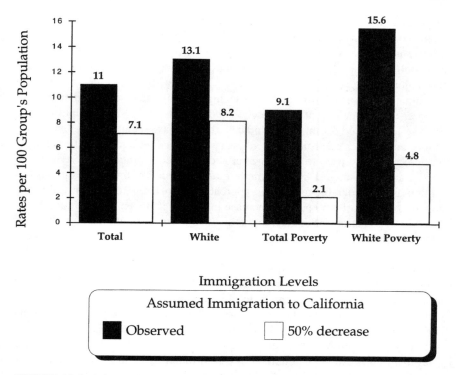

FIGURE 10-8 Arizona, impact on groups, estimated 1985-1990 net domestic migration rates assuming actual/50 percent decrease in California immigration level (ages 25-64 with high school or less education).

migration rate of 15.6 (actual immigration to California) is reduced to 4.8 (assuming the 50 percent reduction of immigration to California). These results for Nevada and Arizona indicate that the spillover effects of immigration to California disproportionately impact on the low-skilled poverty populations in these neighboring states.

IMPLICATIONS

This overview of the impact of recent immigration on population redistribution within the United States has shown that there is a continued concentration of immigrants to selected port-of-entry states and metropolitan areas at the same time the redistribution of internal migrants is more dispersed. Our own studies and those of others suggest that the concentration of immigrants is, in part, a function of their proclivity to locate in areas where there are existing concentrations of persons with like race-ethnic backgrounds and nationalities, and that these tendencies are most pronounced among immigrants with high school educations or less. In contrast, the internal migration processes, at work over the late 1980s and early 1990s, are more responsive to conventional labor market "pushes" and "pulls" and are drawn to state and metropolitan area destinations that are not the major immigrant port-of-entry areas. However, there is clear evidence of accentuated domestic out-migration from high-immigration states and metropolitan areas for persons with high school educations or less. The multivariate analyses conducted for this study indicate that this is associated with low-skilled immigration, after controlling for relevant labor market and amenity variables that are generally used to explain interlabor market migration. Moreover, our impact analyses suggest that the immigration impacts on this domestic out-migration are considerable and would approach a 2-to-1 relationship in California under a scenario of a 50 percent increase in the state's recent immigration level.

The explanation for this demographic displacement may well lie with arguments that immigrants represent labor substitutes for domestic migrants who can take advantage of opportunities in other areas, However, our results are also consistent with other explanations as well. For example, less well-off, longer-term residents in high-immigration areas may be reacting to perceived increases in social costs that may take the form of higher crime rates, reduced services, or increased local taxes that they may take to be a function of recent immigrant flows. In addition, one cannot ignore the possibility that race and ethnic prejudice may enter into decisions of native residents, especially whites, to relocate away from increasingly multiethnic areas in much the same manner that such prejudice prompted "suburban flight" in many American cities in the 1950s and 1960s.

Moreover, our findings suggest broader implications for changes in the social demography of high-immigration areas if recent immigration and internal migration patterns persist. For example, it has been argued that port-of-entry metro areas are taking on a "dual economy" character where large numbers of immigrants, participating in lower-skilled and informal sectors of the labor force, provide complementary activities for more advanced services and corporate headquarters activities among the mostly white-native professional ranks (Mollenkopf and Castells, 1991; Sassen, 1996; Waldinger, 1996). The demographic implications of this scenario become apparent when examining the foreign-born shares and minority shares of different socioeconomic attributes in high-immigration metros (Table 10-8).

For these metropolitan areas, the 1995 foreign-born population comprises a disproportionate share of persons without high school diplomas, in the lower quartile of family income, and of workers in service and unskilled blue collar occupations. The imbalance is even more pronounced in the Los Angeles metropolitan area where, for example, foreign-born residents comprise three-fifths of all persons whose family incomes fall in the bottom quartile, while representing only 23 percent of those in the upper quartile. Over half of service and unskilled blue collar jobs in Los Angeles are taken by foreign-born persons, who account for no more than one-fifth of the managerial and professional jobs.

The divergence in the nativity-class structure for the combined high-immigration metro areas and individual areas, such as Los Angeles and New York, contrasts markedly with the rest of the United States—where the foreign born comprise only 6 percent of persons aged 18 and above and disparities by socioeconomic measures are not nearly as skewed. More contrasts can be made with respect to the minority composition of high-immigration metros and the rest of the United States (Table 10-8, right panel) and on other demographic attributes typically associated with the foreign-born population. The statistics for 1995 point up already sharp disparities with respect to the class-nativity and class-race-ethnic structures between the metropolitan regions that serve as ports of entry and other parts of the United States.

The findings in this chapter suggest that there is a continued concentration of immigration associated with race-ethnicity, country-of-origin groups, and those with high school educations or less that is occurring at the same time that internal migration is redistributing longer-term, native-born migrants to different metropolitan areas and to smaller communities as well as nonmetropolitan territory. The latter movement is, to a large degree, a function of more traditional labor market pushes and pulls, as well as amenities, that are not centered in the same port-of-entry areas in which immigrants are concentrating. However, a significant part of the native-born movement away from high-immigration metropolitan areas, among residents with a high school education or less, has been shown to be related to the levels of recent immigration in those areas when other factors are controlled. Thus, immigration would appear to exert both direct and indirect impacts on redistribution within the United States as a result of its concentration in selected areas and its secondary impact on net domestic out-migration from those areas. To the extent that it is the lower-skilled immigrants (with at most a high school education) who are most associated with both patterns, our results suggest that immigration policies that would select more highly educated immigrants might serve to alleviate immigrant concentration as well as the selective demographic displacement of the native born by immigrants that has been observed over the 1985-1995 period.

Beyond the immediate implications that these concentration and selective displacement patterns hold for local economies and the employment options for less-skilled native-born workers, our findings also suggest that there are broader implications associated with the changing social demographics of high-immigration areas and with the likely widening demographic disparities between areas of high immigration and other parts of the country. More bifurcated race-class labor force structures, the changing demographic profiles of child poverty populations, and widening race-ethnic disparities across state populations are just a few of the social demographic consequences that can result from a con-

TABLE 10-8 1995 Demographic Profiles by Native-Born and Minority Status: Los Angeles CMSA, New York CMSA, the 10 High-Immigration Metro Areas (combined), and Rest of the U.S. Population

	PERCENT FOREIGN BORN-1995				PERCENT MINORITIES*—1995			
	LA Metro	NY Metro	High Immig. Metros	Rest of U.S.	LA Metro	NY Metro	High Immig. Metros	Rest of U.S.
Education**								
College Graduate	21	20	20	8	23	17	19	11
Some College	25	23	21	5	33	26	28	13
High School Graduate	21	24	18	4	41	36	36	18
Less Than High School	56	38	38	7	71	49	56	23
Family Income#								
Top 25%	23	15	17	5	34	20	34	10
Second 25%	34	29	25	4	51	35	51	14
Third 25%	47	34	34	6	63	42	63	19
Bottom 25%	61	47	45	9	75	56	75	31
Age								
Age 18-24	44	23	27	6	71	44	54	24
Age 25-34	46	29	30	7	63	44	48	22
Age 35-44	38	30	28	6	52	36	40	19
Age 45-64	33	30	26	6	42	33	35	15
Age 65+	24	25	22	5	29	18	23	12

Occupations-Men# #							
Mgr & Prof.	19	20	17	5	27	18	21	10
Clerical & Sales	31	23	22	4	47	32	36	14
Service	55	36	40	7	72	51	59	27
Prec. Prod.	48	30	30	5	57	30	40	14
Blue Collar	58	41	40	7	76	52	60	23
Occupations-Women# #							
Mgr & Prof.	20	18	16	4	32	24	26	12
Clerical & Sales	22	17	17	3	44	33	36	16
Service	51	41	38	6	74	56	58	26
Prec. Prod.	52	65	41	6	74	43	54	21
Blue Collar	71	66	53	8	78	62	64	26
Total Ages 18+	38	28	27	6	51	35	40	18

SOURCE: Compiled by author from US Census Bureau 1995 Current Population Survey data (Note: Area definitions for these metro areas are consistent with OMB June, 1990 standards)

*Population not identified as Non-Latino White   # Persons ages 18 and above

**Ages 25-64   # # Ages 16 and above

tinuation of current immigration and internal migration dynamics (Frey, 1997a, 1997b; Frey and Liaw, 1998). The emerging social demographic patterns hold important implications for the nation's social and political geography and deserve further examination and study as consequences of current immigration policies.

APPENDIX A

THE NESTED LOGIT MODEL OF INTERSTATE MIGRATION: METHODOLOGY AND FINDINGS

A two-level nested logit model of interstate migration is applied in this study to the 1985-1990 interstate migration data to assess the effects of low-skilled immigration on U.S.-born Americans with, at most, high school education. The estimated results of this model are an integral part of the impact analysis that is discussed in further detail in Appendix B and in the relevant section of the text. A useful feature of the nested logit model as applied to the current problem is its ability to identify separately the determinants of residents' departure from a state and those of migrants' destination choices. The first section below discusses the general methodology of this model. The second section presents the variables that are used to construct the model. The final section consists of Tables 10-A1 through 10-A6 that present the estimated coefficients for the departure submodel and destination choice submodel, respectively, for the specific age groups 25-29, 30-44, 45-64 as background for the discussion of this model's results in the text. These models are termed the "best models" because, on the basis of extensive preliminary analyses, they represent those in which variables retain sensible and statistically significant coefficients.

Nested Logit Model Methodology

The formulation of the two-level logit model is as follows. For a potential migrant with demographic attributes s and residing in state i, the migration behavior depends on (1) a departure probability $p[i,s]$ at the upper level, and (2) a set of destination choice probabilities, $p[j|i,s]$ for all j not equal to i, at the lower level.[6] Based on a set of reasonable assumptions, these probabilities then become functions of observable explanatory variables in the following two submodels (Kanaraglou et al., 1996).

---

[6] The demographic attributes include detailed age (25-29, 30-34, ..., 60-64), race (white, black, Asian, Hispanic, American Indian), educational attainment (below high school, high school graduation), poverty status (below or above the poverty line), and gender.

Destination Choice Submodel

$$p[j|i,s] = \exp(b'x[j,i,s]) \,/\, \sum_{k\neq i}\{\exp(b'x[k,i,s])\}, \quad j\neq i, \qquad (A1)$$

where x[j,i,s] is a column vector of observable explanatory variables and b' is a row vector of unknown coefficients.

Departure Submodel

$$p[i,s] = \exp(d+c'y[i,s]+u*I[i,s]) \,/\, \{1 + \exp(d+c'y[i,s]+u*I[i,s])\}, \quad (A2)$$

where y[i,s] is another column vector of observable explanatory variables; d, c', and u are unknown coefficients, with u being bounded between 0 and 1; and I[s,i] is the so-called inclusive variable:

$$I[i,s] = \ln(\sum_{k\neq i}\{\exp(b'x[k,i,s])\}), \qquad (A3)$$

where ln is the natural log function.

Assuming that the migration behaviors of all persons in the same cell of the multidimensional migration table depend on the same set of p[i,s] and p[j|i,s], we estimate the unknown coefficients in equations (A1) and (A2) sequentially by the maximum quasi-likelihood method (McCullagh, 1983; Liaw and Ledent, 1987).

Our choice of potentially useful explanatory variables to be considered for inclusion in the model is guided by (1) previous research findings in the literature, (2) the hypotheses we wish to test, and (3) extensive preliminary cross tabulations of the migration data. In constructing a relatively comprehensive model (to be called the best model for simplicity), we include only the explanatory variables that are statistically significant (i.e., those whose t ratios have a magnitude of at least 2.0) and substantively sensible. The data sources for these variables are described in Frey et al. (1996).

The goodness of fit of a given specification of a model is to be measured by

$$\text{Rho-square} = 1 - Lg/Lo, \qquad (A4)$$

where Lg is the maximum quasi-log-likelihood of the given specification and Lo is the maximum quasi-log-likelihood of the corresponding null model (i.e., the destination choice model with c'=0 or the departure model with c'=0). Note that the ceiling of Rho-square is much less than 1.0 so that a value of 0.2 may indicate a very good fit (McFadden, 1974). Another indicator of goodness of fit is

$$\text{Weighted R-square} = 1 - Sg/Sn, \qquad (A5)$$

where Sg is the weighted residual mean square of the given specification, and Sn is the weighted residual mean square of the null model (Liaw and Ledent, 1987). Although the value of weighted R-square tends to be much larger than that of

Rho-square, we choose Rho-square over weighted R-square because we found that the former is more sensitive to changes in the combinations of explanatory variables.

To help evaluate the relative importance of one subset of explanatory variables (say conventional labor market variables) against another subset (say variables representing the effects of foreign immigration), we delete the two subsets of variables in turn from the best model and then compare the resulting decreases in Rho-square: the greater the decrease, the more important the deleted subset of variables.

Definition of the Explanatory Variables Used in This Analysis

Explanatory Variables in the Destination Model

Low-skilled Immigration Rate   For each potential destination, this variable is obtained by dividing the state-specific number of 1985-1990 foreign-born immigrants with high school education or less, aged 15-64, by the 1985 state population, aged 15-64. The unit is "percent per 5 years."

Income   This is the income per capita of a potential destination computed in the following way. First, we adjust the state-specific 1985 and 1989 nominal per capita incomes by the corresponding state-specific cost of living indices of the same years. Second, the 1985 and 1989 adjusted values are then averaged. The unit is $10,000 per person.

Total Employment Growth   For each potential destination, this variable is the state-specific 1985-1989 growth of total civilian employment divided by the 1985 total civilian employment. The unit is "proportion per 4 years."

Service Employment Growth   For each potential destination, this variable is the state-specific 1985-1989 growth of service employment divided by the 1985 service employment. The unit is "proportion per 4 years."

Unemployment Rate   This is the 1985 unemployment rate of a potential destination state. The unit is proportion. Instead of the average value of the 1985-1989 period, we use the 1985 value for the unemployment rate because we believe that among the three labor market variables, it is more subject to the feedback effect of migration.

AFDC and Food Stamp Benefit   For each potential destination, this variable is computed in the following way. First, the state-specific 1985 and 1989 nominal values of the combined AFDC and food stamp benefits per recipient family are adjusted by the corresponding 1985 and 1989 cost of living indices, respectively. Second, the adjusted 1985 and 1989 values are then averaged. The unit is $10,000 per family per year.

Coldness For each potential destination, this variable is defined as a weighted average of the heating degree days of cities with records from 1951 to 1980, using city populations as the weights. The unit is 1,000 degree (F) days.

Hotness For each potential destination, this variable is defined as a weighted average of the cooling degree days of cities with records from 1951 to 1980, using city populations as the weights. The unit is 1,000 degree (F) days.

Violent Crime Rate For each potential destination, this variable is the average of state-specific 1985 and 1989 violent crime rates. The unit is cases per 1,000 residents.

Ln(Distance) This variable is the natural log of the population gravity centers of origin and destination states. The unit is ln(miles).

Contiguity For each potential destination, this is a dummy variable assuming the value of 1 if it shares a common border with the state of origin.

Racial Similarity For the migrants of a specific race, this is the logit of the specific race's proportional share of the potential destination's population in 1985, computed indirectly from the data of the 1990 Census.

Ln(Population Size) For each potential destination, this variable is the natural log of the state-specific 1985 population computed indirectly from the data of the 1990 Census. The unit is Ln(1,000,000 persons).

Explanatory Variables in the Departure Choice Model

All the explanatory variables in the departure choice model that have the same names as those in the destination model are defined in the same way, except that the state in question is the origin rather than a potential destination.

Returning Immigration Rate of U.S.-Born Persons For each origin, this variable is obtained by dividing the state-specific number of 1985-1990 U.S.-born immigrants by the 1985 state population. Because the data come from the 1990 census, individuals less than five years old in 1990 are excluded from both numerator and denominator. The unit is "percent per 5 years."

Non-Native's Share of State Population For each origin, this variable is computed from the data of the 1980 and 1990 censuses in the following way. First, the 1980 and 1990 state-specific numbers of non-natives (i.e., those who were born in other states in the United States) were divided by the corresponding total populations of the state. Second, the two resulting figures are then averaged and transformed into a logit. The reasons for using this variable are (1) that it is well known that non-natives are more migratory than natives (Long, 1988), and (2) that our multidimensional migration table does not have the non-native/native distinction.

Armed Forces' Share of State Employment For each origin, this variable is computed from the data of the 1980 and 1990 censuses in the following way. First, the 1980 and 1990 gender- and state-specific employments in the armed forces were divided by the corresponding total employment. Second, the two resulting figures are then averaged and transformed into a logit. The reasons for using this variable are (1) that members of the armed forces are expected to be more migratory than their civilian counterparts, and (2) that our multidimensional migration table does not have a military/civilian distinction.

Inclusive Variable For each origin, this variable represents the attractiveness of the rest of the United States. Its values are computed according to equation (A3), using the estimated coefficients of the best destination choice model.

TABLE 10-A1   Estimation Result of the Departure Model for U.S.-born Interstate Migrants of the 25-29 Age Group with at most High School Education: 1985-1990

| Explanatory Variable | Best Specification | | Marginal Contribution to the Rho-square |
	Coefficient	T-ratio	
Constant Term	−1.74	−14.5	
1. PUSH EFFECTS OF FOREIGN-BORN IMMIGRANTS			0.0056
Low-skilled Immigration Rate* White	0.30	20.3	
Low-skilled Immigration Rate* Black	0.16	6.2	
Low-skilled Immigration Rate* Indian	0.18	2.9	
Low-skilled Immigration Rate* Poor White	0.15	9.3	
Low-skilled Immigration Rate* Poor Black	0.08	2.1	
Low-skilled Immigration Rate* Poor Hispanic	0.15	2.7	
2. PUSH EFFECTS OF US-BORN IMMIGRANTS			
Returning Immigration Rate of US-Born Persons	0.67	11.2	
3. RETAINING EFFECTS OF WELFARE			0.0018
AFDC&Foodstamp*Poor Black Females	−1.37	−12.5	
AFDC&Foodstamp*Poor Hispanic Females	−0.49	−2.9	
AFDC&Foodstamp*Poor Indian Females	−1.52	−6.4	
4. EFFECTS OF LABOR MARKET VARIABLES			0.0060
Income	−1.20	−10.3	
Income*High School Graduate	−0.41	−9.4	
Civilian Employment Growth	−1.46	−4.3	
Service Employment Growth	−2.40	−7.3	
Service Employment Growth * Below High School	−1.55	−4.8	
5. RETENTION EFFECTS OF RACIAL SIMILARITY			0.0026
Racial Similarity*Black	−0.23	−10.7	
Racial Similarity*Asian	−0.44	−9.3	
Racial Similarity*Hispanic	−0.33	−15.1	
Racial Similarity*Am. Indian	−0.30	−10.4	
6. EFFECTS OF PHYSICAL ENVIRONMENT			0.0007
Coldness of Winter	0.10	7.0	
Hotness of Summer	0.19	8.5	
7. RETENTION EFFECT OF SIZE OF ECUMENE			
Ln (Population Size)	−0.08	−4.0	
8. EFFECTS OF EDUCATION SELECTIVITY			
High School Graduate	—	—	
9. EFFECTS OF POPULATION COMPOSITIONS			
Non-Native's Share of State Population	2.45	17.5	
Armed Forces' Share of State Employment	2.12	7.1	
10. DRAWING POWER OF THE REST OF SYSTEM			0.0020
Inclusive Variable	0.36	14.2	
Rho-Square	0.0275		

TABLE 10-A2   Estimation Result of the Departure Model for U.S.-born Interstate Migrants of the 30-44 Age Group with At Most High School Education: 1985-1990

| Explanatory Variable | Best Specification | | Marginal Contribution to the Rho-square |
	Coefficient	T-ratio	
Constant Term	−3.04	−21.3	
1. PUSH EFFECTS OF FOREIGN-BORN IMMIGRANTS			0.0058
Low-skilled Immigration Rate* White	0.31	30.2	
Low-skilled Immigration Rate* Black	0.24	14.2	
Low-skilled Immigration Rate* Asian	0.16	2.9	
Low-skilled Immigration Rate *Hispanic	0.07	3.3	
Low-skilled Immigration Rate* Indian	0.15	3.7	
Low-skilled Immigration Rate* Poor White	0.23	24.1	
Low-skilled Immigration Rate* Poor Black	0.16	7.1	
Low-skilled Immigration Rate* Poor Hispanic	0.23	6.7	
Low-skilled Immigration Rate*Poor Indian	0.25	4.0	
2. PUSH EFFECTS OF US-BORN IMMIGRANTS			
Returning Immigration Rate of US-Born Persons	0.61	16.9	
3. RETAINING EFFECTS OF WELFARE			0.0012
AFDC&Foodstamp*Poor Black Females	−1.14	−18.1	
AFDC&Foodstamp*Poor Hispanic Females	−0.30	−2.7	
AFDC&Foodstamp*Poor Indian Females	−1.57	−9.7	
4. EFFECTS OF LABOR MARKET VARIABLES			0.0063
Income	−0.79	−7.9	
Income*High School Graduate	−0.39	−4.8	
Civilian Employment Growth	−1.63	−7.6	
Service Employment Growth	−3.22	−14.7	
Service Employment Growth * Below High School	−0.77	−4.2	
Unemployment	1.48	3.2	

TABLE 10-A2   Continued

Explanatory Variable	Best Specification		Marginal Contribution to the Rho-square
	Coefficient	T-ratio	
5. RETENTION EFFECTS OF RACIAL SIMILARITY			0.0020
Racial Similarity*Black	−0.21	−15.1	
Racial Similarity*Asian	−0.41	−11.9	
Racial Similarity*Hispanic	−0.34	−23.6	
Racial Similarity*Am. Indian	−0.37	−20.6	
6. EFFECTS OF PHYSICAL ENVIRONMENT			0.0009
Coldness of Winter	0.11	12.9	
Coldness of Winter*Aged 40-44	0.02	3.5	
Hotness of Summer	0.25	17.2	
7. RETENTION EFFECT OF SIZE OF ECUMENE			
Ln (Population Size)	−0.08	−6.9	
8. EFFECTS OF AGE & EDUCATION SELECTIVITY			
Aged 35-39	−0.14	−11.6	
Aged 40-44	−0.34	−12.6	
High School Graduation	0.36	3.0	
9. EFFECTS OF POPULATION COMPOSITIONS			
Non-Native's Share of State Population	2.61	31.3	
Armed Forces' Share of State Em.* Aged 30-34	0.61	3.3	
10. DRAWING POWER OF THE REST OF SYSTEM			0.0015
Inclusive Variable	0.43	22.5	
Rho-Square	0.0278		

TABLE 10-A3   Estimation Result of the Departure Model for U.S.-born Interstate Migrants of the 45-64 Age Group with At Most High School Education: 1985-1990

Explanatory Variable	Best Specification		Marginal Contribution to the Rho-square
	Coefficient	T-ratio	
Constant Term	–4.82	–47.2	
1. PUSH EFFECTS OF FOREIGN-BORN IMMIGRANTS			0.0059
Low-skilled Immigration Rate* White	0.32	30.3	
Low-skilled Immigration Rate* Black	0.24	12.9	
Low-skilled Immigration Rate *Hispanic	0.08	3.3	
Low-skilled Immigration Rate* Indian	0.10	2.0	
Low-skilled Immigration Rate* Poor White	0.27	25.5	
Low-skilled Immigration Rate* Poor Black	0.26	9.4	
Low-skilled Immigration Rate* Poor Hispanic	0.35	7.5	
Low-skilled Immigration Rate*Poor Indian	0.37	4.8	
2. PUSH EFFECTS OF US-BORN IMMIGRANTS			
Returning Immigration Rate of US-Born Persons	0.12	2.8	
3. RETAINING EFFECTS OF WELFARE			0.0010
AFDC&Foodstamp*Poor Black Females	–1.06	–13.0	
AFDC&Foodstamp*Poor Asian Females	–2.54	–4.1	
AFDC&Foodstamp*Poor Hispanic Females	–1.96	–10.8	
AFDC&Foodstamp*Poor Indian Females	–2.65	–11.4	
4. EFFECTS OF LABOR MARKET VARIABLES			0.0029
Income*High School Graduate	–0.35	–5.2	
Civilian Employment Growth	–1.90	–8.3	
Service Employment Growth	–2.09	–9.3	
Unemployment	3.08	8.0	

TABLE 10-A3 Continued

Explanatory Variable	Best Specification		Marginal Contribution to the Rho-square
	Coefficient	T-ratio	
5. RETENTION EFFECTS OF RACIAL SIMILARITY			0.0013
Racial Similarity*White	−0.05	−4.4	
Racial Similarity*Black	−0.10	−4.9	
Racial Similarity*Asian	−0.38	−10.1	
Racial Similarity*Hispanic	−0.28	−13.4	
Racial Similarity*Am. Indian	−0.36	−17.2	
6. EFFECTS OF PHYSICAL ENVIRONMENT			0.0016
Coldness of Winter	0.12	13.3	
Coldness of Winter*Aged 50-54	0.02	2.2	
Coldness of Winter*Aged 55-59	0.05	6.4	
Coldness of Winter*Aged 60-64	0.08	11.9	
Hotness of Summer	0.21	14.3	
7. RETENTION EFFECT OF SIZE OF ECUMENE			
Ln (Population Size)	−0.06	−5.5	
8. EFFECTS OF AGE & EDUCATION SELECTIVITY			
Aged 50-54	−0.20	−6.1	
Aged 55-59	−0.47	−13.7	
Aged 60-64	−0.71	−20.2	
High School Graduation	0.32	3.1	
9. EFFECTS OF POPULATION COMPOSITIONS			
Non-Native's Share of State Population	2.46	30.5	
10. DRAWING POWER OF THE REST OF SYSTEM			0.0012
Inclusive Variable	0.41	19.8	
Rho-Square	0.0188		

TABLE 10-A4   Estimation Result of Destination Choice Model for U.S.-born Interstate Migrants in the 25-29 Age Group with At Most High School Education: 1985-1990

Explanatory Variable	Best Specification		Marginal Contribution to the Rho-square
	Coefficient	T-ratio	
1. EFFECTS OF FOREIGN-BORN IMMIGRANTS			0.0010
Low-skilled Immigration Rate*	0.09	14.5	
Low-skilled Immigration Rate* Poor White	−0.19	−14.8	
Low-skilled Immigration Rate* Poor Black	−0.21	−8.9	
Low-skilled Immigration Rate* Poor Hispanic	−0.25	−7.4	
Low-skilled Immigration Rate* Poor Indian	−0.43	−7.1	
2. EFFECTS OF AFDC & FOODSTAMP BENEFITS			0.0003
AFDC Benefit* Poor Female	0.82	5.7	
AFDC Benefit* Poor Black Female	1.77	5.6	
AFDC Benefit* Poor Indian Female	3.15	4.0	
3. EFFECTS OF LABOR MARKET VARIABLES			0.0072
Income	0.13	2.1	
Income*High School Education	0.47	6.9	
Civilian Employment Growth	1.76	11.6	
Service Employment Growh	3.18	21.9	
Service Employment Growth* Less Than High School Ed.	0.36	2.1	
4. EFFECTS OF RACIAL ATTRACTIONS			0.0072
Racial Similarity*	0.27	29.5	
Racial Similarity*Black	0.11	6.5	
Racial Similarity*Asian	0.41	4.9	
Racial Similarity*Hispanic	0.12	5.8	
Racial Similarity*Indian	0.29	10.0	
Racial Similarity* Less Than High School Education	−0.06	−5.6	
Racial Similarity*Hispanic*Less Than High School Ed.	0.17	5.7	
5. EFFECTS OF DISTANCE AND CONTIGUITY			
Ln (Distance)	−0.6	−74.0	
Ln (Distance)* Less Than High School Education Contiguity	0.67	49.2	
6. EFFECTS OF SOCIAL & PHYSICAL ENVIROMENT			0.0020
Violent Crime Rate	−2.87	−10.8	
Coldness of Winter	−0.17	−46.7	
7. EFFECT OF ECUMENE SIZE			
Ln (Population Size)	0.76	122.3	
Rho-Square	0.1545		

TABLE 10-A5   Estimation Result of Destination Choice Model for U.S.-born Interstate Migrants in the 30-44 Age Group with At Most High School Education: 1985-1990

Explanatory Variable	Best Specification		Marginal Contribution to the Rho-square
	Coefficient	T-ratio	
1. EFFECTS OF FOREIGN-BORN IMMIGRANTS			0.0006
Low-skilled Immigration Rate*	0.05	10.1	
Low-skilled Immigration Rate* Poor White	−0.16	−16.8	
Low-skilled Immigration Rate* Poor Black	−0.16	−9.3	
Low-skilled Immigration Rate* Poor Hispanic	−0.25	−9.4	
Low-skilled Immigration Rate* Poor Indian	−0.51	−10.6	
2. EFFECTS OF AFDC & FOODSTAMP BENEFITS			0.0001
AFDC Benefit* Poor Female	0.31	2.8	
AFDC Benefit* Poor Black Female	1.53	6.1	
AFDC Benefit* Poor Indian Female	3.35	5.9	
3. EFFECTS OF LABOR MARKET VARIABLES			0.0075
Income	0.47	14.8	
Civilian Employment Growth	2.18	19.2	
Service Employment Growth	3.00	29.6	
4. EFFECTS OF RACIAL ATTRACTIONS			0.0071
Racial Similarity*	0.30	46.6	
Racial Similarity*Black	0.06	4.3	
Racial Similarity*Asian	0.27	3.9	
Racial Similarity*Hispanic	0.12	6.8	
Racial Similarity*American Indian	0.24	11.2	
Racial Similarity* Less Than High School Education	0.05	2.2	
5. EFFECTS OF DISTANCE AND CONTIGUITY			
Ln (Distance)	−0.72	−109.6	
Ln (Distance)* Less Than High School Education	−0.07	−8.5	
Contiguity	0.73	73.2	
6. EFFECTS OF SOCIAL & PHYSICAL ENVIROMENT			0.0071
Violent Crime Rate	−1.22	−6.2	
Coldness of Winter	−0.20	−61.9	
Coldness of Winter*Aged 35-39	−0.02	−6.9	
Coldness of Winter*Aged 40-44	−0.07	−16.9	
7. EFFECT OF ECUMENE SIZE			
Ln (Population Size)	0.71	157.5	
Rho-Square	0.1655		

TABLE 10-A6   Estimation Result of Destination Choice Model for U.S.-born Interstate Migrants in the 45-64 Age Group with At Most High School Education: 1985-1990

Explanatory Variable	Best Specification		Marginal Contribution to the Rho-square
	Coefficient	T-ratio	
1. EFFECTS OF FOREIGN-BORN IMMIGRANTS			0.0010
Low-skilled Immigration Rate* Poor White	−0.20	−14.2	
Low-skilled Immigration Rate* Poor Black	−0.35	−11.4	
Low-skilled Immigration Rate* Poor Asian	−0.43	−1.8	
Low-skilled Immigration Rate* Poor Hispanic	−0.58	−10.2	
Low-skilled Immigration Rate* Poor Indian	−0.72	−8.2	
2. EFFECTS OF AFDC & FOODSTAMP BENEFITS			0.0002
AFDC Benefit* Poor Female	0.31	1.7	
AFDC Benefit* Poor Black Female	1.90	4.3	
AFDC Benefit* Poor Asian Female	8.15	2.4	
AFDC Benefit* Poor Hispanic Female	4.05	4.7	
AFDC Benefit* Poor Indian Female	6.12	6.1	
3. EFFECTS OF LABOR MARKET VARIABLES			0.0156
Income	0.78	22.3	
Civilian Employment Growth	3.05	19.3	
Service Employment Growh	2.24	12.5	
Service Employment Growth* Aged 50-54	0.46	2.2	
Service Employment Growth* Aged 55-59	1.40	6.6	
Service Employment Growth* Aged 60-64	2.39	11.5	
4. EFFECTS OF RACIAL ATTRACTIONS			0.0101
Racial Similarity*	0.50	66.1	
Racial Similarity*Black	−0.12	−6.0	
5. EFFECTS OF DISTANCE AND CONTIGUITY			
Ln (Distance)	−0.68	−65.7	
Ln (Distance) * Less Than High School Education	−0.12	−11.8	
Ln (Distance)* Aged 55-59	−0.03	2.4	
Ln (Distance)* Aged 60-64	0.09	6.8	
Contiguity	0.78	55.6	
6. EFFECTS OF PHYSICAL ENVIROMENT			0.0298
Coldness of Winter	−0.36	−73.6	
Coldness of Winter* Aged 50-54	−0.03	−5.5	
Coldness of Winter* Aged 55-59	−0.09	−13.5	
Coldness of Winter*Aged 60-64	−0.14	−22.6	
7. EFFECT OF ECUMENE SIZE			
Ln (Population Size)	0.64	107.4	
Rho-Square	0.1961		

APPENDIX B

METHODOLOGY FOR IMMIGRATION IMPACT ANALYSIS

Our objective with this impact analysis is to evaluate the impacts of changes in the number of working-aged foreign-born immigrants with, at most, a high school education on the interstate migrations of U.S.-born Americans with, at most, a high school education. These impacts are determined on the basis of the best nested logit models (discussed in Appendix A) that have been constructed from the interstate migration data of the 1985-1990 period. Using the best nested logit models for the age groups 25-29, 30-44, and 45-64, respectively, as inputs, the immigration impact analyses will also be initially disaggregated for these same three age groups. They are later summed to assess the aggregate impact on the U.S.-born persons aged 25-64 with, at most, a high school education. The general methodology for this impact analysis is as follows.

For each of the 25-29, 30-44, and 45-64 age groups, let the estimated destination choice submodel of the best nested logit model be

$$p[j|i,s] = \exp(b'x[j,i,s]) \, / \, \sum_{k \neq i}\{\exp(b'x[k,i,s])\}, \quad j \neq i, \qquad (B1)$$

where $p[j|i,s]$ is the predicted proportion of the out-migrants of state i with the demographic attributes s who select state j as the destination; x[j,i,s] is a column vector of explanatory variables (e.g., the distance between i and j, or the racial similarity between the out-migrants from i and the population of the potential destination j); and b' is a row vector of estimated parameters. Also let the estimated departure submodel be

$$p[i,s] = \exp(d+c'y[i,s]+u*I[i,s]) \, / \, \{1 + \exp(d+c'y[i,s]+u*I[i,s])\}, \quad (B2)$$

where $p[i,s]$ is the predicted proportion of the at-risk population of state I with the demographic attributes s who migrate to the rest of the United States; y[i,s] is another column vector of explanatory variables; d, c', and u are estimated parameters; and $I[i,s]$ is the estimated inclusive variable defined as

$$I[i,s] = \ln(\sum_{k \neq i}\{\exp(b'x[k,i,s])\}), \qquad (B3)$$

where ln is the natural log function.

In both submodels, the variable that allows immigration to impact on the interstate migration of the U.S.-born population is the "low-skilled immigration rate." In the destination choice submodel, this variable is used not only by itself but also as interaction terms with the dummy variables representing the poor U.S.-born Americans with different racial backgrounds. In the departure submodel, it is only used to form interaction terms involving the poverty status and racial backgrounds of the U.S.-born Americans.

To find the "expected net migration" before the number of immigrants is changed, we do the following. We first multiply (1) the at-risk population of each state that has been properly disaggregated according to the attribute vector s (age, race, education, poverty status, and gender) by (2) the product of $p[i,s]$ and $p[j|i,s]$ to generate the origin-by-destination tables of predicted interstate migrants. The formula used is

$$M[i,j,s] = P[i,s] * p[i,s] * p[j|i,s], \quad j \neq i, \tag{B4}$$

where $M[i,j,s]$ is the expected number of migrants with attributes s who move from state I to state j, and $P[i,s]$ is the size of the population with attributes s whose initial state of residence is i. The expected number of in-migrants of each state is obtained from the formula

$$M[.,j] = \sum_{s, i \neq j} \{M[i,j,s]\}. \tag{B5}$$

Similarly, the expected number of out-migrants from each state is computed from the formula

$$M[i,.] = \sum_{s, i \neq j} \{M[i,j,s]\}. \tag{B6}$$

The expected net migration of each state is obtained from the formula

$$N[i] = M[.,I] - M[i,.]. \tag{B7}$$

To study the impact of a change in the national immigration level on interstate migrations, we change each state's assumed value for the variable's "low-skilled immigration rate" to estimate new values for the destination choice and departure submodels in equations (B1), (B2), and (B3) by the scaling factor (F):

$$F = \{(IM[o] + IM[h]) / P[o]\} / (IM[o]/P[o]), \tag{B8}$$

where $IM[o]$ is the original number of immigrants; $IM[h]$ is the change in the number of immigrants; and $P[o]$ is the size of the original at-risk population. The resulting values in equations (B1), (B2), and (B3) are then used in equations (B4) through (B7) to compute the new expected net migration due to the change in immigration.

The *impact* is then computed as (1) the expected net migration after the change in immigration minus (2) the expected net migration before the change. These computations are done separately for the 25-29, 30-44, and 45-64 age groups. The results are then aggregated to obtain the impacts on the 25-64 age interval. Implicit in this method is the assumption that the change in immigration is achieved by the same proportional change in all states' immigration rates.

To study the impact of a change in only California's immigration, we apply the scaling factor from equation (B8) only to California's value of the immigration variable, keeping the values of the variable for all other states unchanged.

The changes in immigration in our simulations involve the following four scenarios.

Scenario I-A. Reduction of the National Number of Immigrants by Approximately One-half

We reduce the national level of immigration by approximately 50 percent (actually 48.85%), which is equivalent to reducing the number of working-aged (age 15-64) immigrants by 1,600,000 and the number of working-aged low-skilled immigrants by 957,000. This translates into scaling the "low-skilled immigration rate" (B8) by a factor of 0.511534.

Scenario II-A. Increase of the National Number of Immigrants by Approximately One-half

We increase the national level of immigration by approximately 50 percent (actually 51.15%), which is equivalent to increasing the number of working-aged (age 15-64) immigrants by 1,600,000 and the number of working-aged low-skilled immigrants by 957,000. This translates into scaling the "low-skilled immigration rate" (B8) by a factor of 1.488466.

Scenario I-B. Reduction of California's Immigrants by Approximately One-half

We reduce California's immigration by approximately 50 percent (actually 52.28%), which is equivalent to reducing the number of California's working-aged (age 15-64) immigrants by 400,000 and the number of California's working-aged low-skilled immigrants by 194,902. This translates into scaling *only* California's "low-skilled immigration rate" by a factor of 0.47176 (B8).

Scenario II-B. Increase of California's Immigrants by Approximately One-half

We increase California's immigration by approximately 50 percent (actually 47.17%), which is equivalent to increasing the number of California's working-aged (age 15-64) immigrants by 400,000 and the number of California's working-aged low-skilled immigrants by 194,902. This translates into scaling *only* California's "low-skilled immigration rate" by a factor of 1.52824 (B8).

ACKNOWLEDGMENTS

This research is funded by the National Institute of Child Health and Human Development project, "The Changing Structure of US Metropolitan Migration" (No. R01-HD297525). We are grateful to Yu Xie, collaborator on this project, for his advice and contributions. We also appreciate the collaboration of Ji-Ping Lin in carrying out the impact analysis. Cathy Sun performed computer programming and Ron Lue Sang prepared maps and graphics.

REFERENCES

Barff, Richard, Mark Ellis, and Michael Reibel
  1995   "The Links between Immigration and Internal Migration in the United States: A Comparison of the 1970s and 1980s." *Working Paper Series No. 1* Dartmouth College, Hanoover, N.H.: Nelson A. Rockefeller Center for the Social Sciences.
Bartel, Ann P.
  1989   "Where Do the New Immigrants Live?" *Journal of Labor Economics* 7(4):371-391.
Bartel, Ann P., and Marianne J. Koch
  1991   "Internal Migration of U.S. Immigrants." Pp. 121-134 in *Immigration Trade and the Labor Market*, J.M. Abowd and R.B. Freeman eds. Chicago: University of Chicago Press.
Bean, Frank D., and Marta Tienda
  1987   *The Hispanic Population of the United States*. New York: Russell Sage Foundation.
Bolton, Nancy
  1993   "Immigration, Migration and the Labor Force of California." *UCLA Business Forecast* (March).
Borjas, George J.
  1994   "The Economics of Immigration." *Journal of Economic Literature*, 32:1667-1717.
Borjas, George J., Richard B. Freeman, and Lawrence F. Katz
  1996   "Searching for the Effect of Immigration on the Labor Market." NBER Working Paper 5454. Cambridge, Mass.: National Bureau of Economic Research.
Bureau of the Census
  1994   *Population Projections for States by Age, Race and Sex, 1993 to 2020*. Current Population Reports P25-1111. Washington, D.C.: U.S. Government Printing Office.
Center for the New West
  1996   *California: A Twenty-first Century Prospectus*. Ontario, Calif.: Center for the New West.
Denton, Nancy, and Douglas S. Massey
  1991   "Patterns of Neighborhood Transition in a Multi-ethnic World: US Metropolitan Areas, 1970-80." *Demography* 28:(1):41-63.
Espenshade, Thomas J., and Charles A. Calhoun
  1993   "An Analysis of Public Opinion toward Undocumented Immigration." *Population Research and Policy Review* 12:189-224.

Filer, Randall K.
1992   "The Effect of Immigrant Arrivals on Migratory Patterns of Native Workers." Pp.245-
        270 in *Immigration and the Work Force*, George J. Borjas and Richard B. Freeman, eds.
        Chicago: University of Chicago Press.
Frey, William H.
1979   "The Changing Impact of White Migration on the Population Compositions of Origin and
        Destination Metropolitan Areas." *Demography* 16:(2):219-238.
Frey, William H.
1994   "The New White Flight." *American Demographics* April:40-48.
Frey, William H.
1995a   "Immigration and Internal Migration 'Flight': A California Case Study." *Population and
        Environment* 16(4):353-375.
Frey, William H.
1995b   "Immigration and Internal Migration 'Flight' from US Metropolitan Areas: Toward a
        New Demographic Balkanization." *Urban Studies* 32(4-5):733-757.
Frey, William H.
1995c   "Immigration Impacts on Internal Migration of the Poor: 1990 Census Evidence for US
        States." *International Journal of Population Geography* 1:51-67.
Frey, William H.
1996   "Immigration, Domestic Migration and Demographic Balkanization in America: New
        Evidence for the 1990s." *Population and Development Review* 22(4):741-763.
Frey, William H.
1997a   "Immigration, Welfare Magnets and the Geography of Child Poverty in the United States."
        Population and Environment 19(1):53-86.
Frey, William H.
1997b   "Emerging Demographic Balkanization: Toward One America or Two?" Research Re-
        port No. 97-410. Ann Arbor: University of Michigan, Population Studies Center.
Frey, William H., and Kao-Lee Liaw
1998   "Immigrant Concentration and Domestic Migrant Dispersal: Is Movement to Non-Metro
        Areas 'White Flight'?" *The Professional Geographer* 50(2).
Frey, William H., and Alden Speare
1988   *Regional and Metropolitan Growth and Decline in the U.S.* New York: Russell Sage.
Frey, William H., Kao-Lee Liaw, Yu Xie, and Marcia J. Carlson
1996   "Interstate Migration of the US Poverty Population: Immigration 'Pushes' and Welfare
        Magnet 'Pulls'." *Population and Environment* 17(6):491-538.
Fuguitt, Glenn V., and Calvin L. Beale
1995   "Recent Trends in Nonmetropolitan Migration: Toward a New Turnaround?" CDE Work-
        ing Paper 95-07. Madison: University of Wisconsin, Center for Demography and Ecology.
Gabriel, Stuart A., Joe P. Mattey, and William L. Wascher
1995   "The Demise of California Reconsidered: Interstate Migration over the Economic Cycle."
        Economic Review, Federal Reserve Bank of California, 2:30-45.
Gober, Patricia
1993   "Americans on the Move." *Population Bulletin*. Washington, D.C: Population Refer-
        ence Bureau.
Immigration and Naturalization Service
1996   *1994-5 Statistical Yearbook of the Immigration and Naturalization Service*. Washington,
        D.C.: U.S. Government Printing Office.
Jennings, Diane
1994   "Job Seekers Making Tracks to Texas Again." *The Dallas Morning News*, September 5, p. 1.

Johnson, Hans, and Richard Lovelady
    1995   *Migration between California and Other States: 1985-1994.* Sacramento: Demographic Research Unit, California Department of Finance.
Johnson, Kenneth M., and Calvin L. Beale
    1995   "The Rural Rebound Revisited." *American Demographics* July:46-54.
Kanaraglou, P.K., L. Liaw, and Y.Y. Papageorgiou
    1996   "An Analysis of Migrating Systems 2. Operational Framework." *Environment and Planning* 18:1039-1060.
Labich, Kenneth
    1994   "The Geography of an Emerging America." *The Survey of Regional Literature* 28:23-28.
Lansing, John B., and Eva Mueller
    1967   *The Geographic Mobility of Labor.* Ann Arbor, Mich.: Survey Research Center, Institute for Social Research.
Lee, Everett S.
    1966   "A Theory of Migration." *Demography* 3:47-57.
Liaw, Kao-Lee
    1990   "Joint Effects of Personal Factors and Ecological Variables on the Interprovincial Migration Pattern of Young Adults in Canada: A Nested Logit Analysis." *Geographical Analysis* 22(3):189-208.
Liaw, Kao-Lee, and Jacques Ledent
    1987   "Nested Logit Model and Maximum Quasi Likelihood Method: A Flexible Methodology for Analyzing Interregional Migration Patterns." *Regional Science and Urban Economics* 17:67-88.
Liaw, Kao-Lee, and William H. Frey
    1996   "Interstate Migration of American Young Adults in 1985-90: An Explanation Using the Nested Logit Model." *Geographical Systems* 3:301-334.
Liaw, Kao-Lee, and William H. Frey
    1998   "Destination Choices of 1985-90 Young Adult Immigrants in the United States: Importance of Race, Education Attainment and Labor Market Forces." *International Journal of Population Geography* 4(1).
Liaw, Kao-Lee, and Atsushi Otomo
    1991   "Inter-prefectural Migration Patterns of Young Adults in Japan: An Explanation Using a Nested Log and Model." *Journal of Population Studies (Japan)* (14):1-20.
Liaw, Kao-Lee, Ji-Ping Lin, and William H. Frey
    1996   "Impacts of Low-skilled Immigration on the Internal Migration of Low-skilled Persons in the United States: An Assessment in a Multivariate Context." Hamilton, Ontario: McMaster University, Department of Geography.
Lieberson, Stanley
    1963   *Ethnic Patterns in American Cities.* New York: The Free Press.
Long, Larry
    1988   *Migration and Residential Mobility in the United States.* New York: Russell Sage.
Long, Larry H., and Alfred Nucci
    1995   "Spatial and Demographic Dynamics of Metropolitan and Nonmetropolitan Territory in the United States." *The International Journal of Population Geography* 1(2):165-182.
Longino, Charles F., Jr.
    1995   *Retirement Migration in America.* Houston: Vacation Publications.
Manson, Donald M., Thomas J. Espenshade, and Thomas Muller
    1985   "Mexican Immigration to Southern California: Issues of Job Competition and Worker Mobility." *The Review of Regional Studies* 15 (Spring):21-33.
Martin, Philip
    1995   "Proposition 187 in California." *International Migration Review* 29:255-263.

Martin, Philip, and Elizabeth Midgley
1994 "Immigration to the United States: Journey to an Uncertain Destination. *Population Bulletin*, Vol. 49, No. 2. Washington, D.C.: Population Reference Bureau.
Martin, Susan Forbes
1993 "The Commission on Immigration Reform." *Migration World* XXI(2):43-44.
Massey, Douglas S., and Nancy Denton
1993 *American Apartheid*. Cambridge, Mass.: Harvard University Press.
Massey, Douglas S., Joaquin Arango, Graeme Hugo, Ali Kouaouci, Adela Pellegrino, and J. Edward Taylor
1994 "An Evaluation of International Migration Theory: The North American Case." *Population and Development Review* 20(4):699-751.
McCullagh, P.
1983 "Quasi-Likelihood Functions. *The Annals of Statistics* 11:59-67.
McFadden, D.
1974 "Conditional Logit Analysis of Qualitative Choice Behavior." In *Frontiers in Econometrics*, P. Zarembka, ed. New York: Academic Press.
McHugh, Kevin E.
1989 "Hispanic Migration and Population Redistribution in the United States." *Professional Geographer* 41(4):429-439.
Miller, Glenn H., Jr.
1994 "People on the Move: Trends and Prospects in District Migration Flows." *Economic Review*, Federal Reserve Bank of Kansas City, Third Quarter, pp. 39-54.
Mollenkopf, John H., and Manuel Castells, eds.
1991 *Dual City: Restructuring New York*. New York: Russell Sage.
Newbold, K. Bruce, and Kao-Lee Liaw
1994 "Return and Onward Interprovincial Migration through Economic Boom and Bust in Canada: from 1976-1981 to 1981-1986." *Geographical Analysis* 26:228-245.
Newman, Kristen E., and Marta Tienda
1994 "The Settlement and Secondary Migration Patterns of Legalized Immigrants: Insights from Administrative Records. Pp. 157-226 in *Immigration and Ethnicity*, B. Edmonston and J.S. Passel, eds. Washington, D.C.: The Urban Institute Press.
Nogle, June Marie
1996 "Immigrants on the Move: How Internal Migration Increases the Concentration of the Foreign Born." *Backgrounder*. Washington, D.C.: Center for Immigration Studies.
Pedraza, Silvia, and Ruben G. Rumbaut
1996 *Origins and Destinites: Immigration, Race and Ethnicity in America*. Belmont, Calif.: Wadsworth.
Sassen, Saskia
1996 "Immigration in Global Cities." Pp. 3-9 in *Proceedings of the International Symposium on Immigration and World Cities*. New York: American Planning Association.
Simon, Julian
1996 "Public Expenditures on Immigrants to the United States, Past and Present." *Population and Development Review* 22(1):99-109.
Spiers, Joseph
1995 "The Economy: Regional Winners and Losers." *Fortune*. August 7, pp. 67-69.
Waldinger, Roger
1996 "Conclusion: Ethnicity and Opportunity in the Plural City." Chap. 15 in *Ethnic Los Angeles,* Roger Waldinger and Mehdi Bozorgmehr, eds. New York: Russell Sage.
Walker, Robert, Mark Ellis, and Richard Barff
1992 "Linked Migration Systems: Immigration and Internal Labor Flows in the United States." *Economic Geography* 68:234-248.

White, Michael J.
  1987   *American Neighborhoods and Residential Differentiation.* New York: Russell Sage.
White, Michael J., and Lori Hunter
  1993   "The Migratory Response of Native-born Workers to the Presence of Immigrants in the Labor Market." Paper presented at the 1993 meeting of the Population Association of America, Cincinnati, April.
White, Michael J., and Yoshie Imai
  1994   "The Impact of Immigration upon Internal Migration." *Population and Environment* 15(3):189-209.
White, Michael J., and Zai Liang
  1994   "The Effect of Immigration on the Internal Migration of the Native-Born Population, 1981-90." Working Paper, Brown University, Population Studies and Training Center, Providence, R.I.

Index

H